STRATEGIC MANAGEMENT
Concepts

A COMPETITIVE ADVANTAGE APPROACH

Editor in Chief: Stephanie Wall
Program Management Lead: Ashely Santora
Program Manager: Sarah Holle
Editorial Assistant: Bernard Ollila
Head of Learning Asset Acquisition, Global Editions:
  Laura Dent
Senior Acquisitions Editor, Global Editions:
  Steven Jackson
Project Editor, Global Editions: Laura Thompson
Assistant Project Editor, Global Editions:
  Paromita Banerjee
Marketing Director: Maggie Moylan
Senior Marketing Manager: Erin Gardner
Senior Production Manufacturing Controller,
  Global Editions: Trudy Kimber
Project Management Lead: Judy Leale
Project Manager: Ann Pulido

Procurement Specialist: Michelle Klein
Art Director, Interior: Kenny Beck
Designer, Interior: Laura Ierardi
Creative Director, Cover: Jayne Conte
Designer, Cover: Bruce Kenselaar
Cover Image: © Nonnakrit/Shutterstock
VP, Director of Digital Strategy & Assessment:
  Paul Gentile
Digital Editor: Brian Surette
Digital Development Manager: Robin Lazrus
Digital Project Manager: Alana Coles
MyLab Product Manager: Joan Waxman
Digital Production Project Manager: Lisa Rinaldi
Media Production Manager, Global Editions:
  Vikram Kumar
Full-Service Project Management and Composition:
  Integra

Credits and acknowledgments borrowed from other sources and reproduced, with permission, in this textbook appear on the appropriate page within text.

Microsoft® and Windows® are registered trademarks of the Microsoft Corporation in the U.S.A. and other countries. Screen shots and icons reprinted with permission from the Microsoft Corporation. This book is not sponsored or endorsed by or affiliated with the Microsoft Corporation.

Pearson Education Limited
Edinburgh Gate
Harlow
Essex CM20 2JE
England
and Associated Companies throughout the world

Visit us on the World Wide Web at:
www.pearsonglobaleditions.com

© Pearson Education Limited 2015

The rights of Fred R. David and Forest R. David to be identified as authors of this work have been asserted by them in accordance with the Copyright, Designs and Patents Act 1988.

Authorized adaptation from the United States edition, entitled Strategic Management: A Competitive Advantage Approach, Concepts, 15th Edition, ISBN 978-0-133-44489-6 by Fred R. David *and* Forest R. David, *published by Pearson Education © 2015.*

ISBN 10: 1-292-01680-9
ISBN 13: 978-1-292-01680-1

British Library Cataloguing-in-Publication Data
A catalogue record for this book is available from the British Library

ARP impression 98

Typeset in 10/12 times Lt Std by integra
Printed and bound by Ashford Colour Press Ltd

STRATEGIC MANAGEMENT
Concepts

FIFTEENTH EDITION

A COMPETITIVE ADVANTAGE APPROACH

GLOBAL EDITION

Fred R. David
Francis Marion University
Florence, South Carolina

Forest R. David
Strategic Planning Consultant

PEARSON

Boston   Columbus   Indianapolis   New York   San Francisco   Upper Saddle River
Amsterdam   Cape Town   Dubai   London   Madrid   Milan   Munich   Paris   Montréal   Toronto
Delhi   Mexico City   São Paulo   Sydney   Hong Kong   Seoul   Singapore   Taipei   Tokyo

Brief Contents

Contents

Cases

Available in the Concepts and Cases version of Strategic Management: A Competitive Advantage Approach

Service Firms

Manufacturing Firms

Welcome Forest, and Thank You:

- For joining me as a coauthor on this 15th edition
- For publishing many strategic management papers and articles with me and other authors
- For your wise strategic-management counsel over many years as this textbook has evolved
- For assisting students for many years through the Strategy Club (www.strategyclub.com) that now also offers your free Excel Student Template
- For developing an outstanding Case MyLab testing feature for this edition
- For preparing the *Chapter Instructor's Manual* for this edition

Preface

Why Adopt This Text?

This textbook is trusted around the world to provide managers the latest skills and concepts needed to effectively formulate and efficiently implement a strategic plan—a game plan, if you will—that can lead to sustainable competitive advantage for any type of business. The Association to Advance Collegiate Schools of Business (AACSB) increasingly advocates a more skills-oriented, practical approach in business books, which the David text provides, rather than a theory-based approach. This textbook meets all AACSB-International guidelines for the strategic-management course at both the graduate and undergraduate levels, and previous editions have been used at more than 500 colleges and universities around the world. We believe you will find this edition to be the best textbook available for communicating both the excitement and value of strategic management. Concise and exceptionally well organized, this text is now published in English, Chinese, Spanish, Thai, German, Japanese, Farsi, Indonesian, Indian, and Arabic. A version in Russian is being negotiated. Not only universities, but also hundreds of companies, organizations, and governmental bodies use this text as a management guide.

In contrast to many other strategic-management textbooks, the David book provides:

1. An effective process for developing a clear strategic plan, rather than simply presenting seminal theories in strategy, and
2. An effective model or flow for actually doing strategic planning.

Eric N. Sims, a professor who in 2013 adopted the David book for his classes at Sonoma State University in California, says:

> "I have read many strategy books. I am going to use the David book. What I like—to steal a line from Alabama coach Nick Saban—is your book teaches 'a process.' I believe at the end of your book, you can actually help a company do strategic planning. In contrast, the other books teach a number of near and far concepts related to strategy."

A recent reviewer of this textbook says:

> "One thing I admire most about the David text is that it follows the fundamental sequence of strategy formulation, implementation, and evaluation. There is a basic flow from vision/mission to internal/external environmental scanning, to strategy development, selection, implementation, and evaluation. This has been, and continues to be, a hallmark of the David text. Many other strategy texts are more disjointed in their presentation, and thus confusing to the student, especially at the undergraduate level."

New Chapter Features

1. The fifteenth edition is 40 percent new and improved from the prior edition.
2. Chapter 2, Outside-USA Strategic Planning, is expanded 30 percent with new coverage of cultural and conceptual strategic-management differences across countries. Doing business globally has become a necessity in most industries. Nearly all strategic decisions today are affected by global issues and concerns.
3. Chapter 3, Ethics/Social Responsibility/Sustainability, is expanded 30 percent, providing extensive new coverage of ethics, workplace romance, and sustainability. This text emphasizes that "good ethics is good business." Unique to strategic-management texts, the sustainability discussion is strengthened in this edition to promote and encourage firms to conduct operations in an environmentally sound manner. Respect for the natural environment has become an important concern for consumers, companies, society, and AACSB-International.

4. An updated Cohesion Case on adidas AG is provided. adidas is one of the most successful, well-known, and best-managed global companies in the world. Students apply strategy concepts to adidas at the end of each chapter through brand new Assurance of Learning Exercises.

5. New or improved Assurance of Learning Exercises appear at the end of all chapters to apply chapter concepts. The exercises prepare students for strategic-management case analysis.

6. A new boxed insert at the beginning of each chapter showcases a company doing strategic management exceptionally well.

7. There are all new examples in all the chapters.

8. There is new narrative on strategic-management theory and concepts in every chapter.

9. On average, 10 new review questions are provided at the end of each chapter.

10. New color photographs bring this new edition to life and illustrate "the practice of strategic management."

11. All current readings at the end of all chapters are new, as new research and theories of seminal thinkers are included. However, practical aspects of strategic management are center stage and the trademark of this text.

12. For the first time ever, the Excel Student Template is provided free at www.strategyclub.com to all students who use this textbook. Widely used for more than a decade by both students and businesses, and improved dramatically just for this edition, the free Excel Student Template enables students to more easily apply strategic-management concepts while engaging in assurance of learning exercises or case analysis. Using the Template, students can devote more time to applying strategy concepts and less time to the mechanics of formatting strategy matrices, tables, and PowerPoints.

13. Every sentence and paragraph has been scrutinized, modified, clarified, deleted, streamlined, updated, and improved to enhance the content and caliber of presentation.

Time-Tested Features

1. This text meets all AACSB-International guidelines that support a practitioner orientation rather than a theory/research approach. This text offers a skills-oriented process for developing a vision and mission statement; performing an external audit; conducting an internal assessment; and formulating, implementing, and evaluating strategies.

2. The author's writing style is concise, conversational, interesting, logical, lively, and supported by numerous current examples.

3. A simple, integrative strategic-management model appears in all chapters and on the inside front cover. The model is widely used by strategic planning consultants and companies worldwide.

4. An exciting, updated Cohesion Case on adidas AG follows Chapter 1 and is revisited at the end of each chapter, allowing students to apply strategic-management concepts and techniques to a real company as chapter material is covered, thus preparing students for case analysis as the course evolves.

5. End-of-chapter Assurance of Learning Exercises apply chapter concepts and techniques in a challenging, meaningful, and enjoyable manner.

6. There is excellent pedagogy, including learning objectives opening each chapter and key terms, current readings, discussion questions, and assurance of learning exercises ending each chapter.

7. There is excellent coverage of strategy formulation issues, such as business ethics, global versus domestic operations, vision and mission, matrix analysis, partnering, joint venturing, competitive analysis, value chain analysis, governance, and matrices for assimilating and evaluating information.

8. There is excellent coverage of strategy implementation issues such as corporate culture, organizational structure, outsourcing, marketing concepts, financial analysis, business ethics, whistleblowing, bribery, pay and performance linkages, and workplace romance.

9. A systematic, analytical "process" is presented that includes nine matrices: IFEM, EFEM, CPM, SWOT, BCG, IE, GRAND, SPACE, and QSPM.
10. Both the chapter material and case material is published in four colors.
11. For the chapter material, an outstanding ancillary package includes a comprehensive Instructor's Manual, Test Bank, TestGen, and Chapter PowerPoints.

Instructor Supplements

At www.pearsonglobaleditions.com/david, instructors can access a variety of resources that accompany this new edition. Registration is easy, please contact your Pearson Sales Representative who will provide you with the access information you need.

If you ever need assistance, our dedicated technical support team is ready to help with the media supplements that accompany this text. Visit http://247.pearsoned.com/ for answers to frequently asked questions and toll-free user support phone numbers.

The following supplements are available to adopting instructors:

- *Chapter Instructor's Manual*
- **Chapter PowerPoints**
- **Test Bank**
- **TestGen**

CourseSmart* Textbooks Online

CourseSmart eTextbooks were developed for students looking to save the cost on required or recommended textbooks. Students simply select their eText by title or author and purchase immediate access to the content for the duration of the course using any major credit card. With a CourseSmart eText, students can search for specific keywords or page numbers, take notes online, print reading assignments that incorporate lecture notes, and bookmark important passages for later review. For more information or to purchase a CourseSmart eTextbook, visit www.coursesmart.com.

Sample of Universities Recently Using This Textbook

Abraham Baldwin Agricultural College

Adelphi University

Akron Institute

Albany State University

Albertus Magnus College

Albright College

Alcorn State University

Alvernia University

Ambassador College

Amberton University

American Intercontinental University—Weston

American International College

American International Continental (AIU) University—Houston

American International University

*This product may not be available in all markets. For more details, please visit www.coursesmart.co.uk or contact your local Pearson representative.

American University

Anderson University

Angelo State University

Aquinas College

Arizona State University—Polytechnic Campus

Art Institute of California

Averett University

Avila University

Azusa Pacific University

Baker College— Flint

Baldwin Wallace College

Barry University

Belhaven University—Jackson

Bellevue University

Belmont Abbey College

Benedictine University

Black Hills State University

Bloomsburg University

Briar Cliff University

Brooklyn College

Broward College—Central

Broward College—North

Broward College—South

Bryant & Stratton—Orchard Park

Buena Vista University—Storm Lake

Caldwell College

California Polytechnic State University

California State University—Sacramento

California State University—San Bernadino

California University of PA

Calumet College

Capella University

Carlow University

Carson-Newman College

Catawba College

Catholic University of America

Cedar Crest College

Central Connecticut State University

Central Michigan University

Central New Mexico Community College

Central Washington University

Chatham University

Chestnut Hill College

Chicago State University

Christian Brothers University

Claflin University

Clarion University of Pennsylvania

Clarkson College

Clatsop Community College

Cleveland State University

College of William & Mary

Colorado State University—Pueblo

Columbia College

Columbia Southern University—Online

Concordia University

Concordia University Wisconsin

Curry College

Cuyahoga Community College

Daniel Webster College

Davis & Elkins College

Delaware State University

Delaware Technology & Community College—Dover

Delaware Technology & Community College—Wilmington

DePaul University—Loop Campus

East Stroudsburg University

Eastern Michigan University

Eastern Oregon University

Eastern Washington University

ECPI College of Technology—Charleston

ECPI Computer Institute

Elmhurst College

Embry-Riddle Aero University—Prescott

Ferrum College

Florida Agricultural & Mechanical University

Florida Southern College

Florida State University

Florida Technical College—Deland

Florida Technical College—Kissimmee

Florida Technical College—Orlando

Fort Valley State College

Francis Marion University

Fresno Pacific University

Frostburg State University

George Fox University

Georgetown College

Georgia Southern University

Georgia Southwestern State University

Hampton University

Harding University

Harris Stowe State University

Herzing College—Madison

Herzing College—New Orleans

Herzing College—Winter Park

Herzing University—Atlanta

High Point University

Highline Community College

Hofstra University

Hood College

Hope International University

Houghton College

Huntingdon College

Indiana University Bloomington

Indiana Wesleyan CAPS

Iona College

Iowa Lakes Community College—Emmetsburg

Jackson Community College

Jackson State University

John Brown University

Johnson & Wales—Charlotte

Johnson & Wales—Colorado

Johnson & Wales—Miami

Johnson & Wales—Rhode Island

Johnson C. Smith University

Kalamazoo College

Kansas State University

Keene State College

Kellogg Community College

La Salle University

Lake Michigan College

Lebanon Valley College

Lee University

Lehman College of CUNY

Liberty University

Limestone College—Gaffney

Lincoln Memorial University

Loyola College Business Center

Loyola College—Chennai

Loyola University—Maryland

Lyndon State College

Madonna University

Manhattan College

Manhattanville College

Marian University—Indiana

Marshall University

Marshall University Graduate College

Marymount University—Arlington

Medgar Evers College

Medical Careers Institute/Newport News

Mercer University—Atlanta

Mercer University—Macon

Miami-Dade College—Homestead

Miami-Dade College—Kendal

Miami-Dade College—North

Miami-Dade College—Wolfson

Michigan State University

Mid-America Christian

Millersville University

Mississippi University for Women

Morgan State University

Morrison College of Reno

Mount Marty College—South Dakota

Mount Mercy University

Mount Wachusett Community College

Mt. Hood Community College

Mt. Vernon Nazarene

MTI Western Business College

Muhlenberg College

Murray State University

New England College

New Mexico State University

New York University

North Carolina Wesleyan College

North Central College

North Central State College

Northwest Arkansas Community College

Northwestern College

Northwood University—Cedar Hill

Notre Dame of Maryland University

Nyack College

Oakland University

Ohio Dominican University

Oklahoma Christian University

Oklahoma State University

Olivet College

Oral Roberts University

Pace University—Pleasantville

Park University

Penn State University—Abington

Penn State University—Hazleton

Pensacola State College

Philadelphia University

Point Park University

Prince George's Community College

Queens College of CUNY

Richard Stockton University

Rider University

Roger Williams University

Saint Edwards University

Saint Leo University

Saint Mary's College

Saint Mary's College—Indiana

Saint Xavier University

San Antonio College

Santa Fe College

Savannah State University

Shippensburg University

Siena Heights University

Southern Nazarene University

Southern New Hampshire University

Southern Oregon University

Southern University—Baton Rouge

Southern Wesleyan University

Southwest Baptist University

Southwest University

St. Bonaventure University

St. Francis University

St. Louis University

St. Martins University

Sterling College

Stevenson University

Strayer University—DC

Texas A&M University—Commerce

Texas A&M University—Texarkana

Texas A&M—San Antonio

Texas Tech University

The College of St. Rose

The Masters College

Tri-County Technical College

Trinity Christian College

Troy State University

Troy University—Dothan

Troy University—Main Campus

Troy University—Montgomery

University Alabama—Birmingham

University Maryland—College Park

University of Arkansas—Fayetteville

University of Findlay

University of Houston—Clearlake

University of Louisiana at Monroe

University of Maine at Augusta

University of Maine—Fort Kent

University of Maryland

University of Massachusetts—Boston Harbor

University of Massachusetts—Dartmouth

University of Miami

University of Michigan—Flint

University of Minnesota—Crookston

University of Mobile

University of Montevallo

University of Nebraska—Omaha

University of Nevada Las Vegas

University of New Orleans

University of North Texas

University of North Texas—Dallas

University of Pikeville

University of Sioux Falls

University of South Florida

University of St. Joseph

University of Tampa

University of Texas—Pan American

University of The Incarnate Word

University of Toledo

Upper Iowa University

Valley City State University

Virginia Community College System

Virginia State University

Virginia Tech

Wagner College

Wake Forest University

Washington University

Webber International University

Webster University

West Chester University

West Liberty University

West Valley College

West Virginia Wesleyan College

Western Connecticut State University

Western Kentucky University

Western Michigan University

Western Washington University

William Jewell College

Williams Baptist College

Winona State University

Winston-Salem State University

WSU Vancouver

Sample of Countries Outside the USA Where This Textbook is Very Widely Used

Mexico, China, Japan, Australia, Singapore, Canada, Indonesia, Pakistan, Iran, Kenya, Congo, Hong Kong, India, England, Argentina, Equador, Zambia, Guam, Italy, Cyprus, Colombia, Philippines, South Africa, Peru, Turkey, Malaysia, and Egypt

Acknowledgments

Many persons have contributed time, energy, ideas, and suggestions for improving this text over 15 editions. The strength of this text is largely attributed to the collective wisdom, work, and experiences of strategic-management professors, researchers, students, and practitioners. Names of particular individuals whose published research is referenced in this edition are listed alphabetically in the Name Index. To all individuals involved in making this text so popular and successful, we are indebted and thankful.

Many special persons and reviewers contributed valuable material and suggestions for this edition. We would like to thank our colleagues and friends at Auburn University, Mississippi State University, East Carolina University, the University of South Carolina, Campbell University, the University of North Carolina at Pembroke, and Francis Marion University. We have taught strategic management at all these universities. Scores of students and professors at these schools helped shape the development of this text. Many thanks go to the following reviewers whose comments shaped the fourteenth and fifteenth editions:

Moses Acquaah, University of North Carolina at Greensboro

Gary L. Arbogast, Glenville State College

Charles M. Byles, Virginia Commonwealth University

Charles J. Capps III, Sam Houston State University

Neil Dworkin, Western Connecticut State University

Jacalyn M. Florn, University of Toledo

John Frankenstein, Brooklyn College/City University of New York

Bill W. Godair, Landmark College, Community College of Vermont

Carol Jacobson, Purdue University

Susan M. Jensen, University of Nebraska at Kearney

Dmitry Khanin, California State University at Fullerton

Thomas E. Kulik, Washington University at St. Louis

Jerrold K. Leong, Oklahoma State University

Trina Lynch-Jackson, Indiana University

Elouise Mintz, Saint Louis University

Raza Mir, William Paterson University

Gerry N. Muuka, Murray State University

Braimoh Oseghale, Fairleigh Dickinson University

Lori Radulovich, Baldwin-Wallace College

Thomas W. Sharkey, University of Toledo

Frederick J. Slack, Indiana University of Pennsylvania

Daniel Slater, Union University

Demetri Tsanacas, Ferrum College

Jill Lynn Vihtelic, Saint Mary's College

Michael W. Wakefield, Colorado State University–Pueblo

Don Wicker, Brazosport College

We want to thank you, the reader, for investing the time and effort to read and study this text. It will help you formulate, implement, and evaluate strategies for any organization with which you become associated. We hope you come to share our enthusiasm for the rich subject area of strategic management and for the systematic learning approach taken in this text. We want to welcome and invite your suggestions, ideas, thoughts, comments, and questions regarding any part of this text or the ancillary materials. Please contact Dr. Fred R. David at the following e-mail freddavid9@gmail.com, or write him at the School of Business, Francis Marion University, Florence, SC 29501. We sincerely appreciate and need your input to continually improve this text in future editions. Your willingness to draw my attention to specific errors or deficiencies in coverage or exposition will especially be appreciated.

Thank you for using this text.

Fred R. David and Forest R. David

Pearson would also like to thank and acknowledge Ivan Ninov, The Emirates Academy of Hospitality Management, and Aykut Arslan, Haliç Üniversitesi, for reviewing the Global Edition.

About the Authors

Fred R. and Forest R. David, a father–son team, have published more than 50 journal articles in outlets such as *Academy of Management Review, Academy of Management Executive, Journal of Applied Psychology, Long Range Planning, International Journal of Management, Journal of Business Strategy*, and *Advanced Management Journal*. Fred and Forest's February 2011 *Business Horizons* article titled "What are Business Schools Doing for Business Today?" is changing the way many business schools view their curricula.

Fred and Forest are coauthors of *Strategic Management: Concepts and Cases* that has been on a two-year revision cycle since 1986 when the first edition was published. This text is among the best-selling strategic-management textbooks in the world. This text has led the field of strategic management for more than two decades in providing an applications, practitioner-approach to the discipline. More than 500 colleges and universities have used this textbook over the years, including Harvard University, Duke University, Carnegie-Mellon University, Johns Hopkins University, the University of Maryland, University of North Carolina, University of Georgia, San Francisco State University, University of South Carolina, Wake Forest University, and countless universities in Japan, China, Australia, Mexico, and the Middle East. For six editions of this book, Forest has been sole author of the *Case Instructor's Manual*, having developed extensive teachers' notes (solutions) for all the cases. Forest is author of the Case MyLab ancillary and the free Excel Student Template that accompany this fifteenth edition.

Fred and Forest actively assist businesses globally in doing strategic planning. They have written and published more than 100 strategic management cases. Fred and Forest were recently keynote speakers at the Pearson International Forum in Monterrey, Mexico. With a PhD in Management from the University of South Carolina, Fred is the TranSouth Professor of Strategic Planning at Francis Marion University (FMU) in Florence, South Carolina. Forest has taught strategic-management courses at Mississippi State University, Campbell University, and FMU.

Fred R. David

Forest R. David

The Case Rationale

Case analysis remains the primary learning vehicle used in most strategic-management classes, for five important reasons:

1. Analyzing cases gives students the opportunity to work in teams to evaluate the internal operations and external issues facing various organizations and to craft strategies that can lead these firms to success. Working in teams gives students practical experience solving problems as part of a group. In the business world, important decisions are generally made within groups; strategic-management students learn to deal with overly aggressive group members and also timid, noncontributing group members. This experience is valuable because strategic-management students are near graduation and soon enter the working world full-time.

2. Analyzing cases enables students to improve their oral and written communication skills as well as their analytical and interpersonal skills by proposing and defending particular courses of action for the case companies.

3. Analyzing cases allows students to view a company, its competitors, and its industry concurrently, thus simulating the complex business world. Through case analysis, students learn how to apply concepts, evaluate situations, formulate strategies, and resolve implementation problems.

4. Analyzing cases allows students to apply concepts learned in many business courses. Students gain experience dealing with a wide range of organizational problems that impact all the business functions.

5. Analyzing cases gives students practice in applying concepts, evaluating situations, formulating a "game plan," and resolving implementation problems in a variety of business and industry settings.

Case MyLab Testing Feature

New to this edition is an enhanced MyLab with some new cases that include gradeable outcomes. This feature assures that the cases are excellent for testing student learning of the key strategic-management concepts, thus serving as a great mechanism for professors to achieve AACSB's Assurance of Learning Objectives. This new testing feature simplifies grading for professors in both traditional and online class settings.

The Case MyLab testing feature includes multiple choice questions for some of the cases, comprised of *Basic* questions that simply test whether the student read the case before class, and *Applied* questions that test the student's ability to apply various strategic-management concepts. In addition, there are *Discussion* questions per case. This testing feature enables professors to determine, before class if desired, whether students 1) read the case in *Basic* terms, and/or 2) are able to *Apply* strategy concepts to resolve issues in the case. For example, the MyLab case *Basic* question may be: In what country is BMW headquartered? Whereas, a MyLab case *Applied* question may be: What are three aspects of the organizational chart given in the BMW case that violate strategic-management guidelines? The Answers to these questions can be found in the *Case Instructor's Manual*.

Case Information Matrix

List of cases available in the Concepts and Cases version of *Strategic Management: A Competitive Advantage Approach*

Case Company	Stock Symbol	Headquarters	URL	Number of Employees	Financials (US$, millions)			Case Year
					Profit	Revenue	%	
COHESION CASE								
adidas Group	ADS	Herzogenaurach, Germany	www.adidas.com	46,300	1,599	19,558	8.2[i]	2013
SERVICE FIRMS								
Ryanair Holdings, plc	RYAAY	Dublin, Ireland	www.ryanair.ie	7,200	413	4,043	10.2	2011
The Emirates Group	n/a	Garhoud, Dubai, UAE	www.theemiratesgroup.com	67,000	986	20,934	4.7[ii]	2013
United Parcel Service, Inc.	UPS	Atlanta, GA, USA	www.ups.com	399,000	869	12,124	7.2	2013
Amazon.com, Inc.	AMZN	Seattle, WA, USA	www.amazon.com	33,700	1,152	34,204	3.3	2011
Netflix, Inc.	NFLX	Los Gatos, CA, USA	www.netflix.com	2,500	160	2,162	7.4	2011
Gap Inc.	GPS	San Fransisco, CA, USA	www.gapinc.com	135,000	1,102	14,197	7.7	2011
Walt Disney Company	DIS	Burbank, CA, USA	www.disney.com	166,000	6,173	42,278	14.6	2013
Staples, Inc.	SPLS	Farmingham, MA, USA	www.staples.com	54,100	881	25,545	3.4	2011
Office Depot Inc.	ODP	Boca Raton, FL, USA	www.officedepot.com	41,000	34	11,633	0.3	2011
Domino's Pizza, Inc.	DPZ	Ann Arbor, MI, USA	www.dominos.com	10,000	112	1,678	6.7	2013
Royal Caribbean Cruises Ltd.	RCL	Miami, FL, USA	www.royalcaribbean.com	57,000	547	6,752	8.1	2011
Carnival Corporation & plc	CCL	Miami, FL, USA	www.carnivalcorp.com	85,200	1,978	14,469	13.6	2011
JPMorgan Chase & Co.	JPM	New York, NY, USA	www.jpmorganchase.com	240,000	21,284	97,031	21.9	2013

Case Company	Stock Symbol	Headquarters	URL	Number of Employees	Financials (US$, millions)			Case Year
					Profit	Revenue	%	
MANUFACTURING FIRMS								
Proctor & Gamble Company	PG	Cincinnati, OH, USA	www.pg.com	127,000	12,736	78,938	16.1	2011
Avon Products, Inc.	AVP	New York, NY, USA	www.avoncompany.com	39,100	314	10,717	2.9	2013
Revlon, Inc.	REV	New York, NY, USA	www.revlon.com	4,800	327	1,321	24.7	2011
L'Oréal SA	LRLCF	Clichy, France	www.loreal.com	72,600	2,867	22,462	12.8	2013
Dr Pepper Snapple Group Inc.	DPS	Plano, TX, USA	www.drpeppersnapple.com	19,000	528	5,636	9.4	2011
Coca-Cola Company	KO	Atlanta, GA, USA	www.coca-colacompany.com	5,200	38	1,442	4.3	2011
Starbucks Corporation	SBUX	Seattle, WA, USA	www.starbucks.com	137,000	945	10,707	8.8	2011
Pearson PLC	PSORF	London, UK	www.pearson.com	37,000	824	8,094	10.2[iii]	2013
Bayerische Motoren Werke (BMW) Group	BMW	Munich, Germany	www.bmwgroup.com	105,000	4,226	79,386	5.3[i]	2013
Apple, Inc.	AAPL	Cupertino, CA, USA	www.apple.com	46,600	14,013	65,225	21.5	2011
Microsoft Corporation	MSFT	Redmond, WA, USA	www.microsoft.com	94,000	16,978	73,723	23.0	2013
Lenovo Group Limited	LNVGY	Beijing, China	www.lenovo.com	27,000	631	33,873	1.9	2013
Netgear, Inc.	NTGR	San Jose, CA, USA	www.netgear.com	850	86	1,271	6.8	2013

[i]Originally reported in EUR – converted at rate of 1EUR = 1.35USD
[ii]Originally reported in AED – converted at rate of 1AED = 0.27USD
[iii]Originally reported in GBP – converted at rate of 1GBP = 1.6USD

Topical Content Areas

	1	2	3	4	5	6	7	8	9	10	11	12	13	14
COHESION CASE														
adidas Group	Y	N	Y	Y	N	Y	N	N	Y	Y	N	N	Y	Y
SERVICE FIRMS														
Ryanair	Y	Y	Y	Y	Y	Y	Y	Y	Y	Y	Y	N	Y	Y
The Emirates Group	Y	Y	Y	Y	N	N	N	N	Y	N	N	N	Y	Y
UPS	Y	Y	Y	Y	Y	Y	Y	Y	Y	N	Y	Y	N	N
Amazon	Y	Y	Y	Y	Y	Y	Y	Y	Y	Y	N	Y	N	N
Netflix	Y	Y	Y	N	Y	Y	Y	Y	Y	Y	N	Y	N	N
Gap	Y	Y	Y	N	Y	Y	Y	Y	Y	Y	N	Y	N	N
Walt Disney	Y	Y	Y	Y	N	N	N	Y	Y	N	N	Y	Y	N
Staples Inc.	Y	Y	Y	Y	Y	Y	Y	Y	Y	N	N	N	Y	N
Office Depot Inc.	Y	Y	Y	Y	Y	Y	Y	Y	Y	Y	Y	N	Y	N
Domino's Pizza Inc.	Y	Y	Y	Y	Y	N	N	N	Y	N	N	Y	N	N
Royal Caribbean Cruises	Y	Y	Y	Y	Y	Y	Y	Y	Y	N	N	Y	N	N
Carnival Corp.	Y	Y	Y	Y	Y	Y	Y	Y	Y	N	N	Y	N	N
JPMorgan Chase & Co.	Y	Y	Y	Y	Y	N	Y	Y	Y	Y	N	Y	N	N

MANUFACTURING FIRMS

	1	2	3	4	5	6	7	8	9	10	11	12	13	14
Proctor and Gamble	Y	Y	Y	Y	Y	N	Y	Y	Y	N	Y	N	Y	N
Avon Products Inc.	Y	Y	Y	Y	N	Y	N	N	Y	Y	Y	Y	N	N
Revlon	Y	Y	Y	Y	N	N	Y	Y	Y	N	N	N	Y	N
L'Oréal	Y	Y	Y	N	N	Y	N	N	Y	N	N	Y	N	Y
Dr Pepper Snapple Group	Y	Y	Y	N	Y	Y	Y	Y	Y	N	Y	N	Y	N
The Coca-Cola Company	Y	Y	Y	Y	Y	Y	Y	Y	Y	N	N	Y	N	N
Starbucks	Y	Y	Y	Y	Y	Y	Y	Y	Y	N	N	N	Y	N
Pearson PLC	Y	Y	Y	N	N	N	N	Y	Y	N	Y	Y	N	Y
BMW	Y	Y	Y	N	N	N	N	N	Y	N	N	Y	N	Y
Apple	Y	Y	Y	Y	Y	N	N	Y	Y	N	N	N	Y	N
Microsoft Corp.	Y	Y	Y	Y	N	N	N	N	Y	N	Y	Y	N	N
Lenovo	Y	Y	Y	N	Y	N	Y	Y	Y	N	N	Y	N	Y
Netgear	Y	Y	Y	N	N	N	N	N	Y	N	Y	Y	N	N

1. Financial Statements Provided?
2. Organizational Chart Provided?
3. Does Company Do Business Outside the United States?
4. Is a Vision or Mission Statement Provided?
5. Business Ethics Issues Included?
6. Sustainability Issues Included?
7. Strategy Formulation Emphasis?
8. Strategy Implementation Emphasis?
9. By-Segment Financial Data Included?
10. Firm Has Declining Revenues?
11. Firm Has Declining Net Income?
12. Case Company Appears in Text for First Time?
13. Case Company Appeared in Prior Edition and Updated Now?
14. Firm Headquartered Outside the United States?

STRATEGIC MANAGEMENT
Concepts

A COMPETITIVE ADVANTAGE APPROACH

Source: © dell/Fotolia

MyManagementLab®

Improve Your Grade!

Over 10 million students improved their results using the Pearson MyLabs.
Visit **mymanagementlab.com** for simulations, tutorials, and end-of-chapter problems.

Strategic Management Essentials

CHAPTER OBJECTIVES

After studying this chapter, you should be able to do the following:

1. Discuss the nature and role of a chief strategy officer (CSO).

2. Describe the strategic-management process.

3. Explain the need for integrating analysis and intuition in strategic management.

4. Define and give examples of key terms in strategic management.

5. Discuss the nature of strategy formulation, implementation, and evaluation activities.

6. Describe the benefits of good strategic management.

7. Discuss the relevance of Sun Tzu's *The Art of War* to strategic management.

8. Discuss how a firm may achieve sustained competitive advantage.

ASSURANCE OF LEARNING EXERCISES

The following exercises are found at the end of this chapter.

When CEOs from the big three U.S. automakers—Ford, General Motors (GM), and Chrysler—showed up a few years ago without a clear strategic plan to ask congressional leaders for bailout monies, they were sent home with instructions to develop a clear strategic plan for the future. Austan Goolsbee, one of President Barack Obama's top economic advisers, said, "Asking for a bailout without a convincing business plan was crazy." Goolsbee also said, "If the three auto CEOs need a bridge, it's got to be a bridge to somewhere, not a bridge to nowhere."[1] This textbook gives the instructions on how to develop a clear strategic plan—a bridge to somewhere rather than nowhere.

This chapter provides an overview of strategic management. It introduces a practical, integrative model of the strategic-management process; it defines basic activities and terms in strategic management.

This chapter also introduces the notion of boxed inserts. A boxed insert at the beginning of each chapter reveals how some firms are doing really well competing in a growing economy. The firms showcased are utilizing excellent strategic management to prosper as their rivals weaken. Each boxed insert examines the strategies of firms doing great amid rising consumer demand and intense price competition. The first company featured for excellent performance is the 5-star airline—Singapore Airlines Limited (SIA).

adidas AG is featured as the new Cohesion Case because it is a well-known global firm undergoing strategic change and is well managed. By working through the adidas AG–related Assurance of Learning Exercises at the end of each chapter, you will be well prepared to develop an effective strategic plan for any company assigned to you this semester. The end-of-chapter exercises apply chapter tools and concepts.

EXCELLENT STRATEGIC MANAGEMENT SHOWCASED

Singapore Airlines

Singapore Airlines Limited (SIA) is the 5-star airline of Singapore. Singapore Airlines operates trans-Pacific flights, including the world's longest non-stop commercial flights from Singapore to Los Angeles and Newark on the Airbus A340-500. In late 2013, the company ceased offering those two long flights although Los Angeles is still served via Tokyo-Narita. The luxury airline has a strong presence in Asia. A member of the Star Alliance, Singapore Airlines carried around 18 million passengers in 2012, up from 16.9 million in 2011.

Singapore Airlines is very well managed strategically. The company has diversified airline-related businesses, such as aircraft handling and engineering, and owns SilkAir that manages regional flights to secondary cities with smaller capacity requirements. Singapore Airlines operates passenger services to more than 60 cities in over 30 countries around the world. Within Asia, passengers can connect to over 30 cities served by SilkAir. The company is the official sponsor of Singapore national football team and has been marketing Singapore Girl as central image to the airline's brand. *Fortune* in 2013 ranked Singapore Airlines as the 31st most admired company in the world outside the United States. In December 2012, Singapore Airlines sold its 49 percent stake in Virgin Atlantic for US$360 million.

In April 2012, Singapore Airlines phased out the 747 from its fleet after 40 years of service. A final round-trip commemorative flight was operated from Singapore to Hong Kong. In December 2012, Singapore Airlines began using the A380 to San Francisco via Hong Kong as a winter seasonal service, but still uses a Boeing 777-300ER for the remainder of the year. In May 2013, Singapore Airlines made a commitment to order 30 Boeing 787-10X to be delivered in 2018-2019 timeframe. In September 2013, Singapore Airlines began using the Airbus A380 on selected flights to and from Shanghai, China.

Singapore Airlines' passenger carriage (measured in revenue passenger kilometers) grew 8.6 percent in August 2013 year-on-year along with a 3.1 percent increase in capacity (measured in available seat kilometers). The company's passenger load factor (PLF) improved by 4.1 percentage points to 82.4 percent as the number of passengers carried in August 2013 increased by 11.7 percent to 1.7 million. Load factors improved across all regions, bolstered by strong leisure travel demand during the Lebaran/Hari Raya holidays, coupled with returning summer traffic. Traffic to West Asia and Africa also saw improvements.

SilkAir's systemwide passenger carriage in August 2013 increased 10.7 percent year-on-year along with a 13.4 percent growth in capacity. For that month, SilkAir's PLF was 1.8 percentage points lower at 71.7 percent. Singapore Airlines' cargo traffic (measured in freight-tonne-kilometres) was 5.7 percent lower in August 2013 year-on-year, while cargo capacity was reduced by 5.0 percent.

What Is Strategic Management?

Once there were two company presidents who competed in the same industry. These two presidents decided to go on a camping trip to discuss a possible merger. They hiked deep into the woods. Suddenly, they came upon a grizzly bear that rose up on its hind legs and snarled. Instantly, the first president took off his knapsack and got out a pair of jogging shoes. The second president said, "Hey, you can't outrun that bear." The first president responded, "Maybe I can't outrun that bear, but I surely can outrun you!" This story captures the notion of strategic management, which is to achieve and maintain competitive advantage.

Defining Strategic Management

Strategic management can be defined as the art and science of formulating, implementing, and evaluating cross-functional decisions that enable an organization to achieve its objectives. As this definition implies, strategic management focuses on integrating management, marketing, finance and accounting, production and operations, research and development, and information systems to achieve organizational success. The term *strategic management* in this text is used synonymously with the term **strategic planning**. The latter term is more often used in the business world, whereas the former is often used in academia. Sometimes the term *strategic management* is used to refer to strategy formulation, implementation, and evaluation and *strategic planning* referring only to strategy formulation. The purpose of strategic management is to exploit and create new and different opportunities for tomorrow; **long-range planning**, in contrast, tries to optimize for tomorrow the trends of today.

The term *strategic planning* originated in the 1950s and was popular between the mid-1960s and the mid-1970s. During these years, strategic planning was widely believed to be the answer for all problems. At the time, much of corporate America was "obsessed" with strategic planning. Following that boom, however, strategic planning was cast aside during the 1980s as various planning models did not yield higher returns. The 1990s, however, brought the revival of strategic planning, and the process is widely practiced today in the business world. Many companies today have a *chief strategy officer (CSO)*.

A strategic plan is, in essence, a company's game plan. Just as a football team needs a good game plan to have a chance for success, a company must have a good strategic plan to compete successfully. Profit margins among firms in most industries are so slim that there is little room for error in the overall strategic plan. A strategic plan results from tough managerial choices among numerous good alternatives, and it signals commitment to specific markets, policies, procedures, and operations in lieu of other, "less desirable" courses of action.

The term *strategic management* is used at many colleges and universities as the title for the capstone course in business administration. This course integrates material from all business courses, and, in addition, introduces new strategic management concepts and techniques being widely used by firms in strategic planning.

Stages of Strategic Management

The **strategic-management process** consists of three stages: strategy formulation, strategy implementation, and strategy evaluation. **Strategy formulation** includes developing a vision and mission, identifying an organization's external opportunities and threats, determining internal strengths and weaknesses, establishing long-term objectives, generating alternative strategies, and choosing particular strategies to pursue. Strategy-formulation issues include deciding what new businesses to enter, what businesses to abandon, whether to expand operations or diversify, whether to enter international markets, whether to merge or form a joint venture, and how to avoid a hostile takeover.

Because no organization has unlimited resources, strategists must decide which alternative strategies will benefit the firm most. Strategy-formulation decisions commit an organization to specific products, markets, resources, and technologies over an extended period of time. Strategies determine long-term competitive advantages. For better or worse, strategic decisions have major multifunctional consequences and enduring effects on an organization. Top managers have the best perspective to understand fully the ramifications of strategy-formulation decisions; they have the authority to commit the resources necessary for implementation.

Strategy implementation requires a firm to establish annual objectives, devise policies, motivate employees, and allocate resources so that formulated strategies can be executed. Strategy implementation includes developing a strategy-supportive culture, creating an effective organizational structure, redirecting marketing efforts, preparing budgets, developing and using information systems, and linking employee compensation to organizational performance.

Strategy implementation often is called the "action stage" of strategic management. Implementing strategy means mobilizing employees and managers to put formulated strategies into action. Often considered to be the most difficult stage in strategic management, strategy implementation requires personal discipline, commitment, and sacrifice. Successful strategy implementation hinges on managers' ability to motivate employees, which is more an art than a science. Strategies formulated but not implemented serve no useful purpose.

Interpersonal skills are especially critical for successful strategy implementation. Strategy-implementation activities affect all employees and managers in an organization. Every division and department must decide on answers to questions such as "What must we do to implement our part of the organization's strategy?" and "How best can we get the job done?" The challenge of implementation is to stimulate managers and employees throughout an organization to work with pride and enthusiasm toward achieving stated objectives.

Strategy evaluation is the final stage in strategic management. Managers desperately need to know when particular strategies are not working well; strategy evaluation is the primary means for obtaining this information. All strategies are subject to future modification because external and internal factors are constantly changing. Three fundamental strategy-evaluation activities are (1) reviewing external and internal factors that are the bases for current strategies, (2) measuring performance, and (3) taking corrective actions. Strategy evaluation is needed because success today is no guarantee of success tomorrow! Success always creates new and different problems; complacent organizations experience demise.

Formulation, implementation, and evaluation of strategy activities occur at three hierarchical levels in a large organization: corporate, divisional or strategic business unit, and functional. By fostering communication and interaction among managers and employees across hierarchical levels, strategic management helps a firm function as a competitive team. Most small businesses and some large businesses do not have divisions or strategic business units; they have only the corporate and functional levels. Nevertheless, managers and employees at these two levels should be actively involved in strategic-management activities.

Peter Drucker says the prime task of strategic management is thinking through the overall mission of a business:

> that is, of asking the question, "What is our business?" This leads to the setting of objectives, the development of strategies, and the making of today's decisions for tomorrow's results. This clearly must be done by a part of the organization that can see the entire business; that can balance objectives and the needs of today against the needs of tomorrow; and that can allocate resources of men and money to key results.[2]

Integrating Intuition and Analysis

Edward Deming once said, *"In God we trust. All others bring data."* The strategic-management process can be described as an objective, logical, systematic approach for making major decisions in an organization. It attempts to organize qualitative and quantitative information in a way that allows effective decisions to be made under conditions of uncertainty. Yet strategic management is not a pure science that lends itself to a nice, neat, one-two-three approach.

Based on past experiences, judgment, and feelings, most people recognize that **intuition** is essential to making good strategic decisions. Intuition is particularly useful for making decisions in situations of great uncertainty or little precedent. It is also helpful when highly interrelated variables exist or when it is necessary to choose from several plausible alternatives. Some managers and owners of businesses profess to have extraordinary abilities for using intuition alone in devising brilliant strategies. For example, Will Durant, who organized GM, was described by Alfred Sloan as "a man who would proceed on a course of action guided solely, as far as I could tell, by some intuitive flash of brilliance. He never felt obliged to make an engineering hunt for the facts. Yet at times, he was astoundingly correct in his judgment."[3] Albert Einstein acknowledged the importance of intuition when he said, "I believe in intuition and inspiration. At times I feel certain that I am right while not knowing the reason. Imagination is more important than knowledge, because knowledge is limited, whereas imagination embraces the entire world."[4]

Although some organizations today may survive and prosper because they have intuitive geniuses managing them, most are not so fortunate. Most organizations can benefit from strategic management, which is based on integrating intuition and analysis in decision making. Choosing an intuitive or analytic approach to decision making is not an either-or proposition. Managers at all levels in an organization inject their intuition and judgment into strategic-management analyses. Analytical thinking and intuitive thinking complement each other.

Operating from the I've-already-made-up-my-mind-don't-bother-me-with-the-facts mode is not management by intuition; it is management by ignorance.[5] Drucker says, "I believe in intuition only if you discipline it. 'Hunch' artists, who make a diagnosis but don't check it out with the facts, are the ones in medicine who kill people, and in management kill businesses."[6] As Henderson notes:

> The accelerating rate of change today is producing a business world in which customary managerial habits in organizations are increasingly inadequate. Experience alone was an adequate guide when changes could be made in small increments. But intuitive and experience-based management philosophies are grossly inadequate when decisions are strategic and have major, irreversible consequences.[7]

In a sense, the strategic-management process is an attempt to duplicate what goes on in the mind of a brilliant, intuitive person who knows the business and assimilates and integrates that knowledge using analysis to formulate effective strategies.

Adapting to Change

The strategic-management process is based on the belief that organizations should continually monitor internal and external events and trends so that timely changes can be made as needed. The rate and magnitude of changes that affect organizations are increasing dramatically, as evidenced by how the global economic recession caught so many firms by surprise. Firms, like organisms, must be "adept at adapting" or they will not survive.

One company trying hard to adapt is the Washington Post Company, best known as publisher of the *Washington Post* newspaper that has a circulation of 525,000 in the Washington, DC area. But the newspaper industry is in decline globally, so the Washington Post Company recently diversified by acquiring Celtic Healthcare, a provider of hospice and home health care facilities in Pennsylvania and Maryland. Treating patients at home instead of paying for hospital stays is a much faster growing industry than selling newspapers. The Washington Post Company also owns Kaplan, a well-known source of test preparation materials, and six TV stations.

To survive, all organizations must astutely identify and adapt to change. The strategic-management process is aimed at allowing organizations to adapt effectively to change over the long run. As Waterman has noted:

> In today's business environment, more than in any preceding era, the only constant is change. Successful organizations effectively manage change, continuously adapting their bureaucracies, strategies, systems, products, and cultures to survive the shocks and prosper from the forces that decimate the competition.[8]

On a political map, the boundaries between countries may be clear, but on a competitive map showing the real flow of financial and industrial activity, the boundaries have largely disappeared. The speedy flow of information has eaten away at national boundaries so that people worldwide readily see for themselves how other people live and work. We have become a borderless world with global citizens, global competitors, global customers, global suppliers, and global distributors! U.S. firms are challenged by large rival companies in many industries. For example, Samsung recently surpassed Apple and Lenovo surpassed HP and Dell in revenues.

The need to adapt to change leads organizations to key strategic-management questions, such as "What kind of business should we become?" "Are we in the right field(s)?" "Should we reshape our business?" "What new competitors are entering our industry?" "What strategies should we pursue?" "How are our customers changing?" "Are new technologies being developed that could put us out of business?"

The Internet promotes endless comparison shopping, which thus enables consumers worldwide to band together to demand discounts. The Internet has transferred power from businesses to individuals. Buyers used to face big obstacles when attempting to get the best price and service, such as limited time and data to compare, but now consumers can quickly scan hundreds of vendor offerings. Both the number of people shopping online and the average amount they spend is increasing dramatically. Digital communication has become the name of the game in marketing. Consumers today are flocking to blogs, sending tweets, watching and posting videos on YouTube, and spending hours on Tumbler, Facebook, Reddit, Instagram, and LinkedIn instead of watching television, listening to the radio, or reading newspapers, and magazines. Facebook and Myspace recently unveiled features that further marry these social sites to the wider Internet. Users on these social sites now can log on to many business shopping sites from their social site so their friends can see what items they have purchased on various shopping sites. Both of these social sites want their members to use their identities to manage *all* their online identities. Most traditional retailers have learned that their online sales can boost in-store sales if they use their websites to promote in-store promotions.

Key Terms in Strategic Management

Before we further discuss strategic management, we should define nine key terms: competitive advantage, strategists, vision and mission statements, external opportunities and threats, internal strengths and weaknesses, long-term objectives, strategies, annual objectives, and policies.

Competitive Advantage

Strategic management is all about gaining and maintaining **competitive advantage**. This term can be defined as "anything that a firm does especially well compared to rival firms." When a firm can do something that rival firms cannot do or owns something that rival firms desire, that can represent a competitive advantage. For example, having ample cash on the firm's balance sheet can provide a major competitive advantage. Some cash-rich firms are buying distressed rivals. Examples of cash-rich (cash as a percentage of total assets) companies today include Priceline.com (63%), Altera (80%), Franklin Resources (51%), Gilead Sciences (57%), and Lorillard (54%). Microsoft, Apple, and Samsung are cash rich, as is the Cohesion Case company, adidas AG.

Having less fixed assets than rival firms also can provide major competitive advantages. For example, Apple has no manufacturing facilities of its own, and rival Sony has 57 electronics factories. Apple relies exclusively on contract manufacturers for production of all of its products, whereas Sony owns its own plants. Less fixed assets has enabled Apple to remain financially lean with virtually no long-term debt. Sony, in contrast, has built up massive debt on its balance sheet.

CEO Paco Underhill of Envirosell says, "Where it used to be a polite war, it's now a 21st-century bar fight, where everybody is competing with everyone else for the customers' money." Shoppers are "trading down," so Nordstrom is taking customers from Neiman Marcus and Saks Fifth Avenue, TJ Maxx and Marshalls are taking customers from most other stores in the mall, and Family Dollar is taking revenues from Walmart.[9] Getting and keeping competitive advantage is essential for long-term success in an organization. In mass retailing, big-box companies such as Walmart, Best Buy, and Sears are losing competitive advantage to smaller stores, so there is a dramatic shift in mass retailing to becoming smaller. As customers shift more to online purchases, less brick and mortar is definitely better for sustaining competitive advantage in retailing. Walmart Express stores of less than 40,000 square feet each, rather than 185,000-square-foot Supercenters, and Office Depot's new 5,000-square-foot stores are examples of smaller is better.

Normally, a firm can sustain a competitive advantage for only a certain period because of rival firms imitating and undermining that advantage. Thus, it is not adequate to simply obtain competitive advantage. A firm must strive to achieve **sustained competitive advantage** by (1) continually adapting to changes in external trends and events and internal capabilities, competencies, and resources; and by (2) effectively formulating, implementing, and evaluating strategies that capitalize on those factors.

An increasing number of companies are gaining a competitive advantage by using the Internet for direct selling and for communication with suppliers, customers, creditors, partners, shareholders, clients, and competitors who may be dispersed globally. E-commerce allows firms to sell products, advertise, purchase supplies, bypass intermediaries, track inventory, eliminate paperwork, and share information. In total, e-commerce is minimizing the expense and cumbersomeness of time, distance, and space in doing business, thus yielding better customer service, greater efficiency, improved products, and higher profitability.

Strategists

Strategists are the individuals most responsible for the success or failure of an organization. Strategists have various job titles, such as chief executive officer, president, owner, chair of the board, executive director, chancellor, dean, or entrepreneur. Jay Conger, professor of organizational behavior at the London Business School and author of *Building Leaders*, says, "All strategists have to be chief learning officers. We are in an extended period of change. If our leaders aren't highly adaptive and great models during this period, then our companies won't adapt either, because ultimately leadership is about being a role model."

Strategists help an organization gather, analyze, and organize information. They track industry and competitive trends, develop forecasting models and scenario analyses, evaluate corporate and divisional performance, spot emerging market opportunities, identify business threats, and develop creative action plans. Strategic planners usually serve in a support or staff role. Usually found in higher levels of management, they typically have considerable authority for decision making in the firm. The CEO is the most visible and critical strategic manager. Any manager who has responsibility for a unit or division, responsibility for profit and loss outcomes, or direct authority over a major piece of the business is a strategic manager (strategist). In the last few years, the position of CSO has emerged as a new addition to the top management ranks of many organizations, including Sun Microsystems, Network Associates, Clarus, Lante, Marimba, Sapient, Commerce One, BBDO, Cadbury Schweppes, General Motors, Ellie Mae, Cendant, Charles Schwab, Tyco, Campbell Soup, Morgan Stanley, and Reed-Elsevier. This corporate officer title represents recognition of the growing importance of strategic planning in business. Franz Koch, the CSO of German sportswear company Puma AG, was recently promoted to CEO of Puma. When asked about his plans for the company, Koch said on a conference call "I plan to just focus on the long-term strategic plan."

Strategists differ as much as organizations themselves, and these differences must be considered in the formulation, implementation, and evaluation of strategies. Some strategists will not consider some types of strategies because of their personal philosophies. Strategists differ in their attitudes, values, ethics, willingness to take risks, concern for social responsibility, concern for profitability, concern for short-run versus long-run aims, and management style. The founder of Hershey Foods, Milton Hershey, built the company to manage an orphanage. From corporate profits, Hershey Foods today cares for about 900 boys and 1,000 girls in its boarding school for pre-K through 12 grade.

Several CSOs who spoke at the CSO Summit in May 2013 in San Francisco were:

Roland Pan at Skype

Mark Achler at Redbox

Jon Berlin at Wells Fargo

Drew Aldrich at Trans-Lux

Ann Neir at Cisco Systems

Jennifer Scott at Virgin Media

Gina Copeland at Mitsubishi Electric

Raj Ratnaker at Tyco Electronics

Tim Johnsone at Hopelink

Nhat Ngo at Omnicell

Daniel Gastel at UBS

Clarence So at Salesforce

Barry Margerum at Plantronics

Vision and Mission Statements

Many organizations today develop a **vision statement** that answers the question "What do we want to become?" Developing a vision statement is often considered the first step in strategic planning, preceding even development of a mission statement. Many vision statements are a single sentence. For example, the vision statement of Stokes Eye Clinic in Florence, South Carolina, is "Our vision is to take care of your vision."

Mission statements are "enduring statements of purpose that distinguish one business from other similar firms. A mission statement identifies the scope of a firm's operations in product and market terms."[10] It addresses the basic question that faces all strategists: "What is our business?" A clear mission statement describes the values and priorities of an organization. Developing a mission statement compels strategists to think about the nature and scope of present operations and to assess the potential attractiveness of future markets and activities. A mission statement broadly charts the future direction of an organization. A mission statement is a constant reminder to its employees of why the organization exists and what the founders envisioned when they put their fame and fortune at risk to breathe life into their dreams.

External Opportunities and Threats

External opportunities and **external threats** refer to economic, social, cultural, demographic, environmental, political, legal, governmental, technological, and competitive trends and events that could significantly benefit or harm an organization in the future. Opportunities and threats are largely beyond the control of a single organization—thus the word *external*. A few opportunities and threats that face many firms are listed here:

- Availability of capital can no longer be taken for granted.
- Consumers expect green operations and products.
- Marketing is moving rapidly to the Internet.
- Commodity food prices are increasing.
- Political unrest in the Middle East is raising oil prices.
- Computer hacker problems are increasing.
- Intense price competition is plaguing most firms.
- Unemployment and underemployment rates remain high globally.
- Interest rates are rising.
- Product life cycles are becoming shorter.
- State and local governments are financially weak.
- Drug cartel-related violence in Mexico.
- Winters are colder and summers hotter than usual.
- Home prices remain exceptionally low.
- Global markets offer the highest growth in revenues.

These types of changes are creating a different type of consumer and consequently a need for different types of products, services, and strategies. Many companies in many industries face the severe external threat of online sales capturing increasing market share in their industry.

Other opportunities and threats may include the passage of a law, the introduction of a new product by a competitor, a national catastrophe, or the declining value of the Euro. A competitor's strength could be a threat. A growing middle class in Africa, rising energy costs, or social media networking could represent an opportunity or a threat.

A basic tenet of strategic management is that firms need to formulate strategies to take advantage of external opportunities and avoid or reduce the impact of external threats. For this reason, identifying, monitoring, and evaluating external opportunities and threats are essential for success. This process of conducting research and gathering and assimilating external information is sometimes called **environmental scanning** or industry analysis. Lobbying is one activity that some organizations use to influence external opportunities and threats.

Internal Strengths and Weaknesses

Internal strengths and **internal weaknesses** are an organization's controllable activities that are performed especially well or poorly. They arise in the management, marketing, finance/accounting, production/operations, research and development (R&D), and management information systems (MIS) activities of a business. Identifying and evaluating organizational strengths and weaknesses in the functional areas of a business is an essential strategic-management activity. Organizations strive to pursue strategies that capitalize on internal strengths and eliminate internal weaknesses.

Strengths and weaknesses are determined relative to competitors. *Relative deficiency or superiority is important information.* Also, strengths and weaknesses can be determined by elements of being rather than performance. For example, a strength may involve ownership of natural resources or a historic reputation for quality. Strengths and weaknesses may be determined relative to a firm's own objectives. For example, high levels of inventory turnover may not be a strength for a firm that seeks never to stock-out.

In performing a strategic-management case analysis, it is important to be as divisional as possible when determining and stating internal strengths and weaknesses. In other words, for a company such as Walmart saying that Sam Club's revenues grew 11 percent in the recent quarter, rather than Walmart couching all of their internal factors in terms of Walmart as a *whole*. This practice will enable strategies to be more effectively formulated because in strategic planning, firms must allocate resources among divisions (segments) of the firm (that is, by product, region, customer, or whatever the various units of the firm are), such as Sam's Club versus Supercenters or Mexico versus Europe at Walmart.

Both internal and external factors should be stated in specific terms to the extent possible, using numbers, percentages, dollars, and ratios, as well as comparisons over time and to rival firms. *Specificity is important because strategies will be formulated and resources allocated based on this information.* The more specific the underlying external and internal factors, the more effectively strategies can be formulated and resources allocated. Determining the numbers takes more time, but survival of the firm often is at stake, so identifying and estimating numbers associated with key factors is essential.

Internal factors can be determined in a number of ways, including computing ratios, measuring performance, and comparing to past periods and industry averages. Various types of surveys also can be developed and administered to examine internal factors such as employee morale, production efficiency, advertising effectiveness, and customer loyalty.

Long-Term Objectives

Objectives can be defined as specific results that an organization seeks to achieve in pursuing its basic mission. Long-term means more than one year. Objectives are essential for organizational success because they provide direction; aid in evaluation; create synergy; reveal priorities; focus coordination; and provide a basis for effective planning, organizing, motivating, and controlling activities. Objectives should be challenging, measurable, consistent, reasonable, and clear. In a multidimensional firm, objectives should be established for the overall company and for each division.

Strategies

Strategies are the means by which **long-term objectives** will be achieved. Business strategies may include geographic expansion, diversification, acquisition, product development, market penetration, retrenchment, divestiture, liquidation, and joint ventures. Strategies currently being pursued by some companies are described in Table 1-1

Strategies are potential actions that require top management decisions and large amounts of the firm's resources. In addition, strategies affect an organization's long-term prosperity, typically for at least five years, and thus are future-oriented. Strategies have multifunctional or multidivisional consequences and require consideration of both the external and internal factors facing the firm.

Annual Objectives

Annual objectives are short-term milestones that organizations must achieve to reach long-term objectives. Like long-term objectives, annual objectives should be measurable, quantitative, challenging, realistic, consistent, and prioritized. They should be established at the corporate, divisional, and functional levels in a large organization. Annual objectives should be stated in terms of management, marketing, finance/accounting, production/operations, R&D, and MIS accomplishments.

TABLE 1-1 Sample Strategies in Action in 2013

Walgreen Company

Do you prefer Walgreen's or CVS? Headquartered in Deerfield, Illinois, Walgreen's is deepening its penetration into the southeastern portion of the USA by acquiring firms such as USA Drug, May's Drug, Med-X, Drug Warehouse, and Super D Drug. At the same time, Walgreen's is expanding globally through acquisition of firms such as U.K pharmacy-led health-and-beauty retailer Alliance Boots GmbH. Perhaps a reason Walgreen's is acquiring firms is that its same-store pharmacy sales have dropped 15 percent in the last year, mainly as a result of selling more generic rather than prescription drugs, and their same-store-overall sales have dropped 10 percent, mainly because of the chain's exit from pharmacy-benefit manager Express Scripts Holding. Of course, their major rival firm, CVS, could also be a key reason why Walgreen's is acquiring other firms—to show net growth, despite lower organic (internal) revenue declines.

Netflix Inc.

Based in Los Gatos, California, the long-time DVD-by-mail provider is struggling to survive as the firm switches from the DVD business to (a) providing Internet-delivered streaming content and (b) expanding to overseas markets. Major rivals to Netflix include News Corp.'s Hulu and Coinstar's Redbox, who are growing rapidly, in the USA. Netflix's overseas efforts are not going well because that strategy requires country-by-country deals to line up video content. In a recent quarter, Netflix lost 850,000 DVD subscribers and added 530,000 movie and TV-show streaming customers. Netflix's international streaming business lost about $400 million in 2012.

Microsoft

Based in Redmond, Washington, Microsoft added 35 retail "pop-up stores" in late 2012 to go with its 30 existing retail stores in the United States and one store in Toronto. This forward integration strategy coincided with Microsoft introducing its first tablet computer, Surface, which unlike Apple's iPad, runs popular Microsoft Office apps such as Word and Excel. The Surface also has an innovative keyboard cover that makes typing easier. In addition to its new retail stores, Microsoft is also selling its new Surface tablet online, but many customers want to touch and see before buying such a product online.

A set of annual objectives is needed for each long-term objective. Annual objectives are especially important in strategy implementation, whereas long-term objectives are particularly important in strategy formulation. Annual objectives represent the basis for allocating resources.

Policies

Policies are the means by which annual objectives will be achieved. Policies include guidelines, rules, and procedures established to support efforts to achieve stated objectives. Policies are guides to decision making and address repetitive or recurring situations.

Policies are most often stated in terms of management, marketing, finance/accounting, production/operations, R&D, and MIS activities. Policies can be established at the corporate level and apply to an entire organization at the divisional level and apply to a single division, or they can be established at the functional level and apply to particular operational activities or departments. Policies, like annual objectives, are especially important in strategy implementation because they outline an organization's expectations of its employees and managers. Policies allow consistency and coordination within and between organizational departments.

Substantial research suggests that a healthier workforce can more effectively and efficiently implement strategies. Smoking has become a heavy burden for Europe's state-run social welfare systems, with smoking-related diseases costing more than $100 billion a year. Smoking also is a huge burden on companies worldwide, so firms are continually implementing policies to curtail smoking. Starbucks in mid-2013 banned smoking within 25 feet of its 7,000 stores not located inside another retail establishment.

Hotel and motels in the United States are rapidly going "smoke-free throughout" with more than 13,000 now having this policy. The American Hotel and Lodging Association says there are 50,800 hotel/motels in the USA with 15 or more rooms. All Marriotts are now nonsmoking. Almost all (except Hertz) car rental companies are exclusively nonsmoking, including Avis, Dollar, Thrifty, and Budget. Most rental car companies charge a $250 cleaning fee if a customer smokes in their rental vehicle. More cigarettes are smoked in Russia per capita (2,786) than any other country in the world, but that country in 2013 instituted strict, mandatory new antismoking policies among all restaurants and bars and government facilities.[11] Sixty percent of men in Russia smoke. Other heavily smoking countries per capita include Japan (1,841), China (1,711), and Indonesia (1,085), compared to the USA (1,028). Excise taxes in Russia on tobacco products are set to rise 135 percent by 2015. About 400,000 Russians die each year as a result of smoking, costing the country 1.5 trillion rubles ($48.1 billion) annually in health-care costs.

The Strategic-Management Model

The strategic-management process can best be studied and applied using a model. Every model represents some kind of process. The framework illustrated in Figure 1-1 with white shading is a widely accepted, comprehensive model of the strategic-management process.[12] This model does not guarantee success, but it does represent a clear and practical approach for formulating, implementing, and evaluating strategies. Relationships among major components of the strategic-management process are shown in the model, which appears in all subsequent chapters with appropriate areas

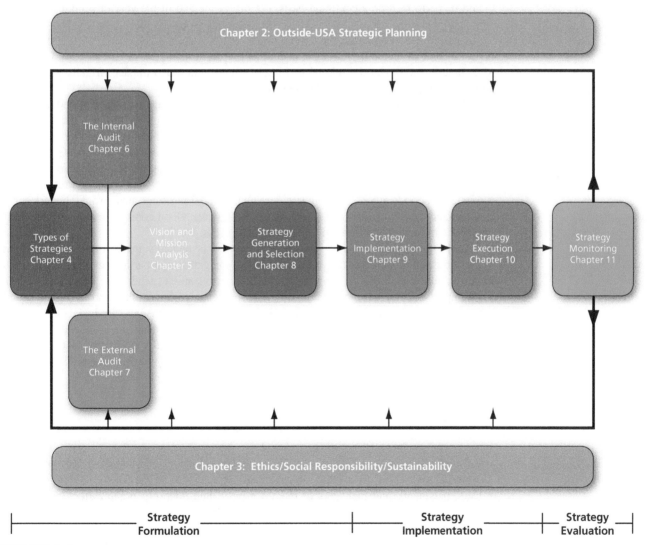

FIGURE 1-1

A Comprehensive Strategic-Management Model

Source: Fred R. David, adapted from "How Companies Define Their Mission," *Long Range Planning* 22, no. 3 (June 1988): 40, © Fred R. David.

shaped to show the particular focus of each chapter. These are three important questions to answer in developing a strategic plan:

> Where are we now?
>
> Where do we want to go?
>
> How are we going to get there?

Identifying an organization's existing vision, mission, objectives, and strategies is the logical starting point for strategic management because a firm's present situation and condition may preclude certain strategies and may even dictate a particular course of action. Every organization has a vision, mission, objectives, and strategy, even if these elements are not consciously designed, written, or communicated. The answer to where an organization is going can be determined largely by where the organization has been!

The strategic-management process is dynamic and continuous. A change in any one of the major components in the model can necessitate a change in any or all of the other components. For instance, African countries coming online could represent a major opportunity and require a change in long-term objectives and strategies; a failure to accomplish annual objectives could require a change in policy; or a major competitor's change in strategy could require a change in the firm's mission. Therefore, strategy formulation, implementation, and evaluation activities should be performed on a continual basis, not just at the end of the year or semiannually. The strategic-management process never really ends.

Note in the **strategic-management model** that business ethics, social responsibility, and environmental sustainability issues impact all activities in the model as discussed in Chapter 3. Also, note in the model that global and international issues also impact virtually all strategic decisions today, as described in detail in Chapter 2.

The strategic-management process is not as cleanly divided and neatly performed in practice as the strategic-management model suggests. Strategists do not go through the process in lockstep fashion. Generally, there is give-and-take among hierarchical levels of an organization. Many organizations conduct formal meetings semiannually to discuss and update the firm's vision, mission, opportunities, threats, strengths, weaknesses, strategies, objectives, policies, and performance. These meetings are commonly held off-premises and are called **retreats**. The rationale for periodically conducting strategic-management meetings away from the work site is to encourage more creativity and candor from participants. Good communication and feedback are needed throughout the strategic-management process.

Application of the strategic-management process is typically more formal in larger and well-established organizations. Formality refers to the extent that participants, responsibilities, authority, duties, and approach are specified. Smaller businesses tend to be less formal. Firms that compete in complex, rapidly changing environments, such as technology companies, tend to be more formal in strategic planning. Firms that have many divisions, products, markets, and technologies also tend to be more formal in applying strategic-management concepts. Greater formality in applying the strategic-management process is usually positively associated with the cost, comprehensiveness, accuracy, and success of planning across all types and sizes of organizations.[13]

Benefits of Strategic Management

Strategic management allows an organization to be more proactive than reactive in shaping its own future; it allows an organization to initiate and influence (rather than just respond to) activities—and thus to exert control over its own destiny. Small business owners, chief executive officers, presidents, and managers of many for-profit and nonprofit organizations have recognized and realized the benefits of strategic management.

Historically, the principal benefit of strategic management has been to help organizations formulate better strategies through the use of a more systematic, logical, and rational approach to strategic choice. This certainly continues to be a major benefit of strategic management, but research studies now indicate that the process, rather than the decision or document, is the more important contribution of strategic management.[14] *Communication is a key to successful strategic management.* Through involvement in the process, in other words, through dialogue

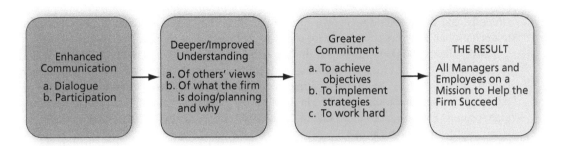

FIGURE 1-2

Benefits to a Firm That Does Strategic Planning

and participation, managers and employees become committed to supporting the organization. Figure 1-2 illustrates this intrinsic benefit of a firm engaging in strategic planning. Note that all firms need all employees "on a mission" to help the firm succeed. Dale McConkey said "plans are less important than planning."

The manner in which strategic management is carried out is thus exceptionally important. A major aim of the process is to achieve understanding and commitment from all managers and employees. Understanding may be the most important benefit of strategic management, followed by commitment. When managers and employees understand what the organization is doing and why, they often feel a part of the firm and become committed to assisting it. This is especially true when employees also understand links between their own compensation and organizational performance. Managers and employees become surprisingly creative and innovative when they understand and support the firm's mission, objectives, and strategies. A great benefit of strategic management, then, is the opportunity that the process provides to empower individuals. **Empowerment** is the act of strengthening employees' sense of effectiveness by encouraging them to participate in decision making and to exercise initiative and imagination, and rewarding them for doing so. William Fulmer said "you want your people to run the business as it if were their own."

Strategic planning is a learning, helping, educating, and supporting process, not merely a paper-shuffling activity among top executives. Strategic-management dialogue is more important than a nicely bound strategic-management document.[15] The worst thing strategists can do is develop strategic plans themselves and then present them to operating managers to execute. Through involvement in the process, line managers become "owners" of the strategy. Ownership of strategies by the people who have to execute them is a key to success!

Although making good strategic decisions is the major responsibility of an organization's owner or chief executive officer, both managers and employees must also be involved in strategy formulation, implementation, and evaluation activities. Participation is a key to gaining commitment for needed changes.

An increasing number of corporations and institutions are using strategic management to make effective decisions. But strategic management is not a guarantee for success; it can be dysfunctional if conducted haphazardly.

Financial Benefits

Research indicates that organizations that use strategic-management concepts are more profitable and successful than those that do not.[16] Businesses using strategic-management concepts show significant improvement in sales, profitability, and productivity compared to firms without systematic planning activities. High-performing firms tend to do systematic planning to prepare for future fluctuations in their external and internal environments. Firms with planning systems more closely resembling strategic-management theory generally exhibit superior long-term financial performance relative to their industry.

High-performing firms seem to make more informed decisions with good anticipation of both short- and long-term consequences. In contrast, firms that perform poorly often engage in activities that are shortsighted and do not reflect good forecasting of future conditions. Strategists of low-performing organizations are often preoccupied with solving internal problems and meeting paperwork deadlines. They typically underestimate their competitors' strengths and overestimate their own firm's strengths. They often attribute weak performance to uncontrollable factors such as a poor economy, technological change, or foreign competition.

More than 100,000 businesses in the USA fail annually. Business failures include bankruptcies, foreclosures, liquidations, and court-mandated receiverships. Although many factors besides a lack of effective strategic management can lead to business failure, the planning concepts and tools described in this text can yield substantial financial benefits for any organization. The business failure rate in the USA fell dramatically in 2012/2013, but rates rose significantly throughout Europe.

Nonfinancial Benefits

Besides helping firms avoid financial demise, strategic management offers other tangible benefits, such as an enhanced awareness of external threats, an improved understanding of competitors' strategies, increased employee productivity, reduced resistance to change, and a clearer understanding of performance–reward relationships. Strategic management enhances the problem-prevention capabilities of organizations because it promotes interaction among managers at all divisional and functional levels. Firms that have nurtured their managers and employees, shared organizational objectives with them, empowered them to help improve the product or service, and recognized their contributions can turn to them for help in a pinch because of this interaction.

In addition to empowering managers and employees, strategic management often brings order and discipline to an otherwise floundering firm. It can be the beginning of an efficient and effective managerial system. Strategic management may renew confidence in the current business strategy or point to the need for corrective actions. The strategic-management process provides a basis for identifying and rationalizing the need for change to all managers and employees of a firm; it helps them view change as an opportunity rather than as a threat. Some nonfinancial benefits of a firm utilizing strategic management, according to Greenley, are increased discipline, improved coordination, enhanced communication, reduced resistance to change, increased forward thinking, improved decision-making, increased synergy, and more effective allocation of time and resources.[17]

Why Some Firms Do No Strategic Planning

Some firms do no strategic planning, and some firms do strategic planning but receive no support from managers and employees. Ten reasons (excuses) often given for poor or no strategic planning in a firm are as follows:

1. No formal training in strategic management
2. No understanding of or appreciation for the benefits of planning
3. No monetary rewards for doing planning
4. No punishment for not planning
5. Too busy "firefighting" (resolving internal crises) to plan ahead
6. To view planning as a waste of time, since no product/service is made
7. Laziness; effective planning takes time and effort; time is money
8. Content with current success; failure to realize that success today is no guarantee for success tomorrow; even Apple Inc. is an example
9. Overconfident
10. Prior bad experience with strategic planning done sometime/somewhere

Pitfalls in Strategic Planning

Strategic planning is an involved, intricate, and complex process that takes an organization into uncharted territory. It does not provide a ready-to-use prescription for success; instead, it takes the organization through a journey and offers a framework for addressing questions and solving problems. Being aware of potential pitfalls and being prepared to address them is essential to success.

Some pitfalls to watch for and avoid in strategic planning are these:

- Using strategic planning to gain control over decisions and resources
- Doing strategic planning only to satisfy accreditation or regulatory requirements
- Too hastily moving from mission development to strategy formulation
- Failing to communicate the plan to employees, who continue working in the dark
- Top managers making many intuitive decisions that conflict with the formal plan
- Top managers not actively supporting the strategic-planning process
- Failing to use plans as a standard for measuring performance
- Delegating planning to a "planner" rather than involving all managers
- Failing to involve key employees in all phases of planning
- Failing to create a collaborative climate supportive of change
- Viewing planning as unnecessary or unimportant
- Becoming so engrossed in current problems that insufficient or no planning is done
- Being so formal in planning that flexibility and creativity are stifled[18]

Guidelines for Effective Strategic Management

Failing to follow certain guidelines in conducting strategic management can foster criticisms of the process and create problems for the organization. Issues such as "Is strategic management in our firm a people process or a paper process?" should be addressed. Some organizations spend an inordinate amount of time developing a strategic plan, but then fail to follow through with effective implementation. Change and results in a firm come through implementation, not through formulation, although effective formulation is critically important for successful implementation. Continual evaluation of strategies is also essential because the world changes so rapidly that existing strategies can need modifying often.

Strategic management must not become a self-perpetuating bureaucratic mechanism. Rather, it must be a self-reflective learning process that familiarizes managers and employees in the organization with key strategic issues and feasible alternatives for resolving those issues. Strategic management must not become ritualistic, stilted, orchestrated, or too formal, predictable, and rigid. Words supported by numbers, rather than numbers supported by words, should represent the medium for explaining strategic issues and organizational responses. A key role of strategists is to facilitate continuous organizational learning and change.

R. T. Lenz offers six guidelines for effective strategic management:

1. Keep the process simple and easily understandable.
2. Eliminate vague planning jargon.
3. Keep the process nonroutine, so vary assignments, team membership, meeting formats, settings, and even the planning calendar.
4. Welcome bad news and encourage devil's advocate thinking.
5. Do not allow technicians to monopolize the planning process.
6. To the extent possible, involve managers from all areas of the firm.[19]

An important guideline for effective strategic management is open-mindedness. A willingness and eagerness to consider new information, new viewpoints, new ideas, and new possibilities is essential; all organizational members must share a spirit of inquiry and learning. Strategists such as chief executive officers, presidents, owners of small businesses, and heads of government agencies must commit themselves to listen to and understand managers' positions well enough to be able to restate those positions to the managers' satisfaction. In addition, managers and employees throughout the firm should be able to describe the strategists' positions to the satisfaction of the strategists. This degree of discipline will promote understanding and learning.

No organization has unlimited resources. No firm can take on an unlimited amount of debt or issue an unlimited amount of stock to raise capital. Therefore, no organization can pursue all the strategies that potentially could benefit the firm. Strategic decisions thus always have to be made to eliminate some courses of action and to allocate organizational resources among others. Most organizations can afford to pursue only a few corporate-level strategies at any given time.

TABLE 1-2 Seventeen Guidelines for the Strategic-Planning Process to Be Effective

1. It should be a people process more than a paper process.
2. It should be a learning process for all managers and employees.
3. It should be words supported by numbers rather than numbers supported by words.
4. It should be simple and nonroutine.
5. It should vary assignments, team memberships, meeting formats, and even the planning calendar.
6. It should challenge the assumptions underlying the current corporate strategy.
7. It should welcome bad news.
8. It should welcome open-mindness and a spirit of inquiry and learning.
9. It should not be a bureaucratic mechanism.
10. It should not become ritualistic, stilted, or orchestrated.
11. It should not be too formal, predictable, or rigid.
12. It should not contain jargon or arcane planning language.
13. It should not be a formal system for control.
14. It should not disregard qualitative information.
15. It should not be controlled by "technicians."
16. Do not pursue too many strategies at once.
17. Continually strengthen the "good ethics is good business" policy.

It is a critical mistake for managers to pursue too many strategies at the same time, thereby spreading the firm's resources so thin that all strategies are jeopardized.

Strategic decisions require trade-offs such as long-range versus short-range considerations or maximizing profits versus increasing shareholders' wealth. There are ethics issues too. Strategy trade-offs require subjective judgments and preferences. In many cases, a lack of objectivity in formulating strategy results in a loss of competitive posture and profitability. Most organizations today recognize that strategic-management concepts and techniques can enhance the effectiveness of decisions. Subjective factors such as attitudes toward risk, concern for social responsibility, and organizational culture will always affect strategy-formulation decisions, but organizations need to be as objective as possible in considering qualitative factors. Table 1-2 summarizes important guidelines for the strategic-planning process to be effective.

Comparing Business and Military Strategy

A strong military heritage underlies the study of strategic management. Terms such as *objectives, mission, strengths*, and *weaknesses* first were formulated to address problems on the battlefield. According to *Webster's New World Dictionary*, strategy is "the science of planning and directing large-scale military operations, of maneuvering forces into the most advantageous position prior to actual engagement with the enemy"[20]. The word *strategy* comes from the Greek *strategos*, which refers to a military general and combines *stratos* (the army) and *ago* (to lead). The history of strategic planning began in the military. A key aim of both business and military strategy is "to gain competitive advantage." In many respects, business strategy is like military strategy, and military strategists have learned much over the centuries that can benefit business strategists today. Both business and military organizations try to use their own strengths to exploit competitors' weaknesses. If an organization's overall strategy is wrong (ineffective), then all the efficiency in the world may not be enough to allow success. Business or military success is generally not the happy result of accidental strategies. Rather, success is the product of both continuous attention to changing external and internal conditions and the formulation and implementation of insightful adaptations to those conditions. The element of surprise provides great competitive advantages in both military and business strategy; information systems that provide data on opponents' or competitors' strategies and resources are also vitally important.

Of course, a fundamental difference between military and business strategy is that business strategy is formulated, implemented, and evaluated with an assumption of *competition*, whereas military strategy is based on an assumption of *conflict*. Nonetheless, military conflict and business competition are so similar that many strategic-management techniques apply equally to both. Business strategists have access to valuable insights that military thinkers have refined over time. Superior strategy formulation and implementation can overcome an opponent's superiority in numbers and resources.

Born in Pella in 356 B.C.E., Alexander the Great was king of Macedon, a state in northern ancient Greece. Tutored by Aristotle until the age of 16, Alexander had created one of the largest empires of the ancient world by the age of 30, stretching from the Ionian Sea to the Himalayas. Alexander was undefeated in battle and is considered one of history's most successful commanders. He became the measure against which military leaders even today compare themselves, and military academies throughout the world still teach his strategies and tactics. Alexander the Great once said: *"Greater is an army of sheep led by a lion, than an army of lions led be a sheep."* This quote reveals the overwhelming importance of an excellent strategic plan for any organization to succeed. The legendary Alabama football coach Bear Bryant once said: *I will defeat the opposing coach's team with my players, but if given a week's notice, I could defeat the opposing coach's team with his players and he take my players.*

Both business and military organizations must adapt to change and constantly improve to be successful. Too often, firms do not change their strategies when their environment and competitive conditions dictate the need to change. Gluck offered a classic military example of this:

> When Napoleon won, it was because his opponents were committed to the strategy, tactics, and organization of earlier wars. When he lost—against Wellington, the Russians, and the Spaniards—it was because he, in turn, used tried-and-true strategies against enemies who thought afresh, who were developing the strategies not of the last war but of the next.[21]

Similarities can be construed from Sun Tzu's writings to the practice of formulating and implementing strategies among businesses today. Table 1-3 provides narrative excerpts from *The Art of War*. As you read through the table, consider which of the principles of war apply to business strategy as companies today compete aggressively to survive and grow.

The Art of War has been applied to many fields well outside of the military. Much of the text is about how to fight wars without actually having to do battle: it gives tips on how to outsmart one's opponent so that physical battle is not necessary. As such, it has found application as a training guide for many competitive endeavors that do not involve actual combat, such as in devising courtroom trial strategy or acquiring a rival company. There are business books applying its lessons to office politics and corporate strategy. Many Japanese companies make the book required reading for their top executives. The book is a popular read among Western business managers who have turned to it for inspiration and advice on how to succeed in competitive business situations.

The Art of War has also been applied in the world of sports. NFL coach Bill Belichick is known to have read the book and used its lessons to gain insights in preparing for games. Australian cricket, as well as Brazilian association football coaches Luis Felipe Scolari and Carolos Alberto Parreira, embraced the text. Scolari made the Brazilian World Cup squad of 2002 study the ancient work during their successful campaign.

Special Note to Students

In performing strategic-management case analysis, emphasize throughout your project, beginning with the first page or slide, where your firm has competitive advantages and disadvantages. More importantly, emphasize throughout how you recommend the firm sustain and grow its competitive advantages and how you recommend the firm overcome its competitive disadvantages. Begin paving the way early for what you ultimately recommend your firm should do over the next three years. The notion of competitive advantage should be integral to the discussion of every page or PowerPoint slide. Therefore, avoid being merely *descriptive* in your written or oral analysis; rather, be *prescriptive*, insightful, and forward-looking throughout your project.

TABLE 1-3 Excerpts from Sun Tzu's *The Art of War* Writings

- War is a matter of vital importance to the state: a matter of life or death, the road either to survival or ruin. Hence, it is imperative that it be studied thoroughly.

- Warfare is based on deception. When near the enemy, make it seem that you are far away; when far away, make it seem that you are near. Hold out baits to lure the enemy. Strike the enemy when he is in disorder. Avoid the enemy when he is stronger. If your opponent is of choleric temper, try to irritate him. If he is arrogant, try to encourage his egotism. If enemy troops are well prepared after reorganization, try to wear them down. If they are united, try to sow dissension among them. Attack the enemy where he is unprepared, and appear where you are not expected. These are the keys to victory for a strategist. It is not possible to formulate them in detail beforehand.

- A speedy victory is the main object in war. If this is long in coming, weapons are blunted and morale depressed. When the army engages in protracted campaigns, the resources of the state will fall short. Thus, while we have heard of stupid haste in war, we have not yet seen a clever operation that was prolonged.

- Generally, in war the best policy is to take a state intact; to ruin it is inferior to this. To capture the enemy's entire army is better than to destroy it; to take intact a regiment, a company, or a squad is better than to destroy it. For to win one hundred victories in one hundred battles is not the epitome of skill. To subdue the enemy without fighting is the supreme excellence. Those skilled in war subdue the enemy's army without battle.

- The art of using troops is this: When ten to the enemy's one, surround him. When five times his strength, attack him. If double his strength, divide him. If equally matched, you may engage him with some good plan. If weaker, be capable of withdrawing. And if in all respects unequal, be capable of eluding him.

- Know your enemy and know yourself, and in a hundred battles you will never be defeated. When you are ignorant of the enemy but know yourself, your chances of winning or losing are equal. If ignorant both of your enemy and of yourself, you are sure to be defeated in every battle.

- He who occupies the field of battle first and awaits his enemy is at ease, and he who comes later to the scene and rushes into the fight is weary. And therefore, those skilled in war bring the enemy to the field of battle and are not brought there by him. Thus, when the enemy is at ease, be able to tire him; when well fed, be able to starve him; when at rest, be able to make him move.

- Analyze the enemy's plans so that you will know his shortcomings as well as his strong points. Agitate him to ascertain the pattern of his movement. Lure him out to reveal his dispositions and to ascertain his position. Launch a probing attack to learn where his strength is abundant and where deficient. It is according to the situation that plans are laid for victory, but the multitude does not comprehend this.

- An army may be likened to water, for just as flowing water avoids the heights and hastens to the lowlands, so an army should avoid strength and strike weakness. And as water shapes its flow in accordance with the ground, so an army manages its victory in accordance with the situation of the enemy. And as water has no constant form, there are in warfare no constant conditions. Thus, one able to win the victory by modifying his tactics in accordance with the enemy situation may be said to be divine.

- If you decide to go into battle, do not announce your intentions or plans. Project "business as usual."

- Unskilled leaders work out their conflicts in courtrooms and battlefields. Brilliant strategists rarely go to battle or to court; they generally achieve their objectives through tactical positioning well in advance of any confrontation.

- When you do decide to challenge another company (or army), much calculating, estimating, analyzing, and positioning bring triumph. Little computation brings defeat.

- Skillful leaders do not let a strategy inhibit creative counter-movement. Nor should commands from those at a distance interfere with spontaneous maneuvering in the immediate situation.

- When a decisive advantage is gained over a rival, skillful leaders do not press on. They hold their position and give their rivals the opportunity to surrender or merge. They do not allow their forces to be damaged by those who have nothing to lose.

- Brilliant strategists forge ahead with illusion, obscuring the area(s) of major confrontation, so that opponents divide their forces in an attempt to defend many areas. Create the appearance of confusion, fear, or vulnerability so the opponent is helplessly drawn toward this illusion of advantage.

Note: Substitute the words *strategy* or *strategic planning* for *war* or *warfare*.

Conclusion

All firms have a strategy, even if it is informal, unstructured, and sporadic. All organizations are heading somewhere, but unfortunately some organizations do not know where they are going. The old saying "If you do not know where you are going, then any road will lead you there!" accents the need for organizations to use strategic-management concepts and techniques. The strategic-management process is becoming more widely used by small firms, large companies, nonprofit institutions, governmental organizations, and multinational conglomerates alike. The process of empowering managers and employees has almost limitless benefits.

Organizations should take a proactive rather than a reactive approach in their industry, and they should strive to influence, anticipate, and initiate rather than just respond to events. The strategic-management process embodies this approach to decision making. It represents a logical, systematic, and objective approach for determining an enterprise's future direction. The stakes are generally too high for strategists to use intuition alone in choosing among alternative courses of action. Successful strategists take the time to think about their businesses, where they are with their businesses, and what they want to be as organizations—and then they implement programs and policies to get from where they are to where they want to be in a reasonable period of time.

It is a known and accepted fact that people and organizations that plan ahead are much more likely to become what they want to become than those that do not plan at all. A good strategist plans and controls his or her plans, whereas a bad strategist never plans and then tries to control people! This textbook is devoted to providing you with the tools necessary to be a good strategist.

Key Terms and Concepts

annual objectives (p. 45)
competitive advantage (p. 42)
empowerment (p. 49)
environmental scanning (p. 44)
external opportunities (p. 44)
external threats (p. 44)
internal strengths (p. 44)
internal weaknesses (p. 44)
intuition (p. 40)
long-range planning (p. 39)
long-term objectives (p. 45)
mission statements (p. 44)
policies (p. 46)

retreats (p. 48)
strategic management (p. 39)
strategic-management model (p. 48)
strategic-management process (p. 39)
strategic planning (p. 39)
strategies (p. 45)
strategists (p. 43)
strategy evaluation (p. 40)
strategy formulation (p. 39)
strategy implementation (p. 40)
sustained competitive advantage (p. 42)
vision statement (p. 44)

Issues for Review and Discussion

1-1. Singapore Airlines has done very well in 2013. Briefly explain whether this strategy will be just as effective going forward.

1-2. Does Singapore Airlines have its strategic plan posted on its website? Should the company do so? Why or why not?

1-3. Compare and contrast the activities involved in strategy formulation versus those involved in strategy implementation.

1-4. Given the political and economic collapse of various Middle Eastern and European countries, identify a list of companies for which gaining and sustaining competitive advantage has permanently changed.

1-5. There is a dramatic shift in mass retailing to become smaller. Give four reasons for this phenomenon, with corporate examples of each.

1-6. Avoid being merely descriptive in your written or oral case analysis; rather, be prescriptive, insightful, and forward-looking throughout your project. Discuss the meaning of this sentence.

1-7. Briefly explain what Dale McConkey means when he says, "plans are less important than planning."

1-8. In terms of developing a strategic plan, explain what Edward Deming means by "In God we trust. All others bring data."

1-9. In an organization, at which three hierarchal levels would strategy formulation, implementation, and evaluation activities occur?

1-10. Explain Einstein's rationale for saying "Imagination is more important than knowledge." Would you agree with Einstein? Why?

1-11. Explain Drucker's statement "I believe in intuition only if you discipline it." Do you agree with it? Give reasons for your answer.

1-12. Strategic management is all about gaining and maintaining competitive advantage. Explain using examples.

1-13. Based on the definition of strategists in Chapter 1, identify the top three strategists that you have personally spoken to, and interacted with.

1-14. Would the collapse of the euro be a major threat, or opportunity, for your college or university? Why? In your opinion, what is the probability of such a collapse?

1-15. Strategic management is not a panacea for success. It can be dysfunctional if conducted haphazardly. Give five examples of potential "haphazard" aspects of the planning process.

1-16. Explain why open-mindedness is an important guideline for effective strategic management.

1-17. Explain how and why firms use social networks these days to gain a competitive advantage.

1-18. Compare and contrast vision statements with mission statements.

1-19. Identify the top 10 external factors that you feel are affecting your university. Rank them with one being most important.

1-20. In order of importance, list six benefits of a firm engaging in strategic management.

1-21. Rank six reasons, in order of their importance, why firms don't have strategic plans.

1-22. Identify six guidelines required while conducting strategic management activities.

1-23. Discuss how relevant you think Sun Tzu's *Art of War* writings are, for firms today, in developing and carrying out a strategic plan.

1-24. Determine the ways and means that your college or university does strategic planning, and report on these efforts to your class.

1-25. Go to the Strategy club website (www.strategyclub.com) and describe the strategic planning products offered.

1-26. Compare and contrast the extent to which strategic-planning concepts are used by companies in your country with those in the United States.

1-27. Would strategy formulation or strategy implementation concepts differ more across countries? Why?

1-28. Compare strategic planning with long range planning.

1-29. Which three activities comprise strategy evaluation? Why is strategy evaluation important, even for successful firms?

1-30. Explain how a firm can achieve sustained competitive advantage.

1-31. Identify and give an overview of three social networking sites that firms are using to gain competitive advantage.

1-32. List four strategists whom you know personally. Rank them on their effectiveness as a leader in their organization.

1-33. List six characteristics of objectives, using examples.

1-34. Conduct an Internet research to determine what percentage of your country's population smoke. What implications does this have for firms in your country?

1-35. List four financial and four nonfinancial benefits of a firm engaging in strategic planning.

1-36. Discuss the comparisons between business strategy and military strategy.

1-37. Briefly explain whether strategic planning should be more of a people-process than a paper process.

1-38. Do you agree with the fact that strategic planning should not be controlled by technicians. Briefly explain the reasons for your answer.

1-39. According to Sun Tzu, warfare is based on deception. Should strategic planning be based on deception? Explain.

1-40. Explain Sun Tzu's statement "Generally, in war the best policy is to take a state intact; to ruin it is inferior to this." Is this true in corporate strategic planning? Explain.

1-41. What is Singapore Airlines' competitive advantage? How can this advantage be sustained?

1-42. Are there any compelling reasons why the external audit, and internal audit, should not be conducted simultaneously?

1-43. Which stage of strategic management do you feel is the most important? Give reasons for your answer.

1-44. Should strategic planning be more open or closed (i.e., hidden or transparent)? Why?

1-45. Discuss the extent to which strategic planning concepts would be applicable to individuals managing their own lives.

MyManagementLab®

Go to **mymanagementlab.com** for the following Assisted-graded writing questions:

1-46. Strengths and weaknesses should be determined relative to competitors, or by elements of being, or relative to a firm's own objectives. Explain.

1-47. What are the three stages in strategic management?

Which stage is more analytical? Which relies most on empowerment to be successful? Which relies most on statistics? Justify your answers.

Current Readings

Foote, Nathaniel, Russell Eisenstat, and Tobias Fredberg. "The Higher-Ambition Leader." *Harvard Business Review* (September 2011): 94.

Frisch, Bob. "Who Really Makes the Big Decisions in Your Company?" *Harvard Business Review* (December 2011): 104.

Gavetti, Giovanni. "The New Psychology of Strategic Leadership." *Harvard Business Review* (July–August 2011): 118.

Isaacson, Walter. "The Real Leadership Lessons of Steve Jobs." *Harvard Business Review* (April 2012): 92.

Lafley, A. G. and Noel M. Tichy. "The Art and Science of Finding the Right CEO." *Harvard Business Review* (October 2011): 66.

Leavy, Brian. "Michael Beer—Higher Ambition Leadership." *Strategy and Leadership* 40, no. 4 (2012): 5–11.

Reeves, Martin and Mike Deimler. "Adaptability: The New Competitive Advantage." *Harvard Business Review* (July–August 2011): 134.

Reeves, Martin, Claire Love, and Philipp Tillmanns. "Your Strategy Needs a Strategy." *Harvard Business Review* (September 2012): 56.

Ronda-Pupo, Guillermo Armando, and Luis Ángel Guerras. "Dynamics of the Evolution of the Strategy Concept 1962–2008: A Co-word Analysis." *Strategic Management Journal* 33, no. 2 (February 2012): 162–188.

Stieger, Daniel, Kurt Matzler, Sayan Chatterjee, and Florian Ladstaetter-Fussenegger. "Democratizing Strategy: How Crowdsourcing Can Be Used for Strategy Dialogues." *Inside CMR* 54, no. 4 (Summer 2012): 44.

Zachary, Miles A., Aaron F. McKenny, Jeremy C. Short, and David J. Ketchen. "Strategy in Motion: Using Motion Pictures to Illustrate Strategic Management Concepts." *Business Horizons* 55, no. 1 (January 2012): 5–10.

Zahra, Shaker A., and Satish Nambisan. "Entrepreneurship and Strategic Thinking in Business Ecosystems." *Business Horizons* 55, no. 3 (May 2012): 219–229.

Zook, Chris, and James Allen. "The Great Repeatable Business Model." *Harvard Business Review* (November 2011): 106.

THE COHESION CASE

adidas Group – 2013

Forest R. and Fred R. David
Francis Marion University
www.adidas-group.com

Headquartered in Herzogenaurach, Germany, adidas AG is a sports apparel and footwear manufacturer and parent company of the adidas Group, which includes the Reebok sportswear company, the TaylorMade-adidas Golf, and Rockport footwear, as well as many other globally-known brands. Besides sports footwear, adidas also produces accessory products such as bags, shirts, watches, eyewear, and other sports- and clothing-related goods. The company is the largest sportswear manufacturer in Europe and the second-largest sportswear manufacturer in the world, with Nike being the first.

The company sells sports shoes, apparel, and equipment, sporting its three-stripe design in 170 countries and focuses on training equipment and apparel for sports such as soccer, basketball, and track athletics, as well as lifestyle goods including SLVR and Y-3 fashion brands. adidas has three segments: Wholesale, Retail, and Other Business. The Wholesale division supplies adidas and Reebok products to retailers globally, while the company's Retail segment operates almost 2,500 Reebok and adidas stores. The Other Business segment includes TaylorMade-adidas Golf, Rockport, Reebok-CCM Hockey, and other brands.

History

At the age of 20, Adolf 'Adi' Dassler was driven by a single idea when he made his first shoe. His vision was to produce the most durable and safest footwear for athletes in different sports. Dassler continued this vision until his death in 1978. His first shoe in 1920 was constructed of canvas due to few materials being available in the post-war period. By the 1930s, Dassler was making 30 different styles of shoes for 11 different sports and employed around 100 workers. After World War II, Dassler found himself once again making shoes with limited materials and in 1947, with only 47 workers, he resurrected shoe manufacturing using canvas and rubber from American fuel tanks. His brother, Rudolf, founded rival company Puma, which is also headquartered in Herzogenaurach. Dassler made the first post-war sports shoes in 1949 and formally registered his company adidas, which is the first three letters of his first and last names. To this day, adidas is still referred to as the "Three Stripes Company."

Perhaps the earliest and greatest pioneer in sports marketing, Dassler garnered many famous athletes to endorse his product, including Jesse Owens, Muhammad Ali, Franz Beckenbauer. The German football team won the 1954 World Cup wearing adidas shoes with screw-in studs, spurring the company to develop and promote many new products for major sporting events.

In January 2006, adidas acquired Reebok International Ltd., furthering the adidas Group as one of the top athletic footwear, apparel, and sports hardware producers in the world. In 2008, adidas entered the English cricket market by sponsoring English batsman Kevin Pietersen. The following year, adidas signed the English player Ian Bell and the Indian Player Ravindra Jadeja as brand spokesmen. The lines under which adidas produces and sells cricket bats currently include Incurza, Pellara, and Libro, and additionally, adidas manufactures the uniforms worn by both the England and the Australia cricket teams.

At the London 2012 Olympic Games, adidas outfitted all volunteers, technical staff, and officials. As the Official Partner of Team GB, adidas provided all British athletes in all Olympic sports with performance products, alongside Licensed and Event-Branded Olympic fan wear in those games.

Second Quarter (Q2) of 2013 Results

For Q2 of 2013, adidas reported growth in their Retail stores segment, but sales declined in their Wholesale and Other Businesses segments. Also for that quarter, adidas' revenues in Western Europe decreased 11 percent compared to the prior year. The company's sales in North America were down 2 percent, mainly due to sales declines at TaylorMade-adidas Golf. In Greater China for Q2, company sales were up 6 percent, while revenues in Other Asian Markets increased 7 percent. For Q2 of 2013, the best performing region for the company was Latin America where sales grew 21 percent.

From a brand perspective, adidas' sales at Reebok grew 11 percent while sales from the company's TaylorMade-adidas Golf segment declined 8 percent. The company's Rockport sales grew 7 percent and Reebok-CCM Hockey sales increased 2 percent.

Overall, adidas' revenues declined 4 percent to €3.383 billion in Q2 of 2013, from €3.517 billion in Q2 of 2012. The operating profit declined 2 percent to €252 million compared to €256 million in 2012. The company's net income grew 4 percent to €172 million (2012: €165 million) and their earnings per share rose to €0.82 (2012: €0.79).

adidas Segments

Wholesale

In 2012, sales in the adidas Wholesale segment grew 2 percent, driven by strong growth at adidas that more than offset sales declines at Reebok. Wholesale's gross profit grew 8 percent to €3.840 billion from €3.570 billion in 2011. Wholesale's operating profit improved 10 percent to €2.965 billion versus €2.690 billion in the prior year. In 2012, adidas' Wholesale segment increased in all regions except North America, where sales were down 9 percent. In 2012, adidas Sport Performance wholesale revenues grew 6 percent mainly a result of double-digit sales increases in the football, running, basketball and outdoor categories. In 2012, Reebok wholesale revenues decreased 28 percent due mainly due to the discontinuation of the NFL license agreement.

Retail

In 2012, adidas' Retail revenues increased 14 percent. The company's Concept stores, factory outlets, concession, and e-commerce corners were all up versus the prior year. The adidas Retail Segmental operating profit increased 22 percent to €724 million versus €593 million in the prior year. Retail sales increased in all regions, especially in the UK, Germany and France. Sales in European Emerging Markets rose 19 percent, with Russia leading the way. Sport Performance revenues grew 11 percent in 2012, Sport Style sales rose 20 percent, Reebok sales rose 12 percent, store sales for the adidas brand rose 7 percent. At year-end 2012, the Retail segment operated 2,446 stores, up 62 stores or 3 percent versus the prior year-end level. Of the total number of stores, 1,353 were adidas and 363 were Reebok branded and there were 730 factory outlets. During 2012, adidas opened 323 new stores, 261 stores were closed and 92 stores were remodeled. In addition in 2012, adidas opened 250 new concept stores, 110 concept stores were closed, 57 concept stores were reclassified as concession corners, and one concept store was reclassified as a factory outlet. As a result, the number of concept stores increased by 82 to 1,437 with 1,171 being adidas brand and 266 Reebok. Also in 2012, sales from adidas and Reebok e-commerce platforms were up 68 percent.

Other Businesses

The Other Businesses revenues increased at a double-digit rate in all regions. Revenues in Western Europe were up 16 percent led by double-digit sales growth at Other Centrally Managed Brands and TaylorMade-adidas Golf. Sales at Reebok-CCM Hockey grew at a low-single-digit rate, and revenues at Rockport declined at a double-digit rate. Sales in European Emerging Markets increased 17 percent led by strong double-digit growth at Rockport. Revenues at Reebok-CCM Hockey and TaylorMade-adidas Golf were up at a high-single- and mid-single-digit rate, respectively. North America revenues rose 19 percent, led by double-digit growth at TaylorMade-adidas Golf and Reebok-CCM Hockey. Revenues in Greater China were up 10 percent while sales in Other Asian Markets grew 12 percent. In Latin America, sales grew 37 percent, as a result of strong double-digit growth at TaylorMade-adidas Golf and Rockport. In 2012, TaylorMade-adidas Golf revenues grew 20 percent and Rockport revenues increased 2 percent. The company's Other Centrally Managed Brands revenues grew 61 percent.

Internal Issues

Vision and Mission

The overall mission of adidas is "to be the leading and most loved sports brand in the world.", whilst adidas' vision for their Retail segment is "to become a top retailer by delivering healthy, sustainable growth with outstanding return on investment." TaylorMade-adidas Golf's mission is "to maintain its status as the world's leading golf company in terms of sales and profitability." Rockport's mission is "to become one of the world's leading leather footwear brands through the innovative combination of contemporary style and engineered comfort."

Organizational Structure

Four young white male executives comprise the top management team at adidas. The individuals are listed below:

1. Herbert Hainer, CEO
2. Glenn Bennett, Director of Global Operations
3. Robin Stalker, CFO
4. Erich Stamminger, Director of Global Brands

Production

Production for almost all of adidas' footwear, apparel and hardware is outsourced to independent third-party suppliers, primarily located in Asia. The company operates ten production and assembly sites in Germany (1), Sweden (1), Finland (1), the USA (4) and Canada (3). In comparison, in 2012, adidas had 337 independent manufacturing partners (2011: 308). The number of suppliers increased throughout all product categories (footwear, apparel and hardware). Among these manufacturing partners, 76 percent were located in Asia, 16 percent in the Americas and 8 percent in Europe. In total, 31 percent of all adidas suppliers were located in China. In fact, 96 percent of adidas' total 2012 footwear volume for adidas, Reebok and adidas Golf was produced in Asia (2011: 97%). Vietnam housed 31 percent of adidas' production and Indonesia had 26 percent. The volume of footwear that adidas sources from Cambodia increased strongly in 2012. Overall for that year, adidas' footwear suppliers produced approximately 244 million pairs of shoes (2011: 245 million pairs), with the largest footwear factory producing about 10 percent of the footwear sourcing volume (2011: 9%). Rockport produced approximately 8 million pairs of footwear in 2012, a decrease of 5 percent from the prior year.

Apparel production in Turkey increases significantly in 2012 as company sourced 84 percent of its total apparel volume from Asia (2011: 83%). Europe remained the second-largest apparel sourcing region, representing 11% of the volume (2011: 11%). The Americas accounted for 5 percent of the volume (2011: 6%). The largest apparel factory produced approximately 10 percent.

R&D

R&D expenses increased 12 percent in 2012 to €128 million (2011: €115 million).

Finance

For the first half of 2013, adidas revenues increased its Retail and Other Businesses (TaylorMade-adidas golf and Rockport) but declined in Wholesale, as indicated in Exhibit 1. The company relies heavily on third-party Wholesale retail channels, including department stores, e-tailers and specialist sports retailers.. Over the past five years, adidas has evolved into a significant retailer itself, operating 2,446 stores for the adidas and Reebok brands worldwide, which comprise the company's Retail segment.

In the first half of 2013, adidas sales grew in all regions except Western Europe, as indicated in Exhibit 2. Revenues in Western Europe decreased 9 percent, as growth in France and Poland was more than offset by double-digit sales declines in the UK, Italy and Spain. In European Emerging Markets, adidas' reported slight sales growth in all countries except Ukraine. Sales in North America grew 1 percent and in Greater China rose 6 percent on a currency-neutral basis. Revenues in Other Asian Markets grew 1 percent, with higher increases in India, South Korea and Australia. In Latin America, adidas' sales grew 16 percent.

EXHIBIT 1 adidas Revenues by Category

	First Half Year 2013	First Half Year 2012	Change y-o-y in euro terms
	€ in millions	€ in millions	in %
Wholesale	4,495	4,727	(5)
Retail	1,589	1,547	3
Other Businesses	1,050	1,067	(2)
Total	**7,134**	**7,341**	**(3)**

Source: adidas First Half Year Report 2013.

EXHIBIT 2 adidas Sales by Region

	First Half Year 2013	First Half Year 2012	Change y-o-y in euro terms
	€ in millions	€ in millions	in %
Western Europe	1,907	2,098	(9)
European Emerging Markets	901	917	(2)
North America	1,716	1,728	(1)
Greater China	781	732	7
Other Asian Markets	1,064	1,162	(8)
Latin America	765	704	9
Total	**7,134**	**7,341**	**(3)**

Source: adidas First Half Year Report 2013.

In the first half of 2013, adidas' net income increased 6 percent to €480 million from €455 million in 2012. Net borrowings at June 30, 2013 amounted to €94 million, a decrease of €223 million, or 70 percent, versus €318 million at the end of June 2012.

Sustainability

For the 13th consecutive year in 2013, adidas was included in the Dow Jones Sustainability Indexes (DJSI) and the FTSE4Good Europe Index, the Vigeo Group's Ethibel Sustainability Index Excellence Europe as well as in the ASPI Eurozone Index. For 2012, adidas was included for the eighth consecutive time in "The Global 100 Most Sustainable Corporations in the World," a list that is revealed each year at the World Economic Forum in Davos, Switzerland. The company is a constituent of the STOXX Global ESG Leaders indices.

Product Areas

Football

As the world's most popular sport, football is a key strategic focus for adidas, and the company puts research and development into technologies for boots, apparel, and footballs at a position of high priority. In late 2013, adidas launched a stream of new and innovative football products for the World Cup. In 2013, adidas reported successes in football, such as brand spokesman Lionel Messi being awarded the FIFA Ballon d´Or as the best player of the year for the fourth time in a row, Chelsea FC won an all-adidas-sponsored final in the UEFA Europa League, and FC Bayern Munich was recently crowned UEFA Champions League winner. At the 2013 FIFA Confederations Cup, four out of eight teams are equipped by adidas, including the World and European Champion Spain, Asian Champion Japan, CONCACAF Champion Mexico and the 2013 Africa Cup winner Nigeria. The Japan team was also the very first team to qualify the 2014 FIFA World Cup in Brazil.

The company expects to achieve record sales of €2 billion in the football category in 2014. As the official sponsor, supplier and licensee of the 2014 FIFA World Cup, to be held in Brazil, and will again supply the official ball of the tournament as well as equipment for officials, referees, and volunteers. Additionally, having extended their partnership with the Union of European Football Associations, adidas will also supply the balls and equipment for the UEFA EURO 2016 tournament. These partnerships continue adidas' 30-year history of sponsoring some of the world's largest sporting events, which also includes the FIFA Confederations Cup and UEFA Champions League. Sponsorship of high-profile events such as these provide adidas with important platforms to assert and showcase their dominance in football.

In 2012 adidas sponsored Spain winning the UEFA EURO 2012 and Chelsea FC becoming the winner of the UEFA Champions League in an all-adidas final against host club FC Bayern Munich. The adizero f50 featuring miCoach has changed the way football is played and how data is analyzed. The introduction of Predator Lethal Zones marked the successful recognition of the Predator family, the most successful boot concept in football history.

Basketball

The company is expanding its market share in the North American and Chinese basketball markets and capitalizing on the growing popularity of the sport in the emerging markets by building brand equity, leveraging its status as the official NBA outfitter, and capitalizing on relationships with some of the most promising stars of the NBA, including Derrick Rose and Dwight Howard. In 2012, adidas Basketball focused on expanding the Derrick Rose signature collection and launched the 269g adizero Crazy Light 2. Also introduced were the D Rose 3.0 basketball shoe and Derrick Rose's first signature apparel collection.

Training

In 2012, adidas introduced several new technologies and product updates, such as the Adipure Trainer 360, a training shoe for men and women offering unrestricted foot movement using lightweight and flexible materials. In 2013, adidas Training introduced the next generation of the ClimaCool and ClimaWarm apparel technologies, featuring advanced fabrics, as well as expanding the Adipure footwear range, to provide athletes with the highest functionality and comfort.

Outdoor

In 1978, climbing legend Reinhold Messner used new adidas boots to reach base camp on his way to becoming the first man to climb Mount Everest without artificial oxygen. Today, adidas offers a wide range of boots for mountaineers, climbers, and hikers, as well as technical footwear, apparel, backpacks and eyewear, sometimes in collaboration with partners such as Gore-Tex, Windstopper, Primaloft and Continental. The adidas Outdoor group has close relationships with the mountain guides from the Alpine Centre in Zermatt, Switzerland, and some of the best climbing and mountaineering athletes from around the world, including world-renowned climbers like Alexander and Thomas Huber, Mayan Smith-Gobat, Dean Potter and Sasha DiGiulian, a rising star in competitive climbing. Special adidas Outdoor offerings include the Terrex Fast R and the HydroterraShandal and the TerrexIcefeather Gore-Tex Pro-Shell jacket. In 2013, adidas Outdoor launched the Terrex Solo Stealth, the first adidas shoe with Stealth rubber designed for technical climbing, where perfect grip is essential.

Sport Style

Street-wear and lifestyle sports fashion now makes up more than 28 percent of adidas brand sales globally. Originals is recognized as a legitimate sports lifestyle brand offering a wide range of products aimed at the 16- to 24-year-old consumer.

Y-3

Y-3 athletic sportswear is elegant and chic. In 2013, the Y-3 portfolio was extended with stores in London, Vienna and Hong Kong and increased emphasis on the Y-3 global e-commerce website.

Porsche Design Sport

Working closely with Porsche Design Sport, adidas creates luxury sportswear that features leading-edge performance technologies. An adidas spokesperson in this category is José Mourinho who showcases the image of Porsche Design Sport. In 2012, the men's collection included apparel, footwear and accessories in the categories of Driving, Golf, Gym, Running, Water and Snow. In 2013, adidas launched its first women's collection and introduced it with the support of its new brand ambassador, tennis player Daniela Hantuchova. New adidas products include the Made in Germany Cleat II and Compound II as well as an exclusive offer of heli-skiing items. Porsche Design Sport is available in Porsche Design stores, adidas Concept Stores and high-end department stores.

SLVR

SLVR is a sportswear clothing product offering that combines comfort and style with advanced fabrics and techniques. In fall 2013, adidas SLVR created a global e-commerce store.

Fitness Brand

The adidas-owned brand Reebok strives to become the leading fitness brand in the world, having helped usher in the aerobics movement years ago with groundbreaking, game-changing products and marketing. While the sporting goods industry and the world have changed considerably since then, Reebok wants to help shift the paradigm and change the perception of fitness, evolving it from a chore to a series of activities and a lifestyle choice. Therefore, Reebok is on a mission to empower people to be "fit for life", supporting them to achieve their full potential in a fun, collaborative and engaging way. In 2013, Reebok significantly expanded its fitness offerings and broadened its communication of what the brand stands for and what it means to wear Reebok.

Studio

In 2013 adidas began its Reebok Studio offerings that include Dance, Yoga and Aerobics product concepts and programmes for women. Dance and Yoga products launched in spring 2013, while Aerobics launched in the second half of 2013. The key dance product is the Dance UR Lead – a technical dance shoe.

TaylorMade-adidas Golf Strategy

The TaylorMade-adidas Golf segment consists of four of the most widely known and respected brands in the sport: TaylorMade, adidas Golf, Adams Golf and Ashworth.

TaylorMade is arguably the market leader in the metal woods and irons categories, and is among the leaders in other golf categories. TaylorMade-adidas Golf is a global leader in golf apparel and is among the top three in footwear sales. In 2012, TaylorMade-adidas Golf acquired Adams Golf, a company that had focused on clubs for game improvement as well as for senior and women golfers in contrast to TaylorMade's focus on younger and lower-handicap golfers. TaylorMade is the clear market leader in metalwoods (drivers, fairway woods and hybrids). The TaylorMadeRocketBallz iron was the best-selling iron in 2012 in the USA. TaylorMade offers wedges such as the ATV (All-Terrain Versatility) wedge, with its innovative sole that makes it highly effective from a wide variety of lies. The ATV was played widely on tour in 2012, and in the USA it rose to be a best-selling wedge at retail during October 2012. TaylorMade's Ghost line of putters sell well, especially the Ghost Spider line introduced in 2013, including the Ghost Spider Daddy Long Legs. In the golf ball category, in 2013, TaylorMade launched its newest tour ball, Lethal, introduced in February 2013, as well as the RocketBallz Urethane, with its three-piece construction and a tour-validated urethane cover priced well below most urethane balls.

Rockport

Rockport shoes are popular globally; 43 percent of the total Rockport revenues in 2012 came from outside Germany. In that year alone, Rockport opened more than 40 stores in Russia/CIS, Japan, South Korea and other markets around the world.

Reebok-CCM Hockey

Reebok-CCM Hockey is a leading designer and marketer of ice hockey equipment and related apparel, equipping more professional hockey players than any other company, including NHL superstars Sidney Crosby and Pavel Datsyuk. Reebok-CCM Hockey is also the official outfitter of the NHL as well as several NCAA and national teams.

Competitors

Columbia Sportswear (COLM)

Headquartered in Portland, Oregon, leading sportswear chain, Columbia Sportswear CompanyColumbia's trademark Bugaboo parka with weatherproof shell sells well globally. Columbia offers many sportswear accessories, boots, and rugged footwear, sold under brands Columbia, Mountain Hardwear, Sorel, and Montrail. Controlled by the Boyle family and run by president and CEO Tim Boyle, Columbia recently strengthened its presence in the growing Indian market by forming a distribution agreement with the New Delhi-based Chogori India Retail Ltd. whereby Chogori will serve as the sole distributor of Columbia's brands in India.

The Indian sportswear industry is growing rapidly as Indians are increasingly taking to outdoor leisure activities. Columbia Sportswear will have to compete with local brands, like Bata, Liberty and Woodland, and international players, like Nike and adidas AG. Columbia's outdoor apparel, footwear and other products are sold in approximately 100 countries. Apart from India, the company has also formed a joint venture with Swire Resources Ltd. in China to expand the company's sales there.

Puma SE

Another rival to adidas is Puma. Both firms are headquartered in Herzogenaurach, Bavaria, Germany primarily because Puma was formed when German brothers Rudi and Adi Dassler feuded and split their family firm into adidas and Puma. Puma designs and makes footwear, apparel, and accessories sold under the Puma, Tretorn, and Cobra Golf labels. While shoes are Puma's primary product line, apparel accounts for a growing portion of sales. Puma has been expanding its athletic apparel styles to include men's golf, sailing, motorsports, and denim items. Puma also operates its own retail stores and controls product distribution in many countries. French luxury-goods giant Keringowns a majority stake in Puma.

Puma owns 25 percent of American brand sports clothing maker Logo Athletic, which is licensed by American professional basketball and association football leagues. In 2013, Puma signed multi-year deals to make kits for the Rangers FC team, the Football League Championship Wolverhampton Wanderers FC, the Serbian Red Star Belgrade, and the Arsenal Football Club.

Nike (NKE)

The world's largest shoe and apparel company, Nike designs, develops, and sells a hundreds of products and services to help in playing basketball and soccer (football), as well as in running, men's and women's training, and other action sports. Nike also markets products for golf, tennis, and walking, and sportswear by Converse and Hurley. Nike sells through thousands of wholesalers but also has more than 800-owned retail stores worldwide, an e-commerce site.

Nike's recent fiscal year ended May 31, 2013 when the company reported that revenues were up 8 percent to $25.3 billion. Nike Brand wholesale revenues increased 8 percent to $18.4 billion, while Direct-to-Consumer (DTC) revenues grew 24 percent to $4.3 billion, driven by 14 percent growth in same store sales and new door expansion. As of May 31, 2013 the Nike Brand had 645 DTC stores in operation as compared to 557 the prior year. Nike reported that revenues for its Other Businesses grew 9 percent. Overall for fiscal 2013, Nike's net income increased 9 percent to $2.5 billion and inventories were $3.4 billion, up 7 percent from the prior year.

Under Armour (UA)

A rising star in the athletic appeal industry, Under Armour is very popular among young athletes. The company has license contracts with some major American universities as a provider of sports appeal and jerseys to their athletic teams. Under Armour develops, markets, and distributes performance apparel, footwear, and accessories for men, women, and youth primarily in the USA and Canada. UA offers products made from moisture-wicking fabrics designed to regulate body temperature regardless of weather conditions. The company provides products in three fit types: compression (tight fitting), fitted (athletic cut), and loose (relaxed) extending across the sporting goods, outdoor, and active lifestyle markets.

Under Armour's footwear offerings include football cleats, baseball, lacrosse, and softball cleats, and slides. The company also provides baseball bats, football, golf, and running gloves, as well as hats, eye wear, bags, and many more sports accessories. Under Armour prides itself on technology and being a good corporate citizen. Three of their main technology marketing tools are HeatGear, ColdGear, and AllSeasonGear.

Callaway Golf (ELY)

Callaway Golf is for sale and adidas is rumored to be interested in acquiring the company. Headquartered in Carlsbad, California and founded in 1982 by Eli Callaway, Callaway Golf sells, designs, and manufactures golf clubs and balls worldwide. The company also sells many accessories such as golf bags, gloves, shoes, and other apparel. Callaway gained an early reputation for producing top quality products with their 1990 introduction of the Big Bertha Driver. Today, Callaway's most innovative breakthrough clubs are sold under the Diablo name. Callaway has produced more than 1,100 United States patents, more than any other golf manufacturer.

Callaway's CEO since March 2012 is Chip Brewer is pursuing a turnaround for the company that has not made an annual profit since 2008. Brewer is seeking to restore profitability by reducing costs, streamlining operations and building market share, Callaway **recently** cut its 2013 revenue forecast for the second time to $810 million, its lowest annual sales in a decade and down from its $850 million projection in January.

Conclusion

Nike in late 2013 wrestled away from adidas the rights to the British athletics team footwear and apparel until 2020, winning the contract after a legal battle involving current supplier adidas. The new agreement includes the world athletics championships to be hosted in London in 2017. "The scale and length of their commitment is significant and demonstrates their confidence in the future of British Athletics," said UK Athletics chief executive Niels de Vos, welcoming the deal with Nike. Media reports said the contract was worth 15 million pounds ($23.44 million), double the current deal. Athletics is enjoying its highest profile in Britain since the 1980s, following the excitement generated by the London Olympicsin 2012, and will remain the kit supplier for the British Olympic team.

A clear strategic plan is needed for adidas' future. Acquisitions may be an effective means to make inroads into Nike's market share, perhaps by acquiring firms such as Callaway Golf, or even maybe Under Armour. Using adidas' financial statements provided at the end of this case, develop projected financial statements for the company given what you would recommend adidas do over the coming three years?

adidas AG Consolidated Statement of Financial Position (IFRS) (€ in millions)

	June 30, 2013	June 30, 2012	Change in %	Dec. 31, 2012
ASSETS				
Cash and cash equivalents	1,197	1,013	18.2	1,670
Short-term financial assets	29	377	(92.2)	265
Accounts receivable	2,029	2,118	(4.2)	1,688
Other current financial assets	239	256	(6.6)	192
Inventories	2,611	2,721	(4.0)	2,486
Income tax receivables	66	57	15.7	76
Other current assets	538	482	11.7	489
Assets classified as held for sale	11	25	55.4	11
Total current assets	**6,720**	**7,049**	**(4.7)**	**6,877**
Property, plant and equipment	1,123	1,003	11.9	1,095
Goodwill	1,288	1,576	(18.3)	1,281
Trademarks	1,496	1,555	(3.8)	1,484
Other intangible assets	157	156	0.5	167
Long-term financial assets	116	103	12.7	112
Other non-current financial assets	23	33	(28.5)	21
Deferred tax assets	504	506	0.3	528
Other non-current assets	98	111	12.8	86
Total non-current assets	**4,805**	**5,043**	**(4.7)**	**4,774**
Total assets	**11,525**	**12,092**	**(4.7)**	**11,651**

(*continued*)

Continued

	June 30, 2013	June 30, 2012	Change in %	Dec. 31, 2012
LIABILITIES AND EQUITY				
Short-term borrowings	163	495	(67.0)	280
Accounts payable	1,746	1,874	(6.9)	1,790
Other current financial liabilities	61	81	(26.2)	83
Income taxes	252	260	(3.1)	275
Other current provisions	462	544	(15.0)	563
Current accrued liabilities	1,123	1,053	6.7	1,084
Other current liabilities	323	319	1.5	299
Liabilities classified as held for sale	—	0	(100.0)	0
Total current liabilities	**4,130**	**4,626**	**(10.7)**	**4,374**
Long-term borrowings	1,158	1,214	(4.6)	1,207
Other non-current financial liabilities	13	6	122.0	17
Pensions and similar obligations	258	215	20.2	251
Deferred tax liabilities	385	424	(9.8)	368
Other non-current provisions	50	48	4.3	69
Non-current accrued liabilities	42	33	28.8	40
Other non-current liabilities	28	35	(23.9)	34
Total non-current liabilities	**1,934**	**1,975**	**(2.2)**	**1,986**
Share capital	209	209	—	209
Reserves	615	909	(32.4)	641
Retained earnings	4,652	4,383	6.2	4,454
Shareholders' equity	**5,476**	**5,501**	**(0.5)**	**5,304**
Non-controlling interests	(13.0)	(10.0)	28.3	(13.0)
Total equity	**5,463**	**5,491**	**(0.5)**	**5,291**
Total liabilities and equity	**11,527**	**12,092**	**(4.7)**	**11,651**

Rounding differences may arise in percentages and totals

adidas AG Consolidated Income Statement (IFRS) (€ in millions)

	First half year 2013	First half year 2012	Change	Second quarter 2013	Second quarter 2012	Change
Net sales	7,134	7,341	(2.8%)	3,383	3,517	(3.8%)
Cost of sales	3,559	3,819	(6.8%)	1,689	1,820	(7.2%)
Gross profit	**3,575**	**3,522**	**1.5%**	**1,694**	**1,697**	**(0.1%)**
(% of net sales)	50.1%	48.0%	2.1pp	50.1%	48.2%	1.8pp
Royalty and commission income	51	52	(1.9%)	26	27	(4.6%)
Other operating income	47	47	(0.4%)	29	22	32.4%
Other operating expenses	2,980	2,956	0.8%	1,497	1,490	0.6%
(% of net sales)	41.8%	40.3%	1.5pp	44.3%	42.4%	1.9pp

Continued

	First half year 2013	First half year 2012	Change	Second quarter 2013	Second quarter 2012	Change
Operating profit	**693**	**665**	**4.2%**	**252**	**256**	**(1.9%)**
(% of net sales)	9.7%	9.1%	0.7pp	7.4%	7.3%	0.1pp
Financial income	10	17	(40.7%)	6	8	(34.5%)
Financial expenses	40	57	(30.2%)	22	29	(29.9%)
Income before taxes	**663**	**625**	**6.2%**	**236**	**235**	**0.4%**
(% of net sales)	9.3%	8.5%	0.8pp	7.0%	6.7%	0.3pp
Income taxes	182	171	6.5%	65	71	(9.6%)
(% of income before taxes)	27.5%	27.4%	0.1pp	27.5%	30.5%	(3.0pp)
Net income	**481**	**454**	**6.0%**	**171**	**164**	**4.8%**
(% of net sales)	6.7%	6.2%	0.6pp	5.1%	4.7%	0.4pp
Net income attributable to shareholders	**480**	**455**	**6.5%**	**172**	**165**	**4.1%**
(% of net sales)	6.7%	6.2%	0.5pp	5.1%	4.7%	0.4pp
Net income attributable to non-controlling interests	**1**	**(1)**	**194.1%**	**(1)**	**(1)**	**71.1%**
Basic earnings per share (in €)	2.29	2.17	5.6%	0.82	0.79	4.1%
Diluted earnings per share (in €)	2.29	2.17	5.6%	0.82	0.79	4.1%

Rounding differences may arise in percentages and totals

Source: http://www.adidas-group.com/en/investors/financial-reports/

ASSURANCE OF LEARNING **EXERCISES**

Assess Singapore Airline's Most Recent Quarterly Performance Data

Purpose

This exercise gives you practice examining the progress a firm is making in executing its strategic plan. Singapore Airlines utilizes excellent strategic management as showcased at the beginning of Chapter 1.

Instructions

Step 1	Go to Singapore Airlines' website. Click on About Us and then Investor Relations.
Step 2	Review Singapore Airlines' most recent quarterly report.
Step 3	Examine the change in performance variables for that most recent quarter versus the prior year-over-year quarter.
Step 4	What strategic changes were made during that quarter? What additional changes in your view are still needed? How is the company doing? What are key problem areas?

Gathering Strategy Information on adidas AG

Purpose

The purpose of this exercise is to get you familiar with strategy terms introduced and defined in Chapter 1. Let's apply these terms to the Cohesion Case on adidas AG.

Instructions

Step 1	Go to the adidas corporate website. Click on Investors and then Financial Reports. Download the most recent *Annual Report*. This document may be quite long, so you may want to copy the document electronically. The *Annual Report* contains excellent information for developing a list of internal strengths and weaknesses for adidas.
Step 2	Go to your college library and make a copy of *Standard & Poor's* Industry Surveys for the athletic footwear and apparel industry. This document will contain excellent information for developing a list of external opportunities and threats facing adidas.
Step 3	Go on the Internet and find and print information about adidas's three major competitors: Nike, Puma, and Callaway Golf.
Step 4	Using the information gathered above, on a separate sheet of paper, list what you consider to be adidas's three major strengths, three major weaknesses, three major opportunities, and three major threats. Each factor listed for this exercise must include a %, #, $, or ratio to reveal some quantified fact or trend. These factors provide the underlying basis for a strategic plan, because a firm strives to take advantage of strengths, improve weaknesses, avoid threats, and capitalize on opportunities. Estimate the #'s as needed.
Step 5	Through class discussion, compare your lists of external and internal factors to those developed by other students and add to your lists of factors. Keep this information for use in later exercises at the end of other chapters.
Step 6	Be mindful that whatever case company is assigned to you and/or your team of students this semester, you can start to update the information on your company by following the steps listed for any publicly held firm.

EXERCISE 1C
Getting Familiar with the Free Excel Student Template

Purpose

This exercise is designed to help strategic management students become familiar with the free Excel student template for the case analysis offered by the authors.

Instructions

Step 1   Go to the Strategy Club's website. Download the free Excel student template.

Step 2   Write a one-page summary summarizing the template and explaining why how the template will benefit you the most in this course.

EXERCISE 1D
Evaluating An Oral Student Presentation

Purpose

Quite often in a strategic management course, a team of students is required to give a 15 to 25 minute case analysis oral presentation. This exercise gives you insight on some do's and don'ts regarding oral presentations.

Instructions

Step 1   Go to Strategy Club's website and watch the student case analysis presentation given there. Critique the presentation. What are four aspects that you liked most and four aspects that you liked least?

EXERCISE 1E
Strategic Planning at Nestlé

Purpose

The purpose of this exercise is to give you experience investigating the strategic plan of large, publicly held firms such as Nestlé SA. An important aspect of formulating a strategic plan is to assess the strategic plans of rival firms. For this exercise, you are on the top management team of M&M Mars, a large chocolate company that competes with Nestlé in the confectionery business worldwide.

Instructions

Step 1   Go to Nestlé's website and review the company's recent *Annual Report*. List as clearly as you can the five major strategies that Nestlé is pursuing worldwide.

Step 2   Go to M&M Mars's website and determine as best you can what the privately held firm is doing worldwide to compete with Nestlé.

Step 3   Write a one-page paper that summarizes your assessment of Nestlé's strategic plan as compared to M&M Mars's strategic plan. Include whether you feel being privately held, as M&M Mars is, enables a firm to conceal its strategic plan from rival firms. Do you feel it is advantageous to keep strategies secret from shareholders, employees, creditors, suppliers, and other stakeholders? What would be the advantages of being publicly held?

EXERCISE 1F
Interviewing Local Strategists

Purpose

This exercise is designed to give you experience learning first hand how strategists in your city/town formulate and implement strategies. This information can be used to compare and contrast concepts presented in this textbook with practices of local strategists. Recall that strategists include owners of businesses, directors of nonprofit organizations, top managers of large firms, CEOs, presidents, and many others.

Instructions

Visit five strategists in your city. Interview them, asking the following questions. Prepare answers and report back to your professor.

1. How do you decide which strategies to implement in this organization?
2. How often do you change strategies or take a fresh look at existing strategies?
3. How many persons assist you in formulating strategies?
4. Does your organization have written mission, vision, and objective statements?
5. Is the strategic planning process in your company more secret or open in regard to process and procedure? Which approach do you feel is best? Why?

Endnotes

1. Kathy Kiely, "Officials Say Auto CEOs Must Be Specific on Plans," *USA Today*, November 24, 2008, 3B.

2. Peter Drucker, *Management: Tasks, Responsibilities, and Practices* (New York: Harper & Row, 1974), 611.

3. Alfred Sloan, Jr., *Adventures of the White Collar Man* (New York: Doubleday, 1941), 104.

4. Quoted in Eugene Raudsepp, "Can You Trust Your Hunches?" *Management Review* 49, no. 4 (April 1960): 7.

5. Stephen Harper, "Intuition: What Separates Executives from Managers," *Business Horizons* 31, no. 5 (September–October 1988): 16.

6. Ron Nelson, "How to Be a Manager," *Success*, July–August 1985, 69.

7. Bruce Henderson, *Henderson on Corporate Strategy* (Boston: Abt Books, 1979), 6.

8. Robert Waterman, Jr., *The Renewal Factor: How the Best Get and Keep the Competitive Edge* (New York: Bantam, 1987). See also *BusinessWeek*, September 14, 1987, 100. Also, see *Academy of Management Executive* 3, no. 2 (May 1989): 115.

9. Jayne O'Donnell, "Shoppers Flock to Discount Stores," *USA Today*, February 25, 2009, B1.

10. John Pearce II and Fred David, "The Bottom Line on Corporate Mission Statements," *Academy of Management Executive* 1, no. 2 (May 1987): 109.

11. Lukas Alpert, "Kremlin Cracks Down on Big Tobacco," *Wall Street Journal* (October 16, 2012): B1.

12. Fred R. David, "How Companies Define Their Mission," *Long Range Planning* 22, no. 1 (February 1989): 91.

13. Jack Pearce and Richard Robinson, *Strategic Management*, 7th ed. (New York: McGraw-Hill, 2000), 8.

14. Ann Langley, "The Roles of Formal Strategic Planning," *Long Range Planning* 21, no. 3 (June 1988): 40.

15. Bernard Reimann, "Getting Value from Strategic Planning," *Planning Review* 16, no. 3 (May–June 1988): 42.

16. G. L. Schwenk and K. Schrader, "Effects of Formal Strategic Planning in Financial Performance in Small Firms: A Meta-Analysis," *Entrepreneurship and Practice* 3, no. 17 (1993): 53–64. Also, C. C. Miller and L. B. Cardinal, "Strategic Planning and Firm

Performance: A Synthesis of More Than Two Decades of Research," *Academy of Management Journal* 6, no. 27 (1994): 1649–1665; Michael Peel and John Bridge, "How Planning and Capital Budgeting Improve SME Performance," *Long Range Planning* 31, no. 6 (October 1998): 848–856; Julia Smith, "Strategies for Start-Ups," *Long Range Planning* 31, no. 6 (October 1998): 857–872.

17. Gordon Greenley, "Does Strategic Planning Improve Company Performance?" *Long Range Planning* 19, no. 2 (April 1986): 106.

18. Adapted from www.des.calstate.edu/limitations.html and www.entarga.com/stratplan/purposes.html

19. R. T. Lenz, "Managing the Evolution of the Strategic Planning Process," *Business Horizons* 30, no. 1 (January–February 1987): 39.

20. *Webster's New World Dictionary*, Year: 1998. Publisher: Pearson plc. Edition: 4th. Edited by Victoria Neufeldt. Pearson purchased this Dictionary from Simon & Schuster in 1998, but sold it to IDG Books in 1999.

21. Frederick Gluck, "Taking the Mystique out of Planning," *Across the Board*, July–August 1985, 59.

MyManagementLab®

Improve Your Grade!

Over 10 million students improved their results using the Pearson MyLabs.
Visit **mymanagementlab.com** for simulations, tutorials, and end-of-chapter problems.

Outside-USA Strategic Planning

CHAPTER OBJECTIVES

After studying this chapter, you should be able to do the following:

1. Discuss the nature and implications of labor union membership across Europe.

2. Discuss income tax rates and practices across countries.

3. Explain the advantages and disadvantages of entering global markets.

4. Discuss protectionism as it impacts the world economy.

5. Explain when and why a firm (or industry) may need to become more or less global in nature to compete.

6. Discuss the global challenge facing U.S. firms.

7. Compare and contrast business culture in the United States with many other countries.

8. Describe how management style varies globally.

9. Discuss communication differences across countries.

10. Discuss Africa as the newest hotspot for business entry.

ASSURANCE OF LEARNING EXERCISES

The following exercises are found at the end of this chapter.

EXERCISE 2A   The adidas Group wants to enter Africa. Help them.

EXERCISE 2B   Assessing Differences in Culture Across Countries

EXERCISE 2C   Honda Motor Company wants to enter the Vietnamese market. Help them.

EXERCISE 2D   Does My University Recruit in Foreign Countries?

As illustrated in Figure 2-1 with white shading, global considerations impact virtually all strategic decisions. The boundaries of countries no longer can define the limits of our imaginations. To see and appreciate the world from the perspective of others has become a matter of survival for businesses. The underpinnings of strategic management hinge on managers gaining an understanding of competitors, markets, prices, suppliers, distributors, governments, creditors, shareholders, and customers worldwide. The price and quality of a firm's products and services must be competitive on a worldwide basis, not just on a local basis. Shareholders expect substantial revenue growth, so doing business globally is one of the best ways to achieve this end. As indicated in the boxed insert, Honda is an example business that has grown dramatically with a well-conceived rollout across the world.

The consulting firm A.T. Kearney reported in mid-2013 that the USA for the first time since 2001 has replaced China as the country with the highest prospects for foreign direct investment (FDI). Brazil is number 3, followed by Canada, India, Australia, Germany, United Kingdom (UK), Mexico, and Singapore. China's allure has dimmed lately due to rising wages, whereas the USA's surge in oil and gas production promises lower energy costs, coupled with high respect for human rights and freedom, and has led to renewed interest in the USA for FDI.

Exports of goods and services from the USA account for only 11 percent of U.S. gross domestic product, so the USA is still largely a domestic, continental economy. What happens inside the USA largely determines the strength of the economic recovery. In contrast, as a percent of gross domestic product (GDP), exports comprise 35.3 percent of the German economy, 24.5 percent of the Chinese economy, and 156 percent of the Singapore economy. Singapore's number is so high because they import oil and other products and then re-export them globally. A point here also is that the USA has substantial room for improvement in doing business globally based on the 11 percent exports to GDP number.

EXCELLENT STRATEGIC MANAGEMENT SHOWCASED

Honda

Honda Motor Company, headquartered in Minato, Tokyo, Japan, is the world's largest motorcycle manufacturer and the world's largest manufacturer of internal combustion engines. Honda was the eighth largest automobile manufacturer in the world. Honda will re-enter Formula One racing in 2015 as an engine supplier to the McLaren team. Honda annually produces and sells thousands of scooters, water pumps, lawn and garden equipment tools, tillers, outboard motors, robotics, jet engines, and solar cells. Honda has about 180,000 employees. In 2013, *Fortune* ranked Honda Motor Company as the 50th most admired company in the world.

In late 2013, Honda moved away from its time-tested nickel-metal hydride batteries to lighter, smaller and more powerful lithium ion chemistry, such as with the 2014 Accord Hybrid. Rival Toyota continues to stick with NMH batteries on its conventional hybrids, citing their reliability and lower cost. However, with its 2014 Accord Hybrid delivering an EPA-certified rating of 50 mpg in city driving, Honda now offers a full three miles per gallon better than the previous "gas economy king," the 47 mpg Ford Fusion Hybrid. The Toyota Camry Hybrid comes in at 43 and the Hyundai Sonata Hybrid at 40.Honda's 2014 Accord Hybrid gets about 10 percent better fuel economy around town than the original Toyota Prius, a dedicated gas-electric model that features a super-aerodynamic, ultralight body. The new hybrid arrived in dealerships in late 2013. The number 50 is significant because only the Prius has ever hit that EPA estimate mark for vehicles not plugged in for charging.

Honda is investing another $215 million in its Ohio operations, pushing the company's total to $2.7 billion in North American operations in only the past three years. The majority of the monies will be spent on an expansion of manufacturing capabilities at the company's Anna, Ohio, Engine Plant, while the remainder is earmarked for a new building in Marysville, Ohio. Honda already has the strongest foothold of any Japanese automaker, and produces more cars with U.S.-sourced parts than any automaker other than General Motors. Nine of Honda's 16 mass-market cars are made with over half American-made parts, according to the survey – that's more than Ford.

Honda is building a new car factory in Brazil, doubling its capacity in that country to 240,000 cars a year. The new factory is being built in Ityrapina, a city of almost 15,000, located approximately 120 miles northwest of Sao Paulo, Brazil's largest city. The existing Honda factory in Brazil is in Sumare, a city of around 100,000, located halfway between Ityrapina and Sao Paulo. The cost of the new factory, including the purchasing of the 1,433 acres it will be located on, is about $435 million. It will employ approximately 2,000 people, and produce the Honda Fit. The new plant should begin operations in 2015.

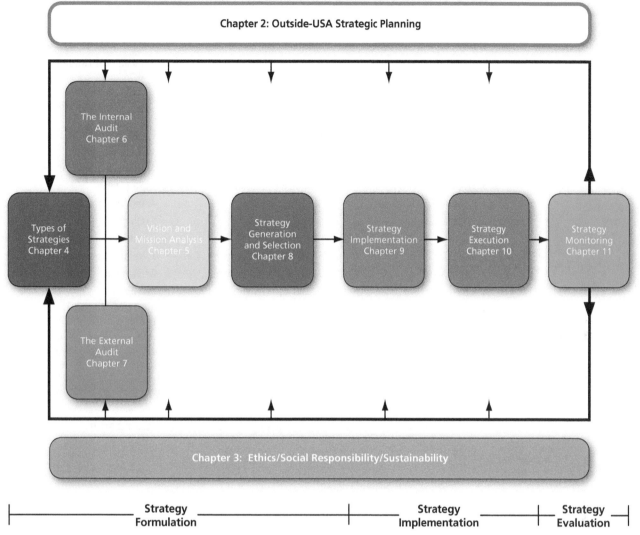

FIGURE 2-1

A Comprehensive Strategic-Management Model

Source: Fred R. David, adapted from "How Companies Define Their Mission," *Long Range Planning* 22, no. 3 (June 1988): 40, © Fred R. David.

A world market has emerged from what previously was a multitude of distinct national markets, and the climate for international business today is more favorable than in years past. Mass communication and high technology have created similar patterns of consumption in diverse cultures worldwide. This means that many companies may find it difficult to survive by relying solely on domestic markets.

It is no exaggeration that in an industry that is, or is rapidly becoming, global, the riskiest possible posture is to remain a domestic competitor. The domestic competitor will watch as more aggressive companies use this growth to capture economies of scale and learning. The domestic competitor will then be faced with an attack on domestic markets using different (and possibly superior) technology, product design, manufacturing, marketing approaches, and economies of scale.[1]

As a point of global reference, the 5 largest companies in nine different countries are listed in Table 2-1. The largest of all 45 companies listed is Walmart, headquartered in Bentonville, Arkansas, and employing 2.1 million people worldwide. *Fortune* annually determines the most admired and least admired companies in the world in terms of "global competitiveness." Table 2-2 reveals the rankings in early 2012.

TABLE 2-1 The Five Largest (by revenue) Companies in Nine Countries (2012)

Britain	India	Japan
1. BP	1. Indian Oil	1. Toyota Motor
2. HSBC Holdings	2. Reliance Industries	2. Japan Post Holdings
3. Lloyds Banking Group	3. Bharat Petroleum	3. Nippon TeleG & TeleP
4. Tesco	4. State Bank of India	4. Hitachi
5. Aviva	5. Hindustan Petroleum	5. Honda Motor
Australia	Brazil	China
1. BHP Billiton	1. Petrobras	1. Sinopec Group
2. Wesfarmers	2. Banco do Brasil	2. China National Petroleum
3. Woolworths	3. Banco Bradesco	3. State Grid
4. Commonwealth Bank	4. Vale	4. Ind. & Com. Bank of China
5. Westpac Banking	5. JBS	5. China Mobile Communi.
USA	Canada	Germany
1. Walmart Stores	1. Manulife Financial	1. Volkswagen
2. ExxonMobil	2. Royal Bank of Canada	2. Daimier
3. Chevron	3. Suncor Energy	3. Allianz
4. Conoco Phillips	4. Power Corp. of Canada	4. E. ON
5. Fannie Mae	5. George Weston	5. Siemens

Source: Based on http://money.cnn.com/magazines/fortune/global500/2011/countries/US.html.

TABLE 2-2 *Fortune's* Most and Least Admired Companies in the World for "Global Competitiveness"

MOST ADMIRED
1. Gas Natural Fenosa
2. McDonald's
3. Nestle
4. Apple
5. IBM
6. Procter & Gamble
7. Philip Morris International
8. Yum Brands
9. Caterpillar
10. RWE

LEAST ADMIRED
1. WellCare Health Plans
2. Universal American
3. Coventry Health Care
4. Amerigroup
5. China South Industries Group
6. Health Net
7. Cracker Barrel Old Country Store
8. Jack in the Box
9. China FAW Group
10. Dongfeng Motor

Source: Based on http://money.cnn.com/magazines/fortune/most-admired/2012/best_worst/best9.html and http://money.cnn.com/magazines/fortune/most-admired/2012/best_worst/worst9.html.

Multinational Organizations

Organizations that conduct business operations across national borders are called **international firms** or **multinational corporations**. The strategic-management process is conceptually the same for multinational firms as for purely domestic firms; however, the process is more complex for international firms as a result of more variables and relationships. The social, cultural, demographic, environmental, political, governmental, legal, technological, and competitive opportunities and threats that face a multinational corporation are almost limitless, and the number and complexity of these factors increase dramatically with the number of products produced and the number of geographic areas served.

More time and effort are required to identify and evaluate external trends and events in multinational corporations than in domestic corporations. Geographic distance, cultural and national differences, and variations in business practices often make communication between domestic headquarters and overseas operations difficult. Strategy implementation can be more difficult because different cultures have different norms, values, and work ethics.

For example, in 2013 Home Depot closed all seven of its remaining big-box stores in China after years of losses. That firm joins a growing list of retailers who stumbled in China by failing to consider local culture and customs. Historically cheap labor, coupled with apartment-based living in China, were two reasons why Home Depot, which entered China in 2006, never gained traction in that country. Mattel and Best Buy are other firms that faltered in China. Yum Brands, which owns Kentucky Fried Chicken and Pizza Hut, obtains almost 50 percent of its revenues from China, but the company's same-store sales in China dropped 4 percent in the fourth quarter of 2012, resulting primarily from thousands of new fast-food restaurants opening in China every year.

Even variables such as unemployment rates vary greatly across countries as indicated in Table 2.3. Note that Spain has the highest and Austria the lowest unemployment rate among the European countries listed. Unemployment rates are a good indicator of consumers' disposable income for purchasing all kinds of things, and the rates are a good indicator of a country's overall financial soundness and attractiveness for doing business.

In late 2012, France lost its triple-A rating by Moody's Investors Service after the S&P Ratings Services delivered a stinging critique of President Francois Hollande's attempts to turn the French economy around. Hollande is trying to shift 20 billion euros from payroll taxes to taxes on consumers, and he is pushing for 25 billion of new taxes to cut the country's deficit to 3 percent of GDP in 2013 from the expected 4.5 percent.

TABLE 2.3 Variations in Unemployment Rates Across Europe (2012)

Country	Unemployment Rate (%)
Spain	25.1
Greece	23.1
Portugal	15.7
Ireland	14.9
Euro-zone average	11.3
Italy	10.7
France	10.3
Finland	7.6
Belgium	7.2
Germany	5.5
Austria	4.5

Source: Based on Eurostat and Gabriele Steinhauser, "Euro Zone Considers Central Budget to Fix Cracks," *Wall Street Journal* (September 26, 2012): A12.

Multinational corporations (MNCs) face unique and diverse risks, such as expropriation of assets, currency losses through exchange rate fluctuations, unfavorable foreign court interpretations of contracts and agreements, social/political disturbances, import/export restrictions, tariffs, and trade barriers. Strategists in MNCs are often confronted with the need to be globally competitive and nationally responsive at the same time. With the rise in world commerce, government and regulatory bodies are more closely monitoring foreign business practices. The U.S. Foreign Corrupt Practices Act, for example, monitors business practices in many areas.

Before entering international markets, firms should scan relevant journals and patent reports, seek the advice of academic and research organizations, participate in international trade fairs, form partnerships, and conduct extensive research to broaden their contacts and diminish the risk of doing business in new markets. Firms can also offset some risks of doing business internationally by obtaining insurance from the U.S. government's Overseas Private Investment Corporation (OPIC).

Advantages and Disadvantages of International Operations

Firms have numerous reasons for formulating and implementing strategies that initiate, continue, or expand involvement in business operations across national borders. Perhaps the greatest advantage is that firms can gain new customers for their products and services, thus increasing revenues. Growth in revenues and profits is a common organizational objective and often an expectation of shareholders because it is a measure of organizational success.

Potential advantages to initiating, continuing, or expanding international operations are as follows:

1. Firms can gain new customers for their products.
2. Foreign operations can absorb excess capacity, reduce unit costs, and spread economic risks over a wider number of markets.
3. Foreign operations can allow firms to establish low-cost production facilities in locations close to raw materials or cheap labor.
4. Competitors in foreign markets may not exist, or competition may be less intense than in domestic markets.
5. Foreign operations may result in reduced tariffs, lower taxes, and favorable political treatment.
6. Joint ventures can enable firms to learn the technology, culture, and business practices of other people and to make contacts with potential customers, suppliers, creditors, and distributors in foreign countries.
7. Economies of scale can be achieved from operation in global rather than solely domestic markets. Larger-scale production and better efficiencies allow higher sales volumes and lower-price offerings.
8. A firm's power and prestige in domestic markets may be significantly enhanced if the firm competes globally. Enhanced prestige can translate into improved negotiating power among creditors, suppliers, distributors, and other important groups.

The availability, depth, and reliability of economic and marketing information in different countries vary extensively, as do industrial structures, business practices, and the number and nature of regional organizations. There are also numerous potential disadvantages of initiating, continuing, or expanding business across national borders, such as the following:

1. Foreign operations could be seized by nationalistic factions.
2. Firms confront different and often little-understood social, cultural, demographic, environmental, political, governmental, legal, technological, economic, and competitive forces when doing business internationally. These forces can make communication difficult in the firm.
3. Weaknesses of competitors in foreign lands are often overestimated, and strengths are often underestimated. Keeping informed about the number and nature of competitors is more difficult when doing business internationally.

4. Language, culture, and value systems differ among countries, which can create barriers to communication and problems managing people.
5. Gaining an understanding of regional organizations such as the European Economic Community, the Latin American Free Trade Area, the International Bank for Reconstruction and Development, and the International Finance Corporation is difficult but is often required in doing business internationally.
6. Dealing with two or more monetary systems can complicate international business operations.

The Global Challenge

Few companies can afford to ignore the presence of international competition. Firms that seem insulated and comfortable today may be vulnerable tomorrow; for example, foreign banks do not yet compete or operate in most of the USA, but this too is changing.

The U.S. economy is becoming much less American. A world economy and monetary system are emerging. Corporations in every corner of the globe are taking advantage of the opportunity to obtain customers globally. Markets are shifting rapidly and in many cases converging in tastes, trends, and prices. Innovative transport systems are accelerating the transfer of technology. Shifts in the nature and location of production systems, especially to China and India, are reducing the response time to changing market conditions. China has more than 1.3 billion residents and a dramatically growing middle class anxious to buy goods and services.

Business in Brazil is booming, with that country having more than a 7 percent annual growth in GDP. The capital of Brazil, Rio de Janeiro, is making massive preparations for the 2016 Summer Olympics, including a $5 billion investment program to extend the subway system, improve railroads, and construct new highways. Two firms in Rio that are growing exponentially are Petrobras, the world's fourth-largest oil producer, and Vale, the world's largest iron-ore mining company. Rio de Janeiro is Brazil's second largest manufacturing center in the country, but its scenic beauty and elaborate port facilities are world renowned.

More and more countries around the world are welcoming foreign investment and capital. As a result, labor markets have steadily become more international. East Asian countries are market leaders in labor-intensive industries, Brazil offers abundant natural resources and rapidly developing markets, and Germany offers skilled labor and technology. The drive to improve the efficiency of global business operations is leading to greater functional specialization. This is not limited to a search for the familiar low-cost labor in Latin America or Asia. Other considerations include the cost of energy, availability of resources, inflation rates, tax rates, and the nature of trade regulations.

Many countries became more protectionist during the recent global economic recession. **Protectionism** refers to countries imposing tariffs, taxes, and regulations on firms outside the country to favor their own companies and people. Most economists argue that protectionism harms the world economy because it inhibits trade among countries and invites retaliation.

Advancements in telecommunications are drawing countries, cultures, and organizations worldwide closer together. Foreign revenue as a percentage of total company revenues already exceeds 50 percent in hundreds of U.S. firms, including ExxonMobil, Gillette, Dow Chemical, Citicorp, Colgate-Palmolive, and Texaco.

A primary reason why most domestic firms do business globally is that growth in demand for goods and services outside the USA is considerably higher than inside. For example, the domestic food industry is growing just 3 percent per year, so Kraft Foods, the second largest food company in the world behind Nestlé, is focusing on foreign acquisitions.

Shareholders and investors expect sustained growth in revenues from firms; satisfactory growth for many firms can only be achieved by capitalizing on demand outside the USA. Joint ventures and partnerships between domestic and foreign firms are becoming the rule rather than the exception!

Fully 95 percent of the world's population lives outside the USA, and this group is growing 70 percent faster than the U.S. population. The lineup of competitors in virtually all industries is global. General Motors, Ford, and Chrysler compete with Toyota and Hyundai.

General Electric and Westinghouse battle Siemens and Mitsubishi. Caterpillar and John Deere compete with Komatsu. Goodyear battles Michelin, Bridgestone/Firestone, and Pirelli. Boeing competes with Airbus. Only a few U.S. industries—such as furniture, printing, retailing, consumer packaged goods, and retail banking—are not yet greatly challenged by foreign competitors. But many products and components in these industries too are now manufactured in foreign countries. International operations can be as simple as exporting a product to a single foreign country or as complex as operating manufacturing, distribution, and marketing facilities in many countries.

Globalization

Based in Wayne, New Jersey, Toys "R" Us is adding 30 new stores in China in 2013–2014 and launching heavy online selling efforts in China. The company knows that a growing middle class in China see playtime as increasingly essential. The firm's focus in China is on "educational toys," such as microscopes and building blocks. Sales of toys in China is growing about 20 percent annually, as increasingly affluent consumers make sure their children have plenty to play with, especially educational toys rather than Barbie Dolls.

Companies growing perhaps even faster than in China or India are those located in Thailand, Vietnam, Philippines, Indonesia, and Singapore in Southeast Asia. A *Wall Street Journal* article (12-4-12, C4) detailed how the growing middle class in these countries are hungry to consume products and services from around the world. The governments of these countries have become stable and are spending heavily on infrastructure projects. African countries too are rapidly becoming attractive for business. GE in mid-2013 began building a huge power plant in Tanzania in East Africa. The International Monetary Fund (IMF) reported in mid-2013 that by 2018, five of the world's fastest growing economies will be in sub-Saharan Africa. The IMF says Africa's economy will grow 5.6 percent in 2013 compared to 3.6 percent worldwide. Shareholders of all companies want high growth; Africa offers high growth.

Globalization is a process of doing business worldwide, so strategic decisions are made based on global profitability of the firm rather than just domestic considerations. A global strategy seeks to meet the needs of customers worldwide, with the highest value at the lowest cost. This may mean locating production in countries with the lowest labor costs or abundant natural resources, locating research and complex engineering centers where skilled scientists and engineers can be found, and locating marketing activities close to the markets to be served.

A **global strategy** includes designing, producing, and marketing products with global needs in mind, instead of considering individual countries alone. A global strategy integrates actions against competitors into a worldwide plan. Today, there are global buyers and sellers and the instant transmission of money and information across continents.

It is clear that different industries become global for different reasons. The need to amortize massive research and development (R&D) investments over many markets is a major reason why the aircraft manufacturing industry became global. Monitoring globalization in one's industry is an important strategic-management activity. Knowing how to use that information for one's competitive advantage is even more important. For example, firms may look around the world for the best technology and select one that has the most promise for the largest number of markets. When firms design a product, they design it to be marketable in as many countries as possible. When firms manufacture a product, they select the lowest-cost source, which may be Japan for semiconductors, Sri Lanka for textiles, Malaysia for simple electronics, and Europe for precision machinery.

Corporate Tax Rates Globally

Corporate tax rates vary considerably across countries and companies. Bermuda has a zero corporate income tax rate. Ireland has a 12.5 corporate tax rate. Many Internet companies have established headquarters and get the bulk of their European revenue in Ireland. For example, although Google has more than 300 employees in France, Google's customers in

France buy ads from Google Ireland Ltd., so Google pays France fees through a marketing agreement, rather than paying the 34 percent corporate tax rate in France. Microsoft has a similar arrangement in France as Google. Tax rates in countries are important in strategic decisions regarding where to build manufacturing facilities or retail stores or even where to acquire other firms. Japan recently cut its corporate tax rate by five percentage points, leaving the USA with the highest corporate tax rate among all nations in the world. Having the highest corporate tax rates is not a good position for the USA because it competes with other nations as a location for investment. High corporate tax rates deter investment in new factories and also provide strong incentives for corporations to avoid and evade taxes. However, it should be pointed out here that a recent *Wall Street Journal* article (7-2-13, p. A4) reported that on average, large, profitable U.S. companies pay a U.S. federal income tax rate of 12.6 percent of their worldwide income, compared to the average individual federal income-tax rate of 7.2 percent.

Since the 1980s, most countries have been steadily lowering their tax rates, but the United States has not cut its top statutory corporate tax rate since 1993. Top combined statutory rates among developed countries, excluding the USA, fell from an average of about 48 percent in the early 1980s to less than 25 percent in 2013.

Even within countries there is significant variation in federal taxes paid. For example, Carnival, the world's largest cruise line company, is incorporated in Panama and pays an effective tax rate of less than 1 percent even though the company is headquartered in Miami, Florida.

To avoid paying U.S. taxes on income made in other countries, many U.S. companies are cash-rich outside the USA but cash-poor inside the USA, and they bring cash back to the USA only as needed. For example in late 2012, Microsoft had $66.6 billion in total cash, but only $8.6 billion in the USA. General Electric had $85.5 billion in total cash, but only $30.7 billion in the USA. Emerson Electric has $2 billion in total cash with almost all of it in Europe and Asia so the firm had to borrow money in the USA rather than bring its cash back and pay a 35 percent corporate USA tax on corporate profits minus whatever ax it has already paid overseas. A *Wall Street Journal* article (12-4-12, p. B1) details this repercussion of the USA having the highest tax rate in the world. The article reveals that Johnson & Johnson keeps virtually all of its $24.5 billion in cash outside the USA, as does Illinois Tool Works Inc. Whirlpool has 85 percent of its cash offshore. Bruce Nolop, former CFO of Pitney Bowes explains it this way: "You end up with the really peculiar result where you are borrowing money in the USA, while you show cash on the balance sheet that is trapped overseas. It is a totally inefficient capital structure." The U.S. tax system, unfortunately for Americans, is structured so that companies can cut their tax bill by shifting income offshore to lower-tax countries.

An increasing number of U.S. companies are reincorporating in foreign countries to reduce their tax burden, and doing this typically by acquiring a foreign firm. Some U.S. firms that recently relocated are Aon Corp., Eaton Corp, Ensco International, D.E. Master Blenders, Transocean Ltd., Noble Corp, Weatherford International Ltd., and Rowan Companies. The 102-year old Eaton Corp. moved its headquarters from Cleveland, Ohio, to downtown Dublin, Ireland, and expects to save about $160 million in taxes annually solely as a result of the move. Critics of the USA tax code also point out that most developed countries tax only domestic earnings, whereas the USA taxes company profits earned abroad.

As indicated in Table 2-4, the top national statutory corporate tax rates in 2012 among sample countries ranged from 10 percent in Serbia to 35 percent in the USA. Note the countries that have a flat tax, which often, on adoption, triggers a surge in foreign direct investment.

Other factors besides the corporate tax rate obviously affect companies' decisions of where to locate plants and facilities and whether to acquire other firms. For example, the large, affluent market and efficient infrastructure in both Germany and Britain attract companies, but the high labor costs and strict labor laws there keep other companies away. The rapidly growing GDP in Brazil and India attracts companies, but violence and political unrest in Middle East countries deter investment. The USA perhaps should lower its rate to reward companies that invest in jobs domestically. Lowering the U.S. corporate tax rate should also reduce unemployment and spur growth domestically.

TABLE 2-4 Corporate Tax Rates Across Countries in 2012 (from high to low)

Country	Corporate Tax Rate (%)
USA	35
Brazil	34
France	33.33
Germany	33
India	30
Mexico	30
Italy	27.5
Japan	25.5
Israel	25
Austria	25
China	25.
Portugal	25
Finland	24.5
U.K.	24
Ukraine	21
Estonia	21
Russia	20
Greece	20
Croatia	20
Libya	20
Netherlands	20
Turkey	20
Poland	19
Czech Republic	19
Hungary	19
Singapore	17
Canada	16.5
Hong Kong	16.5
Romania	16
Latvi	15
Lithuani	15
Ireland	12.5
Serbi	10
Bulgaria	10
Cyprus	10

Source: Based on 11-1-12 information at http://www.worldwide-tax.com/#partthree.

United States versus Foreign Business Cultures

An excellent website to visit on this topic is www.worldbusinessculture.com. There you may select any country in the world and check out how business culture varies in that country vs. other lands. To compete successfully in world markets, U.S. managers must obtain a better knowledge of historical, cultural, and religious forces that motivate and drive people in other countries. In Japan, for example, business relations operate within the context of **Wa**, which stresses group harmony and social cohesion. In China, business behavior revolves around **guanxi**, or personal relations. In South Korea, activities involve concern for **inhwa**, or harmony based on respect of hierarchical relationships, including obedience to authority.[2]

In Europe, it is generally true that the farther north on the continent, the more participatory the management style. Most European workers are unionized and enjoy more frequent vacations and holidays than U.S. workers. A 90-minute lunch break plus 20-minute morning and afternoon breaks are common in European firms. Guaranteed permanent employment is typically a part of employment contracts in Europe. In socialist countries such as France, Belgium, and the United Kingdom, the only grounds for immediate dismissal from work is a criminal offense. A six-month trial period at the beginning of employment is usually part of the contract with a European firm. Many Europeans resent pay-for-performance, commission salaries, and objective measurement and reward systems. This is true especially of workers in southern Europe. Many Europeans also find the notion of team spirit difficult to grasp because the unionized environment has dichotomized worker–management relations throughout Europe.

A weakness of some U.S. firms in competing with Pacific Rim firms is a lack of understanding of Asian cultures, including how Asians think and behave. Spoken Chinese, for example, has more in common with spoken English than with spoken Japanese or Korean. U.S. managers consistently put more weight on being friendly and liked, whereas Asian and European managers often exercise authority without this concern. Americans tend to use first names instantly in business dealings with foreigners, but foreigners find this presumptuous. In Japan, for example, first names are used only among family members and intimate friends; even longtime business associates and coworkers shy away from the use of first names. Table 2-5 lists other cultural differences or pitfalls that U.S. managers need to know about.

U.S. managers have a low tolerance for silence, whereas Asian managers view extended periods of silence as important for organizing and evaluating one's thoughts. U.S. managers are much more action-oriented than their counterparts around the world; they rush to appointments, conferences, and meetings—and then feel the day has been productive. But for many foreign managers, resting, listening, meditating, and thinking is considered productive. Sitting through a conference without talking is unproductive in the United States, but it is viewed as positive in Japan if one's silence helps preserve unity.

U.S. managers place greater emphasis on short-term results than foreign managers. In marketing, for example, Japanese managers strive to achieve "everlasting customers," whereas many Americans strive to make a onetime sale. Marketing managers in Japan see making a sale

TABLE 2-5 Cultural Pitfalls That May Help You Be a Better Manager

- Waving is a serious insult in Greece and Nigeria, particularly if the hand is near someone's face.
- Making a "good-bye" wave in Europe can mean "No," but it means "Come here" in Peru.
- In China, last names are written first.
- A man named Carlos Lopez-Garcia should be addressed as Mr. Lopez in Latin America but as Mr. Garcia in Brazil.
- Breakfast meetings are considered uncivilized in most foreign countries.
- Latin Americans are on average 20 minutes late to business appointments.
- Direct eye contact is impolite in Japan.
- Do not cross your legs in any Arab or many Asian countries—it is rude to show the sole of your shoe.
- In Brazil, touching your thumb and first finger—an American "Okay" sign—is the equivalent of raising your middle finger.
- Nodding or tossing your head back in southern Italy, Malta, Greece, and Tunisia means "No." In India, this body motion means "Yes."
- Snapping your fingers is vulgar in France and Belgium.
- Folding your arms across your chest is a sign of annoyance in Finland.
- In China, leave some food on your plate to show that your host was so generous that you could not finish.
- Do not eat with your left hand when dining with clients from Malaysia or India.
- One form of communication works the same worldwide. It is the smile—so take that along wherever you go.

as the beginning, not the end, of the selling process. This is an important distinction. Japanese managers often criticize U.S. managers for worrying more about shareholders, whom they do not know, than employees, whom they do know. Americans refer to "hourly employees," whereas many Japanese companies still refer to "lifetime employees."

Rose Knotts recently summarized some important cultural differences between U.S. and foreign managers.[3] Awareness and consideration of these differences can enable a manager to be more effective, regardless of his or her own nationality.

1. Americans place an exceptionally high priority on time, viewing time as an asset. Many foreigners place more worth on relationships. This difference results in foreign managers often viewing U.S. managers as "more interested in business than people."

2. Personal touching and distance norms differ around the world. Americans generally stand about three feet from each other when carrying on business conversations, but Arabs and Africans stand about one foot apart. Touching another person with the left hand in business dealings is taboo in some countries.

3. Family roles and relationships vary in different countries. For example, males are valued more than females in some cultures, and peer pressure, work situations, and business interactions reinforce this phenomenon.

4. Business and daily life in some societies are governed by religious factors. Prayer times, holidays, daily events, and dietary restrictions, for example, need to be respected by managers not familiar with these practices in some countries.

5. Time spent with the family and the quality of relationships are more important in some cultures than the personal achievement and accomplishments espoused by the traditional U.S. manager.

6. Many cultures around the world value modesty, team spirit, collectivity, and patience much more than competitiveness and individualism, which are so important in the United States.

7. Punctuality is a valued personal trait when conducting business in the USA, but it is not revered in many of the world's societies. Eating habits also differ dramatically across cultures. For example, belching is acceptable in some countries as evidence of satisfaction with the food that has been prepared. Chinese culture considers it good manners to sample a portion of each food served.

8. To prevent social blunders when meeting with managers from other lands, one must learn and respect the rules of etiquette of others. Sitting on a toilet seat is viewed as unsanitary in most countries, but not in the USA. Leaving food or drink after dining is considered impolite in some countries, but not in China. Bowing instead of shaking hands is customary in many countries. Some cultures view Americans as unsanitary for locating toilet and bathing facilities in the same area, whereas Americans view people of some cultures as unsanitary for not taking a bath or shower every day.

9. Americans often do business with individuals they do not know, unlike businesspersons in many other cultures. In Mexico and Japan, for example, an amicable relationship is often mandatory before conducting business.

In many countries, effective managers are those who are best at negotiating with government bureaucrats rather than those who inspire workers. Many U.S. managers are uncomfortable with nepotism, which are practiced in some countries. The USA defends women from sexual harassment, and defends minorities from discrimination, but not all countries embrace the same values. For example, in Indonesia, in mid-2013, legislators were considering making sex among singles a crime with up to a 5-year prison sentence, and cohabitation a crime with up to 1 year in prison.

U.S. managers in China have to be careful about how they arrange office furniture because Chinese workers believe in **feng shui**, the practice of harnessing natural forces. U.S. managers in Japan have to be careful about **nemaswashio**, whereby Japanese workers expect supervisors to alert them privately of changes rather than informing them in a meeting. Japanese managers have little appreciation for versatility, expecting all managers to be the same. In Japan, "If a nail sticks out, you hit it into the wall," says Brad Lashbrook, an international consultant for Wilson Learning.

Probably the biggest obstacle to the effectiveness of U.S. managers—or managers from any country working in another—is the fact that it is almost impossible to change the attitude of a foreign workforce. "The system drives you; you cannot fight the system or culture," says Bill Parker, president of Phillips Petroleum in Norway.

Communication Differences Across Countries

Americans increasingly interact with managers in other countries, so it is important to understand foreign business cultures. Americans often come across as intrusive, manipulative, and garrulous; this impression may reduce their effectiveness in communication. *Forbes* provided the following cultural hints from Charis Intercultural Training:

1. Italians, Germans, and French generally do not soften up executives with praise before they criticize. Americans do soften up folks, and this practice seems manipulative to Europeans.
2. Israelis are accustomed to fast-paced meetings and have little patience for U.S. informality and small talk.
3. British executives often complain that U.S. executives chatter too much. Informality, egalitarianism, and spontaneity from Americans in business settings jolt many foreigners.
4. Europeans feel they are being treated like children when asked to wear name tags by Americans.
5. Executives in India are used to interrupting one another. Thus, when U.S. executives listen without asking for clarification or posing questions, they are viewed by Indians as not paying attention.
6. When negotiating orally with Malaysian or Japanese executives, it is appropriate to allow periodically for a time of silence. However, no pause is needed when negotiating in Israel.
7. Refrain from asking foreign managers questions such as "How was your weekend?" That is intrusive to foreigners, who tend to regard their business and private lives as totally separate.[4]

Business Culture Across Countries[5]

A recent *USA Today* article (9-24-12, p. 8A) titled "Arab Spring Leaving Women Out in Cold" reveals that the recent changeover of regimes in Middle Eastern countries has unfortunately resulted in arguably less rights for women. Nawal Al Saadawi says for example in Egypt "Things didn't improve for women, and we are going backward." Even in a relatively progressive Middle Eastern country such as Morocco, there is legislation that allows men who rape or have sex with minors to avoid prosecution by wedding their victims. Sexual harassment of women in the streets, according to the article, especially spikes during Muslim holidays. Perhaps the worst country for women's rights is Afghanistan, although Saudi Arabia is quite restrictive. In contrast, South Korea elected its first female president late in 2012. She is Park Geun-hye, the daughter of the general who ruled the country in the 1960s and 1970s. Park joins the following other current female presidents of countries:

> Australia, Julia Gillard
>
> Denmark, Helle Thorning-Schmidt
>
> Germany, Angela Merkel
>
> Iceland, Johanna Sigurdardottir
>
> Switzerland, Eveline Widmer-Schlumpf

Many countries have in the past have had female presidents, including Canada, Chile, Israel, New Zealand, Norway, Slovak Republic, Turkey, and the United Kingdom.

Another recent *USA Today* article (12-4-12, 6B) titled "Europe Tries to Put Women on Boards" reveals that in the UK, 20 percent of senior management is female, but this is higher than in the Netherlands where the percentage is 18, Denmark at 15, or Germany at 13. Germany's upper house of parliament recently approved a bill to guarantee that women make up 20 percent of boards at publicly traded companies by 2018, and 40 percent by 2023. Chancellor Angela Merkel of Germany, however, has said that she prefers voluntary measures over mandatory quotas. In Norway, 40 percent of nonexecutive board members of publicly listed companies are women, which is perhaps best of all countries on the planet.

Mexico—Business Culture

Mexico is an authoritarian society in terms of schools, churches, businesses, and families. Employers seek workers who are agreeable, respectful, and obedient, rather than innovative, creative, and independent. Mexican workers tend to be activity oriented rather than problem solvers. When visitors walk into a Mexican business, they are impressed by the cordial, friendly atmosphere. This is almost always true because Mexicans desire harmony rather than conflict; desire for harmony is part of the social fabric in worker–manager relations. There is a much lower tolerance for adversarial relations or friction at work in Mexico as compared to the USA.

Mexican employers are paternalistic, providing workers with more than a paycheck, but in return they expect allegiance. Weekly food baskets, free meals, free bus service, and free day care are often part of compensation. The ideal working condition for a Mexican worker is the family model, with people all working together, doing their share, according to their designated roles. Mexican workers do not expect or desire a work environment in which self-expression and initiative are encouraged. Whereas U.S. business embodies individualism, achievement, competition, curiosity, pragmatism, informality, spontaneity, and doing more than expected on the job, Mexican businesses stress collectivism, continuity, cooperation, belongingness, formality, and doing exactly what is told.

In Mexico, business associates rarely entertain each other at their homes, which are places reserved exclusively for close friends and family. Business meetings and entertaining are nearly always done at a restaurant. Preserving one's honor, saving face, and looking important are also exceptionally important in Mexico. This is why Mexicans do not accept criticism and change easily; many find it humiliating to acknowledge having made a mistake. A meeting among employees and managers in a business located in Mexico is a forum for giving orders and directions rather than for discussing problems or participating in decision making. Mexican workers want to be closely supervised, cared for, and corrected in a civil manner. Opinions expressed by employees are often regarded as back talk in Mexico. Mexican supervisors are viewed as weak if they explain the rationale for their orders to workers.

Mexicans do not feel compelled to follow rules that are not associated with a particular person in authority they work for or know well. Thus, signs to wear earplugs or safety glasses, or attendance or seniority policies, and even one-way street signs are often ignored. Whereas Americans follow the rules, Mexicans often do not.

Life is slower in Mexico than in the USA. The first priority is often assigned to the last request, rather than to the first. Telephone systems break down. Banks may suddenly not have pesos. Phone repair can take a month. Electricity for an entire plant or town can be down for hours or even days. Business and government offices may open and close at odd hours. Buses and taxis may be hours off schedule. Meeting times for appointments are not rigid. Tardiness is common everywhere. Effectively doing business in Mexico requires knowledge of the Mexican way of life, culture, beliefs, and customs.

In Mexico, when greeting others, it is customary for women to pat each other on the right forearm or shoulder, rather than shaking hands. Men shake hands or, if close friends, use the traditional hug and back slapping upon greeting. If visiting a Mexican home, bring a gift such as flowers or sweets. Avoid marigolds because they symbolize death. Arrive up to 30 minutes late, but definitely not early. Avoid red flowers which have a negative connotation. White flowers are an excellent choice. If you receive a gift, open it immediately and react enthusiastically. At dinner, do not sit until you are invited to and wait to be told where to sit. This is true in most foreign countries and in the USA. Do not begin eating until the hostess starts. Only men give toasts in Mexico. It is also polite to leave some food on your plate after a meal. For business appointments, as opposed to home visits, it is best to arrive on time, although your Mexican counterparts may be up to 30 minutes late. Do not get irritated at their lack of punctuality.

Mexicans often judge or stereotype a person by who introduces them and changing that first impression is difficult in business. Expect to answer questions about personal background, family, and life interests—because Mexicans consider trustworthiness and character to be of upmost importance. Mexicans are status conscious, so business titles and rank are important. Face-to-face meetings are preferred over telephone calls, letters, or e-mail. Negotiations in Mexico include a fair amount of haggling, so do not give a best offer first.

Japan—Business Culture

Japan elected a new prime minister, Shinzo Abe, in December 2012. Abe promises aggressive new monetary policy, big public works spending, and full economic recovery. Walmart believes in Abe because it, under the name Seiyu Ltd., is adding 22 stores in Japan in 2013–2014, to go along with its already 368 stores in Japan. Two trends in Japan driving the Walmart expansion are (1) single-person households, especially among the elderly, are continuing to grow and (2) people have less money to spend. Japanese consumers have traditionally equated discounts with poor quality, but that is changing. Also, Walmart gained much support throughout Japan with its quick response flying in water and food immediately after the earthquake and tsunami hit Japan in 2011.

The Japanese place great importance on group loyalty and consensus, a concept called *Wa*. Nearly all corporate activities in Japan encourage Wa among managers and employees. Wa requires that all members of a group agree and cooperate; this results in constant discussion and compromise. Japanese managers evaluate the potential attractiveness of alternative business decisions in terms of the long-term effect on the group's Wa. This is why silence, used for pondering alternatives, can be a plus in a formal Japanese meeting. Discussions potentially disruptive to Wa are generally conducted in informal settings, such as at a bar, so as to minimize harm to the group's Wa. Entertaining is an important business activity in Japan because it strengthens Wa. Formal meetings are often conducted in informal settings. When confronted with disturbing questions or opinions, Japanese managers tend to remain silent, whereas Americans tend to respond directly, defending themselves through explanation and argument.

Americans have more freedom to control their own fates than do the Japanese. The USA offers more upward mobility to its people, as indicated below:

America is not like Japan and can never be. America's strength is the opposite: It opens its doors and brings the world's disorder in. It tolerates social change that would tear most other societies apart. This openness encourages Americans to adapt as individuals rather than as a group. Americans go west to California to get a new start; they move east to Manhattan to try to make the big time; they move to Vermont or to a farm to get close to the soil. They break away from their parents' religions or values or class; they rediscover their ethnicity. They go to night school; they change their names.[6]

Most Japanese managers are reserved, quiet, distant, introspective, and other oriented, whereas most U.S. managers are talkative, insensitive, impulsive, direct, and individual oriented. Americans often perceive Japanese managers as wasting time and carrying on pointless conversations, whereas U.S. managers often use blunt criticism, ask prying questions, and make quick decisions. These kinds of cultural differences have disrupted many potentially productive Japanese–American business endeavors. Viewing the Japanese communication style as a prototype for all Asian cultures is a stereotype that must be avoided.

In Japan, a person's age and status are of paramount importance, whether in the family unit, the extended family, or a social or business situation. Schoolchildren learn early that the oldest person in the group is to be honored. Older folks are served first and their drinks are poured for them. Greetings in Japan are formal and ritualized. Wait to be introduced because it may be viewed as impolite to introduce yourself, even in a large gathering. Foreigners may shake hands, but the traditional form of greeting is to bow. The deeper you bow, the more respect you show, but at least bow the head slightly in greetings.

In gift giving in Japan, chocolates or small cakes are excellent choices, but do not give lilies, camellias, lotus blossoms, or white flowers because they all are associated with funerals. Do not give potted plants because they encourage sickness, although a bonsai tree is always acceptable. Give items in odd numbers, but avoid the number 9. Gifts are not opened when received. If going to a Japanese home, remove your shoes before entering and put on the slippers left at the doorway. Leave shoes pointing away from the doorway you are about to walk through. If going to the toilet in a Japanese home, put on the toilet slippers and remove them when you exit.

In Japan, when finally seated for dinner, never point the chopsticks. Learn how to use chopsticks before visiting Japan and do not pierce food with chopsticks. Japanese oftentimes slurp their noodles and soup, but mixing other food with rice is inappropriate. Instead of mixing, eat a bit of rice and then a bit of food. To signify that you do not want more rice or drink, leave some in the bowl or glass. Conversation over dinner is generally subdued in Japan because they prefer to savor their food.

Unlike Americans, Japanese prefer to do business on the basis of personal relationships rather than impersonally speaking over the phone or by written correspondence. Therefore, build and maintain relationships by sending greeting, thank you, birthday, and seasonal cards. You need to be a good "correspondent" to effectively do business with the Japanese. Punctuality is important so arrive on time for meetings and be mindful that it may take several meetings to establish a good relationship. The Japanese are looking for a long-term relationship. Always give a small gift as a token of your appreciation, and present it to the most senior person at the end of any meeting.

Like many Asian and African cultures, the Japanese are non-confrontational. They have a difficult time saying "no," so you must be vigilant at observing their nonverbal communication. Rarely refuse a request, no matter how difficult or non-profitable it may appear at the time. In communicating with Japanese, phrase questions so that they can answer *yes*. For example, do you disagree with this? Group decision making and consensus are vitally important. The Japanese often remain silent in meetings for long periods of time and may even close their eyes when they want to listen intently.

Business cards are exchanged in Japan constantly and with excitement. Invest in quality business cards and keep them in pristine condition. Do not write on them. Have one side of your card translated in Japanese and give it to the person with the Japanese side facing the recipient. Business cards are generally given and received with two hands and a slight bow. Examine any business card you receive carefully.

Brazil—Business Culture

In both Brazil and the USA, men greet each other by shaking hands while maintaining steady eye contact. Women greet each other with kisses in Brazil, starting with the left and alternating cheeks. Hugging and backslapping are also common greetings among Brazilian close friends. If a woman wishes to shake hands with a man, she should extend her hand first. Brazilians speak Portuguese. If going to someone's house in Brazil, bring the hostess flowers or a small gift. Orchids are nice, but avoid purple or black, because these are mourning colors. Arrive at least 30 minutes late if your invitation is for dinner and arrive up to an hour late for a party or large gathering. Never arrive early. Brazilians dress with a flair and judge others on their appearance, so even casual dress is more formal than in many other countries. Always err on the side of over-dressing in Brazil rather than under-dressing.

Avoid embarrassing a Brazilian by criticizing an individual publically; that causes that person to lose face with all others at a business meeting, and the person making the criticism also loses face because they have disobeyed the unwritten Brazilian rule. It is considered acceptable, however, to interrupt someone who is speaking. Face-to-face, oral communication is preferred over written communication. As for business agreements, Brazilians insist on drawing up detailed legal contracts. They are more comfortable doing business with and negotiating with people than companies. Therefore, wait for a Brazilian colleagues to raise the business subject. Never rush the prebusiness relationship-building time. Brazilians take their time when negotiating. Use local lawyers and accountants for negotiations because Brazilians resent an outside legal presence.

Appointments are commonly cancelled or changed at the last minute in Brazil, so do not be surprised or get upset. In the cities of Sao Paulo and Brasilia, arrive on time for meetings, but in Rio de Janeiro arrive a few minutes late for a meeting. Do not appear impatient if kept waiting, because relationship building always takes precedence over adhering to a strict schedule. Brazilians pride themselves on dressing well, so men should wear conservative, dark-colored business suits or even three-piece suits for executives. Women should wear suits or dresses that are elegant and feminine with good, quality accessories. And ladies, manicures are expected.

Germany—Business Culture

Business communication in Germany is formal, so the home is a welcome, informal place. Germans take great pride in their home, which is generally neat and tidy inside and out. Only close friends and relatives are invited into the sanctity of a person's house, so consider that an honor if you get that invitation, and bring a gift, such as chocolates or yellow roses or tea roses—but not red roses, which symbolize romantic intentions. Also do not bring carnations, lilies, or chrysanthemums, which in Germany symbolize mourning. If you bring wine to a

German's home, it should be imported, French or Italian. Always arrive on time but never early, and always send a handwritten note the following day to thank your hostess for her hospitality.

When it is time to have dinner, remain standing until invited to sit down. As is custom in many countries, you may be shown to a particular seat. Table manners in Germany are strictly Continental with the fork being held in the left hand and the knife in the right while eating. Do not begin eating until the hostess starts or someone says *guten appetit* ("good appetite"). Wait for the hostess to place her napkin in her lap before doing so yourself and do not rest your elbows on the table. Cut as much of your food with your fork as possible because this compliments the cook by indicating the food is tender. Break bread or rolls apart by hand, but if a loaf is in the middle for all, then touch only what you extract to eat. This sanitary practice is a must in all countries including the USA. Finish everything on your plate and indicate you have finished eating by laying your knife and fork parallel across the right side of your plate, with the fork over the knife.

Germans are like Americans in that they do not need a personal relationship to do business. They are more interested in a businessperson's academic credentials and their company's credentials. A quick, firm handshake is the traditional greeting, even with children. At the office, Germans do not have an open-door policy and often work with their office door closed, so knock and wait to be invited to enter. Appointments are mandatory and should be made one to two weeks in advance. Germans are often direct to the point of bluntness. Punctuality is extremely important in Germany, so if you are going to be delayed, telephone immediately and offer an explanation. It is rude to cancel a meeting at the last minute and this could jeopardize the whole business relationship. German meetings adhere to strict agendas, including starting and ending times. Germans maintain direct eye contact while speaking.

There is a strict protocol to follow in Germany when entering a room—the eldest or highest-ranking person enters first and men enter before women if their age and status are roughly equivalent. Germans are detail oriented and want to understand every innuendo before coming to an agreement. Business decision making is autocratic and held at the top of the company. Final decisions will not be changed and are expected to be implemented by lower-level managers and employees with no questions asked. Americans are more flexible in many respects than Germans.

Egypt—Business Culture

In Egypt, greetings are based on both social class and religion, so follow the lead of others. Handshakes, although limp and prolonged, are the customary greeting among Egyptians of the same sex. Handshakes are always given with a hearty smile and direct eye contact. Once a relationship has developed, it is common to greet with a kiss on one cheek and then the other, while shaking hands, men with men and women with women. In greetings between men and women, the woman will extend her hand first. Otherwise, a man should bow his head in greeting.

If you are invited to an Egyptian's home, remove your shoes before entering, just as you would do in China and Japan. As a gift, bring chocolates, sweets, or pastries to the hostess. Do not give flowers, which are usually reserved for weddings or the ill, unless you know that the host will appreciate them. Always give gifts with the right hand or both hands if the gift is heavy. Gifts are not opened when received. Never sit at a dinner table until the host or hostess tells you where to sit. Eat with the right hand only and compliment the host by taking second helpings. Always show appreciation for the meal. Putting salt or pepper on your food is considered an insult to a cook. This is true to a lesser extent even in the USA. Leave a small amount of food on your plate when you have finished eating. Otherwise your Egyptian host may keep bringing you more food.

Egyptians prefer to do business with those they know and respect, so expect to spend time cultivating a personal relationship before business is conducted. Who you know is more important than what you know in Egypt, so network and cultivate a number of contracts. You should expect to be offered coffee or tea whenever you meet someone in Egypt because this demonstrates hospitality. Even if you do not want the drink, always accept the beverage because declining the offer is viewed as rejecting the person.

In Egypt, appearance is important, so wear, conservative clothes and present yourself well at all times. For Egyptians, direct eye contact is a sign of honesty, so be prepared for overly intense stares. Hierarchy and rank are important. Unlike in Germany, Egyptian business people do have an open-door policy, even when they are in a meeting, so you may experience frequent interruptions as others wander into the room and start a different discussion. It is best that you not try to bring the topic back to the original discussion until the new person leaves. Business meetings generally start after prolonged inquiries about health, family, and such.

Egyptians must know and like you to conduct business. Personal relationships are necessary for long-term business. The highest-ranking person makes decisions, after obtaining group consensus. Decisions are reached after great deliberation. In Egypt, business moves at a slow pace and society is extremely bureaucratic—even in the post-Hosni Mubarak era. Egyptians respect age and experience and engage in a fair amount of haggling. They are tough negotiators and do not like confrontation or having to say *no*. Egyptian women must be careful to cover themselves appropriately. Skirts and dresses should cover the knee and sleeves should cover most of the arm. Women are daily gaining more rights, however, throughout the Middle East, and that is a good thing. In late 2011, women in Saudi Arabia were finally granted the right to vote, but women still are not allowed to drive cars in that country.

China—Business Culture

In China, greetings are formal and the oldest person is always greeted first. Like in the United States, handshakes are the most common form of greeting. Many Chinese will look toward the ground when greeting someone. The Chinese have an excellent sense of humor. They can easily laugh at themselves if they have a comfortable relationship with the other person. In terms of gifts, a food basket makes an excellent gift, but do not give scissors, knives, or other cutting utensils because these objects indicate severing of the relationship. Never give clocks, handkerchiefs, flowers, or straw sandals because they are associated with funerals. Do not wrap gifts in white, blue, or black paper. In China, the number 4 is unlucky, so do not give four of anything. Eight is the luckiest number, so giving eight of something is a great idea.

If invited to a Chinese person's home, consider this a great honor and arrive on time. Remove your shoes before entering the house and bring a small gift to the hostess. Eat heartily to demonstrate that you are enjoying the food. Use chopsticks and wait to be told where to sit. You should try everything that is offered and never eat the last piece from the serving tray. Hold the rice bowl close to your mouth while eating. Do not be offended if a Chinese person makes slurping or belching sounds; it merely indicates that they are enjoying their food.

The Chinese rarely do business with companies or people they do not know. Your position on an organizational chart is extremely important in business relationships. Gender bias is generally not an issue. Meals and social events are not the place for business discussions. There is a demarcation between business and socializing in China, so try to be careful not to intertwine the two.

Like in the USA and Germany, punctuality is important in China. Arriving late to a meeting is an insult and could negatively affect your relationship. Meetings require patience because mobile phones ring frequently and conversations tend to be boisterous. Never ask the Chinese to turn off their mobile phones because this causes you both to lose face. The Chinese are non-confrontational and virtually never overtly say *no*. Rather, they will say "they will think about it" or "they will see." The Chinese are shrewd negotiators, so an initial offer or price should leave room for negotiation.

India—Business Culture

According to United Nations' statistics, India's rate of female participation in the labor force is 34.2 percent, which is quite low, especially because women make up 42 percent of college graduates in India. But Indian women with a college degree are expected to let their careers take a back seat to caring for their husband, children, and elderly parents. "The measures of daughterly guilt are much higher in Indian women than in other countries," says Sylvia Ann Hewlett, president of the Center for Work-Life Policy, a Manhattan think tank, who headed a recent study on the challenges Indian women face in the workplace.[8] Sylvia says, "Since taking care of elderly parents usually becomes a reality later in a woman's career, it takes them out of the workplace just when they should be entering top management roles." That is why gender disparities at Indian companies unfortunately grow more pronounced at higher levels of management.

Like in many Asian cultures, people in India do not like to say *no*, verbally or nonverbally. Rather than disappoint you, they often will say something is not available, will offer you the response that they think you want to hear, or will be vague with you. This behavior should not be considered dishonest. Shaking hands is common in India, especially in the large cities among the more educated who are accustomed to dealing with westerners. Men may shake hands with other men and women may shake hands with other women; however, there are seldom handshakes between men and women because of religious beliefs.

Indians believe that giving gifts eases the transition into the next life. Gifts of cash are common, but do not give frangipani or white flowers because they represent mourning. Yellow, green, and red are lucky colors, so use them to wrap gifts. Because Hindus consider cows to be sacred, do not give gifts made of leather to Hindus. Muslims should not be given gifts made of pigskin or alcoholic products. Gifts are usually not opened when received.

Before entering an Indian's house, take off shoes just as you would in China or Japan. Politely turn down the host's first offer of tea, coffee, or snacks. You will be asked again and again. Saying no to the first invitation is part of the protocol. Be mindful that neither Hindus nor Sikhs eat beef, and many are vegetarians. Muslims do not eat pork or drink alcohol. Lamb, chicken, and fish are the most commonly served main courses. Table manners are somewhat formal, but much Indian food is eaten with the fingers. Like most places in the world, wait to be told where and when to sit at dinner. Women in India typically serve the men and eat later. You may be asked to wash your hands before and after sitting down to a meal. Always use your right hand to eat, whether using utensils or your fingers. Leave a small amount of food on your plate to indicate that you are satisfied. Finishing all your food means that you are still hungry, which as true in Egypt, China, Mexico, and many countries.

Indians prefer to do business with those with whom they have established a relationship built on mutual trust and respect. Punctuality is important. Indians generally do not trust the legal system, and someone's word is often sufficient to reach an agreement. Do not disagree publicly with anyone in India.

Titles such as professor, doctor, or engineer are important in India, as is a person's age, university degree, caste, and profession. Use the right hand to give and receive business cards. Business cards need not be translated into Hindi but always present your business card so the recipient may read the card as it is handed to them. This is a nice, expected gesture in most countries around the world.

Nigeria—Business Culture

With the largest population of any country in Africa and the largest city in Africa (Lagos), Nigeria on the west coast bordering the Gulf of Guinea, is a democratic country with English as its official language. Half of Nigeria's population is under age 18. With a growing economy, Nigeria's constitution guarantees religious freedom. Christians in Nigeria live mostly in the south, whereas Muslims live mostly in the north. Native religions in which people believe in deities, spirits, and ancestor worship are spread throughout Nigeria, as are different languages. Christmas and Easter are national holidays. Muslims observe Ramadan, the Islamic month of fasting, and the two Eids. Working hours in the north often vary from the south, primarily because Muslims do not work on their holy day—Friday.

Endowed with vast quantities of natural resources and being the sixth largest oil-producing nation on the planet, Nigeria has a well-educated and industrious people who are proud of their country. Nigerians are fond of the expression, "When Nigeria sneezes, the rest of Africa catches a cold (except South Africa)." Nigeria re-elected its president in 2011, a zoology professor-turned-president, Goodluck Jonathan.

In Nigeria, extended families are still the backbone of social and business systems. Grandparents, cousins, aunts, uncles, sisters, brothers, and in-laws all work as a unit through life. Hierarchy and seniority within extended families are important; the oldest person in a group is revered and honored, and is greeted and served first. In return, however, the most senior person has the responsibility to make good decisions for the extended family.

The most common greeting in Nigeria is a handshake with a warm, welcoming smile. Muslims will not generally shake hands with members of the opposite sex. Nigerians do not use first names readily, so wait to be invited to do this before engaging. Gift giving is common and even expected, but gifts from a man to a woman must be said to come from the man's mother, wife, sister, or other female relative, never from the man himself. Never rush a greeting because that is extremely rude; rather, spend time inquiring about the other person's general well-being.

Foreigners who take the time to get to know a Nigerian as a person are often welcomed into the Nigerian's inner circle of family and close friends. Nigerians are generally outgoing and friendly, especially in the southwest, where the Yoruba often use humor even during business meetings and serious discussions.

To combat the AIDS epidemic in sub-Saharan Africa, the World Bank is now paying young girls cash to stop accepting gifts and cash from older men in exchange for sex. This "sugar daddy" relationship is common in many African countries and is fueling the AIDS problem because the percent of men aged 30–34 that test positive for HIV is upward of 30 percent in countries such as Zimbabwe. The World Bank has a billboard in the Mbare vegetable market in Harare, Zimbabwe, that reads, "Your future is brighter without a sugar daddy."

Business Climate Across Countries/Continents

The World Bank and the International Finance Corporation annually rank 183 countries in terms of their respective ease of doing business (http://www.doingbusiness.org/rankings). The index ranks nations from 1 (best) to 183 (worst). For each nation, the ranking is calculated as the simple average of the percentile rankings on how easy is it to: (1) start a business, (2) deal with construction permits, (3) register property, (4) get credit, (5) protect investors, (6) pay taxes, (7) trade across borders, (8) enforce contracts, (9) resolving insolvency, and (10) get electricity.

Among all countries on the planet, Morocco improved its ranking most in 2012, climbing 21 places to 94, by simplifying the construction permitting process, easing the administrative burden of tax compliance, and providing greater protections to minority shareholders. Table 2-6 reveals the 2012 Ease of Doing Business rankings for the top 10 nations in various regions of the world. Note for example that Norway is rated the sixth best country on the planet for ease of doing business and Chile is the best country in South America.

Union Membership Across Europe

There is great variation in Europe as per levels of union membership, ranging from 74 percent of employees in Finland and 71 percent in Sweden to 9 percent in Lithuania and 8 percent in France. However, percentage of union membership is not the only indicator of strength because in France for example, unions have repeatedly shown that despite low levels of membership they are able to mobilize workers in mass strikes and demonstrations to great effect.

The average level of union membership across the whole of the European Union (EU), weighted by the numbers employed in the different member states, is 23 percent compared to about 11 percent in the USA. The European average is held down by relatively low levels of membership in some of the larger EU states, Germany with 19 percent, France with 8 percent, Spain with 16 percent, and Poland with 15 percent. The three smallest states, Cyprus, Luxembourg, and Malta, have levels well above the average.

TABLE 2-6 The Top 10 Nations to Do Business With Across Continents

Overall Best	East Asia Pacific	East Europe Central Asia	Latin America Caribbean	Mid-East Africa	South Africa
1. Singapore	Singapore	Georgia	Chile	Saudi Arabia	Mauritius
2. Hong Kong	Hone Kong	Latvia	Peru	UAE	S. Africa
3. New Zealand	Thailand	Macedonia	Colombia	Qatar	Rwanda
4. USA	Malaysia	Lithuania	Puerto Rico	Bahrain	Botswana
5. Denmark	Taiwan	Cyprus	St. Lucia	Tunisia	Ghana
6. Norway	Tonga	Kazakhstan	Mexico	Oman	Nambia
7. United Kingdom	Samoa	Armenia	Antiqua	Kuwait	Zambia
8. South Korea	Solomon Isls.	Montenegro	Panama	Morocco	Seychelles
9. Iceland	Vanuatu	Bulgaria	Dominica	Jordan	Kenya
10. Ireland	Fiji	Azerbajan	Trinidad	Yemen	Ethiopia

Source: Based on information at http://www.doingbusiness.org/rankings in November 2012.

The three Nordic countries of Denmark, Sweden, and Finland are at the top of the table with around 70 percent of all employees in unions. In part this is because, as in Belgium, which also has above average levels of union density, unemployment and other social benefits are normally paid out through the union. High union density in the Nordic countries also reflects an approach that sees union membership as a natural part of employment, as shown by the relatively high proportion of employees (around 53 percent) who are union members in Norway, where unemployment benefits are not paid through the unions.

Central and Eastern Europe nations generally have below average levels of union membership. In Poland for example 16 percent of employees are estimated to be union members. Level of union membership is clearly trending downward all over Europe. Only 8 out of the 27 EU states plus Norway—Belgium, Cyprus, Ireland, Italy, Luxembourg, Malta, Norway and Spain—have seen a gain in union members among the employed in recent years, and in most of these countries. This growth has not kept pace with the overall growth in employment, meaning that union density has drifted downward. The two exceptions appear to be Ireland and Italy where union membership is slowly growing.

African Countries

In 2012, 23 African countries held democratic elections, whereas in 1989 only 3 African countries were considered democracies. Currencies in Africa are stabilizing and many countries are fund-raising to build modern highways, ports, and power grids. African countries are winning over investors as indicated by Zambia raising $750 million in bonds recently, followed by Rwanda, Nigeria, and Kenya doing the same. Yields on some African bonds are only slightly higher than the yield on the debt of some troubled European economies, such as Spain. Investors are looking closely at Africa now in the wake of low interest rates and slow growth elsewhere on the planet.[7]

Many African companies are expanding in Africa, such as South Africa's Shoprite Group in 2013 adding 223 stores in 16 African countries other than South Africa. Shoprite is especially targeting Nigeria and the Congo. Dangote Group, based in Nigeria, is building a cement factory in Zambia, and Togo-based Ecobank Transnational now operates in 32 African countries. Domino's recently opened stores in Nigeria, Egypt, Morocco, and Kenya. Reasons companies are opening outlets in Africa is the rapidly growing middle class and an average GDP growth of 5 percent for the continent through 2017 according to the IMF. Also, the World Bank saying food demand across Africa will double between 2012 and 2020.

Financial troubles in Europe, as well as rioting in the Muslim world, are problems for African currencies, such as the Ghana cedi and the Kenya shilling, which depreciated rapidly in 2012. Perennial challenges remain in Africa, such as lack of reliable roads, phone lines, and power grids, but consumer spending in Africa is expected to double from $500 billion in 2012 to $1 trillion in 2020, creating great opportunities for thousands of firms.[8]

Marriott added its first sub-Saharan Africa hotel in 2013, in the capital of Rwanda, which is Kigali. Rwanda's GDP has grown 8 percent annually since 2004 as their president, Paul Kagame, wants to turn the tiny, landlocked equatorial country into an African Singapore. Marriott previously had 7 hotels in northern Africa (Morocco, Algiers, and Egypt), but none below the Sahara desert. Marriott now plans to build 2 hotels in Ghana, 2 in Nigeria, and 2 in Ethiopia between 2013 and 2015. "Most of Africa is a bit of a blank piece of paper for the hospitality industry," says Alex Kyriakidis, chief of Marriott's Middle East and Africa division. South Africa's Protea Hospitality Group plans to add 9 hotels in 2013–2014 to its 36 African properties outside its home country. All total, 208 new, large hotels were added across Africa in 2012 compared to 159 the prior year. Many firms are globally acquiring firms in Africa, such as India's number-2 tire maker, Apollo Tyres, recently buying South Africa's Dunlop Tyres for $62 million. Apollo plans to triple sales to $6 billion by 2015, with 60 percent of that revenue coming from outside India.

Airlines are beginning to really serve Africa, led by Delta in the USA and Persian Gulf carriers such as Qatar Airways, Emirates, and Etihad Airways. The five largest airports in sub-Saharan Africa ranked by available seats in June 2013 were:

Johannesburg, South Africa (278,392)

Addis Ababa, Ethiopia (167,408)

Khartoum, Sudan (142,408)

Nairobi, Kenya (126,729)

Lagos, Nigeria (120,034)

The McKinsey Global Institute reports that approximately 40 percent of Africans now live in urban areas and the number of households with discretionary income should increase 50 percent by the end of this decade.[9] Graham Allan, CEO of Yum Restaurants International, recently said, "A lot of companies, especially Chinese ones, have invested in Africa; we share the general view that Africa over the next 10 to 20 years will have massive potential." McKinsey & Co. says the number of consumers who can spend beyond bare necessities is greater now in Africa than India. From 2000 to 2009, foreign direct investment in Africa increased 600 percent to $58.56 billion.

Walmart recently acquired South African retailer Massmart Holdings for $4.6 billion, providing the company with 290 stores in 13 African countries: Ghana, Nigeria, Zambia, Botswana, Namibia, South Africa, Lesotho, Mozambique, Zimbabwe, Mauritius, Malawi, Tanzania, and Uganda. The Walmart acquisition paves the way for many firms now viewing Africa as a deal-making destination. For example, HSBC Holdings is trying to acquire a majority stake in Nedbank Group, South Africa's fourth-largest bank, and Nippon Telegraph and Telephone in Japan is buying Africa's largest technology company, Dimension Data. Huge purchases such as these have been a wake-up call to the rest of the world, which now views Africa as a growing, attractive new market.

Table 2-7 provides a summary of the economic situation in 12 African countries. Note that Angola is rated lowest in terms of doing business, whereas South Africa is rated highest. Recent regime changes in Egypt, Tunisia, Libya, and Algeria may spur further investment in Africa as democracy and capitalism strengthens. Many multinational companies are now gaining first mover advantages by engaging Africa at all levels. For example, Nokia and Coca-Cola have distribution networks in nearly every African country. Unilever has a presence in 20 of Africa's 50 countries. Nestlé is in 19 African countries, Barclays is in 12, Societe Generale is in 15, and Standard Chartered Bank is in 14. Africa has about 10 percent of the world's oil reserves, 40 percent of its gold ore, and 85 percent of the world's deposits of chromium and platinum. Africa's population is young, growing, and moving into jobs in the cities. Forty percent of Africans today live in the cities, a proportion close to China and India. *The general stereotype*

TABLE 2-7 Sampling of African Countries— Ease-of-Doing-Business Rankings

	Population in Millions	Ease of Doing Business Among all Countries	Capital City
South Africa	49	35 out of 183	Pretoria
Tunisia	11	46 out of 183	Tunis
Ghana	24	63 out of 183	Accra
Morocco	32	94 out of 183	Rabat
Kenya	39	109 out of 183	Nairobi
Egypt	79	110 out of 183	Cairo
Ethiopia	86	111 out of 183	Addis Ababa
Uganda	33	123 out of 183	Kampala
Nigeria	150	133 out of 183	Abuja
Sudan	41	135 out of 183	Khartoum
Mozambique	22	139 out of 183	Maputo
Angola	13	172 out of 183	Luanda

Source: Based on information at http://www.doingbusiness. org/rankings on November 1, 2012.

of Africa is rapidly changing from subsistence farmers avoiding lions, to millions of smartphone carrying consumers in cities purchasing products.

Africa has the world's largest deposits of platinum, chrome, and diamonds—and many Chinese companies in particular are investing there. Africa's largest food retailer, Shoprite Holdings, has more than 1,000 stores in 17 countries. Shoprite is a potential acquisition target being considered by European retailers Carrefour and Tesco. Diageo PLC sells Guinness beer, Smirnoff vodka, Baileys liqueur, and Johnnie Walker whiskey in more than 40 countries across Africa. Nestlé SA now has more than 25 factories in Africa.

Yum Brands recently doubled the number of Kentucky Fried Chicken (KFC) outlets in Africa to 1,200 and increased its revenue from the continent to almost $2 billion. "Africa wasn't even on our radar screen 10 years ago, but now we see it exploding with opportunity" says David Novak, Yum's chairman and CEO. Yum Brands is excited about Africa's growing middle class, vast population, and improving political stability of most African governments. Yum Brands is especially targeting Nigeria, Namibia, Mozambique, Ghana, Zambia, and South Africa. The company says it wants to reach more of Africa's one billion people than its current customer base of 180 million. But KFC currently has about 45 percent of South Africa's fast-food market, followed by Nando's with 6 percent and McDonald's with 5 percent. KFC is opening 25 new outlets in Ghana in 2013-2014, part of the company's 1,200 KFCs in Africa by year-end 2014.

Ghana recently became Africa's newest oil-producing nation when the 1.5-billion-barrel Jubilee field began pumping oil. Although Ghana's estimated 4 billion barrels of reserves are about a third those of Nigeria, Ghana has a stable political and economic situation. Ethiopia is also doing well economically. SABMiller PLC recently invested $20 million in a manufacturing plant in Ethiopia's large city, Ambo. That factory today produces 40,000 glass bottles of mineral water per hour. Ambo sells for about $6 a bottle in New York restaurants. Ambo water is part of the SABMiller portfolio that includes 45 African beers.[10]

Nairobi, Kenya, is the center of several major telecom companies trying to gain market share in the rapidly growing African cellphone business. Vodafone Safaricom Ltd. dominates the Kenyan telecommunications sector with 77 percent market share, but India's Bharti Airtel Ltd. boosted its market share in the last year to almost 20 percent. There are currently more than 440 million mobile subscribers in Africa generating more than $15 billion in telecom revenue annually. All of Africa is coming online, representing huge opportunities for countless companies. McKinsey & Co. estimates that within five years another 220 million Africans that today can meet only basic needs will join the middle class as consumers.[11] There are more than 950 million people who live in Africa.

China

In late 2012, China's economy began to accelerate after nearly two years of slowing growth. China's industrial production grew 9.6 percent in October 2012, up from a 9.2 percent gain in September. China's GDP grew at 7.4 percent in the third quarter of 2012 year-over-year. Analysts expect continued increasing growth, giving a lift to global economic prospects. Although the USA is the world's largest economy with a GDP of over $15 trillion annually, China recently passed Japan to become the world's second-largest economy with a GDP of about $5.75 trillion annually, compared to Japan's $6 trillion. China, however, is still an emerging economy, as indicated by a per-capita GDP of $10,000, compared to the USA and Japan per-capita GDPs of $48,000 and $47,000, respectively. China's economic (GDP) growth of over 9 percent annually for several decades is, however, much faster than either the USA or Japan. Premier Wen Jiabao recently proclaimed that China's annual GDP growth will be held to 7.0 percent if possible to constrain inflation. Goldman Sachs predicts that China will overtake the USA as the world's largest economy by 2027.

China's rapid growth has created substantial pollution, extensive inequality, and deeply embedded corruption. In fact, China's communist government is concerned that political unrest in the Middle East may spread to China in a "Jasmine Revolution" because the masses in China barely make enough to survive. The World Bank estimates that more than 100 million Chinese citizens, nearly the size of Japan's entire population, live on less than $2 a day—but China's middle class is growing rapidly.

For many decades, low wage rates in China helped keep world prices low on hundreds of products—but that is changing, because all 31 Chinese provinces and regions recently boosted their minimum wage for the second consecutive year. Analysts expect demand for workers in China to outstrip supply by 2014, and this is contributing to rapidly rising wage rates and worldwide inflation. Commercial and industrial development in China's west has turned interior cities such as Chongqing into production centers that compete for labor with coastal factories. According to Credit Suisse in Hong Kong, pay to migrant laborers who fuel China's export industry rose 40 percent in 2010 and 30 percent in 2011, and similar increases are expected in 2012. Average monthly pay in 2009 in Shenzhen on the southern China coast was $235, compared to Seoul's $1,220, Taipei's $888, Ho Chi Minh City's $100, Jakarta's $148, and $47 in Dhaka, Bangladesh.[12]

China has become the biggest trading partner for Australia, Japan, Korea, India, Russia, and South Africa and has replaced the USA as the top export market for Brazil. The world's two fastest-growing major economies, China and India, recently announced that the two countries will more than double their bilateral trade between 2010 and 2015 to $100 billion.[13] China is opening its large consumer markets more to Indian goods. China may soon support India having a permanent seat on the United Nations Security Council. China has long opposed a permanent seat for India. The increased cooperation between China and India is good news for companies worldwide doing business in that part of Asia.

As indicated in Table 2-7, China ranks 91st out of 183 countries in terms of doing business, for a variety of reasons ranging from human rights issues to substantial disregard for copyright, patent, and trademark rules of law. Best Buy and Home Depot are example companies that are closing stores in China. Both firms have not competed well in China as a result of being too "high priced" compared to home-grown, similar businesses. The Chinese are price conscious. In contrast, luxury handbag maker, Coach Inc. has made China the cornerstone of its international strategy as the firm's sales and profits are rising sharply in China. Interestingly, Coach is adding more products for men and opening men's stores in China.

China is gaining a stronger and stronger foothold into Japanese businesses. The five largest recent Chinese investments in Japan are Mitsubishi UFJ Financial (92 billion yen), Canon (74.5 billion yen), Sumitomo Mitsui (57.9 billion yen), Nippon T&T (49.2 billion yen), Mitsubishi (47.8 billion yen), Takeda Pharm (45.4 billion yen), and Sony (41.6 billion yen). The Japanese investment adviser Chibagin Asset Management says China state funds have recently more than doubled their investment in Japan to 1.62 trillion yen in 90 companies.

Note also in Table 2-8 that Singapore is rated the best country on the planet for doing business.

TABLE 2-8 Sampling of Asian Countries— Ease-of-Doing-Business Rankings

	Population in Millions	Ease of Doing Business Among all Countries	Capital City
Singapore	5	1 out of 183	Singapore
South Korea	49	8 out of 183	Seoul
Malaysia	26	18 out of 183	Kuala Lumpur
Thailand	66	19 out of 183	Bangkok
Japan	127	20 out of 183	Tokyo
Taiwan	23	25 out of 183	Taipei
China	1,500	91 out of 183	Beijing
Pakistan	175	105 out of 183	Islamabad
Russia	140	120 out of 183	Moscow
Indonesia	241	129 out of 183	Jakarta
India	1,160	132 out of 183	New Delhi
Philippines	98	136 out of 183	Manila

Source: Based on information at http://www.doingbusiness.org/rankings on November 1, 2012.

Philippines

A highly educated, English speaking country, the Philippines overtook India in early 2011 in call-center jobs, employing 350,000 compared with India's 330,000.[14] Call centers in the Philippines produced $7.4 billion in revenue in 2011, and that figure is growing about 15 percent annually. The Philippines recently also overtook Indonesia as the world's biggest supplier of voice-based call-center services.[15] Citigroup and Chase are just two companies outsourcing customer calls, back-office work, and other operations to the Philippines. A major reason why the Philippines is an attractive place for call centers is the country's overall business culture to "deliver absolutely fantastic service." An associate professor at the City University of Hong Kong, Jane Lockwood, says "Filipinos go out of their way, not just in call centers, but in tourism and events management, to ensure people are well looked after."[16]

As indicated in Table 2-8, the Philippines has about 98 million people, making the country the world's 12th largest in population. Located in Southeast Asia, the Philippines was a founding member of the United Nations and is active in that organization. Filipinos love Americans who rescued them in World War II. Thousands of Filipinos today work all-night shifts to accommodate the normal 8 am-to-5 pm business time zone in the USA. Philippines president Benigno Aquino recently indicated that services outsourced to the Philippines from around the world will generate up to $100 billion in 2020, representing 20 percent of the global offshoring market share.

Unemployment is at 6.9 percent in the Philippines, but under-employment—defined as people who work only part-time or with minimal incomes—is 18 percent. The average per capita income of Filipinos is about $1,790 a year, so hundreds of thousands of Filipinos work outside the country. In fact, the Philippines' economy depends greatly on outside workers sending monies back to the country and also traveling to and from the country.

The television advertising market in the Philippines is nearly $4 billion annually, larger than India's and on par with Indonesia's.[17] Television is the most enjoyed media among the Philippines' 7,100 island people, whereas newspapers are the most important media outlet in India. Television ads comprise 75 percent of advertising spending in the Philippines.

Among major emerging economies, the Philippines has only a 9 percent Internet penetration rate among its population, which is low compared to China (28.9%), Nigeria (28.4%), Mexico (28.3%), and Russia (29.0%). But the Philippines' 9 percent rate is above the Internet penetration rate among Indonesia's population (8.7%) and India's population (5.1%).[18] These percentages reveal the percentage of the country's people that could shop online.

Taiwan

Located off the southeast coast of mainland China, Taiwan has a dynamic, capitalist, export-driven economy with gradually decreasing state involvement in investment and foreign trade. Many large, government-owned banks and industrial firms are being privatized in Taiwan. Real annual growth in GDP has averaged about 8 percent during the past three decades. Exports have provided the primary impetus for industrialization. The trade surplus is substantial, and foreign reserves are the world's fifth largest. As indicated in Table 2-8, Taiwan is rated 25th among all countries in the world for doing business.

Both exports and imports for the year reached record levels, totaling U.S. $274 billion and $251 billion, respectively. Agriculture constitutes only 2 percent of Taiwan's GDP, down from 35 percent in 1952. Some brands from Taiwan that are leaders globally include: Acer, HTC, ASUS, TrendMicro, MasterKong, Want-Want, Maxxis, Giant, Synnex, Transcend, Uni-President, Advantech, D-Link, ZyXel, Merida, Johnson, Gigabyte, CyberLink, Genius, and Depo.

India

India passed a law in late 2011 that for the first time allows foreign firms to own 100 percent of some Indian retail ventures, up from a previous 51 percent. One company taking advantage of this change in the law is IKEA that is opening up 25 new stores in India between 2012 and 2015. Since India's growth in GDP has fallen to below 6 percent, the Indian government began to allow much greater foreign investment especially in Indian retail, airlines, and broadcasting in 2012.[19] The country also greatly reduced the expensive government subsidies on diesel fuel and Indian banks are lowering interest rates also to spur growth.

In late 2012, India instituted a five-year road map to improve it finances, aiming to narrow its budget deficit to 5.3 percent of gross domestic product to 3 percent by 2017. A slowdown in growth to 5 percent in 2012, coupled with massive welfare spending, has led to an unmanageable budget deficit in India. Complicating matters in India are high interest rates and some corruption scandals. The Indian Parliament recently approved higher overseas ownership in their insurance and pension investments sectors of the economy.

The Indian government is slowly improving the country's education system, but an enormous amount of work remains. Only 74 percent of Indian men and 48 percent of Indian women are literate, compared to 96 percent of men and 88 percent of women in China. India's "knowledge economy" employs only about 2.23 million people out of 750 million available.

Prime Minister Manmohan Singh's government has instituted education reforms, so the number of Indian children out of school has dropped greatly from 18 million in 2000. Dropout ratios in primary schools have improved as well. However, at present only 12 percent of India's citizens enter higher education, and the government hopes to increase this to 21 percent by 2017. The Indian Institutes of Technology—a group of universities focused on engineering and technology—are world renowned but offer only a miniscule 7,000 places to students each year. There is elaborate red tape required to establish and operate any business in India. Also, India's tax code is archaic and many new sectors are not even open to foreign direct investment.

India will surpass China as the most populated country in 2030. India's highest density growth and population is in the northwest and east-central areas of the country. India has a literacy rate now of 74 percent, up from 65 percent a decade ago.

Germany

Germany's cars, machinery, and other products are in high demand in Asia, especially China. As Europe's debt crisis has pushed the euro lower, German goods are more competitive abroad. The economic and fiscal crises in Greece, Ireland, Portugal, and Spain have only limited direct impact on Germany's $3.24 trillion economy. There is a growing north-south divide in Europe, with the north doing much better economically than the south. Germany's budget deficit was 3.5 percent in 2010, the first time in years that the country has exceeded the 3 percent limit set by EU budget rules, but that percent is well below the deficit in the USA, the UK, and Japan— so overall the German economy is healthy. Note in Table 2-9 that Germany ranks 22nd out of 183 countries in ease of doing business.

German automobile producers such as Daimler AG, BMW AG, and Volkswagen AG have fallen behind rivals such as GM, Renault SA, and Nissan Motor in mass-producing electric cars. The German companies are playing catch up in this key area of industrial growth, partly because the German government has committed just $688 million in state support for electric battery research and infrastructure projects, such as car-charging stations. That amount is only a small fraction of the U.S. (and Chinese) government support for electric cars. Because one

TABLE 2-9 Sampling of European Countries— Ease-of-Doing-Business Rankings

	Population in Millions	Ease of Doing Business Among All Countries	Capital City
UK	62	7 out of 183	London
Sweden	9	14 out of 183	Stockholm
Germany	83	19 out of 183	Berlin
France	64	29 out of 183	Paris
Czech Republic	11	64 out of 183	Prague
Turkey	77	71 out of 183	Ankara
Italy	59	87 out of 183	Rome
Ukraine	46	152 out of 183	Kiev

Source: Based on information at http://www.doingbusiness.org/rankings on November 1, 2012.

out of seven German jobs is connected to the country's car markers and domestic suppliers, this issue is important. More than 15 percent of German exports stem from the automobile industry. Germany also fallen way behind in electric car lithium-ion battery development and production.

The EU is a single economic bloc with free movement of people, goods, and services among its 27 nations, but in matters such as taxes and labor costs, each country sets its own rules. Businesses entering Europe for the first time need to carefully research the various countries. Belgium, for example, has the highest labor costs in Europe with 53 percent of workers there being unionized, but that percent is only the fifth highest in Europe.

Germany has one of Europe's fastest aging and shrinking populations. Germany now faces shortages of skilled labor and aggressive recruiting from abroad for the country's top engineering and scientific talent.[20] More people emigrate from Germany than relocate to Germany, especially highly educated professionals—partly because Germany has a restrictive labor code and inward-looking hiring practices. Germany might need to follow the lead of Italy, which has the same, albeit more severe, problem but has enacted excellent new laws and incentives to both keep and attract young, highly educated professionals.

Mexico

In late 2012, Mexico elected a new president, Enrique Pena Nieto, who inherits a country with a homicide rate of 24 per 100,000 residents up from 10 per 100,000 in 2006. But homicides in Mexico fell 7 percent in the first nine months of 2012, and Nieto plans to continue his predecessor's war on drug cartels and war on corruption. For example, all 600 municipal policemen in Mexico's business-leading city of Monterrey were fired recently and replaced with Mexican military personnel because of suspected corruption.

Mexico has recently reenergized its automobile manufacturing industry and now is the fourth largest automobile exporter on the planet, behind Germany, Japan, and South Korea. One in 10 cars sold in 2011 in the USA was made in Mexico.[21] Every new taxi in New York City's fleet is made in Mexico. Almost all major automobile producers globally have recently announced plans to build new plants in Mexico, including the upcoming new $1.3 billion Volkswagen plant. An already existing Volkswagen plant in Puebla, Mexico, is the company's largest in North America, with a capacity to produce 2,500 cars a day. "Mexico is extremely competitive," says Carlos Ghosn, Nissan's CEO. Ghosn cites the high productivity of Mexican employees, currency advantages, and the typical $40 per day wage rate for Mexican assembly-line workers, which is approaching the average manufacturing wage in China of $3 per hour. Honda is opening a 3,200-employee factory in 2014 in Mexico to produce its subcompact model Fit. Another key advantage for producing vehicles in Mexico over Europe and Asia is that shipment to the USA takes only a day or two, instead of a few weeks by ship.

No country was hurt more in the last decade by the rise of China than Mexico, but Chinese policy today is to boost wages to boost consumer spending. The Boston Consulting Group estimates that "China's average manufacturing wage exceeded Mexico's in 2012 for the first time, when accounting for differences in productivity; Mexican workers typically produce more per hour than Chinese workers."[22] The average wage plus benefits across Mexico is $3.50 an hour. This fact, coupled with China's rising wages and slowing growth and Mexico's close proximity to the USA, represents a great opportunity for Mexico to recoup some of a lot of the manufacturing prowess it lost in the last decade to China. Viaststems Group, based in St. Louis, recently shifted some of its manufacturing back to Mexico from China. Although Dell Inc. computers are produced by Foxconn in China, U.S. customers can order a customized Dell computer online that is assembled and delivered from a 1,200-acre Foxconn plant near Ciudad Juarez.

Foreign direct investment (FDI) in Mexico in 2013 surged to almost $30 billion, led by automobile manufacturers such as Volkswagen AG building new factories, and auto-parts suppliers such as Delphi Automotive PLC following. Home Depot will soon have 125 stores in Mexico. The FDI surge is expected to last at least through 2018, spurred by low wages, and government policies that allow foreign companies to import raw materials without paying duties or tariffs, a 30 percent corporate tax rate, and rising wages in China. However, note in Table 2-10 that Mexico fell from 35th place to 53rd place in the last two years among all nations in terms of ease of doing business.

TABLE 2-10   **Sampling of North and South American Countries—Ease-of-Doing-Business Rankings**

	Population in Millions	Ease of Doing Business Among all Countries	Capital City
USA	308	4 out of 183	Washington, DC
Canada	34	13 out of 183	Ottawa
Chile	17	39 out of 183	Santiago
Peru	30	41 out of 183	Lima
Mexico	112	53 out of 183	Mexico City
Argentina	41	113 out of 183	Buenos Aires
Brazil	199	126 out of 183	Brasilia
Ecuador	15	130 out of 183	Quito
Bolivia	10	153 out of 183	La Paz
Venezuela	27	177 out of 183	Caracus

Source: Based on information at http://www.doingbusiness.org/rankings on November 1, 2012.

Mexico is especially attractive for manufacturing products that are bulky or costly to transport, so for example, Nissan Motor and Volkswagen AG are planning to build factories in Mexico. The key variable hurting Mexico is drug-related violence since a 2011 United National report says Mexico's homicide rate was 18.1 people per 100,000 compared with a per capita rate of about 5.0 in the USA and 1.1 in China. If Mexico can improve its security situation as it intends, then hundreds of firms may consider moving back there from China (and India).

Special Note to Students

Even the smallest businesses today regularly serve customers globally and gain competitive advantages and economies of scale doing so. Many iconic U.S. businesses, such as Tupperware, obtain more than 80 percent of their revenue from outside the USA. Therefore, in performing a strategic-management case analysis, you must evaluate the scope, magnitude, and nature of what your company is doing globally compared to rival firms. Then, determine what your company should be doing to garner global business. Continuously throughout your presentation or written report, compare your firm to rivals in terms of global business and make recommendations based on careful analysis. Be "prescriptive and insightful" rather than "descriptive and mundane" with every slide presented to pave the way for your specific recommendations with costs regarding global reach of your firm.

Conclusion

The population of the world has surpassed 7 billion. Just as they did for centuries before Columbus reached America, businesses search for new opportunities beyond their national boundaries for centuries to come. There has never been a more internationalized and economically competitive society than today's model. Some U.S. industries, such as textiles, steel, and consumer electronics, are in disarray as a result of the international challenge.

Success in business increasingly depends on offering products and services that are competitive on a world basis, not just on a local basis. If the price and quality of a firm's products and services are not competitive with those available elsewhere in the world, the firm may soon face extinction. Global markets have become a reality in all but the most remote areas of the world. Certainly throughout the USA, even in small towns, firms feel the pressure of world competitors.

This chapter has provided some basic global information that can be essential to consider in developing a strategic plan for any organization. The advantages of engaging in international business may well offset the drawbacks for most firms. It is important in strategic planning to be effective, and the nature of global operations may be the key component in a plan's overall effectiveness.

Key Terms and Concepts

feng shui (p. 86)
global strategy (p. 82)
globalization (p. 82)
guanxi (p. 84)
international firms (p. 79)

inhwa (p. 84)
multinational corporations (p. 79)
nemaswashio (p. 86)
protectionism (p. 81)
Wa (p. 84)

Issues for Review and Discussion

2-1. Honda Motor Company has been very successful in recent years. What percentage of Honda's revenues comes from the United States versus Europe? How does this percentage compare with rival firms?

2-2. Explain why consumption patterns are becoming similar worldwide. What are the strategic implications of this trend?

2-3. What are the advantages and disadvantages of beginning export operations in a foreign country?

2-4. What are the major differences between U.S. and multinational operations that affect strategic management?

2-5. Why is globalization of industries a common factor today?

2-6. Compare and contrast U.S. versus foreign cultures in terms of doing business.

2-7. List six reasons why strategic management is more complex in a multinational firm.

2-8. Do you feel that protectionism is good or bad for the world economy? Why?

2-9. Why are some industries more "global" than others? Discuss.

2-10. *Wa, guanxi* and *inhwa* are important management terms in Japan, China, and Korea respectively. What would be analogous terms to describe American management practices?

2-11. Why do many Europeans also find the notion of "team spirit" in a work environment difficult to grasp?

2-12. In China, *feng shui*, is important in business, whereas in Japan *nemaswashio*, is important. What are analogous American terms and practices?

2-13. Describe the business culture in Mexico.

2-14. Describe the business culture in Japan.

2-15. Compare tax rates in the United States versus other countries. What impact could these differences have on "keeping jobs at home?"

2-16. Discuss the requirements for doing business in India.

2-17. Select four countries. Evaluate Honda Motor Company's operations in those countries.

2-18. Compare business practices and culture in northern Europe with southern Europe.

2-19. Explain how the Arab Spring movement in the Middle East will likely impact Pfizer.

2-20. What five countries in Asia have the highest GDP? What are its implications for adidas?

2-21. Africa is rapidly joining the world economic community. Give 10 examples to justify this.

2-22. Which six African countries do you feel are most attractive for foreign investment?

2-23. Compare business practice and culture in the USA with your own country.

2-24. Explain in your own words the "Special Note to Students" section at the end of the chapter.

2-25. Select three countries in South America. Prepare a one-page summary for each to reveal their attractiveness for foreign direct investment.

2-26. Compare sexual harassment policies and practice across continents and countries.

2-27. Discuss Australia as a continent for doing business in.

2-28. In terms of presenting flowers as business gifts, compare and contrast the practices and customs across six countries.

2-29. Discuss how business etiquette at dinner varies across countries.

MyManagementLab®

Go to **mymanagementlab.com** for the following Assisted-graded writing questions:

2-30. Make a good argument for keeping the statutory corporate tax rate in the United States the highest in the world. Make the counterargument.

2-31. What are the advantages and disadvantages of beginning export operations in a foreign country?

Current Readings

Aguinis, Herman, Harry Joo, Ryan K. Gottfredson. "Performance Management Universals: Think Globally and Act Locally." *Business Horizons* 55, no. 4 (July 2012): 385–392.

Berthon, Pierre R., Leyland F. Pitt, Kirk Plangger, and Daniel Shapiro. "Marketing Meets Web 2.0, Social Media, and Creative Consumers: Implications for International Marketing Strategy." *Business Horizons* 55, no. 3 (May 2012): 261–271.

Bloom, Nicholas, Christos Genakos, Raffaella Sadun, and John Van Reenen. "Management Practices Across Firms and Countries." *The Academy of Management Perspectives 26*, no. 1 (February 2012): 12.

Govindarajan, Vijay and Chris Trimble. "Reverse Innovation: A Global Growth Strategy That Could Pre-empt Disruption at Home." *Strategy and Leadership* 40, no. 5 (2012): 5–11.

Honeycutt, Earl D., Vincent P. Magnini, and Shawn T. Thelen. "Solutions for Customer Complaints About Offshoring and Outsourcing Services." *Business Horizons* 55, no. 1 (January 2012): 33–42.

Ichii, Shigeki, Susumu Hattori, and David Michael. "How to Win in Emerging Markets: Lessons from Japan." *Harvard Business Review* (May 2012): 126.

Ignatius, Adi. "Captain Planet." *Harvard Business Review* (June 2012): 112.

Pagnattaro, Marisa Anne. "Preventing Know-How From Walking Out the Door in China: Protection of Trade Secrets." *Business Horizons* 55, no. 4 (July 2012): 329–337.

Porter, Michael E., and Jan W. Rivkin. "Choosing the USA." *Harvard Business Review* (March 2012): 80.

Ramamurti, Ravi. "Competing with Emerging Market Multinationals." *Business Horizons* 55, no. 3 (May 2012): 241–249.

Thomas, Robert J., Joshua Bellin, Claudy Jules, and Nandani Lynton. "Global Leadership Teams: Diagnosing Three Essential Qualities." *Strategy and Leadership* 40, no. 4 (2012): 25–29.

Underwood, Robert L. "Automotive Foreign Direct Investment in the USA: Economic and Market Consequences of Globalization." *Business Horizons* 55, no. 5 (September 2012): 463–474.

Waldman, David A., Mary Sully de Luque, and Danni Wang. "What Can We Really Learn About Management Practices Across Firms and Countries?" *The Academy of Management Perspectives 26*, no. 1 (February 2012): 34.

ASSURANCE OF LEARNING EXERCISES

EXERCISE 2A
The adidas Group wants to enter Africa. Help them.

Purpose

More and more companies every day decide to begin doing business in Africa. Research is necessary to determine the best strategy for being the first mover in many African countries (i.e., being the first competitor doing business in various countries).

Step 1	Print a map of Africa.
Step 2	Print demographic data on 10 African countries.
Step 3	Gather competitive information regarding the presence of shoe companies doing business in Africa.
Step 4	List in prioritized order eight countries that you would recommend for adidas to enter. Country 1 is your best, and Country 2 is your next best. Based on your research, indicate how many adidas/Reebok/TaylorMade stores you would recommend building over the next three years in each country. List in prioritized order three cities in each of your eight African countries where you believe adidas should build most of its stores.

EXERCISE 2B
Assessing Differences in Culture Across Countries

Purpose

Americans can be more effective in dealing with businesspeople from other countries if they have some awareness and understanding of differences in culture across countries. This is a fun exercise that provides information for your class regarding some of these key differences.

Instructions

Step 1	Identify four individuals who either grew up in a foreign country or have lived in a foreign country for more than one year. Interview those four persons. Try to have four different countries represented. During each interview, develop a list of eight key differences between American style/custom and that particular country's style/custom in terms of various aspects of speaking, meetings, meals, relationships, friendships, and communication that could impact business dealings.
Step 2	Develop a 15-minute PowerPoint presentation for your class and give a talk summarizing your findings. Identify in your talk the persons you interviewed as well as the length of time those persons lived in the respective countries. Give your professor a hard copy of your PowerPoint presentation.

EXERCISE 2C
Honda Motor Company wants to enter the Vietnamese market. Help them.

Purpose

More and more companies every day decide to begin doing business in Vietnam. Research is necessary to determine the best strategy for being competitive in Vietnam. Review the opening chapter boxed insert and Honda Motor Company's website.

Instructions

Step 1	Print off a map of Vietnam.
Step 2	Print off demographic data on 10 cities in Vietnam.
Step 3	Gather competitive information regarding the presence of automobile companies doing business in Vietnam.
Step 4	List in prioritized order the five cities that you would recommend for Honda to expand their business operations into.

EXERCISE 2D
Does My University Recruit in Foreign Countries?

Purpose

A competitive climate is emerging among colleges and universities around the world. Colleges and universities in Europe and Japan are increasingly recruiting U.S. students to offset declining enrollments. Foreign students already make up more than one-third of the student body at many U.S. universities. The purpose of this exercise is to identify particular colleges and universities in foreign countries that represent a competitive threat to your college.

Instructions

Step 1	Select a foreign country. Conduct research to determine the number and nature of colleges and universities in that country. What are the major educational institutions in that country? What programs are those institutions recognized for offering? What percentage of undergraduate and graduate students attending those institutions are citizens of your country? Do these institutions actively recruit students from your country? Are any of the Schools of Business at the various universities AACSB-International accredited?
Step 2	Prepare a report for the class that summarizes your research findings. Present your report to the class.

Notes

1. Frederick Gluck, "Global Competition in the 1990s," *Journal of Business Strategy* (Spring 1983): 22–24.

2. Jon Alston, "Wa, Guanxi, and Inhwa: Managerial Principles in Japan, China and Korea," *Business Horizons* 32, no. 2 (March–April 1989): 26.

3. Rose Knotts, "Cross-Cultural Management: Transformations and Adaptations," *Business Horizons*, January–February 1989, 29–33.

4. Lalita Khosla, "You Say Tomato," *Forbes*, May 21, 2001, 36.

5. Some of the narrative in this section is based on information at: http://www.kwintessential.co.uk/resources/ country-profiles.html and http://www.kwintessential.co.uk/ resources/global-etiquette/.

6. Mehul Srivastava, "Keeping Women on the Job in India," *Bloomberg Businessweek*, March 7–13, 2011, 11–12; Stratford Sherman, "How to Beat the Japanese? *Fortune*, April 10, 1989, 145.

7. Patrick McGroarty, "Debt Investors Put Faith in a More Stable Africa," *Wall Street Journal* (October 24, 2012): C1.

8. Ibid.

9. Julie Jargon, "KFC Savors Potential in Africa," *Wall Street Journal*, December 8, 2010, B1. Peter Wonacott, "A Continent of New Consumers Beckons," *Wall Street Journal*, January 13, 2011, B1.

10. Peter Wonacott, "SABMiller Taps Ethiopia's Holy Water," *Wall Street Journal*, January 13, 2011, B1.

11. Sarah Childress, "Telecom Giants Battle for Kenya," *Wall Street Journal*, January 14, 2011, B1.

12. Sophie Leung and Simon Kennedy with Cotton Timberlake and Chris Burritt, "Global Inflation Starts With Chinese Workers," *Bloomberg Businessweek*, March 7–13, 2011, 9–10.

13. Arpan Mukherjee and Abhrajit Gangopadhyay, "India, China Aim to Double Trade," *Wall Street Journal*, December 17, 2010, A15.

14. Michelle Yun and Kathy Chu, "Philippines May Answer Call," *USA Today*, January 10. 2011, 1–2B.

15. Ibid.

16. James Hookway, "Dollar's Fall Rocks Far-Flung Families," *Wall Street Journal*, February 25, 2011, A12.

17. James Hookway, "High Drama for Philippine TV," *Wall Street Journal*, March 3, 2011, B10.

18. Amol Sharma, "Dot-Coms Begin to Blossom in India," *Wall Street Journal*, April 12, 2011, B1.

19. Rumman Ahmed and Romit Guha, "India Faces Fight Over Foreign Firms," *Wall Street Journal (September* 17, 2012): A12.

20. Vanessa Fuhrmans, "Exodus of Skilled Labor Saps Germany," *Wall Street Journal*, March 11, 2011, A12.

21. Nicholas Casey, "In Mexico, Auto Plants Hit the Gas," *Wall Street Journal* (11-20-12): A1.

22. Luhnow, David and Bob Davis, "For Mexico, an Edge on China," *Wall Street Journal* (September 17, 2012): A12.

3

Source: © contrastwerkstatt/Fotolia

MyManagementLab®

Improve Your Grade!

Over 10 million students improved their results using the Pearson MyLabs.
Visit **mymanagementlab.com** for simulations, tutorials, and end-of-chapter problems.

Ethics/
Social Responsibility/
Sustainability

CHAPTER OBJECTIVES

After studying this chapter, you should be able to do the following:

1. Discuss the ethics of workplace romance.

2. Explain why concern for wildlife is a strategic issue for firms.

3. Explain why good ethics is good business in strategic management.

4. Explain how firms can best ensure that their code of business ethics guides decision making instead of being ignored.

5. Explain why whistle-blowing is important to encourage in a firm.

6. Discuss the nature and role of corporate sustainability reports.

7. Discuss specific ways that firms can be good stewards of the natural environment.

8. Explain ISO 14000 and 14001.

9. Discuss recent trends in bribery law.

ASSURANCE OF LEARNING EXERCISES

The following exercises are found at the end of this chapter.

Although the three sections of this chapter (business ethics, social responsibility, and sustainability) are distinct, the topics are quite related. Many people, for example, consider it unethical for a firm to be socially irresponsible. **Social responsibility** refers to actions an organization takes beyond what is legally required to protect or enhance the well-being of living things. **Sustainability** refers to the extent that an organization's operations and actions protect, mend, and preserve rather than harm or destroy the natural environment. Polluting the environment, for example, is unethical, irresponsible, and in many cases illegal. Business ethics, social responsibility, and sustainability issues therefore are interrelated and impact all areas of the comprehensive strategic-management model, as illustrated in Figure 3-1 with white shading.

Business Ethics

The Institute of Business Ethics (IBE) recently did a study titled "Does Business Ethics Pay?" and concluded that companies displaying a "clear commitment to ethical conduct" consistently outperform companies that do not display ethical conduct. Philippa Foster Black of the IBE stated: "Not only is ethical behavior in business life the right thing to do in principle, it pays off in financial returns." Alan Simpson said: "If you have integrity, nothing else matters. If you don't have integrity, nothing else matters." Table 3-1 provides some results of the IBE study.

EXCELLENT STRATEGIC MANAGEMENT SHOWCASED

Nestlé

Nestlé S.A., headquartered in Vevey, Switzerland, is the largest food company in the world measured by revenues. Nestlé has hundreds of products that include cereals, coffee, dairy products, pet foods, snacks, baby food, and bottled water. Thirty of Nestlé's brands have annual sales of over 1 billion Swiss francs (about $1.1 billion), including Nespresso, Nescafe, Kit Kat, Smarties, Nesquick, Stouffers, Vittel, and Maggi. Nestlé has around 450 factories, operates in 86 countries, and employs around 328,000 people. It is one of the main shareholders of L'Oreal, the world's largest cosmetics company. In April 2012, Nestlé acquired Pfizer's infant-nutrition business for $11.9 billion. In May 2013, Nestlé began a $500 million expansion of its R&D center in Singapore, with a primary focus on health and nutrition.

In order to ensure that various standards within the supply chain maintain a certain level, Nestlé developed the Nestlé Supplier Code. The Code sets out non-negotiable minimum standards which all employees, subcontractors, and suppliers must meet and adhere to whilst doing business with Nestlé. Available in 22 languages on the corporate website, the Nestlé Supplier Code forms an important part of all contracts, orders, and commercial agreements that Nestlé enters into with all 165,000 suppliers and 680,000 farmers that form the Nestlé supply chain. The aim of the Nestlé Supplier Code is to ensure that all the company's suppliers and farmers conduct business in a manner that upholds Nestlé's high values and emphasis on fairness and integrity.

Nestlé's performance for the first half of 2013 was exemplary. The company's profit margins by-region, in the Americas, Europe, and Asia/Oceania/Africa were 17.8, 14.9, and 19.1 percent respectively. The profit margins for Nestle Waters and Nestlé Nutrition were 10 percent and 20 percent respectively. Overall for Nestlé for the first half of 2013, the company generated a positive 4.1 percent organic growth and a 15.1 operating profit margin – both exemplary results.

Regarding Nestlé's by-product financial results for the first of 2013, the company's operating profit margins were all positive, as follows: 1) Powdered and liquid beverages (24%), 2) Water (10.7%), 3) Milk products and ice cream (15.9%), 4) Nutrition & HealthCare (18.6%), 5) Prepared dishes and cooking aids (13.5%), 6) Confectionery (12.7%), and PetCare (19.0%). All of the reported results are also exemplary.

Source: Based on company documents.

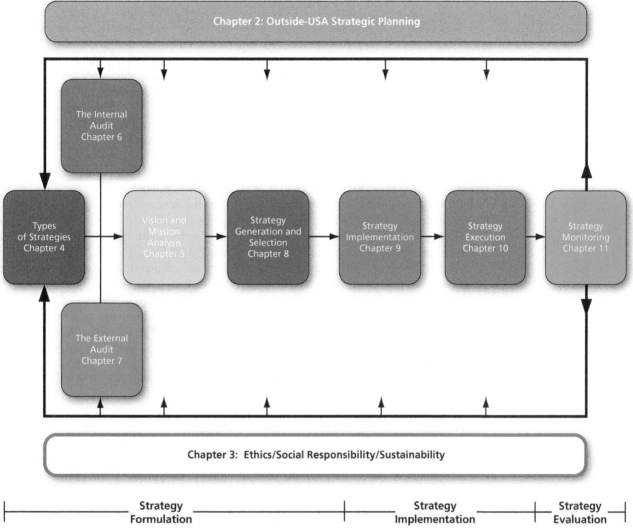

FIGURE 3-1

A Comprehensive Strategic-Management Model

Source: Fred R. David, adapted from "How Companies Define Their Mission," *Long Range Planning* 22, no. 3 (June 1988): 40, © Fred R. David.

Good ethics is good business. Bad ethics can derail even the best strategic plans. This chapter provides an overview of the importance of business ethics in strategic management. **Business ethics** can be defined as principles of conduct within organizations that guide decision making and behavior. Good business ethics is a prerequisite for good strategic management; good ethics is just good business!

TABLE 3-1   Seven Principles of Admirable Business Ethics

---

1. Be trustworthy, because no individual or business wants to do business with an entity they do not trust.
2. Be openminded, continually asking for "ethics-related feedback" from all internal and external stakeholders.
3. Honor all commitments and obligations.
4. Do not misrepresent, exaggerate, or mislead with any print materials.
5. Be visibly a responsible community citizen.
6. Utilize your accounting practices to identify and eliminate questionable activities.
7. Follow the motto: Do unto others as you would have them do unto you.

Source: Based on http://sbinformation.about.com/od/bestpractices/a/businessethics.htm.

A rising tide of consciousness about the importance of business ethics is sweeping the USA and the rest of the world. Strategists such as CEOs and business owners are the individuals primarily responsible for ensuring that high ethical principles are espoused and practiced in an organization. All strategy formulation, implementation, and evaluation decisions have ethical ramifications.

Newspapers and business magazines daily report legal and moral breaches of ethical conduct by both public and private organizations. Being unethical can be expensive. For example, some of the largest payouts for class-action legal fraud suits ever were against Enron ($7.16 billion), WorldCom ($6.16 billion), Cendant ($3.53 billion), Tyco ($2.98 billion), AOL Time Warner ($2.5 billion), Nortel Networks ($2.47 billion), and Royal Ahold ($1.09 billion).

Other business actions considered to be unethical include misleading advertising or labeling, causing environmental harm, poor product or service safety, padding expense accounts, insider trading, dumping banned or flawed products in foreign markets, not providing equal opportunities for women and minorities, overpricing, moving jobs overseas, and sexual harassment.

The Food and Drug Administration (FDA) recently warned both Avon Products and L'Oreal about misleading marketing of certain of its antiwrinkle products. The FDA's position is that Avon and L'Oreal's claims that discuss things like the stimulation of skin cells or reactivating the skin's repair process are not true.

Yahoo!'s CEO Scott Thompson recently was forced to resign as a result of his "resume padding or inflating." J.P. Morgan Chase CEO Jamie Dimon is currently under fire after the investment bank's $2.3 billion trading blunder that has already cost a key deputy her job. Increasingly, executives' and managers' personal and professional decisions are placing them in the cross hairs of angry shareholders, disgruntled employees, and even their own boards of directors—making even the imperious CEO far more vulnerable to personal, public, and corporate missteps than ever before. "Certainly, anybody who is doing something that can be construed as unethical, immoral or greedy is being taken to task," says Paul Dorf of Compensation Resources, a consultant to boards of directors.[1]

Social media and business-centric websites such as glassdoor.com and vault.com as well as disclosure mandates required under Sarbanes-Oxley are just several of many outlets that today quickly spread fact and rumor about the inside dealings of Corporate America, revealing ethical breaches and internal business practices that may never have surfaced before the Internet and a 24/7 media culture. "God forbid anyone who isn't squeaky-clean these days or misrepresents their credentials at the top of the company," says Wendy Patrick, who teaches business ethics at San Diego State University. "Anything embarrassing and you begin to question everything. If they aren't making good decisions in their personal lives, it can bleed over to the way they run their companies."

"The pressure and scrutiny on performance has shortened the tenure of the average CEO from about 10 years to about 5½ years since the 1990s," says John Challenger of consultants Challenger Gray and Christmas. Challenger notes that 42 CEOs were forced out of their jobs in 2011 and that pace is up 5 percent in 2012.[2]

Code of Business Ethics

A new wave of ethics issues related to product safety, employee health, sexual harassment, AIDS in the workplace, smoking, acid rain, affirmative action, waste disposal, foreign business practices, cover-ups, takeover tactics, conflicts of interest, employee privacy, inappropriate gifts, and security of company records has accentuated the need for strategists to develop a clear **code of business ethics**. Internet fraud, hacking into company computers, spreading viruses, and identity theft are other unethical activities that plague every sector of online commerce.

Merely having a code of ethics, however, is not sufficient to ensure ethical business behavior. A code of ethics can be viewed as a public relations gimmick, a set of platitudes, or window dressing. To ensure that the code is read, understood, believed, and remembered, periodic ethics workshops are needed to sensitize people to workplace circumstances in which ethics issues may arise.[3] If employees see examples of punishment for violating the code as well as rewards for upholding the code, this reinforces the importance of a firm's code of ethics. The website www.ethicsweb.ca/codes provides guidelines on how to write an effective code of ethics.

An Ethics Culture

Reverend Billy Graham once said: "When wealth is lost, nothing is lost; when health is lost, something is lost; when character is lost, all is lost." An ethics "culture" needs to permeate organizations! To help create an ethics culture, Citicorp developed a business ethics board game that is played by thousands of employees worldwide. Called "The Word Ethic," this game asks players business ethics questions, such as how do you deal with a customer who offers you football tickets in exchange for a new, backdated IRA? Diana Robertson at the Wharton School of Business believes the game is effective because it is interactive. Many organizations have developed a code-of-conduct manual outlining ethical expectations and giving examples of situations that commonly arise in their businesses.

One reason strategists' salaries are high is that they must take the moral risks of the firm. Strategists are responsible for developing, communicating, and enforcing the code of business ethics for their organizations. Although primary responsibility for ensuring ethical behavior rests with a firm's strategists, an integral part of the responsibility of all managers is to provide ethics leadership by constant example and demonstration. Managers hold positions that enable them to influence and educate many people. This makes managers responsible for developing and implementing ethical decision making. Gellerman and Drucker, respectively, offer some good advice for managers:

> All managers risk giving too much because of what their companies demand from them. But the same superiors, who keep pressing you to do more, or to do it better, or faster, or less expensively, will turn on you should you cross that fuzzy line between right and wrong. They will blame you for exceeding instructions or for ignoring their warnings. The smartest managers already know that the best answer to the question "How far is too far?" is don't try to find out.[4]

> A man (or woman) might know too little, perform poorly, lack judgment and ability, and yet not do too much damage as a manager. But if that person lacks character and integrity—no matter how knowledgeable, how brilliant, how successful—he destroys. He destroys people, the most valuable resource of the enterprise. He destroys spirit. And he destroys performance. This is particularly true of the people at the head of an enterprise because the spirit of an organization is created from the top. If an organization is great in spirit, it is because the spirit of its top people is great. If it decays, it does so because the top rots. As the proverb has it, "Trees die from the top." No one should ever become a strategist unless he or she is willing to have his or her character serve as the model for subordinates.[5]

No society anywhere in the world can compete long or successfully with people stealing from one another or not trusting one another, with every bit of information requiring notarized confirmation, with every disagreement ending up in litigation, or with government having to regulate businesses to keep them honest. Being unethical is a recipe for headaches, inefficiency, and waste. History has proven that the greater the trust and confidence of people in the ethics of an institution or society, the greater its economic strength. Business relationships are built mostly on mutual trust and reputation. Short-term decisions based on greed and questionable ethics will preclude the necessary self-respect to gain the trust of others. More and more firms believe that ethics training and an ethics culture create strategic advantage. Max Killan said: "If business is not based on ethical grounds, it is of no benefit to society, and will, like all other unethical combinations, pass into oblivion."

Whistle-Blowing

Harris Corporation and other firms warn managers and employees that failing to report an ethical violation by others could bring discharge. The Securities and Exchange Commission (SEC) recently strengthened its whistle-blowing policies, virtually mandating that anyone seeing unethical activity report such behavior. **Whistle-blowing** refers to policies that require employees to report any unethical violations they discover or see in the firm.

Whistle-blowers in the corporate world receive up to 25 percent of the proceeds of legal proceedings against firms for wrongdoing. Whistle-blower payouts are becoming more and more common. In late 2012, Brad Birkenfeld, the former Zurich-based UBS AG banker who told the Internal Revenue Service (IRS) how the bank helped thousands of Americans evade taxes, received an IRS award of $104 million, perhaps the largest payout ever for an individual U.S. whistle-blower. The largest bank in Switzerland, UBS's Birkenfeld told IRS agents how UBS bankers came to the USA to woo rich Americans, managed $20 billion of their assets, and helped them cheat the IRS. He pleaded guilty to conspiracy in 2008, a year after reporting the bank's conduct to the Justice Department, U.S. Senate, IRS, and Securities and Exchange Commission. Birkenfeld went briefly to prison for his involvement in the bank scheme, but UBS avoided prosecution in the USA by agreeing to pay $780 million, disclosing data on more than 250 Swiss accounts, and admitting it helped foster tax evasion. It later agreed to hand over data on another 4,450 accounts. Since Birkenfeld came forward, at least 33,000 Americans have voluntarily disclosed offshore accounts to the IRS, generating more than $5 billion.

In October 2012, the IRS in a separate case paid another whistle-blower $38 million which was between 15 and 30 percent of the taxes recovered from another large corporation. The name of this company and the whistle-blower remain completely confidential, proving that the IRS can reward corporate whistle-blowers without ever revealing their identity. Pfizer paid out $2.3 billion in a whistle-blower settlement case and Eli Lilly paid out $1.4 billion. Most firms have internal whistle-blowing incentives and policies and try to keep such matters internal, but recent laws and court cases are shifting disclosure and settlements outside the firm.[6]

An accountant recently tipped off the IRS that his employer was skimping on taxes and received $4.5 million in the first IRS whistle-blower award. The accountant's tip netted the IRS $20 million in taxes and interest from the errant financial-services firm. The award represented a 22 percent cut of the taxes recovered. The IRS program, designed to encourage tips in large-scale cases, mandates awards of 15 to 30 percent of the amount recouped. "It's a win-win for both the government and taxpayers. These are dollars that are being returned to the Treasury that otherwise wouldn't be," said lawyer Eric Young.

Ethics training programs should include messages from the CEO or owner of the business emphasizing ethical business practices, the development and discussion of codes of ethics, and procedures for discussing and reporting unethical behavior. Firms can align ethical and strategic decision making by incorporating ethical considerations into long-term planning, by integrating ethical decision making into the performance appraisal process, by encouraging whistle-blowing or the reporting of unethical practices, and by monitoring departmental and corporate performance regarding ethical issues.

Bribes

Bribery is defined by *Black's Law Dictionary* as the offering, giving, receiving, or soliciting of any item of value to influence the actions of an official or other person in discharge of a public or legal duty. A **bribe** is a gift bestowed to influence a recipient's conduct. The gift may be any money, good, right in action, property, preferment, privilege, emolument, object of value, advantage, or merely a promise or undertaking to induce or influence the action, vote, or influence of a person in an official or public capacity. Bribery is a crime in most countries of the world, including the United States.[7]

The U.S. Foreign Corrupt Practices Act (FCPA) that governs bribery is being enforced more strictly. This act and a new provision in the Dodd-Frank financial-regulation law allows company employees or others who bring cases of financial fraud, such as bribery, to the government's attention to receive up to 30 percent of any sum recovered. Bribery suits against a company also expose the firm to shareholder lawsuits.

In 2012, Pfizer paid $60.2 million to settle a federal investigation into bribery overseas whereby the firm was accused of bribing doctors, hospitals administrators, and regulators in several countries in Europe and Asia to prescribe their medicines. Pfizer allegedly gave doctors in China cellphones and tea sets, while plying Croatian doctors with cash and international trips, and then sought to hide the bribery by recording the payments in accounting records as legitimate expenses.

Avon Products is currently being investigated for bribery charges related to their winning the first direct-sales license awarded by China to a foreign company. Even former Avon CEO Andrea Jung is being interrogated through her attorney Theodore Wells Jr. Avon is also being examined for spending millions of dollars in Brazil and France to consultants hired to assist the company with tax bills in those countries.

A recent (11-15-12) *Wall Street Journal* article titled "Bribery Law Dos and Don'ts" provides a synopsis of the recent 130-page document released by the U.S. Justice Department and the SEC to respond to complaints from companies that ambiguity in the FCPA has forced them to abandon business in high-risk countries and spend millions of dollars investigating themselves.[8] Numerous examples of bribery are given, such as "1) providing a $12,000 birthday trip for a government official from Mexico that incudes visits to wineries and museums" or 2) $10,000 spent on a government official for drinks, dinners, and entertainment."

In mid-2013, the SEC began investigating electronics giant Panasonic for bribery within its subsidiary, Avionics, based in Lake Forest, California. From 2009 to mid-2013, the U.S. Justice Department filed 110 bribery cases and the SEC filed 80 bribery cases.

The United Kingdom's new Bribery Law forbids any company doing any business in the United Kingdom from bribing foreign or domestic officials to gain competitive advantage. The British law is more stringent even than the similar U.S. FCPA. The British Bribery Law carries a maximum 10-year prison sentence for those convicted of bribery. The law stipulates that "failure to prevent bribery" is an offense and stipulates that facilitation payments, or payments to gain access, are not a valid defense to prevent bribery.

Great Britain's Bribery Act applies even to bribes between private businesspersons, and if the individual who makes the payment does not realize the transaction was a bribe, he or she is still liable. The new bribery law is being enforced by Britain's Serious Fraud Office (SFO) and boosts the maximum penalty for bribery to 10 years in prison from 7, and sets no limits on fines. More and more nations are taking a tougher stance against corruption, and companies worldwide are installing elaborate programs to avoid running afoul of the FCPA or the SFO.

Paying bribes is considered both illegal and unethical in the USA, but in some foreign countries, paying bribes and kickbacks is acceptable. Tipping is even considered bribery in some countries. Important antibribery and extortion initiatives are advocated by many organizations, including the World Bank, the International Monetary Fund, the European Union (EU), the Council of Europe, the Organization of American States, the Pacific Basin Economic Council, the Global Coalition for Africa, and the United Nations.

The U.S. Justice Department recently increased its prosecutions of alleged acts of foreign bribery. Businesses have to be much more careful these days. For years, taking business associates to lavish dinners and giving them expensive holiday gifts and even outright cash may have been expected in many countries, such as South Korea and China, but there is now stepped-up enforcement of bribery laws.

The SEC and Justice Department are investigating several pharmaceutical companies, including Merck, AstraZeneca PLC, Bristol-Myers Squibb, and GlaxoSmithKline PLC, for allegedly paying bribes in certain foreign countries to boost sales and speed approvals. Four types of violations are being reviewed: bribing government-employed doctors to purchase drugs; paying company sales agents commissions that are passed along to government doctors; paying hospital committees to approve drug purchases; and paying regulators to win drug approvals. Johnson & Johnson recently paid $70 million to settle allegations that it paid bribes to doctors in Greece, Poland, and Romania to use their surgical implants and to prescribe its drugs. Pfizer paid $60 million to resolve similar probes to win business overseas.

The SEC and the Justice Department are also investigating Hewlett-Packard for allegedly paying Russian government officials bribes to secure a $44.5 million information technology network. Similarly, the engineering giant Siemens AG is being investigated on bribery charges related to a $27 million traffic-control system installed in Moscow, Russia.

The U.S. FCPA prohibits U.S. companies from paying or offering to pay foreign government officials or employees of state companies to gain a business advantage. Under the U.S. Dodd-Frank Act, passed in 2010, employees are encouraged to report possible acts of bribery and whistle-blowers are rewarded between 10 percent and 30 percent of any financial sanctions against companies.

Workplace Romance

Director of the U.S. Central Intelligence Agency (CIA), Gen. David Petraeus abruptly resigned in November 2012, citing workplace romance as the reason. Petraeus wrote in the letter to his staff that he was going to the White House to ask President Obama "for personal reasons" to resign. "After being married for more than 37 years, I showed extremely poor judgment by engaging in an extramarital affair," Petraeus wrote in his letter. "Such behavior is unacceptable, both as a husband and as a leader of an organization such as ours." Petraeus's wife is Holly Petraeus whom he met when he was a cadet at the U.S. Military Academy at West Point.

Just hours after Petraeus resigned, the CEO of Lockheed Martin Corp., Chris Kubasik, was fired for having a "close personal relationship" with a subordinate. The company said the CEO's "improper conduct" violated the company's code of ethics. Kubasik, who is married, had his relationship revealed by a whistle-blower, at which point Lockheed hired external investigators to examine the allegation. Lockheed manufactures numerous military products, so the firm is perhaps more prudent than most in monitoring relationships because spying is a concern within defense firms.

Workplace romance is an intimate relationship between two truly consenting employees, as opposed to *sexual harassment,* which the Equal Employment Opportunity Commission (EEOC) defines broadly as unwelcome sexual advances, requests for sexual favors, and other verbal or physical conduct of a sexual nature. Sexual harassment (and discrimination) is illegal, unethical, and detrimental to any organization and can result in expensive lawsuits, lower morale, and reduced productivity.

Workplace romance between two consenting employees simply happens, so the question is generally not whether to allow the practice, and or even how to prevent it, but rather how best to manage the phenomena. An organization probably should not strictly forbid workplace romance because such a policy could be construed as an invasion of privacy, overbearing, or unnecessary. Some romances actually improve work performance, adding a dynamism and energy that translates into enhanced morale, communication, creativity, and productivity.[9]

However, it is important to note that workplace romance can be detrimental to workplace morale and productivity, for a number of reasons that include:

1. Favoritism complaints can arise.
2. Confidentiality of records can be breached.
3. Reduced quality and quantity of work can become a problem.
4. Personal arguments can lead to work arguments.
5. Whispering secrets can lead to tensions and hostilities among coworkers.
6. Sexual harassment (or discrimination) charges may ensue, either by the involved female or a third party.
7. Conflicts of interest can arise, especially when well being of the partner trumps well-being of the company.

In some states, such as California, managers can be held personally liable for damages that arise from workplace romance. Organizations should establish guidelines or policies that address workplace romance, for at least six reasons:

1. Guidelines can enable the firm to better defend itself against and avoid sexual harassment or discrimination charges.
2. Guidelines can specify reasons (such as the seven listed previously) why workplace romance may not be a good idea.
3. Guidelines can specify resultant penalties for romancing partners if problems arise.
4. Guidelines can promote a professional and fair work atmosphere.
5. Guidelines can help assure compliance with federal, state, and local laws and recent court cases.
6. Lack of any guidelines sends a lackadaisical message throughout the firm.

Workplace romance guidelines should apply to all employees at all levels of the firm and should specify certain situations in which affairs are especially discouraged, such as supervisor and subordinate. Company guidelines or policies in general should discourage workplace romance because "the downside risks generally exceed the upside benefits" for the firm. Best Buy CEO Brian Dunn recently resigned when directors learned of his inappropriate relationship with a young subordinate, a violation of that company's code of ethics. Based in Fremont, California, IGate Corp., fired its CEO, Phaneesh Murthy, in May 2013 for allegedly failing to report a workplace romance relationship that turned into a sexual harassment issue with a subordinate.

Flirting is a step down from workplace romance, but a new full-page *Wall Street Journal* article titled "The New Rules of Flirting" reveal the do's and don'ts of flirting.[10] Flirting is defined by researchers as "romantic behavior that is ambiguous and goal oriented," or said differently, "ambiguous behavior with potential sexual or romantic overtones that is goal-oriented." A few flirting rules given in the article are:

1. Do not flirt with someone you know is looking for a relationship if you are not interested in a new relationship.
2. Do flirt within a relationship that you want to strengthen.
3. Do not flirt to make your partner jealous because this is manipulative behavior.
4. Flirting between power differences, such as boss and employee or professor and student, usually leads to trouble, as many defendants in sexual-harassment complaints know.
5. Do not make physical contact with the person you are flirting with, unless it is within a desired relationship.

Among colleges and universities, the federal Office of Civil Rights (OCR) has stepped up its investigation of sexual harassment cases brought forward by female students against professors. Yale University has been in the news in this regard as well as numerous other institutions currently being investigated. At no charge to the student, the OCR will investigate a female student's claim if evidence is compelling.

A *Wall Street Journal* article recapped U.S. standards regarding boss and subordinate love affairs at work.[11] Only 5 percent of all firms sampled had no restrictions on such relationships; 80 percent of firms have policies that prohibit relationships between a supervisor and a subordinate. Only 4 percent of firms strictly prohibited such relationships, but 39 percent of firms had policies that required individuals to inform their supervisors whenever a romantic relationship begins with a coworker. Only 24 percent of firms required the two persons to be in different departments.

In Europe, romantic relationships at work are largely viewed as private matters and most firms have no policies on the practice. However, European firms are increasingly adopting explicit, U.S.-style sexual harassment laws. The U.S. military strictly bans officers from dating or having sexual relationships with enlistees. At the World Bank, sexual relations between a supervisor and an employee are considered "a de facto conflict of interest which must be resolved to avoid favoritism." World Bank president Paul Wolfowitz recently was forced to resign as a result of a relationship he had with a bank staff person.

A recent *Bloomberg Businessweek* article reports that in the sluggish job market, employees are filing sexual harassment complaints as a way to further their own job security. Many of these filings are increasingly third-party individuals not even directly involved in the relationship but alleging their own job was impacted. Largely the result of the rise of third-party discrimination claims, the EEOC recovers about $500 million on behalf of office romance victims.[12]

Social Responsibility

Fortune annually lists the most admired and least admired companies globally on social responsibility. *Fortune*'s 2012 top three most admired socially responsible companies are GDF Suez, Marquard & Bahls, and RWE. The top three least admired companies are China Railway Group, China Railway Construction, and China State Construction Engineering.[13] Chinese firms dominate the least admired list.

Walmart was socially responsible in the wake of the earthquake and tsunami that devastated Japan in 2011. Following the catastrophe, Walmart quickly mobilized a local relief effort to deliver supplies such as water and flashlights to survivors. Walmart has a history of helping immensely in times of crisis—the retailer was also able to get supplies to people who needed them following Hurricane Katrina.

Some strategists agree with Ralph Nader, who proclaims that organizations have tremendous social obligations. Nader points out, for example, that ExxonMobil has more assets than most countries, and because of this, such firms have an obligation to help society cure its many ills. Other people, however, agree with the economist Milton Friedman, who asserts that organizations have no obligation to do any more for society than is legally required. Friedman may contend that it is irresponsible for a firm to give monies to charity.

Do you agree more with Nader or Friedman? Surely we can all agree that the first social responsibility of any business must be to make enough profit to cover the costs of the future because if this is not achieved, no other social responsibility can be met. Indeed, no social need can be met by the firm if the firm fails.

Strategists should examine social problems in terms of potential costs and benefits to the firm and focus on social issues that could benefit the firm most. For example, should a firm avoid laying off employees so as to protect the employees' livelihood, when that decision may force the firm to liquidate?

Social Policy

The term **social policy** embraces managerial philosophy and thinking at the highest level of the firm, which is why the topic is covered in this textbook. Social policy concerns what responsibilities the firm has to employees, consumers, environmentalists, minorities, communities, shareholders, and other groups. After decades of debate, many firms still struggle to determine appropriate social policies.

The impact of society on business and vice versa is becoming more pronounced each year. Corporate social policy should be designed and articulated during strategy formulation, set and administered during strategy implementation, and reaffirmed or changed during strategy evaluation.[14]

Firms should strive to engage in social activities that have economic benefits. Merck & Co. once developed the drug ivermectin for treating river blindness, a disease caused by a fly-borne parasitic worm endemic in poor tropical areas of Africa, the Middle East, and Latin America. In an unprecedented gesture that reflected its corporate commitment to social responsibility, Merck then made ivermectin available at no cost to medical personnel throughout the world. Merck's action highlights the dilemma of orphan drugs, which offer pharmaceutical companies no economic incentive for profitable development and distribution. Merck did however garner substantial goodwill among its stakeholders for its actions.

Social Policies on Retirement

Some countries around the world are facing severe workforce shortages associated with their aging populations. The percentage of persons age 65 or older exceeds 20 percent in Japan, Italy, and Germany—and will reach 20 percent in 2018 in France. In 2036, the percentage of persons age 65 or older will reach 20 percent in the USA and China. Unlike the USA, Japan is reluctant to rely on large-scale immigration to bolster its workforce. Instead, Japan provides incentives for its elderly to work until ages 65 to 75. Western European countries are doing the opposite, providing incentives for its elderly to retire at ages 55 to 60. The International Labor Organization says 71 percent of Japanese men ages 60 to 64 work, compared to 57 percent of American men and just 17 percent of French men in the same age group.

Sachiko Ichioka, a typical 67-year-old man in Japan, says, "I want to work as long as I'm healthy. The extra money means I can go on trips, and I'm not a burden on my children." Better diet and health care have raised Japan's life expectancy now to 82, the highest in the world. Japanese women are having on average only 1.28 children compared to 2.04 in the USA. Keeping the elderly at work, coupled with reversing the old-fashioned trend of keeping women at home, are Japan's two key remedies for sustaining its workforce in factories and businesses. This prescription for dealing with problems associated with an aging society should be considered by many countries around the world. The Japanese government is phasing in a shift from age 60 to age 65 as the date when a person may begin receiving a pension, and premiums paid by Japanese employees are rising while payouts are falling. Unlike the USA, Japan has no law against discrimination based on age.

Worker productivity increases in Japan are not able to offset declines in number of workers, thus resulting in a decline in overall economic production. Like many countries, Japan does not view immigration as a good way to solve this problem. Japan's shrinking workforce has become such a concern that the government just recently allowed an unspecified number of Indonesian and Filipino nurses and caregivers to work in Japan for two years. The number of working-age

TABLE 3-2   The Best and Worst Companies Globally in Regard to Being Socially Responsible

The Best	The Worst
1. GDF Suez	1. China Railway Group
2. Marquard & Bahls	2. China Railway Construction
3. RWE	3. China State Construction Engineering
4. Altria Group	4. China South Industries Group
5. Starbucks	5. China FAW Group
6. Walt Disney	6. Aviation Industry Corporation of China
7. United Natural Foods	7. Dongfeng Motor
8. Sealed Air	8. MF Global Holdings
9. Chevron	9. China North Industries
10. Whole Foods Market	10. Hon Hai Precision Industry

Sources: Based on http://money.cnn.com/magazines/fortune/most-admired/2012/best_worst/best4.html and http://money.cnn.com/magazines/fortune/most-admired/2012/best_worst/worst4.html.

Japanese—those between ages 15 and 64—is projected to shrink to 70 million by 2030. Using foreign workers is known as *gaikokujin roudousha* in Japanese. Many Filipinos have recently been hired now to work in agriculture and factories throughout Japan.

Fortune's best and worst companies globally in regard to being socially responsible in 2012 are listed in Table 3-2. Note that the 10 worst companies are all based in China.

Environmental Sustainability

In October of every year, three world renowned corporate sustainability rankings are published: (1) the Dow Jones Sustainability Index (DJSI), (2) the Carbon Disclosure Project, and (3) *Newsweek's* "Green" rankings. Regarding the DJSI, some notable companies that were added to the DJSI 2012 Index for being especially sustainable were Microsoft, Target, Hewlett-Packard, and the Canadian National Railway Company. Some notable companies that were kicked out of the 2012 DJSI sustainability rankings were GlaxoSmithKline PLC, Duke Energy, IBM, United Technologies, and Dell.

Launched in 1999, DJSI annually reveals the best corporations in the world in various industries in terms of sustainability. A few of the number-1 (best) companies in the world on sustainability in the DJSI 2012 in their respective industries were: BMW, Unilever NV, Roche Holding AG, Siemens AG, Alcatel-Lucent SA, and Air France-KLM.

The strategies of both companies and countries are increasingly scrutinized and evaluated from a natural environment perspective. Companies such as Walmart now monitor not only the price its vendors offer for products, but also how those products are made in terms of environmental practices, as well as safety and infrastructure soundness particularly of Southeast Asia factories. A growing number of business schools offer separate courses and even a concentration in environmental management.

Businesses must not exploit and decimate the natural environment. Mark Starik at George Washington University says, "Halting and reversing worldwide ecological destruction and deterioration is a strategic issue that needs immediate and substantive attention by all businesses and managers. According to the International Standards Organization (ISO), the word **environment** is defined as "surroundings in which an organization operates, including air, water, land, natural resources, flora, fauna, humans, and their interrelation." This chapter illustrates how many firms are gaining competitive advantage by being good stewards of the natural environment.

Employees, consumers, governments, and society are especially resentful of firms that harm rather than protect the natural environment. Conversely people today are especially appreciative of firms that conduct operations in a way that mends, conserves, and preserves the natural environment. Consumer interest in businesses preserving nature's ecological balance and fostering a clean, healthy environment is high.

No business wants a reputation as being a polluter. A bad sustainability record will hurt the firm in the market, jeopardize its standing in the community, and invite scrutiny by regulators, investors, and environmentalists. Governments increasingly require businesses to behave responsibly and require, for example, that businesses publicly report the pollutants and wastes their facilities produce.

In terms of megawatts of wind power generated by various states in the United States, Iowa's 2,791 recently overtook California's 2,517, but Texas's 7,118 megawatts dwarfs all other states. Minnesota also is making substantial progress in wind power generation. New Jersey recently outfitted 200,000 utility poles with solar panels, which made it the nation's second-largest producer of solar energy behind California. New Jersey is also adding solar panels to corporate rooftops. The state's $514 million solar program doubled its solar capacity to 160 megawatts in 2013. The state's goal is to obtain 3 percent of its electricity from the sun and 12 percent from offshore wind by 2020.

What Is a Sustainability Report?

A sustainability report reveals a firm's operations impact the natural environment. This document discloses to shareholders information about the firm's labor practices, product sourcing, energy efficiency, environmental impact, and business ethics practices.

It is good business for a company to provide a sustainability report annually to the public. With 60,000 suppliers and more than $350 billion in annual sales, Walmart works with its suppliers to make sure they provide such reports. Many firms use the Walmart sustainability report as a benchmark, guideline, and model to follow in preparing their own report.

The Global Reporting Initiative recently issued a set of detailed reporting guidelines specifying what information should go into sustainability reports. The proxy advisory firm Institutional Shareholder Services reports that an increasing number of shareholder groups are pushing firms to provide sustainability information annually. Two companies that released sustainability reports for the first time in 2012 were Hyatt Hotels & Resorts and Las Vegas Sands Corporation. Rival firm Hilton Worldwide does not have a stand-alone sustainability report, but Marriott and Wyndham Worldwide do release annual sustainability reports and of late revealed excellent reductions in energy, water, waste, and carbon dioxide emissions.

Walmart encourages and expects its 1.35 million U.S. employees to adopt what it calls Personal Sustainability Projects, which include such measures as organizing weight-loss or smoking-cessation support groups, biking to work, or starting recycling programs. Employee wellness can be a part of sustainability.

Walmart is installing solar panels on its stores in California and Hawaii, providing as much as 30 percent of the power in some stores. It may go national with solar power if this test works well. Also moving to solar energy is department-store chain Kohl's Corp., which is converting 64 of its 80 California stores to use solar power. There are big subsidies for solar installations in some states.

Home Depot, the world's second largest retailer behind Walmart, recently more than doubled its offering of environmentally friendly products such as all-natural insect repellent. Home Depot has made it much easier for consumers to find its organic products by using special labels similar to Timberland's (the outdoor company) Green Index tags.

Managers and employees of firms must be careful not to become scapegoats blamed for company environmental wrongdoings. Harming the natural environment can be unethical, illegal, and costly. When organizations today face criminal charges for polluting the environment, they increasingly turn on their managers and employees to win leniency. Employee firings and demotions are becoming common in pollution-related legal suits. Managers were fired at Darling International, Inc., and Niagara Mohawk Power Corporation for being indirectly responsible for their firms polluting water. Managers and employees today must be careful not to ignore, conceal, or disregard a pollution problem, or they may find themselves personally liable.

Lack of Standards Changing

A few years ago, firms could get away with placing "green" terminology on their products and labels using such terms as *organic*, *green*, *safe*, *earth-friendly*, *nontoxic*, or *natural* because there were no legal or generally accepted definitions. Today, however, these terms carry much more specific connotations and expectations. Uniform standards defining environmentally responsible company actions are rapidly being incorporated into the legal landscape. It has become more and more difficult for firms to make "green" claims when their actions are not substantive, comprehensive, or even true. Lack of standards once made consumers cynical about corporate environmental claims, but those claims today are increasingly being challenged in courts. Joel Makower says, "One of the main reasons to truly become a green firm is for your employees. They're the first group that needs assurance than any claims you make hold water."[15]

Around the world, political and corporate leaders now realize that the "business green" topic will not go away and in fact is gaining ground rapidly. Strategically, companies more than ever must demonstrate to their customers and stakeholders that their green efforts are substantive and set the firm apart from competitors. A firm's performance facts and figures must back up their rhetoric and be consistent with sustainability standards.

Managing Environmental Affairs in the Firm

The ecological challenge facing all organizations requires managers to formulate strategies that preserve and conserve natural resources and control pollution. Special natural environment issues include ozone depletion, global warming, depletion of rain forests, destruction of animal habitats, protecting endangered species, developing biodegradable products and packages, waste management, clean air, clean water, erosion, destruction of natural resources, and pollution control. Firms increasingly are developing green product lines that are biodegradable or are made from recycled products. Green products sell well.

Managing as if "health of the planet" matters requires an understanding of how international trade, competitiveness, and global resources are connected. Managing environmental affairs can no longer be simply a technical function performed by specialists in a firm; more emphasis must be placed on developing an environmental perspective among all employees and managers of the firm. Many companies are moving environmental affairs from the staff side of the organization to the line side, thus making the corporate environmental group report directly to the chief operating officer. Firms that manage environmental affairs will enhance relations with consumers, regulators, vendors, and other industry players, substantially improving their prospects of success.

Environmental strategies could include developing or acquiring green businesses, divesting or altering environment-damaging businesses, striving to become a low-cost producer through waste minimization and energy conservation, and pursuing a differentiation strategy through green-product features. In addition, firms could include an environmental representative on their board of directors, conduct regular environmental audits, implement bonuses for favorable environmental results, become involved in environmental issues and programs, incorporate environmental values in mission statements, establish environmentally oriented objectives, acquire environmental skills, and provide environmental training programs for company employees and managers.

Preserving the environment should be a permanent part of doing business for the following reasons:

1. Consumer demand for environmentally safe products and packages is high.
2. Public opinion demanding that firms conduct business in ways that preserve the natural environment is strong.
3. Environmental advocacy groups now have more than 20 million Americans as members.
4. Federal and state environmental regulations are changing rapidly and becoming more complex.
5. More lenders are examining the environmental liabilities of businesses seeking loans.
6. Many consumers, suppliers, distributors, and investors shun doing business with environmentally weak firms.
7. Liability suits and fines against firms having environmental problems are on the rise.

More firms are becoming environmentally proactive—doing more than the bare minimum to develop and implement strategies that preserve the environment. The old undesirable alternative of being environmentally reactive—changing practices only when forced to do so by law or consumer pressure—more often today leads to high cleanup costs, liability suits, reduced market share, reduced customer loyalty, and higher medical costs. In contrast, a proactive policy views environmental pressures as opportunities and includes such actions as developing green products and packages, conserving energy, reducing waste, recycling, and creating a corporate culture that is environmentally sensitive.

ISO 14000/14001 Certification

Based in Geneva, Switzerland, the International Organization for Standardization (ISO) is a network of the national standards institutes of 147 countries, with one member per country. ISO is the world's largest developer of sustainability standards. Widely accepted all over the world, ISO standards are voluntary because ISO has no legal authority to enforce their implementation. ISO itself does not regulate or legislate.

Governmental agencies in various countries, such as the Environmental Protection Agency (EPA) in the USA, have adopted ISO standards as part of their regulatory framework, and the standards are the basis of much legislation. Adoptions are sovereign decisions by the regulatory authorities, governments, or companies concerned.

ISO 14000 refers to a series of voluntary standards in the environmental field. The ISO 14000 family of standards concerns the extent to which a firm minimizes harmful effects on the environment caused by its activities and continually monitors and improves its own environmental performance. Included in the ISO 14000 series are the ISO 14001 standards in fields such as environmental auditing, environmental performance evaluation, environmental labeling, and life-cycle assessment.

ISO 14001 is a set of standards adopted by thousands of firms worldwide to certify to their constituencies that they are conducting business in an environmentally friendly manner. ISO 14001 standards offer a universal technical standard for environmental compliance that more and more firms are requiring not only of themselves but also of their suppliers and distributors.

The ISO 14001 standard requires that a community or organization put in place and implement a series of practices and procedures that, when taken together, result in an **environmental management system (EMS)**. ISO 14001 is not a technical standard and as such does not in any way replace technical requirements embodied in statutes or regulations. It also does not set prescribed standards of performance for organizations. Not being certified with ISO 14001 can be a strategic disadvantage for towns, counties, and companies because people today expect organizations to minimize or, even better, to eliminate environmental harm they cause.[16] The major requirements of an EMS under ISO 14001 include the following:

- Show commitments to prevention of pollution, continual improvement in overall environmental performance, and compliance with all applicable statutory and regulatory requirements.
- Identify all aspects of the organization's activities, products, and services that could have a significant impact on the environment, including those that are not regulated.
- Set performance objectives and targets for the management system that link back to three policies: (1) prevention of pollution, (2) continual improvement, and (3) compliance.
- Meet environmental objectives that include training employees, establishing work instructions and practices, and establishing the actual metrics by which the objectives and targets will be measured.
- Conduct an audit operation of the EMS.
- Take corrective actions when deviations from the EMS occur.

Wildlife

In mid-2012, South Korea announced plans to resume whaling despite a 1986 moratorium on commercial whaling. Many countries are upset at these plans, including Australia where the Prime Minister Julia Gillard said: "We are completely opposed to whaling; there's no excuse for scientific whaling." Only a few countries, such as Norway, Japan, and Russia, favor and engage in commercial whaling.

Fairmont Hotels & Resorts in 2012 instituted a policy removing shark fin soup from its menu, following the lead of Shangri-La Hotels & Resorts. Even the Chinese government has recently stopped serving shark fin soup at most official banquets. Studies reveal that many shark species have been reduced 90 percent in recent decades, largely by overfishing for shark fins. The demand for shark fin soup in Asia is arguably the major cause of the alarming decline of blue sharks off the British coast and much of the Atlantic. Scientists from the United Kingdom and Portugal recently tracked sharks and confirm that sharks are being deliberately targeted by fishermen with long-line fishing that can stretch as long as 100 km. The fins are cut off and the bodies discarded onsite. Blue sharks are the most frequently caught shark species, with drastic population declines. Many shark species are now classified as "near-threatened" on the International Union for Conservation of Nature (IUCN) Red List.[17]

The European Parliament in late 2012 voted with an overwhelming 566–47 margin to force all boats in EU waters and EU-registered boats around the world to land sharks with their fins attached and prove the animal had not been thrown back. Uta Bellion of the Pew Environment Group said: "the parliament's vote is a major milestone in ending the wasteful practice of shark finning." EU fisheries chief Maria Damanaki said the law would "ease control and help us eradicate shark finning," which she called cruel to the animals and a vast waste of resources. Sharks are vulnerable to over-exploitation because they mature late and give birth to small numbers of young at a time. Shark fins are in high demand in Asia for soup and alleged cures. Damanaki said some 75 million sharks a year are killed for the use of their fins only, with the EU being the biggest exporter. As a result, the hammerhead shark is as good as extinct in the Mediterranean Sea. Damanaki has compared shark finning to killing elephants only for their tusks.

Arctic sea ice shrank to a record low of 1.32 million square miles (3.41 million square km) in late 2012 according to the National Oceanic and Atmospheric Agency. However, polar bears' designation as a threatened species is being challenged in a U.S. appeals court. A decision is expected in 2013. Alaska and oil companies have argued that Endangered Species Act protections for polar bears diminish opportunities for Alaska energy development. The state has said in its appeals court filing that bears have survived previous warming periods and most populations have grown or remained stable despite shrinkage of ice. The case is *Safari Club International et al v. Ken Salazar et al and Center for Biological Diversity et al*, No. 11-5219.

According to the Convention on the International Trade in Endangered Species (CITES), more than 25,000 elephants are killed each year for their ivory—even though international trade in ivory has been outlawed since 1989.

A recent *Wall Street Journal* article titled "America Gone Wild" talks about how wildlife populations in the USA have experienced an "astonishing resurgence."[18] A drawback of the resurgence is that the total cost of wildlife damage to U.S. crops, landscaping, and infrastructure now exceeds $28 billion a year, including $1.5 billion from deer-vehicle crashes alone.

Solar Power

The Solar Energy Industries Association reported in late 2012 that the USA is on pace to install as much solar power in 2012 as it did in the prior eleven put together, at least 2,500 megawatts, the equivalent of more than two nuclear-power plants. GTM Research says the U.S. solar-power industry grew 71 percent in 2012 and will grow 20 to 40 percent annually through 2016. To cut greenhouse-gas emissions and fight climate change, states such as California have created subsidies for solar power developers and requirements for utilities to buy solar power. China supplies nearly half of the solar panels used globally but two leading U.S. suppliers of solar panels are Solarcity, which has more than 2,000 employees, and Sunrun Inc. Thousands of companies are looking into install solar panels as part of their sustainability efforts.

Table 3-3 reveals the impact that bad environmental policies have on two of nature's many ecosystems.

TABLE 3-3 **Songbirds and Coral Reefs Need Help**

Songbirds

Be a good steward of the natural environment to save our songbirds. Bluebirds are one of 76 songbird species in the USA that have dramatically declined in numbers in the last two decades. Not all birds are considered songbirds, and why birds sing is not clear. Some scientists say they sing when calling for mates or warning of danger, but many scientists now contend that birds sing for sheer pleasure. Songbirds include chickadees, orioles, swallows, mockingbirds, warblers, sparrows, vireos, and the wood thrush. "These birds are telling us there's a problem, something's out of balance in our environment," says Jeff Wells, bird conservation director for the National Audubon Society. Songbirds may be telling us that their air or water is too dirty or that we are destroying too much of their habitat. People collect Picasso paintings and save historic buildings. "Songbirds are part of our natural heritage. Why should we be willing to watch songbirds destroyed any more than allowing a great work of art to be destroyed?" asks Wells. Whatever message songbirds are singing to us today about their natural environment, the message is becoming less and less heard nationwide. Listen when you go outside today. Each of us as individuals, companies, states, and countries should do what we reasonably can to help improve the natural environment for songbirds.[19] A recent study concludes that 67 of the 800 bird species in the USA are endangered, and another 184 species are designated of "conservation concern." The birds of Hawaii are in the greatest peril.

Coral Reefs

Be a good steward of the natural environment to save our coral reefs. The ocean covers more than 71 percent of the earth. The destructive effect of commercial fishing on ocean habitats coupled with increasing pollution runoff into the ocean and global warming of the ocean have decimated fisheries, marine life, and coral reefs around the world. The unfortunate consequence of fishing over the last century has been overfishing, with the principal reasons being politics and greed. Trawl fishing with nets destroys coral reefs and has been compared to catching squirrels by cutting down forests because bottom nets scour and destroy vast areas of the ocean. The great proportion of marine life caught in a trawl is "by-catch" juvenile fish and other life that are killed and discarded. Warming of the ocean as a result of carbon dioxide emissions also kills thousands of acres of coral reefs annually. The total area of fully protected marine habitats in the USA is only about 50 square miles, compared to some 93 million acres of national wildlife refuges and national parks on the nation's land. A healthy ocean is vital to the economic and social future of the nation—and, indeed, all countries of the world. Everything we do on land ends up in the ocean, so we all must become better stewards of this last frontier on earth to sustain human survival and the quality of life.[20]

Special Note to Students

No company or individual wants to do business with someone who is unethical or is insensitive to natural environment concerns. It is no longer just cool to be environmentally proactive, it is expected, and in many respects is the law. Firms are being compared to rival firms every day on sustainability and ethics behavior, actually every minute on Facebook, Twitter, Myspace, LinkedIn, and YouTube. Issues presented in this chapter therefore comprise a competitive advantage or disadvantage for all organizations. Thus, you should include in your case analysis recommendations for your firm to exceed stakeholder expectations on ethics, sustainability, and social responsibility. Make comparisons to rival firms to show how your firm can gain or sustain competitive advantage on these issues. Reveal suggestions for the firm to be a good corporate citizen and promote that for competitive advantage. Be mindful that the first responsibility of any business is to stay in business, so use cost/benefit analysis as needed to present your recommendations effectively.

Conclusion

In a final analysis, ethical standards come out of history and heritage. Our predecessors have left us with an ethical foundation to build on. Even the legendary football coach Vince Lombardi knew that some things were worth more than winning, and he required his players to have three kinds of loyalty: to God, to their families, and to the Green Bay Packers, "in that order." Employees, customers, and shareholders have become less and less tolerant of business ethics violations in firms, and more and more appreciative of model ethical firms. Information-sharing across the Internet increasingly reveals such model firms versus irresponsible firms.

Consumers across the country and around the world appreciate firms that do more than is legally required to be socially responsible. But staying in business while adhering to all laws and regulations must be a primary objective of any business. One of the best ways to be socially responsible is for the firm to proactively conserve and preserve the natural environment. For example, to develop a corporate sustainability report annually is not legally required, but such a report, based on concrete actions, goes a long way toward assuring stakeholders that the firm is worthy of their support. Business ethics, social responsibility, and environmental sustainability are interrelated and key strategic issues facing all organizations.

Key Terms and Concepts

bribe (p. 114)

bribery (p. 114)

business ethics (p. 111)

code of business ethics (p. 112)

environment (p. 119)

environmental management system (EMS) (p. 122)

ISO 14000 (p. 122)

ISO 14001 (p. 122)

sexual harrassment (p. 116)

social policy (p. 118)

social responsibility (p. 110)

sustainability (p. 110)

whistle-blowing (p. 113)

workplace romance (p. 116)

Issues for Review and Discussion

3-1. Nestle SA has done really well in 2011–2013. Visit their corporate website and determine if business ethics and sustainability issues may be key reasons for their success.

3-2. If you owned a small business, would you develop a code of business conduct? If yes, what variables would you include? If no, how would you ensure that ethical business standards were being followed by your employees?

3-3. What is the relationship between personal ethics and business ethics? Are they, or should they be the same?

3-4. How can firms best ensure that their code of business ethics is read, understood, believed, remembered, and acted upon?

3-5. Why is it important not to view the concept of "whistleblowing" as "tattle-telling" or "ratting" on another employee?

3-6. List six desired results of "ethics training programs," in terms of recommended business ethics policies or procedures in the firm.

3-7. Discuss bribery. Would actions such as politicians adding earmarks in legislation, or pharmaceutical salespersons giving away drugs to physicians constitute bribery? Identify three business activities that would constitute bribery and three actions that would not.

3-8. How could a strategist's attitude toward social responsibility affect a firm's strategy? On a 1 to 10 scale, ranging from Nader's view to Friedman's view, what is your attitude toward social responsibility?

3-9. How do social policies on retirement differ in various countries around the world?

3-10. Firms should formulate and implement strategies from an environmental perspective. List eight ways firms can do this.

3-11. Discuss the major requirements of an EMS under ISO 14001.

MyManagementLab®

Go to **mymanagementlab.com** for the following Assisted-graded writing questions:

3-12. Firms should formulate and implement strategies from an environmental perspective. List eight ways firms can do this.

3-13. Discuss the major requirements of an EMS under ISO 14001.

Current Readings

Aguinis, Herman and Ante Glavas. "What We Know and Don't Know About Corporate Social Responsibility: A Review and Research Agenda." *Journal of Management* 38, no. 4 (July 2012): 932.

Barnett, Michael L., and Robert M. Salomon. "Does it pay to be really good? Addressing the shape of the relationship between social and financial performance." *Strategic Management Journal* 33, no. 11 (November 2012): 1304–1320.

Fremeth, Adam R., and Brian K. Richter. "Profiting from Environmental Regulatory Uncertainty: Integrated Strategies for Competitive Advantage." *California Management Review* 54, no. 1 (Fall 2011): 145–165.

Lange, Donald, and Nathan T. Washburn. "Understanding Attributions of Corporate Social Irresponsibility." *The Academy of Management Review 37*, no. 2 (April 2012): 300.

Langvardt, Arlen W. "Business Ethics and Intellectual Property in the Global Marketplace." *Business Horizons* 55, no. 4 (July 2012): 325–327.

Karnani, Aneel. "Doing Well by Doing Good: The Grand Allusion." *California Management Review* 53, no. 2 (Winter 2011): 69–86.

Kleyn, Nicola, Russell Abratt, Kerry Chipp, and Michael Goldman. "Building a Strong Corporate Ethical Identify: Key Findings From Suppliers." *California Management Review* 54, no. 3 (Spring 2012): 61–76.

Langvardt, Arlen W. "Ethical Leadership and the Dual Roles of Examples." *Business Horizons* 55, no. 4 (July 2012): 373–384.

Mayer, David M., Karl Aquino, Rebecca L. Greenbaum, and Maribeth Kuenzi. "Who Displays Ethical Leadership, and Why Does It Matter? An Examination of Antecedents and Consequences of Ethical Leadership." *The Academy of Management Journal 55*, no. 1, February 2012): 151.

Peloza, John, Moritz Loock, James Cerruti, and Micahel Muyot. "Sustainability: How Stakeholder Perceptions Differ from Corporate Reality." *Inside CMR* 55, no. 1 (Fall 2012): 74.

Ramchander, Sanjay, Robert G. Schwebach, and KIM Staking. "The Informational Relevance of Corporate Social Responsibility: Evidence from DS400 Index Reconstitutions." *Strategic Management Journal* 33, no. 3 (March 2012): 303–314.

Rubin, Joel D. "Fairness in Business: Does it Matter, and What Does it Mean?" *Business Horizons* 55, no. 1 (January 2012): 11–15.

Schaubroeck, John M., Sean T. Hannah, Bruce J. Avolio, Steve W. J. Kozlowski, Robert G. Lord, Linda K. Treviño, Nikolaos Dimotakis, and Ann C. Peng. "Embedding Ethical Leadership within and across Organization Levels." *Academy of Management Journal* 55, no. 5 (October 2012): 1053.

Vallaster, Christine, Adam Lindgreen, and François Maon. "Strategically Leveraging Corporate Social Responsibility: A Corporate Branding Perspective." *California Management Review* 54, no. 3 (Spring 2012): 34–60.

Wang, Taiyuan, and Pratima Bansal. "Social Responsibility in New Ventures: Profiting from a Long-term Orientation." *Strategic Management Journal* 33, no. 10 (October 2012): 1135–1153.

Wong, Elaine M., Margaret E. Ormiston, and Philip E. Tetlock. "The Effects of Top Management Team Integrative Complexity and Decentralized Decision Making on Corporate Social Performance." *The Academy of Management Journal 54*, no. 6 (December 2011): 1207.

ASSURANCE OF LEARNING **EXERCISES**

EXERCISE 3A
Sustainability and Nestlé

Purpose

Nestlé is the opening case at the beginning of Chapter 3. Headquartered in Vevey, Switzerland, Nestlé is the largest food company in the world measured by revenues. Nestlé has hundreds of products that include cereals, coffee, dairy products, pet foods, snacks, baby food, and bottled water. Thirty of Nestlé's brands have annual sales of over 1 billion Swiss francs (about $ 1.1 billion), including Nespresso, Nescafé, Kit Kat, Smarties, Nesquick, Stouffers, Vittel, and Maggi. Nestlé has around 450 factories, operates in 86 countries, and employs around 328,000 people.

This exercise can give you practice evaluating a company's sustainability efforts. At the company's website, note the three key sustainability areas the firm engages in are 1) Nutrition, 2) CSV-Water, and 3) Rural Development.

Instructions

Conduct research to evaluate Nestlé's sustainability efforts. Prepare a report for the class giving your assessment of Nestlé's sustainability work versus rival firms.

EXERCISE 3B
How Does My Municipality Compare To Others on Being Pollution-Safe?

Purpose

Sometimes it is difficult to know how safe a particular municipality or county is regarding industrial and agricultural pollutants. A website that provides consumers and businesses excellent information in this regard is http://scorecard.goodguide.com. This type information is often used in assessing where to locate new business operations.

Instructions

Go to http://scorecard.goodguide.com/. Put in your zip code. Print off the information available for your city/county regarding pollutants. Prepare a comparative analysis of your municipality versus state and national norms on pollution issues. Does your locale receive an A, B, C, D, or F?

EXERCISE 3C
Compare adidas AG versus Nike on Social Responsibility

Purpose

This exercise aims to familiarize you with corporate social responsibility programs.

Instructions

Step 1   Go to adidas' Code of Conduct, which is provided within the Corporate Governance section of the corporate website.

Step 2   Go to Nike's corporate website at http://www.nikeinc.com and navigate to the Sustainability section to review Nike's Corporate Responsibility Report.

Step 3   Compare adidas' social responsibility efforts with Nike's. Summarize your findings in a three-page report for your professor.

EXERCISE 3D

How Do You Rate adidas AG's Sustainability Efforts?

Purpose

This exercise aims to familiarize you with corporate sustainability programs.

Instructions

Step 1   Go to http://www.adidas-group.com and click on Sustainability. Review the annual sustainability reports available in this section of the website.

Step 2   On a separate sheet of paper, list six aspects that you like most and six aspects that you like least about adidas' sustainability efforts.

Step 3   Provide a two-page executive summary of your assessment of adidas' sustainability efforts.

EXERCISE 3E

How Do You Rate Nestlé's Sustainability Efforts?

Purpose

This exercise aims to familiarize you with corporate sustainability programs. Review the opening chapter company discussion. Review the material at Nestlé's corporate website. Note that Nestlé recently kept Oxfam's scorecard top slot.

Instructions

Step 1   On a separate sheet of paper, list six aspects that you like most and six aspects that you like least about Nestlé's sustainability efforts.

Step 2   Provide a two-page executive summary of your assessment of Nestlé's sustainability efforts.

EXERCISE 3F

The Ethics of Spying on Competitors

Purpose

This exercise gives you an opportunity to discuss in class ethical and legal issues related to methods being used by many companies to spy on competing firms. Gathering and using information about competitors is an area of strategic management that Japanese firms do more proficiently than American firms.

Instructions

On a separate sheet of paper, write down numbers 1 to 18. For the 18 spying activities that follow, indicate whether or not you believe the activity is ethical or unethical and legal or illegal. Place either an *E* for ethical or *U* for unethical, and either an *L* for legal or an *I* for illegal for each activity. Compare your answers to those of your classmates and discuss any differences.

Step 1   Buying competitors' garbage

Step 2   Dissecting competitors' products

Step 3	Taking competitors' plant tours anonymously
Step 4	Counting tractor-trailer trucks leaving competitors' loading bays
Step 5	Studying aerial photographs of competitors' facilities
Step 6	Analyzing competitors' labor contracts
Step 7	Analyzing competitors' help-wanted ads
Step 8	Quizzing customers and buyers about the sales of competitors'products
Step 9	Infiltrating customers' and competitors' business operations
Step 10	Quizzing suppliers about competitors' level of manufacturing
Step 11	Using customers to buy out phony bids
Step 12	Encouraging key customers to reveal competitive information
Step 13	Quizzing competitors' former employees
Step 14	Interviewing consultants who may have worked with competitors
Step 15	Hiring key managers away from competitors
Step 16	Conducting phony job interviews to get competitors' employees to reveal information
Step 17	Sending engineers to trade meetings to quiz competitors' technical employees
Step 18	Quizzing potential employees who worked for or with competitors

Notes

1. http://www.usatoday.com/money/companies/management/story/2012-05-14/ceo-firings/54964476/1

2. Ibid.

3. Joann Greco, "Privacy—Whose Right Is It Anyhow?" *Journal of Business Strategy*, January–February 2001, 32.

4. Ashby Jones and JoAnn Lublin, "New Law Prompts Blowing Whistle," *Wall Street Journal*, November 1, 2010, B1.

5. Saul Gellerman, "Why 'Good' Managers Make Bad Ethical Choices," *Harvard Business Review* 64, no. 4 (July–August 1986): 88.

6. Peter Drucker, *Management: Tasks, Responsibilities, and Practices* (New York: Harper & Row, 1974), 462, 463.

7. www.wikipedia.org.

8. Joe Palazzolo and Christopher Matthews, "Bribery Law Do's and Don'ts," *Wall Street Journal* (November 15, 2012): B1.

9. http://www.businessknowhow.com/manage/romance.htm

10. Elizabeth Bernstein "The New Rules of Flirting," *Wall Street Journal* (11-13-12): D1.

11. Phred Dvorak, Bob Davis, and Louise Radnofsky, "Firms Confront Boss-Subordinate Love Affairs," *Wall Street Journal*, October 27, 2008, B5.

12. Spencer Morgan, "The End of the Office Affair," *Bloomberg Businessweek*, September 20–26, 2010, 74.

13. http://money.cnn.com/magazines/fortune/most-admired/2012/best_worst/best4.html and http://money.cnn.com/magazines/fortune/most-admired/2012/best_worst/worst4.html.

14. Archie Carroll and Frank Hoy, "Integrating Corporate Social Policy into Strategic Management," *Journal of Business Strategy* 4, no. 3 (Winter 1984): 57.

15. Kerry Hannon, "Businesses' Green Opportunities Are Wide, But Complex," *USA Today*, January 2, 2009, 5B.

16. Adapted from the www.iso14000.com website and the www.epa.gov website.

17. http://www.guardian.co.uk/environment/2012/mar/09/shark-fin-soup-blue-sharks-uk

18. Jim Sterba, "America Gone Wild," *Wall Street Journal* (11-8-12): p. C1.

19. Tom Brook, "Declining Numbers Mute Many Birds' Songs," *USA Today*, September 11, 2001, 4A.

20. John Ogden, "Maintaining Diversity in the Oceans," *Environment*, April 2001, 29–36.

4

MyManagementLab®

Improve Your Grade!

Over 10 million students improved their results using the Pearson MyLabs.
Visit **mymanagementlab.com** for simulations, tutorials, and end-of-chapter problems.

Types of Strategies

CHAPTER OBJECTIVES

After studying this chapter, you should be able to do the following:

1. Define and discuss secondary buyouts and dividend recapitalizations.

2. Identify the benefits and drawbacks of merging with another firm.

3. Discuss the value of establishing long-term objectives.

4. Identify 16 types of business strategies.

5. Identify numerous examples of organizations pursuing different types of strategies.

6. Discuss guidelines when particular strategies are most appropriate to pursue.

7. Discuss Porter's five generic strategies.

8. Describe strategic management in nonprofit, governmental, and small organizations.

9. Discuss the nature and role of joint ventures in strategic planning.

10. Compare and contrast financial with strategic objectives.

11. Discuss the levels of strategies in large versus small firms.

12. Explain the first mover advantages concept.

13. Discuss recent trends in outsourcing and reshoring.

ASSURANCE OF LEARNING EXERCISES

The following exercises are found at the end of this chapter.

EXERCISE 4A   Market Development: Petronas

EXERCISE 4B   Alternative Strategies for Petronas

EXERCISE 4C   Private-Equity Acquisitions

EXERCISE 4D   The strategies of adidas AG: 2013-2015

EXERCISE 4E   Lessons in Doing Business Globally

EXERCISE 4F   Petronas 2013-2015

EXERCISE 4G   What Strategies Are Most Risky?

EXERCISE 4H   Exploring Bankruptcy

EXERCISE 4I   Examining Strategy Articles

EXERCISE 4J   Classifying Some Strategies

Hundreds of companies today, including IBM, Wells Fargo, and General Electric, have embraced strategic planning fully in their quest for higher revenues and profits. Kent Nelson, former chair of UPS, explains why his company has created a new strategic-planning department: "Because we're making bigger bets on investments in technology, we can't afford to spend a whole lot of money in one direction and then find out five years later it was the wrong direction."[1]

This chapter brings strategic management to life with many contemporary examples. Sixteen types of strategies are defined and exemplified, including Michael Porter's generic strategies: cost leadership, differentiation, and focus. Guidelines are presented for determining when each strategy is most appropriate to pursue. An overview of strategic management in nonprofit organizations, governmental agencies, and small firms is provided. As showcased below, Petronas is an example company that for many years has exemplified excellent strategic management.

Long-Term Objectives

Long-term objectives represent the results expected from pursuing certain strategies. Strategies represent the actions to be taken to accomplish long-term objectives. The time frame for objectives and strategies should be consistent, usually from two to five years.

The Nature of Long-Term Objectives

Objectives should be quantitative, measurable, realistic, understandable, challenging, hierarchical, obtainable, and congruent among organizational units. Each objective should also be associated with a timeline. Objectives are commonly stated in terms such as *growth in assets*, *growth in sales*, *profitability*, *market share*, *degree and nature of diversification*, *degree and nature of vertical integration*, *earnings per share*, and *social responsibility*. Clearly established objectives

EXCELLENT STRATEGIC MANAGEMENT SHOWCASED

Petronas

PETRONAS, short for *Petroliam Nasional Berhad*, is a Malaysian oil and gas company, wholly owned by the Government of Malaysia. Headquartered in Kuala Lumpur, PETRONAS owns the entire oil and gas resources in Malaysia and is responsible for developing and adding value to these resources. In 2013, *Fortune* ranked PETRONAS as the 75th largest company in the world, the 19th most profitable company in the world, and the most profitable company in Asia. PETRONAS has business interests in 35 countries and is engaged in a wide spectrum of petroleum activities, including upstream exploration and production of oil and gas as well as downstream oil refining, marketing, and distribution. Revenue derived from PETRONAS provides roughly 45 percent of the Malaysian government's annual budget. PETRONAS was one of the main sponsors of the BMW Sauber Formula One team before sponsoring the Mercedes Grand Prix team. PETRONAS is the main sponsor for the Malaysian Grand Prix and co-sponsors the Chinese Grand Prix.

Among other strategies, PETRONAS is pursuing backward integration by purchasing its own ships to transport its own oil and gas, especially its liquefied natural gas (LNG). PETRONAS is directly procuring new LNG ships to meet its LNG transportation requirements. The strategy will allow PETRONAS to have direct access to LNG shipping capacity at the lowest possible costs. PETRONAS has engaged MISC Bhd to provide Project Management and Technical Consultancy services for the construction of its new LNG ships; MISC's has extensive experience and expertise in the LNG shipping sector and is familiar with PETRONAS' business needs.

PETRONAS since 1975 has awarded 20,600 Malaysian students scholarships, including a total of 400 deserving students in 2013 to pursue their education under its PETRONAS Education Sponsorship Programme (PESP). Scholarship recipients are chosen during rigorous selection days held across Malaysia, and are offered opportunities to take education at overseas institutions or at the Universiti Teknologi PETRONAS in Perak. The aim of PESP is to develop the skills of a pool of young people who meet PETRONAS' business requirements.

TABLE 4-1 **Varying Performance Measures by Organizational Level**

Organizational Level	Basis for Annual Bonus or Merit Pay
Corporate	75% based on long-term objectives
	25% based on annual objectives
Division	50% based on long-term objectives
	50% based on annual objectives
Function	25% based on long-term objectives
	75% based on annual objectives

offer many benefits. They provide direction, allow synergy, aid in evaluation, establish priorities, reduce uncertainty, minimize conflicts, stimulate exertion, and aid in both the allocation of resources and the design of jobs. Objectives provide a basis for consistent decision making by managers whose values and attitudes differ. Objectives serve as standards by which individuals, groups, departments, divisions, and entire organizations can be evaluated.

Long-term objectives are needed at the corporate, divisional, and functional levels of an organization. They are an important measure of managerial performance. Many practitioners and academicians attribute a significant part of U.S. industry's competitive decline to the short-term, rather than long-term, strategy orientation of managers in the USA. Arthur D. Little argues that bonuses or merit pay for managers today must be based to a greater extent on long-term objectives and strategies. An example framework for relating objectives to performance evaluation is provided in Table 4-1. A particular organization could tailor these guidelines to meet its own needs, but incentives should be attached to both long-term and annual objectives.

Without long-term objectives, an organization would drift aimlessly toward some unknown end. It is hard to imagine an organization or individual being successful without clear objectives. You probably have worked hard the last few years striving to achieve an objective to graduate with a business degree. Success only rarely occurs by accident; rather, it is the result of hard work directed toward achieving certain objectives. Table 4-2 reveals the desired characteristics of objectives, while Table 4-3 summarizes the benefits of having clear objectives.

Financial versus Strategic Objectives

Two types of objectives are especially common in organizations: financial and strategic objectives. **Financial objectives** include those associated with growth in revenues, growth in earnings, higher dividends, larger profit margins, greater return on investment, higher earnings per share, a rising stock price, improved cash flow, and so on; whereas **strategic objectives** include things such as a larger market share, quicker on-time delivery than rivals, shorter design-to-market times than rivals, lower costs than rivals, higher product quality than rivals, wider geographic coverage than rivals, achieving technological leadership, consistently getting new or improved products to market ahead of rivals, and so on.

Although financial objectives are especially important in firms, oftentimes there is a trade-off between financial and strategic objectives such that crucial decisions have to be made.

TABLE 4-2 **The Desired Characteristics of Objectives**

1. Quantitative
2. Measurable
3. Realistic
4. Understandable
5. Challenging
6. Hierarchical
7. Obtainable
8. Congruent across departments

TABLE 4-3 The Benefits of Having Clear Objectives

1. Provide direction by revealing expectations
2. Allow synergy
3. Aid in evaluation by serving as standards
4. Establish priorities
5. Reduce uncertainty
6. Minimize conflicts
7. Stimulate exertion
8. Aid in allocation of resources
9. Aid in design of jobs
10. Provide basis for consistent decision making

For example, a firm can do certain things to maximize short-term financial objectives that would harm long-term strategic objectives. To improve financial position in the short run through higher prices may, for example, jeopardize long-term market share. The dangers associated with trading off long-term strategic objectives with near-term bottom-line performance are especially severe if competitors relentlessly pursue increased market share at the expense of short-term profitability. And there are other trade-offs between financial and strategic objectives, related to riskiness of actions, concern for business ethics, need to preserve the natural environment, and social responsibility issues. Both financial and strategic objectives should include both annual and long-term performance targets. Ultimately, the best way to sustain competitive advantage over the long run is to relentlessly pursue strategic objectives that strengthen a firm's business position over rivals. Financial objectives can best be met by focusing first and foremost on achieving strategic objectives that improve a firm's competitiveness and market strength.

Not Managing by Objectives

An unidentified educator once said, "If you think education is expensive, try ignorance." The idea behind this saying also applies to establishing objectives. Strategists should avoid the following alternative ways of "not managing by objectives."

- *Managing by Extrapolation*—adheres to the principle "If it ain't broke, don't fix it." The idea is to keep on doing the same things in the same ways because things are going well.
- *Managing by Crisis*—based on the belief that the true measure of a really good strategist is the ability to solve problems. Because there are plenty of crises and problems to go around for every person and every organization, strategists ought to bring their time and creative energy to bear on solving the most pressing problems of the day. Managing by crisis is actually a form of reacting rather than acting and of letting events dictate the what and when of management decisions.
- *Managing by Subjectives*—built on the idea that there is no general plan for which way to go and what to do; just do the best you can to accomplish what you think should be done. In short, "Do your own thing, the best way you know how" (sometimes referred to as *the mystery approach to decision making* because subordinates are left to figure out what is happening and why).
- *Managing by Hope*—based on the fact that the future is laden with great uncertainty and that if we try and do not succeed, then we hope our second (or third) attempt will succeed. Decisions are predicated on the hope that they will work and that good times are just around the corner, especially if luck and good fortune are on our side![2]

Types of Strategies

The model illustrated in Figure 4-1 provides a conceptual basis for applying strategic management. Defined and exemplified in Table 4-4, alternative strategies that an enterprise could pursue can be categorized into 11 actions: forward integration, backward integration, horizontal integration, market penetration, market development, product development, related diversification,

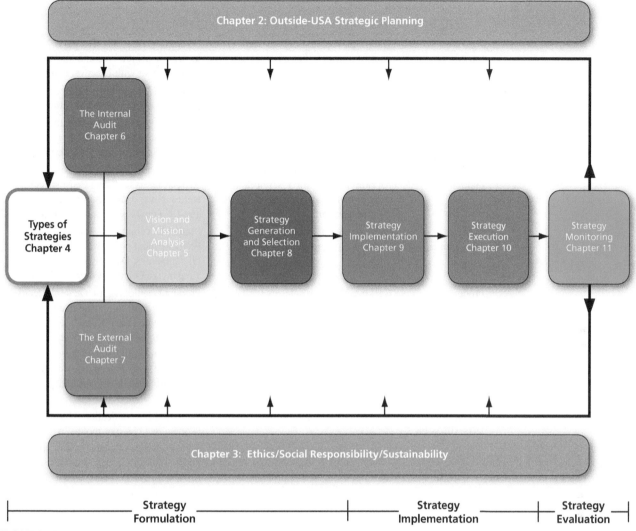

FIGURE 4-1

A Comprehensive Strategic-Management Model

Source: Fred R. David, adapted from "How Companies Define Their Mission," *Long Range Planning* 22, no. 3 (June 1988): 40, © Fred R. David.

unrelated diversification, retrenchment, divestiture, and liquidation. Each alternative strategy has countless variations. For example, market penetration can include adding salespersons, increasing advertising expenditures, couponing, and using similar actions to increase market share in a given geographic area.

Many, if not most, organizations simultaneously pursue a combination of two or more strategies, but a **combination strategy** can be exceptionally risky if carried too far. No organization can afford to pursue all the strategies that might benefit the firm. Difficult decisions must be made. Priority must be established. Organizations, like individuals, have limited resources. Both organizations and individuals must choose among alternative strategies and avoid excessive indebtedness.

Hansen and Smith explain that strategic planning involves "choices that risk resources" and "trade-offs that sacrifice opportunity." In other words, if you have a strategy to go north, then you must buy snowshoes and warm jackets (spend resources) and forgo the opportunity of "faster population growth in southern states." You cannot have a strategy to go north and then take a step east, south, or west "just to be on the safe side." Firms spend resources and focus on a finite number of opportunities in pursuing strategies to achieve an uncertain outcome in the future. Strategic planning is much more than a roll of the dice; it is a wager based on predictions

TABLE 4-4 **Alternative Strategies Defined and Exemplified**

Strategy	Definition	Examples
Forward Integration	Gaining ownership or increased control over distributors or retailers	Forward Integration—PayPal is pushing its service off the Web and into stores via an agreement with Discover card.
Backward Integration	Seeking ownership or increased control of a firm's suppliers	Backward Integration—Fancy Motels Inc. acquiring a furniture manufacturer.
Horizontal Integration	Seeking ownership or increased control over competitors	Horizontal Integration—Britain's GlaxoSmithKline PLC acquired Human Genome Sciences Inc. for $3 billion.
Market Penetration	Seeking increased market share for present products or services in present markets through greater marketing efforts	Market Penetration—PepsiCo is heavily advertising its new Diet Pepsi special-edition silver cans featuring the blue-and-red Pepsi logo in a heart shape.
Market Development	Introducing present products or services into new geographic area	Market Development—China Petrochemical purchased three Canadian oil companies, Daylight Energy, Tanganyika Oil, and Syncrude Canada.
Product Development	Seeking increased sales by improving present products or services or developing new ones	Product Development—General Electric is building new composite material jet engines, whereas rival Pratt & Whitney is developing newly designed jet engines.
Related Diversification	Adding new but related products or services	Related Diversification—The toy retailer, Toys 'R' Us developed a new Wi-Fi tablet computer for children (the Tabeo for $149.99).
Unrelated Diversification	Adding new, unrelated products or services	Unrelated Diversification—Retailer IKEA is opening a chain of motels in Europe.
Retrenchment	Regrouping through cost and asset reduction to reverse declining sales and profit	Retrenchment—Callaway Golf cut 12 percent of its workforce; Deutsche Bank AG cut 1,000 jobs from its investment bank segment.
Divestiture	Selling a division or part of an organization	Divestiture—Dean Foods sold off its WhiteWave-Alpro organic dairy business.
Liquidation	Selling all of a company's assets, in parts, for their tangible worth	Liquidation—Big Sky Farms, one of Canada's biggest hog-producing firms, liquidated.

and hypotheses that are continually tested and refined by knowledge, research, experience, and learning. Survival of the firm itself may hinge on your strategic plan.[3]

Organizations cannot do too many things well because resources and talents get spread thin and competitors gain advantage. In large, diversified companies, a combination strategy is commonly employed when different divisions pursue different strategies. Also, organizations struggling to survive may simultaneously employ a combination of several defensive strategies, such as divestiture, liquidation, and retrenchment.

Levels of Strategies

Strategy making is not just a task for top executives. Middle-and lower-level managers also must be involved in the strategic-planning process to the extent possible. In large firms, there are actually four levels of strategies: corporate, divisional, functional, and operational—as illustrated in Figure 4-2. However, in small firms, there are actually three levels of strategies: company, functional, and operational.

In large firms, the persons primarily responsible for having effective strategies at the various levels include the CEO at the corporate level; the president or executive vice president at the divisional level; the respective chief finance officer (CFO), chief information officer (CIO),

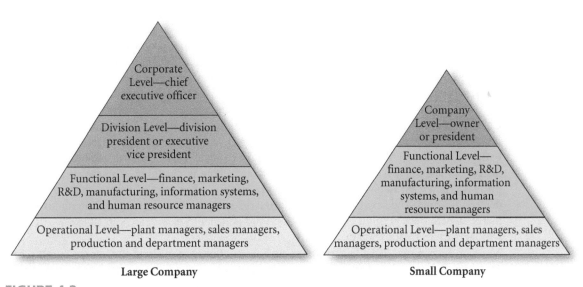

FIGURE 4-2

Levels of Strategies With Persons Most Responsible

human resource manager (HRM), chief marketing officer (CMO), and so on at the functional level; and the plant manager, regional sales manager, and so on at the operational level. In small firms, the persons primarily responsible for having effective strategies at the various levels include the business owner or president at the company level and then the same range of persons at the lower two levels, as with a large firm.

It is important that all managers at all levels participate and understand the firm's strategic plan to help ensure coordination, facilitation, and commitment while avoiding inconsistency, inefficiency, and miscommunication. Plant managers, for example, need to understand and be supportive of the overall strategic plan (game plan), whereas the president and the CEO need to be knowledgeable of strategies being employed in various sales territories and manufacturing plants.

Integration Strategies

The exclusively online men's pants company, Bonobos, now sells menswear wholesale to Nordstrom and in addition is opening its own stores in New York, Palo Alto, Chicago, and other cities. However, shoppers do not walk out of Bonobos stores with anything; the stores are simply for customers to try on the clothing before ordering online.

Forward integration, backward integration, and horizontal integration are sometimes collectively referred to as **vertical integration** strategies. Vertical integration strategies allow a firm to gain control over distributors, suppliers, or competitors.

Forward Integration

Forward integration involves gaining ownership or increased control over distributors or retailers. Increasing numbers of manufacturers (suppliers) today are pursuing a forward integration strategy by establishing websites to directly sell products to consumers. This strategy is causing turmoil in some industries. For example, Amazon is doubling down on forward integration by quietly installing large metal cabinets, called Amazon Lockers, in hundreds of grocery, 7-Eleven, and drugstores that accept the packages for customers for later pickup. This strategy dispels the concern of urban apartment dwellers who fear they will miss an Amazon delivery or have their item stolen. This strategy also combats a growing problem of thieves following UPS and FedEx trucks and stealing packages at doorsteps. Amazon has lockers in the USA and United Kingdom. This strategy entails Amazon emailing customers a code to open the locker holding their merchandise. Curtailing failed deliveries is essential for Amazon because otherwise consumers call customer service, switch to a competitor, or get a replacement item. Amazon pays a small fee each month to store owners where it has lockers.

To combat Amazon's forward integration, Walmart too is pursuing forward integration by launching its Walmart-to-go service in which the company promises same-day delivery in many cities for orders placed online. With that new service, Walmart ships products from its company's stores rather than a warehouse or distribution center. The new Walmart service costs $10 regardless of size of the order.

Ford Motor in 2014–2015 is opening a nationwide network of exclusive Lincoln dealers in China to promote an image of "luxury with simplicity" to compete with China's heavyweight luxury brands, Volkswagen AG's Audi, BMW AG, and Daimler AG's Mercedes-Benz. Jim Farley, Ford Group VP for Global Marketing Sales and Service says that through extensive interviews and surveys the company knows that: "China is changing. Chinese wants to show off less. They want to consume for themselves, not for other people." Ford is hunting for new dealers in China. The new Lincolns will have large back seats, a must in the Chinese luxury-car market where owners often employ drivers. Ford added 115 new dealers in China in 2012 and will increase its total to 500 by 2015.

Samsung in mid-2013 began adding upfront boutiques in all Best Buy stores. For the first time ever, Samsung is recruiting and training thousands of retail workers to staff their new boutiques. This forward integration strategy is a big move for Samsung, who unlike rivals Apple and Microsoft, currently own no retail stores of their own. Samsung is one of Best Buy's top five vendors (suppliers). Also using forward integration, IKEA, the huge furniture retailer, has recently agreed to begin building hotels, i.e. the Moxy brand, with Marriott. Most Moxy hotels will feature rooms prefabricated offsite and then assembled with IKEA furniture.

An effective means of implementing forward integration is **franchising**. Approximately 2,000 companies in about 50 different industries in the USA use franchising to distribute their products or services. Businesses can expand rapidly by franchising because costs and opportunities are spread among many individuals. Total sales by franchises in the United States are annually about $1 trillion.

The International Franchise Association Educational Foundations reports that there are about 800,000 franchise businesses in the USA. However, a growing trend is for franchisees, who for example may operate 10 franchised restaurants, stores, or whatever, to buy out their part of the business from their franchiser (corporate owner). There is a growing rift between franchisees and franchisers as the segment often outperforms the parent. McDonald's today owns only 67 percent of its restaurants, up from 20 percent a decade ago. Restaurant chains are increasingly being pressured to own fewer of their locations. Companies such as McDonald's are using proceeds from the sale of company stores and restaurants to franchisees to buy back company stock, pay higher dividends, and make other investments to benefit shareholders.

Also, McDonald's franchisees in 2012–2013 are opposing the company's remodeling investments, marketing campaigns, and discounting. Mark Kalinowski, lead restaurant analyst at Janney Capital Markets, recently asked 30 McDonald's franchisees to gauge how they felt about what's going on, and some comments were as follows:

- "We are bankrupting the system in the name of 'rebranding' the system!"
- "Major remodel projects are wiping out our cash flow and our equity."
- "Cash flow is trending up, but not as fast as McDonald's cash flow is."
- "We cannot absorb all these costs, do all this discounting, and still pay to remodel our landlord's (McDonald's) building."

McDonald's ironically gets 67 percent of its sales from company-owned restaurants. However, rival fast-food chain Burger King is converting virtually all of its company-owned outlets to franchised operations, with revenue from franchisees going from 30 percent of sales in 2011 to 90 percent in 2015. This change results in more than a 60 percent drop in Burger King revenues in two years since franchisees show revenues on their own personal income statements, but Burger King's operating profit more than doubled during this time. Burger King already has 45 percent of its stores outside the USA, and the company plans to increase that percentage dramatically. Rival Yum Brands owns virtually all of its outside-U.S. restaurants and says that policy gives greater control and benefits if things go well (or bad). In contrast, Burger King has so much long-term debt it has to rely on franchisees for capital.

The following six guidelines indicate when forward integration may be an especially effective strategy:[4]

- When an organization's present distributors are especially expensive, unreliable, or incapable of meeting the firm's distribution needs.
- When the availability of quality distributors is so limited as to offer a competitive advantage to those firms that integrate forward.
- When an organization competes in an industry that is growing and is expected to continue to grow markedly; this is a factor because forward integration reduces an organization's ability to diversify if its basic industry falters.
- When an organization has both the capital and human resources needed to manage the new business of distributing its own products.
- When the advantages of stable production are particularly high; this is a consideration because an organization can increase the predictability of the demand for its output through forward integration.
- When present distributors or retailers have high profit margins; this situation suggests that a company could profitably distribute its own products and price them more competitively by integrating forward.

Backward Integration

In March 2013, Starbucks purchased its first coffee farm—a 600 acre property in Costa Rica. This backward integration strategy was utilized primarily to develop new coffee varieties and to test methods to combat a fungal disease known as coffee rust that plagues the industry. Both manufacturers and retailers purchase needed materials from suppliers. **Backward integration** is a strategy of seeking ownership or increased control of a firm's suppliers. This strategy can be especially appropriate when a firm's current suppliers are unreliable, too costly, or cannot meet the firm's needs.

Campbell Soup recently acquired one of its primary suppliers, Bolthouse Farms, headquartered in Bakersfield, California, for $1.55 billion in an effort to move more aggressively into fresher foods rather than relying so heavily on canned foods. Canned foods, including Campbell's famous soups, are full of preservatives so they will last a long time on shelves, but for an increasing number of consumers, freshness trumps longevity.

Starbucks in early 2014 will open its first company-owned factory to make soluble products such as its VIA Ready Brew and the coffee base for Frappuccinos and many of the company's ready-to-drink beverages. These products are currently made in Colombia, South America, and in Switzerland by third-party manufacturers. Starbucks says this backward integration strategy will enable the company to save on transportation and ensure better quality. The new Starbucks plant is being built in Augusta, Georgia. In addition, Starbucks recently began producing and selling a single-cup coffee brewing machine that will brew coffee, lattes, and espresso in one machine. Some analysts are concerned that consumers may now make their own Starbucks drink at home for one dollar, rather than going to a Starbucks and buying that drink for four dollars.

Priceline.com Inc., recently acquired Kayak Software for $1.8 billion, representing a 29 percent premium over Kayak's closing stock price. Priceline wanted Kayak because that company makes money by referring customers to online travel agencies such as Priceline and rival Expedia. Kayak operated websites and mobile applications for travelers to compare prices for airline, hotel, and rental-car bookings.

Some industries in the USA, such as the automotive and aluminum industries, are reducing their historical pursuit of backward integration. Instead of owning their suppliers, companies negotiate with several outside suppliers. Ford and Chrysler buy more than half of their component parts from outside suppliers such as TRW, Eaton, General Electric (GE), and Johnson Controls. **De-integration** makes sense in industries that have global sources of supply. Companies today shop around, play one seller against another, and go with the best deal.

Global competition is also spurring firms to reduce their number of suppliers and to demand higher levels of service and quality from those they keep. Although traditionally relying on many suppliers to ensure uninterrupted supplies and low prices, U.S. firms now are following the lead of Japanese firms, which have far fewer suppliers and closer, long-term relationships with those few. "Keeping track of so many suppliers is onerous," says Mark Shimelonis, formerly of Xerox.

Seven guidelines when backward integration may be an especially effective strategy are:[5]

* When an organization's present suppliers are especially expensive, unreliable, or incapable of meeting the firm's needs for parts, components, assemblies, or raw materials.
* When the number of suppliers is small and the number of competitors is large.
* When an organization competes in an industry that is growing rapidly; this is a factor because integrative-type strategies (forward, backward, and horizontal) reduce an organization's ability to diversify in a declining industry.
* When an organization has both capital and human resources to manage the new business of supplying its own raw materials.
* When the advantages of stable prices are particularly important; this is a factor because an organization can stabilize the cost of its raw materials and the associated price of its product(s) through backward integration.
* When present suppliers have high profit margins, which suggests that the business of supplying products or services in the given industry is a worthwhile venture.
* When an organization needs to quickly acquire a needed resource.

Horizontal Integration

Horizontal integration refers to a strategy of seeking ownership of or increased control over a firm's competitors. One of the most significant trends in strategic management today is the increased use of horizontal integration as a growth strategy. Mergers, acquisitions, and takeovers among competitors allow for increased economies of scale and enhanced transfer of resources and competencies. Kenneth Davidson makes the following observation about horizontal integration:

> The trend towards horizontal integration seems to reflect strategists' misgivings about their ability to operate many unrelated businesses. Mergers between direct competitors are more likely to create efficiencies than mergers between unrelated businesses, both because there is a greater potential for eliminating duplicate facilities and because the management of the acquiring firm is more likely to understand the business of the target.[6]

Pearson PLC's Penguin book publishing business recently merged with Bertelsmann SE's Random House book publishing division to create a new company named Penguin Random House. This horizontal integration strategy for the two parent firms combines Penguin's 10 percent U.S. book market share with Random House's 20 percent market share into the new joint-venture company. Combining forces allows the new firm to gain more heft in negotiating terms with retailers such as Amazon. Combining forces in the publishing industry is also deemed necessary because publishers' revenue coming from e-books is growing rapidly, to about 18 percent now, compared to 6.3 percent in 2010.

Based in Frankfurt, Germany, Bayer AG actively pursues horizontal integration, having just recently acquired vitamins maker Schiff Nutrition for $1.2 billion, as well as AgraQuest, a maker of biological crop protection and Teva Pharmaceutical Industries' U.S. animal health business. Based in Salt Lake City, Utah, Schiff produces Airborne, as well as many vitamin supplements and nutrition bars.

Sherwin-Williams recently acquired Mexico-based coatings maker Consorcio Comex SA for about $2.34 billion. Sherwin-Williams CEO Chris Connor said: "The transaction will significantly increase our presence in markets where our store count is low and it builds upon our strategy to grow our architectural paint business in the Americas."

Two rival Canadian furniture and appliance retailers, Leon's Furniture Ltd. and Brick Ltd, recently merged. Leon's CEO said: "During these economic times where we have seen multiple American corporations make inroads into our country through acquisitions, it is a pleasure to see two successful Canadian retailers reach an agreement that will better serve Canadian consumers."

In the kidney-dialysis market, the second largest manufacturer, Baxter International, recently acquired the third largest manufacturer, Gambro, based in Sweden, for $4 billion. More than two million patients globally receive some form of kidney dialysis, with treatment rates increasing more than 5 percent annually.

These five guidelines indicate when horizontal integration may be an especially effective strategy:[7]

- When an organization can gain monopolistic characteristics in a particular area or region without being challenged by the federal government for "tending substantially" to reduce competition.
- When an organization competes in a growing industry.
- When increased economies of scale provide major competitive advantages.
- When an organization has both the capital and human talent needed to successfully manage an expanded organization.
- When competitors are faltering as a result of a lack of managerial expertise or a need for particular resources that an organization possesses; note that horizontal integration would not be appropriate if competitors are doing poorly because in that case overall industry sales are declining.

Intensive Strategies

Market penetration, market development, and product development are sometimes referred to as **intensive strategies** because they require intensive efforts if a firm's competitive position with existing products is to improve.

Market Penetration

A **market penetration** strategy seeks to increase market share for present products or services in present markets through greater marketing efforts. This strategy is widely used alone and in combination with other strategies. Market penetration includes increasing the number of salespersons, increasing advertising expenditures, offering extensive sales promotion items, or increasing publicity efforts. Chrysler Group LLC recently launched a new marketing campaign for its redesigned Ram pickup truck that features new technology and improved fuel economy. Chrysler desires to make inroads into the market share of the truck sales leader F-150. Chrysler's new ads feature gruff-voiced actor Sam Elliott promoting Ram trucks over the Chevrolet Silverado and the GMC Sierra trucks.

General Motors in 2013 rolled out its global advertising campaign for its Chevrolet brand in hopes of improving the brand's image globally and halting its market-share slide in the United States. The new tagline for the GM campaign is "Find New Roads" that replaces the lackluster "Chevy Runs Deep" slogan. The new ad campaign is designed to support GM introducing 13 new or refreshed Chevrolet vehicles in the United States in 2013 and another 12 in different regions around the world.

In the 2013 Super Bowl, Anheuser-Busch InBev launched a huge new advertising campaign to coincide with its new Black Crown brand of beer. The prior year, the company had used the Super Bowl to launch its Bud Light Platinum brand. The company believes the Super Bowl is the ideal venue to launch something new because viewers of the game surpass 110 million annually. Black Crown is a golden amber lager that is a little bit darker and a little bit more flavorful than tradition Budweiser lager, and Black Crown has a 6 percent alcohol content rather than 5 percent. Anheuser is especially targeting the 21- to 34-year-old-age group with the new ads and brand.

These five guidelines indicate when market penetration may be an especially effective strategy:[8]

- When current markets are not saturated with a particular product or service.
- When the usage rate of present customers could be increased significantly.
- When the market shares of major competitors have been declining while total industry sales have been increasing.
- When the correlation between dollar sales and dollar marketing expenditures historically has been high.
- When increased economies of scale provide major competitive advantages.

Market Development

Market development involves introducing present products or services into new geographic areas. India is a target for numerous firms to expand geographically. For example, Coca-Cola Company and its bottling partners are investing $5 billion in India between 2013 and 2020 because that country has 1.2 billion people who on average only consume 12 eight-ounce bottles of Coke a year compared with 240 in Brazil and 90 bottles globally. PepsiCo is also expanding aggressively into India (the CEO of PepsiCo is Indra Nooyi who was born in India). The Swedish furniture company, IKEA Group, is investing $1.9 billion in India to open 25 new stores between 2013 and 2018. Seattle-based Starbucks Corp. opened its first store in India in late 2012.

PepsiCo is also expanding aggressively into China and just opened its sixth snack plant in that country, in China's landlocked city of Wuhan. CEO Nooyi at Pepsi said: "China will be the largest consumer market in the next decade, and PepsiCo aims to be the largest food-and-beverage company in that market." The snack-food market in China was about $12 billion in 2012, up 44 percent from 2008. PepsiCo's revenue from emerging markets increased from $8 billion in 2008 to over $25 billion in 2013.

China's Dalian Wanda Group Corp. recently acquired all 346 AMC (AMC Entertainment Holdings) multiplex theaters in the USA and Canada. Valued at $2.6 billion, the acquisition was the largest ever between a Chinese company and the U.S. film industry. AMC was the second-largest theater chain in the USA behind Regal Entertainment. Carmike is another competitor in the theater industry.

These six guidelines indicate when market development may be an especially effective strategy:[9]

- When new channels of distribution are available that are reliable, inexpensive, and of good quality.
- When an organization is successful at what it does.
- When new untapped or unsaturated markets exist.
- When an organization has the needed capital and human resources to manage expanded operations.
- When an organization has excess production capacity.
- When an organization's basic industry is rapidly becoming global in scope.

Product Development

Product development is a strategy that seeks increased sales by improving or modifying present products or services. Product development usually entails large research and development expenditures. Walt Disney Company is quickly developing a Disney Baby line of products and services that it expects to become a powerful baby brand for customers ages zero to two. Bob Chapek, president of Disney Consumer Products, recently said: "This gives Disney the opportunity to reach out to moms when magical moments begin; there is no more special occasion than the birth of a baby." The company plans to create Disney Baby sections in its 200-plus Disney Stores in the USA. Disney Baby online will sell everything from $14 Disney Cuddly Bobysuits to $69 Peeking Pooh Premiere Crib Bumpers.

Microsoft Corp. just released Office 365, an Internet-based (or cloud), subscription-based office system, in conjunction with its new Office 2013. Office 365 represents a culture shift for Microsoft, as web-based software such as Google's Chrome, Android, and Doc and mobile devices undermine the strategic importance of PCs and programs install on them.

Ford Motor is set to release its aluminum body F-150 in 2014, which will cut the weight of that truck by 15 percent or 800 pounds and enable 25 percent lower gas mileage and use of a smaller engine. This is a huge strategic bet by Ford because the F-150 truck accounts for up to a third of their $8 billion operating profit globally. The F-250 and F-350 do not fall under the new emission guidelines so are not being redesigned. Aluminum is more expensive than steel and harder to work with, so Ford is betting that this strategy will work, rather than having the vehicle shut down at stoplights to conserve fuel, or investing as GM is doing for its trucks, in designing more efficient engines. GM and Ford rarely take such divergent strategic paths, but in this case they are. Ford is betting on aluminum and GM is not. The F-Series pickup is Ford's top money-maker and has been the top-selling vehicle of any kind in the USA for 30 years.

Merck is testing a new cancer drug that can unleash the body's immune system's power to fight malignancies. The new drug, known as MK-3475, is among a new class of agents called PD-1 inhibitors, than enable the immune system to destroy cancer cells. Also using product development, Burger King is doubling its offerings of coffee, to include ten items, such as flavored iced coffee and vanilla lattes. Burger King is trying to catch up with rival McDonald's whose specialty coffee line, McCafé, is growing rapidly. Burger King also wants to regain the #2 burger chain in the USA in sales, having lost that ranking to Wendy's.

These five guidelines indicate when product development may be an especially effective strategy to pursue:[10]

- When an organization has successful products that are in the maturity stage of the product life cycle; the idea here is to attract satisfied customers to try new (improved) products as a result of their positive experience with the organization's present products or services.
- When an organization competes in an industry that is characterized by rapid technological developments.
- When major competitors offer better-quality products at comparable prices.
- When an organization competes in a high-growth industry.
- When an organization has especially strong research and development capabilities.

Diversification Strategies

For the first time its 129-year history, Cincinnati-based Kroger began adding clothing to its lineup of products. The new Kroger apparel section in its store in Mansfield, Ohio, includes branded shoes, jewelry, outerwear, and undergarments from Levi, Carhartt, Carter, Skechers, Hanes, Maidenform, and other apparel producers. There is only about a 1 percent profit margin in the grocery business, so Kroger is trying to diversify.

There are two general types of **diversification strategies**: **related diversification** and **unrelated diversification**. Businesses are said to be related when their value chains possesses competitively valuable cross-business strategic fits; businesses are said to be unrelated when their value chains are so dissimilar that no competitively valuable cross-business relationships exist.[11] Most companies favor related diversification strategies to capitalize on synergies as follows:

- Transferring competitively valuable expertise, technological know-how, or other capabilities from one business to another.
- Combining the related activities of separate businesses into a single operation to achieve lower costs.
- Exploiting common use of a well-known brand name.
- Cross-business collaboration to create competitively valuable resource strengths and capabilities.[12]

Diversification strategies are becoming less popular because organizations are finding it more difficult to manage diverse business activities. In the 1960s and 1970s, the trend was to diversify to avoid being dependent on any single industry, but the 1980s saw a general reversal of that thinking. Diversification is now on the retreat. Michael Porter, of the Harvard Business School, says, "Management found it couldn't manage the beast." Hence businesses are selling, or closing, less profitable divisions to focus on core businesses. Although many firms are successful operating in a single industry, new technologies, new products, or fast-shifting buyer preferences can decimate a single business.

Diversification must do more than simply spread business risk across different industries, because shareholders could accomplish this by simply purchasing equity in different firms across different industries or by investing in mutual funds. Diversification makes sense only to the extent the strategy adds more to shareholder value than what shareholders could accomplish acting individually. Thus, the chosen industry for diversification must be attractive enough to yield consistently high returns on investment and offer potential across the operating divisions for synergies greater than those entities could achieve alone.

A few companies today, however, pride themselves on being conglomerates, from small firms such as Pentair Inc. and Blount International to huge companies such as Textron, Allied Signal, Emerson Electric, GE, Viacom, and Samsung. Conglomerates prove that focus and diversity are not always mutually exclusive.

Many strategists contend that firms should "stick to the knitting" and not stray too far from the firms' basic areas of competence. However, diversification is still sometimes an appropriate strategy, especially when the company is competing in an unattractive industry. Hamish Maxwell, Philip Morris's former CEO, says, "We want to become a consumer-products company." Diversification makes sense for Philip Morris because cigarette consumption is declining, product liability suits are a risk, and some investors reject tobacco stocks on principle.

Related Diversification

Firms are generally moving away from diversification to focus. For example, ITT recently divided itself into three separate, specialized companies. ITT once owned everything from Sheraton hotels and Hartford Insurance to the maker of Wonder bread and Hostess Twinkies. About the ITT breakup, analyst Barry Knap said, "Companies generally are not very efficient diversifiers; investors usually can do a better job of that by purchasing stock in a variety of companies."

Bucking the trend however is Berkshire Hathaway, a holding company for diverse companies that include Dairy Queen, Burlington Northern Santa Fe Railroad, and Geico Insurance. Also bucking the trend, Amazon.com continues to diversify and is expected in 2013 to enter the smartphone business, to complement its Kindle e-reader and tablet devices. About 675 smartphones were sold in 2012, up 39 percent from 2011, whereas tablet sales increased 75 percent to 113 million. In another related diversification move in 2012, Amazon acquired mapping app maker UpNext. In addition, analysts expect Amazon to soon enter the mobile payments business and compete with offerings from eBay and Square.

Google in late 2012 entered the cable operator business by providing high-speed Internet and TV service in Kansas City, Missouri, and beyond. This new service entails Google supplying Web connections rather than the services that run on them. Google plans to expand this new service to all markets that Verizon has not entered. Google's new service costs $120 a month and provides 100 times faster Internet service than Time Warner. Google provides less money options but the $120 gets users online file storage space and a Nexus 7 computer tablet that they can use as a remote control, as well as DVR storage of 500 hours of shows, including eight shows simultaneously that can be watched on demand, and more.

IBM recently paid a 42 percent premium (42 percent more than the book value) to acquire Kenexa Corp. for about $1.3 billion, to move more deeply into the online business software applications business. Kenexa was a leading supplier of human-resources software and consulting services that help about 9,000 customers recruit, retain, and develop their employees. This acquisition moved IBM into competition with enterprise-software makers such as SAP AG, that recently acquired a company named Success Factors that competes with Kenexa, and with Oracle Corp., that recently bought human-resources software maker Taleo for $1.9 billion.

Starbucks recently made its largest acquisition ever, acquiring Atlanta-based tea retailer Teavana Holdings for a 54 percent premium over Teavana's closing stock price. Teavana customers tend to be to aficionados, so Starbucks plans to bring its tried-and-true strategy to Teavana, with a tea bar offering customized hot and cold tea drinks. Teavana currently sells most of its tea in loose-leaf form for home consumption.

Six guidelines for when related diversification may be an effective strategy are as follows.[13]

- When an organization competes in a no-growth or a slow-growth industry.
- When adding new, but related, products would significantly enhance the sales of current products.
- When new, but related, products could be offered at highly competitive prices.
- When new, but related, products have seasonal sales levels that counterbalance an organization's existing peaks and valleys.
- When an organization's products are currently in the declining stage of the product's life cycle.
- When an organization has a strong management team.

Unrelated Diversification

Based in Memphis, Tennessee, the huge overnight delivery firm FedEx recently entered the computer repair business offering major corporations with overnight computer repair. FedEx's Todd Taylor, manager of the company's TechConnect computer repair division says "What we offer is unparalleled turnaround time." FedEx's new computer repair service is initially focused on the enterprise market, but the company plans to expand the services to small businesses and consumers in the new future.

An unrelated diversification strategy favors capitalizing on a portfolio of businesses that are capable of delivering excellent financial performance in their respective industries, rather than striving to capitalize on value chain strategic fits among the businesses. Firms that employ unrelated diversification continually search across different industries for companies that can be acquired for a deal and yet have potential to provide a high return on investment. Pursuing unrelated diversification entails being on the hunt to acquire companies whose assets are undervalued, companies that are financially distressed, or companies that have high growth prospects but are short on investment capital. An obvious drawback of unrelated diversification is that the parent firm must have an excellent top management team that plans, organizes, motivates, delegates, and controls effectively. It is much more difficult to manage businesses in many industries than in a single industry. However, some firms are successful pursuing unrelated diversification, such as Walt Disney, which owns ABC, and GE, which owns NBC Universal. GE also produces locomotives, airplanes, appliances, and MRI machines and offers consumer finance, media, entertainment, oil, gas, and lighting products and services.

Numerous hotels are entering the beer brewing business to offer their guests a unique experience at "social" and "happy" hours. Specialty (or craft) beer sales are increasing about 15 percent annually. Four Fairmont hotels for example recently created their own microbrews using honey from on-site beehives. The Four Points by Sheraton in Los Angeles has a new director of brewer relations, a new beer advisory board, and customized in-room beer fridges.

Speaking of hotels and unrelated diversification, perhaps the first underwater hotel on the planet is being built in Dubai by Drydocks World in cooperation with BIG InvestConsult AG. The hotel is to be completed in 2015 and will offer 21 underwater rooms, with big windows looking out into the Persian Gulf, and disc-shaped luxury hotel attached above the water line.

Best Buy recently introduced its own tablet computer, the Insignia Flex, for $250. The new product is available only at Best Buy, the new product is 9.7 inches wide, putting it in the same size category as Apple's iPad and Microsoft's Surface. This is Best Buy's first foray into manufacturing its own electronic devices.

Deutsche Bank recently opened the $4 billion, 3,000-room Cosmopolitan casino on the Las Vegas Strip. The huge German bank was originally just funding the project, but when developers defaulted on their loans, Deutsche decided to finish the last two years of work on the project and own and operate the new casino themselves. The Cosmopolitan features a three-story, crystal-strewn bar meant to evoke the inside of a chandelier. Other financial institutions worldwide perhaps should consider unrelated diversification also by taking over some of their gone-bad projects rather than taking huge losses. Many more firms have failed at unrelated diversification than have succeeded as a result of immense management challenges.

Ten guidelines for when unrelated diversification may be an especially effective strategy are:[14]

- When revenues derived from an organization's current products or services would increase significantly by adding the new, unrelated products.
- When an organization competes in a highly competitive or a no-growth industry, as indicated by low industry profit margins and returns.
- When an organization's present channels of distribution can be used to market the new products to current customers.
- When the new products have countercyclical sales patterns compared to an organization's present products.
- When an organization's basic industry is experiencing declining annual sales and profits.
- When an organization has the capital and managerial talent needed to compete successfully in a new industry.
- When an organization has the opportunity to purchase an unrelated business that is an attractive investment opportunity.

- When there exists financial synergy between the acquired and acquiring firm. (Note that a key difference between related and unrelated diversification is that the former should be based on some commonality in markets, products, or technology, whereas the latter is based more on profit considerations.)
- When existing markets for an organization's present products are saturated.
- When antitrust action could be charged against an organization that historically has concentrated on a single industry.

Defensive Strategies

In addition to integrative, intensive, and diversification strategies, organizations also could pursue retrenchment, divestiture, or liquidation.

Retrenchment

Retrenchment occurs when an organization regroups through cost and asset reduction to reverse declining sales and profits. Sometimes called a *turnaround* or *reorganizational strategy*, retrenchment is designed to fortify an organization's basic distinctive competence. During retrenchment, strategists work with limited resources and face pressure from shareholders, employees, and the media. Retrenchment can entail selling off land and buildings to raise needed cash, pruning product lines, closing marginal businesses, closing obsolete factories, automating processes, reducing the number of employees, and instituting expense control systems.

Cosmetic company Revlon, whose brands include Almay and Mitchum, is closing its manufacturing plant in France and laying off 5 percent of its workforce in 2013 to combat high raw material costs, weakness in Europe, and a slowdown in China. Avon Products Inc. is presently exiting the South Korea and Vietnam markets and laying off 1,500 employees, as new CEO Sheri McCoy tries to stabilize the company, reeling from bribery allegations and falling sales.

In some cases, **bankruptcy** can be an effective type of retrenchment strategy. Bankruptcy can allow a firm to avoid major debt obligations and to void union contracts. There are five major types of bankruptcy: Chapter 7, Chapter 9, Chapter 11, Chapter 12, and Chapter 13.

Chapter 7 bankruptcy is a liquidation procedure used only when a corporation sees no hope of being able to operate successfully or to obtain the necessary creditor agreement. All the organization's assets are sold in parts for their tangible worth. Chapter 7 is also the bankruptcy provision most frequently used by individuals to wipe out many types of unsecured debt. Strauss Auto in 2012 filed Chapter 7 liquidation bankruptcy, after five previous times in its history filing and coming out of Chapter 11 reorganization bankruptcy. This time however, the auto-repair chain is closing its 46 remaining stores and selling its assets for their tangible worth.

Chapter 9 bankruptcy applies to municipalities. Stockton, a river port city of 290,000 in the Central Valley of California, declared Chapter 9 bankruptcy in 2012, to avoid having to close key functions such as their police and fire departments. A judge now, rather than city officials, has control over Stockton's debt-management problems. Stockton has twice in recent years toped *Forbes* magazine's list of "America's most miserable cities." However, the largest municipal (Chapter 9) bankruptcy in U.S. history occurred in 2011 in Birmingham, Alabama (Jefferson County). There were 13 municipal bankruptcies filed in 2011. Detroit, Michigan is eyeing the situation in Stockton to see if it needs to file for bankruptcy.

Chapter 11 bankruptcy allows organizations to reorganize and come back after filing a petition for protection. The Santa Ysabel Resort and Casino located 50 miles north of San Diego filed for Chapter 11 protection in mid-2012 to avoid having to shut down totally. Owned by the local Indian tribe Lipay Nation of Santa Ysabel, the casino owes $9 million to the Yavapai Apache Nation and that tribe needs to collect on their investment. Two military transport airlines declared bankruptcy in 2012, Southern Air and Global Aviation Holdings. Both firms cited the U.S. withdrawal of forces from Afghanistan as the primary reason for their demise.

Based in Mechanicsville, Virginia, the world's largest operator of bowling alleys, AMF Bowling Worldwide, filed for bankruptcy-court protection in late 2012 as the company failed to adapt to customers who shifted from being "blue-collar bowlers in leagues" to middle-class bowlers averse to leagues but who desire attractive amenities and facilities. AMF the last few years was too heavily burdened by debt to financially afford to refurbish its 262 bowling centers in the USA. Mom-and-pop operators and small bowling chains now operate more than 5,000 bowling alleys in the U.S.

Chapter 12 bankruptcy was created by the Family Farmer Bankruptcy Act of 1986. This law became effective in 1987 and provides special relief to family farmers with debt equal to or less than $1.5 million.

Chapter 13 bankruptcy is a reorganization plan similar to Chapter 11, but it is available only to small businesses owned by individuals with unsecured debts of less than $100,000 and secured debts of less than $350,000. The Chapter 13 debtor is allowed to operate the business while a plan is being developed to provide for the successful operation of the business in the future.

Five guidelines for when retrenchment may be an especially effective strategy to pursue are as follows:[15]

- When an organization has a clearly distinctive competence but has failed consistently to meet its objectives and goals over time.
- When an organization is one of the weaker competitors in a given industry.
- When an organization is plagued by inefficiency, low profitability, poor employee morale, and pressure from stockholders to improve performance.
- When an organization has failed to capitalize on external opportunities, minimize external threats, take advantage of internal strengths, and overcome internal weaknesses over time; that is, when the organization's strategic managers have failed (and possibly will be replaced by more competent individuals).
- When an organization has grown so large so quickly that major internal reorganization is needed.

Divestiture

Selling a division or part of an organization is called **divestiture**. Divestiture often is used to raise capital for further strategic acquisitions or investments. Divestiture can be part of an overall retrenchment strategy to rid an organization of businesses that are unprofitable, that require too much capital, or that do not fit well with the firm's other activities. Divestiture has also become a popular strategy for firms to focus on their core businesses and become less diversified. For example, United Technologies recently sold two divisions of its Hamilton Sundstrand pump and air compressor subsidiary to help pay for the company's $16.5 billion acquisition of Goodrich Corp. Owner of the Atlanta Braves baseball team, Liberty Media Corp., recently divested its Starz television network, but retains its large investments in Sirius XM Radio, Live Nation Entertainment, and Barnes & Noble.

New York Times Company (NYTC) recently sold its About.com how-to-website to a rival company, Answers.com, for $270 million. NYTC divested nearly 20 regional newspapers in the last twelve months and also divested its remaining stake in the Boston Red Sox. In addition, NYTC plans to divest *The Boston Globe*, the twenty third largest newspaper in the USA.

Bank of America just sold its overseas wealth-management operations for $880 million to Swiss private-banking specialist Julius Baer Group AG. Since Brian Moynihan became CEO of Bank of America in 2010, he divested more than $50 billion in what he calls noncore assets, dropping Bank of America below J.P. Morgan Chase as the largest bank in the USA.

Time Warner recently divested its magazine division, soon after News Corp. divested its publishing division. The year 2013 exceeded the prior two years in divestitures as firms used the strategy to increase stock price and overall value.

Six guidelines for when divestiture may be an especially effective strategy to pursue follow:[16]

- When an organization has pursued a retrenchment strategy and failed to accomplish needed improvements.
- When a division needs more resources to be competitive than the company can provide.
- When a division is responsible for an organization's overall poor performance.
- When a division is a misfit with the rest of an organization; this can result from radically different markets, customers, managers, employees, values, or needs.
- When a large amount of cash is needed quickly and cannot be obtained reasonably from other sources.
- When government antitrust action threatens an organization.

Liquidation

Selling all of a company's assets, in parts, for their tangible worth is called **liquidation**. Liquidation is a recognition of defeat and consequently can be an emotionally difficult strategy. However, it may be better to cease operating than to continue losing large sums of money. For example, the New York City–based discount retailer of designer clothing, Daffy's, recently liquidated, closing all its 19 stores and selling all its inventory. A family-run business based in Secaucus, New Jersey and founded in 1961, Daffy's decided it could not compete with T.J. Maxx and Marshalls, which had expanded aggressively into New York City. All 1,300 employees of Daffy's received severance pay of 60 days worth of work.

Delta Airlines recently liquidated its 35-year-old regional carrier Comair and sent termination notices to Comair's 1,700 remaining employees. More than 1,000 Comair employees were in the Cincinnati and northern Kentucky region, some 700 of those in Kentucky. Comair had slashed its fleet, flights and workforce in the last seven years and was down to 290 flights a day. Delta decided however that small regional planes are too expensive to fly because they are not as fuel-efficient and are more costly to maintain as the fleet ages. "We just really couldn't get the cost structure to where we wanted to get it," said Don Bornhorst, senior vice president of Delta Connection and a former Comair president. "It ultimately was a cost issue; it wasn't a quality issue with Comair. They're a good airline, great employees, very innovative...we just could not solve the cost issues."

Based in Waltham, Massachusetts, A123 Systems, the electric-car battery manufacturer, filed for bankruptcy recently and then sold all its tangible assets to Johnson Controls. Similarly, solar-panel manufacturer, Solyndra LLC, recently liquidated.

Based in Irving, Texas, Hostess Brands in late 2012 told all 18,000 of its workers that the firm will liquidate in five days unless the union-striking employees returned to work. The union work stoppage basically shut down two-thirds of Hostess' 36 manufacturing plants. Four unions were involved: (1) bakery, (2) confectionary, (3) tobacco workers, and (4) grain millers. The largest union's president, Frank Hurt, said: "I am well aware of the possibility of a liquidation, but our people will only take so much when it comes to cuts to their wages and benefits." The following brands were predicted by the *Wall Street Journal* in May 2013 to disappear in 2014:

J.C. Penney

Barnes & Noble's Nook

Martha Stewart's *Living Magazine*

Living Social (a daily deals website)

Volvo

Olympus cameras

Women's National Basketball Association (WNBA)

Leap Wireless International

Mitsubishi Motors

Road & Track (the automotive magazine)

Thousands of small businesses in Europe and the USA liquidate annually without ever making the news. It is tough to start and successfully operate a small business. In China and Russia, thousands of government-owned businesses liquidate annually as those countries try to privatize and consolidate industries.

These three guidelines indicate when liquidation may be an especially effective strategy to pursue:[17]

- When an organization has pursued both a retrenchment strategy and a divestiture strategy, and neither has been successful.
- When an organization's only alternative is bankruptcy. Liquidation represents an orderly and planned means of obtaining the greatest possible cash for an organization's assets. A company can legally declare bankruptcy first and then liquidate various divisions to raise needed capital.
- When the stockholders of a firm can minimize their losses by selling the organization's assets.

Michael Porter's Five Generic Strategies

Probably the three most widely read books on competitive analysis in the 1980s were Michael Porter's *Competitive Strategy* (1980), *Competitive Advantage* (1985), and *Competitive Advantage of Nations* (1989). According to Porter, strategies allow organizations to gain competitive advantage from three different bases: cost leadership, differentiation, and focus. Porter calls these bases **generic strategies**.

Cost leadership emphasizes producing standardized products at a low per-unit cost for consumers who are price-sensitive. Two alternative types of cost leadership strategies can be defined. Type 1 is a *low-cost* strategy that offers products or services to a wide range of customers at the lowest price available on the market. Type 2 is a *best-value* strategy that offers products or services to a wide range of customers at the best price-value available on the market; the best-value strategy aims to offer customers a range of products or services at the lowest price available compared to a rival's products with similar attributes. Both Type 1 and Type 2 strategies target a large market.

Porter's Type 3 generic strategy is **differentiation**, a strategy aimed at producing products and services considered unique industrywide and directed at consumers who are relatively price-insensitive.

Focus means producing products and services that fulfill the needs of small groups of consumers. Two alternative types of focus strategies are Type 4 and Type 5. Type 4 is a low-cost focus strategy that offers products or services to a small range (niche group) of customers at the lowest price available on the market. Examples of firms that use the Type 4 strategy include Jiffy Lube International and Pizza Hut, as well as local used car dealers and hot dog restaurants. Type 5 is a best-value focus strategy that offers products or services to a small range of customers at the best price-value available on the market. Sometimes called "focused differentiation," the best-value focus strategy aims to offer a niche group of customers products or services that meet their tastes and requirements better than rivals' products do. Both Type 4 and Type 5 focus strategies target a small market. However, the difference is that Type 4 strategies offer products or services to a niche group at the lowest price, whereas Type 5 offers products and services to a niche group at higher prices but loaded with features so the offerings are perceived as the best value. Examples of firms that use the Type 5 strategy include Cannondale (top-of-the-line mountain bikes), Maytag (washing machines), and Lone Star Restaurants (steakhouse), as well as bed-and-breakfast inns and local retail boutiques.

Porter's five strategies imply different organizational arrangements, control procedures, and incentive systems. Larger firms with greater access to resources typically compete on a cost leadership or differentiation basis, whereas smaller firms often compete on a focus basis. Porter's five generic strategies are illustrated in Figure 4-3. Note that a differentiation strategy (Type 3) can be pursued with either a small target market or a large target market. However, it is not effective to pursue a cost leadership strategy in a small market because profits margins are generally too small. Likewise, it is not effective to pursue a focus strategy in a large market because economies of scale would generally favor a low-cost or best-value cost leadership strategy to gain or sustain competitive advantage.

Porter stresses the need for strategists to perform cost-benefit analyses to evaluate "sharing opportunities" among a firm's existing and potential business units. Sharing activities and resources enhances competitive advantage by lowering costs or increasing differentiation. In addition to prompting sharing, Porter stresses the need for firms to effectively "transfer" skills and expertise among autonomous business units to gain competitive advantage. Depending on factors such as type of industry, size of firm, and nature of competition, various strategies could yield advantages in cost leadership, differentiation, and focus.

Cost Leadership Strategies (Type 1 and Type 2)

A primary reason for pursuing forward, backward, and horizontal integration strategies is to gain low-cost or best-value cost leadership benefits. But cost leadership generally must be pursued in conjunction with differentiation. A number of cost elements affect the relative attractiveness of generic strategies, including economies or diseconomies of scale achieved, learning and experience curve effects, the percentage of capacity utilization achieved, and linkages with

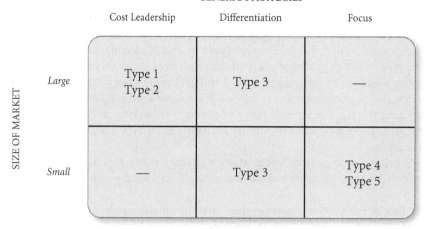

Type 1: Cost Leadership—Low Cost
Type 2: Cost Leadership—Best Value
Type 3: Differentiation
Type 4: Focus—Low Cost
Type 5: Focus—Best Value

FIGURE 4-3

Porter's Five Generic Strategies

Source: Based on Michael E. Porter, *Competitive Strategy: Techniques for Analyzing Industries and Competitors* (New York: Free Press, 1980), 35–40.

suppliers and distributors. Other cost elements to consider in choosing among alternative strategies include the potential for sharing costs and knowledge within the organization, research and development (R&D) costs associated with new product development or modification of existing products, labor costs, tax rates, energy costs, and shipping costs.

Striving to be the low-cost producer in an industry can be especially effective when the market is composed of many price-sensitive buyers, when there are few ways to achieve product differentiation, when buyers do not care much about differences from brand to brand, or when there are a large number of buyers with significant bargaining power. The basic idea is to underprice competitors and thereby gain market share and sales, entirely driving some competitors out of the market. Companies employing a low-cost (Type 1) or best-value (Type 2) cost leadership strategy must achieve their competitive advantage in ways that are difficult for competitors to copy or match. If rivals find it relatively easy or inexpensive to imitate the leader's cost leadership methods, the leaders' advantage will not last long enough to yield a valuable edge in the marketplace. Recall that for a resource to be valuable, it must be either rare, hard to imitate, or not easily substitutable. To employ a cost leadership strategy successfully, a firm must ensure that its total costs across its overall value chain are lower than competitors' total costs. There are two ways to accomplish this:[18]

1. Perform value chain activities more efficiently than rivals and control the factors that drive the costs of value chain activities. Such activities could include altering the plant layout, mastering newly introduced technologies, using common parts or components in different products, simplifying product design, finding ways to operate close to full capacity year-round, and so on.
2. Revamp the firm's overall value chain to eliminate or bypass some cost-producing activities. Such activities could include securing new suppliers or distributors, selling products online, relocating manufacturing facilities, avoiding the use of union labor, and so on.

When employing a cost leadership strategy, a firm must be careful not to use such aggressive price cuts that their own profits are low or nonexistent. Constantly be mindful of cost-saving technological breakthroughs or any other value chain advancements that could erode or destroy the firm's competitive advantage. A Type 1 or Type 2 cost leadership strategy can be especially effective under the following conditions:[19]

1. When price competition among rival sellers is especially vigorous.
2. When the products of rival sellers are essentially identical and supplies are readily available from any of several eager sellers.
3. When there are few ways to achieve product differentiation that have value to buyers.
4. When most buyers use the product in the same ways.
5. When buyers incur low costs in switching their purchases from one seller to another.
6. When buyers are large and have significant power to bargain down prices.
7. When industry newcomers use introductory low prices to attract buyers and build a customer base.

A successful cost leadership strategy usually permeates the entire firm, as evidenced by high efficiency, low overhead, limited perks, intolerance of waste, intensive screening of budget requests, wide spans of control, rewards linked to cost containment, and broad employee participation in cost control efforts. Some risks of pursuing cost leadership are that competitors may imitate the strategy, thus driving overall industry profits down; that technological breakthroughs in the industry may make the strategy ineffective; or that buyer interest may swing to other differentiating features besides price. Several example firms that are well known for their low-cost leadership strategies are Walmart, BIC, McDonald's, Black & Decker, Lincoln Electric, and Briggs & Stratton.

Differentiation Strategies (Type 3)

Different strategies offer different degrees of differentiation. Differentiation does not guarantee competitive advantage, especially if standard products sufficiently meet customer needs or if rapid imitation by competitors is possible. Durable products protected by barriers to quick copying by competitors are best. Successful differentiation can mean greater product flexibility, greater compatibility, lower costs, improved service, less maintenance, greater convenience, or more features. Product development is an example of a strategy that offers the advantages of differentiation.

A differentiation strategy should be pursued only after a careful study of buyers' needs and preferences to determine the feasibility of incorporating one or more differentiating features into a unique product that features the desired attributes. A successful differentiation strategy allows a firm to charge a higher price for its product and to gain customer loyalty because consumers may become strongly attached to the differentiation features. Special features that differentiate one's product can include superior service, spare parts availability, engineering design, product performance, useful life, gas mileage, or ease of use.

A risk of pursuing a differentiation strategy is that the unique product may not be valued highly enough by customers to justify the higher price. When this happens, a cost-leadership strategy easily will defeat a differentiation strategy. Another risk of pursuing a differentiation strategy is that competitors may quickly develop ways to copy the differentiating features. Firms thus must find durable sources of uniqueness that cannot be imitated quickly or cheaply by rival firms.

Common organizational requirements for a successful differentiation strategy include strong coordination among the R&D and marketing functions and substantial amenities to attract scientists and creative people. Firms can pursue a differentiation (Type 3) strategy based on many different competitive aspects. For example, Mountain Dew and root beer have a unique taste; Lowe's, Home Depot, and Walmart offer wide selection and one-stop shopping; Dell Computer and FedEx offer superior service; BMW and Porsche offer engineering design and performance; IBM and Hewlett-Packard offer a wide range of products; and E*Trade and Ameritrade offer Internet convenience. Differentiation opportunities exist or can potentially be developed anywhere along the firm's value chain, including supply chain activities, product R&D activities, production and technological activities, manufacturing activities, human resource management activities, distribution activities, or marketing activities.

The most effective differentiation bases are those that are hard or expensive for rivals to duplicate. Competitors are continually trying to imitate, duplicate, and outperform rivals along any differentiation variable that has yielded competitive advantage. For example, when U.S. Airways cut its prices, Delta quickly followed suit. When Caterpillar instituted its quick-delivery-of-spare-parts policy, John Deere soon followed suit. To the extent that differentiating attributes are tough for rivals to copy, a differentiation strategy will be especially effective, but the sources of uniqueness must be time-consuming, cost prohibitive, and simply too burdensome for rivals to match. A firm, therefore, must be careful when employing a differentiation (Type 3) strategy. Buyers will not pay the higher differentiation price unless their perceived value exceeds the price they are paying.[20] Based on such matters as attractive packaging, extensive advertising, quality of sales presentations, quality of website, list of customers, professionalism, size of the firm, or profitability of the company, perceived value may be more important to customers than actual value.

A Type 3 differentiation strategy can be especially effective under the following conditions:[21]

1. When there are many ways to differentiate the product or service and many buyers perceive these differences as having value.
2. When buyer needs and uses are diverse.
3. When few rival firms are following a similar differentiation approach.
4. When technological change is fast paced and competition revolves around rapidly evolving product features.

Focus Strategies (Type 4 and Type 5)

A successful focus strategy depends on an industry segment that is of sufficient size, has good growth potential, and is not crucial to the success of other major competitors. Strategies such as market penetration and market development offer substantial focusing advantages. Midsize and large firms can effectively pursue focus-based strategies only in conjunction with differentiation or cost leadership–based strategies. All firms in essence follow a differentiated strategy. Because only one firm can differentiate itself with the lowest cost, the remaining firms in the industry must find other ways to differentiate their products.

Focus strategies are most effective when consumers have distinctive preferences or requirements and when rival firms are not attempting to specialize in the same target segment. For example, Clorox Company, which obtains 80 percent of its revenue from the United States, is focusing on brands viewed as environmentally friendly. To refocus, Clorox just sold its auto-care business and acquired personal care company, Burt's Bees, and expanded its Green Works line of household cleaners and Brita water filters. Clorox's CEO Don Knauss loves the United States and is avoiding a costly push into China, Brazil, or India. Knauss's focus is on natural cleaning products, including bleaches and peroxide-based disinfectants for both consumers and hospitals.

Marriott continues to focus on is hotel business by announcing plans to double its hotels in Asia to 260 by 2016, especially growing its China-based hotels to about 125 from 60 and covering nearly 75 percent of Chinese provinces. Reasoning for Marriott's strategy is than Chinese tourists are traveling at home and abroad in dramatically increased numbers, up 21 percent on average year-over-year.

Risks of pursuing a focus strategy include the possibility that numerous competitors will recognize the successful focus strategy and copy it or that consumer preferences will drift toward the product attributes desired by the market as a whole. An organization using a focus strategy may concentrate on a particular group of customers, geographic markets, or on particular product-line segments to serve a well-defined but narrow market better than competitors who serve a broader market.

A low-cost (Type 4) or best-value (Type 5) focus strategy can be especially attractive under the following conditions:[22]

1. When the target market niche is large, profitable, and growing.
2. When industry leaders do not consider the niche to be crucial to their own success.
3. When industry leaders consider it too costly or difficult to meet the specialized needs of the target market niche while taking care of their mainstream customers.
4. When the industry has many different niches and segments, thereby allowing a focuser to pick a competitively attractive niche suited to its own resources.
5. When few, if any, other rivals are attempting to specialize in the same target segment.

Strategies for Competing in Turbulent, High-Velocity Markets

The world is changing more and more rapidly, and consequently industries and firms themselves are changing faster than ever. Some industries are changing so fast that researchers call them **turbulent, high-velocity markets**, such as telecommunications, medical, biotechnology, pharmaceuticals, computer hardware, software, and virtually all Internet-based industries. High-velocity change is clearly becoming more and more the rule rather than the exception, even in such industries as toys, phones, banking, defense, publishing, and communication.

Meeting the challenge of high-velocity change presents the firm with a choice of whether to react, anticipate, or lead the market in terms of its own strategies. To primarily react to changes in the industry would be a defensive strategy used to counter, for example, unexpected shifts in buyer tastes and technological breakthroughs. The react-to-change strategy would not be as effective as the anticipate-change strategy, which would entail devising and following through with plans for dealing with the expected changes. However, firms ideally strive to be in a position to lead the changes in high-velocity markets, whereby they pioneer new and better technologies and products and set industry standards. Being the leader or pioneer of change in a high-velocity market is an aggressive, offensive strategy that includes rushing next-generation products to market ahead of rivals and being continually proactive in shaping the market to one's own benefit. Although a lead-change strategy is best whenever the firm has the resources to pursue this approach, on occasion even the strongest firms in turbulent industries have to employ the react-to-the-market strategy and the anticipate-the-market strategy.

An example turbulent, high-velocity market is the U.S. defense industry, especially with dramatic cuts looming and a shift to higher technology and space defense systems. Based in Hartford, Connecticut, United Technologies, which produces Blackhawk helicopters and a diverse array of other products such as Carrier air conditioners and Otis elevators, recently reduced is sales forecasts. One strategy to compete in a high turbulent industry is to diversify into less turbulent industries. United Technologies continues to diversify, recently acquiring Goodrich Corp. for $16.5 billion, as well as Rolls Royce Holdings PLC's stake in the company's engine joint venture.

Means for Achieving Strategies

Cooperation Among Competitors

In a recent *Wall Street Journal* article titled "Facebook, Yahoo Kiss and Make-Up," these two rival firms, locked for years in bitter patent litigation, revealed what they called a new strategic alliance, which included a patent cross-license, a new advertising partnership, expanded joint distribution, and joint media event coverage.[23]

Strategies that stress cooperation among competitors are being used more. For collaboration between competitors to succeed, both firms must contribute something distinctive, such as technology, distribution, basic research, or manufacturing capacity. But a major risk is that unintended transfers of important skills or technology may occur at organizational levels below where the deal was signed.[24] Information not covered in the formal agreement often gets traded in the day-to-day interactions and dealings of engineers, marketers, and product developers. Firms often give away too much information to rival firms when operating under cooperative agreements! Tighter formal agreements are needed.

Perhaps the best example of rival firms in an industry forming alliances to compete against each other is the airline industry. Today there are three major alliances: Star, SkyTeam, and Oneworld, but other alliances are forming, such as the trans-Atlantic joint venture among American Air, British Air, and Iberia Air formed by Oneworld. There is also a trans-Pacific joint venture among American, Japan Air, United Continental, and All Nippon Air.

The idea of joining forces with a competitor is not easily accepted by Americans, who often view cooperation and partnerships with skepticism and suspicion. Indeed, joint ventures and cooperative arrangements among competitors demand a certain amount of trust if companies are to combat paranoia about whether one firm will injure the other. However, multinational firms are becoming more globally cooperative, and increasing numbers of domestic firms are joining forces with competitive foreign firms to reap mutual benefits. Kathryn Harrigan at Columbia University says, "Within a decade, most companies will be members of teams that compete against each other." Once major rivals, Google's YouTube and Vivendi SA's Universal Music Group have formed a partnership called Vevo to provide a new music-video service. Google provides the technology and Universal Music provides the content, and both firms share the revenues. The two firms now operate the stand-alone site Vevo.com.

U.S. companies often enter alliances primarily to avoid investments, being more interested in reducing the costs and risks of entering new businesses or markets than in acquiring new skills. In contrast, *learning from the partner* is a major reason why Asian and European firms enter into cooperative agreements. U.S. firms, too, should place learning high on the list of reasons to be cooperative with competitors. U.S. companies often form alliances with Asian firms to gain an understanding of their manufacturing excellence, but Asian competence in this area is not easily transferable. Manufacturing excellence is a complex system that includes employee training and involvement, integration with suppliers, statistical process controls, value engineering, and design. In contrast, U.S. know-how in technology and related areas can be imitated more easily. U.S. firms thus need to be careful not to give away more intelligence than they receive in cooperative agreements with rival Asian firms.

Joint Venture and Partnering

Renault SA and British racing-car company Caterham Cars recently developed a joint venture to design, develop, and manufacture a family of sports cars that will be available in 2015. The partnership, named Societe des Automobiles Alpine Caterham, gives the British Formula One race-car maker access to Renault's manufacturing clout.

Joint venture is a popular strategy that occurs when two or more companies form a temporary partnership or consortium for the purpose of capitalizing on some opportunity. Often, the two or more sponsoring firms form a separate organization and have shared equity ownership in the new entity. Other types of **cooperative arrangements** include research and development partnerships, cross-distribution agreements, cross-licensing agreements, cross-manufacturing agreements, and joint-bidding consortia.

Joint ventures and cooperative arrangements are being used increasingly because they allow companies to improve communications and networking, to globalize operations, and to minimize risk. Joint ventures and partnerships are often used to pursue an opportunity that is too complex, uneconomical, or risky for a single firm to pursue alone. Such business creations also are used when achieving and sustaining competitive advantage when an industry requires a broader range of competencies and know-how than any one firm can marshal. Kathryn Rudie Harrigan, summarizes the trend toward increased joint venturing:

> In today's global business environment of scarce resources, rapid rates of technological change, and rising capital requirements, the important question is no longer "Shall we form a joint venture?" Now the question is "Which joint ventures and cooperative arrangements are most appropriate for our needs and expectations?" followed by "How do we manage these ventures most effectively?"[25]

In a global market tied together by the Internet, joint ventures, partnerships, and alliances are proving to be a more effective way to enhance corporate growth than mergers and acquisitions.[26] Strategic partnering takes many forms, including outsourcing, information sharing, joint marketing, and joint research and development. Many companies, such as Eli Lilly, now host partnership training classes for their managers and partners. There are today more than 10,000 joint ventures formed annually, more than all mergers and acquisitions. There are countless examples of successful strategic alliances, such as Internet coverage.

A major reason why firms are using partnering as a means to achieve strategies is globalization. Walmart's successful joint venture with Mexico's Cifra is indicative of how a domestic firm can benefit immensely by partnering with a foreign company to gain substantial presence in that new country. Technology also is a major reason behind the need to form strategic alliances, with the Internet linking widely dispersed partners. The Internet paved the way and legitimized the need for alliances to serve as the primary means for corporate growth. Neiman Marcus and Target recently announced a partnership whereby both firms will offer a limited collection of 50 items from stationery to sporting goods at the same price with all the items carrying both the Target bulls-eye logo and the Neiman Marcus logo. This unusual partnership between a high-end and low-end retailer benefits Neiman by expanding its reach and notoriety, while benefiting Target by raising its overall perceived quality.

Evidence is mounting that firms should use partnering as a means for achieving strategies. However, the sad fact is that most U.S. firms in many industries—such as financial services, forest products, metals, and retailing—still operate in a merger or acquire mode to obtain growth. Partnering is not yet taught at most business schools and is often viewed within companies as a financial issue rather than a strategic issue. However, partnering has become a core competency, a strategic issue of such importance that top management involvement initially and throughout the life of an alliance is vital.[27]

Joint ventures among once rival firms are commonly being used to pursue strategies ranging from retrenchment to market development. Although ventures and partnerships are preferred over mergers as a means for achieving strategies, certainly they are not all successful. The good news is that joint ventures and partnerships are less risky for companies than mergers, but the bad news is that many alliances fail. There are countless examples of failed joint ventures. A few common problems that cause joint ventures to fail are as follows:

1. Managers who must collaborate daily in operating the venture are not involved in forming or shaping the venture.
2. The venture may benefit the partnering companies but may not benefit customers, who then complain about poorer service or criticize the companies in other ways.
3. The venture may not be supported equally by both partners. If supported unequally, problems arise.
4. The venture may begin to compete more with one of the partners than the other.[28]

Six guidelines for when a joint venture may be an especially effective means for pursuing strategies are:[29]

- When a privately-owned organization is forming a joint venture with a publicly-owned organization; there are some advantages to being privately held, such as closed ownership; there are some advantages of being publicly held, such as access to stock issuances as a source of capital. Sometimes, the unique advantages of being privately and publicly held can be synergistically combined in a joint venture.
- When a domestic organization is forming a joint venture with a foreign company; a joint venture can provide a domestic company with the opportunity for obtaining local management in a foreign country, thereby reducing risks such as expropriation and harassment by host country officials.
- When the distinct competencies of two or more firms complement each other especially well.
- When some project is potentially profitable but requires overwhelming resources and risks.
- When two or more smaller firms have trouble competing with a large firm.
- When there exists a need to quickly introduce a new technology.

Merger/Acquisition

As of December 2012, there were 10,346 merger-and-acquisition deals in the USA for the year, a 9 percent increase over the prior year, but an 8 percent decline in terms of the dollar volume. Late in 2012, ConAgra bought Ralcorp for $5 billion and Equity Residential (and AvalonBay) bought Archstone for $6.5 billion.

Merger and acquisition are two commonly used ways to pursue strategies. A **merger** occurs when two organizations of about equal size unite to form one enterprise. An **acquisition** occurs when a large organization purchases (acquires) a smaller firm, or vice versa. When a merger or acquisition is not desired by both parties, it can be called a **takeover** or **hostile takeover**. In contrast, if the acquisition is desired by both firms, it is termed a **friendly merger**. Most mergers are friendly. For example, two Japanese steel producers, Nippon Steel Corp. and Sumitomo Metal Industries Ltd., recently merged in friendly fashion to form the world's second largest steel producer behind ArcelorMittal.

Despite many investment bankers predicting the demise of hostile takeovers because it is difficult to pull off, the number of hostile takeovers are on the rise. For example, Glaxo recently gave Human Genome a deadline to accept their offer or face a hostile takeover. Genomma recently

TABLE 4-5 Key Reasons Why Many Mergers and Acquisitions Fail

- Integration difficulties
- Inadequate evaluation of target
- Large or extraordinary debt
- Inability to achieve synergy
- Too much diversification
- Managers overly focused on acquisitions
- Too large an acquisition
- Difficult to integrate different organizational cultures
- Reduced employee morale due to layoffs and relocations

made an unsolicited offer to acquire Prestige at $16.60 a share and nominated a full slate of directors for election at Prestige's annual shareholder meeting. Prestige's board is not staggered, so Genomma has the chance to push out a majority of Prestige's board, clearing the way for a takeover. Other recent hostile takeovers or attempts include Martin Marietta trying to takeover Vulcan Materials and Westlake Chemical trying to take over Georgia Gulf and Roche's bid for Illumina.

In a rare example of a Chinese company engaging in a hostile takeover, Shanghai-based Cathy Fortune recently bypassed the board of cooper miner Discovery Metals Ltd. with an offer of 830 million Australian dollars. This was a 51 percent premium over the value of Sydney-based Discovery Metals' common stock. China consumes about 40 percent of the world's copper output but historically avoids hostile takeovers altogether.

White knight is a term that refers to a firm that agrees to acquire another firm when that other firm is facing a hostile takeover by some company. For example, Palo Alto, California–based CV Thereapeutics Inc., a heart-drug maker, was fighting a hostile takeover bid by Japan's Astellas Pharma. Then CVT struck a friendly deal to be acquired by Forest City, California–based Gilead Sciences at a higher price of $1.4 billion in cash. Gilead is known for its HIV drugs, so its move into the heart-drug business surprised many analysts.

Not all mergers are effective and successful. For example, even 12 months after PulteGroup bought rival Centex Corp., for $1.3 billion in stock, creating the largest home builder in the USA, PulteGroup's profits were still negative and the company's stock price was 30 percent lower than the week of the acquisition. PulteGroup's dismal performance is in sharp contrast to rival firms such as Toll Brothers and Lennar Corp., whose stock price is up 22 percent during the same period. So a merger between two firms can yield great benefits, but the price and reasoning must be right. Some key reasons why many mergers and acquisitions fail are provided in Table 4-5.

Among mergers, acquisitions, and takeovers in recent years, same-industry combinations have predominated. A general market consolidation is occurring in many industries, especially banking, insurance, defense, and health care, but also in pharmaceuticals, food, airlines, accounting, publishing, computers, retailing, financial services, and biotechnology. For example, there are many potential benefits of merging with or acquiring another firm, as indicated in Table 4-6.

The volume of mergers completed annually worldwide is growing dramatically and exceeds $1 trillion. There are annually more than 10,000 mergers in the USA that total more

TABLE 4-6 Potential Benefits of Merging With or Acquiring Another Firm

- To provide improved capacity utilization
- To make better use of the existing sales force
- To reduce managerial staff
- To gain economies of scale
- To smooth out seasonal trends in sales
- To gain access to new suppliers, distributors, customers, products, and creditors
- To gain new technology
- To reduce tax obligations

than $700 billion. The proliferation of mergers is fueled by companies' drive for market share, efficiency, and pricing power, as well as by globalization, the need for greater economies of scale, reduced regulation and antitrust concerns, the Internet, and e-commerce.

A **leveraged buyout (LBO)** occurs when a corporation's shareholders are bought (hence *buyout*) by the company's management and other private investors using borrowed funds (hence *leverage*). Besides trying to avoid a hostile takeover, other reasons for initiating an LBO are senior management decisions that particular divisions do not fit into an overall corporate strategy, must be sold to raise cash, or receipt of an attractive offering price. An LBO takes a corporation private.

Private-Equity Acquisitions

As stock prices increased and companies became cash-rich in 2012–2013, private-equity (PE) firms such as Kohlberg Kravis Roberts (KKR) jumped aggressively back into the business of acquiring and selling firms. PE firms have unleashed a wave of new initial public offerings (IPO). Apollo Global Management is a large private-equity firm that owns many companies.

The intent of virtually all PE acquisitions is to buy firms at a low price and sell them later at a high price, arguably just good business. Par Pharmaceutical was recently acquired by PE firm TPG for $184 million in cash. Based in Woodcliff Lake, New Jersey, Par's shareholders received $50 in cash for each share, a premium of about 37 percent over the firm's closing stock price.

PE firms increasingly are buying companies from other PE firms, such as Clayton, Dubilier & Rice recently buying David's Bridal from Leonard Green & Partners LP for $1.05 billion. Such PE to PE acquisitions, called **secondary buyouts**, totaled $30 billion in 2012 in the USA compared to $10.5 billion in 2011.

PE firms especially, but other firms also, in 2012 extensively borrowed money, more than $70 billion, at record low interest rates, simply to fund dividend payouts to themselves, a controversial practice known as **dividend recapitalizations**. The previous annual record for dividend recapitalizations, according to S&P's Capital IQ LCD data service, was $40.5 billion in 2010. Critics say dividend recapitalization saddles a company with debt, burdening its operations. One reason for the high 2012 number was the expectation that taxes on dividends would increase in 2013, so the thinking was pay me now.

For all of 2012, the value of private-equity deals by country of investment is given below (in millions $) for the top seven:

1. USA (99.3)
2. UK (23.9)
3. Germany (9.8)
4. China (9.7)
5. Australia (5.2)
6. Canada (4.1)
7. France (4.1)

First Mover Advantages

First mover advantages refer to the benefits a firm may achieve by entering a new market or developing a new product or service prior to rival firms. As indicated in Table 4-7, some advantages of being a first mover include securing access to rare resources, gaining new knowledge of key factors and issues, and carving out market share and a position that is easy to defend and costly for rival firms to overtake. First mover advantages are analogous to taking the high ground first, which puts one in an excellent strategic position to launch aggressive campaigns and to defend territory. Being the first mover can be an excellent strategy when such actions (a) build a firm's image and reputation with buyers, (b) produce cost advantages over rivals in terms of new technologies, new components, new distribution channels, and so on, (c) create strongly loyal customers, and (d) make imitation or duplication by a rival hard or unlikely.

To sustain the competitive advantage gained by being the first mover, a firm needs to be a fast learner. There are, however, risks associated with being the first mover, such as unexpected and unanticipated problems and costs that occur from being the first firm doing business in the new market. Therefore, being a slow mover (also called *fast follower* or *late mover*) can be effective when a firm can easily copy or imitate the lead firm's products or services. If technology is advancing rapidly, slow movers can often leapfrog a first mover's products with improved

TABLE 4-7 Benefits of a Firm Being the First Mover

1. Secure access and commitments to rare resources
2. Gain new knowledge of critical success factors and issues
3. Gain market share and position in the best locations
4. Establish and secure long-term relationships with customers, suppliers, distributors, and investors
5. Gain customer loyalty and commitments

second-generation products. Samsung is an example in the smartphone business. Apple has always been a good example of a first mover firm, although of late Apple is stumbling a bit as Samsung gains momentum.

First mover advantages tend to be greatest when competitors are roughly the same size and possess similar resources. If competitors are not similar in size, then larger competitors can wait while others make initial investments and mistakes and then respond with greater effectiveness and resources. Lenovo has done this of late, as has Volkswagen.

Outsourcing and Reshoring

Business-process outsourcing (BPO) involves companies hiring other companies to take over various parts of their the functional operations, such as human resources, information systems, payroll, accounting, customer service, and even marketing. Companies choose to outsource their functional operations for several reasons: (a) it is less expensive, (b) it allows the firm to focus on its core businesses, and (c) it enables the firm to provide better services. Other advantages of outsourcing are that the strategy (a) allows the firm to align itself with "best-in-world" suppliers who focus on performing the special task, (b) provides the firm flexibility should customer needs shift unexpectedly, and (c) allows the firm to concentrate on other internal value chain activities critical to sustaining competitive advantage. BPO is a means for achieving strategies that are similar to partnering and joint venturing.

Reshoring is the new term that refers to U.S. companies planning to move some of their manufacturing back to the USA. About 14 to 37 percent of U.S. companies plan to *reshore* in 2012–2014 for the following reasons: a desire to get products to market faster and respond rapidly to customer orders; savings from reduced transportation and warehousing; improved quality and protection of intellectual property; pressure to increase U.S. jobs.[30] For example, Google's new Nexus Q music and video player is being manufactured in the USA, something unusual for consumer electronics. GE's website has an "American Jobs Map" that gives details of 14,500 new GE jobs in the USA. A bill named the "Bring Jobs Home Act" is being considered in Congress.

"Made in the USA" is making a comeback. Even Walmart, which pioneered looking globally for the lowest-cost suppliers, is increasing by $50 billion its spending with U.S. suppliers in this decade. U.S. manufacturing is leading the way on superautomated factories that require less labor but more high-tech machines. For example, the 200,000 sq. ft. GE battery plant in Schenectady, NY has only 370 full-time employees but ships batteries around the world. New, high-tech, U.S. factories are leading to extensive "reshoring" in America.

Many firms, such as Dearborn, Michigan–based Visteon Corp. and J.P. Morgan Chase & Co., outsource their computer operations to IBM, which competes with firms such as Electronic Data Systems and Computer Sciences Corp. in the computer outsourcing business. 3M Corp. is outsourcing all of its manufacturing operations to Flextronics International Ltd. of Singapore or Jabil Circuit in Florida. 3M is also outsourcing all design and manufacturing of low-end standardized volume products by building a new design center in Taiwan.

U.S. and European companies for more than a decade have been outsourcing their manufacturing, tech support, and back-office work, but most insisted on keeping research and development activities in-house. However, an ever-growing number of firms today are outsourcing their product design to Asian developers. China and India are becoming increasingly important suppliers of intellectual property.

The details of what work to outsource, to whom, where, and for how much can challenge even the biggest, most sophisticated companies. And some outsourcing deals do not work out, such as the J.P. Morgan Chase deal with IBM and Dow Chemical's deal with Electronic Data Systems. Both outsourcing deals were abandoned after several years. Lehman Brothers Holdings and Dell Inc. both recently reversed decisions to move customer call centers to India after a customer rebellion. India has become a booming place for outsourcing. Outsourcing generally aims to achieve one or more of the following benefits:

- Cost savings: Access lower wages in foreign countries.
- Focus on core business: Focus resources on developing the core business rather than being distracted by other functions.
- Cost restructuring: Outsourcing changes the balance of fixed costs to variable costs by moving the firm more to variable costs. Outsourcing also makes variable costs more predictable.
- Improve quality: Improve quality by contracting out various business functions to specialists.
- Knowledge: Gain access to intellectual property and wider experience and knowledge.
- Contract: Gain access to services within a legally binding contract with financial penalties and legal redress. This is not the case with services performed internally.
- Operational expertise: Gain access to operational best practice that would be too difficult or time consuming to develop in-house.
- Access to talent: Gain access to a larger talent pool and a sustainable source of skills, especially science and engineering.
- Catalyst for change: Use an outsourcing agreement as a catalyst for major change that cannot be achieved alone.
- Enhance capacity for innovation: Use external knowledge to supplement limited in-house capacity for product innovation.
- Reduce time to market: Accelerate development or production of a product through additional capability brought by the supplier.
- Risk management: Manage risk by partnering with an outside firm.
- Tax benefit: Capitalize on tax incentives to locate manufacturing plants to avoid high taxes in various countries.

Strategic Management in Nonprofit and Governmental Organizations

Nonprofit organizations are basically just like for-profit companies except for two major differences: (1) nonprofits do not pay taxes and (2) nonprofits do not have shareholders to provide capital. In virtually all other ways, nonprofits are just like for-profits. Nonprofits have competitors that want to put them out of business. Nonprofits have employees, customers, creditors, suppliers, and distributors as well as financial budgets, income statements, balance sheets, cash flow statements, and so on. Nonprofit organizations embrace strategic planning just as much as for-profit firms, and perhaps even more, because equity capital is not an alternative source of financing.

The strategic-management process is being used effectively by countless nonprofit and governmental organizations, such as the Girl Scouts, Boy Scouts, the Red Cross, chambers of commerce, educational institutions, medical institutions, public utilities, libraries, government agencies, and churches. The nonprofit sector, surprisingly, is by far the largest employer in the USA. Many nonprofit and governmental organizations outperform private firms and corporations on innovativeness, motivation, productivity, and strategic management.

Compared to for-profit firms, nonprofit and governmental organizations may be totally dependent on outside financing. Especially for these organizations, strategic management provides an excellent vehicle for developing and justifying requests for needed financial support.

Educational Institutions

The world of higher education is rapidly moving to massive open online courses (MOOC), with many of the courses being free to anyone with an Internet connection. The American Council on Education, an association for higher education presidents, is considering allowing free, online courses to be eligible for credit toward a degree and eligible for transfer credit. Several companies, including edX, Udacity, Coursera, and the Jack Welch Management Institute, are most associated with MOOCs, but the list is growing weekly.

Educational institutions are more frequently using strategic-management techniques and concepts. Richard Cyert, former president of Carnegie Mellon University, said, "I believe we do a far better job of strategic management than any company I know." Population shifts nationally from the Northeast and Midwest to the Southeast and West are but one factor causing trauma for educational institutions that have not planned for changing enrollments. Ivy League schools in the Northeast are recruiting more heavily in the Southeast and West. This trend represents a significant change in the competitive climate for attracting the best high school graduates each year.

Online college degrees are commonplace and represent a threat to traditional colleges and universities. "You can put the kids to bed and go to law school," says Andrew Rosen, chief operating officer of Kaplan Education Centers, a subsidiary of the Washington Post Company.

Many U.S. colleges and universities have now established campuses outside the USA. For example, Yale University and the National University of Singapore established a joint campus in Singapore in 2013. The institution is Singapore's first liberal-arts college and Yale's first campus outside the Ivy League institution in New Haven, Connecticut.

Medical Organizations

The $200 billion U.S. hospital industry is experiencing declining margins, excess capacity, bureaucratic overburdening, poorly planned and executed diversification strategies, soaring health-care costs, reduced federal support, and high administrator turnover. The seriousness of this problem is accented by a 20 percent annual decline in use by inpatients nationwide. Declining occupancy rates, deregulation, and accelerating growth of health maintenance organizations, preferred provider organizations, urgent care centers, outpatient surgery centers, diagnostic centers, specialized clinics, and group practices are other major threats facing hospitals today. Many private and state-supported medical institutions are in financial trouble as a result of traditionally taking a reactive rather than a proactive approach in dealing with their industry.

Hospitals—originally intended to be warehouses for people dying of tuberculosis, smallpox, cancer, pneumonia, and infectious diseases—are creating new strategies today as advances in the diagnosis and treatment of chronic diseases are undercutting that previous mission. Hospitals are beginning to bring services to the patient as much as bringing the patient to the hospital; health care is more and more being concentrated in the home and in the residential community, not on the hospital campus. Chronic care will require day-treatment facilities, electronic monitoring at home, user-friendly ambulatory services, decentralized service networks, and laboratory testing. A successful hospital strategy for the future will require renewed and deepened collaboration with physicians, who are central to hospitals' well-being, and a reallocation of resources from acute to chronic care in home and community settings.

Current strategies being pursued by many hospitals include creating home health services, establishing nursing homes, and forming rehabilitation centers. Backward integration strategies that some hospitals are pursuing include acquiring ambulance services, waste disposal services, and diagnostic services. Millions of persons annually research medical ailments online, which is causing a dramatic shift in the balance of power between doctor, patient, and hospitals. The number of persons using the Internet to obtain medical information is skyrocketing. A motivated patient using the Internet can gain knowledge on a particular subject far beyond his or her doctor's knowledge because no person can keep up with the results and implications of billions of dollars' worth of medical research reported weekly. Patients today often walk into the doctor's office with a file folder of the latest articles detailing research and treatment options for their ailments.

Governmental Agencies and Departments

Federal, state, county, and municipal agencies and departments, such as police departments, chambers of commerce, forestry associations, and health departments, are responsible for formulating, implementing, and evaluating strategies that use taxpayers' dollars in the most cost-effective way to provide services and programs. Strategic-management concepts are generally required and thus widely used to enable governmental organizations to be more effective and efficient.

Strategists in governmental organizations operate with less strategic autonomy than their counterparts in private firms. Public enterprises generally cannot diversify into unrelated businesses or merge with other firms. Governmental strategists usually enjoy little freedom in altering the organizations' missions or redirecting objectives. Legislators and politicians often have direct or indirect control over major decisions and resources. Strategic issues get discussed and debated in the media and legislatures. Issues become politicized, resulting in fewer strategic choice alternatives. There is now more predictability in the management of public sector enterprises.

Government agencies and departments are finding that their employees get excited about the opportunity to participate in the strategic-management process and thereby have an effect on the organization's mission, objectives, strategies, and policies. In addition, government agencies are using a strategic-management approach to develop and substantiate formal requests for additional funding.

Strategic Management in Small Firms

The reason why "becoming your own boss" has become a national obsession is that entrepreneurs are role models in the USA. Almost everyone wants to own a business—from teens and college students, who are signing up for entrepreneurial courses in record numbers, to those older than age 65, who are forming more companies every year.

Strategic management is vital for large firms' success, but what about small firms? The strategic-management process is just as vital for small companies. From their inception, all organizations have a strategy, even if the strategy just evolves from day-to-day operations. Even if conducted informally or by a single owner or entrepreneur, the strategic-management process can significantly enhance small firms' growth and prosperity. Because an ever-increasing number of men and women in the United States are starting their own businesses, more individuals are becoming strategists. Widespread corporate layoffs have contributed to an explosion in small businesses and new ideas.

Numerous magazine and journal articles have focused on applying strategic-management concepts to small businesses. A major conclusion of these articles is that a lack of strategic-management knowledge is a serious obstacle for many small business owners. Other problems often encountered in applying strategic-management concepts to small businesses are a lack of both sufficient capital to exploit external opportunities and a day-to-day cognitive frame of reference. Research also indicates that strategic management in small firms is more informal than in large firms, but small firms that engage in strategic management outperform those that do not.

Special Note to Students

There are numerous alternative strategies that could benefit any firm, but your strategic management case analysis should result in specific recommendations that you decide will best provide the firm competitive advantages. Because company recommendations with costs comprise the most important pages or slides in your case project, introduce bits of that information early in the presentation as relevant supporting material is presented to justify your expenditures. Your recommendations page(s) itself should therefore be a summary of suggestions mentioned throughout your paper or presentation, rather than being a surprise shock to your reader or audience. You may even want to include with your recommendations insight as to why certain other feasible strategies were not chosen for implementation. That information too should be anchored in the notion of competitive advantage and disadvantage with respect to perceived costs and benefits. If someone asks "what is the difference between recommendations and strategies," respond saying: "Recommendations are alternative strategies actually selected for implementation."

Conclusion

The main appeal of any managerial approach is the expectation that it will enhance organizational performance. This is especially true of strategic management. Through involvement in strategic-management activities, managers and employees achieve a better understanding of an organization's priorities and operations. Strategic management allows organizations to be efficient, but more important, it allows them to be effective. Although strategic management does not guarantee organizational success, the process allows proactive rather than reactive decision making. Strategic management may represent a radical change in philosophy for some organizations, so strategists must be trained to anticipate and constructively respond to questions and issues as they arise. The strategies discussed in this chapter can represent a new beginning for many firms, especially if managers and employees in the organization understand and support the plan for action.

Key Terms and Concepts

acquisition (p. 155)
backward integration (p. 139)
bankruptcy (p. 146)
business-process outsourcing (BPO) (p. 158)
combination strategy (p. 135)
cooperative arrangements (p. 154)
cost leadership (p. 149)
de-integration (p. 139)
differentiation (p. 149)
diversification strategies (p. 143)
divestiture (p. 147)
dividend recapitalizations (p. 157)
financial objectives (p. 133)
first mover advantages (p. 157)
focus (p. 149)
forward integration (p. 137)
franchising (p. 138)
friendly merger (p. 155)
generic strategies (p. 149)
horizontal integration (p. 140)
hostile takeover (p. 155)

integration strategies (p. 137)
intensive strategies (p. 141)
joint venture (p. 154)
leveraged buyout (LBO) (p. 157)
liquidation (p. 148)
long-term objectives (p. 132)
market development (p. 142)
market penetration (p. 141)
merger (p. 155)
product development (p. 142)
related diversification (p. 143)
reshoring (p. 158)
retrenchment (p. 146)
secondary buyouts (p. 157)
strategic objectives (p. 133)
takeover (p. 155)
turbulent, high-velocity markets (p. 153)
unrelated diversification (p. 143)
vertical integration (p. 137)
white knight (p. 156)

Issues for Review and Discussion

4-1. For Petronas, featured at the beginning of the chapter, give a hypothetical strategy for each of the following categories: market penetration, related diversification, divestiture, and retrenchment.

4-2. For Petronas, featured at the beginning of the chapter, give a hypothetical strategy for each of the following categories: market development, unrelated diversification, backward integration, and product development.

4-3. Identify five situations when forward integration is a particularly good strategy.

4-4. What three strategies defined in the chapter do you feel are most widely used by small businesses?

4-5. Should non-profit organizations post their strategic plan on their website? What about corporations? Why?

4-6. Give some guidelines of when divestiture is a particularly effective strategy.

4-7. For adidas, what two strategies do you feel is best for that company to pursue going forward? Why?

4-8. Give some examples of Type 4 and Type 5 focus strategies according to Porter's generic strategy approach.

4-9. List three industries when cooperation among competitors is most likely and explain why.

4-10. Do a Google search on joint ventures. What important new concepts did you learn that were not presented in the chapter?

4-11. Identify three joint ventures that have worked especially well in the past.

4-12. List four important reasons why many mergers and acquisitions fail.

4-13. Explain how strategic management differs in governmental organizations as compared to educational institutions.

4-14. Explain how and why Petronas has been so successful in recent years.

4-15. List six characteristics of objectives and an example of each.

4-16. In order of importance, rank six major benefits of a firm having objectives.

4-17. Give a hypothetical example of forward integration, backward integration, and horizontal integration for Volkswagen.

4-18. Give a hypothetical example of market penetration, market development, and product development for Toyota Motors.

4-19. Give a hypothetical example of related diversification and an example of unrelated diversification for Google.

4-20. Give a hypothetical example of retrenchment and divestiture for Wal-Mart.

4-21. When would market development generally be the preferred strategy over backward or forward integration?

4-22. Why can firms generally not pursue several or many of the strategies presented in this chapter?

4-23. When should a firm diversify?

4-24. List and describe the five types of bankruptcy. If your college or university had to declare bankruptcy, which type would be appropriate?

4-25. Explain why you believe some analysts consider Michael Porter's generic strategies to be too few and too vague.

4-26. Explain the difference between joint ventures and partnerships as a means for achieving various strategies.

4-27. List the pros and cons of a hostile versus friendly takeover of another firm.

4-28. In order of importance, list six reasons why many mergers and acquisitions fail.

4-29. In order of importance, list six potential benefits of two firms merging.

4-30. Give three hypothetical examples of firms being a "first mover."

4-31. List three ways a country could prevent its companies from outsourcing jobs to other countries.

4-32. Explain how strategic planning differs across types and sizes of firms.

4-33. Identify three local businesses in your city. What three strategies do these three firms pursue? List the strategies in order of prevalence.

4-34. What strategies are best for turbulent, high-velocity markets?

4-35. Based on the information given for Petronas, what three strategies are being pursued by the firm?

4-36. Elaborate on this chapter's "Special Note to Students" at the end, in terms of giving a case analysis presentation.

4-37. Identify three companies that use outsourcing effectively. Explain how and why those firms utilize this management approach.

MyManagementLab®

Go to **mymanagementlab.com** for the following Assisted-graded writing questions:

4-38. What are the pros and cons of a firm merging with a rival firm?

4-39. Discuss the nature of as well as the pros and cons of a "friendly merger" versus "hostile takeover" in acquiring another firm. Give an example of each.

Current Readings

Ashkenas, Suzanne Francis, and Rick Heinick. "The Merger Dividend." *Harvard Business Review* (July-August 2011): 126.

Barczak, Gloria, and Kenneth B. Kahn. "Identifying New Product Development Best Practice." *Business Horizons* 55, no. 3 (May 2012): 293–305.

Bouchikhi, Hamid, and John R. Kimberly. "Making Mergers Work." *MITSloan Management Review* 54, no. 1 (Fall 2012): 63.

Fieldstad, Øystein D., Charles C. Snow, and Raymond E. Miles. "The Architecture of Collaboration." *Strategic Management Journal* 33, no. 6 (June 2012): 734–750.

Haleblian, Jerayr, Gerry McNamara, Kalin Kolev, and Bernadine J. Dykes. "Exploring Firm Characteristics that Differentiate Leaders from Followers in Industry Merger Waves: A Competitive Dynamics Perspective." *Strategic Management Journal* 33, no. 9 (September 2012): 1037–1052.

Holweg, Matthias, and Frits K. Pil. "Outsourcing Complex Business Processes: Lessons From An Enterprise Partnership." *California Management Review* 54, no. 3 (Spring 2012): 98–115.

Honeycutt Jr., Earl D., Vincent P. Magnini, and Shawn T. Thelen. "Solutions for customer complaints about offshoring and outsourcing services." *Business Horizons* 55, no. 1 (January–February 2012): 33.

Leavy, Brian. "Collaborative Innovation as the New Imperative—Design Thinking, Value Co-creation and the Power of Pull." *Strategy and Leadership* 40, no. 3 (2012): 25–34.

Muehlfeld, Katrin, Padma Rao Sahib, and Arien Van Witteloostuijn. "A Contextual Theory of Organizational Learning from Failures and Successes: A Study of Acquisition Completion in the Global Newspaper Industry, 1981–2008." *Strategic Management Journal* 33, no. 8 (August 2012): 938–964.

Thomke, Stefan, and Donald Reinertsen. "Six Myths of Product Development." *Harvard Business Review* (May 2012): 84.

Tsai, Wenpin, Kuo-Hsien Su, and Ming-Jer Chen. "Seeing Through the Eyes of a Rival: Competitor Acumen Based on Rival-Centric Perceptions." *The Academy of Management Review 54*, no. 4 (August 2011): 761.

Souder, David, Zeki Simsek, and Scott G. Johnson. "The Differing Effects of Agent and Founder CEOs on the Firm's Market Expansion." *Strategic Management Journal* 33, no. 1 (January 2012): 23–41.

Weigelt, Carmen, and MB Sarkar. "Performance Implications of Outsourcing for Technological Innovations: Managing the Efficiency and Adaptability Trade-off." *Strategic Management Journal* 33, no. 2 (February 2012): 189–216.

Wunker, Stephen. "Better Growth Decisions: Early Mover, Fast Follower or Late Follower?" *Strategy and Leadership* 40, no. 3 (2012): 43–48.

ASSURANCE OF LEARNING EXERCISES

EXERCISE 4A
Market Development: Petronas

Purpose

Petronas is featured in the opening chapter case as a firm that engages in excellent strategic planning. The purpose of this exercise is to give you practice extending a company's global strategy into new geographic regions.

Instructions

Step 1	Visit the Petronas website and review the company's latest *Annual Report*. Especially assess where and in what respect does Petronas do business in Asia, Australia, and the Middle East. Identify six countries that Petronas currently does not do business with.
Step 2	Based on your analysis in Step 1, evaluate the six countries identified in terms of their business culture, environment, and attractiveness for Petronas to begin doing business there.
Step 3	Rank order the six countries identified and evaluated in terms of a proposed plan for Petronas to begin doing business in these places. Prepare a two-page executive summary to support your suggested plan.

EXERCISE 4B
Alternative Strategies for Petronas

Purpose

This exercise will give you practice labeling hypothetical strategies that a firm could pursue.

Instructions

For each of the strategies listed below, identify a hypothetical strategy that you believe may be good for Petronas to pursue. Refer to Chapter 4 for a description of the strategies.

> Forward Integration
> Backward Integration
> Horizontal Integration
> Market Penetration
> Market Development
> Product Development
> Related Diversification
> Unrelated Diversification
> Retrenchment
> Divestiture
> Liquidation

EXERCISE 4C
Private-Equity Acquisitions

Purpose

As stock prices increase and companies become more cash-rich, private-equity firms such as Kohlberg Kravis Roberts (KKR) have jumped aggressively back into the business of acquiring and selling firms. Private-equity firms have unleashed a wave of new initial public offerings (IPOs), such as the IPO of Nielsen Holdings BV, the largest private-equity-backed IPO in the United States in five years. Apollo Global Management is a large private-equity firms that owns many companies. Some private-equity owned firms expected to go public soon include Bank United Inc., Kinder Morgan Inc., and Toys "R" Us Inc.

The purpose of this exercise is to give you practice identifying and evaluating the nature and role of private-equity acquisitions in Europe.

Instructions

Step 1   Identify the top five IPOs in Europe in the last 12 months.
Step 2   Identify the top five private-equity firms in Europe.
Step 3   Prepare a two-page executive summary of the nature and role of private-equity acquisitions in Europe in the last 12 months. Include your expectations over the next 12 months for this activity to increase or decrease across Europe. Give supporting rationales.

EXERCISE 4D
The strategies of adidas AG: 2013-2015

Purpose

In performing strategic management case analysis, you can find information about the company's actual and planned strategies. Comparing what is planned versus what you recommend is an important part of case analysis. Do not recommend what the firm actually plans, unless in-depth analysis of the situation reveals those strategies to be the best among all feasible alternatives. This exercise gives you experience conducting library and Internet research to determine what adidas AG plans to do in 2013-2015.

Instructions

Step 1   Go to Reebok and TaylorMade's websites. Find some recent articles about these subsidiaries and the parent—adidas AG. Review adidas' website also.
Step 2   Prepare a three-page report titled "Strategies Being Pursued By adidas in 2011–2013."

EXERCISE 4E
Lessons in Doing Business Globally

Purpose

The purpose of this exercise is to discover some important lessons learned by local businesses that do business internationally.

Instructions

Contact several local business leaders by telephone. Find at least three firms that engage in international or export operations. Visit the owner or manager of each business in person. Ask the business person to give you several important lessons that his or her firm has learned in globally doing business. Record the lessons on paper and report your findings to the class.

EXERCISE 4F
Petronas 2013-2015

Purpose

In performing strategic management case analysis, you should find information about the company's actual and planned strategies. Comparing what is planned versus what you recommend is an important part of case analysis. Do not recommend what the firm actually plans, unless in-depth analysis of the situation reveals those strategies to be the best among all feasible alternatives. This exercise gives you experience conducting library and Internet research to determine what Petronas plans to do in 2013-2015.

Instructions

Step 1   Go to the Petronas corporate web site. Study the information provided there.
Step 2   Prepare a three-page report titled "Strategies Being Pursued by Petronas in 2013-2015."

EXERCISE 4G
What Strategies Are Most Risky?

Purpose

This exercise encourages you to think about the relative riskiness of various strategies.

Instructions

Step 1   List the strategies defined in Chapter 4 in order of low risk to high risk.
Step 2   Write a synopsis that explains your rankings.

EXERCISE 4H
Exploring Bankruptcy

Purpose

Bankruptcy is becoming more and more common among business firms. This exercise is designed to enhance your knowledge of bankruptcy.

Instructions

Identify five firms in your country that are operating under bankruptcy. Compare and contrast the nature of the bankruptcy among these firms.

EXERCISE 4I
Examining Strategy Articles

Purpose

Strategy articles can be found weekly in journals, magazines, and newspapers. By reading and studying strategy articles, you can gain a better understanding of the strategic management process. Several of the best journals in which to find corporate strategy articles are: *Advanced Management Journal, Business Horizons, Long Range Planning, Journal of Business Strategy,* and *Strategic Management Journal.* These journals are devoted to reporting the results of empirical research in management. They apply strategic management concepts to specific organizations and industries. They introduce new strategic management techniques and provide short case studies on selected firms. Other good journals in which to find strategic management articles are *Harvard Business Review, Sloan Management Review, California Management Review, Academy of Management Review, Academy of Management Journal, Academy of Management Executive, Journal of Management,* and *Journal of Small Business Management.* In addition to journals, many magazines regularly publish articles that focus on business strategies. Several of the best magazines in which to find applied strategy articles are: *Dun's Business Month, Fortune, Forbes, Business Week, Inc,* and *Industry Week.* Newspapers such as *USA Today, Wall Street Journal, New York Times,* and *Barrons* cover strategy events when they occur—for example, a joint venture announcement, a bankruptcy declaration, a new advertising campaign start, acquisition of a company, divestiture of a division, a chief executive officer's hiring or firing, or a hostile takeover attempt. In combination, journal, magazine, and newspaper articles can make the strategic management course more exciting. These sources provide information about the strategies of for-profit and non-profit organizations.

Instructions

Step 1   Go to your college library and find a recent journal article that focuses on a strategic management topic. Select your article from one of the journals listed previously, not from a magazine. Copy the article and bring it to class.
Step 2   Give a three-minute oral report summarizing the most important information in your article. Include comments giving your personal reaction to the article. Pass your article around in class.

EXERCISE 4J
Classifying Some Strategies

Purpose

This exercise can improve your understanding of various strategies by giving you experience classifying strategies. This skill will help you use the strategy-formulation tools presented later. Consider the following 12 (actual or possible) strategies by various firms:

1. Dunkin' Donuts is increasing the number of its U.S. stores from 5,500 to 15,000.
2. Brown-Forman Corp. sold its Hartmann luggage and leather-goods business.
3. Motorola, which makes TVs, acquired Terayon Communication, a supplier of TV equipment.
4. Macy's department stores is adding bistros and Starbucks coffee shops at many of its stores.
5. Dell just allowed Wal-Mart to begin selling its computers. This was its first move away from direct mail order selling of computers.
6. Motorola cut 7,500 additional jobs.
7. Hilton Hotels is building 55 new properties in Russia, the United Kingdom, and Central America.
8. Video-sharing website YouTube launched its services into nine new countries.
9. Cadbury Schweppes PLC is slashing 7,500 jobs, shedding product variations, and closing factories globally.
10. General Electric sold its plastics division for $11.6 million to Saudi Basic Industries Corp. of Saudi Arabia.
11. Cadbury Schweppes PLC, the maker of Trident gum, just bought Turkish gum maker Intergum.
12. Limited Brands is selling its Express and Limited divisions to focus on its Victoria's Secret and Bath & Body Works divisions.

Instructions

Step 1 On a separate sheet of paper, write down numbers 1 to 12. These numbers correspond to the strategies described.
Step 2 What type of strategy best describes the 12 actions cited? Indicate your answers.
Step 3 Exchange papers with a classmate, and grade each other's paper as your instructor gives the right answers.

Notes

1. John Byrne, "Strategic Planning—It's Back," *BusinessWeek*, August 26, 1996, 46.
2. Steven C. Brandt, *Strategic Planning in Emerging Companies* (Reading, MA: Addison-Wesley, 1981). Reprinted with permission of the publisher.
3. F. Hansen and M. Smith, "Crisis in Corporate America: The Role of Strategy," *Business Horizons* (January–February 2003, 9.
4. Adapted from F. R. David, "How Do We Choose Among Alternative Growth Strategies?" *Managerial Planning* 33, no. 4 (January–February 1985): 14–17, 22.
5. Ibid.
6. Kenneth Davidson, "Do Megamergers Make Sense?" *Journal of Business Strategy* 7, no. 3 (Winter 1987): 45.
7. David, "How Do We Choose."
8. Ibid.
9. Ibid.
10. Ibid.
11. Arthur Thompson Jr., A. J. Strickland III, and John Gamble, *Crafting and Executing Strategy: Text and Readings* (New York: McGraw-Hill/Irwin, 2005, 241.
12. Michael E. Porter, *Competitive Strategy: Techniques for Analyzing Industries and Competitors* (New York: Free Press, 1980), 53–57, 318–319.
13. David, "How Do We Choose."
14. Ibid.
15. Ibid.
16. Ibid.
17. Ibid.
18. Michael Porter, *Competitive Advantage* (New York: Free Press, 1985), 97. Also, Arthur Thompson Jr., A. J. Strickland III, and John Gamble, *Crafting and Executing Strategy: Text and Readings* (New York: McGraw-Hill/Irwin, 2005), 117.
19. Arthur Thompson Jr., A. J. Strickland III, and John Gamble, *Crafting and Executing Strategy: Text and Readings* (New York: McGraw-Hill/Irwin, 2005), 125–126.
20. Porter, *Competitive Advantage,* 160–162.
21. Thompson, Strickland, and Gamble, 129–130.
22. Ibid., 134.
23. John Letzing, "Facebook, Yahoo Kiss and Make-Up," *Wall Street Journal* (July 9, 2102): B3.
24. Gary Hamel, Yves Doz, and C. K. Prahalad, "Collaborate with Your Competitors—and Win," *Harvard Business Review* 67, no. 1 (January–February 1989): 133.
25. Kathryn Rudie Harrigan, "Joint Ventures: Linking for a Leap Forward," *Planning Review* 14, no. 4 (July–August 1986): 10.
26. Matthew Schifrin, "Partner or Perish," *Forbes* (May 21, 2001): 26.
27. Ibid., 28.
28. Ibid., 32.
29. David, "How Do We Choose."
30. James Hagerty, "Some Firms Opt to Bring Manufacturing Back to USA," *Wall Street Journal* (July 18, 2012): B8.

5

Source: © Paylessimages/Fotolia

MyManagementLab®

Improve Your Grade!

Over 10 million students improved their results using the Pearson MyLabs.
Visit **mymanagementlab.com** for simulations, tutorials, and end-of-chapter problems.

Vision and Mission Analysis

CHAPTER OBJECTIVES

After studying this chapter, you should be able to do the following:

1. Describe the nature and role of vision and mission statements in strategic management.

2. Discuss why the process of developing a mission statement is as important as the resulting document.

3. Identify the components of mission statements.

4. Discuss how clear vision and mission statements can benefit other strategic-management activities.

5. Evaluate mission statements of different organizations.

6. Write good vision and mission statements.

ASSURANCE OF LEARNING **EXERCISES**

The following exercises are found at the end of this chapter.

This chapter focuses on the concepts and tools needed to evaluate and write business vision and mission statements. A practical framework for developing mission statements is provided. Actual mission statements from large and small organizations and for-profit and nonprofit enterprises are presented and critically examined. The process of creating a vision and mission statement is discussed. The recent economic recession resulted in many firms changing direction and thereby altering their entire vision and mission. For example, Microsoft entered the smartphone business with Nokia, and IBM is focusing more on business analytics.

The boxed insert company examined in this chapter is Samsung which has a clear strategic plan.

We can perhaps best understand vision and mission by focusing on a business when it is first started. In the beginning, a new business is simply a collection of ideas. Starting a new business rests on a set of beliefs that the new organization can offer some product or service to some customers in some geographic area using some type of technology at a profitable price. A new business owner typically believes that the management philosophy of the new enterprise will result in a favorable public image and that this concept of the business can be communicated to, and will be adopted by, important constituencies. When the set of beliefs about a business at its inception is put into writing, the resulting document mirrors the same basic ideas that underlie the vision and mission statements. As a business grows, owners or managers find it necessary to revise the founding set of beliefs, but those original ideas usually are reflected in the revised statements of vision and mission.

Vision and mission statements often can be found in the front of annual reports. They often are displayed throughout a firm's premises and are distributed with company information sent to constituencies. The statements are part of numerous internal reports, such as loan requests, supplier agreements, labor relations contracts, business plans, and customer service agreements.

EXCELLENT STRATEGIC MANAGEMENT SHOWCASED

Samsung

Samsung Electronics Co., Ltd., headquartered in Suwon, South Korea, is the world's largest information company. Samsung has assembly plants and sales networks in 88 countries and employs around 270,000 people. Samsung is the leading smartphone manufacturer, as well as a leading producer of lithium-ion batteries, semiconductors chips, flash memory and hard drive devices, as well as tablet computers. Samsung is the world's largest maker of LCD panels, and the world's largest television manufacturer. In 2013, *Fortune* ranked Samsung as the 12th largest firm in the world, the 12th most profitable, and the 35th most admired company outside the United States.

Samsung's vision statement is posted on their website, as: "Samsung is dedicated to developing innovative technologies and efficient processes that create new markets, enrich people's lives and continue to make Samsung a digital leader." The company's mission statement is called a statement of philosophy and also is given on the corporate website. Samsung does an excellent job in strategic management.

In late 2013, Samsung began mass-producing the industry's first three-dimensional (3D) Vertical NAND (V-NAND) flash memory. The new 3D V-NAND is now used for a wide range of consumer electronics and enterprise applications, including embedded NAND storage and solid state drives (SSDs). In September 2013, Samsung launched a massive global advertising campaign to promote the new Galaxy Note 3 and Galaxy Gear products. Samsung has annual sales of about $190 billion.

Headquartered in Ridgefield Park, New Jersey, Samsung Electronics America (SEA) houses the company's Consumer Business Division (CBD) and Enterprise Business Division (EBD).CBD offers scores of digital products, such as LEDs and plasma TVs, home theater systems and camcorders as well as refrigerators, washers and dryers, ranges, dishwashers, microwave ovens and vacuums. Samsung EBD offers printers, desktop monitors, laptop computers, digital signage, and projectors.

Samsung Telecommunications America (STA), headquartered in Dallas, Texas, offers handheld wireless phones, wireless communications infrastructure systems, fiber optics and enterprise communication systems.

Samsung Semiconductor, Inc. (SSI), headquartered in San Jose, California, is the second largest semiconductor manufacturer in the world and the industry leader in DRAM, NAND Flash, SRAM memory and TFT-LCD panels.

Samsung Information Systems America (SISA), located in Southern California, offers hard disk drives, digital TV technologies, printer software, wireless connectivity and software.

Samsung Austin Semiconductor (SAS), located in Austin, Texas, is the company's only semiconductor manufacturing plant outside Korea. SAS produces NAND Flash memory and Mobile SoC chips.

What Do We Want to Become?

It is especially important for managers and executives in any organization to agree on the basic vision that the firm strives to achieve in the long term. A vision statement should answer the basic question, "What do we want to become?" A clear vision provides the foundation for developing a comprehensive mission statement. Many organizations have both a vision and mission statement, but the vision statement should be established first and foremost. The vision statement should be short, preferably one sentence, and as many managers as possible should have input into developing the statement. Where there is no vision, the people perish (Proverbs 29: 18)

Several example vision statements are provided in Table 5-1.

What Is Our Business?

Current thought on mission statements is based largely on guidelines set forth in the mid-1970s by Peter Drucker, who is often called "the father of modern management" for his pioneering studies at General Motors and for his 22 books and hundreds of articles. *Harvard Business Review* has called Drucker "the preeminent management thinker of our time."

Drucker says that asking the question "What is our business?" is synonymous with asking the question "What is our mission?" An enduring statement of purpose that distinguishes one organization from other similar enterprises, the **mission statement** is a declaration of an organization's "reason for being." It answers the pivotal question "What is our business?" A clear mission statement is essential for effectively establishing objectives and formulating strategies.

Sometimes called a **creed statement**, a statement of purpose, a statement of philosophy, a statement of beliefs, a statement of business principles, or a statement "defining our business," a mission statement reveals what an organization wants to be and whom it wants to serve. All organizations have a reason for being, even if strategists have not consciously transformed this reason into writing. As illustrated with white shading in Figure 5-1, carefully prepared statements of vision and mission are widely recognized by both practitioners and academicians as the first step in strategic management. Drucker has the following to say about mission statements (paraphrased):

TABLE 5-1   Vision Statement Examples

Tyson Foods' vision is to be the world's first choice for protein solutions while maximizing shareholder value. *(Author comment: Good statement, unless Tyson provides nonprotein products)*

General Motors' vision is to be the world leader in transportation products and related services. *(Author comment: Good statement)*

PepsiCo's responsibility is to continually improve all aspects of the world in which we operate—environment, social, economic—creating a better tomorrow than today. *(Author comment: Statement is too vague; it should reveal beverage and food business)*

Dell's vision is to create a company culture where environmental excellence is second nature. *(Author comment: Statement is too vague; it should reveal computer business in some manner; the word environmental is generally used to refer to natural environment so is unclear in its use here)*

The vision of First Reliance Bank is to be recognized as the largest and most profitable bank in South Carolina. *(Author comment: This is a small new bank headquartered in Florence, South Carolina, so this goal is not achievable in five years; the statement is too futuristic)*

Samsonite's vision is to provide innovative solutions for the traveling world. *(Author comment: Statement needs to be more specific, perhaps mention luggage; statement as is could refer to air carriers or cruise lines, which is not good)*

Royal Caribbean's vision is to empower and enable our employees to deliver the best vacation experience for our guests, thereby generating superior returns for our shareholders and enhancing the well-being of our communities. *(Author comment: Statement is good but could end after the word "guests")*

Procter & Gamble's vision is to be, and be recognized as, the best consumer products company in the world. *(Author comment: Statement is too vague and readability is not that good)*

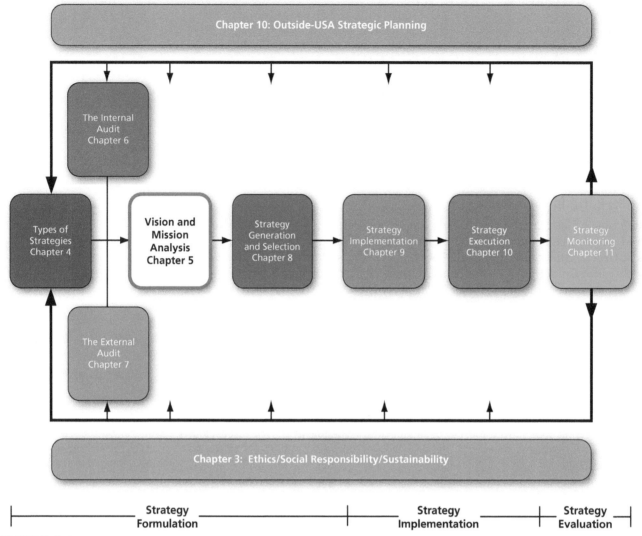

FIGURE 5-1

A Comprehensive Strategic-Management Model

Source: Fred R. David, adapted from "How Companies Define Their Mission," *Long Range Planning* 22, no. 3 (June 1988): 40,
© Fred R. David.

A mission statement is the foundation for priorities, strategies, plans, and work assignments. It is the starting point for the design of jobs and organizational structures. Nothing may seem simpler or more obvious than to know what a company's business is. A lumber mill makes lumber, an airline carries passengers and freight, and a bank lends money. But "What is our business?" is almost always a difficult question and the right answer is usually anything but obvious. The answer to this question is the first responsibility of strategists.[1]

Some strategists spend almost every moment of every day on administrative and tactical concerns, and strategists who rush quickly to establish objectives and implement strategies often overlook the development of a vision and mission statement. This problem is widespread even among large organizations. Many corporations in the USA have not yet developed a formal vision or mission statement. An increasing number of organizations are developing these statements.

Some companies develop mission statements simply because they feel it is fashionable, rather than out of any real commitment. However, as described in this chapter, firms that develop and systematically revisit their vision and mission statements, treat them as living documents, and consider them to be an integral part of the firm's culture realize great benefits. Johnson & Johnson (J&J) is an example firm. J&J managers meet regularly with employees to review, reword, and reaffirm the firm's vision and mission. The entire J&J workforce recognizes the value that top management places on this exercise, and these employees respond accordingly.

Vision versus Mission

Many organizations develop both a mission statement and a vision statement. Whereas the mission statement answers the question "What is our business?" the **vision statement** answers the question "What do we want to become?" Many organizations have both a mission and vision statement.

For many if not most corporations, profit rather than mission or vision is the primary motivator. But profit alone is not enough to motivate people. Profit is perceived negatively by many stakeholders of a firm. For example, employees may see profit as something that they earn and management then uses and even gives away to shareholders. Although this perception is undesired and disturbing to management, it clearly indicates that both profit and vision are needed to motivate a workforce effectively.

When employees and managers together shape or fashion the vision and mission statements for a firm, the resultant documents can reflect the personal visions that managers and employees have in their hearts and minds about their own futures. Shared vision creates a commonality of interests that can lift workers out of the monotony of daily work and put them into a new world of opportunity and challenge.

Vision Statement Analysis

A vision statement should at a minimum reveal the type of business the firm engages. For example, to have a vision that says "to become the best retailing firm in the USA" is not good, because that firm could be selling anything from boats to bunnies.

STARBUCKS PROPOSED VISION STATEMENT

"Starbucks strives to ethically find and roast the highest quality Arabica coffee in the world. With stores around the world, we are the premier roaster and retailer of specialty coffee globally."

STARBUCKS "IMPROVED" VISION STATEMENT

Starbucks' vision is to be the most well-known, specialty coffee, tea, and pastry restaurant in the world, offering sincere customer service, a welcoming atmosphere, and unequaled quality.

STARBUCKS VISION STATEMENT ANALYSIS

- The existing vision statement does not state what the company wants to become. Nor does it acknowledge the firm's movement into specialty tea offerings.
- The improved vision statement reveals the company's aspirations for the future and acknowledges that upscale tea and pastries complement their premium coffee offerings.

The Process of Developing Vision and Mission Statements

As indicated in the strategic-management model, clear vision and mission statements are needed before alternative strategies can be formulated and implemented. As many managers as possible should be involved in the process of developing these statements because, through involvement, people become committed to an organization.

A widely used approach to developing a vision and mission statement is first to select several articles about these statements and ask all managers to read these as background information. Then ask managers themselves to prepare a vision and mission statement for the organization. A facilitator or committee of top managers should then merge these statements into a single document and distribute the draft statements to all managers. A request for modifications, additions, and deletions is needed next, along with a meeting to revise the document. To the extent that all managers have input into and support the final documents, organizations can more easily obtain managers' support for other strategy formulation, implementation, and evaluation activities. Thus, the process of developing a vision and mission statement represents a great opportunity for strategists to obtain needed support from all managers in the firm.

During the process of developing vision and mission statements, some organizations use discussion groups of managers to develop and modify existing statements. Some organizations hire an outside consultant or facilitator to manage the process and help draft the language. Sometimes an outside person with expertise in developing such statements, who has unbiased views, can manage the process more effectively than an internal group or committee of managers. Decisions on how best to communicate the vision and mission to all managers, employees, and external constituencies of an organization are needed when the documents are in final form. Some organizations even develop a videotape to explain the statements and how they were developed.

An article by Campbell and Yeung emphasizes that the process of developing a mission statement should create an "emotional bond" and "sense of mission" between the organization and its employees.[2] Commitment to a company's strategy and intellectual agreement on the strategies to be pursued do not necessarily translate into an emotional bond; hence, strategies that have been formulated may not be implemented. These researchers stress that an emotional bond comes when an individual personally identifies with the underlying values and behavior of a firm, thus turning intellectual agreement and commitment to strategy into a sense of mission. Campbell and Yeung also differentiate between the terms *vision* and *mission*, saying that vision is "a possible and desirable future state of an organization" that includes specific goals, whereas mission is more associated with behavior and the present.

Importance (Benefits) of Vision and Mission Statements

The importance (benefits) of vision and mission statements to effective strategic management is well documented in the literature, although research results are mixed. Rarick and Vitton found that firms with a formalized mission statement have twice the average return on shareholders' equity than those firms without a formalized mission statement have; Bart and Baetz found a positive relationship between mission statements and organizational performance; *BusinessWeek* reports that firms using mission statements have a 30 percent higher return on certain financial measures than those without such statements; however, some studies have found that having a mission statement does not directly contribute positively to financial performance.[3] The extent of manager and employee involvement in developing vision and mission statements can make a difference in business success. This chapter provides guidelines for developing these important documents. In actual practice, wide variations exist in the nature, composition, and use of both vision and mission statements. King and Cleland recommend that organizations carefully develop a written mission statement in order to reap the following benefits:

1. To make sure all employees/managers understand the firm's purpose or reason for being.
2. To provide a basis for prioritization of key internal and external factors utilized to formulate feasible strategies.
3. To provide a basis for the allocation of resources.
4. To provide a basis for organizing work, departments, activities, and segments around a common purpose.[4]

Reuben Mark, former CEO of Colgate, maintains that a clear mission increasingly must make sense internationally. Mark's thoughts on vision are as follows:

When it comes to rallying everyone to the corporate banner, it's essential to push one vision globally rather than trying to drive home different messages in different cultures. The trick is to keep the vision simple but elevated: "We make the world's fastest computers" or "Telephone service for everyone." You're never going to get anyone to charge the machine guns only for financial objectives. It's got to be something that makes people feel better, feel a part of something.[5]

A Resolution of Divergent Views

Another benefit of developing a comprehensive mission statement is that divergent views among managers can be revealed and resolved through the process. The question "What is our business?" can create controversy. Raising the question often reveals differences among strategists in the organization. Individuals who have worked together for a long time and who think they know each other suddenly may realize that they are in fundamental disagreement.

For example, in a college or university, divergent views regarding the relative importance of teaching, research, and service often are expressed during the mission statement development process. Negotiation, compromise, and eventual agreement on important issues are needed before people can focus on more specific strategy-formulation activities.

Considerable disagreement among an organization's strategists over vision and mission statements can cause trouble if not resolved. For example, unresolved disagreement over the business mission was one of the reasons for W. T. Grant's bankruptcy and eventual liquidation. Top executives of the firm, including Ed Staley and Lou Lustenberger, were firmly entrenched in opposing positions that W. T. Grant should be like Kmart or JC Penney respectively. W.T. Grant decided to become a bit like both Kmart and JC Penney; this compromise was a huge strategic mistake. In other words, top executives of W. T. Grant never resolved their vision/mission issue, which ultimately led to the firm's disappearance.[6]

Too often, strategists develop vision and business mission statements only when the organization is in trouble. Of course, it is needed then. Developing and communicating a clear mission during troubled times indeed may have spectacular results and even may reverse decline. However, to wait until an organization is in trouble to develop a vision and mission statement is a gamble that characterizes irresponsible management. According to Drucker, the most important time to ask seriously, "What do we want to become?" and "What is our business?" is when a company has been successful:

Success always obsoletes the very behavior that achieved it, always creates new realities, and always creates new and different problems. Only the fairy tale story ends, "They lived happily ever after." It is never popular to argue with success or to rock the boat. It will not be long before success will turn into failure. Sooner or later, even the most successful answer to the question "What is our business?" becomes obsolete.[7]

In multidivisional organizations, strategists should ensure that divisional units perform strategic-management tasks, including the development of a statement of vision and mission. Each division should involve its own managers and employees in developing a vision and mission statement that is consistent with and supportive of the corporate mission. Ten benefits of having a clear mission and vision are provided in Table 5-2.

An organization that fails to develop a vision statement as well as a comprehensive and inspiring mission statement loses the opportunity to present itself favorably to existing and potential stakeholders. All organizations need customers, employees, and managers, and most firms need creditors, suppliers, and distributors. The vision and mission statements are effective vehicles for communicating with important internal and external stakeholders. The principal benefit of these statements as tools of strategic management is derived from their specification of the ultimate aims of a firm. Vision and mission statements reveal the firm's shared expectations internally among all employees and managers. For external constituencies, the statements reveal the firm's long-term commitment to responsible, ethical action in providing a needed product and/or service for customers.

TABLE 5-2   Ten Benefits of Having a Clear Mission and Vision

1. Achieve clarity of purpose among all managers and employees.
2. Provide a basis for all other strategic planning activities, including internal and external assessment, establishing objectives, developing strategies, choosing among alternative strategies, devising policies, establishing organizational structure, allocating resources, and evaluating performance.
3. Provide direction.
4. Provide a focal point for all stakeholders of the firm.
5. Resolve divergent views among managers.
6. Promote a sense of shared expectations among all managers and employees.
7. Project a sense of worth and intent to all stakeholders.
8. Project an organized, motivated organization worthy of support.
9. Achieve higher organizational performance.
10. Achieve synergy among all managers and employees.

Characteristics of a Mission Statement

A Declaration of Attitude

A mission statement is more than a statement of specific details; it is a declaration of attitude and outlook. It usually is broad in scope for at least two major reasons. First, a good mission statement allows for the generation and consideration of a range of feasible alternative objectives and strategies without unduly stifling management creativity. Excess specificity would limit the potential of creative growth for the organization. However, an overly general statement that does not exclude any strategy alternatives could be dysfunctional. Apple Computer's mission statement, for example, should not open the possibility for diversification into pesticides—or Ford Motor Company's into food processing.

Second, a mission statement needs to be broad to reconcile differences effectively among, and appeal to, an organization's diverse **stakeholders**, the individuals and groups of individuals who have a special stake or claim on the company. Thus, a mission statement should be **reconcilatory**. Stakeholders include employees, managers, stockholders, boards of directors, customers, suppliers, distributors, creditors, governments (local, state, federal, and foreign), unions, competitors, environmental groups, and the general public. Stakeholders affect and are affected by an organization's strategies, yet the claims and concerns of diverse constituencies vary and often conflict. For example, the general public is especially interested in social responsibility, whereas stockholders are more interested in profitability. Claims on any business literally may number in the thousands, and they often include clean air, jobs, taxes, investment opportunities, career opportunities, equal employment opportunities, employee benefits, salaries, wages, clean water, and community services. All stakeholders' claims on an organization cannot be pursued with equal emphasis. A good mission statement indicates the relative attention that an organization will devote to meeting the claims of various stakeholders.

The fine balance between specificity and generality is difficult to achieve, but it is well worth the effort. George Steiner offers the following insight on the need for a mission statement to be broad in scope:

> Most business statements of mission are expressed at high levels of abstraction. Vagueness nevertheless has its virtues. Mission statements are not designed to express concrete ends, but rather to provide motivation, general direction, an image, a tone, and a philosophy to guide the enterprise. An excess of detail could prove counterproductive since concrete specification could be the base for rallying opposition. Precision might stifle creativity in the formulation of an acceptable mission or purpose. Once an aim is cast in concrete, it creates a rigidity in an organization and resists change. Vagueness leaves room for other managers to fill in the details.[8]

As indicated in Table 5-3, in addition to being broad in scope, an effective mission statement should not be too lengthy; recommended length is less than 250 words. An effective mission statement should arouse positive feelings and emotions about an organization; it should be inspiring in the sense that it motivates readers to action. A mission statement should be enduring. All of these are desired characteristics of a statement. An effective mission statement

---

TABLE 5-3   Characteristics of a Mission Statement

1. Broad in scope; do not include monetary amounts, numbers, percentages, ratios, or objectives
2. Less than 250 words in length
3. Inspiring
4. Identify the utility of a firm's products
5. Reveal that the firm is socially responsible
6. Reveal that the firm is environmentally responsible
7. Include nine components customers, products or services, markets, technology, concern for survival/growth/profits, philosophy, self-concept, concern for public image, concern for employees
8. Reconciliatory
9. Enduring

generates the impression that a firm is successful, has direction, and is worthy of time, support, and investment—from all socioeconomic groups of people.

It reflects judgments about future growth directions and strategies that are based on forward-looking external and internal analyses. A business mission should provide useful criteria for selecting among alternative strategies. A clear mission statement provides a basis for generating and screening strategic options. The statement of mission should be dynamic in orientation, allowing judgments about the most promising growth directions and those considered less promising.

A Customer Orientation

A good mission statement describes an organization's purpose, customers, products or services, markets, philosophy, and basic technology. According to Vern McGinnis, a mission statement should (a) define what the organization is and what the organization aspires to be, (b) be limited enough to exclude some ventures and broad enough to allow for creative growth, (c) distinguish a given organization from all others, (d) serve as a framework for evaluating both current and prospective activities, and (e) be stated in terms sufficiently clear to be widely understood throughout the organization.[9]

A good mission statement reflects the anticipations of customers. Rather than developing a product and then trying to find a market, the operating philosophy of organizations should be to identify customers' needs and then provide a product or service to fulfill those needs.

Good mission statements identify the utility of a firm's products to its customers. This is why AT&T's mission statement focuses on communication rather than on telephones; it is why ExxonMobil's mission statement focuses on energy rather than on oil and gas; it is why Union Pacific's mission statement focuses on transportation rather than on railroads; it is why Universal Studios' mission statement focuses on entertainment rather than on movies. A major reason for developing a business mission statement is to attract customers who give meaning to an organization.

The following utility statements are relevant in developing a mission statement:

Do not offer me things.

Do not offer me clothes. Offer me attractive looks.

Do not offer me shoes. Offer me comfort for my feet and the pleasure of walking.

Do not offer me a house. Offer me security, comfort, and a place that is clean and happy.

Do not offer me books. Offer me hours of pleasure and the benefit of knowledge.

Do not offer me CDs. Offer me leisure and the sound of music.

Do not offer me tools. Offer me the benefits and the pleasure that come from making beautiful things.

Do not offer me furniture. Offer me comfort and the quietness of a cozy place.

Do not offer me things. Offer me ideas, emotions, ambience, feelings, and benefits.

Please, do not offer me *things*.

Mission Statement Components

Mission statements can and do vary in length, content, format, and specificity. Most practitioners and academicians of strategic management feel that an effective statement should include these nine **mission statement components**. Because a mission statement is often the most visible and public part of the strategic-management process, it is important that it includes the nine characteristics as summarized in Table 5-3, as well as the following nine components:

1. *Customers*—Who are the firm's customers?
2. *Products or services*—What are the firm's major products or services?
3. *Markets*—Geographically, where does the firm compete?
4. *Technology*—Is the firm technologically current?
5. *Concern for survival, growth, and profitability*—Is the firm committed to growth and financial soundness?
6. *Philosophy*—What are the basic beliefs, values, aspirations, and ethical priorities of the firm?
7. *Self-concept*—What is the firm's distinctive competence or major competitive advantage?
8. *Concern for public image*—Is the firm responsive to social, community, and environmental concerns?
9. *Concern for employees*—Are employees a valuable asset of the firm?[10]

TABLE 5-4   Examples of the Nine Essential Components of a Mission Statement

1. Customers
We believe our first responsibility is to the doctors, nurses, patients, mothers, and all others who use our products and services. (Johnson & Johnson)

To earn our customers' loyalty, we listen to them, anticipate their needs, and act to create value in their eyes. (Lexmark International)

2. Products or Services
AMAX's principal products are molybdenum, coal, iron ore, copper, lead, zinc, petroleum and natural gas, potash, phosphates, nickel, tungsten, silver, gold, and magnesium. (AMAX Engineering Company)

Standard Oil Company (Indiana) is in business to find and produce crude oil, natural gas, and natural gas liquids; to manufacture high-quality products useful to society from these raw materials; and to distribute and market those products and to provide dependable related services to the consuming public at reasonable prices. (Standard Oil Company)

3. Markets
We are dedicated to the total success of Corning Glass Works as a worldwide competitor. (Corning Glass Works)

Our emphasis is on North American markets, although global opportunities will be explored. (Blockway)

4. Technology
Control Data is in the business of applying micro-electronics and computer technology in two general areas: computer-related hardware; and computing-enhancing services, which include computation, information, education, and finance. (Control Data)

We will continually strive to meet the preferences of adult smokers by developing technologies that have the potential to reduce the health risks associated with smoking. (RJ Reynolds)

5. Concern for Survival, Growth, and Profitability
In this respect, the company will conduct its operations prudently and will provide the profits and growth which will assure Hoover's ultimate success. (Hoover Universal)

To serve the worldwide need for knowledge at a fair profit by adhering, evaluating, producing, and distributing valuable information in a way that benefits our customers, employees, other investors, and our society. (McGraw-Hill)

6. Philosophy
Our world-class leadership is dedicated to a management philosophy that holds people above profits. (Johnson Company)

It's all part of the Mary Kay philosophy—a philosophy based on the golden rule.
A spirit of sharing and caring where people give cheerfully of their time, knowledge, and experience. (Mary Kay Cosmetics)

7. Self-Concept
Crown Zellerbach is committed to leapfrogging ongoing competition within 1,000 days by unleashing the constructive and creative abilities and energies of each of its employees. (Crown Zellerbach)

8. Concern for Public Image
To share the world's obligation for the protection of the environment. (Dow Chemical)

To contribute to the economic strength of society and function as a good corporate citizen on a local, state, and national basis in all countries in which we do business. (Pfizer)

9. Concern for Employees
To recruit, develop, motivate, reward, and retain personnel of exceptional ability, character, and dedication by providing good working conditions, superior leadership, compensation on the basis of performance, an attractive benefit program, opportunity for growth, and a high degree of employment security. (Barnes Corporation)

To compensate its employees with remuneration and fringe benefits competitive with other employment opportunities in its geographical area and commensurate with their contributions toward efficient corporate operations. (Public Service Electric & Gas Company)

Excerpts from the mission statements of different organizations are provided in Table 5-4 to exemplify the nine essential mission statement components.

Writing and Evaluating Mission Statements

Perhaps the best way to develop a skill for writing and evaluating mission statements is to study actual company missions. Therefore, the mission statements presented in Table 5-5 are evaluated based on the nine desired components. Note in Table 5-5 that numbers provided in each statement reveal what components are included in the respective documents. Among the statements in Table 5-5, note that the Dell mission statement is the best because it lacks only one component, whereas the L'Oreal statement is the worst, lacking six of the nine recommended components.

There is no one best mission statement for a particular organization, so good judgment is required in evaluating mission statements. Realize that some individuals are more demanding than others in assessing mission statements in this manner. For example, if a statement merely includes the word "customers" without specifying who the customers are, is that satisfactory?

TABLE 5-5   Example Mission Statements

Fleetwood Enterprises will lead the recreational vehicle and manufactured housing industries (2, 7) in providing quality products, with a passion for customer-driven innovation (1). We will emphasize training, embrace diversity and provide growth opportunities for our associates and our dealers (9). We will lead our industries in the application of appropriate technologies (4). We will operate at the highest levels of ethics and compliance with a focus on exemplary corporate governance (6). We will deliver value to our shareholders, positive operating results and industry-leading earnings (5). *(Author comment: Statement lacks two components: Markets and Concern for Public Image)*

We aspire to make **PepsiCo** the world's (3) premier consumer products company, focused on convenient foods and beverages (2) We seek to produce healthy financial rewards for investors (5) as we provide opportunities for growth and enrichment to our employees, (9) our business partners and the communities (8) in which we operate. And in everything we do, we strive to act with honesty, openness, fairness and integrity (6). *(Author comment: Statement lacks three components: Customers, Technology, and Self-Concept)*

We are loyal to **Royal Caribbean** and **Celebrity** and strive for continuous improvement in everything we do. We always provide service with a friendly greeting and a smile (7). We anticipate the needs of our customers and make all efforts to exceed our customers' expectations (1). We take ownership of any problem that is brought to our attention. We engage in conduct that enhances our corporate reputation and employee morale (9). We are committed to act in the highest ethical manner and respect the rights and dignity of others. (6). *(Author comment: Statement lacks five components: Products/Services, Markets, Technology, Concern for Survival/Growth/Profits, Concern for Public Image)*

Dell's mission is to be the most successful computer company (2) in the world (3) at delivering the best customer experience in markets we serve (1). In doing so, Dell will meet customer expectations of highest quality; leading technology (4); competitive pricing; individual and company accountability (6); best-in-class service and support (7); flexible customization capability (7); superior corporate citizenship (8); financial stability (5). *(Author comment: Statement lacks only one component: Concern for Employees)*

Procter & Gamble will provide branded products and services of superior quality and value (7) that improve the lives of the world's (3) consumers. As a result, consumers (1) will reward us with indus-try leadership in sales, profit (5), and value creation, allowing our people (9), our shareholders, and the communities (8) in which we live and work to prosper. *(Author comment: Statement lacks three components: Products/Services, Technology, and Philosophy)*

At **L'Oreal**, we believe that lasting business success is built upon ethical (6) standards which guide growth and on a genuine sense of responsibility to our employees (9), our consumers, our environment and to the communities in which we operate (8). *(Author comment: Statement lacks six components: Customers, Products/Services, Markets, Technology, Concern for Survival/Growth/Profits, Concern for Public Image)*

Note: The numbers in parentheses correspond to the nine components listed on page 178; author comments also refer to those components.

Ideally a statement would provide more than simply inclusion of a single word such as "products" or "employees" regarding a respective component. Why? Because the statement should be informative, inspiring, enduring, and serve to motivate stakeholders to action. Evaluation of a mission statement regarding inclusion of the nine components is just the beginning of the process to assess a statement's overall effectiveness.

Special Note to Students

Recall that gaining and sustaining competitive advantage is the essence of strategic management, so when presenting your vision or mission analysis for the firm, be sure to address the "self-concept" or "distinctive competence" component. Compare your recommended vision or mission statement both with the firm's existing statements and with rival firms' statements to clearly reveal how your recommendations or strategic plan enables the firm to gain and sustain competitive advantage. Thus, your proposed mission statement should certainly include the nine components and nine characteristics, but in your vision or mission discussion, focus on competitive advantage. In other words, be prescriptive, forward-looking, and insightful—couching your vision/mission overview in terms of how you believe the firm can best gain and sustain competitive advantage. Do not be content with merely showing a nine-component comparison of your proposed statement with rival firms' statements, although that would be nice to include in your analysis.

Conclusion

Every organization has a unique purpose and reason for being. This uniqueness should be reflected in vision and mission statements. The nature of a business vision and mission can represent either a competitive advantage or disadvantage for the firm. An organization achieves a heightened sense of purpose when strategists, managers, and employees develop and communicate a clear business vision and mission. Drucker says that developing a clear business vision and mission is the "first responsibility of strategists."

A good mission statement reveals an organization's customers; products or services; markets; technology; concern for survival, growth, and profitability; philosophy; self-concept; concern for public image; and concern for employees. These nine basic components serve as a practical framework for evaluating and writing mission statements. As the first step in strategic management, the vision and mission statements provide direction for all planning activities.

Well-designed vision and mission statements are essential for formulating, implementing, and evaluating strategy. Developing and communicating a clear business vision and mission are the most commonly overlooked tasks in strategic management. Without clear statements of vision and mission, a firm's short-term actions can be counterproductive to long-term interests. Vision and mission statements always should be subject to revision, but, if carefully prepared, they will require infrequent major changes. Organizations usually reexamine their vision and mission statements annually. Effective mission statements stand the test of time.

Vision and mission statements are essential tools for strategists, a fact illustrated in a short story told by Porsche's former CEO Peter Schultz (paraphrased):

> Three guys were at work building a large church. All were doing the same job, but when each was asked what his job was, the answers varied: "Pouring cement," the first replied; "Earning a paycheck," responded the second; "Helping to build a cathedral," said the third. Few of us can build cathedrals. But to the extent we can see the cathedral in whatever cause we are following, the job seems more worthwhile. Good strategists and a clear mission help us find those cathedrals in what otherwise could be dismal issues and empty causes.[11]

Key Terms and Concepts

concern for employees (p. 177)
concern for public image (p. 177)
concern for survival, growth, and profitability (p. 177)
creed statement (p. 171)
customers (p. 177)
markets (p. 177)
mission statement (p. 171)
mission statement components (p. 177)

philosophy (p. 177)
products or services (p. 177)
reconciliatory (p. 176)
self-concept (p. 177)
stakeholders (p. 176)
technology (p. 177)
vision statement (p. 173)

Issues for Review and Discussion

5-1. Develop (or find) a mission statement for Samsung Electronics. Analyze the company's mission statement in light of the guidelines in Chapter 5.

5-2. Summarize Samsung's successful global strategy for the last decade. Can that strategy be as successful in 2014? Explain.

5-3. See if you can find a vision statement for Samsung. If not, write a proposed vision statement for the company.

5-4. Should the mission statement components vary in importance depending on type of business? If yes, how would their relative importance vary for Samsung versus Singapore Airlines?

5-5. List three things you are on a mission to accomplish in the next three years. How relevant is the concept of vision/mission to an individual in their personal and professional life? Explain.

5-6. Conduct a Google search for the key words "mission statement." What are the two best websites in your opinion that provide example mission statements?

5-7. Write a vision statement for your university. Write a vision statement for your School (or College) of Business within the university.

5-8. If you just purchased a 10-employee company, how would you establish a clear vision and mission?

5-9. Identify from the Internet six mission statement examples. Evaluate the six statements and bring your analysis to class.

5-10. How and why could the process of developing a vision and mission statement vary across countries?

5-11. In order of importance, list six benefits of having a clearly defined vision and mission statement.

5-12. Only the fairy story ends "they lived happily ever after." What is the relevance of this statement to the concepts vision and mission statement?

5-13. Explain the meaning, and significance of the term "reconciliatory" in developing mission statements.

5-14. List the nine mission statement components. Give an example of each component for your college or university.

5-15. In order of importance, rank seven characteristics of a mission statement.

5-16. Write a vision and mission statement for a local restaurant in your area.

5-17. Write an excellent sentence for Samsung, which includes four mission statement components.

5-18. Within a given industry, compare the mission statements of three companies in your country versus three competing companies in the United States. How did they differ?

5-19. Does Singapore Airlines have its vision and mission statement posted on its website? Should the company? Why or why not?

5-20. How often do you think a firm's vision and mission statements should be changed? Why?

5-21. Explain how a mission statement can be "reconciliatory." Give an example.

5-22. Do local fast food restaurants need a mission statement posted in their place of business? Why or why not?

5-23. Find 5 mission statements on the Internet. Evaluate the statements in terms of six characteristics.

5-24. Referring to the end of Chapter 5, explain how a team of students should couch their mission statement discussion of slides in a presentation.

5-25. List the four most important characteristics of a mission statement for a small retail store. Explain.

MyManagementLab®

Go to **mymanagementlab.com** for the following Assisted-graded writing questions:

5-26. Explain why a mission statement should not include strategies and objectives.

5-27. List seven characteristics of a mission statement.

5-28. Mymanagementlab Only—comprehensive writing assignment for this chapter.

Current Readings

Bartkus, Barbara, Myron Glassman, and R. Bruce McAfee. "Mission Statements: Are They Smoke and Mirrors?" *Business Horizons* 43, no. 6 (November–December 2000): 23.

Church Mission Statements, http://www.missionstatements.com/church_mission_statements.html.

Collins, David J., and Michael G. Rukstad. "Can You Say What Your Strategy Is?" *Harvard Business Review*, April 2008, 82.

Company Mission Statements, http://www.missionstatements.com/company_mission_statements.html.

Conger, Jay A., and Douglas A. Ready. "Enabling Bold Visions." *MIT Sloan Management Review* 49, no. 2 (Winter 2008): 70.

Day, George S., and Paul Schoemaker. "Peripheral Vision: Sensing and Acting on Weak Signals." *Long Range Planning* 37, no. 2 (April 2004): 117.

Ibarra, Herminia, and Otilia Obodaru. "Women and the Vision Thing." *Harvard Business Review*, January 2009, 62–71.

Lissak, Michael, and Johan Roos. "Be Coherent, Not Visionary." *Long Range Planning* 34, no. 1 (February 2001): 53.

Newsom, Mi Kyong, David A. Collier, and Eric O. Olsen. "Using 'Biztainment' to Gain Competitive Advantage." *Business Horizons*, March–April 2009, 167–166.

Nonprofit Organization Mission Statements, http://www.missionstatements.com/nonprofit_mission_statements.html.

Restaurant Mission Statements, http://www.missionstatements.com/restaurant_mission_statements.html.

School Mission Statements, http://www.missionstatements.com/school_mission_statements.html.

MyManagementLab®

Go to **mymanagementlab.com** for the following Assisted-graded writing questions:

5-26. Explain why a mission statement should not include strategies and objectives.

5-27. List seven characteristics of a mission statement.

Current Readings

Bartkus, Barbara, Myron Glassman, and R. Bruce McAfee. "Mission Statements: Are They Smoke and Mirrors?" *Business Horizons* 43, no. 6 (November–December 2000): 23.

Church Mission Statements, http://www.missionstatements.com/church_mission_statements.html.

Collins, David J., and Michael G. Rukstad. "Can You Say What Your Strategy Is?" *Harvard Business Review*, April 2008, 82.

Company Mission Statements, http://www.missionstatements.com/company_mission_statements.html.

Conger, Jay A., and Douglas A. Ready. "Enabling Bold Visions." *MIT Sloan Management Review* 49, no. 2 (Winter 2008): 70.

Day, George S., and Paul Schoemaker. "Peripheral Vision: Sensing and Acting on Weak Signals." *Long Range Planning* 37, no. 2 (April 2004): 117.

Ibarra, Herminia, and Otilia Obodaru. "Women and the Vision Thing." *Harvard Business Review*, January 2009, 62–71.

Lissak, Michael, and Johan Roos. "Be Coherent, Not Visionary." *Long Range Planning* 34, no. 1 (February 2001): 53.

Newsom, Mi Kyong, David A. Collier, and Eric O. Olsen. "Using 'Biztainment' to Gain Competitive Advantage." *Business Horizons*, March–April 2009, 167–166.

Nonprofit Organization Mission Statements, http://www.missionstatements.com/nonprofit_mission_statements.html.

Restaurant Mission Statements, http://www.missionstatements.com/restaurant_mission_statements.html.

School Mission Statements, http://www.missionstatements.com/school_mission_statements.html.

EXERCISE 5C

Evaluating Mission Statements

Purpose

A business mission statement is an integral part of strategic management. It provides direction for formulating, implementing, and evaluating strategic activities. This exercise will give you practice evaluating mission statements, a skill that is a prerequisite to writing a good mission statement. The mission statement for adidas is given below:

"The adidas Group strives to be the global leader in the sporting goods industry with sports brands built on a passion for sports and a sporting lifestyle. We are dedicated to consistently delivering outstanding financial results. We are innovation and design leaders who seek to help athletes of all skill levels achieve peak performance with every product we bring to market. We are consumer focused and therefore we continuously improve the quality, look, feel and image of our products and our organizational structures to match and exceed consumer expectations and to provide them with the highest value. We are a global organization that is socially and environmentally responsible, creative and financially rewarding for our employees and shareholders. We are committed to continuously strengthening our brands and products to improve our competitive position."

Instructions

Step 1   On a separate sheet of paper, write the nine mission statement components down the left side.

Step 2   Write "yes" or "no" beside each number to indicate whether you feel the adidas mission statement has included the respective component. For any component that you record a "no," write a good sentence to encompass that component.

Step 3   Turn your paper in to your instructor for a classwork grade.

EXERCISE 5D

Evaluating the Mission Statement of Under Armour—a Competitor of adidas AG

Purpose

There is always room for improvement in regard to an existing vision and mission statement. Under Armour was founded in 1996 by former University of Maryland football player Kevin Plank. Under Armour sportswear is designed to keep athletes cool, dry and light throughout the course of a game, practice or workout. The technology behind Under Armour's diverse product assortment is complex, but the advice is simple: wear HeatGear® when it's hot, ColdGear® when it's cold, and AllSeasonGear® between the extremes (www.underarmour.com). Visit the Under Armour website and locate their mission statement.

Instructions

Step 1   On a separate sheet of paper, write the nine mission statement components down the lefthand side.

Step 2   Write "yes" or "no" beside each number to indicate whether you feel the Under Armour mission statement has included the respective component. For any component that you record a "no," write a good sentence to encompass that component.

Step 3   Turn your paper in to your instructor for a classwork grade.

EXERCISE 5E

Selecting the Best Vision and Mission Statements in a Given Industry

Purpose

This exercise is designed to get you familiar with existing vision and mission statements in an industry of your choosing.

Instructions

Identify 10 companies in an industry that you are interested in working in one day. Find the companies' vision and mission statements. Keep searching until you have found five vision statements and five mission statements. The statements do not have to be from the same companies. Rank your five vision statements and your five mission statements in order of attractiveness, with 1 being the best and 5 being the worst.

EXERCISE 5F

Writing an Excellent Vision and Mission Statement for Novartis AG

Purpose

This exercise is designed to give you practice developing from scratch or improving an existing vision and mission statement.

Instructions

Step 1   Go to the Novartis AG website and look for the company's vision statement and mission statement. Recall from Chapter 5 that companies use different names or titles for these documents.

Step 2   Prepare an improved vision and mission statement for Novartis AG whether or not you were able to find these statements on the company's website or in the firm's *Annual Report*.

Notes

1. Peter Drucker, *Management: Tasks, Responsibilities, and Practices* (New York: Harper & Row, 1974), 61.

2. Andrew Campbell and Sally Yeung, "Creating a Sense of Mission," *Long Range Planning* 24, no. 4 (August 1991): 17.

3. Charles Rarick and John Vitton, "Mission Statements Make Cents," *Journal of Business Strategy* 16 (1995): 11. Also, Christopher Bart and Mark Baetz, "The Relationship Between Mission Statements and Firm Performance: An Exploratory Study," *Journal of Management Studies* 35 (1998): 823; "Mission Possible," *Business Week* (August 1999): F12.

4. W. R. King and D. I. Cleland, *Strategic Planning and Policy* (New York: Van Nostrand Reinhold, 1979), 124.

5. Brian Dumaine, "What the Leaders of Tomorrow See," *Fortune*, July 3, 1989, 50.

6. "How W. T. Grant Lost $175 Million Last Year," *Business Week*, February 25, 1975, 75.

7. Drucker, *Management*, 88.

8. John Pearce II, "The Company Mission as a Strategic Tool," *Sloan Management Review* 23, no. 3 (Spring 1982): 74.

9. George Steiner, *Strategic Planning: What Every Manager Must Know* (New York: The Free Press, 1979), 160.

10. Vern McGinnis, "The Mission Statement: A Key Step in Strategic Planning," *Business* 31, no. 6 (November–December 1981): 41.

11. http://ezinearticles.com/?Elements-of-a-Mission-Statement&id=3846671.

Source: © Norman Nick/Fotolia

MyManagementLab®

Improve Your Grade!

More than 10 million students improved their results using the Pearson MyLabs.
Visit **mymanagementlab.com** for simulations, tutorials, and end-of-chapter problems.

The Internal Audit

CHAPTER OBJECTIVES

After studying this chapter, you should be able to do the following:

1. Explain how the nature and role of chief marketing officer has changed.

2. Be able to work out breakeven analysis business problems.

3. Describe how to perform an internal strategic-management audit.

4. Discuss the resource-based view (RBV) in strategic management.

5. Discuss key interrelationships among the functional areas of business.

6. Identify the basic functions or activities that make up management, marketing, finance and accounting, production and operations, research and development, and management information systems.

7. Explain how to determine and prioritize a firm's internal strengths and weaknesses.

8. Explain the importance of financial ratio analysis.

9. Discuss the nature and role of management information systems in strategic management.

10. Develop an internal factor evaluation (IFE) matrix.

11. Explain cost/benefit analysis, value chain analysis, and benchmarking as strategic-management tools.

ASSURANCE OF LEARNING EXERCISES

The following exercises are found at the end of this chapter.

This chapter focuses on identifying and evaluating a firm's strengths and weaknesses in the functional areas of business, including management, marketing, finance and accounting, production and operations, research and development (R&D), and management information systems (MIS). Relationships among these areas of business are examined. Strategic implications of important functional area concepts are examined. The process of performing an internal audit is described. The resource-based view (RBV) of strategic management is introduced as is the value chain analysis (VCA) concept. Volkswagen has done an excellent job in using its strengths to capitalize on external opportunities. Volkswagen is showcased in the opening chapter boxed insert.

The Nature of an Internal Audit

All organizations have strengths and weaknesses in the functional areas of business. No enterprise is equally strong or weak in all areas. Maytag, for example, is known for excellent production and product design, whereas Procter & Gamble is known for superb marketing. Internal strengths and weaknesses, coupled with external opportunities and threats and clear vision and mission statements, provide the basis for establishing objectives and strategies. Objectives and strategies are established with the intention of capitalizing on internal strengths and overcoming weaknesses. The internal-audit part of the strategic-management process is illustrated in Figure 6-1 with white shading.

EXCELLENT STRATEGIC MANAGEMENT SHOWCASED

Volkswagen

Volkswagen (VW) Group is a global automobile manufacturer headquartered in Wolfsburg, Lower Saxony, Germany. The largest German automaker and the third largest automaker in the world, VW produces more than 7 million cars, trucks, and vans annually, including the Beatle, Golf, Passat (trade wind), Jetta (jet stream), Rabbit, and Fox. VW also owns luxury carmakers—AUDI, Lamborghini, Bentley, and Bugatti, and other brands such as SEAT (family cars, Spain) and Škoda (family cars, the Czech Republic). VW owns 49.9 percent of Porsche. VW's American and Chinese version of the Passat won the 2012 Motor Trend Car of the Year. The VW Golf won the 2013 European Car of the Year. In 2013, *Fortune* ranked VW as the 9th largest company in the world, the 6th most profitable, and the 33rd most admired company outside the United States.

In an August 2013 study by the Trendence Institute (TI), the VW Group rose from 4th to 2nd place in the rankings of the most attractive employers in Europe, trailing only USA-based Google. In the study, 320,000 students from 24 European countries were interviewed with regard to their career plans and preferred employers. Ralph Linde, Head of the Volkswagen Group Academy, stated that as well as a trainee scheme for university graduates, Volkswagen also takes great pride in the mentoring and individual career development of each of its employees. This result confirms an April 2013 TI survey with 37,000 German students that revealed that companies in the Volkswagen Group are the most sought-after employers among German students.

For the January through August 2013 period, Volkswagen delivered 3.84 (+3.1 percent) million passenger cars worldwide, doing particularly well in China, where 1.56 (+18.4 percent) million units were delivered, and in Mexico, with 92,100 (+18.3 percent) deliveries. For that period, Audi delivered 1.03 million vehicles worldwide, an increase of 7.2 percent, led by China, where 310,300 (+19.5 percent) Audi vehicles were delivered. Audi deliveries during that period in the United States rose 14.7 percent compared with the same prior-year period, with 101,300 cars sold. VW's sports car manufacturer Porsche, which joined Volkswagen Group on August 1, 2012, delivered 106,800 vehicles in the first eight months of 2013 with the 32,500 units sold in the Asia-Pacific region comprising the largest share of Porsche deliveries. Another 31,400 Porsche's were handed over to customers in the North America region. Also during those eight months, VW's ŠKODA delivered 598,400 (−5.5 percent) vehicles worldwide, while SEAT delivered 234,200 (+11.4 percent) vehicles.

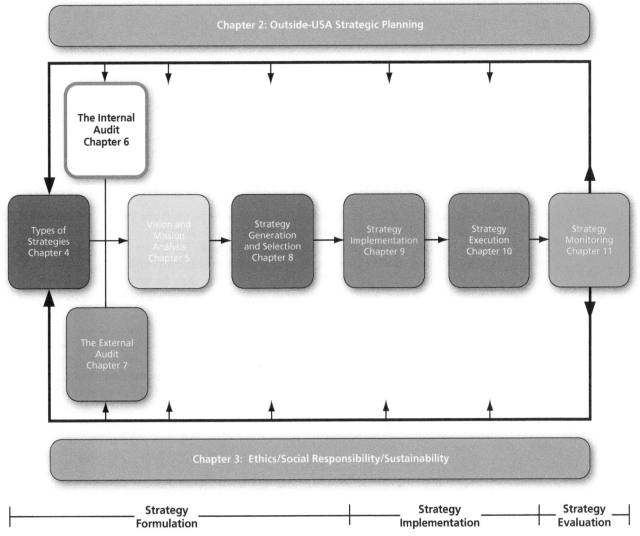

FIGURE 6-1

A Comprehensive Strategic-Management Model

Source: Fred R. David, adapted from "How Companies Define Their Mission," *Long Range Planning* 22, no. 3 (June 1988): 40, © Fred R. David.

Key Internal Forces

It is not possible in a strategic-management text to review in depth all the material presented in courses such as marketing, finance, accounting, management, management information systems, and production and operations; there are many subareas within these functions, such as customer service, warranties, advertising, packaging, and pricing under marketing. But strategic planning must include a detailed assessment of how the firm is doing in all internal areas.

For different types of organizations, such as hospitals, universities, and government agencies, the functional business areas, of course, differ. In a hospital, for example, functional areas may include cardiology, hematology, nursing, maintenance, physician support, and receivables. Functional areas of a university can include athletic programs, placement services, housing, fund-raising, academic research, counseling, and intramural programs. Within large organizations, each division has certain strengths and weaknesses.

A firm's strengths that cannot be easily matched or imitated by competitors are called **distinctive competencies.** Building competitive advantages involves taking advantage of distinctive competencies. Strategies are designed in part to improve on a firm's weaknesses, turning them into strengths—and maybe even into distinctive competencies.

> Weaknesses ⇒ Strenghts ⇒ Distinctive Competencies ⇒ Competitive Advantage

FIGURE 6-2

The Process of Gaining Competitive Advantage in a Firm

Figure 6-2 illustrates that all firms should continually strive to improve on their weaknesses, turning them into strengths, and ultimately developing distinctive competencies that can provide the firm with competitive advantages over rival firms.

The Process of Performing an Internal Audit

The process of performing an **internal audit** closely parallels the process of performing an external audit. Representative managers and employees from throughout the firm need to be involved in determining a firm's strengths and weaknesses. The internal audit requires gathering and assimilating information about the firm's management, marketing, finance and accounting, production and operations, R&D, and MIS operations. Key factors should be prioritized as described in Chapter 7 so that the firm's most important strengths and weaknesses can be determined collectively.

Compared to the external audit, the process of performing an internal audit provides more opportunity for participants to understand how their jobs, departments, and divisions fit into the whole organization. This is a great benefit because managers and employees perform better when they understand how their work affects other areas and activities of the firm. For example, when marketing and manufacturing managers jointly discuss issues related to internal strengths and weaknesses, they gain a better appreciation of the issues, problems, concerns, and needs of all the functional areas. In organizations that do not use strategic management, marketing, finance, and manufacturing managers often do not interact with each other in significant ways. Performing an internal audit thus is an excellent vehicle or forum for improving the process of communication in the organization. **Communication** may be the most important word in management.

Performing an internal audit requires gathering, assimilating, and evaluating information about the firm's operations. Key internal factors, consisting of both strengths and weaknesses, can be identified and prioritized in the manner discussed in Chapter 7. According to William King, a task force of managers from different units of the organization, supported by staff, should be charged with determining the 20 most important strengths and weaknesses that should influence the future of the organization. He says:

> The development of conclusions on the 20 most important organizational strengths and weaknesses can be, as any experienced manager knows, a difficult task, when it involves managers representing various organizational interests and points of view. Developing a 20-page list of strengths and weaknesses could be accomplished relatively easily, but a list of the 20 most important ones involves significant analysis and negotiation. This is true because of the judgments that are required and the impact which such a list will inevitably have as it is used in the formulation, implementation, and evaluation of strategies.[1]

Strategic management is a highly interactive process that requires effective coordination among management, marketing, finance and accounting, production and operations, R&D, and MIS managers. Although the strategic-management process is overseen by strategists, success requires that managers and employees from all functional areas work together to provide ideas and information. Financial managers, for example, may need to restrict the number of feasible options available to operations managers, or R&D managers may develop products for which marketing managers need to set higher objectives. A key to organizational success is effective coordination and understanding among managers from all functional business areas. Through involvement in performing an internal strategic-management audit, managers from different departments and divisions of the firm come to understand the nature and effect of decisions in other functional business areas in their firm. Knowledge of these relationships is critical for effectively establishing objectives and strategies.

A failure to recognize and understand relationships among the functional areas of business can be detrimental to strategic management, and the number of those relationships that must be managed increases dramatically with a firm's size, diversity, geographic dispersion, and the number of products or services offered. Governmental and nonprofit enterprises traditionally have not placed sufficient emphasis on relationships among the business functions. Some firms place too great an emphasis on one function at the expense of others. Ansoff explained:

> During the first fifty years, successful firms focused their energies on optimizing the performance of one of the principal functions: production/operations, R&D, or marketing. Today, due to the growing complexity and dynamism of the environment, success increasingly depends on a judicious combination of several functional influences. This transition from a single function focus to a multifunction focus is essential for successful strategic management.[2]

Financial ratio analysis exemplifies the complexity of relationships among the functional areas of business. A declining return on investment or profit margin ratio could be the result of ineffective marketing, poor management policies, R&D errors, or a weak MIS. The effectiveness of strategy formulation, implementation, and evaluation activities hinges on a clear understanding of how major business functions affect one another. For strategies to succeed, a coordinated effort among all the functional areas of business is needed. In the case of planning, George wrote:

> We may conceptually separate planning for the purpose of theoretical discussion and analysis, but in practice, neither is it a distinct entity nor is it capable of being separated. The planning function is mixed with all other business functions and, like ink once mixed with water, it cannot be set apart. It is spread throughout and is a part of the whole of managing an organization.[3]

The Resource-Based View

Some researchers emphasize the importance of the internal audit part of the strategic-management process by comparing it to the external audit. Robert Grant concluded that the internal audit is more important, saying:

> In a world where customer preferences are volatile, the identity of customers is changing, and the technologies for serving customer requirements are continually evolving, an externally focused orientation does not provide a secure foundation for formulating long-term strategy. When the external environment is in a state of flux, the firm's own resources and capabilities may be a much more stable basis on which to define its identity. Hence, a definition of a business in terms of what it is capable of doing may offer a more durable basis for strategy.[4]

The **resource-based view (RBV)** approach to competitive advantage contends that internal resources are more important for a firm than external factors in achieving and sustaining competitive advantage. In contrast to the Industrial Organization (I/O) theory presented in Chapter 7, proponents of the RBV view contend that organizational performance will primarily be determined by internal resources that can be grouped into three all-encompassing categories: physical resources, human resources, and organizational resources.[5] Physical resources include all plant and equipment, location, technology, raw materials, machines; human resources include all employees, training, experience, intelligence, knowledge, skills, abilities; and organizational resources include firm structure, planning processes, information systems, patents, trademarks, copyrights, databases, and so on. RBV theory asserts that resources are actually what helps a firm exploit opportunities and neutralize threats.

The basic premise of the RBV is that the mix, type, amount, and nature of a firm's internal resources should be considered first and foremost in devising strategies that can lead to sustainable competitive advantage. Managing strategically according to the RBV involves developing and exploiting a firm's unique resources and capabilities, and continually maintaining and strengthening those resources. The theory asserts that it is advantageous for a firm to pursue a strategy that is not currently being implemented by any competing firm. When other firms are unable to duplicate a particular strategy, then the focal firm has a sustainable competitive advantage, according to RBV theorists.

For a resource to be valuable, it must be either (a) rare, (b) hard to imitate, or (c) not easily substitutable. Often called **empirical indicators**, these three characteristics of resources enable a firm to implement strategies that improve its efficiency and effectiveness and lead to a sustainable competitive advantage. The more a resource(s) is rare, nonimitable, and nonsubstitutable, the stronger a firm's competitive advantage will be and the longer it will last.

Rare resources are resources that other competing firms do not possess. If many firms have the same resource, then those firms will likely implement similar strategies, thus giving no one firm a sustainable competitive advantage. This is not to say that resources that are common are not valuable; they do indeed aid the firm in its chance for economic prosperity. However, to sustain a competitive advantage, it is more advantageous if the resource(s) is also rare.

It is also important that these same resources be difficult to imitate. If firms cannot easily gain the resources, say RBV theorists, then those resources will lead to a competitive advantage more so than resources easily imitable. Even if a firm employs resources that are rare, a sustainable competitive advantage may be achieved only if other firms cannot easily obtain these resources.

The third empirical indicator that can make resources a source of competitive advantage is substitutability. Borrowing from Porter's Five-Forces Model, to the degree that there are no viable substitutes, a firm will be able to sustain its competitive advantage. However, even if a competing firm cannot perfectly imitate a firm's resource, it can still obtain a sustainable competitive advantage of its own by obtaining resource substitutes.

RBV has continued to grow in popularity and continues to seek a better understanding of the relationship between resources and sustained competitive advantage in strategic management. However, as alluded to in Chapter 7, one cannot say with any degree of certainty that either external or internal factors will always or even consistently be more important in seeking competitive advantage. Understanding both external and internal factors, and more importantly, understanding the relationships among them, will be the key to effective strategy formulation (discussed in Chapter 8). Because both external and internal factors continually change, strategists seek to identify and take advantage of positive changes and buffer against negative changes in a continuing effort to gain and sustain a firm's competitive advantage. This is the essence and challenge of strategic management, and oftentimes survival of the firm hinges on this work.

Integrating Strategy and Culture

Relationships among a firm's functional business activities perhaps can be exemplified best by focusing on organizational culture, an internal phenomenon that permeates all departments and divisions of an organization. **Organizational culture** can be defined as "a pattern of behavior that has been developed by an organization as it learns to cope with its problem of external adaptation and internal integration, and that has worked well enough to be considered valid and to be taught to new members as the correct way to perceive, think, and feel."[6] This definition emphasizes the importance of matching external with internal factors in making strategic decisions.

Organizational culture captures the subtle, elusive, and largely unconscious forces that shape a workplace. Remarkably resistant to change, culture can represent a major strength or weakness for the firm. It can be an underlying reason for strengths or weaknesses in any of the major business functions.

Defined in Table 6-1, **cultural products** include values, beliefs, rites, rituals, ceremonies, myths, stories, legends, sagas, language, metaphors, symbols, heroes, and heroines. These products or dimensions are levers that strategists can use to influence and direct strategy formulation, implementation, and evaluation activities. An organization's culture compares to an individual's personality in the sense that no two organizations have the same culture and no two individuals have the same personality. Both culture and personality are enduring and can be warm, aggressive, friendly, open, innovative, conservative, liberal, harsh, or likable.

At Google, the culture is informal. Employees are encouraged to wander the halls on employee-sponsored scooters and brainstorm on public whiteboards provided everywhere. In contrast, the culture at Procter & Gamble (P&G) is so rigid that employees jokingly call

TABLE 6-1 Example Cultural Products Defined

Rites	Planned sets of activities that consolidate various forms of cultural expressions into one event.
Ceremonial	Several rites connected together.
Ritual	A standardized set of behaviors used to manage anxieties.
Myth	A narrative of imagined events, usually not supported by facts.
Saga	A historical narrative describing the unique accomplishments of a group and its leaders.
Legend	A handed-down narrative of some wonderful event, usually not supported by facts.
Story	A narrative usually based on true events.
Folktale	A fictional story.
Symbol	Any object, act, event, quality, or relation used to convey meaning.
Language	The manner in which members of a group communicate.
Metaphors	Shorthand of words used to capture a vision or to reinforce old or new values.
Values	Life-directing attitudes that serve as behavioral guidelines.
Belief	An understanding of a particular phenomenon.
Heroes/Heroines	Individuals greatly respected.

Source: Based on H. M. Trice and J. M. Beyer, "Studying Organizational Cultures through Rites and Ceremonials," *Academy of Management Review* 9, no. 4 (October 1984): 655.

themselves "Proctoids." Despite this difference, the two companies are swapping employees and participating in each other's staff training sessions. Why? Because P&G spends more money on advertising than any other company and Google desires more of P&G's $8.7 billion in annual advertising expenses; P&G has come to realize that the next generation of laundry-detergent, toilet-paper, and skin-cream customers now spend more time online than watching TV.

Dimensions of organizational culture permeate all the functional areas of business. It is something of an art to uncover the basic values and beliefs that are deeply buried in an organization's rich collection of stories, language, heroes, and rituals, but cultural products can represent both important strengths and weaknesses. Culture is an aspect of an organization that can no longer be taken for granted in performing an internal strategic-management audit because culture and strategy must work together.

Table 6-2 provides some example (possible) aspects of an organization's culture. Note you could ask employees and managers to rate the degree that the dimension characterizes the firm. When one firm acquires another firm, integrating the two cultures can be important. For example, in Table 6-2, one firm may score mostly 1's (low) and the other firm may score mostly 5's (high), which would present a challenging strategic problem.

The strategic-management process takes place largely within a particular organization's culture. Lorsch found that executives in successful companies are emotionally committed to the firm's culture, but he concluded that culture can inhibit strategic management in two basic ways. First, managers frequently miss the significance of changing external conditions because they are blinded by strongly held beliefs. Second, when a particular culture has been effective in the past, the natural response is to stick with it in the future, even during times of major strategic change.[7] An organization's culture must support the collective commitment of its people to a common purpose. It must foster competence and enthusiasm among managers and employees.

Organizational culture significantly affects business decisions and thus must be evaluated during an internal strategic-management audit. If strategies can capitalize on cultural strengths, such as a strong work ethic or highly ethical beliefs, then management often can swiftly and easily implement changes. However, if the firm's culture is not supportive, strategic changes may be ineffective or even counterproductive. A firm's culture can become antagonistic to new strategies, with the result being confusion and disorientation.

TABLE 6-2 **Fifteen Example (Possible) Aspects of an Organization's Culture**

Dimension	Low	Degree			High
1. Strong work ethic; arrive early and leave late	1	2	3	4	5
2. High ethical beliefs; clear code of business ethics followed	1	2	3	4	5
3. Formal dress; shirt and tie expected	1	2	3	4	5
4. Informal dress; many casual dress days	1	2	3	4	5
5. Socialize together outside of work	1	2	3	4	5
6. Do not question supervisor's decision	1	2	3	4	5
7. Encourage whistle-blowing	1	2	3	4	5
8. Be health conscious; have a wellness program	1	2	3	4	5
9. Allow substantial "working from home"	1	2	3	4	5
10. Encourage creativity, innovation, and open-mindness	1	2	3	4	5
11. Support women and minorities; no glass ceiling	1	2	3	4	5
12. Be highly socially responsible; be philanthropic	1	2	3	4	5
13. Have numerous meetings	1	2	3	4	5
14. Have a participative management style	1	2	3	4	5
15. Preserve the natural environment; have a sustainability program	1	2	3	4	5

An organization's culture should infuse individuals with enthusiasm for implementing strategies. Allarie and Firsirotu emphasized the need to understand culture:

Culture provides an explanation for the insuperable difficulties a firm encounters when it attempts to shift its strategic direction. Not only has the "right" culture become the essence and foundation of corporate excellence, it is also claimed that success or failure of reforms hinges on management's sagacity and ability to change the firm's driving culture in time and in time with required changes in strategies.[8]

The potential value of organizational culture has not been realized fully in the study of strategic management. Ignoring the effect that culture can have on relationships among the functional areas of business can result in barriers to communication, lack of coordination, and an inability to adapt to changing conditions. Some tension between culture and a firm's strategy is inevitable, but the tension should be monitored so that it does not reach a point at which relationships are severed and the culture becomes antagonistic. The resulting disarray among members of the organization would disrupt strategy formulation, implementation, and evaluation. In contrast, a supportive organizational culture can make managing much easier.

Internal strengths and weaknesses associated with a firm's culture sometimes are overlooked because of the interfunctional nature of this phenomenon. It is important, therefore, for strategists to understand their firm as a sociocultural system. Success is often determined by linkages between a firm's culture and strategies. The challenge of strategic management today is to bring about the changes in organizational culture and individual mind-sets that are needed to support the formulation, implementation, and evaluation of strategies.

Management

The **functions of management** consist of five basic activities: planning, organizing, motivating, staffing, and controlling. An overview of these activities is provided in Table 6-3. These activities are important to assess in strategic planning because an organization should continually capitalize on its management strengths and improve on its management weak areas.

Planning

The only thing certain about the future of any organization is change, and **planning** is the essential bridge between the present and the future that increases the likelihood of achieving desired results. Planning is the process by which one determines whether to attempt a task, works out the most effective way of reaching desired objectives, and prepares to overcome

TABLE 6-3 **The Basic Functions of Management**

Function	Description	Stage of Strategic-Management Process When Most Important
Planning	Planning consists of all those managerial activities related to preparing for the future. Specific tasks include forecasting, establishing objectives, devising strategies, developing policies, and setting goals.	Strategy Formulation
Organizing	Organizing includes all those managerial activities that result in a structure of task and authority relationships. Specific areas include organizational design, job specialization, job descriptions, job specifications, span of control, unity of command, coordination, job design, and job analysis.	Strategy Implementation
Motivating	Motivating involves efforts directed toward shaping human behavior. Specific topics include leadership, communication, work groups, behavior modification, delegation of authority, job enrichment, job satisfaction, needs fulfillment, organizational change, employee morale, and managerial morale.	Strategy Implementation
Staffing	Staffing activities are centered on personnel or human resource management. Included are wage and salary administration, employee benefits, interviewing, hiring, firing, training, management development, employee safety, affirmative action, equal employment opportunity, union relations, career development, personnel research, discipline policies, grievance procedures, and public relations.	Strategy Implementation
Controlling	Controlling refers to all those managerial activities directed toward ensuring that actual results are consistent with planned results. Key areas of concern include quality control, financial control, sales control, inventory control, expense control, analysis of variances, rewards, and sanctions.	Strategy Evaluation

unexpected difficulties with adequate resources. Planning is the start of the process by which an individual or business may turn empty dreams into achievements. Planning enables one to avoid the trap of working extremely hard but achieving little.

Planning is an up-front investment in success. Planning helps a firm achieve maximum effect from a given effort. Planning enables a firm to take into account relevant factors and focus on the critical ones. Planning helps ensure that the firm can be prepared for all reasonable eventualities and for all changes that will be needed. Planning enables a firm to gather the resources needed and carry out tasks in the most efficient way possible. Planning enables a firm to conserve its own resources, avoid wasting ecological resources, make a fair profit, and be seen as an effective, useful firm. Planning enables a firm to identify precisely what is to be achieved and to detail precisely the who, what, when, where, why, and how needed to achieve desired objectives. Planning enables a firm to assess whether the effort, costs, and implications associated with achieving desired objectives are warranted.[9] Planning is the cornerstone of effective strategy formulation. But even though it is considered the foundation of management, it is commonly the task that managers neglect most. Planning is essential for successful strategy implementation and strategy evaluation, largely because organizing, motivating, staffing, and controlling activities depend on good planning.

The process of planning must involve managers and employees throughout an organization. The time horizon for planning decreases from two to five years for top-level to less than six months for lower-level managers. The important point is that all managers do planning and should involve subordinates in the process to facilitate employee understanding and commitment.

Planning can have a positive impact on organizational and individual performance. Planning allows an organization to identify and take advantage of external opportunities as well as minimize the impact of external threats. Planning is more than extrapolating from the past and present into the future (long-range planning). It also includes developing a mission, forecasting future events and trends, establishing objectives, and choosing strategies to pursue (strategic planning).

An organization can develop synergy through planning. **Synergy** exists when everyone pulls together as a team that knows what it wants to achieve; synergy is the $2 + 2 = 5$ effect. By establishing and communicating clear objectives, employees and managers can work together toward desired results. Synergy can result in powerful competitive advantages. The strategic-management process itself is aimed at creating synergy in an organization.

Planning allows a firm to adapt to changing markets and thus to shape its own destiny. Strategic management can be viewed as a formal planning process that allows an organization to pursue proactive rather than reactive strategies. Successful organizations strive to control their own futures rather than merely react to external forces and events as they occur. Historically, organisms and organizations that have not adapted to changing conditions have become extinct. Swift adaptation is needed today more than ever because changes in markets, economies, and competitors worldwide are accelerating. Many firms did not adapt to the global recession of late and went out of business.

Organizing

The purpose of **organizing** is to achieve coordinated effort by defining task and authority relationships. Organizing means determining who does what and who reports to whom. There are countless examples in history of well-organized enterprises successfully competing against— and in some cases defeating—much stronger but less-organized firms. A well-organized firm generally has motivated managers and employees who are committed to seeing the organization succeed. Resources are allocated more effectively and used more efficiently in a well-organized firm than in a disorganized firm.

The organizing function of management can be viewed as consisting of three sequential activities: breaking down tasks into jobs (work specialization), combining jobs to form departments (departmentalization), and delegating authority. Breaking down tasks into jobs requires the development of job descriptions and job specifications. These tools clarify for both managers and employees what particular jobs entail. In *The Wealth of Nations*, published in 1776, Adam Smith cited the advantages of work specialization in the manufacture of pins:

> One man draws the wire, another straightens it, a third cuts it, a fourth points it, a fifth grinds it at the top for receiving the head. Ten men working in this manner can produce 48,000 pins in a single day, but if they had all wrought separately and independently, each might at best produce twenty pins in a day.[10]

Combining jobs to form departments results in an organizational structure, span of control, and a chain of command. Changes in strategy often require changes in structure because positions may be created, deleted, or merged. Organizational structure dictates how resources are allocated and how objectives are established in a firm. Allocating resources and establishing objectives geographically, for example, is much different from doing so by product or customer.

The most common forms of departmentalization are functional, divisional, strategic business unit, and matrix. These types of structure are discussed further in Chapter 10.

Delegating authority is an important organizing activity, as evidenced in the old saying "You can tell how good a manager is by observing how his or her department functions when he or she isn't there." Employees today are more educated and more capable of participating in organizational decision making than ever before. In most cases, they expect to be delegated authority and responsibility and to be held accountable for results. Delegation of authority is embedded in the strategic-management process.

Motivating

Motivating can be defined as the process of influencing people to accomplish specific objectives.[11] Motivation explains why some people work hard and others do not. Objectives, strategies, and policies have little chance of succeeding if employees and managers are not motivated to implement strategies once they are formulated. The motivating function of management includes at least four major components: leadership, group dynamics, communication, and organizational change.

When managers and employees of a firm strive to achieve high levels of productivity, this indicates that the firm's strategists are good leaders. Good leaders establish rapport with subordinates, empathize with their needs and concerns, set a good example, and are trustworthy and fair. Leadership includes developing a vision of the firm's future and inspiring people to work hard to achieve that vision. Kirkpatrick and Locke reported that certain traits also characterize effective leaders: knowledge of the business, cognitive ability, self-confidence, honesty, integrity, and drive.[12]Sun Tzu said: "Weak leadership can wreck the soundest strategy."

Research suggests that democratic behavior on the part of leaders results in more positive attitudes toward change and higher productivity than does autocratic behavior. Drucker said:

Leadership is not a magnetic personality. That can just as well be demagoguery. It is not "making friends and influencing people." That is flattery. Leadership is the lifting of a person's vision to higher sights, the raising of a person's performance to a higher standard, the building of a person's personality beyond its normal limitations.[13]

Group dynamics play a major role in employee morale and satisfaction. Informal groups or coalitions form in every organization. The norms of coalitions can range from being positive to negative toward management. It is important, therefore, that strategists identify the composition and nature of informal groups in an organization to facilitate strategy formulation, implementation, and evaluation. Leaders of informal groups are especially important in formulating and implementing strategy changes.

Communication, perhaps the most important word in management, is a major component in motivation. An organization's system of communication determines whether strategies can be implemented successfully. Good two-way communication is vital for gaining support for departmental and divisional objectives and policies. Top-down communication can encourage bottom-up communication. The strategic-management process becomes a lot easier when subordinates are encouraged to discuss their concerns, reveal their problems, provide recommendations, and give suggestions. A primary reason for instituting strategic management is to build and support effective communication networks throughout the firm.

The manager of tomorrow must be able to get his people to commit themselves to the business, whether they are machine operators or junior vice-presidents. The key issue will be empowerment, a term whose strength suggests the need to get beyond merely sharing a little information and a bit of decision making.[14]

Staffing

The management function of **staffing**, also called **personnel management** or **human resource management**, includes activities such as recruiting, interviewing, testing, selecting, orienting, training, developing, caring for, evaluating, rewarding, disciplining, promoting, transferring, demoting, and dismissing employees, as well as managing union relations.

Staffing activities play a major role in strategy-implementation efforts, and for this reason, human resource managers are becoming more actively involved in the strategic-management process. It is important to identify strengths and weaknesses in the staffing area.

The complexity and importance of human resource activities have increased to such a degree that all but the smallest organizations now need a full-time human resource manager. Numerous court cases that directly affect staffing activities are decided each day. Organizations and individuals can be penalized severely for not following federal, state, and local laws and guidelines related to staffing. Line managers simply cannot stay abreast of all the legal developments and requirements regarding staffing. The human resources department coordinates staffing decisions in the firm so that an organization as a whole meets legal requirements. This department also provides needed consistency in administering company rules, wages, policies, and employee benefits as well as collective bargaining with unions.

Human resource management is particularly challenging for international companies. For example, the inability of spouses and children to adapt to new surroundings can be a staffing problem in overseas transfers. The problems include premature returns, job performance slumps, resignations, discharges, low morale, marital discord, and general discontent. Firms such as Ford Motor and ExxonMobil screen and interview spouses and children before assigning persons to overseas positions. 3M Corporation introduces children to peers in the target country and offers spouses educational benefits.

Controlling

The **controlling** function of management includes all of those activities undertaken to ensure that actual operations conform to planned operations. All managers in an organization have controlling responsibilities, such as conducting performance evaluations and taking necessary action to minimize inefficiencies. The controlling function of management is particularly important for effective strategy evaluation. Controlling consists of four basic steps:

1. Establishing performance standards
2. Measuring individual and organizational performance
3. Comparing actual performance to planned performance standards
4. Taking corrective actions

Measuring individual performance is often conducted ineffectively or not at all in organizations. Some reasons for this shortcoming are that evaluations can create confrontations that most managers prefer to avoid, can take more time than most managers are willing to give, and can require skills that many managers lack. No single approach to measuring individual performance is without limitations. For this reason, an organization should examine various methods, such as the graphic rating scale, the behaviorally anchored rating scale, and the critical incident method, and then develop or select a performance-appraisal approach that best suits the firm's needs. Increasingly, firms are striving to link organizational performance with managers' and employees' pay. This topic is discussed further in Chapter 10.

Management Audit Checklist of Questions

The following checklist of questions can help determine specific strengths and weaknesses in the functional area of business. An answer of *no* to any question could indicate a potential weakness, although the strategic significance and implications of negative answers, of course, will vary by organization, industry, and severity of the weakness. Positive or *yes* answers to the checklist questions suggest potential areas of strength.

1. Does the firm use strategic-management concepts?
2. Are company objectives and goals measurable and well communicated?
3. Do managers at all hierarchical levels plan effectively?
4. Do managers delegate authority well?
5. Is the organization's structure appropriate?
6. Are job descriptions and job specifications clear?
7. Is employee morale high?
8. Are employee turnover and absenteeism low?
9. Are organizational reward and control mechanisms effective?

Marketing

Marketing can be described as the process of defining, anticipating, creating, and fulfilling customers' needs and wants for products and services. There are seven basic **functions of marketing**: (1) customer analysis, (2) selling products and services, (3) product and service planning, (4) pricing, (5) distribution, (6) marketing research, and (7) opportunity analysis.[15] Understanding these functions helps strategists identify and evaluate marketing strengths and weaknesses.

Customer Analysis

Customer analysis—the examination and evaluation of consumer needs, desires, and wants—involves administering customer surveys, analyzing consumer information, evaluating market positioning strategies, developing customer profiles, and determining optimal market segmentation strategies. The information generated by customer analysis can be essential in developing an effective mission statement. Customer profiles can reveal the demographic characteristics of an organization's customers. Buyers, sellers, distributors, salespeople, managers, wholesalers, retailers, suppliers, and creditors can all participate in gathering information to successfully identify customers' needs and wants. Successful organizations continually monitor present and potential customers' buying patterns.

Selling Products and Services

Successful strategy implementation generally rests on the ability of an organization to sell some product or service. **Selling** includes many marketing activities, such as advertising, sales promotion, publicity, personal selling, sales force management, customer relations, and dealer relations. These activities are especially critical when a firm pursues a market penetration strategy. The effectiveness of various selling tools for consumer and industrial products varies. Personal selling is most important for industrial goods companies, whereas advertising is most important for consumer goods companies.

For example, the J.M. Smucker Company has $5.5 and 4.8 billion in revenue in 2012 and 2011, respectively, and spent $119 and $115 million in advertising during those two years, comprising 2.1 and 2.4 percent of revenues, respectively. About 3 percent of revenues is normal for companies to spend on advertising although this can vary across industries. J.M. Smucker has a product portfolio that includes coffee, peanut butter, fruit spreads, jams, shortening and oils, baking mixes, canned milk, flour, syrups, pickles, and more. One aspect of ads recently is that they generally take more direct aim at competitors, and this marketing practice is holding true in our bad economic times. Nick Brien at Mediabrands says, "Ads have to get combative in bad times. It's a dog fight, and it's about getting leaner and meaner." Ads are less lavish and glamorous today and are also more interactive. Table 6-4 lists specific characteristics of ads in response to the economic hard times many people nationwide and worldwide are facing.

Marketers spent about $3 million per 30-second advertising spot during the 2012 Super Bowl. Advertising can be expensive, and that is why marketing is a major business function to be studied carefully. Without marketing, even the best products and services have little chance of being successful.

Chief marketing officers (CMOs) such as Eduardo Conrado at Motorola now spend more than 50 percent of their budget on technology to manage activities like online marketing and social media.[16] Marketing is becoming technical with software to track and target customers and manage customer relationships, predict consumer behavior, run online storefronts, analyze social media, manage websites, and craft targeted advertisements. IBM in response to this trend is shifting its attention from CIOs to CMOs as their primary clients.

TABLE 6-4 Desirable Characteristics of Ads Today

1. Take direct aim at competitors; so leaner, meaner, and to the point.
2. Be less lavish and glamorous, requiring less production dollars to develop.
3. Be short and sweet, mostly 10- and 15-second ads rather than longer than 30 seconds.
4. "Make you feel good" or "put you in a good mood" because (a) ads can be more easily avoided than ever and (b) people are experiencing hard times and seek comfort.
5. Be more pervasive such as on buses, elevators, cell phones, and trucks.
6. Appear less on websites as banner ads become the new junk mail.
7. Red will overtake the color orange as the most popular ad color.
8. More than ever emphasize low price and value versus rivals.
9. More than ever emphasize how the product or service will make your life better.

Source: Based on Suzanne Vranica, "Ads to Go Leaner, Meaner in '09," *Wall Street Journal*, January 5, 2009, B8.

The world's largest social network, Facebook may epitomize where the advertising industry is going. Facebook allows a company to "leverage the loyalty" of its best customers. If you have recently gotten engaged and updated your Facebook status, you may start seeing ads from local jewelers who have used Facebook's automated ad system to target you. Facebook enables any firm today to effectively target their exact audience with perfect advertising.[17] In performing a strategic planning analysis, in addition to comparing rival firms' websites, it is important to compare rival firms' Facebook page.

One of the last off-limit advertising outlets has historically been books, but with the proliferation of e-books, marketers are experimenting more and more with advertising to consumers as they read e-books. New ads are being targeted based on the book's content and the demographic profile of the reader. Digital e-book companies such as Wowio and Amazon are trying to insert ads between chapters and along borders of digital pages. Random House says its e-books will soon include ads, but only with author approval.

Determining organizational strengths and weaknesses in the selling function of marketing is an important part of performing an internal strategic-management audit. With regard to advertising products and services on the Internet, a new trend is to base advertising rates exclusively on sales rates. This new accountability contrasts sharply with traditional broadcast and print advertising, which bases rates on the number of persons expected to see a given advertisement. The new cost-per-sale online advertising rates are possible because any website can monitor which user clicks on which advertisement and then can record whether that consumer actually buys the product. If there are no sales, then the advertisement is free.

Product and Service Planning

Product and service planning includes activities such as test marketing; product and brand positioning; devising warranties; packaging; determining product options, features, style, and quality; deleting old products; and providing for customer service. Product and service planning is particularly important when a company is pursuing product development or diversification.

One of the most effective product and service planning techniques is **test marketing.** Test markets allow an organization to test alternative marketing plans and to forecast future sales of new products. In conducting a test market project, an organization must decide how many cities to include, which cities to include, how long to run the test, what information to collect during the test, and what action to take after the test has been completed. Test marketing is used more frequently by consumer goods companies than by industrial goods companies. Test marketing can allow an organization to avoid substantial losses by revealing weak products and ineffective marketing approaches before large-scale production begins.

After extensive test marketing, the chocolate maker Hershey recently launched its first candy in China, a condensed milk candy. The company also opened a new Shanghai-based Asia Innovation Center to test market many potential premium milk type chocolate candies in various Asian countries. Hershey increased its number of stores in China by 32 percent and its sales force by 60 percent in 2013.

Pricing

In late 2012, J.C. Penney abandoned its month-long specials that cut prices of select items by 20 to 29 percent, and instead implemented permanent price cuts on a large amount of merchandise in their stores. Penney's pricing strategy gave consumers two options: everyday low prices and clearance sales on certain items. Penney's price change strategy came as the company's stock price had dropped 40 percent in recent months. To support the new pricing strategy, Penney's began offering free haircuts every Sunday for children aged 5 to 12. Free is a good price and this program exists in 949 of Penney's 1,100 stores totaling about 1 million haircuts per month. "It definitely drove new people and reintroduced J.C. Penney to existing customers who didn't know about the latest changes," said Jan Hodges, senior vice president of Penney's salon services. But in an about-face after losses, Penney's fired CEO Ron Johnson, brought back his predecessor Myron "Mike" Ullman, and began a "we're listening" campaign on Facebook to woo customers back into the stores.

Five major stakeholders affect **pricing** decisions: consumers, governments, suppliers, distributors, and competitors. Sometimes an organization will pursue a forward integration strategy primarily to gain better control over prices charged to consumers. Governments can impose constraints on price fixing, price discrimination, minimum prices, unit pricing, price advertising, and price controls. For example, the Robinson-Patman Act prohibits manufacturers and wholesalers from discriminating in price among channel member purchasers (suppliers and distributors) if competition is injured.

Competing organizations must be careful not to coordinate discounts, credit terms, or condition of sale; not to discuss prices, markups, and costs at trade association meetings; and not to arrange to issue new price lists on the same date, to rotate low bids on contracts, or to uniformly restrict production to maintain high prices. Strategists should view price from both a short-run and a long-run perspective because competitors can copy price changes with relative ease. Often a dominant firm will aggressively match all price cuts by competitors.

With regard to pricing, as the value of the dollar increases, U.S. multinational companies have a choice. They can raise prices in the local currency of a foreign country or risk losing sales and market share. Alternatively, multinational firms can keep prices steady and face reduced profit when their export revenue is reported in the United States in dollars.

Intense price competition, coupled with Internet price-comparative shopping, has reduced profit margins to bare minimum levels for most companies. For example, when Toys 'R' Us introduced its first tablet for kids (the Tabeo) in late 2012 for $149.99, the company's three main competitors instantly reduced their tablet for kids: the Kurlo 7 by Techno Source, the Lexibook by Lexibook Ltd., and the Meep by Oregon Scientific. To help combat Internet comparative shopping, the Tabeo is available only at Toys 'R' Us stores.

Nike raised its shoe and clothing prices by 5 to 10 percent in late 2012 when the company introduced its new LeBron James basketball shoe that sells for $315. That shoe features embedded motion sensors that can measure how high players jump. Even the price of Nike's venerable Converse All-Star sneaker increased to just slightly more than $50. Nike faces rising labor costs in China, where it manufactures a third of its products.

Target Corp. recently joined Best Buy in offering to match online prices of rival retailers. Both companies are seeking to combat "showrooming" by shoppers who check out products in their stores but buy them on rival's websites. Both Target and Best Buy are matching prices from Amazon.com and Walmart.com and Toysrus.com.

Distribution

Distribution includes warehousing, distribution channels, distribution coverage, retail site locations, sales territories, inventory levels and location, transportation carriers, wholesaling, and retailing. Most producers today do not sell their goods directly to consumers. Various marketing entities act as intermediaries; they bear a variety of names such as wholesalers, retailers, brokers, facilitators, agents, vendors—or simply distributors.

Distribution becomes especially important when a firm is striving to implement a market development or forward integration strategy. Some of the most complex and challenging decisions facing a firm concern product distribution. Intermediaries flourish in our economy because many producers lack the financial resources and expertise to carry out direct marketing. Manufacturers who could afford to sell directly to the public often can gain greater returns by expanding and improving their manufacturing operations.

Successful organizations identify and evaluate alternative ways to reach their ultimate market. Possible approaches vary from direct selling to using just one or many wholesalers and retailers. Strengths and weaknesses of each channel alternative should be determined according to economic, control, and adaptive criteria. Organizations should consider the costs and benefits of various wholesaling and retailing options. They must consider the need to motivate and control channel members and the need to adapt to changes in the future. Once a marketing channel is chosen, an organization usually must adhere to it for an extended period of time.

Marketing Research

Marketing research is the systematic gathering, recording, and analyzing of data about problems relating to the marketing of goods and services. Marketing research can uncover critical strengths and weaknesses, and marketing researchers employ numerous scales, instruments, procedures, concepts, and techniques to gather information. Marketing research activities support all of the major business functions of an organization. Organizations that possess excellent marketing research skills have a definite strength in pursuing generic strategies. The president of PepsiCo said,

Looking at the competition is the company's best form of market research. The majority of our strategic successes are ideas that we borrow from the marketplace, usually from a small regional or local competitor. In each case, we spot a promising new idea, improve on it, and then out-execute our competitor.[18]

Cost/Benefit Analysis

The seventh function of marketing is **cost/benefit analysis,** which involves assessing the costs, benefits, and risks associated with marketing decisions. Three steps are required to perform a cost/benefit analysis: (1) compute the total costs associated with a decision, (2) estimate the total benefits from the decision, and (3) compare the total costs with the total benefits. When expected benefits exceed total costs, an opportunity becomes more attractive. Sometimes the variables included in a cost/benefit analysis cannot be quantified or even measured, but usually reasonable estimates can be made to allow the analysis to be performed. One key factor to be considered is risk. Cost/benefit analysis should also be performed when a company is evaluating alternative ways to be socially responsible.

The practice of cost/benefit analysis differs among countries and industries. Some of the main differences include the types of impacts that are included as costs and benefits within appraisals, the extent to which impacts are expressed in monetary terms, and differences in the discount rate. Government agencies across the world rely on a basic set of key cost/benefit indicators, including the following:

1. net present value (NPV)
2. present value of benefits (PVB)
3. present value of costs (PVC)
4. benefit cost ratio (BCR) = PVB / PVC
5. Net benefit = PVB – PVC
6. NPV/k (where k is the level of funds available)[19]

Marketing Audit Checklist of Questions

The following questions about marketing must be examined in strategic planning:

1. Are markets segmented effectively?
2. Is the organization positioned well among competitors?
3. Has the firm's market share been increasing?
4. Are present channels of distribution reliable and cost effective?
5. Does the firm have an effective sales organization?
6. Does the firm conduct market research?
7. Are product quality and customer service good?
8. Are the firm's products and services priced appropriately?
9. Does the firm have an effective promotion, advertising, and publicity strategy?
10. Are marketing, planning, and budgeting effective?
11. Do the firm's marketing managers have adequate experience and training?
12. Is the firm's Internet presence excellent as compared to rivals?

Finance and Accounting

Financial condition is often considered the single best measure of a firm's competitive position and overall attractiveness to investors. Determining an organization's financial strengths and weaknesses is essential to effectively formulating strategies. A firm's liquidity, leverage, working capital, profitability, asset utilization, cash flow, and equity can eliminate some strategies as being feasible alternatives. Financial factors often alter existing strategies and change implementation plans.

Especially good websites from which to obtain financial information about firms are provided in Table 6-5.

Finance and Accounting Functions

According to James Van Horne, the **functions of finance/accounting** comprise three decisions: the investment decision, the financing decision, and the dividend decision.[20] Financial ratio analysis is the most widely used method for determining an organization's strengths and weaknesses

TABLE 6-5 Excellent Websites to Obtain Information on Companies, Including Financial Ratios

1. www.money.msn.com
2. http://finance.yahoo.com
3. www.morningstar.com
4. www.hoovers.com
5. http://globaledge.msu.edu/industries/

in the investment, financing, and dividend areas. Because the functional areas of business are so closely related, financial ratios can signal strengths or weaknesses in management, marketing, production, R&D, and MIS activities. Financial ratios are equally applicable in for-profit and nonprofit organizations. Even though nonprofit organizations obviously would not have return-on-investment or earnings-per-share ratios, they would routinely monitor many other special ratios. For example, a church would monitor the ratio of dollar contributions to number of members, whereas a zoo would monitor dollar food sales to number of visitors. A university would monitor number of students divided by number of professors. Therefore, be creative when performing ratio analysis for nonprofit organizations because they strive to be financially sound just as for-profit firms do. Nonprofit organizations need strategic planning just as much as for-profit firms.

The **investment decision,** also called **capital budgeting,** is the allocation and reallocation of capital and resources to projects, products, assets, and divisions of an organization. Once strategies are formulated, capital budgeting decisions are required to successfully implement strategies. The **financing decision** determines the best capital structure for the firm and includes examining various methods by which the firm can raise capital (for example, by issuing stock, increasing debt, selling assets, or using a combination of these approaches). The financing decision must consider both short-term and long-term needs for working capital. Two key financial ratios that indicate whether a firm's financing decisions have been effective are the debt-to-equity ratio and the debt-to-total-assets ratio.

Dividend decisions concern issues such as the percentage of earnings paid to stockholders, the stability of dividends paid over time, and the repurchase or issuance of stock. Dividend decisions determine the amount of funds that are retained in a firm compared to the amount paid out to stockholders. Three financial ratios that are helpful in evaluating a firm's dividend decisions are the earnings-per-share ratio, the dividends-per-share ratio, and the price-earnings ratio. The benefits of paying dividends to investors must be balanced against the benefits of internally retaining funds, and there is no set formula on how to balance this trade-off. For the reasons listed here, dividends are sometimes paid out even when funds could be better reinvested in the business or when the firm has to obtain outside sources of capital:

1. Paying cash dividends is customary. Failure to do so could be thought of as a stigma. A dividend change is considered a signal about the future.
2. Dividends represent a sales point for investment bankers. Some institutional investors can buy only dividend-paying stocks.
3. Shareholders often demand dividends, even in companies with great opportunities for reinvesting all available funds.
4. A myth exists that paying dividends will result in a higher stock price.

In the second quarter of 2012 alone, 505 U.S. companies boosted their dividends, after 677 firms boosted their dividends in the first quarter. In fact, 70 percent of the stocks in the S&P 500 raised their dividend in 2012. S&P companies are on average today paying out 31 percent of their earnings in the form of dividends, but that is down from 52 percent of earnings in some years.[21]For calendar 2013, companies in the S&P 500 are expected to pay at least $300 billion in dividends, topping 2012's $282 billion. Companies are also buying back their own stock (called Treasury stock) at record levels.

Unlike most firms, RadioShack Corp. recently suspended its 12.5 cents-a-share quarterly dividend, saving $50 million annually to avoid a liquidity crunch as the company seeks to lower its debt. The 91-year-old company has 4,700 stores in towns and cities across the United States and Mexico, but RadioShack is struggling to compete with online-only rivals such as Amazon because customers increasingly order electronics online.

Based in London, BP PLC recently boosted its quarterly dividend 13 percent to $0.09 a share. BP's board, in announcing the increase, said the company has a bright future with its recent $26.8 billion cash-and-shares deal to acquire a 20 percent stake in Russia's state-controlled OAO Rosneft. Despite not yet settling lawsuits related to the Gulf of Mexico Deepwater Horizons oil spill, BP posted a net profit for the three months ended September, 30, 2012, of $5.43 billion, up from $5.04 billion the prior year.

Costco in late 2012 borrowed $3.5 billion just to pay its shareholders a $7 dividend per share, totaling $3 billion. The dividend payout, without the borrowing, would have depleted Costco's cash account. Many companies near the end of 2012 paid "special" dividends, 175 in November 2012 alone or firms paid dividends early, to avoid the expected 2013 substantial increase in taxes on dividends.

Basic Types of Financial Ratios

Financial ratios are computed from an organization's income statement and balance sheet. Computing financial ratios is like taking a picture because the results reflect a situation at just one point in time. Comparing ratios over time and to industry averages is more likely to result in meaningful statistics that can be used to identify and evaluate strengths and weaknesses. Trend analysis, illustrated in Figure 6-3, is a useful technique that incorporates both the time and industry average dimensions of financial ratios. Note that the dotted lines reveal projected ratios. Some websites, such as those provided in Table 6-5, calculate financial ratios and provide data with charts.

Table 6-6 provides a summary of key financial ratios showing how each ratio is calculated and what each ratio measures. However, all the ratios are not significant for all industries and companies. For example, accounts receivable turnover and average collection period are not meaningful to a company that primarily does a cash receipts business. Key financial ratios can be classified into the following five types:

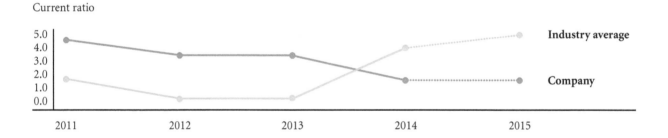

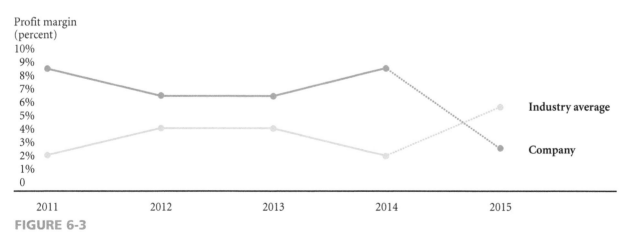

FIGURE 6-3

A Financial Ratio Trend Analysis

1. **Liquidity ratios** measure a firm's ability to meet maturing short-term obligations.

   Current ratio

   Quick (or acid-test) ratio

2. **Leverage ratios** measure the extent to which a firm has been financed by debt.

   Debt-to-total-assets ratio

   Debt-to-equity ratio

   Long-term debt-to-equity ratio

   Times-interest-earned (or coverage) ratio

3. **Activity ratios** measure how effectively a firm is using its resources.

   Inventory turnover

   Fixed assets turnover

   Total assets turnover

   Accounts receivable turnover

   Average collection period

4. **Profitability ratios** measure management's overall effectiveness as shown by the returns generated on sales and investment.

   Gross profit margin

   Operating profit margin

   Net profit margin

   Return on total assets (ROA)

   Return on stockholders' equity (ROE)

   Earnings per share (EPS)

   Price-earnings ratio

5. **Growth ratios** measure the firm's ability to maintain its economic position in the growth of the economy and industry.

   Sales

   Net income

   Earnings per share

   Dividends per share

Financial ratio analysis must go beyond the actual calculation and interpretation of ratios. The analysis should be conducted on three separate fronts:

1. *How has each ratio changed over time?* This information provides a means of evaluating historical trends. It is important to note whether each ratio has been historically increasing, decreasing, or nearly constant. For example, a 10 percent profit margin could be bad if the trend has been down 20 percent each of the last three years. But a 10 percent profit margin could be excellent if the trend has been up, up, up. Therefore, calculate the percentage change in each ratio from one year to the next to assess historical financial performance on that dimension. Identify and examine large percent changes in a financial ratio from one year to the next.
2. *How does each ratio compare to industry norms?* A firm's inventory turnover ratio may appear impressive at first glance but may pale when compared to industry standards or norms. Industries can differ dramatically on certain ratios. For example grocery companies, such as Kroger, have a high inventory turnover whereas automobile dealerships have a lower turnover. Therefore, comparison of a firm's ratios within its particular industry can be essential in determining strength and weakness.

TABLE 6-6 A Summary of Key Financial Ratios

Ratio	How Calculated	What It Measures
Liquidity Ratios		
Current Ratio	$\dfrac{\text{Current assets}}{\text{Current liabilities}}$	The extent to which a firm can meet its short-term obligations
Quick Ratio	$\dfrac{\text{Current assets minus inventory}}{\text{Current liabilities}}$	The extent to which a firm can meet its short-term obligations without relying on the sale of its inventories
Leverage Ratios		
Debt-to-Total-Assets Ratio	$\dfrac{\text{Total debt}}{\text{Total assets}}$	The percentage of total funds that are provided by creditors
Debt-to-Equity Ratio	$\dfrac{\text{Total debt}}{\text{Total stackholders' equity}}$	The percentage of total funds provided by creditors versus by owners
Long-Term Debt-to-Equity Ratio	$\dfrac{\text{Long-term debt}}{\text{Total stackholders' equity}}$	The balance between debt and equity in a firm's long-term capital structure
Times-Interest-Earned Ratio	$\dfrac{\text{Profits before interest and taxes}}{\text{Total interest charges}}$	The extent to which earnings can decline without the firm becoming unable to meet its annual interest costs
Activity Ratios		
Inventory Turnover	$\dfrac{\text{Sales}}{\text{Inventory of finished goods}}$	Whether a firm holds excessive stocks of inventories and whether a firm is slowly selling its inventories compared to the industry average
Fixed Assets Turnover	$\dfrac{\text{Sales}}{\text{Fixed assets}}$	Sales productivity and plant and equipment utilization
Total Assets Turnover	$\dfrac{\text{Sales}}{\text{Total assets}}$	Whether a firm is generating a sufficient volume of business for the size of its asset investment
Accounts Receivable Turnover	$\dfrac{\text{Annual credit sales}}{\text{Accounts receivable}}$	The average length of time it takes a firm to collect credit sales (in percentage terms)
Average Collection Period	$\dfrac{\text{Accounts receivable}}{\text{Total credit sales/365 days}}$	The average length of time it takes a firm to collect on credit sales (in days)
Profitability Ratios		
Gross Profit Margin	$\dfrac{\text{Sales minus cost of goods sold}}{\text{Sales}}$	The total margin available to cover operating expenses and yield a profit
Operating Profit Margin	$\dfrac{\text{Earnings before interest and taxes EBIT}}{\text{Sales}}$	Profitability without concern for taxes and interest
Net Profit Margin	$\dfrac{\text{Net income}}{\text{Sales}}$	After-tax profits per dollar of sales
Return on Total Assets (ROA)	$\dfrac{\text{Net income}}{\text{Total assets}}$	After-tax profits per dollar of assets; this ratio is also called return on investment (ROI)
Return on Stockholders' Equity (ROE)		After-tax profits per dollar of stockholders' investment in the firm
Earnings Per Share (EPS)	$\dfrac{\text{Net income}}{\text{Number of shares of common stock outstanding}}$	Earnings available to the owners of common stock
Price-Earnings Ratio	$\dfrac{\text{Market price per share}}{\text{Earnings per share}}$	Attractiveness of firm on equity markets
Growth Ratios		
Sales	Annual percentage growth in total sales	Firm's growth rate in sales
Net Income	Annual percentage growth in profits	Firm's growth rate in profits
Earnings Per Share	Annual percentage growth in EPS	Firm's growth rate in EPS
Dividends Per Share	Annual percentage growth in dividends per share	Firm's growth rate in dividends per share

3. *How does each ratio compare with key competitors?* Oftentimes competition is more intense between several competitors in a given industry or location than across all rival firms in the industry. When this is true, financial ratio analysis should include comparison to those key competitors. For example, if a firm's profitability ratio is trending up over time and compares favorably to the industry average, but it is trending down relative to its leading competitor, there may be reason for concern.

Financial ratio analysis is not without some limitations. First of all, financial ratios are based on accounting data, and firms differ in their treatment of such items as depreciation, inventory valuation, R&D expenditures, pension plan costs, mergers, and taxes. Also, seasonal factors can influence comparative ratios. Therefore, conformity to industry composite ratios does not establish with certainty that a firm is performing normally or that it is well managed. Likewise, departures from industry averages do not always indicate that a firm is doing especially well or badly. For example, a high inventory turnover ratio could indicate efficient inventory management and a strong working capital position, but it also could indicate a serious inventory shortage and a weak working capital position.

Another limitation of financial ratios in terms of including them as key internal factors in the upcoming IFE Matrix is that financial ratios are not very "actionable" in terms of revealing potential strategies needed, i.e. since they generally are based on performance of the overall firm. For example, to include as a key internal factor that the firm's "current ratio increased from 1.8 to 2.1" is not as "actionable" as "the firm's fragrance division revenues increased 18 percent in Africa in 2013." Chapter 7 discusses the importance of selecting "actionable" key factors, both externally and internally, upon which to formulate strategies. Selecting "actionable" key factors, both externally and internally, upon which to formulate strategies is important.

A firm's financial condition depends not only on the functions of finance, but also on many other factors that include (1) management, marketing, management production and operations, R&D, and MIS; (2) actions by competitors, suppliers, distributors, creditors, customers, and shareholders; and (3) economic, social, cultural, demographic, environmental, political, governmental, legal, and technological trends.

Breakeven Analysis

Because consumers remain price sensitive, many firms have lowered prices to compete. As a firm lowers prices, its **breakeven (BE) point** in terms of units sold increases, as illustrated in Figure 6-4. The breakeven point can be defined as the quantity of units that a firm must sell for its total revenues (TR) to equal its total costs (TC). Note that the before and after chart in Figure 6-4 reveals that the TR line rotates to the right with a decrease in price, thus increasing the quantity (Q) that must be sold just to break even. Increasing the breakeven point is thus a huge drawback of lowering prices. Of course when rivals are lowering prices, a firm may have to lower prices anyway to compete. However, the breakeven concept should be kept in mind because it is so important, especially in recessionary times.

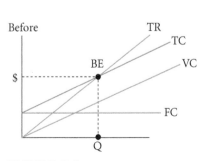
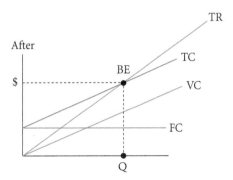

FIGURE 6-4

A Before and After Breakeven Chart When Prices Are Lowered

Notice in Figure 6-5 that increasing fixed costs (FC) also raises a firm's breakeven quantity. Note the before and after chart in Figure 6-5 reveals that adding fixed costs such as more stores, or more plants, or even more advertising as part of a strategic plan raises the TC line, which makes the intersection of the TC and TR lines at a point farther down the Quantity axis. Increasing a firm's FC thus significantly raises the quantity of goods that must be sold to break even. This is not just theory for the sake of theory. Firms with less fixed costs, such as Apple and Amazon.com, have lower breakeven points, which give them a decided competitive advantage in harsh economic times. Figure 6-5 reveals that adding **fixed costs (FC),** such as plant, equipment, stores, advertising, and land, may be detrimental whenever there is doubt that significantly more units can be sold to offset those expenditures.

Firms must be cognizant of the fact that lowering prices and adding fixed costs could be a catastrophic double whammy because the firm's breakeven quantity needed to be sold is increased dramatically. Figure 6-6 illustrates this double whammy. Note how far the breakeven point shifts with both a price decrease and an increase in fixed costs. If a firm does not break-even, then it will of course incur losses, and losses are not good, especially sustained losses.

Finally, note in Figures 6-4, 6-5, and 6-6 that **variable costs (VC),** such as labor and materials, when increased, have the effect of raising the breakeven point, too. Raising VC is reflected by the VC line shifting left or becoming steeper. When the TR line remains constant, the effect of increasing VC is to increase TC, which increases the point at which TR = TC = BE.

The formula for calculating breakeven point is BE Quantity = TFC divided by (price – VC). In other words, the quantity or units of product that need to be sold for a firm to breakeven is total fixed costs divided by (price per unit – variable costs per unit). A breakeven problem is given in Table 6-7.

Suffice it to say here that various strategies can have dramatically beneficial or harmful effects on the firm's financial condition because of the concept of breakeven analysis.

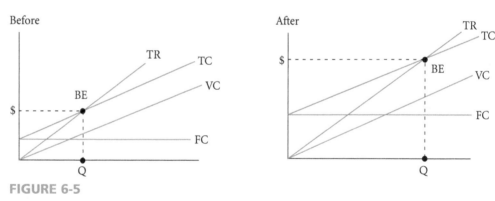

FIGURE 6-5

A Before and After Breakeven Chart When Fixed Costs Are Increased

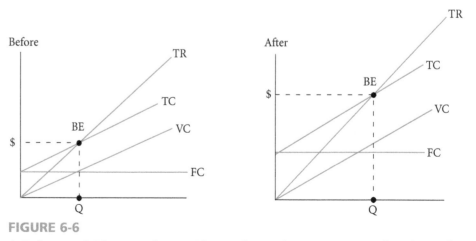

FIGURE 6-6

A Before and After Breakeven Chart When Prices Are Lowered and Fixed Costs Are Increased

TABLE 6-7 Applying Breakeven Analysis for Joy's Day Care

Seeing a need for childcare in her town, Joy is considering opening her own day-care service. Joy's Day Care needs to be affordable, so Joy would like to care for each child for $12 a day. But Joy also wants to make money. Joy needs to know how many children she will have to watch per day to make money. Joy gathered the following information about her potential new business.

- The month of June has 20 workdays, Monday through Friday for 4 weeks.
- Insurance and rent on her business will be $200 and $400, respectively, per month.
- Expenses per student per day will be snacks (2 @ $1.00) + meals (2 @ $3.00).

Joy's Analysis

Breakeven = Operating Expenses ÷ ($12.00 – $8.00)

Breakeven = $600 ÷ $4.00 Breakeven = 150 units (children) in June.

Because there are 20 days in June, Joy must watch 150 ÷ 20 = 7.5 kids, or 8 children every day to make a profit.

Joy's Conclusion

Thanks to breakeven analysis, Joy is pondering whether or not she can care for 8 children daily. Instead of abruptly opening the business, Joy is now considering adding a helper for $50 per day and charging $20 per student per day. How many students now would Joy have to care for to make a profit under this scenario? (Answer 6.6 = 7) What do you think would be an ideal scenario for Joy in planning for her new business?

There are some limitations of breakeven analysis, including the following points:

1. Breakeven analysis is only a supply side (i.e., costs only) analysis because it tells you nothing about what sales are likely to be for the product at various prices.
2. It assumes that fixed costs are constant. Although this is true in the short run, an increase in the scale of production will cause fixed costs to rise.
3. It assumes average variable costs are constant per unit of output, at least in the range of likely quantities of sales.
4. It assumes that the quantity of goods produced is equal to the quantity of goods sold (i.e., there is no change in beginning or ending inventory).
5. In multiproduct companies, it assumes that the relative proportions of each product sold and produced are constant (i.e., the sales mix is constant).[22]

Finance and Accounting Audit Checklist

The following finance and accounting questions, like the similar questions about marketing and management previously, should be examined:

1. Where is the firm financially strong and weak as indicated by financial ratio analyses?
2. Can the firm raise needed short-term capital?
3. Can the firm raise needed long-term capital through debt or equity?
4. Does the firm have sufficient working capital?
5. Are capital budgeting procedures effective?
6. Are dividend payout policies reasonable?
7. Does the firm have good relations with its investors and stockholders?
8. Are the firm's financial managers experienced and well trained?
9. Is the firm's debt situation excellent?

Production and Operations

The extent to which a manufacturing plant's output reaches its potential output is called **capacity utilization,** a key strategic variable. The higher the capacity utilization the better because otherwise equipment may sit idle. The estimated plant capacity utilization in Europe for the major auto producers is Volkswagen (84%), Renault (77%), Peugeot (73%), Ford (66%), GM (60%), and Fiat (55%).[23]

The **production/operations function** of a business consists of all those activities that transform inputs into goods and services. Production and operations management deals with inputs, transformations, and outputs that vary across industries and markets. A manufacturing operation transforms or converts inputs such as raw materials, labor, capital, machines, and facilities into finished goods and services. As indicated in Table 6-8, Roger Schroeder suggested

TABLE 6-8 **The Basic Functions (Decisions) Within Production/Operations**

Decision Areas	Example Decisions
1. Process	These decisions include choice of technology, facility layout, process flow analysis, facility location, line balancing, process control, and transportation analysis. Distances from raw materials to production sites to customers are a major consideration.
2. Capacity	These decisions include forecasting, facilities planning, aggregate planning, scheduling, capacity planning, and queuing analysis. Capacity utilization is a major consideration.
3. Inventory	These decisions involve managing the level of raw materials, work-in-process, and finished goods, especially considering what to order, when to order, how much to order, and materials handling.
4. Workforce	These decisions involve managing the skilled, unskilled, clerical, and managerial employees by caring for job design, work measurement, job enrichment, work standards, and motivation techniques.
5. Quality	These decisions are aimed at ensuring that high-quality goods and services are produced by caring for quality control, sampling, testing, quality assurance, and cost control.

Source: Based on R. Schroeder, *Operations Management* (New York: McGraw-Hill, 1981), 12.

that production and operations management comprises five functions or decision areas: process, capacity, inventory, workforce, and quality.

Production and operations activities often represent the largest part of an organization's human and capital assets. In most industries, the major costs of producing a product or service are incurred within operations, so production and operations can have great value as a competitive weapon in a company's overall strategy. Strengths and weaknesses in the five functions of production can mean the success or failure of an enterprise.

Many production and operations managers are finding that cross-training of employees can help their firms respond faster to changing markets. Cross-training of workers can increase efficiency, quality, productivity, and job satisfaction. For example, at General Motors' Detroit gear and axle plant, costs related to product defects were reduced 400 percent in 2 years as a result of cross-training workers. As shown in Table 6-9, James Dilworth outlined implications of several types of strategic decisions that a company might make.

A magazine that had been printed since 1933, *Newsweek*, ended its print edition of the magazine on December 31, 2012, after suffering through years of declining profits and falling subscriptions. Now only an all digital-tablet version, *Newsweek Global*, is available with a paid subscription. As a result of this strategic decision, *Newsweek* is laying off employees and closing production facilities both in the USA and abroad. Among the USA's three icon weekly magazines, *Time, Newsweek,* and *U.S. News and World Report*, only *Time* now remains in print version. The weekly cost to publish and distribute the print version of *Newsweek* was $42 million. The top 10 print magazines by circulation in 2012 are:

1. *AARP Magazine* (22,528,478)
2. *AARP Bulletin* (22,283,411)
3. *Game Informer* (8,169,524)
4. *Better Homes and Gardens* (7,617,038)
5. *Reader's Digest* (5,577,717)
6. *Good Housekeeping* (4,346,757)
7. *National Geographic* (4,232,205)
8. *Family Circle* (4,100,977)
9. *People* (3,563,035)
10. *Woman's Day* (3,449,692)

A current trend that is accelerating among U.S. manufacturers is to extend the payment term on monies owed to suppliers. Procter & Gamble is leading the way on this trend, freeing

TABLE 6-9 Implications of Various Strategies on Production and Operations

Various Strategies	Implications
1. Low-cost provider	Creates high barriers to entry
	Creates larger market
	Requires longer production runs and fewer product changes
2. A high-quality provider	Requires more quality-assurance efforts
	Requires more expensive equipment
	Requires highly skilled workers and higher wages
3. Provide great customer service	Requires more service people, service parts, and equipment
	Requires rapid response to customer needs or changes in customer tastes
	Requires a higher inventory investment
4. Be the first to introduce new products	Has higher research and development costs
	Has high retraining and tooling costs
5. Become highly automated	Requires high capital investment
	Reduces flexibility
	May affect labor relations
	Makes maintenance more crucial
6. Minimize layoffs	Serves the security needs of employees and may develop employee loyalty
	Helps to attract and retain highly skilled employees

Source: Based on: J. Dilworth, *Production and Operations Management: Manufacturing and Nonmanufacturing,* 2nd ed. Copyright © 1983 by Random House, Inc.

up nearly $2 billion in cash annually by delaying payments to suppliers. Hundreds of other firms are doing the same, including Unilever and even retailers such as Walmart and Kohl's.

Another trend among U.S. manufacturers and retailers regarding suppliers is to quit doing business with unsafe factories, such as the one in Bangladesh that recently collapsed and killed 1,100 people. Walmart has publicly blacklisted 250 Bangladeshi suppliers found to have safety problems.

Production and Operations Audit Checklist

Questions such as the following should be examined:

1. Are supplies of raw materials, parts, and subassemblies reliable and reasonable?
2. Are facilities, equipment, machinery, and offices in good condition?
3. Are inventory-control policies and procedures effective?
4. Are quality-control policies and procedures effective?
5. Are facilities, resources, and markets strategically located?
6. Does the firm have technological competencies?

Research and Development

The fifth major area of internal operations that should be examined for specific strengths and weaknesses is **research and development (R&D).** Many firms today conduct no R&D, and yet many other companies depend on successful R&D activities for survival. Firms pursuing a product development strategy especially need to have a strong R&D orientation. Founded in 1897 and headquartered in Orrville, Ohio, J.M. Smucker Company had $5.5 and 4.8 billion in revenue in 2012 and 2011, and spent $21.9 and $20.9 million in R&D during those two years, comprising 0.39 and 0.43 percent of revenues, respectively. In contrast, Microsoft had revenues of $73.7 and $69.9 billion in 2012 and 2011 and spent $9.8 and $9.0 billion on R&D, comprising 13.3 and 12.9 percent of revenues respectively. High-tech firms such as Microsoft spend a much larger proportion of their revenues on R&D.

Huawei Technologies, the world's largest supplier of telecom equipment, increased its R&D spending by 25 percent in 2012 to $4.7 billion, almost equal to rival Ericsson's R&D expenditures of $4.8 billion. A key decision for many firms is whether to be a "first mover" or a "late follower," i.e. spending heavily on R&D to be the first to develop radically new products, or alternatively spending less on R&D by imitating/duplicating/improving upon products once rival firms develop them.

Organizations invest in R&D because they believe that such an investment will lead to a superior product or service and will give them competitive advantages. R&D expenditures are directed at developing new products before competitors do, at improving product quality, or at improving manufacturing processes to reduce costs.

Effective management of the R&D function requires a strategic and operational partnership between R&D and the other vital business functions. A spirit of partnership and mutual trust between general and R&D managers is evident in the best-managed firms today. Managers in these firms jointly explore; assess; and decide the what, when, where, why, and how much of R&D. Priorities, costs, benefits, risks, and rewards associated with R&D activities are discussed openly and shared. The overall mission of R&D thus has become broad based, including supporting existing businesses, helping launch new businesses, developing new products, improving product quality, improving manufacturing efficiency, and deepening or broadening the company's technological capabilities.[24]

The best-managed firms today seek to organize R&D activities in a way that breaks the isolation of R&D from the rest of the company and promotes a spirit of partnership between R&D managers and other managers in the firm. R&D decisions and plans must be integrated and coordinated across departments and divisions by having the departments share experiences and information. The strategic-management process facilitates this cross-functional approach to managing the R&D function.

R&D spending in the USA was $418.6 billion in 2012 and is expected to increase only 1.2 percent to $423.7 billion in 2013. The inflation-adjusted R&D spending for 2013 actually is expected to decline 0.7 percent. In comparison, the number-2 R&D spending country, China, spent $197.3 billion in 2012, but it is annually increasing its expenditure 10 to 12 percent. According to the Battelle Memorial Institute, China will achieve parity with the USA in R&D spending in 2022.

Internal and External Research and Development

Cost distributions among R&D activities vary by company and industry, but total R&D costs generally do not exceed manufacturing and marketing start-up costs. Four approaches to determining R&D budget allocations commonly are used: (1) financing as many project proposals as possible, (2) using a percentage-of-sales method, (3) budgeting about the same amount that competitors spend for R&D, or (4) deciding how many successful new products are needed and working backward to estimate the required R&D investment.

R&D in organizations can take two basic forms: (1) internal R&D, in which an organization operates its own R&D department, or (2) contract R&D, in which a firm hires independent researchers or independent agencies to develop specific products. Many companies use both approaches to develop new products. A widely used approach for obtaining outside R&D assistance is to pursue a joint venture with another firm. R&D strengths (capabilities) and weaknesses (limitations) play a major role in strategy formulation and strategy implementation.

Most firms have no choice but to continually develop new and improved products because of changing consumer needs and tastes, new technologies, shortened product life cycles, and increased domestic and foreign competition. A shortage of ideas for new products, increased global competition, increased market segmentation, strong special-interest groups, and increased government regulations are several factors making the successful development of new products more and more difficult, costly, and risky. In the pharmaceutical industry, for example, only one out of every few thousand drugs created in the laboratory ends up on pharmacists' shelves. Scarpello, Boulton, and Hofer emphasized that different strategies require different R&D capabilities:

> The focus of R&D efforts can vary greatly depending on a firm's competitive strategy. Some corporations attempt to be market leaders and innovators of new products, while others are satisfied to be market followers and developers of currently available products. The basic skills required to support these strategies will vary, depending on whether R&D becomes the driving force behind competitive strategy. In cases where new product introduction is the driving force for strategy, R&D activities must be extensive.[25]

Research and Development Audit

Questions such as the following should be asked in performing an R&D audit:

1. Does the firm have R&D facilities? Are they adequate?
2. If outside R&D firms are used, are they cost-effective?
3. Are the organization's R&D personnel well qualified?
4. Are R&D resources allocated effectively?
5. Are management information and computer systems adequate?
6. Is communication between R&D and other organizational units effective?
7. Are present products technologically competitive?

Management Information Systems

Billions of bits of information are now "in the cloud." Information ties all business functions together and provides the basis for all managerial decisions. It is the cornerstone of all organizations. Information represents a major source of competitive management advantage or disadvantage. Assessing a firm's internal strengths and weaknesses in information systems is a critical dimension of performing an internal audit.

A MIS's purpose is to improve the performance of an enterprise by improving the quality of managerial decisions. An effective information system thus collects, codes, stores, synthesizes, and presents information in such a manner that it answers important operating and strategic questions. The heart of an information system is a database containing the kinds of records and data important to managers.

A **management information system (MIS)** receives raw material from both the external and internal evaluation of an organization. It gathers data about marketing, finance, production, and personnel matters internally, and social, cultural, demographic, environmental, economic, political, governmental, legal, technological, and competitive factors externally. Data are integrated in ways needed to support managerial decision making.

There is a logical flow of material in an information system, whereby data are input to the system and transformed into output. Outputs include computer printouts, written reports, tables, charts, graphs, checks, purchase orders, invoices, inventory records, payroll accounts, and a variety of other documents. Payoffs from alternative strategies can be calculated and estimated. **Data** becomes **information** only when it is evaluated, filtered, condensed, analyzed, and organized for a specific purpose, problem, individual, or time.

Management Information Systems Audit

Questions such as the following should be asked when conducting this audit:

1. Do all managers in the firm use the information system to make decisions?
2. Is there a chief information officer or director of information systems position in the firm?
3. Are data in the information system updated regularly?
4. Do managers from all functional areas of the firm contribute input to the information system?
5. Are there effective passwords for entry into the firm's information system?
6. Are strategists of the firm familiar with the information systems of rival firms?
7. Is the information system user-friendly?
8. Do all users of the information system understand the competitive advantages that information can provide firms?
9. Are computer training workshops provided for users of the information system?
10. Is the firm's information system continually being improved in content and user-friendliness?

Value Chain Analysis

According to Porter, the business of a firm can best be described as a value chain, in which total revenues minus total costs of all activities undertaken to develop and market a product or service yields value. All firms in a given industry have a similar value chain, which includes activities such as obtaining raw materials, designing products, building manufacturing facilities, developing cooperative agreements, and providing customer service. A firm will be profitable as long as total revenues exceed the total costs incurred in creating and delivering the product or service. Firms should strive to understand not only their own value chain operations but also their competitors', suppliers', and distributors' value chains.

Value chain analysis (VCA) refers to the process whereby a firm determines the costs associated with organizational activities from purchasing raw materials to manufacturing product(s) to marketing those products. VCA aims to identify where low-cost advantages or disadvantages exist anywhere along the value chain from raw material to customer service activities. VCA can enable a firm to better identify its own strengths and weaknesses, especially as compared to competitors' value chain analyses and their own data examined over time.

Substantial judgment may be required in performing a VCA because different items along the value chain may impact other items positively or negatively, so there exist complex interrelationships. For example, exceptional customer service may be especially expensive yet may reduce the costs of returns and increase revenues. Cost and price differences among rival firms can have their origins in activities performed by suppliers, distributors, creditors, or even shareholders. Despite the complexity of VCA, the initial step in implementing this procedure is to divide a firm's operations into specific activities or business processes. Then the analyst attempts to attach a cost to each discrete activity, and the costs could be in terms of both time and money. Finally, the analyst converts the cost data into information by looking for competitive cost strengths and weaknesses that may yield competitive advantage or disadvantage. Conducting a VCA is supportive of the RBV's examination of a firm's assets and capabilities as sources of distinctive competence.

When a major competitor or new market entrant offers products or services at low prices, this may be because that firm has substantially lower value chain costs or perhaps the rival firm is just waging a desperate attempt to gain sales or market share. Thus, VCA can be critically important for a firm in monitoring whether its prices and costs are competitive. An example value chain is illustrated in Figure 6-7. There can be more than a hundred particular value-creating activities associated with the business of producing and marketing a product or service, and each one of the activities can represent a competitive advantage or disadvantage for the firm. The combined costs of all the various activities in a company's value chain define the firm's cost of doing business. Firms should determine where cost advantages and disadvantages in their value chain occur *relative* to the value chain of rival firms.

Value chains differ immensely across industries and firms. Whereas a paper products company, such as Stone Container, would include on its value chain timber farming, logging, pulp mills, and papermaking, a company such as Hewlett-Packard would include programming, peripherals, software, hardware, and laptops. A motel would include food, housekeeping, check-in and check-out operations, website, reservations system, and so on. However, all firms should use VCA to develop and nurture a core competence and convert this competence into a distinctive competence. A **core competence** is a VCA that a firm performs especially well. When a core competence evolves into a major competitive advantage, then it is called a distinctive competence. Figure 6-8 illustrates this process.

More and more companies are using VCA to gain and sustain competitive advantage by being especially efficient and effective along various parts of the value chain. For example, Walmart has built powerful value advantages by focusing on exceptionally tight inventory control and volume purchasing of products. Computer companies in contrast compete aggressively along the distribution end of the value chain. Price competitiveness is a key component of competitiveness for both mass retailers and computer firms.

Benchmarking

Benchmarking is an analytical tool used to determine whether a firm's VCA are competitive compared to rivals and thus conducive to winning in the marketplace. Benchmarking entails measuring costs of value chain activities across an industry to determine "best practices" among competing firms for the purpose of duplicating or improving on those best practices. Benchmarking enables a firm to take action to improve its competitiveness by identifying (and improving on) value chain activities where rival firms have comparative advantages in cost, service, reputation, or operation.

Supplier Costs ——— |
    Raw materials ——— |
    Fuel ——— |
    Energy ——— |
    Transportation ——— |
    Truck drivers ——— |
    Truck maintenance ——— |
    Component parts ——— |
    Inspection ——— |
    Storing ——— |
    Warehouse ——— |
Production Costs ——— |
    Inventory system ——— |
    Receiving ——— |
    Plant layout ——— |
    Maintenance ——— |
    Plant location ——— |
    Computer ——— |
    R&D ——— |
    Cost accounting ——— |
Distribution Costs ——— |
    Loading ——— |
    Shipping ——— |
    Budgeting ——— |
    Personnel ——— |
    Internet ——— |
    Trucking ——— |
    Railroads ——— |
    Fuel ——— |
    Maintenance ——— |
Sales and Marketing Costs ——— |
    Salespersons ——— |
    Website ——— |
    Internet ——— |
    Publicity ——— |
    Promotion ——— |
    Advertising ——— |
    Transportation ——— |
    Food and lodging ——— |
Customer Service Costs ——— |
    Postage ——— |
    Phone ——— |
    Internet ——— |
    Warranty ——— |
Management Costs ——— |
    Human resources ——— |
    Administration ——— |
    Employee benefits ——— |
    Labor relations ——— |
    Managers ——— |
    Employees ——— |
    Finance and legal ——— |

FIGURE 6-7

An Example Value Chain for a Typical Manufacturing Firm

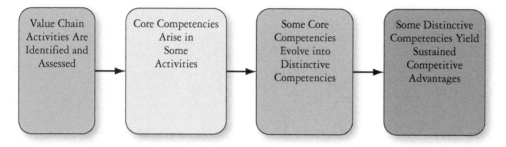

FIGURE 6-8

Transforming Value Chain Activities into Sustained Competitive Advantage

A comprehensive survey on benchmarking was recently commissioned by the Global Benchmarking Network, a network of benchmarking centers representing 22 countries. More than 450 organizations responded from over 40 countries. The results showed that:

1. Mission and vision statements along with customer (client) surveys are the most used (77 percent of organizations) of 20 improvement tools, followed by SWOT analysis (72 percent), and informal benchmarking (68 percent). Performance benchmarking was used by 49 percent and best practice benchmarking by 39 percent.
2. The tools that are likely to increase in popularity the most over the next three years are performance benchmarking, informal benchmarking, SWOT, and best practice benchmarking. More than 60 percent of organizations not currently using these tools indicated they are likely to use them in the next three years.[26]

The hardest part of benchmarking can be gaining access to other firms' VCA with associated costs. Typical sources of benchmarking information, however, include published reports, trade publications, suppliers, distributors, customers, partners, creditors, shareholders, lobbyists, and willing rival firms. Some rival firms share benchmarking data. However, the International Benchmarking Clearinghouse provides guidelines to help ensure that restraint of trade, price fixing, bid rigging, bribery, and other improper business conduct do not arise between participating firms.

Because of the popularity of benchmarking today, numerous consulting firms such as Accenture, AT Kearney, Best Practices Benchmarking & Consulting, as well as the Strategic Planning Institute's Council on Benchmarking, gather benchmarking data, conduct benchmarking studies, and distribute benchmark information without identifying the sources.

The Internal Factor Evaluation Matrix

A summary step in conducting an internal strategic-management audit is to construct an **Internal Factor Evaluation (IFE) Matrix**. This strategy-formulation tool summarizes and evaluates the major strengths and weaknesses in the functional areas of a business, and it also provides a basis for identifying and evaluating relationships among those areas. Intuitive judgments are required in developing an IFE Matrix, so the appearance of a scientific approach should not be interpreted to mean this is an all-powerful technique. A thorough understanding of the factors included is more important than the actual numbers. Similar to the EFE Matrix and CPM described in Chapter 7, an IFE Matrix can be developed in five steps:

1. List key internal factors as identified in the internal-audit process. Use a total of 20 internal factors, including both strengths and weaknesses. List strengths first and then weaknesses. Be as specific as possible, using percentages, ratios, and comparative numbers. Recall that Edward Deming said: "In God we trust. Everyone else bring data." Include "actionable" factors that can provide insight regarding strategies to pursue. For example, the factor "our Quick Ratio is 2.1 vs. industry average of 1.8" is not actionable, whereas the factor "our chocolate division's ROI increased from 8 to 15 percent in South America" is actionable.
2. Assign a weight that ranges from 0.0 (not important) to 1.0 (all-important) to each factor. The weight assigned to a given factor indicates the relative importance of the factor to being successful in the firm's industry. Regardless of whether a key factor is an internal strength

or weakness, factors considered to have the greatest effect on organizational performance should be assigned the highest weights. The sum of all weights must equal 1.0.

3. Assign a 1-to-4 rating to each factor to indicate whether that factor represents a major weakness (rating = 1), a minor weakness (rating = 2) a minor strength (rating = 3), or a major strength (rating = 4). Note that strengths must receive a 3 or 4 rating and weaknesses must receive a 1 or 2 rating. Ratings are thus company-based, whereas the weights in step 2 are industry-based.

4. Multiply each factor's weight by its rating to determine a weighted score for each variable.

5. Sum the weighted scores for each variable to determine the total weighted score for the organization.

Regardless of how many factors are included in an IFE Matrix, the total weighted score can range from a low of 1.0 to a high of 4.0, with the average score being 2.5. Total weighted scores well below 2.5 characterize organizations that are weak internally, whereas scores significantly above 2.5 indicate a strong internal position. Like the EFE Matrix, an IFE Matrix should include 20 key factors. The number of factors has no effect on the range of total weighted scores because the weights always sum to 1.0.

When a key internal factor is both a strength and a weakness, the factor may be included twice in the IFE Matrix, and a weight and rating assigned to each statement. For example, the Playboy logo both helps and hurts Playboy Enterprises; the logo attracts customers to *Playboy* magazine, but it keeps the Playboy cable channel out of many markets. Be as quantitative as possible when stating factors. Use monetary amounts, percentages, numbers, and ratios to the extent possible.

An example IFE Matrix is provided in Table 6-10 for a retail computer store. Note that the two most important factors to be successful in the retail computer store business are "revenues from repair/service in the store" and "location of the store." Also note that the store is doing best on "average customer purchase amount" and "in-store technical support." The store is having major problems with its carpet, bathroom, paint, and checkout procedures. Note also that the matrix contains substantial quantitative data rather than vague statements; this is excellent. Overall, this store

TABLE 6-10 A Sample Internal Factor Evaluation Matrix for a Retail Computer Store

Key Internal Factors	Weight	Rating	Weighted Score
Strengths			
1. Inventory turnover increased from 5.8 to 6.7	0.05	3	0.15
2. Average customer purchase increased from $97 to $128	0.07	4	0.28
3. Employee morale is excellent	0.10	3	0.30
4. In-store promotions resulted in 20 percent increase in sales	0.05	3	0.15
5. Newspaper advertising expenditures increased 10 percent	0.02	3	0.06
6. Revenues from repair/service segment of store up 16 percent	0.15	3	0.45
7. In-store technical support personnel have MIS college degrees	0.05	4	0.20
8. Store's debt-to-total assets ratio declined to 34 percent	0.03	3	0.09
9. Revenues per employee up 19 percent	0.02	3	0.06
Weaknesses			
1. Revenues from software segment of store down 12 percent	0.10	2	0.20
2. Location of store negatively impacted by new Highway 34	0.15	2	0.30
3. Carpet and paint in store somewhat in disrepair	0.02	1	0.02
4. Bathroom in store needs refurbishing	0.02	1	0.02
5. Revenues from businesses down 8 percent	0.04	1	0.04
6. Store has no website	0.05	2	0.10
7. Supplier on-time delivery increased to 2.4 days	0.03	1	0.03
8. Often customers have to wait to check out	0.05	1	0.05
Total	**1.00**		**2.50**

TABLE 6-11 An Actual IFE Matrix for Fresenius, Inc.

Strengths	Weight	Rating	WScore
1. Sales and earnings per share have not declined a single year for 10 years	0.09	4	0.36
2. Fresenius Medical Care is the market leader in dialysis services and products	0.09	4	0.36
3. Trading volume increased by 17 percent in 2011	0.05	3	0.15
4. Dividends were just raised for the 20th consecutive year	0.06	4	0.24
5. Financial analysts ratings show 23 "buy," 2 "hold," and no "sell"	0.06	3	0.18
6. Has a renown training school for nurses and other health workers	0.03	3	0.09
7. DAX30 ranking in market capitalization steadily improving	0.05	4	0.20
8. Fresenius Medical increased worldwide clinics by 6 percent	0.03	3	0.09
9. Fresenius Helios is the second largest private hospital operators in Germany	0.06	3	0.18
10. Diversified 4 business segments in different healthcare sectors	0.05	3	0.15
Weaknesses			
1. Quick Ratio of 0.65 shows a lack of ability to cover cash needs	0.07	2	0.14
2. Group sales decreased by 4 percent in North America	0.03	2	0.06
3. Group debt increased by 9 percent	0.05	1	0.05
4. Fresenius Biotech has a negative EBIT of approx. $–38.6 million	0.05	2	0.10
5. Decrease of 21% in operating cash flow from 2010 to 2011	0.08	1	0.08
6. Fresenius Helios dropped 3.1 billion euro takeover of rival Rhoen-Klinikum on September 3, 2012, because of rival hospital operators blocking the merger	0.01	2	0.02
7. Fresenius Vamed made no material acquisitions	0.02	2	0.04
8. No racial diversity on management and supervisory boards	0.04	2	0.08
9. Healthcare Group board members and committees comprised of all males	0.04	1	0.04
10. Only one female in all top management	0.04	1	0.04
Total	**1.0**		**2.65**

receives a 2.5 total weighted score, which on a 1-to-4 scale is exactly average/halfway, indicating there is definitely room for improvement in store operations, strategies, policies, and procedures.

The IFE Matrix provides important information for strategy formulation. For example, this retail computer store might want to hire another checkout person and repair its carpet, paint, and bathroom problems. Also, the store may want to increase advertising for its repair/services, because that is a really important (weight 0.15) factor to being successful in this business.

Headquartered in Germany and specializing in kidney dialysis, Fresenius provides healthcare products and services in about 100 countries. Fresenius owns and operates 2,800 dialysis clinics and many other healthcare facilities. Table 6-11 provides an actual IFE matrix created for Fresenius in late 2012. As indicated in Table 6-11, Fresenius is financially strong, but needs to include women and minorities in its management.

In multidivisional firms, each autonomous division or strategic business unit should construct an IFE Matrix. Divisional matrices then can be integrated to develop an overall corporate IFE Matrix. Be as divisional as possible when developing a corporate IFE Matrix. Also, in developing an IFE Matrix, do not allow more than 30 percent of the key factors to be financial ratios because financial ratios are generally the result of many other factors so it is difficult to know what particular strategies should be considered based on financial ratios. For example, a firm would have no insight on whether to sell in Brazil or South Africa to take advantage of a high corporate ROI ratio.

Special Note to Students

It can be debated whether external or internal factors are more important in strategic planning, but there is no debate regarding the fact that gaining and sustaining competitive advantage is the essence or purpose of strategic planning. In the internal portion of your case analysis, emphasize how and why your internal strengths and weaknesses can be leveraged to both gain competitive advantage and overcome competitive disadvantage, in light of the direction you are taking the firm. Maintain your project's upbeat, insightful, and forward-thinking demeanor during the internal assessment, rather than being mundane, descriptive, and vague. Focus on how your firm's resources, capabilities, structure, and strategies, with your recommended improvements, can lead the firm to prosperity. Although the numbers absolutely must be there, must be accurate, and must be reasonable, do not bore a live audience or class with overreliance on numbers. Periodically throughout your presentation or written analysis, refer to your recommendations, explaining how your plan of action will improve the firm's weaknesses and capitalize on strengths in light of anticipated competitor countermoves. Keep your audience's attention, interest, and suspense, rather than "reading" to them or "defining" ratios for them.

Conclusion

Management, marketing, finance and accounting, production and operations, R&D, and MIS represent the core operations of most businesses. A strategic-management audit of a firm's internal operations is vital to organizational health. Many companies still prefer to be judged solely on their bottom-line performance. However, an increasing number of successful organizations are using the internal audit to gain competitive advantages over rival firms.

Systematic methodologies for performing strength-weakness assessments are not well developed in the strategic-management literature, but it is clear that strategists must identify and evaluate internal strengths and weaknesses to effectively formulate and choose among alternative strategies. The EFE Matrix, CPM, IFE Matrix, and clear statements of vision and mission provide the basic information needed to successfully formulate competitive strategies. The process of performing an internal audit represents an opportunity for managers and employees throughout the organization to participate in determining the future of the firm. Involvement in the process can energize and mobilize managers and employees.

Key Terms and Concepts

activity ratios (p. 205)
benchmarking (p. 214)
breakeven (BE) point (p. 207)
capacity utilization (p. 209)
capital budgeting (p. 203)
communication (p. 190)
controlling (p. 198)
core competence (p. 214)
cost/benefit analysis (p. 202)
cultural products (p. 192)
customer analysis (p. 199)
data (p. 213)
distinctive competencies (p. 189)
distribution (p. 201)
dividend decisions (p. 203)
empirical indicators (p. 192)
financial ratio analysis (p. 191)
fixed costs (FC) (p. 208)
financing decision (p. 203)
functions of finance/accounting (p. 202)
functions of management (p. 194)
functions of marketing (p. 194)
growth ratios (p. 205)
human resource management (p. 197)
information (p. 213)

internal audit (p. 190)
internal factor evaluation (IFE) matrix (p. 216)
investment decision (p. 203)
leverage ratios (p. 205)
liquidity ratios (p. 205)
management information system
    (MIS) (p. 213)
marketing research (p. 201)
motivating (p. 197)
organizational culture (p. 192)
organizing (p. 196)
personnel management (p. 197)
planning (p. 194)
pricing (p. 200)
product and service planning (p. 200)
production/operations function (p. 209)
profitability ratios (p. 205)
research and development (R&D) (p. 211)
resource-based view (RBV) (p. 191)
selling (p. 199)
staffing (p. 197)
synergy (p. 196)
test marketing (p. 200)
value chain analysis (VCA) (p. 214)
variable costs (VC) (p. 208)

Issues for Review and Discussion

6-1. Volkswagen (VW) Group has been very successful in the last decade. Research VW and see if they have strategic planning. Create a report of your findings for your class.

6-2. Visit VW's corporate website. See the list of top executives for VW and create an organizational chart for VW.

6-3. Given the fifteen examples of (possible) aspects of an organization's culture as presented in the chapter, rate a company you are very familiar with in terms of the extent each culture item exists. Explain.

6-4. Rank the seven functions of marketing in order of importance for a small hardware business.

6-5. Develop a quantitative problem to show your understanding of cost/benefit analysis.

6-6. Develop a quantitative problem to show that you understand breakeven analysis.

6-7. For VW, determine their most recent dividend payout amount per share. How has that amount changed over the last 12 months?

6-8. List some advantages and disadvantages of a company paying dividends versus reinvesting that money in the company, and striving for stock price increase as the primary way to reward investors.

6-9. Illustrate a breakeven chart for VW. Explain how it may work for the organization.

6-10. VW has historically spent more on R&D than almost any other automobile company in the world. What are the major advantages and disadvantages of this strategy?

6-11. Perform a value chain analysis for an organization of your choice.

6-12. Discuss the relationship between benchmarking and value chain analysis.

6-13. Explain why the ratings in an IFE Matrix should be 4 or 3 for strengths, and 1 or 2 for weaknesses as compared to the EFE Matrix—where the ratings should be 1, 2, 3, or 4 anywhere among both the opportunities and threats.

6-14. Compare the financial ratio analysis for VW on the four different websites identified in the chapter. Which site do you like best? Why?

6-15. Conduct a Google search for value chain analysis. In a two-page report, expand on the concepts presented in the chapter.

6-16. What competitive advantages would Amazon have over Wal-Mart stores in doing business outside the United States?

6-17. How could the "process of performing an internal audit" differ across countries, given varying global management styles?

6-18. Why is sole reliance on financial ratios an ineffective means of deriving internal strengths and weaknesses?

6-19. Give an example of two resources for a fast-food chain that you believe meet the three "empirical indicators" criteria.

6-20. Prepare a culture assessment table, as presented in the chapter, for a local business that you are familiar with.

In other words, rate that business on all 15 culture criteria presented. What are the implications of your ratings on the strategic planning process within that firm?

6-21. Why is human resource management particularly challenging for international firms?

6-22. List some specific characteristics of advertisements, in the wake of a lingering recession in Europe.

6-23. How do changes in the value of the dollar affect pricing of products of global firms?

6-24. Historically, what has been the attitude of technology firms toward paying dividends? Give some examples.

6-25. Describe Singapore as a place to locate or start a business.

6-26. Visit the strategyclub website, and describe the strategic planning products offered.

6-27. Develop a value chain analysis for a large global firm and its primary rival firm.

6-28. Identify four major strengths and weaknesses each, of your college or university. Rank each factor in terms of importance.

6-29. Look up financial information about VW. Identify three financial ratios where the firm is weak and three financial ratios the firm is strong.

6-30. What five cultural products do you feel are most important? Justify your selections.

6-31. Rate the company where you work, or would like to work, on the 15 aspects of culture listed in the chapter.

6-32. Develop a breakeven chart for a company, which simultaneously lays off employees and closes facilities.

6-33. Financial ratio analysis should be conducted on three separate fronts. What are these fronts and which is most important?

6-34. Explain breakeven analysis using three graphs that show changes in breakeven given: 1) a change in price, 2) a change in advertising expenditures, and 3) a change in labor costs.

6-35. Why is breakeven analysis such an important strategic planning concept?

6-36. What are the basic functions of production/operations in a large manufacturing company? Why are these factors important in an internal strategic management audit?

6-37. Explain benchmarking.

6-38. Go to the www.strategyclub.com website and review the benefits of using the free excel template.

6-39. For the adidas Cohesion Case, what do you consider to be the company's four major strengths and four major weaknesses?

6-40. Prepare a financial ratio analysis for adidas. Include comparative ratios for adidas.

6-41. Explain how adidas could utilize breakeven analysis.

6-42. Explain how top executives of adidas could utilize Porter's Five Forces Model to aid the firm in strategic planning.

6-43. Since adidas and Puma are based in the same city, could this close proximity benefit or hinder the two firms 1) cooperating with each other on R&D, or 2) gathering and assimilating competitive intelligence on the other firm?

6-44. Since adidas is so divisional, how could the company best develop a corporate IFE Matrix for various divisional IFE Matrices?

6-45. When is it more important to capitalize on strengths than improve on weaknesses in strategic planning?

6-46. Explain what 20 internal factors is a recommended number to include in an IFE Matrix, rather than 10 or 40 total.

6-47. Do you think the RBV view or the I/O theorists view is more important/accurate in performing a strategic analysis? What would be important implications for a business?

MyManagementLab®

Go to **mymanagementlab.com** for the following Assisted-graded writing questions:

6-48. List three ways that financial ratios should be compared or used. Which of the three comparisons do you feel is most important? Why?

6-49. Would you ever pay out dividends when your firm's annual net profit is negative? Why? What effect could this have on a firm's strategies?

Current Readings

Arora, Ashish and Anand Nandkumar. "Insecure Advantage? Markets for Technology and the Value of Resources for Entrepreneurial Ventures." *Strategic Management Journal* 33, no. 3 (March 2012): 231–251.

Browning, Tyson R., Sanders, and Nada R. "Can Innovation Be Lean?" *California Management Review* 54, no. 4 (Summer 2012): 5–19.

Knott, Anne Marie. "The Trillion-Dollar R&D Fix." *Harvard Business Review* (May 2012): 76.

Lemper, Timothy A. "The Critical Role of Timing in Managing Intellectual Property." *Business Horizons* 55, no. 4 (July 2012): 339–347.

Lindenberg, Siegwart, and Nicolai J. Foss. "Managing Joint Production Motivation: The Role of Goal Framing and Governance Mechanisms." *The Academy of Management Review* 36, no. 3 (July 2011): 500.

Mossholder, Kevin W., Hettie A. Richardson, and Randall P. Settoon. "Human Resource Systems and Helping in Organizations: A Relational Perspective." *The Academy of Management Review* 36, no. 1 (January 2011): 33.

Rader, David. "How Cloud Computing Maximizes Growth Opportunities for a Firm Challenging Established Rivals." *Strategy and Leadership* 40, no. 4 (2012): 36–43.

Turner, Karynne L., and Mona V. Makhija. "The Role of Individuals in the Information Processing Perspective." *Strategic Management Journal* 33, no. 6 (June 2012): 661–680.

Watkins, Michael D. "How Managers Become Leaders." *Harvard Business Review* (June 2012): 64.

ASSURANCE OF LEARNING EXERCISES

EXERCISE 6A
Develop a Corporate IFE Matrix for Volkswagen Group

Purpose
Volkswagen Group is featured in the opening chapter case as a firm that engages in excellent strategic planning. VW has four major geographic business segments. Each of these divisions of VW would preparetheir own IFE Matrices, which would be assimilated to develop an overall corporate IFE Matrix.

This exercise gives you practice developing divisional IFE Matrices and assimilating those into an overall corporate IFE Matrix.

Instructions
Step 1	Review VW's most recent *Annual Report* in regards to the company's four geographic business segments, which are North America, South America, Asia-Pacific, and Europe.
Step 2	Review the latest S&P *Industry Survey* for companies that produce and market automobiles.
Step 3	Develop a divisional IFE Matrix for each of VW's business segments.
Step 4	Assimilate your divisional IFE Matrices into an overall corporate IFE Matrix for VW.

EXERCISE 6B
Should VW Deploy More Resources or Less Outside of the USA?

Purpose

As indicated in the opening chapter boxed insert, VW receives more revenue from outside its home base of Europe than from inside Europe. This exercise gives you practice analyzing this domestic versus global revenue base so that more effective strategies can be formulated and implemented.

Instructions

Step 1   Go the VW's website and review the company's most recent *Annual Report*. Be careful to note the financial, management, and marketing information available for each geographic region. Let all regions outside Europe, for purposes of this exercise, be referred to as Global, and Europe be referred to as domestic for VW.

Step 2   Go to www.finance.yahoo.com and review the last 45 days of Headlines for VW. Take note of public information related to VW as well as to GM, Ford, Honda, and Toyota.

Step 3   Prepare a 3-page executive summary to reveal whether you feel VW should be placing more or less emphasis on operations outside of Europe. Provide supporting tables, #'s, ratios, and narrative.

EXERCISE 6C
Apply Breakeven Analysis

Purpose

Breakeven analysis is one of the simplest yet underused analytical tools in management. It helps to provide a dynamic view of the relationships between sales, costs and profits. A better understanding of breakeven analysis can enable an organization to formulate and implement strategies more effectively.

This exercise will show you how to calculate breakeven points mathematically. The formula for calculating breakeven point is BE Quantity = TFC/P – VC. In other words, the Quantity (Q) or units of product that need to be sold for a firm to breakeven is Total Fixed Costs divided by (Price per Unit 2 Variable Costs per Unit).

Instructions

Step 1   Lets say an airplane company has Fixed Costs of $100 million and Variable Costs per Unit of $2 million. Planes sell for $3 million each. What is the company's breakeven point in terms of the number of planes that need to be sold just to breakeven?

Step 2   If the airplane company wants to make a profit of $99 million annually, how many planes will it have to sell?

Step 3   If the company can sell 200 airplanes in a year, how much annual profit will the firm make?

EXERCISE 6D
Performing a Financial Ratio Analysis for adidas AG

Purpose

Financial ratio analysis is one of the best techniques for identifying and evaluating internal strengths and weaknesses. Potential investors and current shareholders look closely at firms' financial ratios, making detailed comparisons to industry averages and to previous periods of time. Financial ratio analysis provides vital input information for developing an IFE Matrix.

Instructions

Step 1   On a separate sheet of paper, write down numbers 1 to 20. Referring to adidas AG's income statement and balance sheet, calculate 20 financial ratios for 2013.

Step 2   In a second column, indicate whether you consider each ratio to be a strength, weakness, or neutral factor for adidas.

EXERCISE 6E
Constructing an IFE Matrix for adidas AG

Purpose

This exercise will give you experience developing an IFE Matrix. Identifying and prioritizing factors to include in an IFE Matrix fosters communication among functional and divisional managers.

Preparing an IFE Matrix allows human resource, marketing, production/operations, finance/accounting, R&D, and management information systems managers to articulate their concerns and thoughts regarding the business condition of the firm. This results in an improved collective understanding of the business.

Instructions

Step 1   Join with two other individuals to form a three-person team. Develop a IFE Matrix for adidas. Be sure to include information on Reebok and TaylorMade.

Step 2   Compare your team's IFE Matrix to other teams' IFE Matrices. Discuss any major differences.

Step 3   What strategies do you think would allow adidas to capitalize on its major strengths? What strategies would allow adidas to improve upon its major weaknesses?

EXERCISE 6F

Analyzing Your College or University's Internal Strategic Situation

Purpose

This exercise is excellent for doing together as a class.

Instructions

As a class, determine your college or university's major internal strengths and weaknesses. List 10 strengths and 10 weaknesses. Then, get everyone in class to rank order their factors with 1 being most important and 10 being least important. Then, gather up everyone's paper, count the numbers, and in that manner create a prioritized list of the key internal strengths and weaknesses facing your college.

Notes

1. Reprinted by permission of the publisher from "Integrating Strength–Weakness Analysis into Strategic Planning," by William King, *Journal of Business Research* 2, no. 4: 481. Copyright 1983 by Elsevier Science Publishing Co., Inc.

2. Igor Ansoff, "Strategic Management of Technology" *Journal of Business Strategy* 7, no. 3 (Winter 1987): 38.

3. Claude George Jr., *The History of Management Thought*, 2nd ed. (Upper Saddle River, NJ: Prentice-Hall, 1972), 174.

4. Robert Grant, "The Resource-Based Theory of Competitive Advantage: Implications for Strategy Formulation," *California Management Review*, Spring 1991, 116.

5. J. B. Barney, "Firm Resources and Sustained Competitive Advantage," *Journal of Management* 17 (1991): 99–120; J. B. Barney, "The Resource-Based Theory of the Firm," *Organizational Science* 7 (1996): 469; J. B. Barney, "Is the Resource-Based 'View' a Useful Perspective for Strategic Management Research? Yes." *Academy of Management Review* 26, no. 1 (2001): 41–56.

6. Edgar Schein, *Organizational Culture and Leadership* (San Francisco: Jossey-Bass, 1985), 9.

7. John Lorsch, "Managing Culture: The Invisible Barrier to Strategic Change," *California Management Review* 28, no. 2 (1986): 95–109.

8. Y. Allarie and M. Firsirotu, "How to Implement Radical Strategies in Large Organizations," *Sloan Management Review* (Spring 1985): 19.

9. www.mindtools.com/plfailpl.html

10. Adam Smith, *The Wealth of Nations* (New York: Modern Library, 1937), 3–4.

11. Richard Daft, *Management*, 3rd ed. (Orlando, FL: Dryden Press, 1993), 512.

12. Shelley Kirkpatrick and Edwin Locke, "Leadership: Do Traits Matter?" *Academy of Management Executive* 5, no. 2 (May 1991): 48.

13. Peter Drucker, *Management Tasks, Responsibilities, and Practice* (New York: Harper & Row, 1973), 463.

14. Brian Dumaine, "What the Leaders of Tomorrow See," *Fortune*, July 3, 1989, 51.

15. J. Evans and B. Bergman, *Marketing* (New York: Macmillan, 1982), 17.

16. Spencer Ante, "As Economy Cools, IBM Furthers Focus on Marketers," *Wall Street Journal* (July 18, 2012): B3.

17. Brad Stone, "See Your Friends," *Bloomberg Businessweek* (September 27–October 3, 2010): 65–69.

18. Quoted in Robert Waterman, Jr., "The Renewal Factor," *BusinessWeek*, September 14, 1987, 108.

19. http://en.wikipedia.org/wiki/Cost-benefit_analysis

20. J. Van Horne, *Financial Management and Policy* (Upper Saddle River, N.J.: Prentice-Hall, 1974), 10.

21. Matt Krantz, "Today's Fat Dividends are Getting Even Heftier," *Wall Street Journal* (August 6, 2012): 3B.

22. http://en.wikipedia.org/wiki/Break-even_(economics).

23. Andrew Peaple, "Fiat's Struggle With Italian Job Threatens American Promise," *Wall Street Journal* (September 28, 2012): C10.

24. Philip Rousebl, Kamal Saad, and Tamara Erickson, "The Evolution of Third Generation R&D," *Planning Review* 19, no. 2 (March–April 1991): 18–26.

25. Vida Scarpello, William Boulton, and Charles Hofer, "Reintegrating R&D into Business Strategy," *Journal of Business Strategy* 6, no. 4 (Spring 1986): 50–51.

26. http://en.wikipedia.org/wiki/Benchmarking.

7

Source: © industrieblick/Fotolia

MyManagementLab®

Improve Your Grade!

Over 10 million students improved their results using the Pearson MyLabs.
Visit **mymanagementlab.com** for simulations, tutorials, and end-of-chapter problems.

The External Audit

CHAPTER OBJECTIVES

After studying this chapter, you should be able to do the following:

1. Discuss the nature and role of labor unions in the USA as a corporate strategic issue.

2. Describe how to conduct an external strategic-management audit.

3. Discuss 10 major external forces that affect organizations: economic, social, cultural, demographic, environmental, political, governmental, legal, technological, and competitive.

4. Describe key sources of external information.

5. Discuss important forecasting tools used in strategic management.

6. Discuss the importance of monitoring external trends and events.

7. Explain how to develop an EFE Matrix.

8. Explain how to develop a Competitive Profile Matrix.

9. Discuss the importance of gathering competitive intelligence.

10. Discuss market commonality and resource similarity in relation to competitive analysis.

ASSURANCE OF LEARNING EXERCISES

The following exercises are found at the end of this chapter.

This chapter examines the tools and concepts needed to conduct an external strategic management audit (sometimes called **environmental scanning** or **industry analysis**). An **external audit** focuses on identifying and evaluating trends and events beyond the control of a single firm, such as increased foreign competition, population shifts to coastal areas of the USA, an aging society, and taxing Internet sales. An external audit reveals key opportunities and threats confronting an organization so that managers can formulate strategies to take advantage of the opportunities and avoid or reduce the impact of threats. This chapter presents a practical framework for gathering, assimilating, and analyzing external information. The Industrial Organization (I/O) view of strategic management is introduced.

The Chapter 7 boxed insert company pursuing strategies based on an excellent external strategic analysis is Michelin.

The Nature of an External Audit

The purpose of an external audit is to develop a finite list of opportunities that could benefit a firm and threats that should be avoided. As the term *finite* suggests, the external audit is not aimed at developing an exhaustive list of every possible factor that could influence the business; rather, it is aimed at identifying key variables that offer actionable responses. Firms should be able to respond either offensively or defensively to the factors by formulating strategies that take advantage of external opportunities or that minimize the impact of potential threats. Figure 7-1 illustrates with white shading how the external audit fits into the strategic-management process.

EXCELLENT STRATEGIC MANAGEMENT SHOWCASED

Michelin

Michelin is a huge tire manufacturer headquartered in Clemont-Ferrand in the Auvergne region of France. A major rival is Bridgestone. Michelin owns BFGoodrich, Kleber, Riken, Komoran, and the Uniroyal tire brands, as well as the Warrior brand in China. Michelin produces more than 175 million tires annually for all kinds of vehicles, supplying new and replacement tires to the passenger car and truck markets. The company is also a world leader in aircraft and earthmover tires. Additionally, Michelin is also known in the culinary world for its Red Guide reference books and restaurant star awards. The company publishes about 10 million maps and travel guides per year.

In 2014, Michelin will bring to market two new enduro bicycle tires, reentering the bike racing business. To provide mountain bike riders with high-performance tires, Michelin has partnered with two famous bikers: Fabien Barel, three-time world downhill champion, and Pierre Edouard Ferry, free ride champion. These two bikers have worked closely with Michelin Group engineers for two and a half years to design and develop the new Michelin bike tires.

In late 2013, production began on the new Porsche 918 Spyder. Michelin will be the only tire supplier for this new hybrid supercar, of which only 918 units are being produced. Michelin's new Pilot Sport Cup 2 is the only tire certified for two new high-powered sports cars- the Ferrari 458 Speciale and the Porsche 918 Spyder. Michelin's Pilot Sport 3 tires are equip the new Peugeot 308, making that car more energy efficient while delivering outstanding safety, handling and longevity. For the Peugeot 208 HYbrid FE, Michelin developed a range of Tall and Narrow tires with a longer rim diameter and better performance.

In late 2013, Kepler Cheuvreux, Jean-Dominique Senard, Chief Executive Officer of Michelin, revealed the six major Michelin Performance and Responsibility objectives for 2020 (paraphrased):

1. Increase durability and effectiveness of our products by at least 10% compared with 2010, while using fewer raw materials to produce.
2. Become more environmentally friendly by improving the energy efficiency of our plants and reducing our carbon footprint.
3. Annually deliver €1 billion in structural free cash flow per year and generate at least a 15% return on capital.
4. Develop and implement programs to improve employee engagement, well-being and development.
5. Deploy employee-driven outreach programs and create local jobs to continuously improve our public relations in communities.
6. Develop and promote improved recycling solutions to the extent possible.

Source: Based on the company website and press releases.

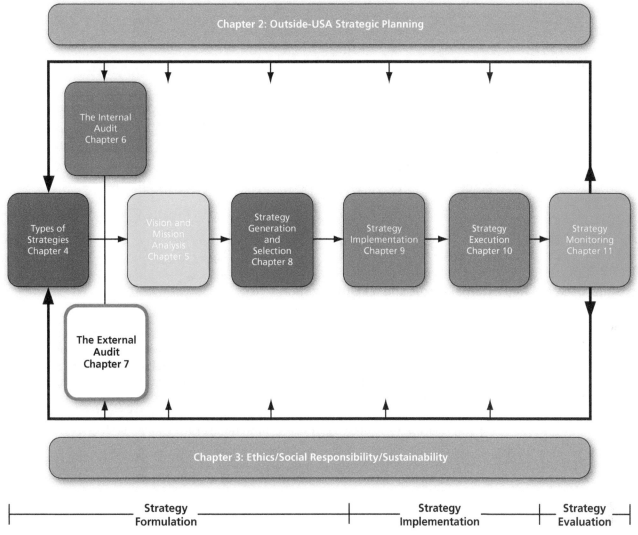

FIGURE 7-1

A Comprehensive Strategic-Management Model

Source: Fred R. David, adapted from "How Companies Define Their Mission," *Long Range Planning* 22, no. 3 (June 1988): 40, © Fred R. David.

Key External Forces

External forces can be divided into five broad categories: (1) economic forces; (2) social, cultural, demographic, and natural environment forces; (3) political, governmental, and legal forces; (4) technological forces; and (5) competitive forces. Relationships among these forces and an organization are depicted in Figure 7-2. External trends and events, such as rising food prices and people in African countries coming online, significantly affect products, services, markets, and organizations worldwide. IMPORTANT NOTE: WHEN IDENTIFYING AND PRIORITIZING KEY EXTERNAL FACTORS IN STRATEGIC PLANNING, MAKE SURE THE FACTORS SELECTED ARE SPECIFIC, IE QUANTIFIED TO THE EXTENT POSSIBLE; PERHAPS MORE IMPORTANTLY MAKE SURE THE FACTORS SELECTED ARE *ACTIONABLE*, IE MEANINGFUL IN TERMS OF HAVING STRATEGIC IMPLICATIONS. For example, regarding *actionable*, to say "the stock market is rising" is not actionable because there is no apparent strategy that the firm could formulate to capitalize on that factor. In contrast, a factor such as "the GDP of Brazil is 6.8 percent" is actionable because the firm should perhaps open 100 new stores in Brazil. In other words, select factors that will be helpful in deciding what to recommend the firm to do, rather than selecting nebulous factors.

Changes in external forces translate into changes in consumer demand for both industrial and consumer products and services. External forces affect the types of products developed,

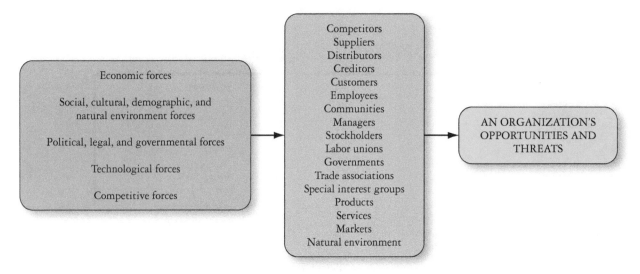

FIGURE 7-2

Relationships Between Key External Forces and an Organization

the nature of positioning and market segmentation strategies, the type of services offered, and the choice of businesses to acquire or sell. External forces directly affect both suppliers and distributors. Identifying and evaluating external opportunities and threats enables organizations to develop a clear mission, to design strategies to achieve long-term objectives, and to develop policies to achieve annual objectives.

The increasing complexity of business today is evidenced by more countries developing the capacity and will to compete aggressively in world markets. Foreign businesses and countries are willing to learn, adapt, innovate, and invent to compete successfully in the marketplace. There are more competitive new technologies in Asia today than ever before, as recently introduced for example by Lenovo in China and Samsung in South Korea.

The Process of Performing an External Audit

The process of performing an external audit must involve as many managers and employees as possible. As emphasized in Chapter 1 and Chapter 5, involvement in the strategic-management process can lead to understanding and commitment from organizational members. Individuals appreciate having the opportunity to contribute ideas and to gain a better understanding of their firm's industry, competitors, and markets.

To perform an external audit, a company first must gather competitive intelligence and information about economic, social, cultural, demographic, environmental, political, governmental, legal, and technological trends. Individuals can be asked to monitor various sources of information, such as key magazines, trade journals, and newspapers. These persons can submit periodic scanning reports to a committee of managers charged with performing the external audit. This approach provides a continuous stream of timely strategic information and involves many individuals in the external-audit process. The Internet provides another source for gathering strategic information, as do corporate, university, and public libraries. Suppliers, distributors, salespersons, customers, and competitors represent other sources of vital information.

Once information is gathered, it should be assimilated and evaluated. A meeting or series of meetings of managers is needed to collectively identify the most important opportunities and threats facing the firm. These key external factors should be listed on flip charts or a chalkboard. A prioritized list of these factors could be obtained by requesting that all managers rank the factors identified, from 1 for the most important opportunity or threat to 20 for the least important opportunity or threat. These key external factors can vary over time and by industry. Relationships with suppliers or distributors are often a critical success factor. Other variables commonly used include market share, breadth of competing products, world economies, foreign affiliates, proprietary and key account advantages, price competitiveness, technological advancements, population shifts, interest rates, and pollution abatement.

Freund emphasized that these key external factors should be (a) important to achieving long-term and annual objectives, (b) measurable, (c) applicable to all competing firms, and (d) hierarchical in the sense that some will pertain to the overall company and others will be more narrowly focused on functional or divisional areas. A final list of the most important key external factors should be communicated and distributed widely in the organization. Both opportunities and threats can be key external factors.[1]

The Industrial Organization (I/O) View

The **Industrial Organization (I/O)** approach to competitive advantage advocates that external (industry) factors are more important than internal factors in a firm for achieving competitive advantage. Proponents of the I/O view, such as Michael Porter, contend that organizational performance will be primarily determined by industry forces. Porter's Five-Forces Model, presented later in this chapter, is an example of the I/O perspective, which focuses on analyzing external forces and industry variables as a basis for getting and keeping competitive advantage. Competitive advantage is determined largely by competitive positioning within an industry, according to I/O advocates. Managing strategically from the I/O perspective entails firms striving to compete in attractive industries, avoiding weak or faltering industries, and gaining a full understanding of key external factor relationships within that attractive industry. I/O research provides important contributions to our understanding of how to gain competitive advantage.

I/O theorists contend that external factors and the industry in which a firm competes has a stronger influence on the firm's performance than do the internal functional issues in marketing, finance, and the like. Firm performance, they contend, is based more on industry properties such as economies of scale, barriers to market entry, product differentiation, the economy, and level of competitiveness than on internal resources, capabilities, structure, and operations. The USA's recent economic recovery having such a positive impact on both strong and weak firms adds credence to the notion that external forces are more important than internal.

The I/O view has enhanced the understanding of strategic management. However, it is not a question of whether external or internal factors are more important in gaining and maintaining competitive advantage. Effective integration and understanding of *both* external and internal factors is the key to securing and keeping a competitive advantage. In fact, as discussed in Chapter 8, matching key external opportunities and threats with key internal strengths and weaknesses provides the basis for successful strategy formulation.

Economic Forces

The lingering high underemployment rate in the USA bodes well for discount firms ranging from Dollar Tree to TJ Maxx to Walmart to Subway, but hurts thousands of traditional priced retailers in many industries. The Dow Jones Industrial Average is over 15,000, corporate profits are high, dividend increases are up sharply, and emerging markets are growing. Yet, job growth is still stymied, home prices remain low, and millions of people work for minimum wages or are either unemployed or underemployed. As a result of droughts, commodity prices are up sharply, especially food, which is contributing to rising inflation fears. Many firms are switching to the extent possible to part-time rather than full-time employees to avoid having to pay health benefits. Consumer spending is rebounding. Much of Europe lingers in a recession.

Economic factors have a direct impact on the potential attractiveness of various strategies. For example, with interest rates, funds needed for capital expansion are less costly. As interest rates rise, discretionary income declines, and the demand for discretionary goods falls. When stock prices increase, the desirability of equity as a source of capital for market development increases. When the market rises, consumer and business wealth expands. A summary of economic variables that often represent opportunities and threats for organizations is provided in Table 7-1.

To take advantage of Canada's robust economy and eager-to-spend people, many firms are aggressively expanding operations into Canada, including TJX opening many Marshalls stores, Target opening stores, Walmart opening supercenters, and Tanger Outlet Factory Centers

TABLE 7-1 Key Economic Variables to Be Monitored

Shift to a service economy in the USA	Import/export factors
Availability of credit	Demand shifts for different categories of goods and services
Level of disposable income	Income differences by region and consumer groups
Propensity of people to spend	Price fluctuations
Interest rates	Export of labor and capital from the USA
Inflation rates	Monetary policies
Money market rates	Fiscal policies
Federal government budget deficits	Tax rates
Gross domestic product trend	European Economic Community (EEC) policies
Consumption patterns	Organization of Petroleum Exporting Countries (OPEC) policies
Unemployment trends	Coalitions of Lesser Developed Countries (LDC) policies
Worker productivity levels	
Value of the dollar in world markets	
Stock market trends	
Foreign countries' economic conditions	

opening new stores. "Canada is one of the most economically prosperous countries in the world," said Howard Davidowitz, chairman of Davidowitz & Associates, a retail consultancy and investment banking firm. "It has a stable currency, it did not have a banking crisis and it did not spend itself into insanity."

Trends in the dollar's value have significant and unequal effects on companies in different industries and in different locations. For example, the pharmaceutical, tourism, entertainment, motor vehicle, aerospace, and forest products industries benefit greatly when the dollar falls against the yen and euro. Agricultural and petroleum industries are hurt by the dollar's rise against the currencies of Mexico, Brazil, Venezuela, and Australia. Generally, a strong or high dollar makes U.S. goods more expensive in overseas markets. This worsens the U.S. trade deficit. When the value of the dollar falls, tourism-oriented firms benefit because Americans do not travel abroad as much when the value of the dollar is low; rather, foreigners visit and vacation more in the United States.

A low value of the dollar means lower imports and higher exports; it helps U.S. companies' competitiveness in world markets. A falling dollar makes U.S. goods cheaper to foreign consumers and combats deflation by pushing up prices of imports. A low value of the dollar benefits the U.S. economy in many ways. First, it helps stave off the risks of deflation in the USA and also reduces the U.S. trade deficit. In addition, a low value of the dollar raises the foreign sales and profits of domestic firms, thanks to dollar-induced gains, and encourages foreign countries to lower interest rates and loosen fiscal policy, which stimulates worldwide economic expansion. Some sectors, such as consumer staples, energy, materials, technology, and health care, especially benefit from a low value of the dollar. Manufacturers in many domestic industries in fact benefit because of a weak dollar, which forces foreign rivals to raise prices and extinguish discounts. Domestic firms with big overseas sales, such as McDonald's, greatly benefit from a weak dollar. Table 7-2 lists some advantages and disadvantages of a weak U.S. dollar for U.S. firms.

In contrast to rivals Nissan Motor and Honda Motor, Mazda Motor Corp. based in Hiroshima, Japan, has a strategy to produce more than 80 percent of its vehicles in Japan and export them rather than building manufacturing plants globally. Even if the value of the dollar weakens to 77 yen, Mazda says it can make a profit on its CX-5 vehicles. But with the dollar at 79 yen, Honda and Nissan say they must keep moving production abroad and will do so until or unless the dollar climbs back to at least 100 yen. Thus, value of the dollar versus the Japanese yen is an important factor in strategic planning among Japanese firms.

The value of the dollar changes some every day, but generally in 2012–2013 the value of the dollar was strong and thus profits of U.S. companies with revenue from abroad were lowered on average 6 to 7 percent. Why the lowered profits? Because, for example, 100 euros earned in Europe, when translated back to U.S. dollars for reporting purposes, the 100 euros is worth

TABLE 7-2 Advantages and Disadvantages of a Weak Dollar for Domestic Firms

Advantages	Disadvantages
1. Leads to more exports	1. Can lead to inflation
2. Leads to lower imports	2. Can cause rise in oil prices
3. Makes U.S. goods cheaper to foreign consumers	3. Can weaken U.S. government
4. Combats deflation by pushing up prices of imports	4. Makes it unattractive for Americans to travel globally
5. Can contribute to rise in stock prices in short run	5. Can contribute to fall in stock prices in long run
6. Encourages foreign countries to lower interest rates	
7. Raises the revenues and profits of firms that do business outside the USA	
8. Forces foreign firms to raise prices	
9. Reduces the U.S. trade deficit	
10. Encourages firms to globalize	
11. Encourages foreigners to visit the United States	

maybe $75. To combat this "loss," some companies try to raise prices in their European or Mexican stores, but that carries a risk of alienating shoppers, angering retailers, and giving local competitors a price edge. Some advantages of a strong dollar however are that companies with substantial outside U.S. operations see their overseas expenses, such as salaries paid in euros, become cheaper. Another advantage of a strong dollar is that it gives U.S. companies greater firepower for international acquisitions. Another advantage of a strong dollar is that companies that import benefit from greater buying power because their dollars now go further overseas.

A recent *Wall Street Journal* article (12-4-12, B4) explains the unfavorable foreign-exchange rate environment plaguing U.S. firms. For example, the starch and sweetener maker Ingredion Inc.'s earnings were reduced by 20 cents per share recently by weakness in the Brazilian real, Argentine peso, British pound, and the euro. Similarly, General Motors reported that its third quarter 2012 sales were reduced by about $1.3 billion as a result of weakness in the European euro, Russian ruble, Hungarian forint, South Korean won, South African rand, Canadian dollar, and Mexican pesos.

Social, Cultural, Demographic, and Natural Environment Forces

Asian Americans are now the best-educated, highest-earning, and fastest-growing racial group in the United States.[2] The number of Asian Americans in the United States grew by 46 percent between 2000 and 2010, with Chinese Americans becoming by far the largest group. The median U.S. household income is $49.8K, with Asian American's median being $66K, compared to whites $54K, Hispanics $40K, and African Americans $33.3K.[3]

The U.S. Fish and Wildlife Service reported in late 2012 that 11 percent more Americans (ages 16 and older) fished and 9 percent more hunted in 2011 than in 2006. The report also revealed that among children aged 6 to 15, 13 percent more hunted and 2 percent more fished during the same period. A variety of reasons account for the shift back to "doing outdoor things," but this trend is excellent news for thousands of sporting goods companies.

Social, cultural, demographic, and environmental changes have a major impact on virtually all products, services, markets, and customers. Small, large, for-profit, and nonprofit organizations in all industries are being staggered and challenged by the opportunities and threats arising from changes in social, cultural, demographic, and environmental variables. In every way, the United States is much different today than it was yesterday, and tomorrow promises even greater changes.

The USA is getting older and less white. The oldest among the 76 million baby boomers in the USA plan to retire soon, and this has lawmakers and younger taxpayers deeply concerned about who will pay their Social Security, Medicare, and Medicaid. Individuals age 65 and older in the USA as a percentage of the population, will rise to 18.5 percent by 2025. The oldest USA veteran is Richard Everton of East Austin, Texas, who is 108; the oldest USA woman is 114, Teralean Talley of Inkster, Michigan.

By 2075, the USA will have no racial or ethnic majority. This forecast is aggravating tensions over issues such as immigration and affirmative action. Hawaii, California, and New Mexico already have no majority race or ethnic group

The population of the world recently surpassed 7 billion; the USA has slightly more than 310 million people. That leaves billions of people outside the USA who may be interested in the products and services produced through domestic firms. Remaining solely domestic is an increasingly risky strategy, especially as the world population continues to grow to an estimated 8 billion in 2028 and 9 billion in 2054.

Social, cultural, demographic, and environmental trends are shaping the way Americans live, work, produce, and consume. New trends are creating a different type of consumer and, consequently, a need for different products, different services, and different strategies. There are now more U.S. households with people living alone or with unrelated people than there are households consisting of married couples with children. U.S. households are making more and more purchases online.

The trend toward an older USA is good news for restaurants, hotels, airlines, cruise lines, tours, resorts, theme parks, luxury products and services, recreational vehicles, home builders, furniture producers, computer manufacturers, travel services, pharmaceutical firms, automakers, and funeral homes. Older Americans are especially interested in health care, financial services, travel, crime prevention, and leisure. The world's longest-living people are the Japanese, with Japanese women living to 86.3 years and men living to 80.1 years on average. By 2050, the Census Bureau projects that the number of Americans age 100 and older will increase to over 834,000 from just under 100,000 centenarians in the USA in 2000. Americans age 65 and over will increase from 12.6 percent of the U.S. population in 2000 to 20.0 percent by the year 2050. The aging U.S. population affects the strategic orientation of nearly all organizations.

The historical trend of people moving from the Northeast and Midwest to the Sunbelt and West has dramatically slowed. Hard number data related to this trend can represent key opportunities for many firms and thus can be essential for successful strategy formulation, including where to locate new plants and distribution centers and where to focus marketing efforts.

A summary of important social, cultural, demographic, and environmental variables that represent opportunities or threats for virtually all organizations is given in Table 7-3.

Political, Governmental, and Legal Forces

Figure 7-3 reveals the USA county-by-county presidential election results for the 2012 Barack Obama versus Mitt Romney election, with the red being Republican and the blue being Democratic. The red indicates counties that had a Republican majority vote result, but much of this land is sparsely inhabited. President Obama and the Democrats won both the popular vote and the Electoral College count. Various industries, such as aerospace, and all their supplier firms, typically support and lobby for Republicans, whereas other industries, such as automotive and all their supplier firms, generally support Democrats. National, state, and local elections impact businesses, with ongoing healthy debate concerning the pros and cons of each party's agenda for business. Should firms take stances on political issues?

Political issues and stances do matter for business, especially in today's world of instant tweeting and e-mailing. For example, Starbucks' recent support of same-sex marriage in its home state of Washington was praised by a number of prominent rights activists. Maine, Maryland, Minnesota, Washington, Massachusetts, New York, California, and a few other states all allow same-sex marriage. But the Seattle-based coffee chain's outspoken opponents, such as the National Organization for Marriage (NOM), has vowed to make Starbucks (along with other companies that support same-sex marriage) pay a "price" for this stance. "Middle Eastern countries are hostile to lesbian, gay, bisexual and transgender (LGBT)

TABLE 7-3 Key Social, Cultural, Demographic, and Natural Environment Variables

Childbearing rates	Attitudes toward retirement
Number of special-interest groups	Attitudes toward leisure time
Number of marriages	Attitudes toward product quality
Number of divorces	Attitudes toward customer service
Number of births	Pollution control
Number of deaths	Attitudes toward foreign peoples
Immigration and emigration rates	Energy conservation
Social Security programs	Social programs
Life expectancy rates	Number of churches
Per capita income	Number of church members
Location of retailing, manufacturing, and service businesses	Social responsibility
Attitudes toward business	Attitudes toward careers
Lifestyles	Population changes by race, age, sex, and level of affluence
Traffic congestion	Attitudes toward authority
Inner-city environments	Population changes by city, county, state, region, and country
Average disposable income	
Trust in government	Value placed on leisure time
Attitudes toward government	Regional changes in tastes and preferences
Attitudes toward work	Number of women and minority workers
Buying habits	Number of high school and college graduates by geographic area
Ethical concerns	
Attitudes toward saving	Recycling
Sex roles	Waste management
Attitudes toward investing	Air pollution
Racial equality	Water pollution
Use of birth control	Ozone depletion
Average level of education	Endangered species
Government regulation	

rights. So for example, in Qatar, in the Middle East, we've begun working to make sure that there's some price to be paid for this," Brian Brown of the NOM said. "These are not countries that look kindly on same-sex marriage. And this is where Starbucks wants to expand, as well as India." In essence, the question needs to be asked, should firms take stances on contentious social issues?

Beginning in 2014, U.S. businesses will have to offer workers a minimum level in medical insurance or pay a penalty starting at $2,000 for each worker. This is part of the so-called Obamacare legislation. So, thousands of U.S. businesses, such as Pillar Hotels & Resorts, are transitioning to having a larger percentage of their workforce being comprised of part-time workers rather than full-time employees. Pillar Hotels owns Sheraton, Fairfield Inns, Hampton Inns, and Holiday Inns.

A political debate still rages in the USA regarding sales taxes on the Internet. Walmart, Target, and other large retailers are pressuring state governments to collect sales taxes from Amazon.com. Big brick-and-mortar retailers are backing a coalition called the Alliance for Main Street Fairness, which is leading political efforts to change sales-tax laws in more than a dozen states. Walmart's executive Raul Vazquez says, "The rules today don't allow brick-and-mortar retailers to compete evenly with online retailers, and that needs to be addressed."

Federal, state, local, and foreign governments are major regulators, deregulators, subsidizers, employers, and customers of organizations. Political, governmental, and legal factors, therefore, can represent key opportunities or threats for both small and large organizations. Political unrest in the Middle East threatens to raise oil prices globally, which could cause inflation. The political

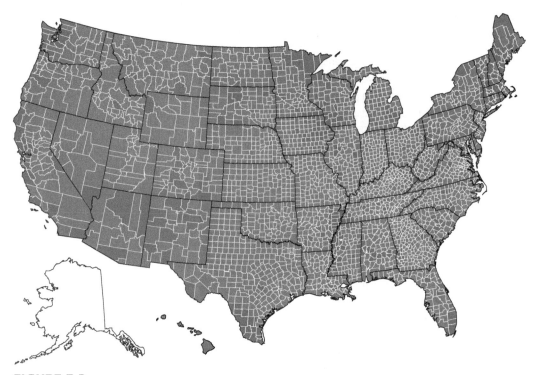

FIGURE 7-3

County-by County USA 2012 Presidential Results (red = Republican; blue = Democrat)

overthrow of monarchies in Egypt, Tunisia, Yemen, and Libya has spread to Syria and even Turkey because people in all nations desire liberty and freedom rather than oppression and suppression.

For industries and firms that depend heavily on government contracts or subsidies, political forecasts can be the most important part of an external audit. Changes in patent laws, antitrust legislation, tax rates, and lobbying activities can affect firms significantly. The increasing global interdependence among economies, markets, governments, and organizations makes it imperative that firms consider the possible impact of political variables on the formulation and implementation of competitive strategies.

The Marketplace Fairness Act (MFA) in the U.S. Senate and the Marketplace Equity Act (MEA) in the U.S. House are likely to pass in 2013, basically reversing the 1992 Supreme Court decision exempting many online retailers from collecting state sales taxes unless they had a physical presence in the state, such as a warehouse. But as online sales boom, states continue to suffer severe budget shortfalls and brick-and-mortar companies cannot compete with online firms, so legislation to tax online sales is expected to pass soon.

Many countries worldwide are resorting to protectionism to safeguard their own industries. European Union (EU) nations, for example, have tightened their own trade rules and resumed subsidies for various of their own industries while barring imports from certain other countries. The EU recently restricted imports of U.S. chicken and beef. India is increasing tariffs on foreign steel. Russia perhaps has instituted the most protectionist measures by raising tariffs on most imports and subsidizing its own exports. Russia even imposed a new toll on trucks from the EU, Switzerland, and Turkmenistan. Despite these measures taken by other countries, the USA has largely refrained from "Buy American" policies and protectionist measures, although there are increased tariffs on French cheese and Italian water. Many economists say trade constraints will make it harder for global economic growth.

Labor Unions

The extent that a state is unionized can be a significant political factor in strategic planning decisions as related to manufacturing plant location and other operational matters. The size of U.S. labor unions has fallen sharply in the last decade as a result in large part of erosion of the U.S. manufacturing base.

Huge declines of late in receipts of federal, state, and municipal governments has contributed to a sharp decline in the membership of public-sector unions. Organized public-sector labor issues are being debated in many state legislatures. State governments seek concessions, the most drastic of which may be the abolition of collective bargaining rights. Wisconsin recently passed a law eliminating most collective-bargaining rights for the state's public-employee unions. That law sets a precedent that many other states may follow to curb union rights as a way to help state budgets become solvent. Ohio is close to passing a similar bill curbing union rights for 400,000 public workers.

According to the U.S. Bureau of Labor Statistics, the union membership rate (the percent of wage and salary workers who were members of a union) in the USA was 11.8 percent in 2011, down slightly from 11.9 percent the prior year. The number of wage and salary workers belonging to unions, at 14.8 million, also showed little movement over the year. By comparison, in 1983, the union membership rate was 20.1 percent and there were 17.7 million union workers. Highlights from the Bureau's 2011 data are as follows:

- Public-sector workers had a union membership rate (37.0 percent) more than five times higher than that of private-sector workers (6.9 percent).
- Workers in education, training, and library occupations had the highest unionization rate, at 36.8 percent, whereas the lowest rate occurred in sales and related occupations (3.0 percent).
- Black workers were more likely to be union members than were white, Asian, or Hispanic workers.
- Among states, New York continued to have the highest union membership rate (24.1 percent) and North Carolina again had the lowest rate (2.9 percent).

In Europe, German-based Lufthansa AG recently cancelled two-thirds of its airline flights as a result of an anticipated strike by its cabin crew. The union UFO represents 18,000 Lufthansa cabin-crew members who want higher wages, but Lufthansa says their average flight attendant' salary is 52,492 euros compared with 23,680 euros at rival firm Air Berlin PLC. Similarly, British Airways recently was hammered by the cabin-crew union Unite, costing the airline about $250 million.

Local, state, and federal laws; regulatory agencies; and special-interest groups can have a major impact on the strategies of small, large, for-profit, and nonprofit organizations. Many companies have altered or abandoned strategies in the past because of political or governmental actions. In the academic world, as state budgets have dropped in recent years, so too has state support for colleges and universities. Resulting from the decline in monies received from the state, many institutions of higher learning are doing more fund-raising on their own—naming buildings and classrooms, for example, for donors. A summary of political, governmental, and legal variables that can represent key opportunities or threats to organizations is provided in Table 7-4.

TABLE 7-4 Some Political, Governmental, and Legal Variables

Government regulations or deregulations	Sino American relationships
Changes in tax laws	Russian American relationships
Special tariffs	European American relationships
Political action committees	African American relationships
Voter participation rates	Import–export regulations
Number, severity, and location of government protests	Government fiscal and monetary policy changes
Number of patents	Political conditions in foreign countries
Changes in patent laws	Special local, state, and federal laws
Environmental protection laws	Lobbying activities
Level of defense expenditures	Size of government budgets
Legislation on equal employment	World oil, currency, and labor markets
Level of government subsidies	Location and severity of terrorist activities
Antitrust legislation	Local, state, and national elections

Technological Forces

The **Internet** has changed the nature of opportunities and threats by altering the life cycles of products, increasing the speed of distribution, creating new products and services, erasing limitations of traditional geographic markets, and changing the historical trade-off between production standardization and flexibility. The Internet has lowered entry barriers and redefined the relationship between industries and various suppliers, creditors, customers, and competitors.

Papa John's International a few years ago received more than 50 percent of all its pizza orders through its website, up from 30 percent in 2011 and far more than the industry average of 10 percent. Technology is a key to Papa John's success as it strives to compete with Domino's Pizza and Pizza Hut. Papa John's new website is interactive, where customers can see a picture of their pizza as they decide upon toppings. Papa John's new loyalty program, called Papa Points, is promoted heavily through its new website.

Google's Nexus 7 tablet computer and Apple's iPhone 5 released in late 2012 worldwide provide a reminder of the kind of competition that has left Japan's consumer electronics makers struggling to survive. Japanese firms such as Sony Corp., Panasonic Corp. and Sharp Corp. once dominated the electronics business. Sharp's new restructuring plan involves the firm cutting more than 10,000 jobs, cutting wages, and selling plants in Mexico, China, and Malaysia.

According to media consultant BIA/Kelsey, small and midsize businesses in the USA spent about $1.3 billion in 2011 on online reputation management tools and services. Those figures grew to about $1.6 billion in 2012 and are expected to grow to $2.5 billion by 2016 according to the firm. Further, the firm says about 57 percent of small and midsize businesses in the USA monitor online content about their businesses, with 71 percent using free, do-it-yourself software. In general, monitoring of online reviews about your business, large or small, has become a burdensome but an essential task, especially given emergence of social-media channels, such as Twitter, that empowers opinionated customers. Research is clear that benign neglect of a company's online reputation could quickly hurt sales, especially given the new normal behavior of customers consulting their smartphones for even the smallest of purchases.[4]

To effectively capitalize on e-commerce, a number of organizations are establishing two new positions in their firms: **chief information officer (CIO)** and **chief technology officer (CTO)**. This trend reflects the growing importance of **information technology (IT)** in strategic management. A CIO and CTO work together to ensure that information needed to formulate, implement, and evaluate strategies is available where and when it is needed. These individuals are responsible for developing, maintaining, and updating a company's information database. The CIO is more a manager, managing the firm's relationship with stakeholders; the CTO is more a technician, focusing on technical issues such as data acquisition, data processing, decision-support systems, and software and hardware acquisition.

Technological forces represent major opportunities and threats that must be considered in formulating strategies. Technological advancements can dramatically affect organizations' products, services, markets, suppliers, distributors, competitors, customers, manufacturing processes, marketing practices, and competitive position. Technological advancements can create new markets, result in a proliferation of new and improved products, change the relative competitive cost positions in an industry, and render existing products and services obsolete. Technological changes can reduce or eliminate cost barriers between businesses, create shorter production runs, create shortages in technical skills, and result in changing values and expectations of employees, managers, and customers. Technological advancements can create new competitive advantages that are more powerful than existing advantages. No company or industry today is insulated against emerging technological developments. In high-tech industries, identification and evaluation of key technological opportunities and threats can be the most important part of the external strategic-management audit.

Organizations that traditionally have limited technology expenditures to what they can fund after meeting marketing and financial requirements urgently need a reversal in thinking. The pace of technological change is increasing and literally wiping out businesses every day. An emerging consensus holds that technology management is one of the key responsibilities of strategists. Firms should pursue strategies that take advantage of technological opportunities to achieve sustainable, competitive advantages in the marketplace.

In practice, critical decisions about technology too often are delegated to lower organizational levels or are made without an understanding of their strategic implications. Many strategists spend countless hours determining market share, positioning products in terms of features and price, forecasting sales and market size, and monitoring distributors; yet too often, technology does not receive the same respect.

Not all sectors of the economy are affected equally by technological developments. The communications, electronics, aeronautics, and pharmaceutical industries are much more volatile than the textile, forestry, and metals industries.

Competitive Forces

An important part of an external audit is identifying rival firms and determining their strengths, weaknesses, capabilities, opportunities, threats, objectives, and strategies. George Salk said: "If you're not faster than your competitor, you're in a tenuous position, and if you're only half as fast, you're terminal."

Collecting and evaluating information on competitors is essential for successful strategy formulation. Identifying major competitors is not always easy because many firms have divisions that compete in different industries. Many multidivisional firms do not provide sales and profit information on a divisional basis for competitive reasons. Also, privately-held firms do not publish any financial or marketing information. Addressing questions about competitors such as those presented in Table 7-5 is important in performing an external audit.

Competition in virtually all industries can be described as intense—and sometimes as cut-throat. For example, Walgreens and CVS pharmacies are located generally across the street from each other and battle each other every day on price and customer service. Most automobile dealerships also are located close to each other. Dollar General, based in Goodlettsville, Tennessee, and Family Dollar, based in Matthews, North Carolina, compete intensely on price to attract customers away from each other and away from Walmart.

Seven characteristics describe the most competitive companies:

1. Strive to continually increase market share.
2. Use the vision/mission as a guide for all decisions.
3. Realize that the old adage "if it's not broke, don't fix it" has been replaced by "whether its broke or not, fix it;" in other words, continually strive to improve everything about the firm
4. Continually adapt, innovate, improve – especially when the firm is successful.
5. Strive to grow through acquisition whenever possible
6. Hire and retain the best employees and managers possible
7. Strive to stay cost-competitive on a global basis.[5]

TABLE 7-5 Key Questions About Competitors

---

1. What are the major competitors' strengths?
2. What are the major competitors' weaknesses?
3. What are the major competitors' objectives and strategies?
4. How will the major competitors most likely respond to current economic, social, cultural, demographic, environmental, political, governmental, legal, technological, and competitive trends affecting our industry?
5. How vulnerable are the major competitors to our alternative company strategies?
6. How vulnerable are our alternative strategies to successful counterattack by our major competitors?
7. How are our products or services positioned relative to major competitors?
8. To what extent are new firms entering and old firms leaving this industry?
9. What key factors have resulted in our present competitive position in this industry?
10. How have the sales and profit rankings of major competitors in the industry changed over recent years? Why have these rankings changed that way?
11. What is the nature of supplier and distributor relationships in this industry?
12. To what extent could substitute products or services be a threat to competitors in this industry?

Competitive Intelligence Programs

What is competitive intelligence? **Competitive intelligence (CI)**, as formally defined by the Society of Competitive Intelligence Professionals (SCIP), is a systematic and ethical process for gathering and analyzing information about the competition's activities and general business trends to further a business's own goals (SCIP website).

Good competitive intelligence in business, as in the military, is one of the keys to success. The more information and knowledge a firm can obtain about its competitors, the more likely it is that it can formulate and implement effective strategies. Major competitors' weaknesses can represent external opportunities; major competitors' strengths may represent key threats.

Various legal and ethical ways to obtain competitive intelligence include the following:

- Hire top executives from rival firms
- Reverse engineer rival firms' products
- Use surveys and interviews of customers, suppliers, and distributors
- Conduct drive by and on-site visits to rival firm operations
- Search online databases
- Contact government agencies for public information about rival firms
- Systematically monitor relevant trade publications, magazines, and newspapers
- Include gathering competitive intelligence in the job description of salespersons

Many U.S. executives grew up in times when U.S. firms dominated foreign competitors so much that gathering CI did not seem worth the effort. Too many of these executives still cling to these attitudes—to the detriment of their organizations today. Even most MBA programs do not offer a course in competitive and business intelligence, thus reinforcing this attitude. As a consequence, three strong misperceptions about business intelligence prevail among U.S. executives today:

1. Running an intelligence program requires lots of people, computers, and other resources.
2. Collecting intelligence about competitors violates antitrust laws; business intelligence equals espionage.
3. Intelligence gathering is an unethical business practice.[6]

Any discussions with a competitor about price, market, or geography intentions could violate antitrust statutes. However, this fact must not lure a firm into underestimating the need for and benefits of systematically collecting information about competitors for strategic planning purposes. The Internet is an excellent medium for gathering CI. Information gathering from employees, managers, suppliers, distributors, customers, creditors, and consultants also can make the difference between having superior or just average intelligence and overall competitiveness.

Firms need an effective CI program. The three basic objectives of a CI program are (1) to provide a general understanding of an industry and its competitors, (2) to identify areas in which competitors are vulnerable and to assess the impact strategic actions would have on competitors, and (3) to identify potential moves that a competitor might make that would endanger a firm's position in the market.[7] Competitive information is equally applicable for strategy formulation, implementation, and evaluation decisions. An effective CI program allows all areas of a firm to access consistent and verifiable information in making decisions. All members of an organization—from the CEO to custodians—are valuable intelligence agents and should feel themselves to be a part of the CI process. Special characteristics of a successful CI program include flexibility, usefulness, timeliness, and cross-functional cooperation.

The increasing emphasis on **competitive analysis** in the USA is evidenced by corporations putting this function on their organizational charts under job titles such as Director of Competitive Analysis, Competitive Strategy Manager, Director of Information Services, or Associate Director of Competitive Assessment. The responsibilities of a **director of competitive analysis** include planning, collecting data, analyzing data, facilitating the process of gathering and analyzing data, disseminating intelligence on a timely basis, researching special issues, and recognizing what information is important and who needs to know. CI is not corporate espionage because 95 percent of the information a company needs to make strategic decisions is available and accessible to the public. Sources of competitive information include trade journals, want ads, newspaper articles, and government filings, as well as customers, suppliers, distributors, competitors themselves, and the Internet.

Unethical tactics such as bribery, wiretapping, and computer hacking should never be used to obtain information. All the information you could wish for can be collected without resorting to unethical tactics.

Market Commonality and Resource Similarity

By definition, competitors are firms that offer similar products and services in the same market. Markets can be geographic or product areas or segments. For example, in the insurance industry the markets are broken down into commercial/consumer, health/life, or Europe/Asia. Researchers use the terms *market commonality* and *resource similarity* to study rivalry among competitors. **Market commonality** can be defined as the number and significance of markets that a firm competes in with rivals.[8] **Resource similarity** is the extent to which the type and amount of a firm's internal resources are comparable to a rival.[9] One way to analyze competitiveness between two or among several firms is to investigate market commonality and resource similarity issues while looking for areas of potential competitive advantage along each firm's value chain.

Competitive Analysis: Porter's Five-Forces Model

Wayne Calloway said: "Nothing focuses the mind better than the constant sight of a competitor that wants to wipe you off the map." As illustrated in Figure 7-4, **Porter's Five-Forces Model** of competitive analysis is a widely used approach for developing strategies in many industries. The intensity of competition among firms varies widely across industries. Table 7-6 reveals the average gross profit margin and earnings per share for firms in different industries. Note the substantial variation among industries. For example, note that industry profit margins range from 20.5 to 2.3 percent, whereas industry return on equity (ROE) values range from 23.2 to 8.9. Note that bookstores have the lowest average profit margin (2.3), which implies fierce competition in that industry. Intensity of competition is highest in lower-return industries. The collective impact of competitive forces is so brutal in some industries that the market is clearly "unattractive" from a profit-making standpoint. Rivalry among existing firms is severe, new rivals can enter the industry with relative ease, and both suppliers and customers can exercise considerable bargaining leverage. According to Porter, the nature of competitiveness in a given industry can be viewed as a composite of five forces:

1. Rivalry among competing firms
2. Potential entry of new competitors
3. Potential development of substitute products
4. Bargaining power of suppliers
5. Bargaining power of consumers

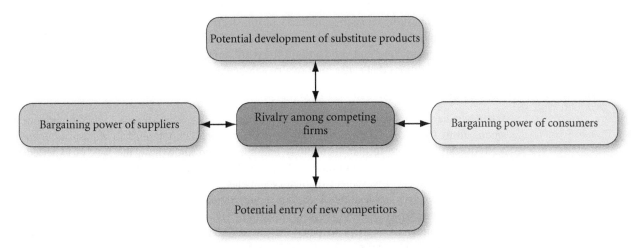

FIGURE 7-4

The Five-Forces Model of Competition

TABLE 7-6 **Competitiveness Across a Few Industries (late 2013 data)**

	Profit Margin (%)	EPS ($)
Pharmaceutical	20.5	20.3
Telecommunications	8.0	14.1
Fragrances/Cosmetics	9.8	22.6
Banking	16.1	8.9
Bookstores	2.3	10.5
Food Manufacturers	6.6	19.3
Oil and Gas	6.1	15.7
Airlines	2.5	23.2
Machinery/Construction	7.2	21.6
Paper Products	7.6	10.6

Source: Based on information at www.finance.yahoo.com retrieved on May 10, 2011.

The following three steps for using Porter's Five-Forces Model can indicate whether competition in a given industry is such that the firm can make an acceptable profit:

1. Identify key aspects or elements of each competitive force that impact the firm.
2. Evaluate how strong and important each element is for the firm.
3. Decide whether the collective strength of the elements is worth the firm entering or staying in the industry.

Rivalry Among Competing Firms

Rivalry among competing firms is usually the most powerful of the five competitive forces. The strategies pursued by one firm can be successful only to the extent that they provide competitive advantage over the strategies pursued by rival firms. Changes in strategy by one firm may be met with retaliatory countermoves, such as lowering prices, enhancing quality, adding features, providing services, extending warranties, and increasing advertising.

The intensity of rivalry among competing firms tends to increase as the number of competitors increases, as competitors become more equal in size and capability, as demand for the industry's products declines, and as price cutting becomes common. Rivalry also increases when consumers can switch brands easily; when barriers to leaving the market are high; when fixed costs are high; when the product is perishable; when consumer demand is growing slowly or declines such that rivals have excess capacity or inventory; when the products being sold are commodities (not easily differentiated, such as gasoline); when rival firms are diverse in strategies, origins, and culture; and when mergers and acquisitions are common in the industry. As rivalry among competing firms intensifies, industry profits decline, in some cases to the point where an industry becomes inherently unattractive. When rival firms sense weakness, typically they will intensify both marketing and production efforts to capitalize on the "opportunity." Table 7-7 summarizes conditions that cause high rivalry among competing firms.

Potential Entry of New Competitors

Whenever new firms can easily enter a particular industry, the intensity of competitiveness among firms increases. Barriers to entry, however, can include the need to gain economies of scale quickly, the need to gain technology and specialized know-how, the lack of experience, strong customer loyalty, strong brand preferences, large capital requirements, lack of adequate distribution channels, government regulatory policies, tariffs, lack of access to raw materials, possession of patents, undesirable locations, counterattack by entrenched firms, and potential saturation of the market.

Despite numerous barriers to entry, new firms sometimes enter industries with higher-quality products, lower prices, and substantial marketing resources. The strategist's job, therefore, is to identify potential new firms entering the market, to monitor the new rival firms' strategies, to counterattack as needed, and to capitalize on existing strengths and opportunities.

TABLE 7-7 Conditions That Cause High Rivalry Among Competing Firms

1. High number of competing firms
2. Similar size of firms competing
3. Similar capability of firms competing
4. Falling demand for the industry's products
5. Falling product or service prices in the industry
6. When consumers can switch brands easily
7. When barriers to leaving the market are high
8. When barriers to entering the market are low
9. When fixed costs are high among firms competing
10. When the product is perishable
11. When rivals have excess capacity
12. When consumer demand is falling
13. When rivals have excess inventory
14. When rivals sell similar products/services
15. When mergers are common in the industry

When the threat of new firms entering the market is strong, incumbent firms generally fortify their positions and take actions to deter new entrants, such as lowering prices, extending warranties, adding features, or offering financing specials.

Walt Disney is rapidly building its Shanghai Disneyland $4.4 billion complex set to open in China in 2016, complete with hotels, restaurants, retail shops and other amenities. However, a rival firm, DreamWorks Animation SKG, is now building a $3.1 billion entertainment district named Dream Center in Shanghai right beside Disneyland and says its facility will also open in 2016. Although expensive to build, theme parks are becoming more popular globally. Time Warner's Warner Brothers is building Harry Potter attractions around the world, including a converted movie studio outside London.

Potential Development of Substitute Products

In many industries, firms are in close competition with producers of substitute products in other industries. Examples are plastic container producers competing with glass, paperboard, and aluminum can producers, and acetaminophen manufacturers competing with other manufacturers of pain and headache remedies. The presence of substitute products puts a ceiling on the price that can be charged before consumers will switch to the substitute product. Price ceilings equate to profit ceilings and more intense competition among rivals. Producers of eyeglasses and contact lenses, for example, face increasing competitive pressures from laser eye surgery. Producers of sugar face similar pressures from artificial sweeteners. Newspapers and magazines face substitute-product competitive pressures from the Internet and 24-hour cable television. The magnitude of competitive pressure derived from the development of substitute products is generally evidenced by rivals' plans for expanding production capacity, as well as by their sales and profit growth numbers.

Competitive pressures arising from substitute products increase as the relative price of substitute products declines and as consumers' costs of switching decrease. The competitive strength of substitute products is best measured by the inroads into the market share those products obtain, as well as those firms' plans for increased capacity and market penetration.

For example, circulation of U.S. newspapers continues to drop drastically, with the exception of the *Wall Street Journal, USA Today,* and a few others. The growing popularity of free news on the web and more timely news online are two key factors negatively impacting traditional papers such as the *New York Times*, *Los Angeles Times*, and others.

Bargaining Power of Suppliers

The bargaining power of suppliers affects the intensity of competition in an industry, especially when there are few suppliers, when there are few good substitute raw materials, or when the cost of switching raw materials is especially high. It is often in the best interest of both suppliers and producers to assist each other with reasonable prices, improved quality, development of new services, just-in-time deliveries, and reduced inventory costs, thus enhancing long-term profitability for all concerned.

Firms may pursue a backward integration strategy to gain control or ownership of suppliers. This strategy is especially effective when suppliers are unreliable, too costly, or not capable of meeting a firm's needs on a consistent basis. Firms generally can negotiate more favorable terms with suppliers when backward integration is a commonly used strategy among rival firms in an industry.

However, in many industries it is more economical to use outside suppliers of component parts than to self-manufacture the items. This is true, for example, in the outdoor power equipment industry, where producers of lawn mowers, rotary tillers, leaf blowers, and edgers such as Murray generally obtain their small engines from outside manufacturers such as Briggs & Stratton that specialize in such engines and have huge economies of scale.

In more and more industries, sellers are forging strategic partnerships with select suppliers in efforts to (a) reduce inventory and logistics costs (e.g., through just-in-time deliveries); (b) speed the availability of next-generation components; (c) enhance the quality of the parts and components being supplied and reduce defect rates; and (d) squeeze out important cost savings for both themselves and their suppliers.[10]

Bargaining Power of Consumers

When customers are concentrated or large in number or buy in volume, their bargaining power represents a major force affecting the intensity of competition in an industry. Rival firms may offer extended warranties or special services to gain customer loyalty whenever the bargaining power of consumers is substantial. Bargaining power of consumers also is higher when the products being purchased are standard or undifferentiated. When this is the case, consumers often can negotiate selling price, warranty coverage, and accessory packages to a greater extent.

The bargaining power of consumers can be the most important force affecting competitive advantage. Consumers gain increasing bargaining power under the following circumstances:

1. If they can inexpensively switch to competing brands or substitutes
2. If they are particularly important to the seller
3. If sellers are struggling in the face of falling consumer demand
4. If they are informed about sellers' products, prices, and costs
5. If they have discretion in whether and when they purchase the product[11]

Sources of External Information

A wealth of strategic information is available to organizations from both published and unpublished sources. Unpublished sources include customer surveys, market research, speeches at professional and shareholders' meetings, television programs, interviews, and conversations with stakeholders. Published sources of strategic information include periodicals, journals, reports, government documents, abstracts, books, directories, newspapers, and manuals. A company website is usually an excellent place to start to find information about a firm, particularly on the Investor Relations web pages.

There are many excellent websites for gathering strategic information, but five that the author uses routinely are:

1. www.money.msn.com
2. http://finance.yahoo.com
3. www.hoovers.com
4. http://globaledge.msu.edu/industries/
5. www.monrningstar.com

An excellent source of industry information is provided by Michigan State University at http://globaledge.msu.edu/industries/. Industry Profiles provided at that site are an excellent source for information, news, events, and statistical data for any industry. In addition to a wealth of indices, risk assessments, and interactive trade information, a wide array of global resources are provided.

Most college libraries subscribe to Standard & Poor's (S&P's) *Industry Surveys*. These documents are exceptionally up-to-date and give valuable information about many different industries. Each report is authored by a Standard & Poor's industry research analyst and includes the following sections:

1. Current Environment
2. Industry Trends
3. How the Industry Operates
4. Key Industry Ratios and Statistics
5. How to Analyze a Company
6. Glossary of Industry Terms
7. Additional Industry Information
8. References
9. Comparative Company Financial Analysis

Forecasting Tools and Techniques

Forecasts are educated assumptions about future trends and events. Forecasting is a complex activity because of factors such as technological innovation, cultural changes, new products, improved services, stronger competitors, shifts in government priorities, changing social values, unstable economic conditions, and unforeseen events. Managers often must rely on published forecasts to effectively identify key external opportunities and threats.

A sense of the future permeates all action and underlies every decision a person makes. People eat expecting to be satisfied and nourished in the future. People sleep assuming that in the future they will feel rested. They invest energy, money, and time because they believe their efforts will be rewarded in the future. They build highways assuming that automobiles and trucks will need them in the future. Parents educate children on the basis of forecasts that they will need certain skills, attitudes, and knowledge when they grow up. The truth is we all make implicit forecasts throughout our daily lives. The question, therefore, is not whether we should forecast but rather how we can best forecast to enable us to move beyond our ordinarily unarticulated assumptions about the future. Can we obtain information and then make educated assumptions (forecasts) to better guide our current decisions to achieve a more desirable future state of affairs? Assumptions must be made based on facts, figures, trends, and research. Strive for the firm's assumptions to be more accurate than rival firm's assumptions.

Sometimes organizations must develop their own projections. Most organizations forecast (project) their own revenues and profits annually. Organizations sometimes forecast market share or customer loyalty in local areas. Because forecasting is so important in strategic management and because the ability to forecast (in contrast to the ability to use a forecast) is essential, selected forecasting tools are examined further here.

Forecasting tools can be broadly categorized into two groups: quantitative techniques and qualitative techniques. Quantitative forecasts are most appropriate when historical data are available and when the relationships among key variables are expected to remain the same in the future. **Linear regression**, for example, is based on the assumption that the future will be just like the past—which, of course, it never is. As historical relationships become less stable, quantitative forecasts become less accurate.

No forecast is perfect, and some forecasts are even wildly inaccurate. This fact accents the need for strategists to devote sufficient time and effort to study the underlying bases for published forecasts and to develop internal forecasts of their own. Key external opportunities and threats can be effectively identified only through good forecasts. Accurate forecasts can provide major competitive advantages for organizations. Accurate forecasts are vital to the strategic-management process and to the success of organizations.

Making Assumptions

Planning would be impossible without assumptions. McConkey defines assumptions as the "best present estimates of the impact of major external factors, over which the manager has little if any control, but which may exert a significant impact on performance or the ability to achieve desired results."[12] Strategists are faced with countless variables and imponderables that can be neither controlled nor predicted with 100 percent accuracy. Wild guesses should never be made in formulating strategies, but reasonable assumptions based on available information must *always* be made.

By identifying future occurrences that could have a major effect on the firm and by making reasonable assumptions about those factors, strategists can carry the strategic-management process forward. Assumptions are needed only for future trends and events that are most likely to have a significant effect on the company's business. Based on the best information at the time, assumptions serve as checkpoints on the validity of strategies. If future occurrences deviate significantly from assumptions, strategists know that corrective actions may be needed. Without reasonable assumptions, the strategy-formulation process could not proceed effectively. Firms that have the best information generally make the most accurate assumptions, which can lead to major competitive advantages.

Industry Analysis: The External Factor Evaluation Matrix

An **external factor evaluation (EFE) matrix** allows strategists to summarize and evaluate economic, social, cultural, demographic, environmental, political, governmental, legal, technological, and competitive information. Illustrated in Table 7-8, the EFE Matrix can be developed in five steps:

1. List key external factors as identified in the external-audit process. Include a total of 20 factors, including both opportunities and threats that affect the firm and its industry. List the opportunities first and then the threats. Be as specific as possible, using percentages, ratios, and comparative numbers whenever possible. Recall that Edward Deming said: "In God we trust. Everyone else bring data." In addition, utilize "*actionable*" factors as defined earlier in this chapter.
2. Assign to each factor a weight that ranges from 0.0 (not important) to 1.0 (very important). The weight indicates the relative importance of that factor to being successful in the firm's industry. Opportunities often receive higher weights than threats, but threats can receive high weights if they are especially severe or threatening. Appropriate weights can be determined by comparing successful with unsuccessful competitors or by discussing the factor and reaching a group consensus. The sum of all weights assigned to the factors must equal 1.0.
3. Assign a rating between 1 and 4 to each key external factor to indicate how effectively the firm's current strategies respond to the factor, where 4 = *the response is superior*, 3 = *the response is above average*, 2 = *the response is average*, and 1 = *the response is poor*. Ratings are based on effectiveness of the firm's strategies. Ratings are thus company-based, whereas the weights in Step 2 are industry-based. It is important to note that both threats and opportunities can receive a 1, 2, 3, or 4.
4. Multiply each factor's weight by its rating to determine a weighted score.
5. Sum the weighted scores for each variable to determine the total weighted score for the organization.

Regardless of the number of key opportunities and threats included in an EFE Matrix, the highest possible total weighted score for an organization is 4.0 and the lowest possible total weighted score is 1.0. The average total weighted score is 2.5. A total weighted score of 4.0 indicates that an organization is responding in an outstanding way to existing opportunities and threats in its industry. In other words, the firm's strategies effectively take advantage of existing opportunities and minimize the potential adverse effects of external threats. A total score of 1.0 indicates that the firm's strategies are not capitalizing on opportunities or avoiding external threats.

An example of an EFE Matrix is provided in Table 7-8 for a local 10-theater cinema complex. Note that the most important factor to being successful in this business is "Trend toward healthy eating eroding concession sales" as indicated by the 0.12 weight. Also note that the local cinema is doing excellent in regard to handling two factors, "TDB University is expanding 6 percent annually" and "Trend toward healthy eating eroding concession sales." Perhaps the cinema is placing flyers on campus and also adding yogurt and healthy drinks to its concession menu. Note that you may have a 1, 2, 3, or 4 anywhere down the Rating column. Note also that the factors are stated in quantitative terms to the extent possible, rather than being stated in vague terms. Quantify the factors as much as possible in constructing an EFE Matrix. Note also that all the factors are "actionable" instead of being something like "the economy is bad." Finally, note that the total weighted score of 2.58 is above the average (midpoint) of 2.5, so this cinema business is doing pretty well, taking advantage of the

TABLE 7-8 EFE Matrix for a Local 10-Theater Cinema Complex

Key External Factors	Weight	Rating	Weighted Score
Opportunities			
1. Rowan County is growing 8 percent annually in population	0.05	3	0.15
2. TDB University is expanding 6 percent annually	0.08	4	0.32
3. Major competitor across town recently ceased operations	0.08	3	0.24
4. Demand for going to cinema growing 10 percent annually	0.07	2	0.14
5. Two new neighborhoods being developed within 3 miles	0.09	1	0.09
6. Disposable income among citizens grew 5 percent in prior year	0.06	3	0.18
7. Unemployment rate in county declined to 3.1 percent	0.03	2	0.06
Threats			
8. Trend toward healthy eating eroding concession sales	0.12	4	0.48
9. Demand for online movies and DVDs growing 10 percent annually	0.06	2	0.12
10. Commercial property adjacent to cinemas for sale	0.06	3	0.18
11. TDB University installing an on-campus movie theater	0.04	3	0.12
12. County and city property taxes increasing 25 percent this year	0.08	2	0.16
13. Local religious groups object to R-rated movies being shown	0.04	3	0.12
14. Movies rented from local Blockbuster store up 12 percent	0.08	2	0.16
15. Movies rented last quarter from Time Warner up 15 percent	0.06	1	0.06
Total	**1.00**		**2.58**

external opportunities and avoiding the threats facing the firm. There is definitely room for improvement, though, because the highest total weighted score would be 4.0. As indicated by ratings of 1, this business needs to capitalize more on the "two new neighborhoods nearby" opportunity and the "movies rented from Time Warner" threat. Note also that there are many percentage-based factors among the group. Be quantitative to the extent possible! Note also that the ratings range from 1 to 4 on both the opportunities and threats.

An EFE Matrix for Netflix is provided in Table 7-9. Note that the most important external factors for Netflix were the growth in Internet users globally as indicated by a weight of 0.08. Netflix's total weighted score of 2.73 is good but not excellent.

The Competitive Profile Matrix

The **Competitive Profile Matrix (CPM)** identifies a firm's major competitors and its particular strengths and weaknesses in relation to a sample firm's strategic position. The weights and total weighted scores in both a CPM and an EFE have the same meaning. However, *critical success factors* in a CPM include both internal and external issues; therefore, the ratings refer to strengths and weaknesses, where 4 = major strength, 3 = minor strength, 2 = minor weakness, and 1 = major weakness. The critical success factors in a CPM are not grouped into opportunities and threats as they are in an EFE. In a CPM, the ratings and total weighted scores for rival firms can be compared to the sample firm. This comparative analysis provides important internal strategic information. Avoid assigning the same rating to firms included in your CPM analysis.

A sample CPM is provided in Table 7-10. In this example, the two most important factors to being successful in the industry are "advertising" and "global expansion," as indicated by weights of 0.20. If there were no weight column in this analysis, note that each factor then would be equally important. Thus, having a weight column makes for a more robust analysis because it enables the analyst to assign higher and lower numbers to capture perceived or actual levels of importance. Note in Table 7-10 that Company 1 is strongest on "product quality," as indicated by a rating of 4, whereas Company 2 is strongest on "advertising." Overall, Company 1 is strongest, as indicated by the total weighted score of 3.15 and Company 3 is weakest.

TABLE 7-9 **An Actual EFE Matrix for Netflix**

Opportunities	Weight	Rating	WScore
1. Netflix has 30 million members globally. Millions more would like Netflix.	0.07	2	.14
2. Movie ticket prices rose 3 percent in 2012.	0.04	2	.08
3. Blockbuster closed 30 percent of its stores in 2012.	0.06	4	.24
Number of Internet users globally increased from 2.4 billion in mid-2012 to over 3.0 billion in 2013.	0.08	4	.32
4. The introduction of smart TVs is enabling online content to be viewed faster and without gaming consoles.	0.06	3	.18
5. Average cable bills nationwide increased 5.8 percent.	0.05	2	.10
6. The average price of a DVD is $25 and rising.	0.04	2	.08
7. Percentage of Americans who play computer & video games is 72 percent.	0.03	3	.09
8. Once you start a movie stream on Blockbuster, you only have 24 hours to watch as any number of times.	0.05	4	.20
9. Smartphone usage is growing 20 percent annually.	0.02	3	.06
Threats			
1. Unemployment exceeds 10 percent in many areas.	0.04	2	.08
2. Blockbuster has new movie and television titles available 28 days before Redbox and Netflix.	0.05	4	.20
3. Blockbuster offers disc-only plans, stream-only plans, and combination plans.	0.04	3	.12
4. Blockbuster offers unlimited rentals-by-mail *and* in-store exchanges.	0.06	2	.12
5. Redbox installed about 6,000 kiosks in Canada in 2012.	0.05	3	.15
6. Netflix's streaming content licensing costs rose from $180 million in 2010 to a huge $1.98 billion in 2012.	0.06	4	.24
7. Coinstar is partnering with Verizon to enter the streaming market.	0.07	2	.14
8. YouTube has an agreement with Paramount to stream movies through their website.	0.05	2	.10
9. Increase in online activity increases the threat of identity theft.	0.03	1	.04
10. Amazon, Apple, and Hulu enter the movie streaming business.	0.05	3	.15
Total	**1.00**		**2.73**

Other than the critical success factors listed in the example CPM, factors often included in this analysis include breadth of product line, effectiveness of sales distribution, proprietary or patent advantages, location of facilities, production capacity and efficiency, experience, union relations, technological advantages, and e-commerce expertise.

Just because one firm receives a 3.20 overall rating and another receives a 2.80 in a CPM, it does not necessarily follow that the first firm is precisely 14.3 percent better than the second, but it does suggest that the first firm is better in some areas. Regarding weights in a CPM, EFEM, or IFEM, 0.08 is 33 percent higher than 0.06, so even small differences can reveal important perceptions regarding the relative importance of various factors. The aim with numbers is to assimilate and evaluate information in a meaningful way that aids in decision-making.

Another CPM is provided in Table 7-11. Note that Company 2 has the best product quality and management experience; Company 3 has the best market share and inventory system; and Company 1 has the best price as indicated by the ratings. Again, avoid assigning duplicate ratings on any row in a CPM.

TABLE 7-10 An Example Competitive Profile Matrix

Critical Success Factors	Weight	Company 1 Rating	Company 1 Score	Company 2 Rating	Company 2 Score	Company 3 Rating	Company 3 Score
Advertising	0.20	1	0.20	4	0.80	3	0.60
Product Quality	0.10	4	0.40	3	0.30	2	0.20
Price Competitiveness	0.10	3	0.30	2	0.20	1	0.10
Management	0.10	4	0.40	3	0.20	1	0.10
Financial Position	0.15	4	0.60	2	0.30	3	0.45
Customer Loyalty	0.10	4	0.40	3	0.30	2	0.20
Global Expansion	0.20	4	0.80	1	0.20	2	0.40
Market Share	0.05	1	0.05	4	0.20	3	0.15
Total	**1.00**		**3.15**		**2.50**		**2.20**

Note: The ratings values are as follows: 1 = major weakness, 2 = minor weakness, 3 = minor strength, 4 = major strength. As indicated by the total weighted score of 2.50, Competitor 2 is weakest. Only eight critical success factors are included for simplicity; this is too few in actuality.

An example CPM for Royal Caribbean Cruises (RCC) is provided in Table 7-12. Note that RCC's main rival is Carnival Corporation. Having 40 ships in its fleet, RCC is the world's second-largest cruise line operator, after Carnival, which has 100 ships. RCC owns Celebrity Cruises, Pullmantur Cruises, Azamara Club Cruises, and CDF Croisieres de France. Carnival recently ordered a brand new ship (being built by Fincantieri) to be the largest cruise ship ever built, having a passenger capacity of 4,000 and a tonnage of 135,000, and scheduled for delivery in 2016. Note in the CPM that Carnival has a much better financial position than RCC, but RCC has the nicest ships as of year 2013, led by its Oasis ship.

Special Note To Students

In developing and presenting your external assessment for the firm, be mindful that gaining and sustaining competitive advantage is the overriding purpose of developing the opportunity and threat lists, value chain, EFEM, and CPM. During this section of your written or oral project, emphasize how and why particular factors can yield competitive advantage for the firm. In

TABLE 7-11 Another Example Competitive Profile Matrix

Critical Success Factors	Weight	Company 1 Rating	Company 1 Weighted Score	Company 2 Rating	Company 2 Weighted Score	Company 3 Rating	Company 3 Weighted Score
Market Share	0.15	3	0.45	2	0.30	4	0.60
Inventory System	0.08	2	0.16	1	0.08	4	0.32
Financial Position	0.10	2	0.20	3	0.30	4	0.40
Product Quality	0.08	3	0.24	4	0.32	2	0.16
Consumer Loyalty	0.02	3	0.06	1	0.02	4	0.08
Sales Distribution	0.10	3	0.30	2	0.20	4	0.40
Global Expansion	0.15	3	0.45	2	0.30	4	0.60
Organization Structure	0.05	3	0.15	4	0.20	2	0.10
Production Capacity	0.04	3	0.12	2	0.08	4	0.16
E-commerce	0.10	3	0.30	1	0.10	4	0.40
Customer Service	0.10	3	0.30	2	0.20	4	0.40
Price Competitive	0.02	4	0.08	1	0.02	3	0.06
Management Experience	0.01	2	0.02	4	0.04	3	0.03
Total	**1.00**		**2.83**		**2.16**		**3.69**

TABLE 7-12 A Competitive Profile Matrix for Royal Caribbean Cruises

Critical Success Factors	Weight	RCC Rating	RCC Score	Carnival Corp Rating	Carnival Corp Score
Advertising	0.20	2	0.40	4	0.80
Quality of Ships	0.20	4	0.80	2	0.40
Price Competitiveness	0.15	3	0.45	4	0.60
Management	0.15	3	0.45	2	0.30
Financial Position	0.05	1	0.05	4	0.20
Customer Loyalty	0.15	2	0.30	4	0.60
Global Expansion	0.05	.	.15	3	0.15
Market Share	0.05	1	0.05	4	0.20
Total	**1.00**		**2.65**		**3.25**

other words, instead of robotically going through the weights and ratings (which by the way are critically important), highlight various factors in light of where you are leading the firm. Make it abundantly clear in your discussion how your firm, with your suggestions, can subdue rival firms or at least profitably compete with them. Showcase during this section of your project the key underlying reasons how and why your firm can prosper among rivals. Remember to be *prescriptive*, rather than *descriptive*, in the manner that you present your entire project. If presenting your project orally, be self-confident and passionate rather than timid and uninterested. Definitely "bring the data" throughout your project because "vagueness" is the most common downfall of students in case analyses.

Conclusion

Increasing turbulence in markets and industries around the world means the external audit has become an explicit and vital part of the strategic-management process. This chapter provides a framework for collecting and evaluating economic, social, cultural, demographic, environmental, political, governmental, legal, technological, and competitive information. Firms that do not mobilize and empower their managers and employees to identify, monitor, forecast, and evaluate key external forces may fail to anticipate emerging opportunities and threats and, consequently, may pursue ineffective strategies, miss opportunities, and invite organizational demise. Firms not taking advantage of e-commerce and social media networks are technologically falling behind.

A major responsibility of strategists is to ensure development of an effective external-audit system. This includes using information technology to devise a competitive intelligence system that works. The external-audit approach described in this chapter can be used effectively by any size or type of organization. Typically, the external-audit process is more informal in small firms, but the need to understand key trends and events is no less important for these firms. The EFE Matrix and Porter's Five-Forces Model can help strategists evaluate the market and industry, but these tools must be accompanied by good intuitive judgment. Multinational firms especially need a systematic and effective external-audit system because external forces among foreign countries vary so greatly.

Key Terms and Concepts

actionable factors (p. 227)
chief information officer (CIO) (p. 236)
chief technology officer (CTO) (p. 236)

competitive analysis (p. 238)
competitive intelligence (CI) (p. 238)
competitive profile matrix (CPM) (p. 245)

director of competitive analysis (p. 238)
environmental scanning (p. 226)
external audit (p. 226)
external factor evaluation (EFE)
   matrix (p. 244)
external forces (p. 227)
Industrial Organization (I/O) (p. 229)

industry analysis (p. 226)
information technology (IT) (p. 236)
Internet (p. 236)
linear regression (p. 243)
market commonality (p. 239)
Porter's Five-Forces Model (p. 239)
resource similarity (p. 239)

Issues for Review and Discussion

7-1. Michelin has been very successful in the last decade. In your opinion, what strategy changes would Michelin need in 2014?

7-2. Of the many competitors it has, which firm do you think worries Michelin most about? Why? Prepare a CPM that includes Michelin and the rival firm you identified.

7-3. A political debate, raging in the United States, concerns sales taxes on the Internet. Most states do not collect a sales tax. Brick and mortar businesses think this is unfair. How does the situation in Europe compare with the United States, in terms of sales tax on items purchased online? What is the strategic implication for companies?

7-4. The size of American labor unions have fallen sharply in the last decade, mostly due to the erosion of the U.S. manufacturing base. How does the situation in Europe compare to the United States in this regard? What is the strategic implication for companies?

7-5. List four reasons why some countries in Europe are struggling economically in comparison to Asian countries. What is the strategic implication for companies?

7-6. Does the Arab Spring—unfolding in the Middle East—represent more of an opportunity or threat to companies? Explain.

7-7. Identify two companies that you think would have a 1.5 total weighted score on their EFE Matrix. Why? Identify two companies that would have a 3.5 total weighted score on their EFE Matrix. Why?

7-8. Summarize what Chapter 7 says at the end, regarding competitive advantage whenever someone is presenting an EFE Matrix and CPM as part of a case analysis or strategic plan.

7-9. List the 10 key external forces that give rise to opportunities and threats. Give a specific example of each force, for your college or university.

7-10. Give four reasons why you agree or do not agree with I/O theorists.

7-11. Regarding economic variables, list in order of importance six specific factors that you feel greatly impact your college or university.

7-12. Explain why U.S.-based firms, such as McDonald's, greatly benefit from a weak dollar.

7-13. Regarding social, cultural, demographic, and natural environment variables, list in order of importance six specific factors that you feel most greatly impact your college or university.

7-14. Regarding political, governmental, and legal variables, list in order of importance six specific factors that you feel most greatly impact your college or university.

7-15. Explain how wireless technology is impacting four industries.

7-16. Discuss the pros and cons of gathering and assimilating competitive intelligence.

7-17. Using Porter's Five-Forces Model, explain competitiveness for a local fast food restaurant.

7-18. Identify an industry in which "bargaining power of suppliers" is the most important factor among Porter's variables.

7-19. Develop an EFE Matrix for your college or university.

7-20. Distinguish between ratings and weights in an EFE Matrix.

7-21. List 10 external trends or facts pertaining specifically to your country that would impact companies in your city.

7-22. Develop a CPM for a company that you or your parents have been employed.

7-23. Discuss the ethics of gathering competitive intelligence.

7-24. Discuss the ethics of cooperating with rival firms.

7-25. Contact your college library. Ask if they have the S&P Industry Surveys in hardcopy in the library. If they do, print out the relevant report for a company that you familiar with.

7-26. Your boss develops an EFE Matrix that includes 54 factors. How would you suggest reducing the number of factors to 20?

7-27. List the 10 external areas that give rise to opportunities and threats. Give an example of each for IBM.

7-28. Compare the ratings in an EFE Matrix with those in a CPM in terms of meaning and definition.

7-29. Discuss the I/O view or approach to strategic planning.

7-30. List in order of importance what you feel are the six major advantages of a weak dollar for a U.S.-based firm.

7-31. List in order of importance what you feel are the six major advantages of a weak euro for a European-based firm headquartered in a country that has the euro as its currency.

7-32. Cooperating with competitors is becoming more common. What are the advantages and disadvantages of this for a company?

7-33. Regarding sources of external information, visit the www.finance.yahoo.com website and enter IBM; click on Headlines, and identify three major new initiatives the company has undertaken.

7-34. Differentiate between making assumptions and making wild guesses about future opportunities, and threats facing business firms.

7-35. Explain how the external assessment would, or should be different for non-profit organizations versus corporations.

7-36. Apply Porter's Five-Forces Model to IBM. What strategic implications arise in that analysis?

7-37. Compare and contrast competitive intelligence programs across several organizations that you are familiar with.

MyManagementLab®

Go to **mymanagementlab.com** for the following Assisted-graded writing questions:

7-38. Describe the "process of performing an external audit" in an organization doing strategic planning for the first time.

7-39. Compare and contrast the duties and responsibilities of a CIO with a CTO in a large firm.

Current Readings

Allio, Robert J. and Liam Fahey. "Joan Magretta: What Executives can Learn from Revisiting Michael Porter." *Strategy and Leadership* 40, no. 3 (2012): 5–10.

Berchicci, Luca, Glen Dowell, and Andrew A. King. "Environmental Capabilities and Corporate Strategy: Exploring Acquisitions Among US Manufacturing Firms." *Strategic Management Journal* 33, no. 9 (September 2012): 1053–1071.

Berman, Saul J. "Digital Transformation: Opportunities to Create New Business Models." *Strategy and Leadership* 40, no. 3 (2012): 16–24.

Kim, Kwang-Ho and Wenpin Tsai. "Social Comparison Among Competing Firms." *Strategic Management Journal* 33, no. 2 (February 2012): 115–136.

Pacheco-de-Almeida, Gonçalo and Peter B. Zemsky. "Some Like it Free: Innovators' Strategic Use of Disclosure to Slow Down Competition." *Strategic Management Journal* 33, no. 7 (July 2012): 773–793.

ASSURANCE OF LEARNING EXERCISES

EXERCISE 7A
Michelin and Africa: An External Assessment

Purpose
Michelin is featured in the opening chapter case as a firm that engages in excellent strategic planning. This exercise gives you practice conducting an external strategic management audit to determine if Africa is the new, best place for Michelin to produce and market products and services. For example, considerable underground mining occurs in much of Africa. The new MICHELIN XTXL tire is available in 25-inch for underground mining vehicles. The new tires offer enhanced safety and productivity and are available in sizes 26.5R25 and 29.5R25. Tests indicate that the new tires offer increases of 10 percent in longevity, 20 percent in puncture resistance, and 30 percent in load capacity.

Instructions

Step 1	Research the business climate in 10 African countries.
Step 2	Prepare an EFE Matrix for Michelin based solely on the opportunities and threats that Michelin will face in doing business in the 10 African countries you chose.
Step 3	Based on your research, list the 10 African countries you selected in rank order of attractiveness for Michelin to focus efforts upon. Give a one-sentence rationale for each country's ranking.

EXERCISE 7B

Preparing a CPM for Michelin Based on Countries Rather than Companies

Purpose

Countries are similar to companies in that they compete with each other for investment dollars and economic development.

Instructions

Step 1   Revisit the research you collected and analyzed in the above exercise.

Step 2   Prepare a CPM that reveals your assessment of 6 African countries in terms of their relative strengths and weaknesses across what you deem to be the most critical success factors.

EXERCISE 7C

Develop Divisional Michelin EFE Matrices

Purpose

Michelin has five major geographic divisions: Europe, North America, Asia, South America, Africa/India/Middle-East. The company faces fierce but different competitors in each segment.

The external opportunities and threats that Michelin faces are different in each geographic segment, so each segment prepares its own list of key external success factors. This external analysis is critically important in strategic planning because a firm needs to exploit opportunities and avoid or at least mitigate threats.

The purpose of this exercise is to develop divisional EFE Matrices that Michelin could use in developing an overall corporate EFE Matrix.

Instructions

Step 1   Go to Michelin's website. Review the company's most recent *Annual Report*.

Step 2   Determine and review Michelin's major geographic segments.

Step 3   Conduct research to determine what you believe are the four major threats and the four major opportunities critical to strategic planning within Michelin's geographic segments. Review the relevant *Standard and Poor's* Industry Survey documents for each segment.

Step 4   Develop divisional EFE Matrices for Michelin. Work within a team of students if your instructor so requests but you will need an EFE Matrix for each segment.

Step 5   Prioritize the 20 threats and the 20 opportunities developed in the prior step so that corporate Michelin top executives can better develop a corporate EFE Matrix.

Step 6   Let's say Michelin has their operations segmented by Domestic versus Global. Based on your research, prepare an EFE Matrix for Michelin's domestic operations and another EFE Matrix for Michelin's Global Operations. Let Europe be Domestic and all other regions be Global.

EXERCISE 7D

Developing an EFE Matrix for adidas AG

Purpose

This exercise will provide practice developing an EFE Matrix. An EFE Matrix summarizes the results of an external audit. This is an important tool widely used by strategists.

Instructions

Step 1   Join with two other students in class and jointly prepare an EFE Matrix for adidas AG. Refer back to the Cohesion Case and to Exercise 1B, if necessary, to identify external opportunities and threats. Use the information in the *Standard and Poor's* Industry Surveys that you copied as part of Assurance of Learning Exercise 1B. Be sure not to include strategies as opportunities, but do include as many monetary amounts, percentages, numbers, and ratios as possible.

Step 2   All three-person teams participating in this exercise should record their EFE total weighted scores on the board. Put your initials after your score to identify it as your teams.

Step 3   Compare the total weighted scores. Which team's score came closest to the instructor's answer? Discuss reasons for variation in the scores reported on the board.

EXERCISE 7E
The External Assessment

Purpose

This exercise will help you become familiar with important sources of external information available in your college or university library. A key part of preparing an external audit is searching the Internet and examining published sources of information for relevant economic, social, cultural, demographic, environmental, political, governmental, legal, technological, and competitive trends and events. External opportunities and threats must be identified and evaluated before strategies can be formulated effectively.

Instructions

Step 1   Select an American company or business where you recently purchased a product or previously have worked. Conduct an external audit for this company. Find opportunities and threats in recent issues of newspapers and magazines. Search for information using the Internet. Use the following websites: http://marketwatch.multexinvestor.com; www.hoovers.com; http://moneycentral.msn.com; http://finance.yahoo.com; www.clearstation.com; https://us.etrade.com/e/t/invest/markets

Step 2   On a separate sheet of paper, list 10 opportunities and 10 threats that face this company. Be specific in stating each factor.

Step 3   Include a bibliography to reveal where you found the information.

Step 4   Write a three-page summary of your findings, and submit it to your instructor.

EXERCISE 7F
Developing a CPM for Michelin

Purpose

Monitoring competitors' performance and strategies is a key aspect of an external audit. This exercise is designed to give you practice evaluating the competitive position of organizations in a given industry and assimilating that information in the form of a CPM.

Instructions

Step 1   Gather information about Michelin Corporation. Turn back to the opening chapter boxed insert and review this information.

Step 2   On a separate sheet of paper, prepare a CPM that includes Michelin and its two leading competitors: Bridgestone Corporation, and Goodyear Tire and Rubber Company.

Step 3   Turn in your CPM for a classwork grade.

EXERCISE 7G
Developing a CPM for adidas AG

Purpose

Monitoring competitors' performance and strategies is a key aspect of an external audit. This exercise is designed to give you practice evaluating the competitive position of organizations in a given industry and assimilating that information in the form of a CPM.

Instructions

Step 1   Gather information from Assurance of Learning Exercise 1B. Also, turn back to the Cohesion Case and review the section on competitors.

Step 2   On a separate sheet of paper, prepare a CPM that includes Nike, Puma, Under Armour, and Callaway Golf.

Step 3   Turn in your CPM for a classwork grade.

EXERCISE 7H

Analyzing Your College or University's External Strategic Situation

Purpose

This exercise is excellent for doing together as a class.

Instructions

As a class, determine your college or university's major external opportunities and threats. List 10 opportunities and 10 threats. Then, get everyone in class to rank order their factors with 1 being most important and 10 being least important. Then, gather up everyone's paper, count the numbers, and in that manner create a prioritized list of the key external opportunities and threats facing your college.

Notes

1. York Freund, "Critical Success Factors," *Planning Review* 16, no. 4 (July–August 1988): 20.

2. Lee Siegel, "Rise of the Tiger Nation," *Wall Street Journal* (October 27, 2012): C1.

3. Siegel, "Rise of the Tiger Nation."

4. Roger Yu, "Online Rep Crucial for Small Companies," USA Today (October 30, 2012): 5B.

5. Bill Saporito, "Companies That Compete Best," Fortune, May 22, 1989, 36.

6. Kenneth Sawka, "Demystifying Business Intelligence," *Management Review* (October 1996): 49.

7. John Prescott and Daniel Smith, "The Largest Survey of 'Leading-Edge' Competitor Intelligence Managers," *Planning Review* 17, no. 3 (May–June 1989): 6–13.

8. M. J. Chen, "Competitor Analysis and Interfirm Rivalry: Toward a Theoretical Integration," *Academy of Management Review* 21 (1996): 106.

9. S. Jayachandran, J. Gimeno, and P. R. Varadarajan, "Theory of Multimarket Competition: A Synthesis and Implications for Marketing Strategy," *Journal of Marketing* 63, 3 (1999): 59; and M. J. Chen. "Competitor Analysis and Interfirm Rivalry: Toward a Theoretical Integration," *Academy of Management Review* 21 (1996): 107–108.

10. Arthur Thompson, Jr., A. J. Strickland III, and John Gamble, Crafting and Executing Strategy: Text and Readings (New York: McGraw-Hill/Irwin, 2005), 63.

11. Michael E. Porter, Competitive Strategy: Techniques for Analyzing Industries and Competitors (New York: Free Press, 1980), 24–27.

12. Dale McConkey, "Planning in a Changing Environment," Business Horizons 31, no. 5 (September–October 1988): 67.

8

Source: © motorlka/Fotolia

MyManagementLab®

Improve Your Grade!

Over 10 million students improved their results using the Pearson MyLabs.
Visit **mymanagementlab.com** for simulations, tutorials, and end-of-chapter problems.

Strategy Generation and Selection

CHAPTER OBJECTIVES

After studying this chapter, you should be able to do the following:

1. Describe a three-stage framework for choosing among alternative strategies.

2. Explain how to develop a Strengths-Weaknesses-Opportunities-Threats (SWOT) Matrix, Strategic Position and Action Evaluation (SPACE) Matrix, Boston Consulting Group (BCG) Matrix, Internal-External (IE) Matrix, and Quantitative Strategic Planning Matrix (QSPM).

3. Identify important behavioral, political, ethical, and social responsibility considerations in strategy analysis and choice.

4. Discuss the role of intuition in strategic analysis and choice.

5. Discuss the role of organizational culture in strategic analysis and choice.

6. Discuss the role of a board of directors in choosing among alternative strategies.

ASSURANCE OF LEARNING EXERCISES

The following exercises are found at the end of this chapter.

Strategy analysis and choice largely involve making subjective decisions based on objective information. This chapter introduces important concepts that can help strategists generate feasible alternatives, evaluate those alternatives, and choose a specific course of action. Behavioral aspects of strategy formulation are described, including politics, culture, ethics, and social responsibility considerations. Modern tools for formulating strategies are described, and the appropriate role of a board of directors is discussed. As showcased below, Unilever is an example company pursuing an excellent strategic plan.

The Nature of Strategy Analysis and Choice

As indicated by Figure 8-1 with white shading, this chapter focuses on generating and evaluating alternative strategies, as well as selecting strategies to pursue. Strategy analysis and choice seek to determine alternative courses of action that could best enable the firm to achieve its mission and objectives. The firm's present strategies, objectives, vision, and mission, coupled with the external and internal audit information, provide a basis for generating and evaluating feasible alternative strategies. This systematic approach is the best way to avoid a crisis. Rudin's Law states: "When a crisis forces choosing among alternatives, most people choose the worst possible one."

Unless a desperate situation confronts the firm, alternative strategies will likely represent incremental steps that move the firm from its present position to a desired future position. Alternative strategies do not come out of the wild blue yonder; they are derived from the firm's vision, mission, objectives, external audit, and internal audit; they are consistent with, or build on, past strategies that have worked well.

The Process of Generating and Selecting Strategies

Strategists never consider all feasible alternatives that could benefit the firm because there are an infinite number of possible actions and an infinite number of ways to implement those actions. Therefore, a manageable set of the most attractive alternative strategies must be developed. The advantages, disadvantages, trade-offs, costs, and benefits of these strategies should be determined. This section discusses the process that many firms use to determine an appropriate set

EXCELLENT STRATEGIC MANAGEMENT SHOWCASED

Unilever

Unilever, the world's third-largest consumer goods company behind Procter & Gamble and Nestle, is an Anglo–Dutch company whose products include foods, beverages, cleaning agents and personal care products. Unilever is a dual listed company consisting of Unilever N.V. based in Rotterdam, Netherlands, and Unilever PLC based in London – but both companies have the same directors and operate as a single business. Some of Unilever's best selling among its 450 brands are Aviance, Ben & Jerry's, Dove, Flora/Becel, Heartbrand ice creams, Hellmann's, Knorr, Lipton, Lux/Radox, Omo/Surf, Sunsilk, Toni & Guy, VO5, and PG Tips. In December 2012, Unilever began phasing out by 2015 the use of microplastics in their personal care products.

In January 2013, Unilever divested its Skippy peanut butter brand, together with related manufacturing facilities in Little Rock, Arkansas, United States and Weifang, China, to Hormel Foods for approximately $700 million. In July 2013, Unilever increased its stake in its Indian unit, Hindustan Unilever, to 67 percent for around €2.45 billion.

In August 2013, Unilever signed an agreement for the sale of its Wish-Bone and Western dressings brands to Pinnacle Foods Inc. for $580 million, subject to regulatory approval. In 2013, *Fortune* ranked Unilever as the 39th most admired company in the world outside the United States.

In September 2013, Unilever acquired T2, a premium Australian tea company that generated sales approaching AUS$57 million for the 12-month period ending June 30 2013. Unilever is the largest tea company in the world. T2 operates 40 stores and its range of fragrant teas and tea wares from around the world are also sold through some of the best restaurants in the country.

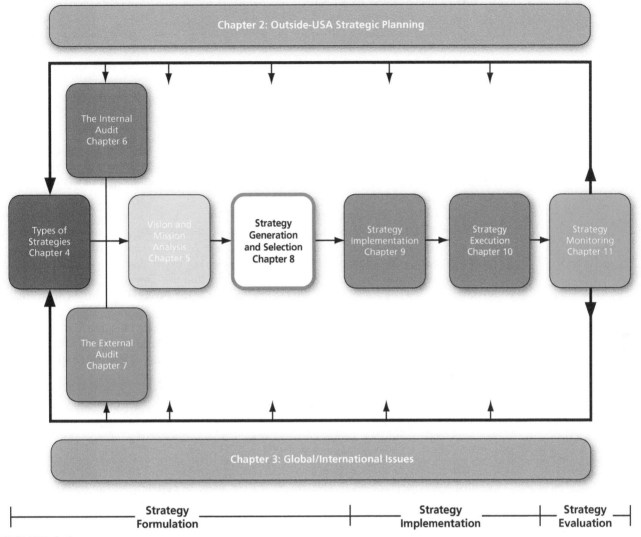

FIGURE 8-1

A Comprehensive Strategic-Management Model

Source: Fred R. David, adapted from "How Companies Define Their Mission," *Long Range Planning* 22, no. 3 (June 1988): 40, © Fred R. David.

of alternative strategies. Recommendations (strategies selected to pursue) come from alternative strategies formulated.

Identifying and evaluating alternative strategies should involve many of the managers and employees who previously assembled the organizational vision and mission statements, performed the external audit, and conducted the internal audit. Representatives from each department and division of the firm should be included in this process, as was the case in previous strategy-formulation activities. Recall that involvement provides the best opportunity for managers and employees to gain an understanding of what the firm is doing and why and to become committed to helping the firm accomplish its objectives.

All participants in the strategy analysis and choice activity should have the firm's external and internal audit information available. This information, coupled with the firm's mission statement, will help participants crystallize in their own minds particular strategies that they believe could benefit the firm most. Creativity should be encouraged in this thought process.

Alternative strategies proposed by participants should be considered and discussed in a meeting or series of meetings. Proposed strategies should be listed in writing. When all feasible strategies identified by participants are given and understood, the strategies should be ranked in order of attractiveness by all participants, with 1 = should not be implemented, 2 = possibly should be implemented, 3 = probably should be implemented, and 4 = definitely should be implemented. This process will result in a prioritized list of best strategies that reflects the collective wisdom of the group.

A Comprehensive Strategy-Formulation Analytical Framework

Important strategy-formulation techniques can be integrated into a three-stage decision-making framework, as shown in Figure 8-2. The tools presented in this framework are applicable to all sizes and types of organizations and can help strategists identify, evaluate, and select strategies.

Stage 1 of the formulation framework consists of the EFE Matrix, the IFE Matrix, and the Competitive Profile Matrix (CPM). Called the **input stage**, Stage 1 summarizes the basic input information needed to formulate strategies. Stage 2, called the **matching stage**, focuses on generating feasible alternative strategies by aligning key external and internal factors. Stage 2 techniques include the Strengths-Weaknesses-Opportunities-Threats (SWOT) Matrix, the Strategic Position and Action Evaluation (SPACE) Matrix, the Boston Consulting Group (BCG) Matrix, the Internal-External (IE) Matrix, and the Grand Strategy Matrix. Stage 3, called the **decision stage**, involves a single technique, the Quantitative Strategic Planning Matrix (QSPM). A QSPM uses input information from Stage 1 to objectively evaluate feasible alternative strategies identified in Stage 2. A QSPM reveals the relative attractiveness of alternative strategies and thus provides objective basis for selecting specific strategies.

All nine techniques included in the **strategy-formulation framework** require the integration of intuition and analysis. Autonomous divisions in an organization commonly use strategy-formulation techniques to develop strategies and objectives. Divisional analyses provide a basis for identifying, evaluating, and selecting among alternative corporate-level strategies.

Strategists themselves, not analytic tools, are always responsible and accountable for strategic decisions. Lenz emphasized that the shift from a words-oriented to a numbers-oriented planning process can give rise to a false sense of certainty; it can reduce dialogue, discussion, and argument as a means for exploring understandings, testing assumptions, and fostering organizational learning.[1] Strategists, therefore, must be wary of this possibility and use analytical tools to facilitate, rather than to diminish, communication. Without objective information and analysis, personal biases, politics, emotions, personalities, and **halo error** (the tendency to put too much weight on a single factor) unfortunately may play a dominant role in the strategy-formulation process.

STAGE 1: THE INPUT STAGE		
External Factor Evaluation (EFE) Matrix	Competitive Profile Matrix (CPM)	Internal Factor Evaluation (IFE) Matrix

STAGE 2: THE MATCHING STAGE				
Strengths-Weaknesses-Opportunities-Threats (SWOT) Matrix	Strategic Position and Action Evaluation (SPACE) Matrix	Boston Consulting Group (BCG) Matrix	Internal-External (IE) Matrix	Grand Strategy Matrix

STAGE 3: THE DECISION STAGE
Quantitative Strategic Planning Matrix (QSPM)

FIGURE 8-2

The Strategy-Formulation Analytical Framework

The Input Stage

Procedures for developing an EFE Matrix, an IFE Matrix, and a CPM were presented in Chapters 6 and 7. The information derived from these three matrices provides basic input information for the matching and decision stage matrices described later in this chapter.

The input tools require strategists to quantify subjectivity during early stages of the strategy-formulation process. Making small decisions in the input matrices regarding the relative importance of external and internal factors allows strategists to more effectively generate and evaluate alternative strategies. Good intuitive judgment is always needed in determining appropriate weights and ratings.

The Matching Stage

Strategy is sometimes defined as the match an organization makes between its internal resources and skills and the opportunities and risks created by its external factors.[2] The matching stage of the strategy-formulation framework consists of five techniques that can be used in any sequence: the SWOT Matrix, the SPACE Matrix, the BCG Matrix, the IE Matrix, and the Grand Strategy Matrix. These tools rely on information derived from the input stage to match external opportunities and threats with internal strengths and weaknesses. **Matching** external and internal critical success factors is the key to effectively generating feasible alternative strategies. For example, a firm with excess working capital (an internal strength) could take advantage of the cell phone industry's 20 percent annual growth rate (an external opportunity) by acquiring Cellfone, Inc., a firm in the cell phone industry. This example portrays simple one-to-one matching. In most situations, external and internal relationships are more complex, and the matching requires multiple alignments for each strategy generated. Successful matching of key external and internal factors depends upon those underlying key factors being both *specific* and *actionable*. The basic concept of matching is illustrated in Table 8-1.

Any organization, whether military, product-oriented, service-oriented, governmental, or even athletic, must develop and execute good strategies to win. A good offense without a good defense, or vice versa, usually leads to defeat. Developing strategies that use strengths to capitalize on opportunities could be considered an offense, whereas strategies designed to improve on weaknesses while avoiding threats could be termed defensive. Every organization has some external opportunities and threats and internal strengths and weaknesses that can be aligned to formulate feasible alternative strategies.

The SWOT Matrix

The **Strengths-Weaknesses-Opportunities-Threats (SWOT) Matrix** is an important matching tool that helps managers develop four types of strategies: SO (strengths-opportunities) strategies, WO (weaknesses-opportunities) strategies, ST (strengths-threats) strategies, and WT (weaknesses-threats) strategies.[3] Matching key external and internal factors is the most difficult part of developing a SWOT Matrix and requires good judgment—and there is no one best set of matches. Note in Table 8-1 that the first, second, third, and fourth strategies are SO, WO, ST, and WT strategies, respectively.

TABLE 8-1 **Matching Key External and Internal Factors to Formulate Alternative Strategies**

Key Internal Factor	Key External Factor	Resultant Strategy
Excess working capital (an internal strength)	+ 20 percent annual growth in the cell phone industry (an external opportunity)	= Acquire Cellfone, Inc.
Insufficient capacity (an internal weakness)	+ Exit of two major foreign competitors from the industry (an external opportunity)	= Pursue horizontal integration by buying competitors' facilities
Strong research and development expertise (an internal strength)	+ Decreasing numbers of younger adults (an external threat)	= Develop new products for older adults
Poor employee morale (an internal weakness)	+ Rising health-care costs (an external threat)	= Develop a new wellness program

SO strategies use a firm's internal strengths to take advantage of external opportunities. All managers would like their organization to be in a position in which internal strengths can be used to take advantage of external trends and events. Organizations generally will pursue WO, ST, or WT strategies to get into a situation in which they can apply SO strategies. When a firm has major weaknesses, it will strive to overcome them and make them strengths. When an organization faces major threats, it will seek to avoid them to concentrate on opportunities.

WO strategies aim at improving internal weaknesses by taking advantage of external opportunities. Sometimes key external opportunities exist, but a firm has internal weaknesses that prevent it from exploiting those opportunities. For example, there may be a high demand for electronic devices to control the amount and timing of fuel injection in automobile engines (opportunity), but a certain auto parts manufacturer may lack the technology required for producing these devices (weakness). One possible WO strategy would be to acquire this technology by forming a joint venture with a firm having competency in this area. An alternative WO strategy would be to hire and train people with the required technical capabilities.

ST strategies use a firm's strengths to avoid or reduce the impact of external threats. This does not mean that a strong organization should always meet threats in the external environment head-on. An example ST strategy occurred when Texas Instruments used an excellent legal department (a strength) to collect nearly $700 million in damages and royalties from nine Japanese and Korean firms that infringed on patents for semiconductor memory chips (threat). Rival firms that copy ideas, innovations, and patented products are a major threat in many industries. This is still a major problem for U.S. firms selling products in China.

WT strategies are defensive tactics directed at reducing internal weakness and avoiding external threats. An organization faced with numerous external threats and internal weaknesses may indeed be in a precarious position. In fact, such a firm may have to fight for its survival, merge, retrench, declare bankruptcy, or choose liquidation.

A schematic representation of the SWOT Matrix is provided in Figure 8-3. Note that a SWOT Matrix is composed of nine cells. As shown, there are four key factor cells, four strategy cells, and one cell that is always left blank (the upper-left cell). The four strategy cells, labeled *SO*, *WO*, *ST*, and *WT*, are developed after completing four key factor cells, labeled *S*, *W*, *O*, and *T*. There are eight steps involved in constructing a SWOT Matrix:

1. List the firm's key external opportunities.
2. List the firm's key external threats.
3. List the firm's key internal strengths.
4. List the firm's key internal weaknesses.
5. Match internal strengths with external opportunities, and record the resultant SO strategies in the appropriate cell.
6. Match internal weaknesses with external opportunities, and record the resultant WO strategies.
7. Match internal strengths with external threats, and record the resultant ST strategies.
8. Match internal weaknesses with external threats, and record the resultant WT strategies.

Some important aspects of a SWOT Matrix are evidenced in Figure 8-3. For example, note that both the internal and external factors and the SO, ST, WO, and WT strategies are stated in quantitative terms to the extent possible. This is important. For example, regarding the second SO number-2 and ST number-1 strategies, if the analyst just said, "Add new repair and service persons," the reader might think that 20 new repair and service persons are needed. Actually only two are needed. Always *be specific* to the extent possible in stating factors and strategies.

It is also important to include the "S1, O2" type notation after each strategy in a SWOT Matrix. This notation reveals the rationale for each alternative strategy. Strategies do not rise out of the blue. Note in Figure 8-3 how this notation reveals the internal and external factors that were matched to formulate desirable strategies. For example, note that this retail computer store business may need to "purchase land to build new store" because a new Highway 34 will make its location less desirable. The notation (W2, O2) and (S8, T3) in Figure 8-3 exemplifies this matching process.

The purpose of each Stage 2 matching tool is to generate feasible alternative strategies, not to select or determine which strategies are best. Not all of the strategies developed in the SWOT Matrix, therefore, will be selected for implementation.

The strategy-formulation guidelines provided in Chapter 4 can enhance the process of matching key external and internal factors. For example, when an organization has both the

	Strengths	Weaknesses
	1. Inventory turnover up 5.8 to 6.7 2. Average customer purchase up $97 to $128 3. Employee morale is excellent 4. In-store promotions = 20 percent increase in sales 5. Newspaper advertising expenditures down 10 percent 6. Revenues from repair and service in store up 16 percent 7. In-store technical support persons have MIS degrees 8. Store's debt-to-total-assets ratio down 34 percent	1. Software revenues in store down 12 percent 2. Location of store hurt by new Hwy 34 3. Carpet and paint in store in disrepair 4. Bathroom in store needs refurbishing 5. Total store revenues down 8 percent 6. Store has no website 7. Supplier on-time-delivery up to 2.4 days 8. Customer checkout process too slow 9. Revenues per employee up 19 percent
Opportunities	**SO Strategies**	**WO Strategies**
1. Population of city growing 10 percent 2. Rival computer store opening one mile away 3. Vehicle traffic passing store up 12 percent 4. Vendors average six new products a year 5. Senior citizen use of computers up 8 percent 6. Small business growth in area up 10 percent 7. Desire for websites up 18 percent by realtors 8. Desire for websites up 12 percent by small firms	1. Add four new in-store promotions monthly (S4, O3) 2. Add two new repair and service persons (S6, O5) 3. Send flyer to all seniors over age 55 (S5, O5)	1. Purchase land to build new store (W2, O2) 2. Install new carpet, paint, and bath (W3, W4, O1) 3. Up website services by 50 percent (W6, O7, O8) 4. Launch mailout to all realtors in city (W5, O7)
Threats	**ST Strategies**	**WT Strategies**
1. Best Buy opening new store in one year nearby 2. Local university offers computer repair 3. New bypass Hwy 34 in 1 year will divert traffic 4. New mall being built nearby 5. Gas prices up 14 percent 6. Vendors raising prices 8 percent	1. Hire two more repair persons and market these new services (S6, S7, T1) 2. Purchase land to build new store (S8, T3) 3. Raise out-of-store service calls from $60 to $80 (S6, T5)	1. Hire two new cashiers (W8, T1, T4) 2. Install new carpet, paint, and bath (W3, W4, T1)

FIGURE 8-3

A SWOT Matrix for a Retail Computer Store

capital and human resources needed to distribute its own products (internal strength) and distributors are unreliable, costly, or incapable of meeting the firm's needs (external threat), forward integration can be an attractive ST strategy. When a firm has excess production capacity (internal weakness) and its basic industry is experiencing declining annual sales and profits (external threat), related diversification can be an effective WT strategy.

Although the SWOT matrix is widely used in strategic planning, the analysis does have some limitations.[4] First, SWOT does not show how to achieve a competitive advantage, so it must not be an end in itself. The matrix should be the starting point for a discussion on how proposed strategies could be implemented as well as cost-benefit considerations that ultimately could lead to competitive advantage. Second, SWOT is a static assessment (or snapshot) in time.

A SWOT matrix can be like studying a single frame of a motion picture where you see the lead characters and the setting but have no clue as to the plot. As circumstances, capabilities, threats, and strategies change, the dynamics of a competitive environment may not be revealed in a single matrix. Third, SWOT analysis may lead the firm to overemphasize a single internal or external factor in formulating strategies. There are interrelationships among the key internal and external factors that SWOT does not reveal that may be important in devising strategies.

The Strategic Position and Action Evaluation (SPACE) Matrix

The **Strategic Position and Action Evaluation (SPACE) Matrix**, another important Stage 2 matching tool, is illustrated in Figure 8-4. Its four-quadrant framework indicates whether aggressive, conservative, defensive, or competitive strategies are most appropriate for a given organization. The axes of the SPACE Matrix represent two internal dimensions (**financial position [FP]** and **competitive position [CP]**) and two external dimensions (**stability position [SP]** and **industry position [IP]**). These four factors are perhaps the most important determinants of an organization's overall strategic position.[5]

It is helpful here to elaborate upon the difference between the SP and IP axes. SP refers to the volatility of profits and revenues for firms in a given industry. SP volatility (stability) is based on the expected impact of changes in core external factors such as technology, economy, demographic, seasonality, etc.) The higher frequency and magnitude of the changes the more unstable on SP. An industry can be stable or unstable on SP, yet high or low on IP. The smartphone industry for example would be unstable on SP yet high growth on IP, whereas the carbonated beverage industry would be stable on SP yet low growth on IP.

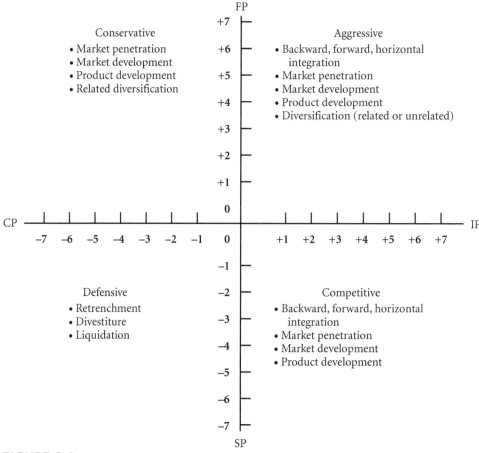

FIGURE 8-4

The SPACE Matrix

Source: Based on H. Rowe, R. Mason, and K. Dickel, *Strategic Management and Business Policy: A Methodological Approach* (Reading, MA: Addison-Wesley Publishing Co. Inc., © 1982), 155.

Depending on the type of organization, numerous variables could make up each of the dimensions represented on the axes of the SPACE Matrix. Factors that were included in the firm's EFE and IFE matrices should be considered in developing a SPACE Matrix. Other variables commonly included are given in Table 8-2. For example, return on investment, leverage, liquidity, working capital, and cash flow are commonly considered to be determining factors of an organization's financial strength. Like the SWOT Matrix, the SPACE Matrix should be both tailored to the particular organization being studied and based on factual information as much as possible.

The steps required to develop a SPACE Matrix are as follows:

1. Select a set of variables to define financial position (FP), competitive position (CP), stability position (SP), and industry position (IP).
2. Assign a numerical value ranging from +1 (worst) to +7 (best) to each of the variables that make up the FP and IP dimensions. Assign a numerical value ranging from –1 (best) to –7 (worst) to each of the variables that make up the SP and CP dimensions. On the FP and CP axes, make comparison to competitors. On the IP and SP axes, make comparison to other industries.
3. Compute an average score for FP, CP, IP, and SP by summing the values given to the variables of each dimension and then by dividing by the number of variables included in the respective dimension.
4. Plot the average scores for FP, IP, SP, and CP on the appropriate axis in the SPACE Matrix.
5. Add the two scores on the *x*-axis and plot the resultant point on X. Add the two scores on the *y*-axis and plot the resultant point on Y. Plot the intersection of the new *xy* point.
6. Draw a **directional vector** from the origin of the SPACE Matrix through the new intersection point. This vector reveals the type of strategies recommended for the organization: aggressive, competitive, defensive, or conservative.

Some examples of strategy profiles that can emerge from a SPACE analysis are shown in Figure 8-5. The directional vector associated with each profile suggests the type of strategies to pursue: aggressive, conservative, defensive, or competitive. When a firm's directional vector is located in the **aggressive quadrant** (upper-right quadrant) of the SPACE Matrix, an organization is in an excellent position to use its internal strengths to (a) take advantage of external opportunities, (b) overcome internal weaknesses, and (c) avoid external threats. Therefore, market penetration, market

TABLE 8-2 Example Factors That Make Up the SPACE Matrix Axes

Internal Strategic Position	External Strategic Position
Financial Position (FP)	*Stability Position (SP)*
Return on investment	Technological changes
Leverage	Rate of inflation
Liquidity	Demand variability
Working capital	Price range of competing products
Cash flow	Barriers to entry into market
Inventory turnover	Competitive pressure
Earnings per share	Ease of exit from market
Price earnings ratio	Price elasticity of demand
	Risk involved in business
Competitive Position (CP)	*Industry Position (IP)*
Market share	Growth potential
Product quality	Profit potential
Product life cycle	Financial stability
Customer loyalty	Extent leveraged
Capacity utilization	Resource utilization
Technological know-how	Ease of entry into market
Control over suppliers and distributors	Productivity, capacity utilization

Source: Based on H. Rowe, R. Mason, and K. Dickel, *Strategic Management and Business Policy: A Methodological Approach* (Reading, MA: Addison-Wesley Publishing Co. Inc., © 1982), 155–156.

development, product development, backward integration, forward integration, horizontal integration, or diversification, can be feasible, depending on the specific circumstances that face the firm.

When a particular company is known, the analyst must be much more specific in terms of recommended strategies. For example, instead of saying market penetration is a recommended

Aggressive Profiles

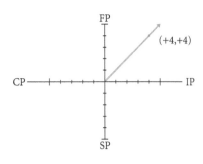

A financially strong firm that has achieved major competitive advantages in a growing and stable industry

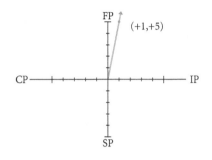

A firm whose financial strength is a dominating factor in the industry

Conservative Profiles

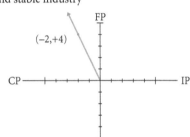

A firm that has achieved financial strength in a stable industry that is not growing; the firm has few competitive advantages

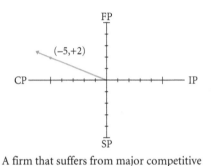

A firm that suffers from major competitive disadvantages in an industry that is technologically stable but declining in sales

Competitive Profiles

A firm with major competitive advantages in a high-growth industry

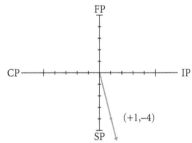

An organization that is competing fairly well in an unstable industry

Defensive Profiles

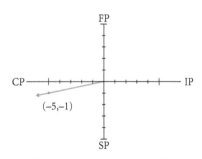

A firm that has a very weak competitive position in a negative growth, stable industry

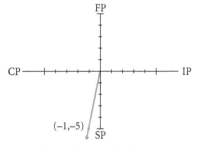

A financially troubled firm in a very unstable industry

FIGURE 8-5

Example Strategy Profiles

Source: Based on H. Rowe, R. Mason, and K. Dickel, *Strategic Management and Business Policy: A Methodological Approach* (Reading, MA: Addison-Wesley Publishing Co. Inc., © 1982), 155.

strategy when your vector goes in the conservative quadrant, say that adding 34 new stores in India is a recommended strategy. This is an important point for students doing case analyses because a particular company is generally known, and terms such as *market development* are too vague to use. That term could refer to adding a manufacturing plant in Thailand or Mexico or South Africa—*so students—be specific to the extent possible regarding implications of all the matrices presented in this chapter. Not being specific can be disastrous in this course. Avoid terms like expand, increase, decrease, grow—be much more specific than that!*

The directional vector may appear in the **conservative quadrant** (upper-left quadrant) of the SPACE Matrix, which implies staying close to the firm's basic competencies and not taking excessive risks. Conservative strategies most often include market penetration, market development, product development, and related diversification. The directional vector may be located in the lower-left or **defensive quadrant** of the SPACE Matrix, which suggests that the firm should focus on rectifying internal weaknesses and avoiding external threats. Defensive strategies include retrenchment, divestiture, liquidation, and related diversification. Finally, the directional vector may be located in the lower-right or **competitive quadrant** of the SPACE Matrix, indicating competitive strategies. Competitive strategies include backward, forward, and horizontal integration; market penetration; market development; and product development.

A SPACE Matrix analysis for a bank is provided in Table 8-3. Note that competitive type strategies are recommended. A SPACE Matrix for Hewlett-Packard (HP) is given in

TABLE 8-3 A SPACE Matrix for a Bank

Financial Position (FP)	Ratings
The bank's primary capital ratio is 7.23 percent, which is 1.23 percentage points over the generally required ratio of 6 percent.	1.0
The bank's return on assets is negative 0.77, compared to a bank industry average ratio of positive 0.70.	1.0
The bank's net income was $183 million, down 9 percent from a year previously.	3.0
The bank's revenues increased 7 percent to $3.46 billion.	4.0
	9.0

Industry Position (IP)	
Deregulation provides geographic and product freedom.	4.0
Deregulation increases competition in the banking industry.	2.0
Pennsylvania's interstate banking law allows the bank to acquire other banks in New Jersey, Ohio, Kentucky, the District of Columbia, and West Virginia.	4.0
	10.0

Stability Position (SP)	
Less-developed countries are experiencing high inflation and political instability.	−4.0
Headquartered in Pittsburgh, the bank historically has been heavily dependent on the steel, oil, and gas industries. These industries are depressed.	−5.0
Banking deregulation has created instability throughout the industry.	−4.0
	−13.0

Competitive Position (CP)	
The bank provides data processing services for more than 450 institutions in 38 states.	−2.0
Superregional banks, international banks, and nonbanks are becoming increasingly competitive.	−5.0
The bank has a large customer base.	−2.0
	−9.0

Conclusion

SP Average is −13.0 ÷ 3 = −4.33   IP Average is +10.0 ÷ 3 = 3.33

CP Average is −9.0 ÷ 3 = −3.00   FP Average is +9.0 ÷ 4 = 2.25

Directional Vector Coordinates: x-axis: −3.00 + (+3.33) = +0.33

y-axis: −4.33 + (+2.25) = −2.08

The bank should pursue competitive strategies.

TABLE 8-4   An Actual SPACE Matrix for Hewlett-Packard

Internal Analysis		External Analysis	
Financial Position (FP)		Stability Position (SP)	
Return on Investment (ROI)	1	Rate of Inflation	−2
Leverage	4	Technological Changes	−6
Liquidity	2	Price Elasticity of Demand	−3
Working Capital	1	Competitive Pressure	−7
Cash Flow	2	Barriers to Entry into Market	−4
Financial Position (FP) Average	**2**	**Stability Position (SP) Average**	**−4.4**
Internal Analysis		External Analysis	
Competitive Position (CP)		Industry Position (IP)	
Market Share	−7	Growth Potential	6
Product Quality	−2	Financial Stability	2
Customer Loyalty	−3	Ease of Entry into Market	4
Technological Know-how	−4	Resource Utilization	1
Control over Suppliers/Distributors	−5	Profit Potential	2
Competitive Position (CP) Average	**−4.2**	**Industry Position (IP) Average**	**3.0**

2.0 + (−4.4) = −2.4 y-axis
3.0 + (−4.2) = −1.2 x-axis
Coordinate (−1.2, −2.4)
Conclusion: Vector points in defensive quadrant

Table 8-4 followed by the Krispy Kreme Donuts SPACE diagram in Figure 8-6. Note that HP is in a precarious defensive position, struggling to compete against Apple, Dell, and Amazon.

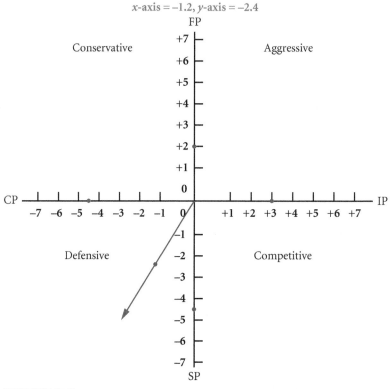

x-axis = −1.2, y-axis = −2.4

FIGURE 8-6

A SPACE Matrix for Krispy Kreme

The Boston Consulting Group (BCG) Matrix

Based in Boston and having 1,713 employees, the Boston Consulting Group (BCG) is a large consulting firm that endured the recent economic downturn without laying off any employees and in 2010 hired the most new consultants ever. BCG ranks number 2 in *Fortune*'s recent list of the "100 Best Companies To Work For."

Autonomous divisions (or profit centers) of an organization make up what is called a **business portfolio**. When a firm's divisions compete in different industries, a separate strategy often must be developed for each business. The Boston Consulting Group (BCG) Matrix and the Internal-External (IE) Matrix are designed specifically to enhance a multidivisional firm's efforts to formulate strategies. (BCG is a private management consulting firm based in Boston that currently employs about 4,400 consultants in 40 countries.)

In a *Form 10K* or *Annual Report*, some companies do not disclose financial information by segment, in which case a BCG portfolio analysis may not be possible by persons external to the firm. Reasons to disclose by-division financial information in the author's view, however, more than offset the reasons not to disclose, as indicated in Table 8-5.

The BCG Matrix graphically portrays differences among divisions in terms of relative market share position and industry growth rate. The BCG Matrix allows a multidivisional organization to manage its portfolio of businesses by examining the relative market share position and the industry growth rate of each division relative to all other divisions in the organization. **Relative market share position** is defined as the ratio of a division's own market share (or revenues) in a particular industry to the market share (or revenues) held by the largest rival firm in that industry. Note in Table 8-6 that other variables can be used in this analysis besides revenues. For example, number of stores, or number of restaurants, or in the airline industry number of airplanes could be used for comparative purposes to determine relative market share position. Relative market share position for Enterprise Rent-a-Car based on number of locations is 6,187/6,187 = 1.00 as indicated in Table 8-6. Enterprise is the largest rental car company and its circle in a BCG Matrix would be somewhere along the far left axis.

Relative market share position is given on the *x*-axis of the BCG Matrix. The midpoint on the *x*-axis usually is set at 0.50, corresponding to a division that has half the market share of the leading firm in the industry. The *y*-axis represents the industry growth rate in sales, measured in percentage terms. The growth rate percentages on the *y*-axis could range from −20 to +20 percent, with 0.0 being the midpoint. The average annual increase in revenues for several leading firms in the industry would be a good estimate of the value. Also, various sources such as the S&P Industry Survey would provide this value. These numerical ranges on the *x*- and *y*-axes are often used, but other numerical values could be

TABLE 8-5 Reasons to (or Not to) Disclose Financial Information by Segment (by Division)

Reasons to Disclose	Reasons Not to Disclose
1. Transparency is a good thing in today's world of Sarbanes-Oxley	1. Can become free competitive information for rival firms
2. Investors will better understand the firm, which can lead to greater support	2. Can hide performance failures
3. Managers and employees will better understand the firm, which should lead to greater commitment	3. Can reduce rivalry among segments
4. Disclosure enhances the communication process both within the firm and with outsiders	

TABLE 8-6   Market Share Data for Selected Industries

Hard Cider (consumption growing rapidly; has about 5 percent alcohol; consumed 50/50 by men/women versus 80/20 men/women for beer; sweeter than beer); *WSJ*, 8-15-12, B9—Top hard cider brands in the USA in millions of liters sold in 2011.

Brand	Liters	Owner
Woodchuck Cider	14.1	Vermont Hard Cider
Strongbow Cider	6.9	Heineken NV
Hornsby's Cider	6.8	C&C Group PLC
Magners	6.2	C&C Group PLC
Ace Cider	2.1	California Cider Co.
Crispin Cider	1.0	MillerCoors LLC
Michelob Cider	1.0	Anheuser-Busch InBev NV
Angry Orchard Cider	1.0	Boston Beer Co. (maker of Sam Adams lager)
Other Ciders	60.9	
Total	100.0	

USA Car Rental Industry (*USA Today*, 8-28-12, p. 1B)

Brand	Number of Cars	Number of Locations	Airport Market Share (%)
Enterprise	920K	6,187	34
Hertz/Advantage/ Dollar Thrifty	438K	2,945	37
Avis/Budget	285K	2,300	26
Other	106K	978	03
TOTAL	1,749K	2,410	

Smartphones in the USA (*USA Today*, 10-18-12, p. 4B)

Brand	Market Share (%)
Apple	37.3
Samsung	27.0
LG	7.9
Motorola	6.7

Note: Ireland's C&C Group PLC is trying to acquire Vermont Hard Cider, maker of the best-selling Woodchuck cider. For many Americans until the mid-19th century, hard cider was the go-to alcoholic beverage, until drinkers turned to beer. Today in the USA, hard cider represents less than 0.5 percent of beer consumption, compared to the UK where it is closer to 15 percent. But hard cider, which has an alcohol content of about 5 percent like beer, is mounting a comeback in the USA.

established as deemed appropriate for particular organizations, such as -10 to +10 percent on the *y*-axis.

The basic BCG Matrix appears in Figure 8-7. Each circle represents a separate division. The size of the circle corresponds to the proportion of corporate revenue generated by that business unit, and the pie slice indicates the proportion of corporate profits generated by that division. Divisions located in Quadrant I of the BCG Matrix are called "Question Marks," those located in Quadrant II are called "Stars," those located in Quadrant III are called "Cash Cows," and those divisions located in Quadrant IV are called "Dogs."

- *Question Marks*—Divisions in Quadrant I have a low relative market share position, yet they compete in a high-growth industry. Generally these firms' cash needs are high and their cash generation is low. These businesses are called **question marks** because the organization must decide whether to strengthen them by pursuing an intensive

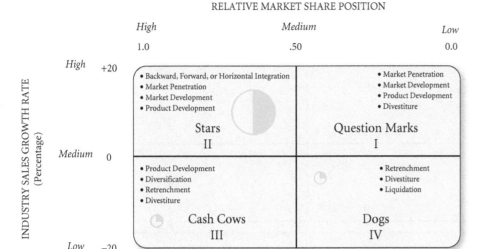

RELATIVE MARKET SHARE POSITION

FIGURE 8-7

The BCG Matrix

Source: Based on the BCG Portfolio Matrix from the Product Portfolio Matrix, © 1970, The Boston Consulting Group.

strategy (market penetration, market development, or product development) or to sell them.

- *Stars*—Quadrant II businesses (**stars**) represent the organization's best long-run opportunities for growth and profitability. Divisions with a high relative market share and a high industry growth rate should receive substantial investment to maintain or strengthen their dominant positions. Forward, backward, and horizontal integration; market penetration; market development; and product development are appropriate strategies for these divisions to consider, as indicated in Figure 8-7.
- *Cash Cows*—Divisions positioned in Quadrant III have a high relative market share position but compete in a low-growth industry. Called **cash cows** because they generate cash in excess of their needs, they are often milked. Many of today's cash cows were yesterday's stars. Cash cow divisions should be managed to maintain their strong position for as long as possible. Product development or diversification may be attractive strategies for strong cash cows. However, as a cash cow division becomes weak, retrenchment or divestiture can become more appropriate.
- *Dogs*—Quadrant IV divisions of the organization have a low relative market share position and compete in a slow- or no-market-growth industry; they are **dogs** in the firm's portfolio. Because of their weak internal and external position, these businesses are often liquidated, divested, or trimmed down through retrenchment. When a division first becomes a dog, retrenchment can be the best strategy to pursue because many Dogs have bounced back, after strenuous asset and cost reduction, to become viable, profitable divisions.

The major benefit of the BCG Matrix is that it draws attention to the cash flow, investment characteristics, and needs of an organization's various divisions. The divisions of many firms evolve over time: dogs become question marks, question marks become stars, stars become cash cows, and cash cows become dogs in an ongoing counterclockwise motion. Less frequently, stars become question marks, question marks become dogs, dogs become cash cows, and cash cows become stars (in a clockwise motion). In some organizations, no cyclical motion is apparent. Over time, organizations should strive to achieve a portfolio of divisions that are stars.

An example BCG Matrix is provided in Figure 8-8, which illustrates an organization composed of five divisions with annual sales ranging from $5,000 to $60,000. Division 1 has

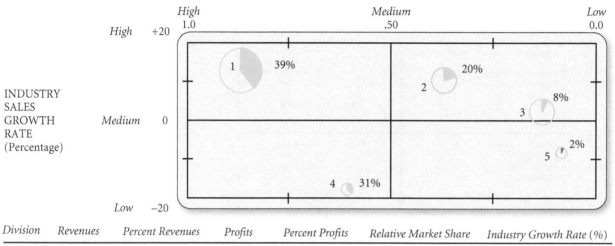

Division	Revenues	Percent Revenues	Profits	Percent Profits	Relative Market Share	Industry Growth Rate (%)
1	$60,000	37	$10,000	39	.80	+15
2	40,000	24	5,000	20	.40	+10
3	40,000	24	2,000	8	.10	+1
4	20,000	12	8,000	31	.60	−20
5	5,000	3	500	2	.05	−10
Total	$165,000	100	$25,500	100	—	—

FIGURE 8-8

An Example BCG Matrix

the greatest sales volume, so the circle representing that division is the largest one in the matrix. The circle corresponding to Division 5 is the smallest because its sales volume ($5,000) is least among all the divisions. The pie slices within the circles reveal the percent of corporate profits contributed by each division. As shown, Division 1 contributes the highest profit percentage, 39 percent, as indicated by 39 percent of the area within circle 1 being shaded. Notice in the diagram that Division 1 is considered a star, Division 2 is a question mark, Division 3 is also a question mark, Division 4 is a cash cow, and Division 5 is a dog.

The BCG Matrix, like all analytical techniques, has some limitations. For example, viewing every business as a star, cash cow, dog, or question mark is an oversimplification; many businesses fall right in the middle of the BCG Matrix and thus are not easily classified. Furthermore, the BCG Matrix does not reflect whether or not various divisions or their industries are growing over time; that is, the matrix has no temporal qualities, but rather it is a snapshot of an organization at a given point in time. Finally, other variables besides relative market share position and industry growth rate in sales, such as size of the market and competitive advantages, are important in making strategic decisions about various divisions.

An example BCG Matrix is provided in Figure 8-9. Note in Figure 8-9 that Division 5 had an operating loss of $188 million. Take note how the percent profit column is still calculated because oftentimes a firm will have a division that incurs a loss for a year. In terms of the pie slice in circle 5 of the diagram, note that it is a *different color* from the positive profit segments in the other circles.

The Internal-External (IE) Matrix

The **Internal-External (IE) Matrix** positions an organization's various divisions in a nine-cell display, illustrated in Figure 8-10. The IE Matrix is similar to the BCG Matrix in that both tools involve plotting organization divisions in a schematic diagram; this is why they are both called "portfolio matrices." Also, the size of each circle represents the percentage sales contribution of each division, and pie slices reveal the percentage profit contribution of each division in both the BCG and IE Matrix.

RELATIVE MARKET SHARE POSITION (RMSP)

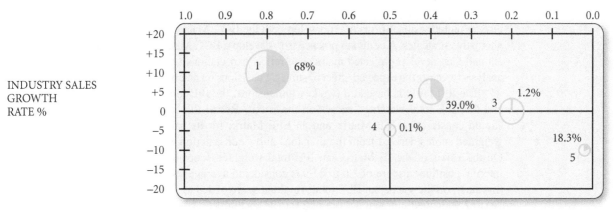

Division	$ Sales (millions)	% Sales	$ Profits (millions)	% Profits	RMSP	IG Rate %
1.	$5,139	51.5	$799	68.0	0.8	10
2.	2,556	25.6	400	39.0	0.4	05
3.	1,749	17.5	12	1.2	0.2	00
4.	493	4.9	4	0.1	0.5	−05
5.	42	0.5	−188	(18.3)	.02	−10
Total	**$9,979**	**100.0**	**$1,027**	**100.0**		

FIGURE 8-9

An Example BCG Matrix

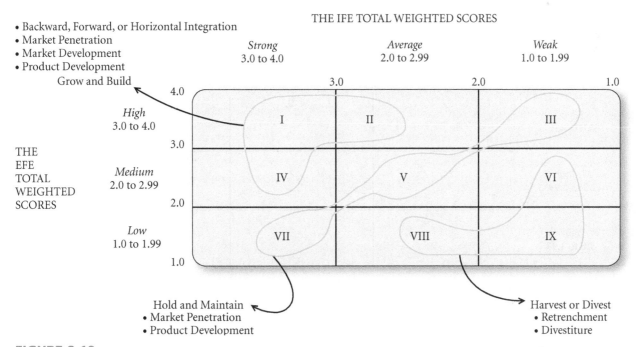

FIGURE 8-10

The Internal–External (IE) Matrix

Source: Based on: The IE Matrix was developed from the General Electric (GE) Business Screen Matrix. For a description of the GE Matrix, see Michael Allen, "Diagramming GE's Planning for What's WATT," in R. Allio and M. Pennington, eds., *Corporate Planning: Techniques and Applications* 1 par; New York: AMACOM, 1979.

But there are some important differences between the BCG Matrix and the IE Matrix. First, the axes are different. Also, the IE Matrix requires more information about the divisions than the BCG Matrix. Furthermore, the strategic implications of each matrix are different. For these reasons, strategists in multidivisional firms often develop both the BCG Matrix and the IE Matrix in formulating alternative strategies. A common practice is to develop a BCG Matrix and an IE Matrix for the present and then develop projected matrices to reflect expectations of the future. This before-and-after analysis forecasts the expected effect of strategic decisions on an organization's portfolio of divisions.

The IE Matrix is based on two key dimensions: the IFE total weighted scores on the *x*-axis and the EFE total weighted scores on the *y*-axis. Recall that each division of an organization should construct an IFE Matrix and an EFE Matrix for its part of the organization. The total weighted scores derived from the divisions allow construction of the corporate-level IE Matrix. On the *x*-axis of the IE Matrix, an IFE total weighted score of 1.0 to 1.99 represents a weak internal position; a score of 2.0 to 2.99 is considered average; and a score of 3.0 to 4.0 is strong. Similarly, on the *y*-axis, an EFE total weighted score of 1.0 to 1.99 is considered low; a score of 2.0 to 2.99 is medium; and a score of 3.0 to 4.0 is high.

The IE Matrix can be divided into three major regions that have different strategy implications. First, the prescription for divisions that fall into cells I, II, or IV can be described as *grow and build*. Intensive (market penetration, market development, and product development) or integrative (backward integration, forward integration, and horizontal integration) strategies can be most appropriate for these divisions. Second, divisions that fall into cells III, V, or VII can be managed best with *hold and maintain* strategies; market penetration and product development are two commonly employed strategies for these types of divisions. Third, a common prescription for divisions that fall into cells VI, VIII, or IX is *harvest or divest*. Successful organizations are able to achieve a portfolio of businesses positioned in or around cell I in the IE Matrix.

An example of a completed IE Matrix is given in Figure 8-11, which depicts an organization composed of four divisions. As indicated by the positioning of the circles, *grow and build* strategies are appropriate for Division 1, Division 2, and Division 3. Division 4 is a candidate for *harvest or divest*. Division 2 contributes the greatest percentage of company sales and thus is represented by the largest circle. Division 1 contributes the greatest proportion of total profits; it has the largest-percentage pie slice.

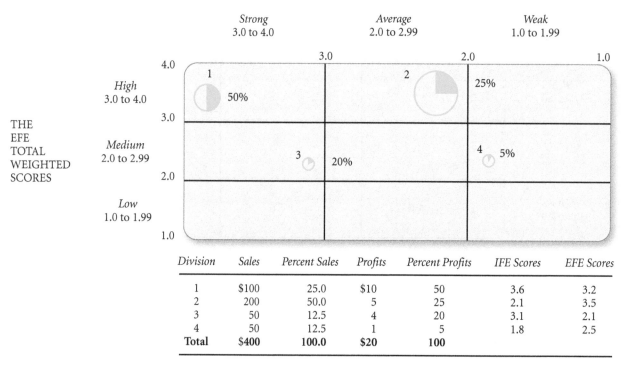

THE IFE TOTAL WEIGHTED SCORES

Division	Sales	Percent Sales	Profits	Percent Profits	IFE Scores	EFE Scores
1	$100	25.0	$10	50	3.6	3.2
2	200	50.0	5	25	2.1	3.5
3	50	12.5	4	20	3.1	2.1
4	50	12.5	1	5	1.8	2.5
Total	$400	100.0	$20	100		

FIGURE 8-11

An Example IE Matrix

THE IFE TOTAL WEIGHTED SCORES

| | Strong 3.0 to 4.0 | Average 2.0 to 2.99 | Weak 1.0 to 1.99 |

THE EFE TOTAL WEIGHTED SCORES

High 3.0 to 4.0

Medium 2.0 to 2.99

Low 1.0 to 1.99

(I 16%) (II) (III 5 4%)
(IV 59% 3) (V 4 2%) (VI)
(VII) (VIII 19%) (IX)

Grow and Build

Segments	$ Revenue	% Revenue	$ Profit	% Profit	EFE Scores	IFE Scores
1.	$7,868	71.5%	$3,000	59%	2.5	3
2.	1,241	11.3%	1,000	19%	2	2
3.	1,578	14.3%	800	16%	3	3
4.	90	0.8%	100	2%	2.5	2.5
5.	223	2.1%	200	4%	3	2
Total	**$11,000**	**100%**	**$5,100**	**100%**	—	—

FIGURE 8-12

The IE Matrix

As indicated in Figure 8-12, the IE Matrix has five product segments. Note that Division 1 has the largest revenues (as indicated by the largest circle) and the largest profits (as indicated by the largest pie slice) in the matrix. It is common for organizations to develop both geographic and product-based IE Matrices to more effectively formulate strategies and allocate resources among divisions. In addition, firms often prepare an IE (or BCG) Matrix for competitors. Furthermore, firms will often prepare "before and after" IE (or BCG) Matrices to reveal the situation at present versus the expected situation after one year. This latter idea minimizes the limitation of these matrices being a "snapshot in time." In performing case analysis, feel free to estimate the IFE and EFE scores for the various divisions based upon your research into the company and industry—rather than preparing a separate IE Matrix for each division.

The Grand Strategy Matrix

In addition to the SWOT Matrix, SPACE Matrix, BCG Matrix, and IE Matrix, the **Grand Strategy Matrix** has become a popular tool for formulating alternative strategies. All organizations can be positioned in one of the Grand Strategy Matrix's four strategy quadrants. A firm's divisions likewise could be positioned. As illustrated in Figure 8-13, the Grand Strategy Matrix is based on two evaluative dimensions: competitive position and market (industry) growth. Any industry whose annual growth in sales exceeds 5 percent could be considered to have rapid growth. Appropriate strategies for an organization to consider are listed in sequential order of attractiveness in each quadrant of the matrix.

Firms located in Quadrant I of the Grand Strategy Matrix are in an excellent strategic position. For these firms, continued concentration on current markets (market penetration and market development) and products (product development) is an appropriate strategy. It is unwise for a Quadrant I firm to shift notably from its established competitive advantages. When a Quadrant I organization has excessive resources, then backward, forward, or horizontal integration may be effective strategies. When a Quadrant I firm is too heavily committed to a single product, then

FIGURE 8-13

The Grand Strategy Matrix

Source: Based on Roland Christensen, Norman Berg, and Malcolm Salter, *Policy Formulation and Administration* (Homewood, IL: Richard D. Irwin, 1976), 16–18.

related diversification may reduce the risks associated with a narrow product line. Quadrant I firms can afford to take advantage of external opportunities in several areas. They can take risks aggressively when necessary.

Firms positioned in Quadrant II need to evaluate their present approach to the marketplace seriously. Although their industry is growing, they are unable to compete effectively, and they need to determine why the firm's current approach is ineffective and how the company can best change to improve its competitiveness. Because Quadrant II firms are in a rapid-market-growth industry, an intensive strategy (as opposed to integrative or diversification) is usually the first option that should be considered. However, if the firm is lacking a distinctive competence or competitive advantage, then horizontal integration is often a desirable alternative. As a last resort, divestiture or liquidation should be considered. Divestiture can provide funds needed to acquire other businesses or buy back shares of stock.

Quadrant III organizations compete in slow-growth industries and have weak competitive positions. These firms must make some drastic changes quickly to avoid further decline and possible liquidation. Extensive cost and asset reduction (retrenchment) should be pursued first. An alternative strategy is to shift resources away from the current business into different areas (diversify). If all else fails, the final options for Quadrant III businesses are divestiture or liquidation.

Finally, Quadrant IV businesses have a strong competitive position but are in a slow-growth industry. These firms have the strength to launch diversified programs into more promising growth areas: Quadrant IV firms have characteristically high cash-flow levels and limited internal growth needs and often can pursue related or unrelated diversification successfully. Quadrant IV firms also may pursue joint ventures.

Students: Even with the Grand Strategy Matrix, be sure to state your alternative strategies in *specific* terms whenever a particular company is known. Avoid using terms such as divestiture for example. Rather, specify the exact division to be sold. Also, be sure to use the free excel student template at www.strategyclub.com if you like.

The Decision Stage

Analysis and intuition provide a basis for making strategy-formulation decisions. The matching techniques just discussed reveal feasible alternative strategies. Many of these strategies will likely have been proposed by managers and employees participating in the strategy analysis and choice activity. Any additional strategies resulting from the matching analyses could be discussed and added to the list of feasible alternative options. As indicated previously in this chapter, participants could rate these strategies on a 1-to-4-scale so that a prioritized list of the best strategies could be achieved.

The Quantitative Strategic Planning Matrix (QSPM)

Other than ranking strategies to achieve the prioritized list, there is only one analytical technique in the literature designed to determine the relative attractiveness of feasible alternative actions. This technique is the **Quantitative Strategic Planning Matrix (QSPM)**, which comprises Stage 3 of the strategy-formulation analytical framework.[6] This technique objectively indicates which alternative strategies are best. The QSPM uses input from Stage 1 analyses and matching results from Stage 2 analyses to decide objectively among alternative strategies. That is, the EFE Matrix, IFE Matrix, and CPM that comprise Stage 1, coupled with the SWOT Matrix, SPACE Matrix, BCG Matrix, IE Matrix, and Grand Strategy Matrix that comprise Stage 2, provide the needed information for setting up the QSPM (Stage 3). The QSPM is a tool that allows strategists to evaluate alternative strategies objectively, based on previously identified external and internal key success factors. Like other strategy-formulation analytical tools, the QSPM requires good intuitive judgment.

The basic format of the QSPM is illustrated in Table 8-7. Note that the left column of a QSPM consists of key external and internal factors (from Stage 1), and the top row consists of feasible alternative strategies (from Stage 2). Specifically, the left column of a QSPM consists of information obtained directly from the EFE Matrix and IFE Matrix. In a column adjacent to the key success factors, the respective weights received by each factor in the EFE Matrix and the IFE Matrix are recorded.

The top row of a QSPM consists of alternative strategies derived from the SWOT Matrix, SPACE Matrix, BCG Matrix, IE Matrix, and Grand Strategy Matrix. These matching tools usually generate similar feasible alternatives. However, not every strategy suggested by the matching techniques has to be evaluated in a QSPM. Strategists should compare several viable alternative strategies in a QSPM. Make sure your strategies are stated in specific terms, such

TABLE 8-7   The Quantitative Strategic Planning Matrix—QSPM

Key Factors	Weight	Strategic Alternatives		
		Strategy 1	Strategy 2	Strategy 3
Key External Factors				
Economy				
Political/Legal/Governmental				
Social/Cultural/Demographic/Environmental				
Technological				
Competitive				
Key Internal Factors				
Management				
Marketing				
Finance/Accounting				
Production/Operations				
Research and Development				
Management Information Systems				

as "Open 275 new stores in Indonesia" rather than "Expand globally" or "Open new stores in Africa." In Chapter 9, you will see that a dollar value must be established for each recommended strategy; it would be impossible to establish a dollar value for "expand globally."

Conceptually, the QSPM determines the relative attractiveness of various strategies based on the extent to which key external and internal critical success factors are capitalized on or improved. The relative attractiveness of each strategy within a set of alternatives is computed by determining the cumulative impact of each external and internal critical success factor. Any number of sets of alternative strategies can be included in the QSPM, and any number of strategies can make up a given set, but only strategies within a given set are evaluated relative to each other. For example, one set of strategies may include diversification, whereas another set may include issuing stock and selling a division to raise needed capital. These two sets of strategies are totally different, and the QSPM evaluates strategies only within sets. Note in Table 8-7 that three strategies are included, and they make up just one set.

A QSPM for a retail computer store is provided in Table 8-8. This example illustrates all the components of the QSPM: strategic alternatives, key factors, weights, attractiveness scores (AS), total attractiveness scores (TAS), and the sum total attractiveness score. The three new terms just introduced—(1) attractiveness scores, (2) total attractiveness scores, and (3) the sum total attractiveness score—are defined and explained as the six steps required to develop a QSPM are discussed:

Step 1: *Make a list of the firm's key external opportunities and threats and internal strengths and weaknesses in the left column of the QSPM.* This information should be taken directly from the EFE Matrix and IFE Matrix. A minimum of 10 external key success factors and 10 internal key success factors should be included in the QSPM.

Step 2: *Assign weights to each key external and internal factor.* These weights are identical to those in the EFE Matrix and the IFE Matrix. The weights are presented in a straight column just to the right of the external and internal critical success factors.

Step 3: *Examine the Stage 2 (matching) matrices, and identify alternative strategies that the organization should consider implementing.* Record these strategies in the top row of the QSPM. Group the strategies into mutually exclusive sets if possible.

Step 4: *Determine the Attractiveness Scores (AS)* defined as numerical values that indicate the relative attractiveness of each strategy in a given set of alternatives. **Attractiveness Scores (AS)** are determined by examining each key external or internal factor, one at a time, and asking the question "Does this factor affect the choice of strategies being made?" If the answer to this question is yes, then the strategies should be compared relative to that key factor. Specifically, AS should be assigned to each strategy to indicate the relative attractiveness of one strategy over others, considering the particular factor. The range for AS is 1 = not attractive, 2 = somewhat attractive, 3 = reasonably attractive, and 4 = highly attractive. By attractive, we mean the extent that one strategy, compared to others, enables the firm to either capitalize on the strength, improve on the weakness, exploit the opportunity, or avoid the threat. Work row by row in developing a QSPM. If the answer to the previous question is *no*, indicating that the respective key factor has no effect upon the specific choice being made, then do not assign AS to the strategies in that set. Use a dash to indicate that the key factor does not affect the choice being made. *Note:* If you assign an AS score to one strategy, then assign an AS score(s) to the other. In other words, if one strategy receives a dash, then all others must receive a dash in a given row.

Step 5: *Compute the Total Attractiveness Scores.* **Total Attractiveness Scores (TAS)** are defined as the product of multiplying the weights (Step 2) by the AS (Step 4) in each row. The TAS indicate the relative attractiveness of each alternative strategy, considering only the impact of the adjacent external or internal critical success factor. The higher the TAS, the more attractive the strategic alternative (considering only the adjacent critical success factor).

TABLE 8-8   A QSPM for a Retail Computer Store

| Key Factors | Weight | STRATEGIC ALTERNATIVES | | | |
| | | 1 Buy New Land and Build New Larger Store | | 2 Fully Renovate Existing Store | |
		AS	TAS	AS	TAS
Opportunities					
1. Population of city growing 10 percent	0.10	4	0.40	2	0.20
2. Rival computer store opening one mile away	0.10	2	0.20	4	0.40
3. Vehicle traffic passing store up 12 percent	0.08	1	0.08	4	0.32
4. Vendors average six new products/year	0.05	—		—	
5. Senior citizen use of computers up 8 percent	0.05	—		—	
6. Small business growth in area up 10 percent	0.10	—		—	
7. Desire for websites up 18 percent by realtors	0.06	—		—	
8. Desire for websites up 12 percent by small firms	0.06	—		—	
Threats					
1. Best Buy opening new store nearby in one year	0.15	4	0.60	3	0.45
2. Local university offers computer repair	0.08	—		—	
3. New bypass for Hwy 34 in one year will divert traffic	0.12	4	0.48	1	0.12
4. New mall being built nearby	0.08	2	0.16	4	0.32
5. Gas prices up 14 percent	0.04	—		—	
6. Vendors raising prices 8 percent	0.03	—		—	
Total	**1.00**				
Strengths					
1. Inventory turnover increased from 5.8 to 6.7	0.05	—		—	
2. Average customer purchase increased from $97 to $128	0.07	2	0.14	4	0.28
3. Employee morale is excellent	0.10	—		—	
4. In-store promotions resulted in 20 percent increase in sales	0.05	—		—	
5. Newspaper advertising expenditures increased 10 percent	0.02	—		—	
6. Revenues from repair/service segment of store up 16 percent	0.15	4	0.60	3	0.45
7. In-store technical support personnel have MIS college degrees	0.05	—		—	
8. Store's debt-to-total-assets ratio declined to 34 percent	0.03	4	0.12	2	0.06
9. Revenues per employee up 19 percent	0.02	—		—	
Weaknesses					
1. Revenues from software segment of store down 12 percent	0.10	—		—	
2. Location of store negatively impacted by new Hwy 34	0.15	4	0.60	1	0.15
3. Carpet and paint in store somewhat in disrepair	0.02	1	0.02	4	0.08
4. Bathroom in store needs refurbishing	0.02	1	0.02	4	0.08
5. Revenues from businesses down 8%	0.04	3	0.12	4	0.16
6. Store has no website	0.05	—		—	
7. Supplier on-time delivery increased to 2.4 days	0.03	—		—	
8. Often customers have to wait to check out	0.05	2	0.10	4	0.20
Total	**1.00**		**3.64**		**3.27**

Step 6: ***Compute the Sum Total Attractiveness Score.*** Add TAS in each strategy column of the QSPM. The **Sum Total Attractiveness Scores (STAS)** reveal which strategy is most attractive in each set of alternatives. Higher scores indicate more attractive strategies, considering all the relevant external and internal factors that could affect the strategic decisions. The magnitude of the difference between the STAS in a given set of strategic alternatives indicates the relative desirability of one strategy over another.

In Table 8-8, two alternative strategies—(1) buy new land and build new larger store and (2) fully renovate existing store—are being considered by a computer retail store. Note by sum total attractiveness scores of 3.64 versus 3.27 that the analysis indicates the business should buy new land and build a new larger store. Note the use of dashes to indicate which factors do not affect the strategy choice being considered. If a particular factor affects one strategy but not the other, it affects the choice being made, so AS should be recorded for both strategies. Never rate one strategy and not the other. Note also in Table 8-8 that there are no double 1's, 2's, 3's, or 4's in a row. Never duplicate scores in a row. Never work column by column; always prepare a QSPM working row by row. If you have more than one strategy in the QSPM, then let the AS scores range from 1 to "the number of strategies being evaluated." This will enable you to have a different AS score for each strategy. These are all important guidelines to follow in developing a QSPM. In actual practice, the store did purchase the new land and build a new store; the business also did some minor refurbishing until the new store was operational.

There should be a rationale for each AS score assigned. Note in Table 8-8 in the first row that the "city population growing 10 percent annually" opportunity could be capitalized on best by Strategy 1, "building the new, larger store," so an AS score of 4 was assigned to Strategy 1. AS scores, therefore, are not mere guesses; they should be rational, defensible, and reasonable.

An example QSPM is given in Table 8-9. Note in the actual QSPM for Starbucks in Table 8-9 that many rows are not rated, indicating that the particular factor does not significantly impact the choice to be made. This is good procedure. Also, notice in Table 8-9 that the 3 and 4 ratings given to the Strategy 2 "Open 400 Stores in the Middle East, Asia/Africa" versus Strategy 1 and indicate that Strategy 2 is a better choice given most of the factors. Working row by row is also good procedure. In addition, notice in Table 8-9 that many rows are not rated at all, indicating the particular factor will not impact the choice between Strategy 1 and 2. Leaving perhaps half of the rows blank in this manner is also good procedure. Finally, note in Table 8-9, that Strategy 2 is better for Starbucks as indicated by a STAS of 2.41.

TABLE 8-9   An Actual QSPM for Starbucks (2013)

		Strategy 1		Strategy 2	
		Open 100 Stores on U.S. College Campuses		Open 400 Stores in Middle East Asia/Africa	
	WT.	AS	TAS	AS	TAS
Strengths					
1. 22 percent of revenue comes from its international unit.	0.04	1	0.4	4	0.16
2. Net income grew to $333.1M for the recent quarter.	0.03	–	–	–	–
3. Total revenue grew to $3.30B from $2.92B.	0.04	–	–	–	–
4. Sales at global restaurants open at least 13 months rose 6 percent.	0.04	1	0.04	3	0.12
5. Starbucks earned a 100 percent HRC rating for the fourth consecutive year.	0.03	–	–	–	–
6. Starbucks global comparable store sales also increased 6 percent.	0.04	1	0.04	3	0.12
7. Starbucks revenues reached $166.9M in the Asian-Pacific region for 2011's last quarter (up 38 percent from a year earlier).	0.04	1	0.04	4	0.16
8. Starbucks only buys coffee grown at elevations higher than 2,600 feet because those beans are of better quality.	0.05	–	–	–	–
9. Starbucks employs more than 650 people to provide technology solutions.	0.04	–	–	–	–
10. Starbucks buys Evolution Fresh Inc. (a high end juice maker) for $30M.	0.05	–	–	–	–
11. Starbucks market share is 32.6 percent.	0.04	–	–	–	–
12. Starbucks sells 8.2 million coffee drinks on average each day in the United States.	0.04	4	0.16	1	0.04

(continued)

		Strategy 1 Open 100 Stores on U.S. College Campuses		Strategy 2 Open 400 Stores in Middle East Asia/ Africa	
	WT.	AS	TAS	AS	TAS
Weaknesses					
13. Starbucks rose prices in the Northeast and Sunbelt by about 1 percent.	0.04	3	0.12	1	0.04
14. Starbucks rose prices in 500 Chinese mainland stores. Coffee prices will increase by 1 to 2 yuan (16 to 32 U.S. cents).	0.04	1	0.04	3	0.12
15. Starbucks reward cardholders protest firm charging for soy milk and flavored syrups.	0.05	–	–	–	–
16. Starbucks does not offer the same type and quality tea as would be served in India.	0.04	1	0.04	2	0.08
17. After 63 Starbucks were opened in France, the firm has never turned a profit there.	0.06	–	–	–	–
18. Sales for Starbucks in Europe open at least 13 months only rose 2 percent whereas in the United States had a 9 percent and Asia had a 20 percent growth.	0.06	–	–	–	–
19. Starbucks reputation takes a big hit among British consumers after a report showed they paid no tax on sales of 1.2 billion pounds in years past after telling the taxman it made no profit but told investors it was a profitable unit.	0.03	–	–	–	–
20. Starbucks comes in second place to Dunkin Donuts on Brand Keys 2012 Customer Loyalty Engagement Index.	0.04	–	–	–	–
Opportunities					
21. 80 percent of U.S. adults are concerned about weight.	0.04	–	–	–	–
22. 45 percent of cell phone users have a smart phone.	0.04	–	–	–	–
23. China's projected GDP is $7.9 trillion.	0.02	2	0.04	4	0.08
24. U.S. projected GDP is $15.6 trillion.	0.02	4	0.08	2	0.04
25. Arabica coffee's futures price fell to a 17-month low after the likelihood of a record global crop in 2012–2013.	0.04	2	0.08	3	0.12
26. Since 2005 China's market for specialized coffee shops has tripled.	0.05	1	0.05	4	0.20
27. Tea is the second most consumed beverage in the world, behind bottled water.	0.04	1	0.04	4	0.16
28. India's tea industry accounts for 31 percent of global production.	0.04	1	0.04	4	0.16
29. Dunkin' Donuts comparable stores sales growth was 5.1 percent in 2011 versus Starbucks 8 percent.	0.02	–	–	–	–
30. The domestic coffee market in India is growing by 25 percent annually.	0.02	–	–	–	–
Threats					
31. The European debt crisis causes the demand for coffee to falter in various countries; down 6.7 percent, 2.6 percent, and 1.6 percent in Britain, Spain, and Italy, respectively.	0.05	2	0.10	4	0.20
32. Consumer confidence index fell to 60.6 in August from 65.4 in July.	0.03	3	0.09	1	0.03
33. China's per capital GDP in 2011 was $5,184.	0.04	1	0.04	4	0.16
34. An estimated 30 to 50 million American adults are lactose intolerant.	0.04	–	–	–	–
35. Dunkin' Donuts opens outlets in the U.S. Northeast, South, and Mid-Atlantic at 10 college campuses.	0.03	4	0.12	1	0.03
36. Dunkin' Donuts announces its company's goal of doubling U.S. store presence over 20 years.	0.03	4	0.12	1	0.03
37. McDonald's Asia/Pacific, Middle East and Africa division had a 1.4 percent increase in comparable sales.	0.04	1	0.04	4	0.16
38. McDonald's had total revenues of $27B for fiscal 2011 compared to Starbucks $11.7B.	0.04	2	0.08	3	0.12
39. McDonald's takes 7th place in Interbrand's Best Global Brands 2012 while Starbucks comes in 88th place.	0.02	1	0.02	4	0.08
40. Select McDonald's stores in the United States and Europe are providing iPads for customers to use while they are in the store.	0.04	–	–	–	–
TOTAL	**1.00**		**1.82**		**2.41**

Positive Features and Limitations of the QSPM

A positive feature of the QSPM is that sets of strategies can be examined sequentially or simultaneously. For example, corporate-level strategies could be evaluated first, followed by division-level strategies, and then function-level strategies. There is no limit to the number of strategies that can be evaluated or the number of sets of strategies that can be examined at once using the QSPM.

Another positive feature of the QSPM is that it requires strategists to integrate pertinent external and internal factors into the decision process. Developing a QSPM makes it less likely that key factors will be overlooked or weighted inappropriately. A QSPM draws attention to important relationships that affect strategy decisions. Although developing a QSPM requires a number of subjective decisions, making small decisions along the way enhances the probability that the final strategic decisions will be best for the organization. A QSPM can be used by small and large, for-profit and nonprofit organizations.

The QSPM is not without some limitations. First, it always requires intuitive judgments and educated assumptions. The ratings and attractiveness scores require judgmental decisions, even though they should be based on objective information. Discussion among strategists, managers, and employees throughout the strategy-formulation process, including development of a QSPM, is constructive and improves strategic decisions. Constructive discussion during strategy analysis and choice may arise because of genuine differences of interpretation of information and varying opinions. Another limitation of the QSPM is that it can be only as good as the prerequisite information and matching analyses upon which it is based.

Cultural Aspects of Strategy Choice

All organizations have a culture. **Culture** includes the set of shared values, beliefs, attitudes, customs, norms, personalities, heroes, and heroines that describe a firm. Culture is the unique way an organization does business. It is the human dimension that creates solidarity and meaning, and it inspires commitment and productivity in an organization when strategy changes are made. All human beings have a basic need to make sense of the world, to feel in control, and to make meaning. When events threaten meaning, individuals react defensively. Managers and employees may even sabotage new strategies in an effort to recapture the status quo.

It is beneficial to view strategic management from a cultural perspective because success often rests on the degree of support that strategies receive from a firm's culture. If a firm's strategies are supported by cultural products such as values, beliefs, rites, rituals, ceremonies, stories, symbols, language, heroes, and heroines, then managers often can implement changes swiftly and easily. However, if a supportive culture does not exist and is not cultivated, then strategy changes may be ineffective or even counterproductive. A firm's culture can become antagonistic to new strategies, and the result of that antagonism may be confusion and disarray.

Strategies that require fewer cultural changes may be more attractive because extensive changes can take considerable time and effort. Whenever two firms merge, it becomes especially important to evaluate and consider culture-strategy linkages.

Culture provides an explanation for the difficulties a firm encounters when it attempts to shift its strategic direction, as the following statement explains:

> Not only has the "right" corporate culture become the essence and foundation of corporate excellence, but success or failure of needed corporate reforms hinges on management's sagacity and ability to change the firm's driving culture in time and in tune with required changes in strategies.[8]

The Politics of Strategy Choice

All organizations are political. Unless managed, political maneuvering consumes valuable time, subverts organizational objectives, diverts human energy, and results in the loss of some valuable employees. Sometimes political biases and personal preferences get unduly embedded in strategy choice decisions. Internal politics affect the choice of strategies in all organizations. The hierarchy of command in an organization, combined with the career aspirations of different people and the need to allocate scarce resources, guarantees the formation of coalitions of individuals who strive to take care of themselves first and the organization second, third, or fourth. Coalitions of individuals often form around key strategy issues that face an enterprise. A major responsibility of strategists is to guide the development of coalitions, to nurture an overall team concept, and to gain the support of key individuals and groups of individuals.

In the absence of objective analyses, strategy decisions too often are based on the politics of the moment. With development of improved strategy-formation tools, political factors become less important in making strategic decisions. In the absence of objectivity, political factors sometimes dictate strategies, and this is unfortunate. Managing political relationships is an integral part of building enthusiasm and esprit de corps in an organization.

A classic study of strategic management in nine large corporations examined the political tactics of successful and unsuccessful strategists.[9] Successful strategists were found to let weakly supported ideas and proposals die through inaction and to establish additional hurdles or tests for strongly supported ideas considered unacceptable but not openly opposed. Successful strategists kept a low political profile on unacceptable proposals and strived to let most negative decisions come from subordinates or a group consensus, thereby reserving their personal vetoes for big issues and crucial moments. Successful strategists did a lot of chatting and informal questioning to stay abreast of how things were progressing and to know when to intervene. They led strategy but did not dictate it. They gave few orders, announced few decisions, depended heavily on informal questioning, and sought to probe and clarify until a consensus emerged.

Successful strategists generously and visibly rewarded key thrusts that succeeded. They assigned responsibility for major new thrusts to **champions**, the individuals most strongly identified with the idea or product and whose futures were linked to its success. They stayed alert to the symbolic impact of their own actions and statements so as not to send false signals that could stimulate movements in unwanted directions.

Successful strategists ensured that all major power bases within an organization were represented in, or had access to, top management. They interjected new faces and new views into considerations of major changes. This is important because new employees and managers generally have more enthusiasm and drive than employees who have been with the firm a long time. New employees do not see the world the same old way; nor do they act as screens against changes. Successful strategists minimized their own political exposure on highly controversial issues and in circumstances in which major opposition from key power centers was likely. In combination, these findings provide a basis for managing political relationships in an organization.

Because strategies must be effective in the marketplace and capable of gaining internal commitment, the following tactics used by politicians for centuries can aid strategists:

1. Achieving desired results is more important that imposing a particular method, so consider various methods and choose, whenever possible, the one(s) that will afford the greatest commitment from employees/managers.
2. Achieving satisfactory results with a popular strategy is generally better than trying to achieve optimal results with an unpopular strategy.
3. An effective way to gain commitment and achieve desired results is oftentimes to shift from specific to general issues and concerns.
4. An effective way to gain commitment and achieve desired results is oftentimes to shift from short-term to long-term issues and concerns.
5. Middle level managers must be genuinely involved in and supportive of strategic decisions, because successful implementation will hinge on their support.[10]

Governance Issues

A "director," according to Webster's Dictionary, is "one of a group of persons entrusted with the overall direction of a corporate enterprise." A **board of directors** is a group of individuals who are elected by the ownership of a corporation to have oversight and guidance over management and who look out for shareholders' interests. The act of oversight and direction is referred to as **governance**. The National Association of Corporate Directors defines governance as "the characteristic of ensuring that long-term strategic objectives and plans are established and that the proper management structure is in place to achieve those objectives, while at the same time making sure that the structure functions to maintain the corporation's integrity, reputation, and responsibility to its various constituencies." Boards are being held accountable for the entire performance of the firm. Boards of directors are increasingly sued by shareholders for mismanaging their interests. New accounting rules in the USA and Europe now enhance corporate-governance codes and require much more extensive financial disclosure among publicly held firms. The roles and duties of a board of directors can be divided into four broad categories, as indicated in Table 8-10.

Shareholders today are wary of boards of directors. Shareholders of hundreds of firms are demanding that their boards do a better job of governing corporate America.[11] New compensation policies are needed as well as direct shareholder involvement in some director activities. For example, boards could require CEOs to groom possible replacements from inside the firm because exorbitant compensation is most often paid to new CEOs coming from outside the firm.

Most boards of directors globally have ended their image as rubber-stamping friends of CEOs. Boards are more autonomous than ever and continually mindful of and responsive to legal and institutional-investor scrutiny. Boards are more cognizant of auditing and compliance issues and more reluctant to approve excessive compensation and perks. Boards stay much more abreast today of public scandals that attract shareholder and media attention. Increasingly,

TABLE 8-10   Board of Director Duties and Responsibilities

1. CONTROL AND OVERSIGHT OVER MANAGEMENT
   a. Select the Chief Executive Officer (CEO).
   b. Sanction the CEO's team.
   c. Provide the CEO with a forum.
   d. Ensure managerial competency.
   e. Evaluate management's performance.
   f. Set management's salary levels, including fringe benefits.
   g. Guarantee managerial integrity through continuous auditing.
   h. Chart the corporate course.
   i. Devise and revise policies to be implemented by management.

2. ADHERENCE TO LEGAL PRESCRIPTIONS
   a. Keep abreast of new laws.
   b. Ensure the entire organization fulfills legal prescriptions.
   c. Pass bylaws and related resolutions.
   d. Select new directors.
   e. Approve capital budgets.
   f. Authorize borrowing, new stock issues, bonds, and so on.

3. CONSIDERATION OF STAKEHOLDERS' INTERESTS
   a. Monitor product quality.
   b. Facilitate upward progression in employee quality of work life.
   c. Review labor policies and practices.
   d. Improve the customer climate.
   e. Keep community relations at the highest level.
   f. Use influence to better governmental, professional association, and educational contacts.
   g. Maintain good public image.

4. ADVANCEMENT OF STOCKHOLDERS' RIGHTS
   a. Preserve stockholders' equity.
   b. Stimulate corporate growth so that the firm will survive and flourish.
   c. Guard against equity dilution.
   d. Ensure equitable stockholder representation.
   e. Inform stockholders through letters, reports, and meetings.
   f. Declare proper dividends.
   g. Guarantee corporate survival.

boards of directors monitor and review executive performance carefully without favoritism to executives, representing shareholders rather than the CEO. Boards are more proactive today, whereas in years past they were oftentimes merely reactive. These are all reasons why the chair of the board of directors should not also serve as the firm's CEO.[12]

Shareholders are also upset at boards for allowing CEOs to receive huge end-of-year bonuses when the firm's stock price drops drastically during the year.[13] For example, Chesapeake Energy Corp. and its board of directors came under fire from shareholders for paying Chairman and CEO Aubrey McClendon $112 million as the firm's stock price plummeted. Investor Jeffrey Bronchick wrote in a letter to the Chesapeake board that the CEO's compensation was a "near perfect illustration of the complete collapse of appropriate corporate governance."

Until recently, boards of directors did most of their work sitting around polished wooden tables. However, Hewlett-Packard's directors, among many others, now log on to their own special board website twice a week and conduct business based on extensive confidential briefing information posted there by the firm's top management team. Then the board members meet face-to-face and fully informed every two months to discuss the biggest issues facing the firm. Even the decision of whether to locate operations in countries with low corporate tax rates would be reviewed by a board of directors. New board involvement policies are aimed at curtailing lawsuits against board members. For example, there were 740 lawsuits filed in 2012 against directors regarding merger deals. The Federal Deposit Insurance Corporation (FDIC) filed 23 lawsuits against directors in 2012, compared to 16 in 2011 and just 2 in 2010.

Today, boards of directors are composed mostly of outsiders who are becoming more involved in organizations' strategic management. The trend in the USA is toward much greater board member accountability with smaller boards, now averaging 12 members rather than 18 as they did a few years ago. *BusinessWeek* recently evaluated the boards of most large U.S. companies and provided the following "principles of good governance":

1. Never have more than two of the firm's executives (current or past) on the board.
2. Never allow a firm's executives to be the board's audit, compensation, or nominating committees.
3. Require all board members to own a large amount of the firm's equity.
4. Require all board members to attend at least 75 percent of all meetings.
5. Require the board to meet annually to evaluate its own performance, without the CEO, COO, or top management in attendance.
6. Never allow the CEO to be Chairperson of the Board.
7. Never allow interlocking directorships (where a director or CEO sits on another director's board).[14]

Jeff Sonnerfeld, associate dean of the Yale School of Management, says, "Boards of directors are now rolling up their sleeves and becoming much more closely involved with management decision making." Company CEOs and boards are required to personally certify financial statements; company loans to company executives and directors are illegal; and there is faster reporting of insider stock transactions.

Just as directors place more emphasis on staying informed about an organization's health and operations, they are also taking a more active role in ensuring that publicly issued documents are accurate representations of a firm's status. Failure to accept responsibility for auditing or evaluating a firm's strategy is considered a serious breach of a director's duties. Stockholders, government agencies, and customers are filing legal suits against directors for fraud, omissions, inaccurate disclosures, lack of due diligence, and culpable ignorance about a firm's operations with increasing frequency. Liability insurance for directors has become exceptionally expensive and has caused numerous directors to resign.

The Sarbanes-Oxley Act resulted in scores of boardroom overhauls among publicly traded companies. The jobs of chief executive and chairman are now held by separate persons, and board audit committees must now have at least one financial expert as a member. Board audit committees now meet 10 or more times per year, rather than three or four times as they did prior to the act. The act put an end to the "country club" atmosphere of most boards and has shifted power from CEOs to directors. Although aimed at public companies, the act has also had a similar impact on privately owned companies.[15]

In Sweden, a new law requires 25 percent female representation in boardrooms. The Norwegian government has passed a similar law that requires 40 percent of corporate director seats to go to women. In the USA, women currently hold about 13 percent of board seats at S&P 500 firms and 10 percent at S&P 1,500 firms. The Investor Responsibility Research Center in Washington, D.C., reports that minorities hold just 8.8 percent of board seats of S&P 1,500 companies. Progressive firms realize that women and minorities ask different questions and make different suggestions in boardrooms than white men, which is helpful because women and minorities comprise much of the consumer base everywhere.

The European Union (EU) Justice Commissioner Viviane Reding introduced in late 2012 contentious legislation requiring publicly traded companies across the EU to fill at least 40 percent of board positions with women by 2020, or be hit with sanctions to be decided by the EU countries.

A direct response to increased pressure on directors to stay informed and execute their responsibilities is that audit committees are becoming commonplace. A board of directors should conduct an annual strategy audit in much the same fashion that it reviews the annual financial audit. In performing such an audit, a board could work jointly with operating management and/or seek outside counsel. Boards should play a role beyond that of performing a strategic audit. They should provide greater input and advice in the strategy-formulation process to ensure that strategists are providing for the long-term needs of the firm. This is being done through the formation of three particular board committees: nominating committees to propose candidates for the board and senior officers of the firm; compensation committees to evaluate the performance of top executives and determine the terms and conditions of their employment; and audit committees to give board-level attention to company accounting and financial policies and performance.

Special Note to Students

Your SWOT, SPACE, BCG, IE, Grand, and QSPM need to be developed accurately, but in covering those matrices in an oral presentation, focus more on the implications of those analyses than the nuts-and-bolts calculations. In other words, as you go through those matrices in a presentation, your goal is not to prove to the class that you did the calculations correctly. They expect accuracy and clarity and certainly you should have that covered. It is the implications of each matrix that your audience will be most interested in, so use these matrices to pave the way for your recommendations with costs, which generally come just a page or two deeper into the project. A good rule of thumb is to spend at least an equal amount of time on the implications as the actual calculations of each matrix when presented. This approach will improve the delivery aspect of your presentation or paper by maintaining the high interest level of your audience. Focusing on implications rather than calculations will also encourage questions from the audience when you finish. Questions on completion are a good thing. Silence on completion is a bad thing because silence could mean your audience was asleep, disinterested, or did not feel you did a good job. Also, utilize the free excel student template at www.strategyclub.com as needed.

Conclusion

The essence of strategy formulation is an assessment of whether an organization is doing the right things and how it can be more effective in what it does. Every organization should be wary of becoming a prisoner of its own strategy because even the best strategies become obsolete sooner or later. Regular reappraisal of strategy helps management avoid complacency. Objectives and strategies should be consciously developed and coordinated and should not merely evolve out of day-to-day operating decisions.

An organization with no sense of direction and no coherent strategy precipitates its own demise. When an organization does not know where it wants to go, it usually ends up some place it does not want to be. Every organization needs to consciously establish and communicate clear objectives and strategies.

Modern strategy-formulation tools and concepts are described in this chapter and integrated into a practical three-stage framework. Tools such as the SWOT Matrix, SPACE Matrix, BCG Matrix, IE Matrix, and QSPM can significantly enhance the quality of strategic decisions, but they should never be used to dictate the choice of strategies. Behavioral, cultural, and political aspects of strategy generation and selection are always important to consider and manage. Because of increased legal pressure from outside groups, boards of directors are assuming a more active role in strategy analysis and choice. This is a positive trend for organizations.

Key Terms and Concepts

aggressive quadrant (p. 263)
attractiveness scores (AS) (p. 276)
board of directors (p. 281)
Boston Consulting Group (BCG) matrix (p. 267)
business portfolio (p. 267)
cash cows (p. 269)
champions (p. 281)
competitive position (CP) (p. 262)
competitive quadrant (p. 265)
conservative quadrant (p. 265)
culture (p. 280)
decision stage (p. 258)
defensive quadrant (p. 265)
directional vector (p. 263)
dogs (p. 269)
financial position (FP) (p. 262)
governance (p. 281)
Grand Strategy Matrix (p. 273)
halo error (p. 258)
industry position (IP) (p. 262)

input stage (p. 258)
internal-external (IE) matrix (p. 270)
matching (p. 259)
matching stage (p. 258)
Quantitative Strategic Planning Matrix (QSPM) (p. 275)
question marks (p. 268)
relative market share position (p. 267)
SO strategies (p. 260)
stability position (SP) (p. 262)
stars (p. 269)
Strategic Position and Action Evaluation (SPACE) Matrix (p. 262)
strategy-formulation analytical framework (p. 258)
Strengths-Weaknesses Opportunities-Threats (SWOT) Matrix (p. 259)
ST strategies (p. 260)
Sum Total Attractiveness Scores (STAS) (p. 278)
Total Attractiveness Scores (TAS) (p. 276)
WO strategies (p. 260)
WT strategies (p. 260)

Issues for Review and Discussion

8-1. Unilever has done really well for decades. How does Unilever do so well? How can they continue to prosper?

8-2. Give an internal and external strength of Unilever. Show how those two factors are related to reveal a feasible alternative strategy.

8-3. What do you believe are the three major external opportunities that Unilever faces?

8-4. Develop a SPACE Matrix for Unilever. Explain the implications of your Matrix.

8-5. Develop a BCG Matrix for Unilever. Explain the implications of your Matrix.

8-6. Develop a QSPM for Unilever that includes two strategies, six internal factors, and six external factors. What strategy appears to be best for Unilever to pursue?

8-7. Do a Google search using the key terms "boards of directors." What new information did you learn that was not given in the chapter?

8-8. In preparing a SPACE Matrix, which axis would the European political and economic unrest fall under?

8-9. In preparing a BCG Matrix, what would be the best range for the IGR axis as applied to the beverage industry?

8-10. List four reasons why the IE Matrix is widely considered to be superior to the BCG Matrix.

8-11. Is there a limit to the number of strategies that could be examined in a QSPM? Why?

8-12. Go to adidas' website and examine what you can find about the company's board of directors. Evaluate adidas' board based on guidelines presented in the chapter.

8-13. Explain why the CEO of a firm should not also be chairperson of the board of directors.

8-14. In preparing a QSPM, what should be done if the TAS for each strategy turn out to be identical?

8-15. Summarize in your own words the "Special Note to Students" section, given at the end of the chapter.

8-16. Develop a Grand Strategy Matrix for Unilever and include one rival firm.

8-17. Explain what should be done if the SPACE vector coordinate point is (0,0).

8-18. On QSPM, why should you work row by row instead of column by column?

8-19. When constructing a SPACE Matrix, would it be appropriate to use a 1 to 10 scale for all axes?

8-20. If Unilever has the leading market share in Russia, where along the top axis of a BCG would their Russia Operations be plotted?

8-21. Develop a SWOT Matrix for yourself.

8-22. Why is "matching" internal with external factors such an important strategic management activity?

8-23. Illustrate the strategy formulation framework that includes three stages and nine analytical tools. Which stage and tool do you feel is most important? Why?

8-24. Develop an example SWOT Matrix for your college or university with two items in each quadrant. Make sure your strategies clearly exemplify "matching" and show this with (S1, T2) type notation.

8-25. Develop an example SPACE Matrix for a global company that you are familiar with. Include two factors for each of the four axes (SP, IP, SP, and CP).

8-26. What would be an appropriate SP rating for Unilever?

8-27. Discuss the pros and cons of divulging divisional information to stakeholders.

8-28. Develop an example BCG Matrix for a company that has three divisions with revenues of 4, 8, and 12 and profits of 5, 3, and 2, respectively.

8-29. Develop a SPACE Matrix for a firm that is a weak competitor competing in a slow growing and unstable industry. Label axes and quadrants clearly.

8-30. Discuss the limitations of a BCG analysis and the limitations of a SPACE analysis.

8-31. Prepare an IE Matrix for a company with two divisions that have 30 and 60 in revenues to go with 10 and 15 in profits.

8-32. Develop a Grand Strategy Matrix with two example companies in each quadrant, i.e., companies that you know something about and that you would place in those quadrants.

8-33. Develop a QSPM for yourself—given two strategies: 1) go to graduate school or 2) begin working full-time.

8-34. Would a QSPM analysis be useful without the weight column? Why or why not?

8-35. Discuss the characteristics of successful strategists in terms of political factions within the firm.

8-36. In order of attractiveness to you, rank the political tactics presented in Chapter 8.

8-37. For a business in your city, list in order of importance the top eight board-of-director duties and responsibilities listed in the chapter.

8-38. Discuss the pros and cons of Sweden's new board-of-director rule regarding women.

8-39. Develop a SPACE Matrix for your college or university.

8-40. Develop a BCG Matrix for your college or university.

8-41. Explain the limitations of the BCG, SPACE, and SWOT.

8-42. Develop a QSPM for a local company that you are familiar with.

8-43. Write a short essay that reveals your recommendations to firms, regarding disclosure of financial information.

8-44. Explain why a before and after BCG and IE analysis can be useful in presenting a strategic plan for consideration.

8-45. Find an example of a company, on the Internet, which has both a Cash Cow and a Question Mark division.

8-46. Regarding a Grand Strategy Matrix, identify two companies that would be located in your judgment in each quadrant—identify eight firms total.

8-47. For a non-profit company, list in order of importance the top 10 board-of-director duties and responsibilities.

8-48. Regarding the principles of good governance in the chapter, list in order of importance the top seven guidelines.

MyManagementLab®

Go to **mymanagementlab.com** for the following Assisted-graded writing questions:

8-49. Explain the steps involved in developing a QSPM.

8-50. How are the SWOT Matrix, SPACE Matrix, BCG Matrix, IE Matrix, and Grand Strategy Matrix similar? How are they different?

Current Readings

Arms, Hanjo, Mathias Wiecher, and Valeska Kleiderman. "Dynamic Models for Managing Big Decisions." *Strategy and Leadership* 40, no. 5 (2012): 39–46.

Blettner, Daniela P., Fernando R. Chaddad, and Richard A. Bettis. "The CEO Performance Effect: Statistical Issues and a Complex Fit Perspective." *Strategic Management Journal* 33, no. 8 (August 2012): 986–999.

Connelly, Brian L., and Erik J. Van Slyke. "The Power and Peril of Board Interlocks." *Business Horizons* 55, no. 5 (September 2012): 403–408.

Donaldson, Thomas. "The Epistemic Fault Line in Corporate Governance" *The Academy of Management Review 37,* no. 2 (April 2012): 256.

Fernhaber, Stephanie A., and Pankaj C. Patel. "How do young firms manage product portfolio complexity? The role of absorptive capacity and ambidexterity." *Strategic Management Journal* 33, no. 13 (December 2012): 1516–1539.

He, Jinyu, and Zhi Huang. "Board Informal Hierarchy and Firm Financial Performance: Exploring a Tacit Structure Guiding Boardroom Interactions." *The Academy of Management Journal 54,* no. 6 (December 2011): 1119.

Joseph, John, and William Ocasio. "Architecture, Attention, and Adaptation in the Multibusiness Firm: General Electric from 1951 to 2001." *Strategic Management Journal* 33, no. 6 (June 2012): 633–660.

Kiron, David, Pamela Kirk Prentice, and Renee Boucher Ferguson. "Innovating With Analytics." *MITSloan Management Review* 54, no. 1 (Fall 2012): 47.

Walls, Judith L., Pascual Berrone, and Phillip H. Phan. "Corporate Governance and Environmental Performance: Is There Really a Link?" *Strategic Management Journal* 33, no. 8 (August 2012): 885-913.

Walter, Jorge, Franz W. Kellermanns, and Christoph Lechner. "Decision Making Within and Between Organizations: Rationality, Politics and Alliance Performance." *Journal of Management* 38, no. 5 (September 2012): 1582.

ASSURANCE OF LEARNING **EXERCISES**

EXERCISE 8A
Should Unilever Penetrate Southeast Asia Further?

Purpose

Unilever is featured in the opening chapter case as a firm that engages in excellent strategic planning. Unilever is the world's third-largest consumer goods company (behind Procter & Gamble and Nestlé). Some of Unilever's best selling brands are Aviance, Ben & Jerry's, Dove, Flora/Becel, Hellmann's, Knorr, Lipton, Lux/Radox, Omo/Surf, Sunsilk, Toni & Guy, VO5, Wall's, and PG Tips.

The purpose of this exercise is to give you experience investigating a particular region of the world to determine whether a firm should expand more deeply into that region of the world.

Unilever has recently began construction of a new factory in Yangon, Myanmar, and by 2015 expects to provide direct and indirect employment for over 2,000 people in Myanmar. The company currently employs close to 200 Myanmar employees at its factory in Thailand, of which a number are being moved back to Myanmar to help kick-start its operations in the country.

Instructions

Step 1	Go to Unilever's corporate website and download the company's most recent *Annual Report*. Examine the narrative and tables related to their operations in Southeast Asia.
Step 2	Research the competitive climate and business culture of Myanmar and two other countries in Southeast Asia as well as the operations of rival Nestlé.
Step 3	Develop six recommendations for Unilever based on your assessment of their present and potential operations in Southeast Asia.

EXERCISE 8B
Perform a SWOT Analysis for Unilever's Global Operations

Purpose

Unilever's global and domestic business segments could be required annually to submit a SWOT analysis to corporate top executives who merge divisional analyses into an overall corporate analysis. This exercise will give you practice performing a SWOT analysis.

Instructions

Step 1   Review Unilever's global operations as described in the company's most recent *Annual Report*. Unilever recently acquired 82 percent of the Russia-based beauty company Kalina.

Step 2   Review industry and competitive information pertaining to Unilever's global operations, especially as compared to rival Procter & Gamble.

Step 3   Join with two other students in class. Together, develop a global SWOT Matrix for Unilever's global business segment. Follow all the SWOT guidelines provided in the chapter, including (S4, T3)-type notation at the end of each strategy. Include three strategies in each of the four (SO, ST, WT, WO) quadrants. Avoid generic strategy terms such as Forward Integration.

Step 4   Turn in your team-developed SWOT Matrix to your professor for a classwork grade.

EXERCISE 8C
Preparing a BCG Matrix for Unilever

Purpose

This exercise will give you practice preparing both a by-product and a by-region -based BCG Matrix. Unilever has four major product segments of the company: Personal Care, Food, Refreshment, and Home Care. The company also has three major geographic segments: Europe, The Americas, and Asia/AMET/RUB.

Instructions

Step 1   Review Unilever's global operations as described in the company's most recent *Annual Report* and *Form 10K*.

Step 2   Prepare an up-to-date BCG matrices for Unilever's 1) four product categories and 2) three geographic divisions.

Step 3   Write a two-page executive summary to reveal the strategic implications of your analyses.

EXERCISE 8D
Developing a SWOT Matrix for adidas AG

Purpose

The most widely used strategy formulation technique among firms worldwide is the SWOT Matrix. This exercise requires development of a SWOT Matrix for adidas. Matching key external and internal factors in a SWOT Matrix requires good intuitive and conceptual skills. You will improve with practice in developing a SWOT Matrix.

Instructions

Recall from Exercise 1B that you already may have determined adidas' external opportunities/threats and internal strengths/weaknesses. This information could be used to complete this exercise. Follow the steps outlined as follows:

Step 1   On a separate sheet of paper, construct a large nine-cell diagram that will represent your SWOT Matrix. Appropriately label the cells.

Step 2   Appropriately record adidas' opportunities/threats and strengths/weaknesses in your diagram.

Step 3   Match external and internal factors to generate feasible alternative strategies for adidas. Record SO, WO, ST, and WT strategies in appropriate cells of the SWOT Matrix. Use the proper notation to indicate the rationale for the strategies. Try to include four strategies in each of the four strategy cells.

Step 4   Compare your SWOT Matrix to another students' SWOT Matrices. Discuss any major differences.

EXERCISE 8E
Developing a SPACE Matrix for adidas AG

Purpose
Should adidas pursue aggressive, conservative, competitive, or defensive strategies? Develop a SPACE Matrix for adidas to answer this question. Elaborate on the strategic implications of your directional vector. Be specific in terms of strategies that could benefit adidas.

Instructions

Step 1   Join with two other persons in your class and develop a joint SPACE Matrix for adidas.
Step 2   Diagram your SPACE Matrix on the board. Compare your Matrix with other teams' matrices.
Step 3   Discuss the implications of your SPACE Matrix.

EXERCISE 8F
Developing a BCG Matrix for adidas AG

Purpose
Portfolio matrices are widely used by multidivisional organizations to help identify and select strategies to pursue. A BCG analysis identifies particular divisions that should receive fewer resources than others. It may identify some divisions to be divested. This exercise can give you practice developing a BCG Matrix.

Instructions

Step 1   Place the following five column headings at the top of a separate sheet of paper: Divisions, Revenues, Profits, Relative Market Share Position, and Industry Growth Rate. Down the far left of your page, list adidas, Reebok, and TaylorMade. Turn back to the Cohesion Case and find information to fill in all the cells in your data table.
Step 2   Complete two BCG Matrices for adidas: 1) Include Reebok, TaylorMade, and adidas and 2) include Geographic Regions of the World.
Step 3   Compare your BCG Matrix to other students' matrices. Discuss any major differences.

EXERCISE 8G
Developing a QSPM for adidas AG

Purpose
This exercise can give you practice developing a Quantitative Strategic Planning Matrix (QSPM) to determine the relative attractiveness of various strategic alternatives.

Instructions

Step 1   Join with two other students in class to develop a joint QSPM for adidas.
Step 2   Go to the board and record your strategies and their Sum Total Attractiveness Scores. Compare your team's strategies and sum total attractiveness scores to those of other teams. Be sure not to assign the same AS score in a given row. Recall that dashes should be inserted all the way across a given row when used.
Step 3   Discuss any major differences.

EXERCISE 8H
Developing a SWOT Matrix for Unilever

Purpose
The most widely used strategy formulation technique among American firms is the SWOT Matrix. This exercise requires development of a SWOT Matrix for Unilever. Matching key external and internal factors in a SWOT Matrix requires good intuitive and conceptual skills. You will improve with practice in developing a SWOT Matrix.

Instructions

Step 1   On a separate sheet of paper, construct a large nine-cell diagram that will represent your SWOT matrix. Appropriately label the cells.

Step 2   Determine six opportunities and six threats, and six strengths and six weaknesses for Unilever.

Step 3   Match external and internal factors to generate feasible alternative strategies for Unilever. Record SO, WO, ST, and WT strategies in appropriate cells of the SWOT Matrix. Use the proper notation to indicate the rationale for the strategies. Try to include two strategies in each of the four strategy cells. Compare your SWOT Matrix to another student's SWOT Matrix. Discuss any major differences.

EXERCISE 8I
Developing a SPACE Matrix for Unilever

Purpose

Should Unilever pursue aggressive, conservative, competitive, or defensive strategies? Develop a SPACE Matrix for Unilever to answer this question. Elaborate on the strategic implications of your directional vector. Be specific in terms of strategies that could benefit Unilever.

Instructions

Step 1   Join with two other persons in class and develop a joint SPACE Matrix for Unilever.

Step 2   Diagram your SPACE Matrix on the board. Compare your matrix with other teams' matrices.

Step 3   Discuss the implications of your SPACE Matrix.

EXERCISE 8J
Developing a BCG Matrix for your College or University

Purpose

Portfolio matrices are widely used by multidivisional organizations to help identify and select strategies to pursue. A BCG analysis identifies particular divisions that should receive fewer resources than others; or it may identify some divisions to be divested. This exercise can give you practice developing a BCG Matrix for a college or university.

Instructions

Step 1   Place the following five column headings at the top of a separate sheet of paper: Divisions, Revenues, Profits, Relative Market Share Position, and Industry Growth Rate. Down the far left of your page, list Schools at your college.

Step 2   Complete two BCG Matrices for your college or university. Include the School of Business, the School of Education, and the School of Nursing—or any other three Schools.

Step 3   Compare your BCG Matrix to other students' Matrices. Discuss any major differences.

EXERCISE 8K
Developing a QSPM for a Company that You Are Familiar With

Purpose

This exercise can give you practice developing a Quantitative Strategic Planning Matrix (QSPM) to determine the relative attractiveness of various strategic alternatives.

Instructions

Step 1   Join with two other students in class to develop a joint QSPM for a company that all of you are familiar with.

Step 2   Record your strategies and their Sum Total Attractiveness Scores. Compare your team's strategies and sum total attractiveness scores to those of other teams. Be sure not to assign the same AS score in a given row. Recall that dashes should be inserted all the way across a given row when used. Discuss any major differences.

EXERCISE 8L
Formulating Individual Strategies

Purpose

Individuals and organizations are alike in many ways. Each has competitors, and each should plan for the future. Every individual and organization faces some external opportunities and threats and has some internal strengths and weaknesses. Both individuals and organizations establish objectives and allocate resources. These and other similarities make it possible for individuals to use many strategic-management concepts and tools. This exercise is designed to demonstrate how the SWOT Matrix can be used by individuals to plan their futures. As one nears completion of a college degree and begins interviewing for jobs, planning can be particularly important.

Instructions

On a separate sheet of paper, construct a SWOT Matrix. Include what you consider to be your major external opportunities, your major external threats, your major strengths, and your major weaknesses. An internal weakness may be a low grade point average. An external opportunity may be that your university offers a graduate program that interests you. Match key external and internal factors by recording in the appropriate cell of the matrix alternative strategies or actions that would allow you to capitalize upon your strengths, overcome your weaknesses, take advantage of your external opportunities, and minimize the impact of external threats. Be sure to use the appropriate matching notation in the strategy cells of the matrix. Because every individual (and organization) is unique, there is no one right answer to this exercise.

EXERCISE 8M
The Mach Test

Purpose

The purpose of this exercise is to enhance your understanding and awareness of the impact that behavioural and political factors can have on strategy analysis and choice.

Instructions

Step 1   On a separate sheet of paper, write down numbers 1 to 10. For each of the 10 statements given as follows, record a *1, 2, 3, 4,* or *5* to indicate your attitude, where

1 = I disagree a lot.
2 = I disagree a little.
3 = My attitude is neutral.
4 = I agree a little.
5 = I agree a lot.

1. The best way to handle people is to tell them what they want to hear.
2. When you ask someone to do something for you, it is best to give the real reason for wanting it, rather than a reason that might carry more weight.
3. Anyone who completely trusts anyone else is asking for trouble.
4. It is hard to get ahead without cutting corners here and there.
5. It is safest to assume that all people have a vicious streak, and it will come out when they are given a chance.
6. One should take action only when it is morally right.
7. Most people are basically good and kind.
8. There is no excuse for lying to someone else.
9. Most people forget more easily the death of their father than the loss of their property.
10. Generally speaking, people won't work hard unless they're forced to do so.

Step 2   Add up the numbers you recorded beside statements 1, 3, 4, 5, 9, and 10. This sum is Subtotal One. For the other four statements, reverse the numbers you recorded, so a 5 becomes a *1, 4* becomes *2, 2* becomes *4, 1* becomes *5,* and *3* remains *3.* Then add those four numbers to get Subtotal Two. Finally, add Subtotal One and Subtotal Two to get your Final Score.

Your Final Score

Your Final Score is your Machiavellian Score. Machiavellian principles are defined in a dictionary as "manipulative, dishonest, deceiving, and favoring political expediency over morality." These tactics are not desirable, are not ethical, and are not recommended in the strategic management process! You may, however, encounter some highly Machiavellian individuals in your career, so beware. It is important for strategists not to manipulate others in the pursuit of organizational objectives. Individuals today recognize and resent manipulative tactics more than ever before. The National Opinion Research Center used this short quiz in a random sample of U.S. adults and found the national average Final Score to be 25.[1] The higher your score, the more Machiavellian (manipulative) you tend to be. The following scale is descriptive of individual scores on this test:

- Below 16: Never uses manipulation as a tool.
- 16 to 20: Rarely uses manipulation as a tool.
- 21 to 25: Sometimes uses manipulation as a tool.
- 26 to 30: Often uses manipulation as a tool.
- Over 30: Always uses manipulation as a tool.

Test Development

The Mach (Machiavellian) test was developed by Dr. Richard Christie, whose research suggests the following tendencies:

1. Men generally are more Machiavellian than women.
2. There is no significant difference between high Machs and low Machs on measures of intelligence or ability.
3. Although high Machs are detached from others, they are detached in a pathological sense.
4. Machiavellian scores are not statistically related to authoritarian values.
5. High Machs tend to be in professions that emphasize the control and manipulation of individuals—for example law, psychiatry, and behavioral science.
6. Machiavellianism is not significantly related to major demographic characteristics such as educational level or marital status.
7. High Machs tend to come from a city or have urban backgrounds.
8. Older adults tend to have lower Mach scores than younger adults.[2]

Notes

1. Richard Christie and Florence Geis, *Studies in Machiavellianism* (Orlando, FL: Academic Press, 1970). Material in this exercise adapted with permission of the authors and Academic Press.
2. Ibid. 82–83.

Notes

1. R. T. Lenz, "Managing the Evolution of the Strategic Planning Process," *Business Horizons* 30, no. 1 (January–February 1987): 37.

2. Robert Grant, "The Resource-Based Theory of Competitive Advantage: Implications for Strategy Formulation," *California Management Review*, Spring 1991, 114.

3. Heinz Weihrich, "The TOWS Matrix: A Tool for Situational Analysis," *Long Range Planning* 15, no. 2 (April 1982): 61. *Note:* Although Dr. Weihrich first modified SWOT analysis to form the TOWS matrix, the acronym SWOT is much more widely used than TOWS in practice.

4. Greg Dess, G. T. Lumpkin, and Alan Eisner, *Strategic Management: Text and Cases* (New York: McGraw-Hill/ Irwin, 2006), 72.

5. Adapted from H. Rowe, R. Mason, and K. Dickel, *Strategic Management and Business Policy:*

A Methodological Approach (Reading, MA: Addison-Wesley, 1982), 155–156.

6. Fred David, "The Strategic Planning Matrix—A Quantitative Approach," *Long Range Planning* 19, no. 5 (October 1986): 102; Andre Gib and Robert Margulies, "Making Competitive Intelligence Relevant to the User," *Planning Review* 19, no. 3 (May–June 1991): 21.

7. Fred David, "Computer-Assisted Strategic Planning in Small Businesses," *Journal of Systems Management* 36, no. 7 (July 1985): 24–34.

8. Y. Allarie and M. Firsirotu, "How to Implement Radical Strategies in Large Organizations," *Sloan Management Review* 26, no. 3 (Spring 1985): 19. Another excellent article is P. Shrivastava, "Integrating Strategy Formulation with Organizational Culture," *Journal of Business Strategy* 5, no. 3 (Winter 1985): 103–111.

9. James Brian Quinn, *Strategies for Changes: Logical Incrementalism* (Homewood, IL: Richard D. Irwin, 1980), 128–145. These political tactics are listed in A. Thompson and A. Strickland, *Strategic Management: Concepts and Cases* (Plano, TX: Business Publications, 1984), 261.

10. William Guth and Ian MacMillan, "Strategy Implementation Versus Middle Management Self-Interest," *Strategic Management Journal* 7, no. 4 (July–August 1986): 321.

11. Joann Lublin, "Corporate Directors' Group Gives Repair Plan to Boards," *Wall Street Journal*, March 24, 2009, B4.

12. http://www.usatoday.com/money/companies/management/story/2012-05-14/ceo-firings/54964476/1.

13. Phred Dvorak, "Poor Year Doesn't Stop CEO Bonuses," *Wall Street Journal*, March 18, 2009, B1.

14. Louis Lavelle, "The Best and Worst Boards," *BusinessWeek*, October 7, 2002, 104–110.

15. Matt Murray, "Private Companies Also Feel Pressure to Clean Up Acts," *Wall Street Journal*, July 22, 2003, B1.

9

Source: © hansenn/Fotolia

MyManagementLab®

Improve Your Grade!

More than 10 million students improved their results using the Pearson MyLabs.
Visit **mymanagementlab.com** for simulations, tutorials, and end-of-chapter problems.

Strategy Implementation

CHAPTER OBJECTIVES

After studying this chapter, you should be able to do the following:

1. Develop effective perceptual maps to position rival firms.

2. Develop effective perceptual maps to identify market segments and demand voids.

3. Determine the cash worth of any business.

4. Explain market segmentation and product positioning as strategy-implementation tools.

5. Discuss procedures for determining the worth of a business.

6. Develop projected financial statements to reveal the impact of strategy recommendations.

7. Perform EPS-EBIT analysis to evaluate the attractiveness of debt versus stock as a source of capital to implement strategies.

8. Discuss the nature and role of research and development in strategy implementation.

9. Explain how management information systems can determine the success of strategy-implementation efforts.

10. Explain business analytics and data mining.

ASSURANCE OF LEARNING **EXERCISES**

The following exercises are found at the end of this chapter.

Strategies have no chance of being implemented successfully in organizations that do not market goods and services well, in firms that cannot raise needed working capital, in firms that produce technologically inferior products, or in firms that have a weak information system. This chapter examines marketing, finance and accounting, research and development (R&D), and management information systems (MIS) issues that are central to effective strategy implementation. Special topics include market segmentation, market positioning, evaluating the worth of a business, determining to what extent debt or stock should be used as a source of capital, developing projected financial statements, contracting R&D outside the firm, and creating an information support system. Manager and employee involvement and participation are essential for success in marketing, finance and accounting, R&D, and MIS activities.

The Nature of Strategy Implementation

The quarterback can call the best play possible in the huddle, but that does not mean the play will go for a touchdown. The team may even lose yardage unless the play is executed (implemented) well. Less than 10 percent of strategies formulated are successfully implemented! There are many reasons for this low success rate, including failing to appropriately segment markets, paying too much for a new acquisition, and falling behind competitors in R&D. Royal Dutch Shell implements strategies especially well.

Strategy implementation directly affects the lives of plant managers, division managers, department managers, sales managers, product managers, project managers, personnel managers, staff managers, supervisors, and all employees. In some situations, individuals may not have participated in the strategy-formulation process at all and may not appreciate, understand, or even accept the work and thought that went into strategy formulation. There may even be foot dragging or resistance on their part. Managers and employees who do not understand the business and are not committed to the business may attempt to sabotage strategy-implementation efforts in hopes that the organization will return to its old ways. The strategy-implementation stage of the strategic-management process is highlighted in Figure 9-1 as illustrated with white shading.

EXCELLENT STRATEGIC MANAGEMENT SHOWCASED

Royal Dutch Shell

Royal Dutch Shell plc is the largest oil and gas company in the world and the largest firm globally. *Fortune*, in 2013, also ranked Shell as the 7th most profitable firm in the world. Incorporated in the United Kingdom but headquartered in the Netherlands, Shell has worldwide reserves of the equivalent of 14.2 billion barrels of oil. Most of Shell's crude oil is produced in Nigeria, Oman, and the UK, but Shell is also investing heavily in the Athabasca Oil Sands Project, which converts oil sands in Alberta to synthetic oil. Shell operates 44,000 gas stations, the world's largest retail fuel network, in more than 90 countries. Vertically integrated, Shell explores, produces, refines, transports, and sells oil related products and chemicals.

Shell's CEO, Peter Voser, is to retire at the end of March 2014, marking the end of 29 years with the Company. He is being replaced with Ben van Beurden, age 55, who has been Shell's Downstream Director since January 2013. Ben's promotion came after a comprehensive assessment and review of internal and external candidates led by the Board Nomination and Succession Committee. Ben joined Shell in 1983 and has held a number of positions in both the Upstream and Downstream businesses, working in the Netherlands, Africa, Malaysia, USA and, most recently, the UK. A Dutch national, Ben graduated with a Master's Degree in Chemical Engineering from Delft University of Technology, the Netherlands.

Royal Dutch Shell plc in September 2013 purchased as Treasury Stock 921,881 "B" Shares of its own stock at a price of 2159.15 pence per share. Following the purchase, the remaining number of "A" Shares of Royal Dutch Shell plc was 3,821,611,712 and the remaining number of "B" Shares of Shell plc was 2,509,794,307.

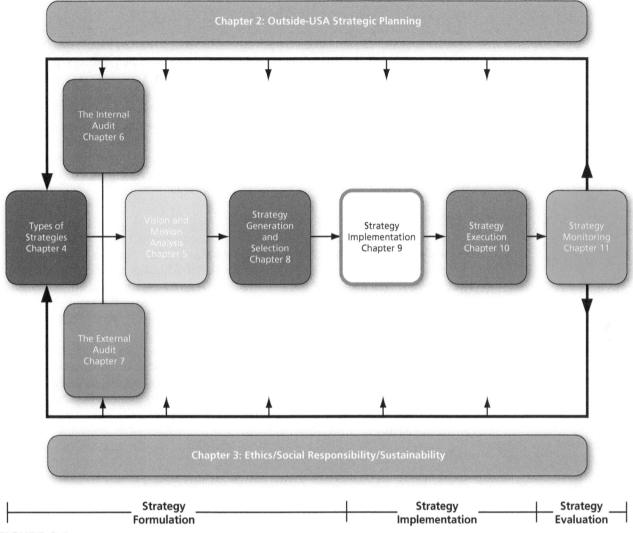

FIGURE 9-1

A Comprehensive Strategic-Management Model

Source: Fred R. David, adapted from "How Companies Define Their Mission," *Long Range Planning* 22, no. 3 (June 1988): 40, © Fred R. David.

Current Marketing Issues

Countless marketing variables affect the success or failure of strategy implementation efforts. Some example marketing decisions that may require policies are as follows:

1. How to make advertisements more interactive to be more effective
2. How to best take advantage of Facebook and Twitter conservations about the company and industry
3. To use exclusive dealerships or multiple channels of distribution
4. To use heavy, light, or no TV advertising versus online advertising
5. To limit (or not) the share of business done with a single customer
6. To be a price leader or a price follower
7. To offer a complete or limited warranty
8. To reward salespeople based on straight salary, straight commission, or a combination salary and commission

Marketing is more about building a two-way relationship with consumers than just informing consumers about a product or service. Marketers today must get their customers involved in their company website and solicit suggestions from customers in terms of product development, customer service, and ideas. The online community is much quicker, cheaper, and effective than traditional focus groups and surveys.

Companies and organizations should encourage their employees to create **wikis**—websites that allow users to add, delete, and edit content regarding frequently asked questions and information across the firm's whole value chain of activities. The most common wiki is Wikipedia, but wikis are user-generated content. Anyone can change the content in a wiki but the group and other editors can change the content submitted.

Firms should provide incentives to customers to share their thoughts, opinions, and experiences on the company website. Encourage customers to network among themselves on topics of their choosing on the company website. So the company website must not be all about the company—it must be all about the customer too. Perhaps offer points or discounts for customers who provide ideas and suggestions. This practice will not only encourage participation but will allow both the company and other customers to interact with "experts."

New Principles of Marketing

A business or organization's website must provide clear and simple instructions for customers to set up a blog or contribute to a wiki. Customers trust each others' opinions more than a company's marketing pitch, and the more they talk freely, the more the firm can learn how to improve its product, service, and marketing. Marketers today monitor blogs daily to determine, evaluate, and influence opinions being formed by customers. Customers must not feel like they are a captive audience for advertising at a firm's website. Table 9-1 provides new principles of marketing according to Parise, Guinan, and Weinberg.[1]

Wells Fargo and Bank of America **tweet** customers, meaning they post messages of 140 characters or less on Twitter.com to describe features of bank products. Some banks are placing marketing videos on YouTube. UMB Financial of Kansas City, Missouri, tweets about everything from the bank's financial stability to the industry's prospects. Steve Furman, Discover's director of e-commerce, says the appeal of social networking is that it provides "pure, instant" communication with customers.[2]

PepsiCo recently established a "Mission Control" staffed with social marketing employees promoting the company's long-time product Gatorade, which had been on a three-year sales slide. PepsiCo staffs Mission Control 24/7 to tweet encouragement to high-school athletes and respond to Facebook questions.[3] Whenever anybody uses Twitter or Facebook to comment on Gatorade, that message pops up on a screen in Mission Control and a PepsiCo employee joins that person's social circle. PepsiCo is a leading company that tracks social media, tracks online-ad traffic, heads off potential crises, builds support for products, and monitors consumer behavior in depth. Gatorade is under intense pressure from Coca-Cola's Powerade, whose sales are increasing in contrast to Gatorade's sales decreasing.

Although the exponential increase in social networking and business online has created huge opportunities for marketers, it also has produced some severe threats. Perhaps the greatest threat is that any kind of negative publicity travels fast online. For example, Taco Bell suffered from its ads that featured asking 50 Cent (aka Curtis Jackson) if he would change his name to 79 Cent or 89 Cent for a day in exchange for a $10,000 donation to charity. Seemingly minor ethical and

TABLE 9-1 The New Principles of Marketing

1. Do not just talk at consumers—work with them throughout the marketing process.
2. Give consumers a reason to participate.
3. Listen to—and join—the conversation outside your company's website.
4. Resist the temptation to sell, sell, sell. Instead attract, attract, attract.
5. Do not control online conversations; let it flow freely.
6. Find a "marketing technologist," a person who has three excellent skill sets (marketing, technology, and social interaction).
7. Embrace instant messaging and chatting.

Source: Based on Salvatore Parise, Patricia Guinan, and Bruce Weinberg, "The Secrets of Marketing in a Web 2.0 World," *Wall Street Journal*, December 15, 2008, R1.

TABLE 9-10 Projected Whole Foods Market Income Statements (in millions)

	2010	2011	2012
Revenue (a)	$9,005.8	12,584.0	17,860.0
Cost of Goods Sold	5,870.4	7,550.0	10,716.0
Gross Profit	3,135.4	5,034.0	7,144.0
Gross Profit Margin (b)	34.8%	40%	40%
SG&A Expense (c)	2,697.4	3,782.0	4,109.0
Depreciation & Amortization	275.6	290	310.0
Operating Income	438.0	1,252.0	3,035.0
Operating Margin	4.9%	9.9%	16.9%
Nonoperating Income	6.9	0	0
Nonoperating Expenses	(33.0)	0	0
Income Before Taxes	411.8	1,252.0	3,035.0
Income Taxes (d)	165.9	504.0	1,223.0
Net Income After Taxes	245.8	748.0	1,812.0
Net Income	$245.8	748.0	1,812.0
Dividends	5.4	175.0	180.0
Retained Earnings	$240.4	573.0	1,632.0

(a) $60.89 million per new store + 10% increase for all stores, so in 2011 we have $60.89 × 40 = $2,435 + 9,005 = $11,440 + 10% = $12,584. In 2012 we have $60.89 × 60 = 3,653 + 12,584 = $16,237 + 10% = $17,860.
(b) increases to 40% due to better inventory control; note that 5,034/12,584 = 40% and 7,144/17,860 = 40%.
(c) same 29.9% of revenue + $20 million per year, new ad campaign; note that $12,584 × .299 + $20 = $3,782.
(d) same 40.3% rate as in 2010.

Financial budgets have some limitations. First, budgetary programs can become so detailed that they are cumbersome and overly expensive. Overbudgeting or underbudgeting can cause problems. Second, financial budgets can become a substitute for objectives. A budget is a tool and not an end in itself. Third, budgets can hide inefficiencies if based solely on precedent rather than on periodic evaluation of circumstances and standards. Finally, budgets are sometimes used as instruments of tyranny that result in frustration, resentment, absenteeism, and high turnover. To minimize the effect of this last concern, managers should increase the participation of subordinates in preparing budgets.

Company Valuation

Evaluating the worth of a business is central to strategy implementation because integrative, intensive, and diversification strategies are often implemented by acquiring other firms. Other strategies, such as retrenchment and divestiture, may result in the sale of a division of an organization or of the firm itself. Thousands of transactions occur each year in which businesses are bought or sold in the USA. In all these cases, it is necessary to establish the financial worth or cash value of a business to successfully implement strategies.

All the various methods for determining a business's worth can be grouped into three main approaches: what a firm owns, what a firm earns, or what a firm will bring in the market. But it is important to realize that valuation is not an exact science. The valuation of a firm's worth is based on financial facts, but common sense and intuitive judgment must enter into the process. It is difficult to assign a monetary value to some factors—such as a loyal customer base, a history of growth, legal suits pending, dedicated employees, a favorable lease, a bad credit rating, or good patents—that may not be reflected in a firm's financial statements. Also, different valuation methods will yield different totals for a firm's worth, and no prescribed approach is best for a certain situation. Evaluating the worth of a business truly requires both qualitative and quantitative skills.

TABLE 9-11 Projected Whole Foods Market Balance Sheets (in millions)

	2010	2011	2012
Assets			
Current Assets			
Cash	$132.0	$1,55.3	$3,260.3
Net Receivables	133.3	140.0	160.0
Inventories	323.5	330.0	360.0
Other Current Assets	572.7	0	0
Total Current Assets	1,161.5	2,020.3	3,580.3
Net Fixed Assets (a)	1,886.1	2,138.0	2,516.0
Other Noncurrent Assets	938.9	0	0
Total Assets	**$3,986.5**	**$4,159.3**	**$6,296.3**
Liabilities			
Current Liabilities			
Accounts Payable	213.2	300.0	400.0
Short-Term Debt	0.4	0	0
Other Current Liabilities	534.3	0	0
Total Current Liabilities	747.9	300.0	400.0
Long-Term Debt (b)	508.3	708.0	908.0
Other Noncurrent Liabilities	357.0	0	0
Total Liabilities	1,613.2	1,008.0	1,308.0
Shareholders' Equity			
Common Stock (c)	500.0	505.0	510.0
Additional-paid-in-capital (d)	1,247.7	1,474.7	1,674.7
Retained Earnings (e)	598.6	1,171.6	2,803.6
Total Shareholders' Equity	2,373.3	3151.3	4,988.3
Total Liabilities and SE	**$3,986.5**	**$4,159.3**	**$6,296.3**
Shares Outstanding (in thousands) (f)	172,033	177,033	182,033

(a) $6.3 M per store × 40 stores = 252 + 1,886 = 2,138; 6.3 × 60 = 378 + 2,139 = 2,516
(b) $200 M to be raised by debt annually
(c) add 5 M new shares annually since $40 per share and need $200 M to be raised by equity annually
(d) add $200 M annually thru stock issuance
(e) $ 598.6 + $ 573.0 = $1,171.6 + 1,632.0 = $2,803.6
(f) stock price = $40, $200 M needed per year thru equity, so 5 M new shares to be issued annually; thus 172,033 + 5 M = 177,033

The first approach in evaluating the worth of a business is determining its net worth or stockholders' equity. Net worth represents the sum of common stock, additional paid-in capital, and retained earnings. After calculating net worth, subtract an appropriate amount for goodwill and intangibles. Whereas intangibles include copyrights, patents, and trademarks, goodwill arises only if a firm acquires another firm and pays more than the book value for that firm.

It should be noted that FASB Rule 142 requires companies to admit once a year if the premiums they paid for acquisitions, called **goodwill**, were a waste of money. Goodwill is not a good thing to have on a balance sheet. Note in Table 9-13 that J.M. Smucker's $Goodwill to $Total Assets is a really high 33.5 percent, indicating that a third of the company's assets are "Goodwill," which is not good.

The second approach to measuring the value of a firm grows out of the belief that the worth of any business should be based largely on the future benefits its owners may derive through net profits. A conservative rule of thumb is to establish a business's worth as five times the firm's current annual profit. A five-year average profit level could also be used. When using this approach, remember that firms normally suppress earnings in their financial statements to minimize taxes.

TABLE 9-12 Six-Month Cash Budget for the Toddler Toy Company in 2015

Cash Budget (in thousands)	July	Aug.	Sept.	Oct.	Nov.	Dec.	Jan.
Receipts							
Collections	$12,000	$21,000	$31,000	$35,000	$22,000	$18,000	$11,000
Payments							
Purchases	14,000	21,000	28,000	14,000	14,000	7,000	
Wages and Salaries	1,500	2,000	2,500	1,500	1,500	1,000	
Rent	500	500	500	500	500	500	
Other Expenses	200	300	400	200	—	100	
Taxes	—	8,000	—	—	—	—	
Payment on Machine	—	—	10,000	—	—	—	
Total Payments	$16,200	$31,800	$41,400	$16,200	$16,000	$8,600	
Net Cash Gain (Loss) During Month	–4,200	–10,800	–10,400	18,800	6,000	9,400	
Cash at Start of Month if No Borrowing Is Done	6,000	1,800	–9,000	–19,400	-600	5,400	
Cumulative Cash (Cash at start plus gains or minus losses)	1,800	–9,000	–19,400	–600	5,400	14,800	
Less Desired Level of Cash	–5,000	–5,000	–5,000	–5,000	–5,000	–5,000	
Total Loans Outstanding to Maintain $5,000 Cash Balance	$3,200	$14,000	$24,400	$5,600	—	—	
Surplus Cash	—	—	—	—	400	9,800	

TABLE 9-13 Company Worth Analysis for J.M. Smucker, Microsoft Corp., and Zale Corp. (in millions, except stock price and EPS)

Input Data	J.M. Smucker	Microsoft Corp.	Zale Corp.
$ Shareholders' Equity (SE)	5,163	66,363	178
$ Net Income (NI)	460	17,000	–27
$ Stock Price (SP)	80	30	7
$ EPS	4.08	2.00	–.90
# of Shares Outstanding	109	8,330	32
$ Goodwill	3,050	13,542	100
$ Intangibles	3,190	3,170	0
$ Total Assets	9,115	121,271	1,171
Company Worth Analyses			
1. SE – Goodwill – Intangibles	$977	$49,741	$78
2. Net Income x 5	2,300	85,000	0
3. (SP / EPS) x NI	9,019	225,000	0
4. # of Shares Out x Stock Price	8,720	251,400	224
5. Four Method Average	$4,765	$161,285	$151
$ Goodwill / $ Total Assets	33.5%	11.1%	8.5%

The third approach is called the **price-earnings ratio method**. To use this method, divide the market price of the firm's common stock by the annual earnings per share and multiply this number by the firm's average net income for the past five years.

The fourth method can be called the **outstanding shares method**. To use this method, simply multiply the number of shares outstanding by the market price per share. If the purchase price is more than this amount, the additional dollars are called a **premium**. The outstanding shares method may be called the "**market value**" or "**market capitalization**" or "**book value**" of the firm. The premium is a per-share dollar amount that a person or firm is willing to pay beyond the book value of the firm to control (acquire) the other company. Bristol-Myers Squibb recently offered $31 a share to acquire Amylin Pharmaceuticals and that offer represented a 9.9 percent premium over Amylin's closing stock price the day of the offer. WellPoint, the second-largest insurer in the USA, recently acquired Amerigroup for $92 per share in cash, which was a whopping 43 percent premium to Amerigroup's closing stock price of $64.34. Amerigroup's stock soared 38 percent to $88.79 the day after the offer.

Table 9-13 provides the cash value analyses for three companies—J.M. Smucker, Microsoft Corp., and Zale Corp.—for fiscal year-end 2012. Notice that there is significant variation among the four methods used to determine cash value. For example, the worth of J.M. Smucker ranged from minus $1,077 to $9.019 billion. Obviously, if you were selling your company, you would seek the larger values, whereas if purchasing a company you would seek the lower values. In practice, substantial negotiation takes place in reaching a final compromise (or averaged) amount. Also recognize that if a firm's net income is negative, theoretically the approaches involving that figure would result in a negative number, implying that the firm would pay you to acquire them. Of course, you obtain all of the firm's debt and liabilities in an acquisition, so theoretically this would be possible.

Hewlett-Packard, Boston Scientific, Frontier Communications, and Republic Services (unfortunately for them) carry more goodwill on their balance sheet than their market (or book) value. This is a signal that their goodwill should be "written down," which means "reduced and recorded as an expense on the income statement." Nasdaq OMX Group's $5.1 billion in goodwill exceeds its $3.9 billion market capitalization by a precarious 31 percent. Jack Ciesielski, publisher of Analyst's Accounting Observer, says: "Writing down goodwill is an admission that the company screwed up when it budgeted what an acquired firm is worth." Sometimes it is OK to pay more for a company than its book value if the firm has technology or patents you need or economies of scale you desire or even to reduce competitive pricing pressure, but, like buying a house, paying a "premium" for a company is almost always not a good thing. Acquiring at a "discount" is far better for shareholders.

Because goodwill write-down accounting rules involve projections and judgments, companies have leeway for when to write down goodwill, and by how much. Microsoft for example in 2012 wrote down (reduced) their goodwill $6.2 billion, basically admitting that their previous acquisition of online-advertising firm aQuantive Inc. for $6.3 billion was ill advised—now recording that amount as an expense. Analysts expect Hewlett-Packard to soon write down some (or all) of the $6.6 billion in goodwill among the $10.1 billion total that they recently paid for British software maker Autonomy PLC.[10]

If the purchase price is less than the stock price times number of shares outstanding, rather than more, that difference is called a **discount**. For example, when Clayton Doubilier & Rice LLC recently acquired Emergency Medical Services (EMS) Corp. for $2.9 billion, a 9.4 percent discount below EMS's stock price of $64.00.

Business evaluations are becoming routine in many situations. Businesses have many strategy-implementation reasons for determining their worth in addition to preparing to be sold or to buy other companies. Employee plans, taxes, retirement packages, mergers, acquisitions, expansion plans, banking relationships, death of a principal, divorce, partnership agreements, and IRS audits are other reasons for a periodic valuation. It is just good business to have a reasonable understanding of what a firm is worth. This knowledge protects the interests of all parties involved.

Ryan Brewer, an assistant professor of finance at Indiana University-Purdue University Columbus, recently calculated the monetary value of top college football teams. Brewer examined each program's revenues and expenses and made cash-flow adjustments, risk assessments and growth projections for each school. Brewer's results for 69 college programs are provided in Table 9-14. Note that Texas was the most valuable college football program in 2012, followed by Michigan. Interestingly, all of these programs are "nonprofit." As a point of reference, the NFL's Jacksonville Jaguars sold in late 2011 for about $760 million.

TABLE 9-14 The Monetary Value of Various College Football Programs

Sticker Shock The value, in millions, of major-conference college-football programs, plus Notre Dame and BYU:

Rank	SCHOOL	VALUE	Rank	SCHOOL	VALUE	Rank	SCHOOL	VALUE	Rank	SCHOOL	VALUE
1	Texas	$761.7	19	Oregon	$264.6	37	Virginia	$146.3	55	Mississippi St.	$99.3
2	Michigan	$731.9	20	Washington	$259.9	38	Purdue	$145.1	56	Maryland	$96.0
3	Florida	$599.7	21	Michigan St.	$224.8	39	N.C. State	$143.0	57	California	$92.6
4	Notre Dame	$597.4	22	Texas Tech	$211.0	40	Indiana	$142.7	58	Syracuse	$91.4
5	Ohio St.	$586.6	23	Oklahoma St.	$209.1	41	Iowa St.	$140.3	59	Texas Christian	$76.6
6	Auburn	$508.1	24	Kansas St.	$207.1	42	Minnesota	$139.7	60	Louisville	$75.4
7	Georgia	$481.8	25	Colorado	$202.9	43	BYU	$136.1	61	Washington St.	$73.4
8	Alabama	$476.0	26	Kentucky	$202.7	44	Arizona	$126.8	62	Baylor	$71.3
9	LSU	$471.7	27	Clemson	$201.8	45	UCLA	$125.8	63	Rutgers	$64.1
10	Oklahoma	$454.7	28	USC	$197.8	46	Utah	$119.7	64	Duke	$62.0
11	Iowa	$384.4	29	Georgia Tech	$188.4	47	Oregon St.	$118.8	65	Pittsburgh	$59.6
12	Tennessee	$364.6	30	Virginia Tech	$171.5	48	Illinois	$117.3	66	Vanderbilt	$57.3
13	Nebraska	$360.1	31	Arizona St.	$164.6	49	Mississippi	$111.7	67	Missouri	$56.4
14	Arkansas	$332.0	32	West Virginia	$159.4	50	Boston College	$110.2	68	Cincinnati	$48.9
15	S.Carolina	$311.9	33	Florida St.	$159.0	51	Kansas	$103.4	69	Temple	$46.9
16	Penn St.	$300.8	34	Miami(Fla.)	$157.7	52	Connecticut	$101.8			
17	Wisconsin	$296.1	35	Northwestern	$148.8	53	South Florida	$101.2			
18	Texas A&M	$278.5	36	Stanford	$148.7	54	North Carolina	$99.8			

Source: Ryan Brewer, Indiana University-Purdue University Columbus.
Note: Excludes Wake Forest; based on information at http://online.wsj.com/article/SB10001424127887324391104578225802183417888.html.

Deciding Whether to Go Public

Hundreds of companies in 2012 held **initial public offerings (IPOs)** to move from being private to being public. These firms took advantage of high stock market prices. For example, some recent IPOs include computer-network-security firm Palo Alto Networks Inc., search engine Kayak Software Corp., guitar maker Fender Musical Instruments, discount retailer Five Below, and pharmaceutical developer Durata Therapeutics, health-food retailer Natural Grocers by vitamin Cottage, software firm E2open, and Chuy's Holdings, a U.S.-based operator of Mexican restaurants. MGM Holdings, parent of the film studio Metro-Goldwyn-Mayer, just hired Goldman Sachs Group to develop a public stock offering for the company. MGM hopes its new "Hobbit" and "Skyfall" movies will help its pending IPO.

Groupon, the firm that offers daily deals on services, went public in November 2011 at $20 per share or $13 billion in market capitalization, but less than a year later Groupon stock was selling for $6.00 per share and the company's market capitalization had dropped to less than $5 billion. Zynga and Facebook's recent IPO's also turned sour quite quickly.

Going public means selling off a percentage of a company to others to raise capital; consequently, it dilutes the owners' control of the firm. Going public is not recommended for companies with less than $10 million in sales because the initial costs can be too high for the firm to generate sufficient cash flow to make going public worthwhile. One dollar in four is the average total cost paid to lawyers, accountants, and underwriters when an initial stock issuance is under $1 million; $1 in $20 will go to cover these costs for issuances over $20 million.

In addition to initial costs involved with a stock offering, there are costs and obligations associated with reporting and management in a publicly held firm. For firms with more than $10 million in sales, going public can provide major advantages. It can allow the firm to raise capital to develop new products, build plants, expand, grow, and market products and services more effectively.

Research and Development (R&D) Issues

In terms of "Innovation," *Fortune* recently ranked the following companies as best in the world. Note that Apple retained its number-1 ranking from the prior year.

Rank	Company
1	Apple
2	Sistema
3	GDF Suez
4	Limited Brands
5	Qualcomm
6*	Enterprise Products Partners
6*	Koc Holding
8	Amazon.com
9	Sealed Air
10	Nike

Source: Based on http://money.cnn.com/magazines/fortune/most-admired/2012/best_worst/best1.html.

Research and development (R&D) personnel can play an integral part in strategy implementation. These individuals are generally charged with developing new products and improving old products in a way that will allow effective strategy implementation. R&D employees and managers perform tasks that include transferring complex technology, adjusting processes to local raw materials, adapting processes to local markets, and altering products to particular tastes and specifications. Strategies such as product development, market penetration, and related diversification require that new products be successfully developed and that old products be significantly improved.

Technological improvements that affect consumer and industrial products and services shorten product life cycles. Companies in virtually every industry are relying on the development of new products and services to fuel profitability and growth.[11] Surveys suggest that the most successful organizations use an R&D strategy that ties external opportunities to internal strengths and is linked with objectives. Well-formulated R&D policies match market opportunities with internal capabilities. R&D policies can enhance strategy implementation efforts to:

1. Emphasize product or process improvements.
2. Stress basic or applied research.
3. Be leaders or followers in R&D.
4. Develop robotics or manual-type processes.
5. Spend a high, average, or low amount of money on R&D.
6. Perform R&D within the firm or to contract R&D to outside firms.
7. Use university researchers or private-sector researchers.

R&D policy among rival firms often varies dramatically. For example, Pfizer spends only about $5 billion annually on R&D even though the firm has about $70 billion in annual revenues, whereas rival Merck spends about $10 billion annually on R&D with annual revenue of about $50 billion. Underlying this difference in strategy between the two pharmaceutical giants is a philosophical disagreement over the merits of heavy investment to discover new drugs versus waiting for others to spend the money and discover and then follow up with similar products. Pfizer and Merck "are going in different directions," said Les Funtleyder, portfolio manager of the Miller Tabak Health Care Transformation mutual fund.

There must be effective interactions between R&D departments and other functional departments in implementing different types of generic business strategies. Conflicts between marketing, finance and accounting, R&D, and information systems departments can be minimized with clear policies and objectives. Table 9-15 gives some examples of R&D activities that could be required for successful implementation of various strategies. Many U.S. utility, energy, and automotive companies are employing their R&D departments to determine how the firm can effectively reduce its gas emissions.

TABLE 9-15 Research and Development Involvement in Selected Strategy-Implementation Situations

Type of Organization	Strategy Being Implemented	R&D Activity
Pharmaceutical company	Product development	Test the effects of a new drug on different subgroups.
Boat manufacturer	Related diversification	Test the performance of various keel designs under various conditions.
Plastic container manufacturer	Market penetration	Develop a biodegradable container.
Electronics company	Market development	Develop a telecommunications system in a foreign country.

Many firms wrestle with the decision to acquire R&D expertise from external firms or to develop R&D expertise internally. The following guidelines can be used to help make this decision:

1. If the rate of technical progress is slow, the rate of market growth is moderate, and there are significant barriers to possible new entrants, then in-house R&D is the preferred solution. The reason is that R&D, if successful, will result in a temporary product or process monopoly that the company can exploit.
2. If technology is changing rapidly and the market is growing slowly, then a major effort in R&D may be risky because it may lead to the development of an ultimately obsolete technology or one for which there is no market.
3. If technology is changing slowly but the market is growing quickly, there generally is not enough time for in-house development. The prescribed approach is to obtain R&D expertise on an exclusive or nonexclusive basis from an outside firm.
4. If both technical progress and market growth are fast, R&D expertise should be obtained through acquisition of a well-established firm in the industry.[12]

There are at least three major R&D approaches for implementing strategies. The first strategy is to be the first firm to market new technological products. This is a glamorous and exciting strategy but also a dangerous one. Even Apple found this to be dangerous as per Samsung. Firms such as 3M and General Electric have been successful with this approach, but many other pioneering firms have fallen, with rival firms seizing the initiative.

A second R&D approach is to be an innovative imitator of successful products, thus minimizing the risks and costs of start-up. This approach entails allowing a pioneer firm to develop the first version of the new product and to demonstrate that a market exists. Then, laggard firms develop a similar product. This strategy requires excellent R&D and marketing personnel.

A third R&D strategy is to be a low-cost producer by mass-producing products similar to but less expensive than products recently introduced. As a new product is accepted by customers, price becomes increasingly important in the buying decision. Also, mass marketing replaces personal selling as the dominant selling strategy. This R&D strategy requires substantial investment in plant and equipment but fewer expenditures in R&D than the two approaches described previously. Dell and Lenovo have utilized this third approach to gain competitive advantage.

R&D activities among U.S. firms need to be more closely aligned to business objectives. There needs to be expanded communication between R&D managers and strategists. Corporations are experimenting with various methods to achieve this improved communication climate, including different roles and reporting arrangements for managers and new methods to reduce the time it takes research ideas to become reality.

Perhaps the most current trend in R&D management has been lifting the veil of secrecy whereby firms, even major competitors, are joining forces to develop new products. Collaboration is on the rise as a result of new competitive pressures, rising research costs, increasing regulatory issues, and accelerated product development schedules. Companies not only are working more closely with each other on R&D, but they are also turning to consortia at universities for their R&D needs. More than 600 research consortia are now in operation in the USA.

Management Information Systems (MIS) Issues

Firms that gather, assimilate, and evaluate external and internal information most effectively are gaining competitive advantages over other firms. Having an effective **management information system (MIS)** may be the most important factor in differentiating successful from unsuccessful firms. The process of strategic management is facilitated immensely in firms that have an effective information system.

Information collection, retrieval, and storage can be used to create competitive advantages in ways such as cross-selling to customers, monitoring suppliers, keeping managers and employees informed, coordinating activities among divisions, and managing funds. Like inventory and human resources, information is now recognized as a valuable organizational asset that can be controlled and managed. Firms that implement strategies using the best information will reap competitive advantages in the twenty-first century.

A good information system can allow a firm to reduce costs. For example, online orders from salespersons to production facilities can shorten materials ordering time and reduce inventory costs. Direct communications between suppliers, manufacturers, marketers, and customers can link together elements of the value chain as though they were one organization. Improved quality and service often result from an improved information system.

Firms must increasingly be concerned about computer hackers and take specific measures to secure and safeguard corporate communications, files, orders, and business conducted over the Internet. Thousands of companies today are plagued by computer hackers who include disgruntled employees, competitors, bored teens, sociopaths, thieves, spies, and hired agents. Computer vulnerability is a giant, expensive headache.

Headquartered in Short Hills, New Jersey, Dun & Bradstreet is an example company that has an excellent information system. Every D&B customer and client in the world has a separate nine-digit number. The database of more than 200 million businesses worldwide contains of information associated with each number. The D-U-N-S # has become so widely used that it is like a business Social Security number. D&B reaps great competitive advantages from its information system.

In many firms, information technology is doing away with the workplace and allowing employees to work at home or anywhere, anytime. The mobile concept of work allows employees to work the traditional 9-to-5 workday across any of the 24 time zones around the globe. Affordable desktop videoconferencing software allows employees to "beam in" whenever needed. Any manager or employee who travels a lot away from the office is a good candidate for working at home rather than in an office provided by the firm. Salespersons or consultants are good examples, but any person whose job largely involves talking to others or handling information could easily operate at home with the proper MIS.[13]

Business Analytics

Business analytics is a MIS technique that involves using software to mine huge volumes of data to help executives make decisions. Sometimes called predictive analytics, machine learning, or data mining, this software enables a researcher to assess and use the aggregate experience of an organization, a priceless strategic asset for a firm. The history of a firm's interaction with its customers, suppliers, distributors, employees, rival firms, and more can all be tapped with **data mining** to generate predictive models. Business analytics is similar to the actuarial methods used by insurance companies to rate customers by the chance of positive or negative outcomes. Every business is basically a risk management endeavor! Therefore, like insurance companies, all businesses can benefit from measuring, tracking, and computing the risk associated with hundreds of strategic and tactical decisions made everyday. Business analytics enables a company to benefit from measuring and managing risk.

As more and more products become commoditized (so similar as to be indistinguishable), competitive advantage more and more hinges on improvements to business processes. Business analytics can provide a firm with proprietary business intelligence regarding, for example, which segment(s) of customers choose your firm versus those who defer, delay, or defect to a competitor and why. Business analytics can reveal where competitors are weak so that marketing and sales activities can be directly targeted to take advantage of resultant opportunities (knowledge).

In addition to understanding consumer behavior better, which yields more effective and efficient marketing, business analytics also is being used to slash expenses by, for example, withholding retention offers from customers who are going to stay with the firm anyway, or managing fraudulent transactions involving invoices, credit care purchases, tax returns insurance claims, mobile phone calls, online ad clicks, and more.

A key distinguishing feature of business analytics is that it is predictive rather than retrospective, in that it enables a firm to learn from experience and to make current and future decisions based on prior information. Deriving robust predictive models from data mining to support hundreds of commonly occurring business decisions is the essence of learning from experience. The mathematical models associated with business analytics can dramatically enhance decision making at all organizational levels and all stages of strategic management. In a sense, art becomes science with business analytics resulting from the mathematical generalization of thousands, millions, or even billions of prior data points to discover patterns of behavior for optimizing the deployment of resources.

IBM's former CEO Samuel Palmisano announced that IBM is moving aggressively into business analytics, trying to overtake Oracle's market share lead.[14] IBM's annual business analytics revenues of about $40 billion are growing about 15 percent every quarter compared to the industry growing about 15 percent annually. IBM's acquisition of SPSS for $1.2 billion, among other recent acquisitions, launched the firm heavily into the business analytics consulting business. Microsoft currently has a software program called PowerPivot that offers data-mining capability in a spreadsheet-like way, but this is not nearly as powerful as business analytics software. IBM recently completed a business analytics project for the New York City Fire Department whereby buildings in the city were assessed for risk.

Special Note to Students

Regardless of your business major, be sure to capitalize on that special knowledge in delivering your strategic management case analysis. Whenever the opportunity arises in your oral or written project, reveal how your firm can gain and sustain competitive advantage using your marketing, finance and accounting, or MIS recommendations. Continuously compare your firm to rivals and draw insights and conclusions so that your recommendations come across as well conceived. Never shy away from the EPS/EBIT or projected financial statement analyses because your audience must be convinced that what you recommend is financially feasible and worth the dollars to be spent. Spend sufficient time on the nuts-and-bolts of those analyses, so fellow students (and your professor) will be assured that you did them correctly and reasonably. Too often, when students rush at the end, it means their financial statements are overly optimistic or incorrectly developed—so avoid that issue. The marketing, finance and accounting, and MIS aspects of your recommended strategies must ultimately work together to gain and sustain competitive advantage for the firm—so point that out frequently. By the way, the free student excel template at www.strategyclub.com can help immensely in performing EPS-EBIT analysis.

Conclusion

Successful strategy implementation depends on cooperation among all functional and divisional managers in an organization. Marketing departments are commonly charged with implementing strategies that require significant increases in sales revenues in new areas and with new or improved products. Finance and accounting managers must devise effective strategy-implementation approaches at low cost and minimum risk to that firm. R&D managers have to transfer complex technologies or develop new technologies to successfully implement strategies. Information systems managers are being called upon more and more to provide leadership and training for all individuals in the firm. The nature and role of marketing, finance and accounting, R&D, and MIS activities, coupled with the management activities described in Chapter 10, largely determine organizational success.

Key Terms and Concepts

book value (p. 318)

business analytics (p. 322)

cash budget (p. 314)

data mining (p. 322)

demand void (p. 303)

discount (p. 318)

EPS/EBIT analysis (p. 305)

financial budget (p. 313)

goodwill (p. 316)

initial public offering (IPO) (p. 319)

management information system (MIS) (p. 322)

market capitalization (p. 318)

market segment (p. 303)

market segmentation (p. 299)

market value (p. 318)

marketing mix variables (p. 300)

multidimensional scaling (p. 302)

outstanding shares method (p. 317)

perceptual mapping (p. 303)

premium (p. 318)

price-earnings ratio method (p. 317)

product positioning (p. 299)

projected financial statement analysis (p. 310)

research and development (R&D) (p. 320)

treasury stock (p. 307)

tweet (p. 298)

vacant niche (p. 302)

wikis (p. 298)

Issues for Review and Discussion

9-1. Royal Dutch Shell plc has been successful for decades. Analyze their year-end 2013 financials. List six points that best summarize Shell's performance in 2013.

9-2. Explain how to develop an advertising strategy.

9-3. Illustrate a product-positioning map for Royal Dutch Shell. Include three rival firms in your matrix.

9-4. Illustrate a product-positioning map for your college or university.

9-5. List and explain the advantages and disadvantages of using debt versus equity, as a means of raising capital.

9-6. In order of importance, list the limitations of the EPS/EBIT analysis.

9-7. Consider the Cohesion Case on adidas AG. Calculate that company's tax rate, which is a common calculation needed in performing EPS/EBIT analysis.

9-8. Review the website of a company that you are familiar with. Discuss the extent to which that organization has instituted the new principles of marketing according to Parise, Guinan, and Weinberg.

9-9. For companies in general, identify and discuss three opportunities and three threats associated with social networking activities on the Internet.

9-10. Do you agree or disagree with the following statement? Explain your reasoning. "Television viewers are passive viewers of ads whereas Internet users take an active role in choosing what to look at—so customers on the Internet are tougher for marketers to reach."

9-11. How important or relevant do you believe purpose-based marketing is for organizations today?

9-12. Why is it essential for organizations to segment markets and target particular groups of consumers?

9-13. Explain how, and why the Internet makes market segmentation easier?

9-14. A product-positioning rule given in the chapter is that "when there are only two competitors, the middle becomes the preferred strategic position." Illustrate this for the cruise ship industry where two firms, Carnival and Royal Caribbean, dominate. Illustrate this for the commercial airliner building industry where Boeing and Airbus dominate.

9-15. How would dividends affect an EPS/EBIT analysis? Would it be correct to refer to "earnings after taxes, interest, and dividends" as retained earnings for a given year?

9-16. In performing an EPS/EBIT analysis, where does the first row of (EBIT) numbers come from?

9-17. In performing an EPS/EBIT analysis, where does the tax rate percentage come from?

9-18. What amount of dividends did Royal Dutch Shell pay in 2013? How much of 2013's earnings did Shell reinvest back into the company?

9-19. Show algebraically that the price earnings ratio formula is identical to the number of shares outstanding multiplied by the stock price formula. Why are the values obtained from these two methods sometimes different?

9-20. In accounting terms, distinguish between intangibles and goodwill on a balance sheet. Why do these two items generally stay the same on projected financial statements?

9-21. What are the three major R&D approaches to implementing strategies? Which approach would you prefer as owner of a small software company? Why?

9-22. Explain in your own words the process of developing projected financial statement analysis.

9-23. In developing projected financial statements, why should the preparer not use historical percentages too heavily?

9-24. Explain five methods for determining the cash value of a company.

9-25. Given the seven R&D policies mentioned in the chapter, which four do you feel would be best for Audi to utilize? Why?

9-26. Illustrate an EPS/EBIT chart that reflects negative EPS values.

9-27. Define a vacant niche using an example.

9-28. Define and give an example of wikis and tweets.

9-29. List the marketing mix variables. Give an example of each.

9-30. Show algebraically that the price earnings ratio method of calculating the cash value of a company is identical to the number of shares outstanding multiplied by the stock price method.

9-31. Define, and give an example of, goodwill and intangibles.

9-32. Differentiate between capital surplus and additional paid in capital on a balance sheet.

9-33. What transaction is the link between the projected income statement and the projected balance sheet?

9-34. Explain the benefits of a before-and-after product-positioning map.

9-35. Explain how HP should conduct market segmentation.

9-36. Determine the cash value of HP using the methods described in this chapter.

MyManagementLab®

Go to **mymanagementlab.com** for the following Assisted-graded writing questions:

9-37. Why is it essential for organizations to segment markets and target particular groups of consumers?

9-38. Explain how you would estimate the total worth of a business.

Current Readings

Aaker, David A. "Win the Brand Relevance Battle and then Build Competitor Barriers." *California Management Review* 54, no. 2 (Winter 2012): 43–57.

Balmer, John M. T. "Corporate Brand Management Imperatives: Custodianship, Credibility, and Calibration." *California Management Review* 54, no. 3 (Spring 2012): 6–33.

Crittenden, Victoria L., William F. Crittenden. "Strategic Marketing in a Changing World." *Business Horizons* 55, no. 3 (May 2012): 215–217.

Denning, Stephen. "From Maximizing Shareholder Value to Delighting the Customer." *Strategy and Leadership* 40, no. 4 (2012): 12–16.

Fox, Justin, and Jay W. Lorsch. "What Good Are Shareholders?" *Harvard Business Review* (July-August 2012): 48.

Guillén, Mauro F., and Esteban Garcia-Canal. "Execution as Strategy." *Harvard Business Review* (October 2012): 103.

Kumar, V., and Rohan Mirchandani. "Increasing the ROI of Social Media Marketing." *MIT Sloan Management Review* 54, no. 1 (Fall 2012): 55.

Muller, Amy, Nate Hutchins, and Miguel Cardoso Pinto. "Applying Open Innovation Where Your Company Needs It Most." *Strategy and Leadership* 40, no. 3 (2012): 35–42.

Quigley, Timothy J., and Donald C. Hambrick. "When the Former CEO Stays on as Board Chair: Effects on Successor Discretion, Strategic Change, and Performance." *Strategic Management Journal* 33, no. 7 (July 2012): 834–859.

ASSURANCE OF LEARNING **EXERCISES**

EXERCISE 9A

Preparing an EPS/EBIT Analysis for Royal Dutch Shell plc

Purpose

Shell is featured in the opening chapter case as a firm that engages in excellent strategic planning. Shell is both the largest oil and gas company in the world and the largest firm globally, according to *Fortune*, who in 2013 also ranked Shell as the 7th most profitable firm in the world. Incorporated in the United Kingdom but headquartered in the Netherlands, Shell has worldwide reserves of 14.2 billion barrels of oil equivalent.

An important part of effective strategic management is wisely using debt versus equity for raising capital. This exercise gives you practice preparing an EPS/EBIT analysis for a company to determine whether debt versus equity or some combination of the two is best for the firm to expand and grow.

Instructions

Step 1	Shell needs to raise $1billion to acquire a rival firm in Southeast Asia.
Step 2	Prepare an EPS/EBIT analysis to determine whether Shell should use stock or debt to raise the needed capital.
Step 3	Prepare a two-page executive summary to provide justification for your financing decision.

EXERCISE 9B
Developing a Product-Positioning Map for adidas AG

Purpose

Organizations continually monitor how their products and services are positioned relative to competitors. This information is especially useful for marketing managers, but is also used by other managers and strategists.

Instructions

Step 1   On a separate sheet of paper, develop two product-positioning maps that include Reebok, adidas, Nike, Puma, Converse, and Under Armour. Let one map focus on athletic footwear and one map focus on apparel.

Step 2   At the board, diagram your product-positioning maps.

Step 3   Compare your product-positioning maps with those diagrammed by other students. Discuss any major differences.

EXERCISE 9C
Performing an EPS/EBIT Analysis for adidas AG

Purpose

An EPS/EBIT analysis is one of the most widely used techniques for determining the extent that debt and/or stock should be used to finance strategies to be implemented. This exercise can give you practice performing EPS/EBIT analysis.

Instructions

In order to expand into Africa, adidas needs to raise $1 billion. Determine whether adidas should use all debt, all stock, or a 50–50 combination of debt and stock to finance this market-development strategy. Assume a 20 percent tax rate, 5 percent interest rate, adidas stock price of $30 per share, and an annual dividend of $0.50 per share of common stock. The EBIT range for 2011 is between $1.0 billion and $2 billion. A total of 500 million shares of common stock are outstanding. Develop an EPS/EBIT chart to reflect your analysis.

EXERCISE 9D
Preparing Projected Financial Statements for adidas AG

Purpose

This exercise is designed to give you experience preparing projected financial statements. Pro forma analysis is a central strategy-implementation technique because it allows managers to anticipate and evaluate the expected results of various strategy-implementation approaches.

Instructions

Step 1   Work with a classmate. Develop a 2014 projected income statement and balance sheet for adidas. Assume that adidas plans to raise $900 million in 2014 to begin serving Africa, and plans to obtain 50 percent financing from a bank and 50 percent financing from a stock issuance. Make other assumptions as needed, and state them clearly in written form. Use adidas' website as needed.

Step 2   Compute adidas' current ratio, debt-to-equity ratio, and return on investment for 2012 and 2013. How do your 2014 projected ratios compare to the 2012 and 2013 ratios? Why is it important to make this comparison?

Step 3   Bring your projected statements to class and discuss any problems or questions you encountered.

Step 4   Compare your projected statements to the statements of other students. What major differences exist between your analysis and the work of other students?

Determining the Cash Value of adidas AG

Purpose

It is simply good business practice to periodically determine the financial worth or cash value of your company. This exercise gives you practice determining the total worth of a company using several methods. Use data as given in the Cohesion Case or the data from the adidas website.

Instructions

Step 1   Calculate the financial worth of adidas based on four methods: 1) the net worth or stockholders' equity, 2) the future value of adidas' earnings, 3) the price-earnings ratio, and 4) the outstanding shares method. In dollars, how much is adidas worth?

Step 2   Compare your analyses and conclusions with those of other students.

Developing a Product-Positioning Map for My College

Purpose

Organizations continually monitor how their products and services are positioned relative to competitors. This information is especially useful for marketing managers, but is also used by other managers and strategists.

Instructions

Step 1   On a separate sheet of paper, develop a product-positioning map for your college or university.

Step 2   At the board, diagram your product-positioning map. Compare your product-positioning map with those diagrammed by other students. Discuss any major differences.

Do Banks Require Projected Financial Statements?

Purpose

This exercise will allow you to explore the practical importance and use of projected financial statements among banks in your city.

Instructions

Contact several local banks and ask managers about the nature and role of projected financial statements in determining whether to make commercial loans to businesses. Report back to your class on your findings.

Notes

1. Salvatore Parise, Patricia Guinan, and Bruce Weinberg, "The Secrets of Marketing in a Web 2.0 World," *Wall Street Journal*, December 15, 2008, R1.

2. Kathy Chu and Kim Thai, "Banks Jump on Twitter Wagon," *USA Today*, May 12, 2009, B1.

3. Valerie Bauerlein, "Gatorade's Mission: Sell More Drinks," *Wall Street Journal*, September 14, 2010, B6.

4. Susanne Vranica, "Veteran Marketer Promotes a New Kind of Selling," *Wall Street Journal*, October 31, 2008, B4.

5. Gupta, Sunil, and Donald R. Lehmann, *Managing Customers as Investments: The Strategic Value of Customers in the Long Run* ("Customer Retention" section) (Upper Saddle River, NJ: Pearson Education/ Wharton School Publishing, 2005).

6. Shayndi Raice, "Facebook to Target Ads Based on App Usage," *Wall Street Journal* (July 7, 2012): B3.

7. Ralph Biggadike, "The Contributions of Marketing to Strategic Management," *Academy of Management Review* 6, no. 4 (October 1981): 627.

8. Patrick McGee, "Corporate Debt Has Allure," *Wall Street Journal* (August 3, 2012): C1.

9. Michael Rapoport, "Pro Forma Is a Hard Habit to Break," *Wall Street Journal*, September 18, 2003, B3A.

10. Scott Thurm, "Buyers Beware: The Goodwill Games," *Wall Street Journal* (August 14, 2012): B1.

11. Amy Merrick, "U.S. Research Spending to Rise Only 3.2 Percent," *Wall Street Journal*, December 28, 2001, A2.

12. Pier Abetti, "Technology: A Key Strategic Resource," *Management Review* 78, no. 2 (February 1989): 38.

13. Adapted from Edward Baig, "Welcome to the Officeless Office," *Businessweek*, June 26, 1995.

14. Spencer Ante, "IBM Ready for Close-Up," *Wall Street Journal*, January 18, 2011, B4.

10

Source: © apops/Fotolia

MyManagementLab®

Improve Your Grade!

Over 10 million students improved their results using the Pearson MyLabs.
Visit **mymanagementlab.com** for simulations, tutorials, and end-of-chapter problems.

Strategy Execution

CHAPTER OBJECTIVES

After studying this chapter, you should be able to do the following:

1. Construct an effective organizational chart.

2. Explain why corporate wellness has become so important in strategic planning.

3. Explain why strategy implementation is more difficult than strategy formulation.

4. Discuss the importance of annual objectives and policies in achieving organizational commitment for strategies to be implemented.

5. Explain why organizational structure is so important in strategy implementation.

6. Compare and contrast restructuring and reengineering.

7. Describe the relationship between production/operations and strategy implementation.

8. Explain how a firm can effectively link performance and pay to strategies.

9. Discuss employee stock ownership plans (ESOPs) as a strategic-management concept.

10. Describe how to modify an organizational culture to support new strategies.

ASSURANCE OF LEARNING **EXERCISES**

The following exercises are found at the end of this chapter.

The strategic-management process does not end on deciding what strategy or strategies to pursue. There must be a translation of strategic thought into strategic action. This translation is much easier if managers and employees of the firm understand the business, feel a part of the company, and through involvement in strategy-formulation activities have become committed to helping the organization succeed. Without understanding and commitment, strategy-implementation efforts face major problems. Vince Lombardi said: "The best game plan in the world never blocked or tackled anybody."

Implementing strategy affects an organization from top to bottom, including all the functional and divisional areas of a business. This chapter focuses on management issues most central to implementing strategies in 2014–2015 and Chapter 9 focuses on marketing, finance/accounting, R&D, and management information systems issues. Accenture is an example firm with excellent management practices.

> Even the most technically perfect strategic plan will serve little purpose if it is not implemented. Many organizations tend to spend an inordinate amount of time, money, and effort on developing the strategic plan, treating the means and circumstances under which it will be implemented as afterthoughts! Change comes through implementation and evaluation, not through the plan. A technically imperfect plan that is implemented well will achieve more than the perfect plan that never gets off the paper on which it is typed.[1]

The Nature of Strategy Implementation

The strategy-implementation stage of strategic management is revealed in Figure 10-1, as illustrated with white shading. Successful strategy formulation does not guarantee successful strategy implementation. It is always more difficult to do something (strategy implementation) than to say you are going to do it (strategy formulation)! Although inextricably linked, strategy

---

EXCELLENT STRATEGIC MANAGEMENT SHOWCASED

Accenture

Accenture plc, headquartered in Dublin, Ireland, is the world's largest consulting firm measured by revenues. As of August 2013, the company has approximately 266,000 employees serving clients in more than 120 countries. India is the single largest employee base for Accenture, with the headcount being close to 100,000, compared to about 50,000 in the United States.

In 2013, *Fortune* ranked Accenture as the 44th most admired company in the world outside the United States. As most consulting firms, Accenture operates in a matrix structure. The first axis is dedicated to the operating groups, or industries of its clients. Accenture's has five Operating Groups that comprise 39 industry subgroups.

The five Operating Groups are:

- Communications, Media & Technology
- Financial Services
- Products
- Resources
- Health & Public Service.

In September 2013, Accenture acquired AMS Research headquartered in Fairfax, Virginia. Accenture made the acquisition to strategically expand its U.S. defense business in the growing military health market, especially desiring to better serve the U.S. Department of Defense (DoD).

Accenture offers DoD extensive experience in providing electronic health records, healthcare integration, interoperability. AMS has more than three decades of government experience and expertise in healthcare IT, information solutions and services, data analytics, cloud, data warehousing, human capital management and benefit solutions and agile software development.

Also in September 2013, YSPay, one of the leading payment services providers in China, began using a new mobile payments solution developed with Accenture. The new product allows YSPay customers – consumers, banks and merchants – to process payments with any type of mobile phone. YSPay is using the Accenture Mobility platform to connect with banks via China Union Pay – China's bank card association. Accenture is also providing application outsourcing services to YSPay, including the ongoing maintenance of the platform and any future enhancements agreed by both parties, allowing YSPay to keep its internal resources focused on core business activities.

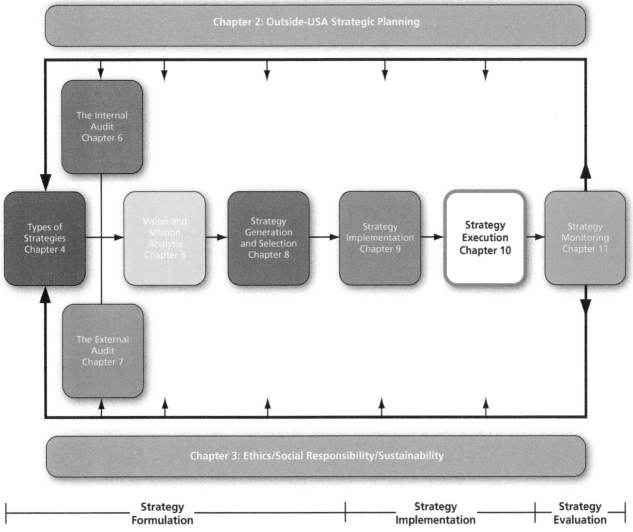

FIGURE 10-1

Comprehensive Strategic-Management Model

Source: Fred R. David, adapted from "How Companies Define Their Mission," *Long Range Planning* 22, no. 3 (June 1988): 40, © Fred R. David.

implementation is fundamentally different from strategy formulation. Strategy formulation and implementation can be contrasted in the following ways:

- Strategy formulation is positioning forces before the action.
- Strategy implementation is managing forces during the action.
- Strategy formulation focuses on effectiveness.
- Strategy implementation focuses on efficiency.
- Strategy formulation is primarily an intellectual process.
- Strategy implementation is primarily an operational process.
- Strategy formulation requires good intuitive and analytical skills.
- Strategy implementation requires special motivation and leadership skills.
- Strategy formulation requires coordination among a few individuals.
- Strategy implementation requires coordination among many individuals.

Strategy-formulation concepts and tools do not differ greatly for small, large, for-profit, or nonprofit organizations. However, strategy implementation varies substantially among different types and sizes of organizations. Implementing strategies requires such actions as altering sales territories, adding new departments, closing facilities, hiring new employees, changing an organization's pricing strategy, developing financial budgets, developing new employee benefits, establishing cost-control procedures, changing advertising strategies, building new facilities, training new employees, transferring managers among divisions, and building a better management information system. These types of activities obviously differ greatly among manufacturing, service, and governmental organizations.

Management Perspectives

In terms of "Quality of Management," *Fortune* recently ranked the following companies as best in the world:

Rank	Company
1	Koc Holding
2	McDonald's
3	Apple
4	Philip Morris International
5	Costco Wholesale
6	JP Morgan Chase
7	Wyndham Worldwide
8	Sysco
9	Walt Disney
10	TJX

Source: Based on: http://money.cnn.com/magazines/fortune/mostadmired/2012/best_worst/best5.html.

In all but the smallest organizations, the transition from strategy formulation to strategy implementation requires a shift in responsibility from strategists to divisional and functional managers. Implementation problems can arise because of this shift in responsibility, especially if strategy-formulation decisions come as a surprise to middle- and lower-level managers. Managers and employees are motivated more by perceived self-interests than by organizational interests, unless the two coincide. This is a primary reason why divisional and functional managers should be involved as much as possible in strategy-formulation and strategy-implementation activities.

As indicated in Table 10-1, management issues central to strategy implementation include establishing annual objectives, devising policies, allocating resources, altering an existing organizational structure, restructuring and reengineering, revising reward and incentive plans,

TABLE 10-1 Some Management Issues Central to Strategy Implementation

Establish annual objectives
Devise policies
Allocate resources
Alter an existing organizational structure
Restructure and reengineer
Revise reward and incentive plans
Minimize resistance to change
Match managers with strategy
Develop a strategy-supportive culture
Adapt production and operations processes
Develop an effective human resources function
Downsize and furlough as needed
Link performance and pay to strategies

minimizing resistance to change, matching managers with strategy, developing a strategy-supportive culture, adapting production and operations processes, developing an effective human resources function, and, if necessary, downsizing. Management changes are necessarily more extensive when strategies to be implemented move a firm in a major new direction.

Managers and employees throughout an organization should participate early and directly in strategy-implementation decisions. Their role in strategy implementation should build on prior involvement in strategy-formulation activities. Strategists' genuine personal commitment to implementation is a necessary and powerful motivational force for managers and employees. Too often, strategists are too busy to actively support strategy-implementation efforts, and their lack of interest can be detrimental to organizational success. The rationale for objectives and strategies should be understood and clearly communicated throughout an organization. Major competitors' accomplishments, products, plans, actions, and performance should be apparent to all organizational members. Major external opportunities and threats should be clear, and managers' and employees' questions should be answered. Top-down flow of communication is essential for developing bottom-up support.

Firms need to develop a competitor focus at all hierarchical levels by gathering and widely distributing competitive intelligence; every employee should be able to benchmark her or his efforts against best-in-class competitors so that the challenge becomes personal. For example, Starbucks Corp. recently instituted "lean production/operations" at its 11,000+ U.S. stores. This system eliminates idle employee time and unnecessary employee motions, such as walking, reaching, and bending. Starbucks says 30 percent of employees' time is motion and the company wants to reduce that. They say "motion and work are two different things."

Annual Objectives

Establishing annual objectives is a decentralized activity that directly involves all managers in an organization. Active participation in establishing annual objectives can lead to acceptance and commitment. **Annual objectives** are essential for strategy implementation because they (a) represent the basis for allocating resources; (b) are a primary mechanism for evaluating managers; (c) are the major instrument for monitoring progress toward achieving long-term objectives; and (d) establish organizational, divisional, and departmental priorities. Considerable time and effort should be devoted to ensuring that annual objectives are well conceived, consistent with long-term objectives, and supportive of strategies to be implemented. Approving, revising, or rejecting annual objectives is much more than a rubber-stamp activity. The purpose of annual objectives can be summarized as follows:

> Annual objectives serve as guidelines for action, directing and channeling efforts and activities of organization members. They provide a source of legitimacy in an enterprise by justifying activities to stakeholders. They serve as standards of performance. They serve as an important source of employee motivation and identification. They give incentives for managers and employees to perform. They provide a basis for organizational design.[2]

Clearly stated and communicated objectives are critical to success in all types and sizes of firms. Annual objectives, stated in terms of profitability, growth, and market share by business segment, geographic area, customer groups, and product, are common in organizations. Figure 10-2 illustrates how the Stamus Company could establish annual objectives based on long-term objectives. Table 10-2 reveals associated revenue figures that correspond to the objectives outlined in Figure 10-2. Note that, according to plan, the Stamus Company will slightly exceed its long-term objective of doubling company revenues between 2012 and 2014.

Figure 10-2 also reflects how a hierarchy of annual objectives can be established based on an organization's structure. Objectives should be consistent across hierarchical levels and form a network of supportive aims. **Horizontal consistency of objectives** is as important as **vertical consistency of objectives**. For instance, it would not be effective for manufacturing to achieve more than its annual objective of units produced if marketing could not sell the additional units.

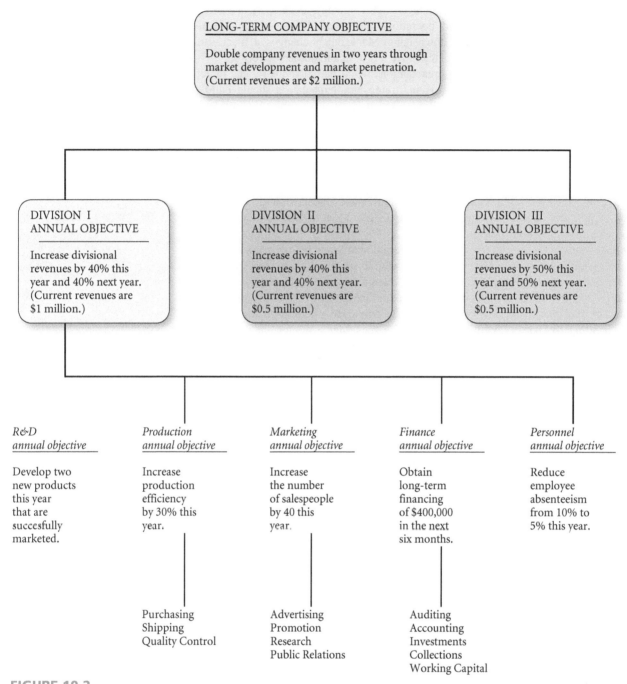

FIGURE 10-2

The Stamus Company's Hierarchy of Aims

Annual objectives should be measurable, consistent, reasonable, challenging, clear, communicated throughout the organization, characterized by an appropriate time dimension, and accompanied by commensurate rewards and sanctions. Too often, objectives are stated in generalities, with little operational usefulness. Annual objectives, such as "to improve communication" or "to improve performance," are not clear, specific, or measurable. Objectives should state quantity, quality, cost, and time—and also be verifiable. Terms and phrases such as *maximize, minimize, as soon as possible,* and *adequate* should be avoided.

Annual objectives should be compatible with employees' and managers' values and supported by clearly stated policies. More of something is not always better. Improved quality or

TABLE 10-2 **The Stamus Company's Revenue Expectations (in $millions)**

	2012	2013	2014
Division I Revenues	1.0	1.400	1.960
Division II Revenues	0.5	0.700	0.980
Division III Revenues	0.5	0.750	1.125
Total Company Revenues	**2.0**	**2.850**	**4.065**

reduced cost may, for example, be more important than quantity. It is important to tie rewards and sanctions to annual objectives so that employees and managers understand that achieving objectives is critical to successful strategy implementation. Clear annual objectives do not guarantee successful strategy implementation, but they do increase the likelihood that personal and organizational aims can be accomplished. Overemphasis on achieving objectives can result in undesirable conduct, such as faking the numbers, distorting the records, and letting objectives become ends in themselves. Managers must be alert to these potential problems.

Policies

Changes in a firm's strategic direction do not occur automatically. On a day-to-day basis, policies are needed to make a strategy work. Policies facilitate solving recurring problems and guide the implementation of strategy. Broadly defined, **policy** refers to specific guidelines, methods, procedures, rules, forms, and administrative practices established to support and encourage work toward stated goals. Policies are instruments for strategy implementation. Policies set boundaries, constraints, and limits on the kinds of administrative actions that can be taken to reward and sanction behavior; they clarify what can and cannot be done in pursuit of an organization's objectives. For example, Carnival's *Paradise* ship has a no smoking policy anywhere, anytime aboard ship. It was the first cruise ship to ban smoking comprehensively. Another example of corporate policy relates to surfing the Web while at work. About 40 percent of companies today do not have a formal policy preventing employees from surfing the Internet, but software is being marketed now that allows firms to monitor how, when, where, and how long various employees use the Internet at work.

Policies let both employees and managers know what is expected of them, thereby increasing the likelihood that strategies will be implemented successfully. They provide a basis for management control, allow coordination across organizational units, and reduce the amount of time managers spend making decisions. Policies also clarify what work is to be done and by whom. They promote delegation of decision making to appropriate managerial levels where various problems usually arise. Many organizations have a policy manual that serves to guide and direct behavior. Walmart has a policy that it calls the "10 Foot" Rule, whereby customers can find assistance within 10 feet of anywhere in the store. This is a welcomed policy in Japan, where Walmart is trying to gain a foothold; 58 percent of all retailers in Japan are mom-and-pop stores and consumers historically have had to pay "top yen" rather than "discounted prices" for merchandise.

Policies can apply to all divisions and departments (for example, "We are an equal opportunity employer"). Some policies apply to a single department ("Employees in this department must take at least one training and development course each year"). Whatever their scope and form, policies serve as a mechanism for implementing strategies and obtaining objectives. Policies should be stated in writing whenever possible. They represent the means for carrying out strategic decisions. Examples of policies that support a company strategy, a divisional objective, and a departmental objective are given in Table 10-3.

Some example issues that may require a management policy are provided in Table 10-4.

TABLE 10-3 **A Hierarchy of Policies**

Company Strategy
Acquire a chain of retail stores to meet our sales growth and profitability objectives.
Supporting Policies
1. "All stores will be open from 8 a.m. to 8 p.m. Monday through Saturday." (This policy could increase retail sales if stores currently are open only 40 hours a week.)
2. "All stores must submit a Monthly Control Data Report." (This policy could reduce expense-to-sales ratios.)
3. "All stores must support company advertising by contributing 5 percent of their total monthly revenues for this purpose." (This policy could allow the company to establish a national reputation.)
4. "All stores must adhere to the uniform pricing guidelines set forth in the Company Handbook." (This policy could help assure customers that the company offers a consistent product in terms of price and quality in all its stores.)

Divisional Objective
Increase the division's revenues from $10 million in 2014 to $15 million in 2015.
Supporting Policies
1. "Beginning in January 2014, each one of this division's salespersons must file a weekly activity report that includes the number of calls made, the number of miles traveled, the number of units sold, the dollar volume sold, and the number of new accounts opened." (This policy could ensure that salespersons do not place too great an emphasis in certain areas.)
2. "Beginning in January 2014, this division will return to its employees 5 percent of its gross revenues in the form of a Christmas bonus." (This policy could increase employee productivity.)
3. "Beginning in January 2014, inventory levels carried in warehouses will be decreased by 30 percent in accordance with a just-in-time (JIT) manufacturing approach." (This policy could reduce production expenses and thus free funds for increased marketing efforts.)

Production Department Objective
Increase production from 20,000 units in 2014 to 30,000 units in 2015.
Supporting Policies
1. "Beginning in January 2014, employees will have the option of working up to 20 hours of overtime per week." (This policy could minimize the need to hire additional employees.)
2. "Beginning in January 2014, perfect attendance awards in the amount of $100 will be given to all employees who do not miss a workday in a given year." (This policy could decrease absenteeism and increase productivity.)
3. "Beginning in January 2014, new equipment must be leased rather than purchased." (This policy could reduce tax liabilities and thus allow more funds to be invested in modernizing production processes.)

TABLE 10-4 **Some Issues That May Require a Management Policy**

- To offer extensive or limited management development workshops and seminars
- To centralize or decentralize employee-training activities
- To recruit through employment agencies, college campuses, or newspapers
- To promote from within or to hire from the outside
- To promote on the basis of merit or on the basis of seniority
- To tie executive compensation to long-term or annual objectives
- To offer numerous or few employee benefits
- To negotiate directly or indirectly with labor unions
- To delegate authority for large expenditures or to centrally retain this authority
- To allow much, some, or no overtime work
- To establish a high- or low-safety stock of inventory
- To use one or more suppliers
- To buy, lease, or rent new production equipment
- To greatly or somewhat stress quality control
- To establish many or only a few production standards
- To operate one, two, or three shifts
- To discourage using insider information for personal gain
- To discourage sexual harassment
- To discourage smoking at work
- To discourage insider trading
- To discourage moonlighting

Resource Allocation

Resource allocation is a central management activity that allows for strategy execution. In organizations that do not use a strategic-management approach to decision making, resource allocation is often based on political or personal factors. Strategic management enables resources to be allocated according to priorities established by annual objectives.

All organizations have at least four types of resources that can be used to achieve desired objectives: financial resources, physical resources, human resources, and technological resources. Allocating resources to particular divisions and departments does not mean that strategies will be successfully implemented. A number of factors commonly prohibit effective resource allocation, including an overprotection of resources, too great an emphasis on short-run financial criteria, organizational politics, vague strategy targets, a reluctance to take risks, and a lack of sufficient knowledge.

Below the corporate level, there often exists an absence of systematic thinking about resources allocated and strategies of the firm. Yavitz and Newman explain why:

> Managers normally have many more tasks than they can do. Managers must allocate time and resources among these tasks. Pressure builds up. Expenses are too high. The CEO wants a good financial report for the third quarter. Strategy formulation and implementation activities often get deferred. Today's problems soak up available energies and resources. Scrambled accounts and budgets fail to reveal the shift in allocation away from strategic needs to currently squeaking wheels.[3]

The real value of any resource allocation program lies in the resulting accomplishment of an organization's objectives. Effective resource allocation does not guarantee successful strategy implementation because programs, personnel, controls, and commitment must breathe life into the resources provided. Strategic management itself is sometimes referred to as a "resource allocation process."

Managing Conflict

Interdependency of objectives and competition for limited resources often leads to conflict. **Conflict** can be defined as a disagreement between two or more parties on one or more issues. Establishing annual objectives can lead to conflict because individuals have different expectations and perceptions, schedules create pressure, personalities are incompatible, and misunderstandings between line managers (such as production supervisors) and staff managers (such as human resource specialists) occur. For example, a collection manager's objective of reducing bad debts by 50 percent in a given year may conflict with a divisional objective to increase sales by 20 percent.

Establishing objectives can lead to conflict because managers and strategists must make trade-offs, such as whether to emphasize short-term profits or long-term growth, profit margin or market share, market penetration or market development, growth or stability, high risk or low risk, and social responsiveness or profit maximization. Trade-offs are necessary because no firm has sufficient resources to pursue all strategies that would benefit the firm. Table 10-5 reveals some important management trade-off decisions required in strategy implementation.

Conflict is unavoidable in organizations, so it is important that conflict be managed and resolved before dysfunctional consequences affect organizational performance. Conflict is not always bad. An absence of conflict can signal indifference and apathy. Conflict can serve to energize opposing groups into action and may help managers identify problems. General George Patton once said: "If everyone is thinking alike, then somebody isn't thinking."

Various approaches for managing and resolving conflict can be classified into three categories: avoidance, defusion, and confrontation. **Avoidance** includes such actions as ignoring the problem in hopes that the conflict will resolve itself or physically separating the conflicting individuals (or groups). **Defusion** can include playing down differences between conflicting parties while accentuating similarities and common interests, compromising so that there is neither a clear winner nor loser, resorting to majority rule, appealing to a higher authority, or redesigning present positions. **Confrontation** is exemplified by exchanging members of conflicting parties so that each can gain an appreciation of the other's point of view or holding a meeting at which conflicting parties present their views and work through their differences.

TABLE 10-5 Some Management Trade-Off Decisions Required in Strategy Implementation

To emphasize short-term profits or long-term growth

To emphasize profit margin or market share

To emphasize market development or market penetration

To lay off or furlough

To seek growth or stability

To take high risk or low risk

To be more socially responsible or more profitable

To outsource jobs or pay more to keep jobs at home

To acquire externally or to build internally

To restructure or reengineer

To use leverage or equity to raise funds

To use part-time or full-time employees

Matching Structure with Strategy

Changes in strategy often require changes in the way an organization is structured, for two major reasons. First, structure largely dictates how objectives and policies will be established. For example, objectives and policies established under a geographic organizational structure are couched in geographic terms. Objectives and policies are stated largely in terms of products in an organization whose structure is based on product groups. The structural format for developing objectives and policies can significantly impact all other strategy-implementation activities.

The second major reason why changes in strategy often require changes in structure is that structure dictates how resources will be allocated. If an organization's structure is based on customer groups, then resources will be allocated in that manner. Similarly, if an organization's structure is set up along functional business lines, then resources are allocated by functional areas. Unless new or revised strategies place emphasis in the same areas as old strategies, structural reorientation commonly becomes a part of strategy implementation.

Alfred Chandler promoted the notion that "changes in strategy lead to changes in organizational structure." Structure should be designed to facilitate the strategic pursuit of a firm and, therefore, follow strategy. Without a strategy or reasons for being (mission), companies find it difficult to design an effective structure. Chandler found a particular structure sequence to be repeated often as organizations grow and change strategy over time.

There is no one optimal organizational design or structure for a given strategy or type of organization. What is appropriate for one organization may not be appropriate for a similar firm, although successful firms in a given industry do tend to organize themselves in a similar way. For example, consumer goods companies tend to emulate the divisional structure-by-product form of organization. Small firms tend to be functionally structured (centralized). Medium-sized firms tend to be divisionally structured (decentralized). Large firms tend to use a **strategic business unit (SBU) structure** or matrix structure. As organizations grow, their structures generally change from simple to complex as a result of concatenation, or the linking together of several basic strategies.

Numerous external and internal forces affect an organization; no firm could change its structure in response to every one of these forces because to do so would lead to chaos. However, when a firm changes its strategy, the existing organizational structure may become ineffective. As indicated in Table 10-6, symptoms of an ineffective organizational structure include too many levels of management, too many meetings attended by too many people, too much attention being directed toward solving interdepartmental conflicts, too large a span of control, and too many unachieved objectives. Changes in structure can facilitate strategy-implementation efforts, but changes in structure should not be expected to make a bad strategy good, to make bad managers good, or to make bad products sell.

TABLE 10-6 Symptoms of an Ineffective Organizational Structure

1. Too many levels of management
2. Too many meetings attended by too many people
3. Too much attention being directed toward solving interdepartmental conflicts
4. Too large a span of control
5. Too many unachieved objectives
6. Declining corporate or business performance
7. Losing ground to rival firms
8. Revenue or earnings divided by number of employees or number of managers is low compared to rival firms

Structure undeniably can and does influence strategy. Strategies formulated must be workable, so if a certain new strategy required massive structural changes it would not be an attractive choice. In this way, structure can shape the choice of strategies. But a more important concern is determining what types of structural changes are needed to implement new strategies and how these changes can best be accomplished. There are seven basic types of organizational structure: functional, divisional by geographic area, divisional by product, divisional by customer, divisional process, strategic business unit (SBU), and matrix.

The Functional Structure

The most widely used structure is the functional or centralized type because this structure is the simplest and least expensive of the seven alternatives. A **functional structure** groups tasks and activities by business function, such as production and operations, marketing, finance and accounting, research and development, and management information systems. A university may structure its activities by major functions that include academic affairs, student services, alumni relations, athletics, maintenance, and accounting. Besides being simple and inexpensive, a functional structure also promotes specialization of labor, encourages efficient use of managerial and technical talent, minimizes the need for an elaborate control system, and allows rapid decision making.

Some disadvantages of a functional structure are that it forces accountability to the top, minimizes career development opportunities, and is sometimes characterized by low employee morale, line or staff conflicts, poor delegation of authority, and inadequate planning for products and markets.

A functional structure often leads to short-term and narrow thinking that may undermine what is best for the firm as a whole. For example, the research and development department may strive to overdesign products and components to achieve technical elegance, whereas manufacturing may argue for low-frills products that can be mass produced more easily. Thus, communication is often not as good in a functional structure. Schein gives an example of a communication problem in a functional structure:

The word "marketing" will mean product development to the engineer, studying customers through market research to the product manager, merchandising to the salesperson, and constant change in design to the manufacturing manager. Then when these managers try to work together, they often attribute disagreements to personalities and fail to notice the deeper, shared assumptions that vary and dictate how each function thinks.[4]

Most large companies have abandoned the functional structure in favor of decentralization and improved accountability. However, a large company that still operates from a functional type organizational design is Southwest Airlines, headquartered in Dallas, Texas. As illustrated in Figure 10-3, Southwest has only five top executives and no divisions, even though the firm operates 700 aircraft serving 72 cities in 37 states.

Table 10-7 summarizes the advantages and disadvantages of a functional organizational structure.

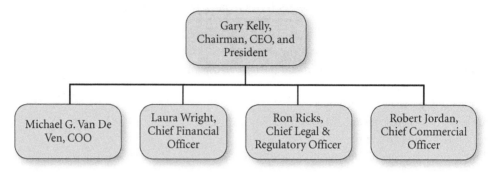

FIGURE 10-3

Southwest Airlines' Functional Organizational Chart

Source: Based on company documents.

The Divisional Structure

The **divisional structure** or **decentralized structure** is the second most common type used by U.S. businesses. As a small organization grows, it has more difficulty managing different products and services in different markets. Some form of divisional structure generally becomes necessary to motivate employees, control operations, and compete successfully in diverse locations. The divisional structure can be organized in one of four ways: *by geographic area*, *by product* or *service*, *by customer*, or *by process*. With a divisional structure, functional activities are performed both centrally and in each separate division.

Sun Microsystems recently reduced the number of its business units from seven to four. Kodak recently reduced its number of business units from seven by-customer divisions to five by-product divisions. As consumption patterns become increasingly similar worldwide, a by-product structure is becoming more effective than a by-customer or a by-geographic type divisional structure. In the restructuring, Kodak eliminated its global operations division and distributed those responsibilities across the new by-product divisions.

A divisional structure has some clear advantages. First and perhaps foremost, accountability is clear. That is, divisional managers can be held responsible for sales and profit levels. Because a divisional structure is based on extensive delegation of authority, managers and employees can easily see the results of their good or bad performances. As a result, employee morale is generally higher in a divisional structure than it is in a centralized structure. Other advantages of the divisional design are that it creates career development opportunities for managers, allows local control of situations, leads to a competitive climate within an organization, and allows new businesses and products to be added easily.

The divisional design is not without some limitations, however. Perhaps the most important limitation is that a divisional structure is costly, for a number of reasons. First, each division requires functional specialists who must be paid. Second, there exists some duplication of staff

TABLE 10-7 Advantages and Disadvantages of a Functional Organizational Structure

Advantages	Disadvantages
1. Simple and inexpensive	1. Accountability forced to the top
2. Capitalizes on specialization of business activities such as marketing and finance	2. Delegation of authority and responsibility not encouraged
3. Minimizes need for elaborate control system	3. Minimizes career development
4. Allows for rapid decision making	4. Low employee and manager morale
	5. Inadequate planning for products and markets
	6. Leads to short-term, narrow thinking
	7. Leads to communication problems

TABLE 10-8 Advantages and Disadvantages of a Divisional Organizational Structure

Advantages	Disadvantages
1. Accountability is clear	1. Can be costly
2. Allows local control of local situations	2. Duplication of functional activities
3. Creates career development chances	3. Requires a skilled management force
4. Promotes delegation of authority	4. Requires an elaborate control system
5. Leads to competitive climate internally	5. Competition among divisions can become so intense as to be dysfunctional
6. Allows easy adding of new products or regions	6. Can lead to limited sharing of ideas and resources
7. Allows strict control and attention to products, customers, or regions	7. Some regions, products, or customers may receive special treatment

services, facilities, and personnel; for instance, functional specialists are also needed centrally (at headquarters) to coordinate divisional activities. Third, managers must be well qualified because the divisional design forces delegation of authority; better-qualified individuals require higher salaries. A divisional structure can also be costly because it requires an elaborate, headquarters-driven control system. Fourth, competition between divisions may become so intense that it is dysfunctional and leads to limited sharing of ideas and resources for the common good of the firm. Table 10-8 summarizes the advantages and disadvantages of divisional organizational structure.

Ghoshal and Bartlett, two leading scholars in strategic management, note the following:

As their label clearly warns, divisions divide. The divisional model fragments companies' resources; it creates vertical communication channels that insulate business units and prevents them from sharing their strengths with one another. Consequently, the whole of the corporation is often less than the sum of its parts. A final limitation of the divisional design is that certain regions, products, or customers may sometimes receive special treatment, and it may be difficult to maintain consistent, companywide practices. Nonetheless, for most large organizations and many small firms, the advantages of a divisional structure more than offset the potential limitations.[5]

A *divisional structure by geographic area* is appropriate for organizations whose strategies need to be tailored to fit the particular needs and characteristics of customers in different geographic areas. This type of structure can be most appropriate for organizations that have similar branch facilities located in widely dispersed areas. A divisional structure by geographic area allows local participation in decision making and improved coordination within a region. Hershey Foods is an example company organized using the divisional-by-region type of structure, as illustrated in Figure 10-4. Analysts contend that this type of structure may not be best for Hershey because consumption patterns for candy are quite similar worldwide. An alternative—and perhaps better—type of structure for Hershey would be divisional by product because the company produces, and sells three types of products worldwide: (1) chocolate, (2) nonchocolate, and (3) grocery.

The *divisional structure by product (or services)* is most effective for implementing strategies when specific products or services need special emphasis. Also, this type of structure is widely used when an organization offers only a few products or services or when an organization's products or services differ substantially. The divisional structure allows strict control over and attention to product lines, but it may also require a more skilled management force and reduced top management control. General Motors, DuPont, Microsoft, and Procter & Gamble use a divisional structure by product to implement strategies. Microsoft introduced its new Surface Tablet for $499 in late 2012. The Surface is being sold online and in Microsoft retail stores, but not in stores such as Best Buy or Walmart, or even Amazon. Microsoft's divisional-by-product organizational structure is illustrated in Figure 10-5.

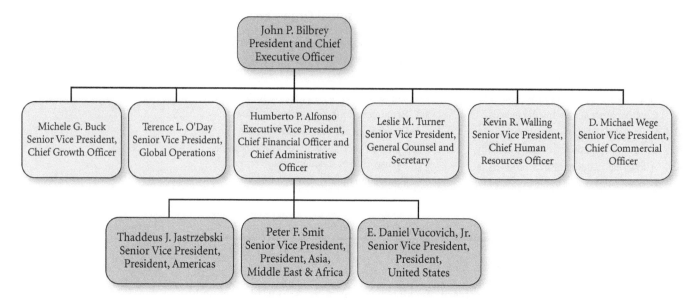

FIGURE 10-4

Hershey Foods' Divisional-by-Region Organizational Chart

Source: Based on company documents.

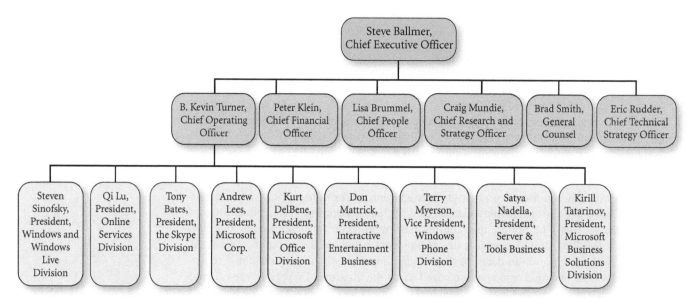

FIGURE 10-5

Microsoft's Divisional-by-Product Organizational Structure

Source: Based on company documents.

When a few major customers are of paramount importance and many different services are provided to these customers, then a *divisional structure by customer* can be the most effective way to implement strategies. This structure allows an organization to cater effectively to the requirements of clearly defined customer groups. For example, book publishing companies often organize their activities around customer groups, such as colleges, secondary schools, and private commercial schools. Some airline companies have two major customer divisions: passengers and freight or cargo services. Utility companies often use (1) commercial, (2) residential, and (3) industrial as their divisions by customer.

A *divisional structure by process* is similar to a functional structure, because activities are organized according to the way work is actually performed. However, a key difference between these two designs is that functional departments are not accountable for profits or revenues, whereas divisional process departments are evaluated on these criteria. An example of a divisional structure by process is a manufacturing business organized into six divisions: electrical work, glass cutting, welding, grinding, painting, and foundry work. In this case, all operations related to these specific processes would be grouped under the separate divisions. Each process (division) would be responsible for generating revenues and profits. The divisional structure by process can be particularly effective in achieving objectives when distinct production processes represent the thrust of competitiveness in an industry. Halliburton's organizational chart illustrated on the next page features aspects of the division-by-process design.

The Strategic Business Unit (SBU) Structure

As the number, size, and diversity of divisions in an organization increase, controlling and evaluating divisional operations become increasingly difficult for strategists. Increases in sales often are not accompanied by similar increases in profitability. The span of control becomes too large at top levels of the firm. For example, in a large conglomerate organization composed of 90 divisions, such as ConAgra, the chief executive officer could have difficulty even remembering the first names of divisional presidents. In multidivisional organizations, an SBU structure can greatly facilitate strategy-implementation efforts. ConAgra has put its many divisions into three primary SBUs: (1) food service (restaurants), (2) retail (grocery stores), and (3) agricultural products.

The SBU structure groups similar divisions into SBUs and delegates authority and responsibility for each unit to a senior executive who reports directly to the chief executive officer. This change in structure can facilitate strategy implementation by improving coordination between similar divisions and channeling accountability to distinct business units. In a 100-division conglomerate, the divisions could perhaps be regrouped into 10 SBUs according to certain common characteristics, such as competing in the same industry, being located in the same area, or having the same customers.

Two disadvantages of an SBU structure are that it requires an additional layer of management, which increases salary expenses. Also, the role of the group vice president is often ambiguous. However, these limitations often do not outweigh the advantages of improved coordination and accountability. Another advantage of the SBU structure is that it makes the tasks of planning and control by the corporate office more manageable.

News Corp. recently reorganized its operations into two SBUs: (1) Entertainment, which includes 20th Century Fox, Fox Broadcast News, and the Fox News Channel, and (2) Publishing, which includes The *Wall Street Journal*, *Times of London*, *The Sun* newspaper, *The Australian* newspaper, and HarperCollins book publishing. News Corp.'s Chairman and CEO, Rupert Murdoch, is retaining his family's 40 percent voting stake in what may result in two separate companies. Estimated 2014 revenue in billions of dollars by division within the Publishing SBU is as follows:

Australia newspapers (2.19)

Dow Jones (2.07)

U.K. newspapers (1.34)

Book publishing (1.25)

Marketing services (0.97)

Fox Sports (0.62)

REA Group (0.37)

NY Post, other (0.30)

Education business (0.12)

Apparently to groom a new CEO, Coca-Cola recently streamlined its organizational structure by converting to three SBUs: (1) The Americas Beverages headed by Cahillane, (2) Outside-The-Americas Beverages headed by Bozer, and (3) Outside-The-Americas Bottlers headed by Finan. Coke CEO Muhtar Kent said "Consolidating leadership under the three groups

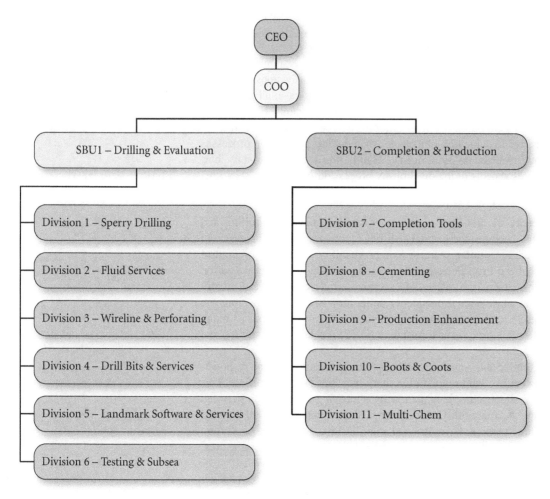

FIGURE 10-6

Halliburton Company's SBU Organizational Chart

Source: Based on http://www.halliburton.com/AboutUs/default.aspx?pageid=2458&navid=966.

will streamline reporting lines and intensify our focus on key markets." Either Mr. Cahillane and Mr. Bozer are expected to replace Mr. Kent as CEO sometime in the future, although Mr. Kent says: "As long as I'm having fun, my health allows me to continue and I'm generating good returns for our shareholders, and importantly as long as I'm smiling, which is important in anything you do, then I will continue."[6]

An excellent example of an SBU organizational chart is the one posted at the Halliburton Company website and shown in Figure 10-6. Note that six division executives report to the Drilling and Evaluation top executive, whereas five division heads report to the Completion and Production top executive. It is interesting and somewhat unusual that the 11 Halliburton divisions are organized by process rather than by geographic region or product.

The Matrix Structure

A **matrix structure** is the most complex of all designs because it depends on both vertical and horizontal flows of authority and communication (hence the term *matrix*). In contrast, functional and divisional structures depend primarily on vertical flows of authority and communication. A matrix structure can result in higher overhead because it creates more management positions. Other disadvantages of a matrix structure that contribute to overall complexity include dual lines of budget authority (a violation of the unity-of-command principle), dual sources of reward and punishment, shared authority, dual reporting channels, and a need for an extensive and effective communication system.

Despite its complexity, the matrix structure is widely used in many industries, including construction, health care, research, and defense. As indicated in Table 10-9, some advantages of a

TABLE 10-9 Advantages and Disadvantages of a Matrix Structure

Advantages	Disadvantages
1. Project objectives are clear	1. Requires excellent vertical and horizontal flows of communication
2. Employees can clearly see results of their work	2. Costly because creates more manager positions
3. Shutting down a project is easily accomplished	3. Violates unity of command principle
4. Facilitates uses of special equipment, personnel, and facilities	4. Creates dual lines of budget authority
5. Functional resources are shared instead of duplicated as in a divisional structure	5. Creates dual sources of reward and punishment
	6. Creates shared authority and reporting
	7. Requires mutual trust and understanding

matrix structure are that project objectives are clear, there are many channels of communication, workers can see the visible results of their work, and shutting down a project can be accomplished relatively easily. Another advantage of a matrix structure is that it facilitates the use of specialized personnel, equipment, and facilities. Functional resources are shared in a matrix structure, rather than duplicated as in a divisional structure. Individuals with a high degree of expertise can divide their time as needed among projects, and they in turn develop their own skills and competencies more than in other structures.

A typical matrix structure is illustrated in Figure 10-7. Note that the letters (A through Z4) refer to managers. For example, if you were manager A, you would be responsible for financial aspects of Project 1, and you would have two bosses: the Project 1 Manager on site and the CFO off site.

For a matrix structure to be effective, organizations need participative planning, training, clear mutual understanding of roles and responsibilities, excellent internal communication, and mutual trust and confidence. The matrix structure is being used more frequently by U.S. businesses because firms are pursuing strategies that add new products, customer groups, and technology to their range of activities. Out of these changes are coming product managers, functional managers, and geographic-area managers, all of whom have important strategic responsibilities. When several variables, such as product, customer, technology, geography, functional area, and line of business, have roughly equal strategic priorities, a matrix organization can be an effective structural form.

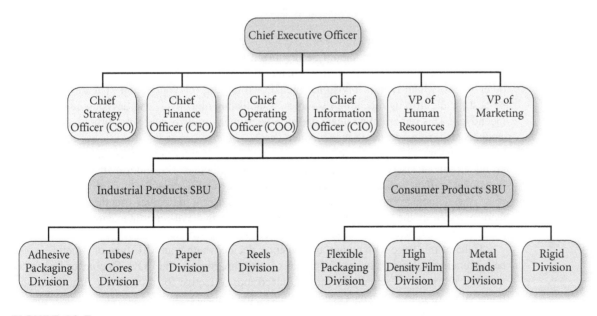

FIGURE 10-7

An Example Matrix Structure

Some Do's and Don'ts in Developing Organizational Charts

Students analyzing strategic-management cases are often asked to revise and develop a firm's organizational structure. This section provides some basic guidelines for this endeavor. There are some basic do's and don'ts in regard to devising or constructing organizational charts, especially for midsize to large firms. First of all, reserve the title CEO for the top executive of the firm. Don't use the title "president" for the top person; use it for the division top managers if there are divisions within the firm. Also, do not use the title "president" for functional business executives. They should have the title "chief," or "vice president," or "manager," or "officer," such as "Chief Information Officer," or "VP of Human Resources." Further, do not recommend a dual title (such as "CEO and president") for just one executive. Do not let a single individual be both chairman of the board, although Pfizer's CEO, Ian Read, is also chairman of the board. And Comverse Technology recently named Charles Burdick its president, chief executive officer, and chairman of the board. Actually, "chairperson" is much better than "chairman" for this title.

A significant movement among corporate America is to split the chairperson of the board and the CEO positions in publicly held companies.[7] The movement includes asking the New York Stock Exchange and Nasdaq to adopt listing rules that would require separate positions. About 50 percent of companies in the S&P 500 stock index have separate positions, up from 22 percent in 2002, but this still leaves plenty of room for improvement. Among European and Asian companies, the split in these two positions is much more common. For example, 79 percent of British companies split the positions, and all German and Dutch companies split the position. South Korea's Samsung Electronics in mid-2013 dissolved its COO position in favor of dual CEO's—but this practice in not common or popular in the USA.

Directly below the CEO, it is best to have a COO (chief operating officer) with any division presidents reporting directly to the COO. On the same level as the COO and also reporting to the CEO, draw in your functional business executives, such as a CFO (chief financial officer), VP of human resources, a CSO (chief strategy officer), a CIO (chief information officer), a CMO (chief marketing officer), a VP of R&D, a VP of legal affairs, an investment relations officer, maintenance officer, and so on. Note in Figure 10-8 that these positions are labeled and placed appropriately. Note that a controller or treasurer would normally report to the CFO.

In developing an organizational chart, avoid having a particular person reporting to more than one person in the chain of command. This would violate the unity-of-command principle of management that "every employee should have just one boss." Also, do not have the CFO, CIO, CSO, human resource officer, or other functional positions report to the COO. All these positions report directly to the CEO.

A key consideration in devising an organizational structure concerns the divisions. Note whether the divisions (if any) of a firm presently are established based on geography, customer, product, or process. If the firm's organizational chart is not available, you often can devise a chart based on the titles of executives. An important case analysis activity is for you to decide how the divisions of a firm should be organized for maximum effectiveness. Even if the firm presently has no divisions, determine whether the firm would operate better with divisions. In other words, which type of divisional breakdown do you (or your group or team) feel would be best for the firm in allocating resources, establishing objectives, and devising compensation incentives? This important strategic decision faces many midsize and large firms (and teams of students analyzing a strategic-management case).

As consumption patterns become more and more similar worldwide, the divisional-by-product form of structure is increasingly the most effective. Be mindful that all firms have functional staff below their top executive and often readily provide this information, so be wary of concluding prematurely that a particular firm uses a functional structure. If you see the word *president* in the titles of executives, coupled with financial-reporting segments, such as by product or geographic region, then the firm is divisionally structured.

If the firm is large with numerous divisions, decide whether an SBU type of structure would be more appropriate to reduce the span of control reporting to the COO. One never knows for sure if a proposed or actual structure is indeed most effective for a particular firm. Declining financial performance signals a need for altering the structure.

Some important guidelines to follow in devising organizational charts for companies are provided in Table 10-10.

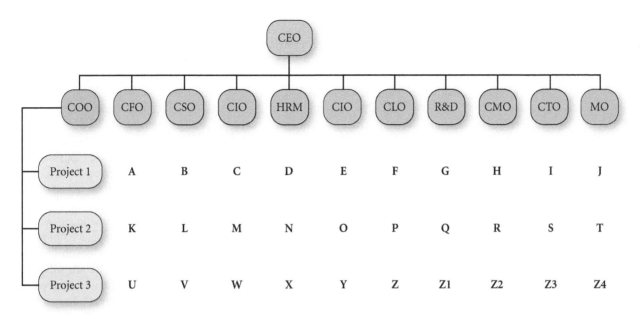

Note: Titles spelled out as follows.

Chief Executive Officer (CEO)
Chief Finance Officer (CFO)
Chief Strategy Officer (CSO)
Chief Information Officer (CIO)
Human Resources Manager (HRM)
Chief Operating Officer (COO)
Chief Legal Officer (CLO)
Research & Development Officer (R&D)
Chief Marketing Officer (CMO)
Chief Technology Officer (CTO)
Competitive Intelligence Officer (CIO)
Maintenance Officer (MO)

FIGURE 10-8

Typical Top Managers of a Large Firm

TABLE 10-10 **Fifteen Guidelines for Developing an Organizational Chart**

1. Instead of chairman of the board, make it chairperson of the board.
2. Make sure the board of directors reveals diversity in race, ethnicity, gender, and age.
3. Make sure the chair of the board is not also the CEO or president of the company.
4. Make sure the CEO of the firm does not also carry the title *president*.
5. Reserve the title *president* for the division heads of the firm.
6. Make sure the firm has a COO.
7. Make sure only presidents of divisions report to the COO.
8. Make sure functional executives such as CFO, CIO, CMO, CSO, R&D, CLO, CTO, and HRM report to the CEO, not the COO.
9. Make sure every executive has one boss, so lines in the chart should be drawn accordingly, assuring unity of command.
10. Make sure span of control is reasonable, probably no more than 10 persons reporting to any other person.
11. Make sure diversity in race, ethnicity, gender, and age is well represented among corporate executives.
12. Avoid a functional type structure for all but the smallest firms.
13. Decentralize, using some form of divisional structure, whenever possible.
14. Use an SBU type structure for large, multidivisional firms.
15. Make sure executive titles match product names as best possible in division-by-product and SBU-designated firms.

Restructuring

Restructuring and reengineering are becoming commonplace on the corporate landscape across the USA and Europe. **Restructuring**—also called **downsizing**, **rightsizing**, or **delayering**—involves reducing the size of the firm in terms of number of employees, number of divisions or units, and number of hierarchical levels in the firm's organizational structure. This reduction in size is intended to improve both efficiency and effectiveness. Restructuring is concerned primarily with shareholder well-being rather than employee well-being.

The lingering recession in Europe has forced many companies there to downsize, laying off managers and employees. This practice was historically rare in Europe because labor unions and laws required lengthy negotiations or huge severance checks before workers could be terminated. In contrast to the USA, labor union executives of large European firms sit on most boards of directors.

Job security in European companies is slowly moving toward a U.S. scenario, in which firms lay off almost at will. From banks in Milan to factories in Mannheim, European employers are starting to show people the door in an effort to streamline operations, increase efficiency, and compete against already slim and trim U.S. firms. Massive U.S.-style layoffs are still rare in Europe, but unemployment rates throughout the continent are rising quite rapidly. European firms still prefer to downsize by attrition and retirement rather than by blanket layoffs because of culture, laws, and unions.

In contrast, reengineering is concerned more with employee and customer well-being than shareholder well-being. **Reengineering**—also called *process management*, *process innovation*, or *process redesign*—involves reconfiguring or redesigning work, jobs, and processes for the purpose of improving cost, quality, service, and speed. Reengineering does not usually affect the organizational structure or chart, nor does it imply job loss or employee layoffs. Whereas restructuring is concerned with eliminating or establishing, shrinking or enlarging, and moving organizational departments and divisions, the focus of reengineering is changing the way work is actually carried out. Reengineering is characterized by many tactical (short-term, business-function-specific) decisions, whereas restructuring is characterized by strategic (long-term, affecting all business functions) decisions.

Developed by Motorola in 1986 and made famous by CEO Jack Welch at General Electric and more recently by Robert Nardelli, former CEO of Home Depot, **Six Sigma** is a quality-boosting process improvement technique that entails training several key persons in the firm in the techniques to monitor, measure, and improve processes and eliminate defects. Six Sigma has been widely applied across industries from retailing to financial services. CEO Dave Cote at Honeywell and CEO Jeff Immelt at General Electric spurred acceptance of Six Sigma, which aims to improve work processes and eliminate waste by training "select" employees who are given judo titles such as Master Black Belts, Black Belts, and Green Belts. Target Corp. claims more than $100 million in savings over the past six years resulting from its Six Sigma program.

Six Sigma was criticized in a *Wall Street Journal* article that cited many example firms whose stock price fell for a number of years after adoption of Six Sigma. The technique's reliance on the special group of trained employees is problematic and its use within retail firms such as Home Depot has not been as successful as in manufacturing firms.[8]

Restructuring

Firms often employ restructuring when various ratios appear out of line with competitors as determined through benchmarking exercises. Recall that **benchmarking** simply involves comparing a firm against the best firms in the industry on a wide variety of performance-related criteria. Some benchmarking ratios commonly used in rationalizing the need for restructuring are headcount-to-sales-volume, or corporate-staff-to-operating-employees, or span-of-control figures.

The primary benefit sought from restructuring is cost reduction. For some highly bureaucratic firms, restructuring can actually rescue the firm from global competition and demise. But the downside of restructuring can be reduced employee commitment, creativity, and innovation that accompanies the uncertainty and trauma associated with pending and actual employee layoffs. Avon Products recently restructured partly as a result of corruption investigations in its

Russia and Brazil operations. The company reduced its six commercial business units down to two—(1) Developed Markets and (2) Developing Markets—in essence going to a divisional by geographic region type structure. Avon has been reporting lower sales and profits amid missteps in key markets. Former CEO Andrea Jung installed five new regional heads and new presidents in Avon's U.S. and Russia markets.

Employers today are looking for people who can do things, not for people who make other people do things. Restructuring in many firms has made a manager's job an invisible, thankless role. More workers today are self-managed, entrepreneurs, interpreneurs, or team-managed. Managers today need to be counselors, motivators, financial advisors, and psychologists. They also run the risk of becoming technologically behind in their areas of expertise. "Dilbert" cartoons sometimes portray managers as enemies or as morons.

Linking Performance and Pay to Strategies

With so many people out of work and executive salaries so large, politicians are more and more giving shareholders greater control over executive pay. The Dodd-Frank Wall Street Reform and Consumer Protection Act grants shareholders advisory votes on compensation. A recent *Bloomberg Businessweek* article says companies should install five policies to improve their compensation practices:

1. Provide full transparency to all stakeholders. Novartis does an excellent job on this.
2. Reward long-term performance with long-term pay, rather than annual incentives. ExxonMobil does an excellent job on this.
3. Base executive compensation on actual company performance, rather than on stock price. Target, for example, bases executive pay on same-store sales growth rather than stock price.
4. Extend the time-horizon for bonuses. Replace short-term with long-term incentives. Goldman Sachs does an excellent job on this.
5. Increase equity between workers and executives. Delete many special perks and benefits for executives. Be more consistent across levels, although employees with greater responsibility must receive greater compensation.[10]

As firms acquire other firms in other countries, these pay differences can cause resentment and even turmoil. Larger pay packages of U.S. CEOs are socially less acceptable in many other countries. For example, in Japan, seniority rather than performance is the key factor in determining pay, and harmony among managers is emphasized over individual excellence.

How can an organization's reward system be more closely linked to strategic performance? How can decisions on salary increases, promotions, merit pay, and bonuses be more closely aligned to support the long-term strategic objectives of the organization? There are no widely accepted answers to these questions, but a dual bonus system based on both annual objectives and long-term objectives is becoming common. The percentage of a manager's annual bonus attributable to short-term versus long-term results should vary by hierarchical level in the organization. It is important that bonuses not be based solely on short-term results because such a system ignores long-term company strategies and objectives.

Many companies have recently instituted policies to allow their shareholders to vote on executive compensation policies. Aflac was the first U.S. corporation to voluntarily give shareholders an advisory vote on executive compensation. Aflac did this back in 2007. Apple did this in 2008, as did H&R Block. Several companies that instituted say-on-pay policies more recently were Ingersoll-Rand, Verizon, Motorola, Occidental Petroleum, and Hewlett-Packard. These new policies underscore how the financial crisis and shareholder outrage about top executive pay has affected compensation practice. None of the shareholder votes are binding on the companies, however, at least not so far. The U.S. House of Representatives recently passed a bill to formalize this shareholder tactic, which is gaining steam across the country as a means to combat exorbitant executive pay.

In an effort to cut costs and increase productivity, more and more Japanese companies are switching from seniority-based pay to performance-based approaches. Toyota has switched to a full merit system for 20,000 of its 70,000 white-collar workers. Fujitsu, Sony, Matsushita

Electric Industrial, and Kao also have switched to merit pay systems. This switching is hurting morale at some Japanese companies, which have trained workers for decades to cooperate rather than to compete and to work in groups rather than individually.

Richard Brown, CEO of Electronic Data Systems (EDS), once said,

> You have to start with an appraisal system that gives genuine feedback and differentiates performance. Some call it ranking people. That seems a little harsh. But you can't have a manager checking a box that says you're either stupendous, magnificent, very good, good, or average. Concise, constructive feedback is the fuel workers use to get better. A company that doesn't differentiate performance risks losing its best people.[11]

Profit sharing is another widely used form of incentive compensation. More than 30 percent of U.S. companies have profit-sharing plans, but critics emphasize that too many factors affect profits for this to be a good criterion. Taxes, pricing, or an acquisition would wipe out profits, for example. Also, firms try to minimize profits in a sense to reduce taxes.

For employee (rather than executive) bonuses and incentives, only 16 percent of U.S. companies are now using stock price, down from 29 percent in 2009.[12] Instead, companies are using profit in order to more closely link employees' incentives to spending and budget decisions. PepsiCo, for example, recently began using profit and cash flow instead of stock price to focus managers on profit and cash-flow targets. PepsiCo's CFO, Hugh Johnston, said: "The change allows our employees to make decisions about spending and profit trade-offs themselves, rather than simply being handed a budget to follow; it's something they can wrap their arms around and say, 'Now I understand how I can impact PepsiCo's stock price.'" PepsiCo's new compensation system based on profit enabled the company to lower its capital spending to 4.5 percent of sales in 2012, down from an historical average of about 5.5 percent. For upper-level executives, stock price is still the major variable used for compensation incentives, but for mid-and-lower level managers and employees, stock price is dependent on too many extraneous variables for it to be an effective compensation variable.

The good news for shareholders is that in 2013, over 50 percent of CEO compensation was directly associated with the performance of the firm, rather than salary—up from 35 percent in 2009 (*WSJ*, 3-21-13, p. B1). Note below that Indra Nooyi of PepsiCo was the third highest paid women CEO in 2012 in the USA:

1. Irene Rosenfeld at Kraft ($21.9M)
2. Debra Cafaro at Ventas ($18.5M)
3. Indra Nooyi at PepsiCo ($17.1M)
4. Meg Whitman at HP ($16.5M)
5. Ellen Kullman at DuPont ($15.9M)
6. Angela Braly at WellPoint ($13.3M)

Still another criterion widely used to link performance and pay to strategies is gain sharing. **Gain sharing** requires employees or departments to establish performance targets; if actual results exceed objectives, all members get bonuses. More than 26 percent of U.S. companies use some form of gain sharing; about 75 percent of gain-sharing plans have been adopted since 1980. Carrier, a subsidiary of United Technologies, has had excellent success with gain sharing in its six plants in Syracuse, New York; Firestone's tire plant in Wilson, North Carolina, has experienced similar success with gain sharing.

Criteria such as sales, profit, production efficiency, quality, and safety could also serve as bases for an effective **bonus system**. If an organization meets certain understood, agreed-on profit objectives, every member of the enterprise should share in the harvest. A bonus system can be an effective tool for motivating individuals to support strategy-implementation efforts. BankAmerica, for example, recently overhauled its incentive system to link pay to sales of the bank's most profitable products and services. Branch managers receive a base salary plus a bonus based both on the number of new customers and on sales of bank products. Every employee in each branch is also eligible for a bonus if the branch exceeds its goals. Thomas Peterson, a top BankAmerica executive, says, "We want to make people responsible for meeting their goals, so we pay incentives on sales, not on controlling costs or on being sure the parking lot is swept."

Five tests are often used to determine whether a performance-pay plan will benefit an organization:

1. ***Does the plan capture attention?*** Are people talking more about their activities and taking pride in early successes under the plan?
2. ***Do employees understand the plan?*** Can participants explain how it works and what they need to do to earn the incentive?
3. ***Is the plan improving communication?*** Do employees know more than they used to about the company's mission, plans, and objectives?
4. ***Does the plan pay out when it should?*** Are incentives being paid for desired results—and being withheld when objectives are not met?
5. ***Is the company or unit performing better?*** Are profits up? Has market share grown? Have gains resulted in part from the incentives?[13]

In addition to a dual bonus system, a combination of reward strategy incentives, such as salary raises, stock options, fringe benefits, promotions, praise, recognition, criticism, fear, increased job autonomy, and awards, can be used to encourage managers and employees to push hard for successful strategic implementation. The range of options for getting people, departments, and divisions to actively support strategy-implementation activities in a particular organization is almost limitless. Merck, for example, recently gave each of its 37,000 employees a 10-year option to buy 100 shares of Merck stock at a set price of $127. Steven Darien, Merck's vice president of human resources, says, "We needed to find ways to get everyone in the workforce on board in terms of our goals and objectives. Company executives will begin meeting with all Merck workers to explore ways in which employees can contribute more."

Managing Resistance to Change

No organization or individual can escape change. But the thought of change raises anxieties because people fear economic loss, inconvenience, uncertainty, and a break in normal social patterns. Almost any change in structure, technology, people, or strategies has the potential to disrupt comfortable interaction patterns. For this reason, people resist change. The strategic-management process itself can impose major changes on individuals and processes. Reorienting an organization to get people to think and act strategically is not an easy task.

Resistance to change can be considered the single greatest threat to successful strategy implementation. Resistance regularly occurs in organizations in the form of sabotaging production machines, absenteeism, filing unfounded grievances, and an unwillingness to cooperate. People often resist strategy implementation because they do not understand what is happening or why changes are taking place. In that case, employees may simply need accurate information. Successful strategy implementation hinges on managers' ability to develop an organizational climate conducive to change. Change must be viewed as an opportunity rather than as a threat by managers and employees.

Resistance to change can emerge at any stage or level of the strategy-implementation process. Although there are various approaches for implementing changes, three commonly used strategies are a force change strategy, an educative change strategy, and a rational or self-interest change strategy. A **force change strategy** involves giving orders and enforcing those orders; this strategy has the advantage of being fast, but it is plagued by low commitment and high resistance. The **educative change strategy** is one that presents information to convince people of the need for change; the disadvantage of an educative change strategy is that implementation becomes slow and difficult. However, this type of strategy evokes greater commitment and less resistance than does the force change strategy. Finally, a **rational change strategy** or **self-interest change strategy** is one that attempts to convince individuals that the change is to their personal advantage. When this appeal is successful, strategy implementation can be relatively easy. However, implementation changes are seldom to everyone's advantage.

The rational change strategy is the most desirable, so this approach is examined a bit further. Managers can improve the likelihood of successfully implementing change by carefully designing change efforts. Jack Duncan described a rational or self-interest change strategy as consisting of four steps. First, employees are invited to participate in the process of change and in the details of transition; participation allows everyone to give opinions, to feel a part of the change process, and to identify their own self-interests regarding the recommended change. Second, some motivation or incentive to change is required; self-interest can be the most important motivator. Third, communication is needed so that people can understand the purpose for the changes. Giving and receiving feedback is the fourth step: everyone enjoys knowing how things are going and how much progress is being made.[14]

Because of diverse external and internal forces, change is a fact of life in organizations. The rate, speed, magnitude, and direction of changes vary over time by industry and organization. Strategists should strive to create a work environment in which change is recognized as necessary and beneficial so that individuals can more easily adapt to change. Adopting a strategic-management approach to decision making can itself require major changes in the philosophy and operations of a firm.

Strategists can take a number of positive actions to minimize managers' and employees' resistance to change. For example, individuals who will be affected by a change should be involved in the decision to make the change and in decisions about how to implement the change. Strategists should anticipate changes and develop and offer training and development workshops so that managers and employees can adapt to those changes. They also need to effectively communicate the need for changes. The strategic-management process can be described as a process of managing change.

Organizational change should be viewed today as a continuous process rather than as a project or event. The most successful organizations today continuously adapt to changes in the competitive environment, which themselves continue to change at an accelerating rate. It is not sufficient today to simply react to change. Managers need to anticipate change and ideally be the creator of change. Viewing change as a continuous process is in stark contrast to an old management doctrine regarding change, which was to unfreeze behavior, change the behavior, and then refreeze the new behavior. The new "continuous organizational change" philosophy should mirror the popular "continuous quality improvement philosophy."

Creating a Strategy-Supportive Culture

Strategists should strive to preserve, emphasize, and build on aspects of an existing **culture** that support proposed new strategies. Aspects of an existing culture that are antagonistic to a proposed strategy should be identified and changed. Substantial research indicates that new strategies are often market-driven and dictated by competitive forces. For this reason, changing a firm's culture to fit a new strategy is usually more effective than changing a strategy to fit an existing culture. As indicated in Table 10-11, numerous techniques are available to alter

TABLE 10-11 Ways and Means for Altering an Organization's Culture

1. Recruitment
2. Training
3. Transfer
4. Promotion
5. Restructuring
6. Reengineering
7. Role modeling
8. Positive reinforcement
9. Mentoring
10. Revising vision and/or mission
11. Redesigning physical spaces/facades
12. Altering reward system
13. Altering organizational policies, procedures, and practices

an organization's culture, including recruitment, training, transfer, promotion, restructure of an organization's design, role modeling, positive reinforcement, and mentoring.

Schein indicated that the following elements are most useful in linking culture to strategy:

1. Formal statements of organizational philosophy, charters, creeds, materials used for recruitment and selection, and socialization
2. Designing of physical spaces, facades, and buildings
3. Deliberate role modeling, teaching, and coaching by leaders
4. Explicit reward and status system and promotion criteria
5. Stories, legends, myths, and parables about key people and events
6. What leaders pay attention to, measure, and control
7. Leader reactions to critical incidents and organizational crises
8. How the organization is designed and structured
9. Organizational systems and procedures
10. Criteria used for recruitment, selection, promotion, leveling off, retirement, and "excommunication" of people[15]

When Volkswagen AG acquired Porsche in late 2012, there was concern that the 75-year-old Volkswagen Chairman and patriarch, Ferdinand Piech's autocratic style would be at odds with Porsche's corporate culture. Porsche had for a long time placed a premium on individual effort among its engineers and designers, often encouraging competition among groups to come up with new design ideas and innovations. Time will tell if Volkswagen and Porsche can meld their cultures into a competitive advantage.

In the personal and religious side of life, the impact of loss and change is easy to see.[16] Memories of loss and change often haunt individuals and organizations for years. Ibsen wrote, "Rob the average man of his life illusion and you rob him of his happiness at the same stroke."[17] When attachments to a culture are severed in an organization's attempt to change direction, employees and managers often experience deep feelings of grief. This phenomenon commonly occurs when external conditions dictate the need for a new strategy. Managers and employees often struggle to find meaning in a situation that changed many years before. Some people find comfort in memories; others find solace in the present. Weak linkages between strategic management and organizational culture can jeopardize performance and success. Deal and Kennedy emphasized that making strategic changes in an organization always threatens a culture:

> People form strong attachments to heroes, legends, the rituals of daily life, the hoopla of extravaganza and ceremonies, and all the symbols of the workplace. Change strips relationships and leaves employees confused, insecure, and often angry. Unless something can be done to provide support for transitions from old to new, the force of a culture can neutralize and emasculate strategy changes.[18]

Production and Operations Concerns When Implementing Strategies

Apple employs thousands of its own workers in China, but about 700,000 assembly workers at manufacturing contractors like Foxconn put together Apple products. It would be almost impossible to bring those jobs to the USA for at least three reasons. First of all, Foxconn—China's largest private employer and the manufacturer of an estimated 40 percent of the world's consumer electronic devices—pays its assembly workers far less than U.S. labor laws would allow. A typical salary is about $18 a day. Secondly, unlike U.S. plants, Foxconn and other Chinese manufacturing operations house employees in dormitories and can send hundreds of thousands of workers to the assembly lines at a moment's notice. On the lines, workers are subjected to what most Americans would consider unbearable long hours and tough working conditions. That system gives tech companies the efficiency needed to race products out the door, so speed is a bigger factor than pay. Finally, most of the component suppliers for Apple and other technology giants are also

TABLE 10-12 Production Management and Strategy Implementation

Type of Organization	Strategy Being Implemented	Production System Adjustments
Hospital	Adding a cancer center (Product Development)	Purchase specialized equipment and add specialized people.
Bank	Adding 10 new branches (Market Development)	Perform site location analysis.
Beer brewery	Purchasing a barley farm operation (Backward Integration)	Revise the inventory control system.
Steel manufacturer	Acquiring a fast-food chain (Unrelated Diversification)	Improve the quality control system.
Computer company	Purchasing a retail distribution chain (Forward Integration)	Alter the shipping, packaging, and transportation systems.

in China or other Asian countries. That geographic clustering gives companies the flexibility to change a product design at the last minute and still ship on time.

Production and operations capabilities, limitations, and policies can significantly enhance or inhibit the attainment of objectives. Production processes typically constitute more than 70 percent of a firm's total assets. A major part of the strategy-implementation process takes place at the production site. Production-related decisions on plant size, plant location, product design, choice of equipment, kind of tooling, size of inventory, inventory control, quality control, cost control, use of standards, job specialization, employee training, equipment and resource utilization, shipping and packaging, and technological innovation can have a dramatic impact on the success or failure of strategy-implementation efforts.

Examples of adjustments in production systems that could be required to implement various strategies are provided in Table 10-12 for both for-profit and nonprofit organizations. For instance, note that when a bank formulates and selects a strategy to add 10 new branches, a production-related implementation concern is site location. The largest bicycle company in the USA, Huffy, recently ended its own production of bikes and now contracts out those services to Asian and Mexican manufacturers. Huffy focuses instead on the design, marketing, and distribution of bikes, but it no longer produces bikes itself. The Dayton, Ohio, company closed its plants in Ohio, Missouri, and Mississippi.

Just-in-time (JIT) production approaches have withstood the test of time. JIT significantly reduces the costs of implementing strategies. With JIT, parts and materials are delivered to a production site just as they are needed, rather than being stockpiled as a hedge against later deliveries. Harley-Davidson reports that at one plant alone, JIT freed $22 million previously tied up in inventory and greatly reduced reorder lead time.

Factors that should be studied before locating production facilities include the availability of major resources, the prevailing wage rates in the area, transportation costs related to shipping and receiving, the location of major markets, political risks in the area or country, and the availability of trainable employees. Some of these factors explain why many manufacturing operations in China are moving back to Mexico, or to Vietnam, or even back to the USA.

Human Resource Concerns When Implementing Strategies

More and more companies are instituting furloughs to cut costs as an alternative to laying off employees. **Furloughs** are temporary layoffs and even white-collar managers are being given furloughs, once confined to blue-collar workers. A few organizations furloughing professional workers include Gulfstream Aerospace, Media General, Gannett, the University of Maryland, Clemson University, and Spansion. Most companies are still using temporary and part-time workers rather than hiring full-time employees, which suggests that high unemployment rates may be a long-term trend. More and more companies may follow Harley-Davidson's lead

TABLE 10-13 Labor Cost-Saving Tactics

Salary freeze

Hiring freeze

Salary reductions

Reduce employee benefits

Raise employee contribution to health-care premiums

Reduce employee 401(k)/403(b) match

Reduce employee workweek

Mandatory furlough

Voluntary furlough

Hire temporary instead of full-time employees

Hire contract employees instead of full-time employees

Volunteer buyouts (Walt Disney is doing this)

Halt production for three days a week (Toyota Motor is doing this)

Layoffs

Early retirement

Reducing or eliminating bonuses

Source: Based on Dana Mattioli, "Employers Make Cuts Despite Belief Upturn Is Near," *Wall Street Journal*, April 23, 2009, B4.

when that firm signed a new union contract recently that creates a tier of "casual workers" with no benefits and no minimum number of hours, allowing Harley to call up workers only as needed.[20] Table 10-13 lists ways that companies today are reducing labor costs to stay financially sound.

A well-designed strategic-management system can fail if insufficient attention is given to the human resource dimension. Human resource problems that arise when businesses implement strategies can usually be traced to one of three causes: (1) disruption of social and political structures, (2) failure to match individuals' aptitudes with implementation tasks, and (3) inadequate top management support for implementation activities.[21]

Strategy implementation poses a threat to many managers and employees in an organization. New power and status relationships are anticipated and realized. New formal and informal groups' values, beliefs, and priorities may be largely unknown. Managers and employees may become engaged in resistance behavior as their roles, prerogatives, and power in the firm change. Disruption of social and political structures that accompany strategy execution must be anticipated and considered during strategy formulation and managed during strategy implementation.

A concern in matching managers with strategy is that jobs have specific and relatively static responsibilities, although people are dynamic in their personal development. Commonly used methods that match managers with strategies to be implemented include transferring managers, developing leadership workshops, offering career development activities, promotions, job enlargement, and job enrichment.

A number of other guidelines can help ensure that human relationships facilitate rather than disrupt strategy-implementation efforts. Specifically, managers should do a lot of chatting and informal questioning to stay abreast of how things are progressing and to know when to intervene. Managers can build support for strategy-implementation efforts by giving few orders, announcing few decisions, depending heavily on informal questioning, and seeking to probe and clarify until a consensus emerges. Key thrusts that succeed should be rewarded generously and visibly.

Perhaps the best method for preventing and overcoming human resource problems in strategic management is to actively involve as many managers and employees as possible in the process. Although time consuming, this approach builds understanding, trust, commitment, and ownership and reduces resentment and hostility. The true potential of strategy formulation and implementation resides in people.

Employee Stock Ownership Plans (ESOPs)

An ESOP is a tax-qualified, defined-contribution, employee-benefit plan whereby employees purchase stock of the company through borrowed money or cash contributions. ESOPs empower employees to work as owners; this is a primary reason why the number of ESOPs have grown dramatically to more than 10,000 firms covering more than 14 million employees. ESOPs now control more than $600 billion in corporate stock in the USA.

Some ESOP companies include:

- W. L. Gore & Associates—maker of medical and industrial products as well as Gore-Tex
- Herman Miller—famous for making innovative office furniture
- KCI—a civil engineering firm
- HCSS—a software manufacturer for the heavy construction industry

Besides reducing worker alienation and stimulating productivity, ESOPs allow firms other benefits, such as substantial tax savings. Principal, interest, and dividend payments on ESOP-funded debt are tax deductible. Banks lend money to ESOPs at interest rates below prime. This money can be repaid in pretax dollars, lowering the debt service as much as 30 percent in some cases. "The ownership culture really makes a difference, when management is a facilitator, not a dictator," says Corey Rosen, executive director of the National Center for Employee Ownership. Fifteen employee-owned companies are listed in Table 10-14.

If an ESOP owns more than 50 percent of the firm, those who lend money to the ESOP are taxed on only 50 percent of the income received on the loans. ESOPs are not for every firm, however, because the initial legal, accounting, actuarial, and appraisal fees to set up an ESOP are about $50,000 for a small or midsized firm, with annual administration expenses of about $15,000. Analysts say ESOPs also do not work well in firms that have fluctuating payrolls and profits. Human resource managers in many firms conduct preliminary research to determine the desirability of an ESOP, and then they facilitate its establishment and administration if benefits outweigh the costs.

Wyatt Cafeterias, a southwestern U.S. operator of 120 cafeterias, also adopted the ESOP concept to prevent a hostile takeover. Employee productivity at Wyatt greatly increased since the ESOP began, as illustrated in the following quote:

The key employee in our entire organization is the person serving the customer on the cafeteria line. We now tell the tea cart server, "Don't wait for the manager to tell you how to do your job better or how to provide better service. You take care of it." Sure,

TABLE 10-14 Fourteen Example ESOP Firms

Firm	Headquarters Location
Publix Supermarkets	Florida
Tribune Company	Illinois
Lifetouch	Minnesota
John Lewis Partnership	United Kingdom
Mondragon Cooperative	Spain
Houchens Industries	Kentucky
Amsted Industries	Illinois
Mast General Store	North Carolina
HDR, Inc.	Nebraska
Yoke's Fresh Market	Washington
SPARTA, Inc.	California
Hy-Vee	Iowa
Bi-Mart	Washington
Ferrellgas Partners	Kansas

we're looking for productivity increases, but since we began pushing decisions down to the level of people who deal directly with customers, we've discovered an awesome side effect—suddenly the work crews have this "happy to be here" attitude that the customers really love.[22]

Balancing Work Life and Home Life

More women earn both undergraduate and graduate degrees in the USA than men, but a wage disparity still persists between men and women at all education levels.[23] Women on average make 25 percent less than men. The average age today for women to get married in the USA is 30 for those with a college degree, and 26 for those with just a high school degree. About 29 percent of both men and women in the USA today have a college degree, whereas in 1970 only 8 percent of women and 14 percent of men had college degrees.

A recent article in *Wall Street Journal* (12-5-12, A3) revealed that in the USA, women now hold 33.4 percent of legal jobs, including lawyers, judges, magistrates, and other judicial employees, up from 29.2 percent in 2000. Also, the percentage of women physicians and surgeons rose to 32.4 percent from 26.8 percent during that time. This is great news; however, the bad news is that the median salary for women lawyers is $90,000 versus $122,000 for men, and the median salary for female physicians is $112,128 versus $186,916 for men.

Globally, it is widely acknowledged that the best countries for working women are Norway, Sweden, Finland, and Denmark—that often rate above the USA. According to the World Economic Forum's 2012 report on the global gender gap overall, the USA ranked number 22 overall, and on wage equality, the USA ranked number 61 behind Madagascar, Cambodia, and Guyana. In that report, women in the USA make on average 67 percent of what men make, compared, for example, to 73 percent in Canada. Unmarried women in fact make more than men in many countries. Married women with children, however, usually make considerably lower than men.

Work and family strategies have become so popular among companies today that the strategies now represent a competitive advantage for those firms that offer such benefits as elder care assistance, flexible scheduling, job sharing, adoption benefits, an on-site summer camp, employee help lines, pet care, and even lawn service referrals. New corporate titles such as work and life coordinator and director of diversity are becoming common.

Working Mother magazine annually published its listing of "The 100 Best Companies for Working Mothers" (www.workingmother.com). Three especially important variables used in the ranking were availability of flextime, advancement opportunities, and equitable distribution of benefits among companies. Other important criteria are compressed weeks, telecommuting, job sharing, childcare facilities, maternity leave for both parents, mentoring, career development, and promotion for women. *Working Mother's* top 10 best companies for working women in 2012 are provided in Table 10-15. *Working Mother* also conducts extensive research to determine the best U.S. firms for women of color.

A corporate objective to become more lean and mean must today include consideration for the fact that a good home life contributes immensely to a good work life. The work and family issue is no longer just a women's issue. Some specific measures that firms are taking to address this issue are providing spouse relocation assistance as an employee benefit; providing company resources for family recreational and educational use; establishing employee country clubs, such as those at IBM and Bethlehem Steel; and creating family and work interaction opportunities. A study by Joseph Pleck of Wheaton College found that in companies that do not offer paternity leave for fathers as a benefit, most men take short, informal paternity leaves anyway by combining vacation time and sick days.

Some organizations have developed family days, when family members are invited into the workplace, taken on plant or office tours, dined by management, and given a chance to see exactly what other family members do each day. Family days are inexpensive and increase the employee's pride in working for the organization. Flexible working hours during the week are another human resource response to the need for individuals to balance work life and home life. The work and family topic is being made part of the agenda at meetings and thus is being discussed in many organizations.

TABLE 10-15 Top Ten Companies for Working Women

1. Bank of America—allows employees to define how they work.
2. Deloitte—grants employees four unpaid weeks off annually.
3. Ernst & Young (E&Y)—up to 75 percent of its employees work outside E&Y offices. Breastfeeding moms may rely on lactation rooms at most sites.
4. General Mills—women head five of the seven U.S. retail divisions.
5. Grant Thornton—offers 8 weeks of paid maternity leave and numerous flexible work options.
6. IBM—offers outstanding assistance to children of employees through its Special Care for Children program.
7. KPMG—employees may take 26 (job guaranteed, partially paid) weeks off following the birth or adoption of a child.
8. Procter & Gamble (P&G)—all P&G office employees may adjust the times that they start or finish work by two hours either way; 47 percent of all P&G hires in 2011 were women. Breastfeeding moms may rely on lactation rooms at most sites.
9. PricewaterhouseCoopers—many female partners go through the Breakthrough Leadership Development Program and achieve top executive positions.
10. WellStar Health System—has an in-house concierge service to help moms get things done.

Source: Based on 2012: http://www.workingmother.com/best-company-list/129110/7271.

There is great room for improvement in removing the glass ceiling domestically, especially considering that women make up 47 percent of the U.S. labor force. **Glass ceiling** refers to the invisible barrier in many firms that bars women and minorities from top-level management positions. The USA is a leader globally in promoting women and minorities into mid- and top-level managerial positions in business. Only 4.0 percent of Fortune 500 firms have a woman CEO. Table 10-16 gives the 21 Fortune 500 Women CEOs in 2013. These women are wonderful role models for women around the world.

TABLE 10-16 Fortune 500 Women CEOs in 2013

CEO	Company
Angela Braly	WellPoint
Patricia Woertz	Archer Daniels Midland
Marissa Mayer	Yahoo!
Indra Nooyi	PepsiCo
Irene Rosenfeld	Kraft Foods
Carol Meyrowitz	TJX
Virginia Rometty	IBM
Debra Reed	Sempra Energy
Deanna Mulligan	Guardian Life Insurance
Sherilyn McCoy	Avon Products
Denise Morrison	Campbell Soup
Maggie Wilderotter	Frontier Communications
Meg Whitman	Hewlett-Packard
Ilene Gordon	Corn Products
Heather Bresch	Mylan
Gracia Martore	Gannett
Ellen Kullman	DuPont
Ursula Burns	Xerox
Kathleen Mazzarella	Graybar Electric
Beth Mooney	Key Corp
Marillyn Hewson	Lockheed Martin Corp

Benefits of a Diverse Workforce

CEO Rosalind Brewer, the first African American and first woman to lead a Walmart business unit, is turning Walmart's SAM's Club into a $100 billion business. After taking over of SAM'S in 2012, Brewer says SAM's is raising membership fees, building stores in metropolitan areas instead of rural towns, adding brands like Eddie Bauer, Nautica, and Lucky Brand Jeans that differential SAM's from Walmart and other discount retailers. Brewer is also opening SAM's stores earlier to capture small businesspersons who buy the morning of their day's business. CEO Brewer is doing a great job trying to gain ground on Costco Wholesale, which logged nearly double the sales of SAM's Club in 2012.

In late 2012, when CEO Chris Kubasik at Lockheed Martin was fired for having an "improper" relationship with a fellow employee, a long-time Lockheed Martin female executive, Marillyn Hewson, was appointed as the company's new CEO. Three of the six largest Pentagon contractors now have female CEO's. Lockheed Martin is the world's largest defense contractor.

Advertising agencies are an example industry transitioning from being specialist Hispanic, African American, and Asian agencies to becoming multicultural, generalist agencies. Leading executives of culturally specialized agencies are defecting in large numbers to generalist agencies as companies increasingly embrace multicultural marketing using multicultural ad agencies. Companies such as Burger King are shifting their Hispanic and African American ad agencies to generalist firms such as Crispin. Church's Chicken says pooling everything at a generalist agency helps reinforce the multicultural component of its overall market strategy.[24]

In Latin and South America, the number of women in high office has increased dramatically in recent years. Brazil recently elected its first woman president, Dilma Rouseff. Both Argentina and Chile already have a woman president, Cristina Kirchner and Michelle Bachelet, respectively. Regarding the percent of national congressional seats held by women, Argentina has 38.3 percent followed by Honduras with 23.4 percent, as compared to Europe with 20.0 percent, Nordic countries at 41.6 percent, and Arab states at 11.1 percent.[25] Women now make up 53 percent of the work force in Latin and South America.

A recent study by McKinsey & Co. in Asia revealed that Asian companies' average return on equity improves from 15 percent to 22 percent when more and more women hold high-level positions.[26] Wang Jin at McKinsey says: "Women tend to be stronger in terms of collaboration and people development, while men tend to be stronger in individual decision making. By having more women at the senior level, companies are helping to improve organizational health as well as financial performance."[27] The percentage of women on corporate boards in Australia increased from 8.3 in 2010 to 14 percent in 2012.[28] Malaysia and South Korea are also making excellent progress integrating women into upper levels of management and subsidizing companies that build child-care facilities and help women juggle work and family life. In contrast, women in India still are expected to care for their family and extended family; also in India women often unfortunately have an abortion if they know their fetus is a girl. Overall in Asia, women comprise only 6 percent of corporate board seats, compared to 17 percent in Europe and 15 percent in the USA.

An organization can perhaps be most effective when its workforce mirrors the diversity of its customers. For global companies, this goal can be optimistic, but it is a worthwhile goal.

Corporate Wellness Programs

Recent articles detail how companies such as Johnson & Johnson (J&J), Lowe's Home-Improvement, the supermarket chain H-E-B, and Healthwise report impressive returns on investment of comprehensive, well-run employee wellness programs, sometimes as high as six to one.[29] A recent study by Fidelity Investments and the National Business Group on Health reports that nearly 90 percent of employers today offer some kind of wellness incentives or prizes to employees who "get healthier," up from 59 percent in 2009. For example, JetBlue Airways offers employees money—$25 for teeth cleanings and $400 for completing an Ironman triathlon, etc. Furniture company, KI, has all its employees divided into four groups based on "healthiness" with the most-healthy people paying $1,000 less on health insurance premiums than the least-healthy employees.

According to the 2013 National Survey of Employer-Sponsored Health Plans, the percentage of large employers (500+ employees) that offer lower health insurance premiums to nonsmokers increased from 9 percent in 2009 to 15 percent in 2012 (*WSJ*, 2-10-R5). In addition, 42 percent of large firms now offer onsite exercise or yoga classes, and 35 percent offer onsite Weight Watchers programs. J&J estimates that wellness programs have cumulatively saved the company $250 million on health-care costs over the past decade. All J&J facilities around the world are tobacco free. At the software firm SAS Institute headquartered in Cary, North Carolina, voluntary turnover of employees has dropped to just 4 percent, largely, the firm says, due to its effective wellness program. On the SAS main campus, 70 percent of employees use the recreation center at least twice a week. SAS is number 3 among *Fortune*'s "100 Best Companies to Work For." At Healthwise, CEO Don Kemper's personal commitment to wellness permeates the entire culture of the firm, from monthly staff meetings to an annual Wellness Day. Lowe's offers employees a monthly $50 discount on medical insurance if they pledge that they and covered dependents will not use any tobacco products.

Chevron is also a model corporate wellness company that sponsors many internal and external wellness activities. Chevron and other companies such as Biltmore that provide exemplary wellness programs think beyond diet and exercise and focus also on stress management by assisting employees with such issues as divorce, serious illness, death and grief recovery, child rearing, and care of aging parents. Biltmore's two-day health fairs twice a year focus on physical, financial, and spiritual wellness. At Lowe's headquarters, an impressive spiral staircase in the lobby makes climbing the stairs more appealing than riding the elevator. Such practices as "providing abundant bicycle racks," "conducting walking meetings," and "offering five minute stress breaks" are becoming common at companies to promote a corporate wellness culture.

Whole Foods Market headquartered in Austin, Texas, is another outstanding corporate wellness company with their employees receiving a 30 percent discount card on all products sold in their stores "if they maintain and document a healthy lifestyle." In addition, Wegman's Food Markets, headquartered in Rochester, New York, is another supermarket chain with an excellent corporate wellness program. More than 11,000 of Wegman's 39,000 employees recently took part in a challenge to eat five cups of fruit and vegetables and walk up to 10,000 steps a day for eight weeks. Wegman recently ranked number 4 among *Fortune*'s "100 Best Companies to Work For."

Firms are striving to lower the accelerating costs of employees' health-care insurance premiums. Many firms such as Scotts Miracle-Gro Company (based in Marysville, Ohio), IBM, and Microsoft are implementing wellness programs, requiring employees to get healthier or pay higher insurance premiums. Employees that do get healthier win bonuses, free trips, and pay lower premiums; nonconforming employees pay higher premiums and receive no "healthy" benefits. Wellness of employees has become a strategic issue for many firms. Most firms require a health examination as a part of an employment application, and healthiness is more and more becoming a hiring factor. Michael Porter, coauthor of *Redefining Health Care*, says, "We have this notion that you can gorge on hot dogs, be in a pie-eating contest, and drink every day, and society will take care of you. We can't afford to let individuals drive up company costs because they're not willing to address their own health problems."

Wellness programs provide counseling to employees and seek lifestyle changes to achieve healthier living. For example, trans fats are a major cause of heart disease. Near elimination of trans fats in one's diet will reduce one's risk for heart attack. Saturated fats are also bad, so one should avoid eating too much red meat and dairy products, which are high in saturated fats. Seven key lifestyle habits listed in Table 10-17 may significantly improve health and longevity. Boston Market recently removed all salt shakers off tables in its 476 restaurants. The company is also reducing salt by 20 percent in its rotisserie chicken, macaroni and cheese, and mashed potatoes. CEO George Michel says Boston Market will reduce salt levels by 15 percent menu-wide by the end of 2014. Pepper shakers remain on tables at Boston Market.

TABLE 10-17 The Key to Staying Healthy, Living to 100, and Being a "Well" Employee

1. Eat nutritiously—eat a variety of fruits and vegetables daily because they have ingredients that the body uses to repair and strengthen itself.
2. Stay hydrated—drink plenty of water to aid the body in eliminating toxins and to enable body organs to function efficiently; the body is mostly water.
3. Get plenty of rest—the body repairs itself during rest, so get at least seven hours of sleep nightly, preferably eight hours.
4. Get plenty of exercise—exercise vigorously at least 30 minutes daily so the body can release toxins and strengthen vital organs.
5. Reduce stress—the body's immune system is weakened when one is under stress, making the body vulnerable to many ailments, so keep stress to a minimum.
6. Do not smoke—smoking kills, no doubt about it anymore.
7. Take vitamin supplements—consult your physician, but because it is difficult for diet alone to supply all the nutrients and vitamins needed, supplements can be helpful in achieving good health and longevity.

Source: Based on Lauren Etter, "Trans Fats: Will They Get Shelved?" *Wall Street Journal*, December 8, 2006, A6; Joel Fuhrman, MD, *Eat to Live* (Boston: Little, Brown, 2003).

Special Note to Students

An integral part of managing a firm is continually and systematically seeking to gain and sustain competitive advantage through effective planning, organizing, motivating, staffing, and controlling. Rival firms engage in these same activities, so emphasize in your strategic-management case analysis how your firm implementing your recommendations will outperform rival firms. Remember to be prescriptive rather than descriptive on every page or slide in your project, meaning to be insightful, forward-looking, and analytical rather than just describing operations. It is easy to *describe* a company but is difficult to *analyze* a company. Strategic-management case analysis is about *analyzing* a company and its industry, uncovering ways and means for the firm to best gain and sustain competitive advantage. So communicate throughout your project how your firm, and especially your recommendations, will lead to improved growth and profitability versus rival firms. Avoid vagueness and generalities throughout your project, as your audience or reader seeks great ideas backed up by great analyses. Be analytical and prescriptive rather than vague and descriptive in highlighting every slide you show an audience.

Conclusion

Successful strategy formulation does not at all guarantee successful strategy implementation. Although inextricably interdependent, strategy formulation and strategy implementation are characteristically different. In a single word, strategy implementation means *change*. It is widely agreed that "the real work begins after strategies are formulated." Successful strategy implementation requires the support of, as well as discipline and hard work, from motivated managers and employees. It is sometimes frightening to think that a single individual can irreparably sabotage strategy-implementation efforts.

Formulating the right strategies is not enough because managers and employees must be motivated to implement those strategies. Management issues considered central to strategy implementation include matching organizational structure with strategy, linking performance and pay to strategies, creating an organizational climate conducive to change, managing political relationships, creating a strategy-supportive culture, adapting production and operations processes, and managing human resources. Establishing annual objectives, devising policies, and allocating resources are central strategy-implementation activities common to all organizations. Depending on the size and type of the organization, other management issues could be equally important to successful strategy implementation.

Key Terms and Concepts

annual objectives (p. 335)

avoidance (p. 339)

benchmarking (p. 350)

bonus system (p. 352)

conflict (p. 339)

confrontation (p. 339)

culture (p. 354)

decentralized structure (p. 342)

defusion (p. 339)

delayering (p. 350)

divisional structure by geographic area, product, customer, or process (p. 342)

downsizing (p. 350)

educative change strategy (p. 353)

employee stock ownership plans (ESOP) (p. 358)

establishing annual objectives (p. 335)

force change strategy (p. 353)

functional structure (p. 341)

furloughs (p. 356)

gain sharing (p. 352)

glass ceiling (p. 360)

horizontal consistency of objectives (p. 335)

just-in-time (JIT) (p. 356)

matrix structure (p. 346)

policy (p. 337)

profit sharing (p. 352)

rational change strategy (p. 353)

reengineering (p. 350)

resistance to change (p. 353)

resource allocation (p. 339)

restructuring (p. 350)

rightsizing (p. 350)

self-interest change strategy (p. 353)

Six Sigma (p. 350)

strategic business unit (SBU) structure (p. 340)

vertical consistency of objectives (p. 335)

Issues for Review and Discussion

10-1. Accenture is a strong firm, globally. What are the three major threats you see that face Accenture in your country?

10-2. In order of importance, list the six management issues you feel are most central to strategy implementation. Briefly explain your answer.

10-3. List the five major benefits of a firm that has clearly defined its annual objectives.

10-4. Which approach to conflict resolution would you use to resolve a disagreement between top-level managers, regarding a firm's strategic plan?

10-5. Illustrate a functional organizational chart.

10-6. Create a diagram for a divisional organizational chart.

10-7. Draw a strategic business unit organizational chart.

10-8. Illustrate a matrix organizational chart.

10-9. List ten "do's and don'ts" regarding development of organizational charts.

10-10. Compare and contrast restructuring and reengineering.

10-11. Describe five ways a firm could link performance and pay, to strategies.

10-12. List, in order of importance, eight ways and means for altering an organization's culture. Explain your answer.

10-13. Why are so many firms today installing corporate wellness programs?

10-14. Discuss how business attitudes towards "balancing work life and home life" vary across three countries that you are familiar with.

10-15. Discuss the glass ceiling in your country versus the United States.

10-16. Discuss ESOPs in your country compared to the United States.

10-17. In order of importance, in your opinion, list six advantages of a matrix organizational structure.

10-18. Determine whether your college or university has a corporate wellness program. Provide examples of policies that could be used to implement such a program.

10-19. Do you think horizontal consistency of objectives is as important as vertical consistency? Explain using an example.

10-20. Define policies. Give four examples of policies for a bank.

10-21. Discuss your preference on each of the trade-off decisions required for strategy implementation. Explain why.

10-22. List three categories or approaches for conflict resolution. Which approach would you use for a salesperson who has had a disagreement with a client, regarding value of a property to be listed for sale?

10-23. In order of importance, list six symptoms of an ineffective organizational structure.

10-24. Explain why the functional organizational structure is the most widely used around the world.

10-25. List the advantages and disadvantages of a functional versus divisional structure.

10-26. How should a firm decide between a divisional-by-product versus divisional-by-geographic region type organizational chart?

10-27. A divisional-structure-by-process organizational chart is quite uncommon. Give two examples of the type of companies where this would be appropriate.

10-28. Illustrate a matrix-type structure for a hospital.

10-29. Compare and contrast restructuring with reengineering.

10-30. Explain why it is so important to link performance and pay to strategies.

10-31. Describe five tests that are often used to determine whether a performance-pay plan will benefit an organization.

10-32. Describe three commonly used strategies to minimize employee resistance to change. Which approach would you most often use? Why?

10-33. Give a hypothetical example of each labor cost-saving tactic listed in the chapter.

10-34. Use the Internet to find five companies in your country, which operate based on an ESOP. Present your list to the class.

10-35. Provide the advantages and disadvantages of a firm operating based on an ESOP.

10-36. Visit www.workingmother.com and find five examples of firms, which are best suited for working mothers, and that have business locations in your city.

10-37. There were only 12 *Fortune* 500 women CEOs in 2009. Conduct an Internet research to identify five companies in your country that have women CEOs. Why are there so few women CEOs?

10-38. List four benefits of having a diverse workforce.

10-39. Explain why corporate wellness programs are becoming increasingly popular.

10-40. Define and give an example of Six Sigma.

10-41. Define a glass ceiling. Provide an example.

10-42. How many divisions would a firm have to have for you to recommend an SBU type structure? Why?

10-43. Explain when a matrix type structure may be the most effective for an organization.

10-44. How would you link compensation of your employees to performance of your business?

MyManagementLab®

Go to **mymanagementlab.com** for the following Assisted-graded writing questions:

10-45. What are the two major disadvantages of an SBU-type organizational structure? What are the two major advantages? At what point in a firm's growth do you feel the advantages offset the disadvantages? Explain.

10-46. Would you recommend a divisional structure by geographic area, product, customer, or process for a medium-sized bank in your local area? Why?

Current Readings

Allio, Michael K. "Strategic Dashboards: Designing and Deploying Them to Improve Implementation." *Strategy and Leadership* 40, no. 5 (2012): 24–31.

Beeson, John, and Anna Marie Valerio. "The Executive Leadership Imperative: A New Perspective on How Companies and Executives Can Accelerate the Development of Women Leaders." *Business Horizons* 55, no. 5 (September 2012): 417–425.

Campbell, Benjamin A. Campbell, Russell Coff, and David Kryscynski. "Rethinking Sustained Competitive Advantage from Human Capital." *The Academy of Management Review 37*, no. 3 (July 2012): 376.

Csaszar, Felipe A. "Organizational Structure as a Determinant of Performance: Evidence from Mutual Funds." *Strategic Management Journal* 33, no. 6 (June 2012): 611–632.

Chng, Daniel Han Ming, Matthew S. Rodgers, Eric Shih, and Xiao-Bing Song. "When does incentive compensation motivate managerial behaviors? An experimental investigation of the fit between incentive compensation, executive core self-evaluation, and firm performance." *Strategic Management Journal* 33, no. 12 (December 2012): 1343–1362.

Davis, Paul J. "A Model for Strategy Implementation and Conflict Resolution in the Franchise Business." *Strategy and Leadership* 40, no. 5 (2012): 32–38.

Denning, Stephen. "Gary Hamel: Managing While Under the Influence of Innovation." *Strategy and Leadership* 40, no. 5 (2012): 12–18.

Dezsö, Cristian L., and David Gaddis Ross. "Does Female Representation in Top Management Improve Firm Performance? A Panel Data Investigation." *Strategic Management Journal* 33, no. 9 (September 2012): 1072–1089.

Fulmer, C. Ashley, and Michele J. Gelfand. "At What Level (and in Whom) We Trust: Trust Across Multiple Organization Levels." *Journal of Management* 38, no. 4 (July 2012): 1167.

Gulati, Ranjay, Phanish Puranam, and Michael Tushman. "Meta-Organization Design: Rethinking Design in Interorganizational and Community Contexts." *Strategic Management Journal* 33, no. 6 (June 2012): 571–586.

Karim, Samina, and Charles Williams. "Structural Knowledge: How Executive Experience with Structural Composition Affects Intrafirm Mobility and Unit Reconfiguration." *Strategic Management Journal* 33, no. 6 (June 2012): 681–709.

Katzenbach, Jon R., Ilona Steffen, and Caroline Kronley. "Cultural Change That Sticks." *Harvard Business Review* (July-August 2012): 110.

King, Eden B., Jeremy F. Dawson, Michael A. West, Veronica L. Gilrane, Chad I. Peddie, and Lucy Bastin. "Why Organizational and Community Diversity Matter: Representativeness and the Emergence of Incivility and Organizational Performance." *The Academy of Management Journal 54*, no. 6 (December 2011): 1103.

Larkin, Ian, Lamar Pierce, and Francesca Gino. "The Psychological Costs of Pay-for-Performance: Implications for the Strategic Compensation of Employees." *Strategic Management Journal* 33, no. 10 (October 2012): 1194–1214.

Lechner, Christoph, and Steven W. Floyd. "Group Influence Activities and the Performance of Strategic Initiatives." *Strategic Management Journal* 33, no. 5 (May 2012): 478–495.

Prats, Julia, Marc Sosna, and S. Ramakrishna Velamuri. "Managing in Different Growth Contexts." *California Management Review* 54, no. 4 (Summer 2012): 118–142.

Puranam, Phanish, Marlo Raveendran, and Thorbjorn Knudsen. "Organization Design: The Epistemic Interdependence Perspective." *The Academy of Management Review 37*, no. 3 (July 2012): 419.

Wulf, Julie. "The Flattened Firm: Not as Advertised." *Inside CMR* 55, no. 1 (Fall 2012): 5.

ASSURANCE OF LEARNING **EXERCISES**

EXERCISE 10A
Developing an Organizational Chart for Accenture plc

Purpose

Accenture is featured in the opening chapter case as a firm that engages in excellent strategic planning. Accenture plc, headquartered in Dublin, Ireland, is the world's largest consulting firm measured by revenues. As of August 2013, the company has approximately 266,000 employees serving clients in more than 120 countries. India is the single largest employee base for Accenture, with the headcount being close to 100,000, compared to about 50,000 in the United States.

This exercise gives you practice developing an organizational chart.

Instructions

Step 1   Visit Accenture's website. Review the company's most recent *Annual Report*. Note the list of top managers of the firm.

Step 2   Develop an organizational chart for Accenture based on the titles of their top executives.

Step 3   Develop a recommended organizational chart for Accenture based on the guidelines presented in Chapter 10.

EXERCISE 10B
Assessing Accenture's Philanthrophy Efforts

Purpose

Accenture recently awarded Quest Alliance India an additional grant of US$623,000 to help Quest provide approximately 3,000 disadvantaged young people with career and workplace skills. The grant brings Accenture's direct support to Quest Alliance India to more than US$950,000 since 2009. This exercise gives you practice comparing a company's philanthrophy efforts vs its major rivals.

Instructions

Step 1   Visit Accenture's website and click on the Citizenship and Values hotlink. Review Accenture's sustainability efforts.

Step 2   Identify Accenture's major competitors.

Step 3   Compare and contrast Accenture's sustainability efforts versus its two major competitors.

EXERCISE 10C
Revising adidas AG's Organizational Chart

Purpose

Developing and altering organizational charts is an important skill for strategists to possess. This exercise can improve your skill in altering an organization's hierarchical structure in response to new strategies being formed.

Instructions

Step 1   Develop an organizational chart for adidas. On a separate sheet of paper, answer the following questions:
1. What type of organizational chart have you illustrated for adidas?
2. What improvements could you recommend for the adidas organizational chart?
Give your reasoning for each suggestion.

Step 2   Now consider the following:
1. What aspects of your adidas chart do you especially like?
2. What type of organizational chart do you believe would best suit adidas? Why?

EXERCISE 10D
Exploring Objectives

Purpose

The purpose of this exercise is to bridge the gap between key topics in Chapter 10 versus what companies are doing in your area with regard to having clearly defined objectives.

Instructions

Do sufficient research to discover five businesses in your local area that have clearly defined objectives. Discuss the nature and role of objectives in these firms.

EXERCISE 10E

Understanding My University's Culture

Purpose

It is something of an art to uncover the basic values and beliefs that are buried deeply in an organization's rich collection of stories, language, heroes, heroines, and rituals. Yet culture can be the most important factor in implementing strategies.

Instructions

Step 1	On a separate sheet of paper, list the following terms: hero/heroine, belief, metaphor, language, value, symbol, story, legend, saga, folktale, myth, ceremony, rite, and ritual.
Step 2	For your college or university, give examples of each term. If necessary, speak with faculty, staff, alumni, administration, or fellow students of the institution to identify examples of each term.
Step 3	Report your findings to the class. Tell the class how you feel regarding cultural products being consciously used to help implement strategies.

Notes

1. Dale McConkey, "Planning in a Changing Environment," *Business Horizons*, September–October 1988, 66.

2. A. G. Bedeian, and W. F. Glueck, *Management*, 3rd ed. (Chicago: The Dryden Press, 1983), 212.

3. Boris Yavitz and William Newman, *Strategy in Action: The Execution, Politics, and Payoff of Business Planning* (New York: The Free Press, 1982), 195.

4. E. H. Schein, "Three Cultures of Management: The Key to Organizational Learning," *Sloan Management Review* 38, 1 (1996): 9–20.

5. S. Ghoshal, and C. A. Bartlett, "Changing the Role of Management: Beyond Structure to Processes." *Harvard Business Review* 73, 1 (1995): 88.

6. Mike Ester, "Coca-Cola Starts a Horse Race for Next CEO," *Wall Street Journal* (July 31, 2012): B1.

7. Joann Lublin, "Chairman-CEO Split Gains Allies," *Wall Street Journal*, March 30, 2009, B4.

8. Karen Richardson, "The 'Six Sigma' Factor for Home Depot," *Wall Street Journal*, January 4, 2007, C3.

9. "Want to Be a Manager? Many People Say No, Calling Job Miserable," *Wall Street Journal*, April 4, 1997, 1;

Stephanie Armour, "Management Loses Its Allure," *USA Today*, October 10, 1997, 1B.

10. Bill George, "Executive Pay: Rebuilding Trust in an Era of Rage," *Bloomberg Businessweek*, September 13–19, 2010, 56.

11. Richard Brown, "Outsider CEO: Inspiring Change with Force and Grace," *USA Today* (July 19, 1999): 3B.

12. Emily Chasan, "Stock Loses Some Sway on Pay," *Wall Street Journal* (October 30, 2012): B4.

13. Yavitz and Newman, 58.

14. Jack Duncan, *Management* (New York: Random House, 1983): 381–390.

15. E. H. Schein, "The Role of the Founder in Creating Organizational Culture," *Organizational Dynamics* (Summer 1983): 13–28.

16. T. Deal and A. Kennedy, "Culture: A New Look Through Old Lenses," *Journal of Applied Behavioral Science* 19, no. 4 (1983): 498–504.

17. H. Ibsen, "The Wild Duck," in O. G. Brochett and L. Brochett (eds.), *Plays for the Theater* (New York: Holt, Rinehart & Winston, 1967); R. Pascale, "The Paradox

of 'Corporate Culture': Reconciling Ourselves to Socialization," *California Management Review* 28, no. 2 (1985): 26, 37–40.

18. T. Deal and A. Kennedy, *Corporate Cultures: The Rites and Rituals of Corporate Life* (Reading, MA: Addison-Wesley, 1982): 256.

19. Robert Stobaugh, and Piero Telesio, "Match Manufacturing Policies and Product Strategy," *Harvard Business Review* 61, no. 2 (March–April 1983): 113.

20. Sudeep Reddy, "Employers Increasingly Rely on Temps, Part-Timers," *Wall Street Journal*, October 11, 2010, A4.

21. R. T. Lenz and Marjorie Lyles, "Managing Human Resource Problems in Strategy Planning Systems," *Journal of Business Strategy* 60, no. 4 (Spring 1986): 58.

22. J. Warren Henry, "ESOPs with Productivity Payoffs," *Journal of Business Strategy* (July–August 1989): 33.

23. Conor Dougherty, "Strides by Women, Still a Wage Gap," *Wall Street Journal*, March 1, 2011, A3. Also, David Jackson and Mimi Hall, "Women Gain in Education and Longevity," *USA Today*, March 2, 2011, 5A.

24. Suzanne Vranica, "Ad Firms Heed Diversity," *Wall Street Journal*, November 29, 2010, B7.

25. Paulo Prada, "Women Ascend in Latin America," *Wall Street Journal*, December 24, 2010, A10.

26. Kathy Chu, "Asian Women Fight Barriers," *Wall Street Journal* (July 2, 2012): B4.

27. Ibid.

28. Ibid.

29. Berry, Leonard L., Ann Mirabito, and William Baun, "What's The Hard Return On Employee Wellness Programs?" *Harvard Business Review*, December 2010, 104–112. Also, Jen Wieczner, "Your Company Wants to Make You Healthy." *Wall Street Journal*, April 9, 2013, R6.

MyManagementLab®

Improve Your Grade!

More than 10 million students improved their results using the Pearson MyLabs.
Visit **mymanagementlab.com** for simulations, tutorials, and end-of-chapter problems.

Strategy Monitoring

CHAPTER OBJECTIVES

After studying this chapter, you should be able to do the following:

1. Describe a practical framework for evaluating strategies.

2. Explain why strategy evaluation is complex, sensitive, and yet essential for organizational success.

3. Discuss the importance of contingency planning in strategy evaluation.

4. Explain the role of auditing in strategy evaluation.

5. Describe and develop a Balanced Scorecard.

6. Discuss three 21st-century challenges in strategic management.

ASSURANCE OF LEARNING EXERCISES

The following exercises are found at the end of this chapter.

EXERCISE 11A Evaluating BHP Billiton's Strategies

EXERCISE 11B Preparing a Strategy-Evaluation Report for adidas AG

EXERCISE 11C Preparing a Balanced Scorecard for adidas AG

EXERCISE 11D Evaluate My University's Strategies

The best formulated and best implemented strategies become obsolete as a firm's external and internal environments change. It is essential, therefore, that strategists systematically review, evaluate, and control the execution of strategies. This chapter presents a framework that can guide managers' efforts to evaluate strategic-management activities, to make sure they are working, and to make timely changes. Guidelines are presented for formulating, implementing, and evaluating strategies. BHP Billiton is an example company that has reinvented itself a number of times by continually evaluating its strategies and taking bold corrective actions to continue growing.

The Nature of Strategy Evaluation

The strategic-management process results in decisions that can have significant, long-lasting consequences. Erroneous strategic decisions can inflict severe penalties and can be exceedingly difficult, if not impossible, to reverse. Most strategists agree, therefore, that strategy evaluation is vital to an organization's well-being; timely evaluations can alert management to problems or potential problems before a situation becomes critical. Strategy evaluation includes three basic activities: (1) examining the underlying bases of a firm's strategy, (2) comparing expected results with actual results, and (3) taking corrective actions to ensure that performance conforms to plans. The strategy-evaluation stage of the strategic-management process is illustrated in Figure 11-1 with white shading.

Adequate and timely feedback is the cornerstone of effective strategy evaluation. Strategy evaluation can be no better than the information on which it is based. Too much pressure from top managers may result in lower managers contriving numbers they think will be satisfactory.

Strategy evaluation can be a complex and sensitive undertaking. Too much emphasis on evaluating strategies may be expensive and counterproductive. No one likes to be evaluated too closely! The more managers attempt to evaluate the behavior of others, the less control they have. Yet too little or no evaluation can create even worse problems. Strategy evaluation is essential to ensure that stated objectives are being achieved.

EXCELLENT STRATEGIC MANAGEMENT SHOWCASED

BHP Billiton

BHP Billiton is a large Australian multinational mining and petroleum company headquartered in Melbourne. BHP has major offices in London. BHP is arguably the world's largest mining company and among the top ten largest companies in the world measured by market capitalization. *Fortune* in 2013 ranked BHP as the 115th largest company in the world and the 20th most profitable. The Melbourne side of the firm is BHP Billiton Limited; the London side is BHP Billiton Plc.

BHP is among the world's top producers of iron ore, coal, aluminum, copper, manganese, nickel, silver, uranium, and potash. BHP also has crude oil and natural gas holdings. BHP may soon divest its diamond assets. BHP recently paid $4.75 billion in cash to Chesapeake Energy for all of the company's shale assets and 487,000 acres (1,970 km²) of mineral rights leases and 420 miles (680 km) of pipeline located in north central Arkansas in the USA. The wells on the mineral leases are producing about 415 million cubic feet of natural gas per day. BHP plans to spend $800 million to $1 billion a year over 10 years to develop the field and triple production.

BHP recently acquired Petrohawk Energy in the USA for $12.1 billion in cash, considerably expanding its shale natural gas resources.

In 2012, BHP ceased operations at its $20 billion Olympic Dam copper and uranium mine expansion project in South Australia, as a result of falling commodity prices and slowing global economic growth. The company just sold its Yeelirrie Uranium Project to Canadian Cameco for about $430 million as part of a broader move to step away from resource expansion in Australia.

In August 2013, BHP announced the vesting outcomes for the five-year long-term incentive plan (LTIP) awards for their top executives. For awards to be granted, BHP had to deliver a total shareholder return (TSR) that exceeded the TSR of a group of peer companies by an average of 5.5 percent per year for five years, or 30.7 percent in total compounded over a five year performance period. For the performance period that ended June 30, 2013, the TSR for peer companies was negative 44.0 percent, compared to BHP's negative 9.4 percent. Thus, BHP top executives received the awards.

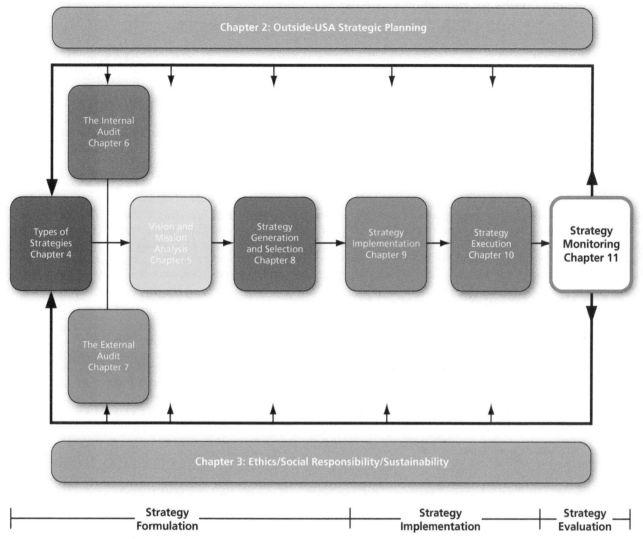

FIGURE 11-1

A Comprehensive Strategic-Management Model

Source: Fred R. David, adapted from "How Companies Define Their Mission," *Long Range Planning* 22, no. 3 (June 1988): 40, © Fred R. David.

In many organizations, strategy evaluation is simply an appraisal of how well an organization has performed. Have the firm's assets increased? Has there been an increase in profitability? Have sales increased? Have productivity levels increased? Have profit margin, return on investment, and earnings-per-share ratios increased? Some firms argue that their strategy must have been correct if the answers to these types of questions are affirmative. Well, the strategy or strategies may have been correct, but this type of reasoning can be misleading because strategy evaluation must have both a long-run and short-run focus. Strategies often do not affect short-term operating results until it is too late to make needed changes.

It is impossible to demonstrate conclusively that a particular strategy is optimal or even to guarantee that it will work. One can, however, evaluate it for critical flaws. Richard Rumelt offered four criteria that could be used to evaluate a strategy: consistency, consonance, feasibility, and advantage. Described in Table 11-1, **consonance** and **advantage** are mostly based on a firm's external assessment, whereas **consistency** and **feasibility** are largely based on an internal assessment.

Strategy evaluation is important because organizations face dynamic environments in which key external and internal factors often change quickly and dramatically. Success today is no guarantee of success tomorrow! Joseph Stalin was a ruthless leader (from 1928 on) and premier

TABLE 11-1 Rumelt's Criteria for Evaluating Strategies

Consistency

A strategy should not present inconsistent goals and policies. Organizational conflict and interdepartmental bickering are often symptoms of managerial disorder, but these problems may also be a sign of strategic inconsistency. Three guidelines help determine if organizational problems are the result of inconsistencies in strategy:

- If managerial problems continue despite changes in personnel and if they tend to be issue-based rather than people-based, then strategies may be inconsistent.
- If success for one organizational department means, or is interpreted to mean, failure for another department, then strategies may be inconsistent.
- If policy problems and issues continue to be brought to the top for resolution, then strategies may be inconsistent.

Consonance

Consonance refers to the need for strategists to examine *sets of trends*, as well as individual trends, in evaluating strategies. A strategy must represent an adaptive response to the external environment and to the critical changes occurring within it. One difficulty in matching a firm's key internal and external factors in the formulation of strategy is that most trends are the result of interactions among other trends. For example, the daycare explosion came about as a combined result of many trends that included a rise in the average level of education, increased inflation, and an increase in women in the workforce. Although single economic or demographic trends might appear steady for many years, there are waves of change going on at the interaction level.

Feasibility

A strategy must neither overtax available resources nor create unsolvable subproblems. The final broad test of strategy is its feasibility; that is, can the strategy be attempted within the physical, human, and financial resources of the enterprise? The financial resources of a business are the easiest to quantify and are normally the first limitation against which strategy is evaluated. It is sometimes forgotten, however, that innovative approaches to financing are often possible. Devices, such as captive subsidiaries, sale-leaseback arrangements, and tying plant mortgages to long-term contracts, have all been used effectively to help win key positions in suddenly expanding industries. A less quantifiable, but actually more rigid, limitation on strategic choice is that imposed by individual and organizational capabilities. In evaluating a strategy, it is important to examine whether an organization has demonstrated in the past that it possesses the abilities, competencies, skills, and talents needed to carry out a given strategy.

Advantage

A strategy must provide for the creation or maintenance of a competitive advantage in a selected area of activity. Competitive advantages normally are the result of superiority in one of three areas: (1) resources, (2) skills, or (3) position. The idea that the positioning of one's resources can enhance their combined effectiveness is familiar to military theorists, chess players, and diplomats. Position can also play a crucial role in an organization's strategy. Once gained, a good position is defensible—meaning that it is so costly to capture that rivals are deterred from full-scale attacks. Positional advantage tends to be self-sustaining as long as the key internal and environmental factors that underlie it remain stable. This is why entrenched firms can be almost impossible to unseat, even if their raw skill levels are only average. Although not all positional advantages are associated with size, it is true that larger organizations tend to operate in markets and use procedures that turn their size into advantage, whereas smaller firms seek product or market positions that exploit other types of advantage. The principal characteristic of good position is that it permits the firm to obtain advantage from policies that would not similarly benefit rivals without the same position. Therefore, in evaluating strategy, organizations should examine the nature of positional advantages associated with a given strategy.

Source: Adapted from Richard Rumelt, "The Evaluation of Business Strategy," in W. F. Glueck (ed.), *Business Policy and Strategic Management* (New York: McGraw-Hill, 1980), 359–367. Used with permission.

(from 1941 on) of the Soviet Union until his death in 1953. A famous quote from Stalin was: *History shows that there are no invincible armies.* This quote reveals that even the mightiest, most successful firms must continually evaluate their strategies and be wary of rival firms. An organization should never be lulled into complacency with success. Countless firms have thrived one year only to struggle for survival the following year. Peter Drucker said: Unless strategy evaluation is performed seriously and systematically, and unless strategists are willing to act on the results, energy will be used up defending yesterday."

Demise can come quickly. For example, the large clothing retailer J.C. Penney, based in Plano, Texas, was profitable and fine, until they hired CEO Ron Johnson in November 2011. Johnson implemented a new strategic plan at Penney's that included doing away with coupons, promotions, and discounting in favor of his "fair and square pricing" policy, building branded boutiques stores-within stores, replacing their chief marketing officer, Michael Francis, with himself, adding more celebrity brands and high-tech features to attract younger customers, exiting from the outlet business, and extensive, expensive remodeling. Johnson envisioned all Penney stores to have tables with iPads for customers to use, and activities for kids such as making greeting cards, and even Pilates and yoga classes within stores.[1] Moody's Investors Service downgraded Penney's long-term debt two notches to Ba3 from Ba1 in August 2012; Penney's is still unprofitable in late 2013.

Another example of quick demise is Hewlett-Packard, which delivered an $8.9 billion loss in its fiscal third quarter of 2012 as the firm's revenue dropped to $29.7 billion. Consumers are flocking in the millions to tablets and away from desktop and laptop computers, crushing HP who had not anticipated such as swift switch in consumer preferences. This consumer trend is also crushing another U.S. icon company, Intel, which reported a 14-percent drop in third-quarter 2012 profits.

Strategy evaluation is becoming increasingly difficult with the passage of time, for many reasons. Domestic and world economies were more stable in years past, product life cycles were longer, product development cycles were longer, technological advancement was slower, change occurred less frequently, there were fewer competitors, foreign companies were weak, and there were more regulated industries. Other reasons why strategy evaluation is more difficult today include the following trends:

1. A dramatic increase in the environment's complexity
2. The increasing difficulty of predicting the future with accuracy
3. The increasing number of variables
4. The rapid rate of obsolescence of even the best plans
5. The increase in the number of both domestic and world events affecting organizations
6. The decreasing time span for which planning can be done with any degree of certainty[2]

A fundamental problem facing managers today is how to control employees effectively in light of modern organizational demands for greater flexibility, innovation, creativity, and initiative from employees.[3] How can managers today ensure that empowered employees acting in an entrepreneurial manner do not put the well-being of the business at risk? The potential costs to companies in terms of damaged reputations, fines, missed opportunities, and diversion of management's attention are enormous.

When empowered employees are held accountable for and pressured to achieve specific goals and are given wide latitude in their actions to achieve them, there can be dysfunctional behavior. For example, Nordstrom, the upscale fashion retailer known for outstanding customer service, was subjected to lawsuits and fines when employees underreported hours worked to increase their sales per hour—the company's primary performance criterion.

The Process of Evaluating Strategies

Strategy evaluation is necessary for all sizes and kinds of organizations. Strategy evaluation should initiate managerial questioning of expectations and assumptions, should trigger a review of objectives and values, and should stimulate creativity in generating alternatives and formulating criteria of evaluation.[4] Regardless of the size of the organization, a certain amount of **management by wandering around** at all levels is essential to effective strategy evaluation. Strategy-evaluation activities should be performed on a continuing basis, rather than at the end of specified periods of time or just after problems occur. Waiting until the end of the year, for example, could result in a firm *closing the barn door after the horses have already escaped.*

Evaluating strategies on a continuous rather than on a periodic basis allows benchmarks of progress to be established and more effectively monitored. Some strategies take years to implement; consequently, associated results may not become apparent for years. Successful strategies combine patience with a willingness to promptly take corrective actions when necessary. There always comes a time when corrective actions are needed in an organization! Centuries ago, a writer (perhaps Solomon) made the following observations about change:

There is a time for everything,

A time to be born and a time to die,

A time to plant and a time to uproot,

A time to kill and a time to heal,

A time to tear down and a time to build,

> A time to weep and a time to laugh,
>
> A time to mourn and a time to dance,
>
> A time to scatter stones and a time to gather them,
>
> A time to embrace and a time to refrain,
>
> A time to search and a time to give up,
>
> A time to keep and a time to throw away,
>
> A time to tear and a time to mend,
>
> A time to be silent and a time to speak,
>
> A time to love and a time to hate,
>
> A time for war and a time for peace.[5]

Managers and employees of the firm should be continually aware of progress being made toward achieving the firm's objectives. As key success factors change, organizational members should be involved in determining appropriate corrective actions. If assumptions and expectations deviate significantly from forecasts, then the firm should renew strategy-formulation activities, perhaps sooner than planned. In strategy evaluation, like strategy formulation and strategy implementation, people make the difference. Through involvement in the process of evaluating strategies, managers and employees become committed to keeping the firm moving steadily toward achieving objectives.

A Strategy-Evaluation Framework

Table 11-2 summarizes strategy-evaluation activities in terms of key questions that should be addressed, alternative answers to those questions, and appropriate actions for an organization to take. Notice that corrective actions are almost always needed except when (1) external and internal factors have not significantly changed and (2) the firm is progressing satisfactorily toward achieving stated objectives. Relationships among strategy-evaluation activities are illustrated in Figure 11-2.

Reviewing Bases of Strategy

As shown in Figure 11-2, **reviewing the underlying bases of an organization's strategy** could be approached by developing a revised EFE Matrix and IFE Matrix. A **revised IFE Matrix** should focus on changes in the organization's management, marketing, finance and accounting, production and operations, research and development (R&D), and management information systems (MIS) strengths and weaknesses. A **revised EFE Matrix** should indicate how effective

TABLE 11-2 A Strategy-Evaluation Assessment Matrix

Have Major Changes Occurred in the Firm's Internal Strategic Position?	Have Major Changes Occurred in the Firm's External Strategic Position?	Has the Firm Progressed Satisfactorily Toward Achieving Its Stated Objectives?	Result
No	No	No	Take corrective actions
Yes	Yes	Yes	Take corrective actions
Yes	Yes	No	Take corrective actions
Yes	No	Yes	Take corrective actions
Yes	No	No	Take corrective actions
No	Yes	Yes	Take corrective actions
No	Yes	No	Take corrective actions
No	No	Yes	Continue present strategic course

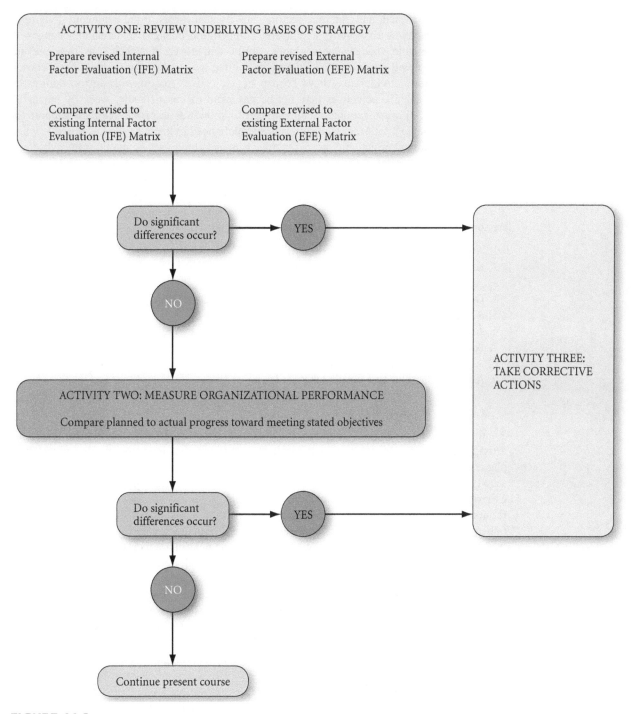

FIGURE 11-2

A Strategy-Evaluation Framework

a firm's strategies have been in response to key opportunities and threats. This analysis could also address such questions as the following:

1. How have competitors reacted to our strategies?
2. How have competitors' strategies changed?
3. Have major competitors' strengths and weaknesses changed?
4. Why are competitors making certain strategic changes?
5. Why are some competitors' strategies more successful than others?
6. How satisfied are our competitors with their present market positions and profitability?
7. How far can our major competitors be pushed before retaliating?
8. How could we more effectively cooperate with our competitors?

Numerous external and internal factors can prevent firms from achieving long-term and annual objectives. Externally, actions by competitors, changes in demand, changes in technology, economic changes, demographic shifts, and governmental actions may prevent objectives from being accomplished. Internally, ineffective strategies may have been chosen or implementation activities may have been poor. Objectives may have been too optimistic. Thus, failure to achieve objectives may not be the result of unsatisfactory work by managers and employees. All organizational members need to know this to encourage their support for strategy-evaluation activities. Organizations desperately need to know as soon as possible when their strategies are not effective. Sometimes managers and employees on the front lines discover this well before strategists.

External opportunities and threats and internal strengths and weaknesses that represent the bases of current strategies should continually be monitored for change. It is not really a question of *whether* these factors will change but rather *when* they will change and in what ways. Here are some key questions to address in evaluating strategies:

1. Are our internal strengths still strengths?
2. Have we added other internal strengths? If so, what are they?
3. Are our internal weaknesses still weaknesses?
4. Do we now have other internal weaknesses? If so, what are they?
5. Are our external opportunities still opportunities?
6. Are there now other external opportunities? If so, what are they?
7. Are our external threats still threats?
8. Are there now other external threats? If so, what are they?
9. Are we vulnerable to a hostile takeover?

Measuring Organizational Performance

Another important strategy-evaluation activity is **measuring organizational performance**. This activity includes comparing expected results to actual results, investigating deviations from plans, evaluating individual performance, and examining progress being made toward meeting stated objectives. Both long-term and annual objectives are commonly used in this process. Criteria for evaluating strategies should be measurable and easily verifiable. Criteria that predict results may be more important than those that reveal what already has happened. For example, rather than simply being informed that sales in the last quarter were 20 percent under what was expected, strategists need to know that sales in the next quarter may be 20 percent below standard unless some action is taken to counter the trend. Really effective control requires accurate forecasting.

Failure to make satisfactory progress toward accomplishing long-term or annual objectives signals a need for corrective actions. Many factors, such as unreasonable policies, unexpected turns in the economy, unreliable suppliers or distributors, or ineffective strategies, can result in unsatisfactory progress toward meeting objectives. Problems can result from ineffectiveness (not doing the right things) or inefficiency (poorly doing the right things).

Many variables can and should be included in measuring organizational performance. As indicated in Table 11-3, typically a favorable or unfavorable variance is recorded monthly, quarterly, and annually, and resultant actions needed are then determined.

Determining which objectives are most important in the evaluation of strategies can be difficult. Strategy evaluation is based on both quantitative and qualitative criteria. Selecting the exact set of criteria for evaluating strategies depends on a particular organization's size, industry, strategies, and management philosophy. An organization pursuing a retrenchment strategy, for example, could have an entirely different set of evaluative criteria from an organization pursuing a market-development strategy. Quantitative criteria commonly used to evaluate strategies are financial ratios, often monitored for each segment of the firm. Strategists use ratios to make three critical comparisons: (1) comparing the firm's performance over different time periods, (2) comparing the firm's performance to competitors', and (3) comparing the firm's performance to industry averages.

Some potential problems are associated with using only quantitative criteria for evaluating strategies. First, most quantitative criteria are geared to annual objectives rather than long-term objectives. Also, different accounting methods can provide different results on

TABLE 11-3 A Sample Framework for Measuring Organizational Performance

Factor	Actual Result	Expected Result	Variance	Action Needed
Corporate Revenues				
Corporate Profits				
Corporate ROI				
Region 1 Revenues				
Region 1 Profits				
Region 1 ROI				
Region 2 Revenues				
Region 2 Profits				
Region 2 ROI				
Product 1 Revenues				
Product 1 Profits				
Product 1 ROI				
Product 2 Revenues				
Product 2 Profits				
Product 2 ROI				

ROI, return on investment.

many quantitative criteria. Third, intuitive judgments are almost always involved in deriving quantitative criteria. Thus, qualitative criteria are also important in evaluating strategies. Human factors such as high absenteeism and turnover rates, poor production quality and quantity rates, or low employee satisfaction can be underlying causes of declining performance. Marketing, finance and accounting, R&D, or MIS factors can also cause financial problems.

Some additional key questions that reveal the need for qualitative or intuitive judgments in strategy evaluation are as follows:

1. How good is the firm's balance of investments between high-risk and low-risk projects?
2. How good is the firm's balance of investments between long-term and short-term projects?
3. How good is the firm's balance of investments between slow-growing markets and fast-growing markets?
4. How good is the firm's balance of investments among different divisions?
5. To what extent are the firm's alternative strategies socially responsible?
6. What are the relationships among the firm's key internal and external strategic factors?
7. How are major competitors likely to respond to particular strategies?

Taking Corrective Actions

The final strategy-evaluation activity, **taking corrective actions**, requires making changes to competitively reposition a firm for the future. As indicated in Table 11-4, examples of changes that may be needed are altering an organization's structure, replacing one or more key individuals, selling a division, or revising a business mission. Other changes could include establishing or revising objectives, devising new policies, issuing stock to raise capital, adding additional salespersons, differently allocating resources, or developing new performance incentives. Taking corrective actions does not necessarily mean that existing strategies will be abandoned or even that new strategies must be formulated.

The probabilities and possibilities for incorrect or inappropriate actions increase geometrically with an arithmetic increase in personnel. Any person directing an overall undertaking must check on the actions of the participants as well as the results that they have achieved. If either the actions or results do not comply with preconceived or planned achievements, then corrective actions are needed.[6]

TABLE 11-4 Corrective Actions Possibly Needed to Correct Unfavorable Variances

1. Alter the firm's structure
2. Replace one or more key individuals
3. Divest a division
4. Alter the firm's vision or mission
5. Revise objectives
6. Alter strategies
7. Devise new policies
8. Install new performance incentives
9. Raise capital with stock or debt
10. Add or terminate salespersons, employees, or managers
11. Allocate resources differently
12. Outsource (or rein in) business functions

The largest office-supplies chain in the USA with 2,295 stores globally and 1,500 in the USA, Staples, is taking corrective actions to try to survive in the big-box office-supply store business. Many analysts say it is too little too late, but Staples is reducing its U.S. store space by 15 percent between 2013 and 2015 and is opening smaller stores more focused on mobile applications. Especially hurting Staples (and OfficeMax and Office Depot) are trends such as: (a) consumers prefer to purchase office supplies online (cheaper) from rivals such as Amazon, and (b) there is falling demand for office supplies since handheld devices such as the iPad have reduced demand for personal computers, printers, and even paper. Staples does own a fleet of vehicles that can deliver orders for free the next day, as compared to Amazon that only offers free two-day deliveries to members paying $79 a year to be part of Amazon Prime.

No organization can survive as an island; no organization can escape change. Taking corrective actions is necessary to keep an organization on track toward achieving stated objectives. In his thought-provoking books *Future Shock* and *The Third Wave*, Alvin Toffler argued that business environments are becoming so dynamic and complex that they threaten people and organizations with **future shock**, which occurs when the nature, types, and speed of changes overpower an individual's or organization's ability and capacity to adapt. Strategy evaluation enhances an organization's ability to adapt successfully to changing circumstances.

Taking corrective actions raises employees' and managers' anxieties. Research suggests that participation in strategy-evaluation activities is one of the best ways to overcome individuals' resistance to change. According to Erez and Kanfer, individuals accept change best when they have a cognitive understanding of the changes, a sense of control over the situation, and an awareness that necessary actions are going to be taken to implement the changes.[7]

Strategy evaluation can lead to strategy-formulation changes, strategy-implementation changes, both formulation and implementation changes, or no changes at all. Strategists cannot escape having to revise strategies and implementation approaches sooner or later. Hussey and Langham offered the following insight on taking corrective actions:

Resistance to change is often emotionally based and not easily overcome by rational argument. Resistance may be based on such feelings as loss of status, implied criticism of present competence, fear of failure in the new situation, annoyance at not being consulted, lack of understanding of the need for change, or insecurity in changing from well-known and fixed methods. It is necessary, therefore, to overcome such resistance by creating situations of participation and full explanation when changes are envisaged.[8]

Corrective actions should place an organization in a better position to capitalize on internal strengths; to take advantage of key external opportunities; to avoid, reduce, or mitigate external threats; and to improve internal weaknesses. Corrective actions should have a proper time horizon and an appropriate amount of risk. They should be internally consistent and socially responsible. Perhaps most important, corrective actions strengthen an organization's competitive position in its basic industry. Continuous strategy evaluation keeps strategists close to the pulse of an organization and provides information needed for an effective strategic-management system. Carter Bayles described the benefits of strategy evaluation as follows:

> Evaluation activities may renew confidence in the current business strategy or point to the need for actions to correct some weaknesses, such as erosion of product superiority or technological edge. In many cases, the benefits of strategy evaluation are much more far-reaching, for the outcome of the process may be a fundamentally new strategy that will lead, even in a business that is already turning a respectable profit, to substantially increased earnings. It is this possibility that justifies strategy evaluation, for the payoff can be very large.[9]

The Balanced Scorecard

Developed in 1993 by Harvard Business School professors Robert Kaplan and David Norton, and refined continually through today, the Balanced Scorecard is a strategy evaluation and control technique. **Balanced Scorecard** derives its name from the perceived need of firms to "balance" financial measures that are oftentimes used exclusively in strategy evaluation and control with nonfinancial measures such as product quality and customer service. An effective Balanced Scorecard contains a carefully chosen combination of strategic and financial objectives tailored to the company's business.

As a tool to manage and evaluate strategy, the Balanced Scorecard is currently in use at Sears, United Parcel Service, 3M Corporation, Heinz, and hundreds of other firms. For example, 3M Corporation has a financial objective to achieve annual growth in earnings per share of 10 percent or better, as well as a strategic objective to have at least 30 percent of sales come from products introduced in the past four years. The overall aim of the Balanced Scorecard is to "balance" shareholder objectives with customer and operational objectives. Obviously, these sets of objectives interrelate and many even conflict. For example, customers want low price and high service, which may conflict with shareholders' desire for a high return on their investment. The Balanced Scorecard concept is consistent with the notions of continuous improvement in management (CIM) and total quality management (TQM).

The Balanced Scorecard basic premise is that firms should establish objectives and evaluate strategies on criteria other than financial measures. Financial measures and ratios are vitally important in strategic planning, but of equal importance are factors such as customer service, employee morale, product quality, pollution abatement, business ethics, social responsibility, community involvement, and other such items. In conjunction with financial measures, these "softer" factors comprise an integral part of both the objective-setting process and the strategy-evaluation process. A Balanced Scorecard for a firm is simply a listing of all key objectives to work toward, along with an associated time dimension of when each objective is to be accomplished, as well as a primary responsibility or contact person, department, or division for each objective.

The Balanced Scorecard is an important strategy-evaluation tool. It is a process that allows firms to evaluate strategies from four perspectives: financial performance, customer knowledge, internal business processes, and learning and growth. The *Balanced Scorecard* analysis requires that firms seek answers to the following questions and use that information, in conjunction with financial measures, to adequately and more effectively evaluate strategies being implemented:

1. How well is the firm continually improving and creating value along measures such as innovation, technological leadership, product quality, operational process efficiencies, and so on?
2. How well is the firm sustaining and even improving on its core competencies and competitive advantages?
3. How satisfied are the firm's customers?

A sample Balanced Scorecard is provided in Table 11-5. Notice that the firm examines six key issues in evaluating its strategies: (1) Customers, (2) Managers/Employees, (3) Operations/Processes, (4) Community/Social Responsibility, (5) Business Ethics/Natural Environment, and (6) Financial. The basic form of a Balanced Scorecard may differ for different organizations. The Balanced Scorecard approach to strategy evaluation aims to balance long-term with short-term concerns, to balance financial with nonfinancial concerns, and to balance internal

TABLE 11-5 **An Example Balanced Scorecard**

Area of Objectives	Measure or Target	Time Expectation	Primary Responsibility
Customers			
1.			
2.			
3.			
4.			
Managers/Employees			
1.			
2.			
3.			
4.			
Operations/Processes			
1.			
2.			
3.			
4.			
Community/Social Responsibility			
1.			
2.			
3.			
4.			
Business Ethics/Natural Environment			
1.			
2.			
3.			
4.			
Financial			
1.			
2.			
3.			
4.			

with external concerns. The Balanced Scorecard would be constructed differently, that is, adapted to particular firms in various industries with the underlying theme or thrust being the same, which is to evaluate the firm's strategies based on both key quantitative and qualitative measures.

The Balanced Scorecard Institute has a Certification Program that includes two levels of certification: Balanced Scorecard Master Professional (BSMP) and Balanced Scorecard Professional (BSP), both of which are offered in association with George Washington University and are achievable through public workshop participation. The website for this program is http://www.balancedscorecard.org/.

Published Sources of Strategy-Evaluation Information

A number of publications are helpful in evaluating a firm's strategies. For example, *Fortune* annually identifies and evaluates the Fortune 1,000 (the largest manufacturers) and the Fortune 50 (the largest retailers, transportation companies, utilities, banks, insurance companies, and diversified financial corporations in the USA). *Fortune* ranks the best and worst

TABLE 11-6 The Most and Least Admired Companies in Management Quality in Various Industries in 2012

Most Admired	Least Admired
Koc Holding	Sears Holdings
McDonald's	China South Industries Group
Apple	MF Global Holdings
Philip Morris International	NewPage Holding
Costco Wholesale	Gas Natural Fenosa
J.P. Morgan Chase	Yahoo!
Wyndham Worldwide	AMR
Sysco	GDF Suez
Walt Disney	Dongfeng MG
	China FAW Group

Source: Based on information accessed November 1, 2012 at http://money.cnn.com/magazines/fortune/most-admired/2012/best_worst/best5.html.

performers on various factors, such as return on investment, sales volume, and profitability. *Fortune* annually publishes its strategy-evaluation research in an article titled "World's Most Admired Companies." Nine key attributes serve as evaluative criteria: people management; innovativeness; products quality; financial soundness; social responsibility; use of assets; long-term investment; global competitiveness; and quality of management. *Fortune's* 2012 evaluation in Table 11-6 reveals the firms most admired (best managed) in their industry.

Businessweek, Industry Week, and *Dun's Business Month* periodically publish detailed evaluations of U.S. businesses and industries. Although published sources of strategy-evaluation information focus primarily on large, publicly held businesses, the comparative ratios and related information are widely used to evaluate small businesses and privately owned firms as well.

Characteristics of an Effective Evaluation System

Strategy evaluation must meet several basic requirements to be effective. First, strategy-evaluation activities must be economical; too much information can be just as bad as too little information, and too many controls can do more harm than good. Strategy-evaluation activities also should be meaningful; they should specifically relate to a firm's objectives. They should provide managers with useful information about tasks over which they have control and influence. Strategy-evaluation activities should provide timely information; on occasion and in some areas, managers may daily need information. For example, when a firm has diversified by acquiring another firm, evaluative information may be needed frequently. However, in an R&D department, daily or even weekly evaluative information could be dysfunctional. Approximate information that is timely is generally more desirable as a basis for strategy evaluation than accurate information that does not depict the present. Frequent measurement and rapid reporting may frustrate control rather than give better control. The time dimension of control must coincide with the time span of the event being measured.

Strategy evaluation should be designed to provide a true picture of what is happening. For example, in a severe economic downturn, productivity and profitability ratios may drop alarmingly, although employees and managers are actually working harder. Strategy evaluations should fairly portray this type of situation. Information derived from the strategy-evaluation process should facilitate action and should be directed to those individuals in the organization who need to take action based on it. Managers commonly ignore evaluative reports that are provided only for informational purposes; not all managers need to receive all reports. Controls need to be action-oriented rather than information-oriented.

The strategy-evaluation process should not dominate decisions; it should foster mutual understanding, trust, and common sense. No department should fail to cooperate with another in evaluating strategies. Strategy evaluations should be simple, not too cumbersome, and not too restrictive. Complex strategy-evaluation systems often confuse people and accomplish little. The test of an effective evaluation system is its usefulness, not its complexity.

Large organizations require a more elaborate and detailed strategy-evaluation system because it is more difficult to coordinate efforts among different divisions and functional areas. Managers in small companies often communicate daily with each other and their employees and do not need extensive evaluative reporting systems. Familiarity with local environments usually makes gathering and evaluating information much easier for small organizations than for large businesses. But the key to an effective strategy-evaluation system may be the ability to convince participants that failure to accomplish certain objectives within a prescribed time is not necessarily a reflection of their performance.

There is no one ideal strategy-evaluation system. The unique characteristics of an organization, including its size, management style, purpose, problems, and strengths, can determine a strategy-evaluation and control system's final design. Robert Waterman offered the following observation about successful organizations' strategy-evaluation and control systems:

> Successful companies treat facts as friends and controls as liberating. Morgan Guaranty and Wells Fargo not only survive but thrive in the troubled waters of bank deregulation, because their strategy evaluation and control systems are sound, their risk is contained, and they know themselves and the competitive situation so well. Successful companies have a voracious hunger for facts. They see information where others see only data. Successful companies maintain tight, accurate financial controls. Their people don't regard controls as an imposition of autocracy but as the benign checks and balances that allow them to be creative and free.[10]

Contingency Planning

A basic premise of good strategic management is that firms plan ways to deal with unfavorable and favorable events before they occur. Too many organizations prepare contingency plans just for unfavorable events; this is a mistake, because both minimizing threats and capitalizing on opportunities can improve a firm's competitive position.

Regardless of how carefully strategies are formulated, implemented, and evaluated, unforeseen events, such as strikes, boycotts, natural disasters, arrival of foreign competitors, and government actions, can make a strategy obsolete. To minimize the impact of potential threats, organizations should develop contingency plans as part of their strategy-evaluation process. **Contingency plans** can be defined as alternative plans that can be put into effect if certain key events do not occur as expected. Only high-priority areas require the insurance of contingency plans. Strategists cannot and should not try to cover all bases by planning for all possible contingencies. But in any case, contingency plans should be as simple as possible.

Some contingency plans commonly established by firms include the following:

1. If a major competitor withdraws from particular markets as intelligence reports indicate, what actions should our firm take?
2. If our sales objectives are not reached, what actions should our firm take to avoid profit losses?
3. If demand for our new product exceeds plans, what actions should our firm take to meet the higher demand?
4. If certain disasters occur—such as loss of computer capabilities; a hostile takeover attempt; loss of patent protection; or destruction of manufacturing facilities because of earthquakes, tornadoes, or hurricanes—what actions should our firm take?
5. If a new technological advancement makes our new product obsolete sooner than expected, what actions should our firm take?

Too many organizations discard alternative strategies not selected for implementation although the work devoted to analyzing these options would render valuable information. Alternative strategies not selected for implementation can serve as contingency plans in case the strategy or strategies selected do not work. U.S. companies and governments are increasingly considering nuclear-generated electricity as the most efficient means of power generation. Many contingency plans certainly call for nuclear power rather than for coal- and gas-derived electricity.

When strategy-evaluation activities reveal the need for a major change quickly, an appropriate contingency plan can be executed in a timely way. Contingency plans can promote a strategist's ability to respond quickly to key changes in the internal and external bases of an organization's current strategy. For example, if underlying assumptions about the economy turn out to be wrong and contingency plans are ready, then managers can make appropriate changes promptly.

In some cases, external or internal conditions present unexpected opportunities. When such opportunities occur, contingency plans could allow an organization to quickly capitalize on them. Linneman and Chandran reported that contingency planning gave users, such as DuPont, Dow Chemical, Consolidated Foods, and Emerson Electric, three major benefits: (1) It permitted quick response to change, (2) it prevented panic in crisis situations, and (3) it made managers more adaptable by encouraging them to appreciate just how variable the future can be. They suggested that effective contingency planning involves a five-step process:

1. Identify both good and bad events that could jeopardize strategies.
2. Determine when the good and bad events are likely to occur.
3. Determine the expected pros and cons of each contingency event.
4. Develop contingency plans for key contingency events.
5. Determine early warning trigger points key contingency events.[11]

Auditing

A frequently used tool in strategy evaluation is the audit. **Auditing** is defined by the American Accounting Association (AAA) as "a systematic process of objectively obtaining and evaluating evidence regarding assertions about economic actions and events to ascertain the degree of correspondence between these assertions and established criteria, and communicating the results to interested users."[12]

Auditors examine the financial statement of firms to determine whether they have been prepared according to *generally accepted accounting principles* (**GAAP**) and whether they fairly represent the activities of the firm. Independent auditors use a set of standards called *generally accepted auditing standards (***GAAS***)*. Public accounting firms often have a consulting arm that provides strategy-evaluation services.

The new era of *international financial reporting standards (***IFRS***)* appears unstoppable, and businesses need to go ahead and get ready to use IFRS. Many U.S. companies now report their finances using both the old GAAP and the new IFRS. "If companies don't prepare, if they don't start three years in advance," warns business professor Donna Street at the University of Dayton, "they're going to be in big trouble." GAAP standards comprised 25,000 pages, whereas IFRS comprises only 5,000 pages, so in that sense IFRS is less cumbersome.

This accounting switch from GAAP to IFRS in the United States is going to cost businesses millions of dollars in fees and upgraded software systems and training. U.S. CPAs need to study global accounting principles intensely, and business schools should go ahead and begin teaching students the new accounting standards. Most large accounting firms and multinational firms favor the switch to IFRS saying it will simplify accounting, make it easier for investors to compare firms across countries, and make it easier to raise capital globally. But many smaller firms oppose the upcoming change say it will be too costly; some firms are uneasy about the idea of giving an international body the authority to write accounting rules for the USA. Some firms also would pay higher taxes because last in, first out (LIFO) inventory methods are not allowed under IFRS.[13] The International Accounting Standards Board (IASB) has publicly expressed "regret" over the USA's slowness in adopting IFRS.

The U.S. Chamber of Commerce supports a change, saying it will lead to much more cross-border commerce and will help the USA compete in the world economy. Already the European Union and 113 nations have adopted or soon plan to use international rules, including Australia, China, India, Mexico, and Canada. So the USA likely will also adopt IFRS rules, but this switch could unleash a legal and regulatory nightmare. A few U.S. multinational firms already use IFRS for their foreign subsidiaries, such as United Technologies (UT). UT derives more than 60 percent of its revenues from abroad and is already training its entire staff to use IFRS.

Movement to IFRS from GAAP encompasses a company's entire operations, including auditing, oversight, cash management, taxes, technology, software, investing, acquiring, merging, importing, exporting, pension planning, and partnering. Switching from GAAP to IFRS is also likely to be plagued by gaping differences in business customs, financial regulations, tax laws, politics, and other factors. One critic of the upcoming switch is Charles Niemeier of the Public Company Accounting Oversight Board, who says the switch "has the potential to be a Tower of Babel," costing firms millions when they do not even have thousands to spend.

Others say the switch will help U.S. companies raise capital abroad and do business with firms abroad. Perhaps the biggest upside of the switch is that IFRS rules are more streamlined and less complex than GAAP. Lenovo is a big advocate of IFRS as they desire to be a world company rather than a U.S. or Chinese company, so the faster the switch to IFRS, the better for them. The bottom line is that IFRS is coming to the United States, sooner rather than later, so we all need to gear up for this switch as soon as possible.

21st-Century Challenges in Strategic Management

Three particular challenges or decisions that face all strategists today are (1) deciding whether the process should be more an art or a science, (2) deciding whether strategies should be visible or hidden from stakeholders, and (3) deciding whether the process should be more top-down or bottom-up in their firm.[14]

The Art or Science Issue

This textbook is consistent with most of the strategy literature in advocating that strategic management be viewed more as a science than an art. This perspective contends that firms need to systematically assess their external and internal environments, conduct research, carefully evaluate the pros and cons of various alternatives, perform analyses, and then decide on a particular course of action. In contrast, Mintzberg's notion of "crafting" strategies embodies the artistic model, which suggests that strategic decision making be based primarily on holistic thinking, intuition, creativity, and imagination.[15] Mintzberg and his followers reject strategies that result from objective analysis, preferring instead subjective imagination. "Strategy scientists" reject strategies that emerge from emotion, hunch, creativity, and politics. Proponents of the artistic view often consider strategic planning exercises to be time poorly spent. The Mintzberg philosophy insists on informality, whereas strategy scientists (and this text) insist on more formality. Mintzberg refers to strategic planning as an "emergent" process whereas strategy scientists use the term *deliberate* process.[16]

The answer to the art-versus-science question is one that strategists must decide for themselves, and certainly the two approaches are not mutually exclusive. In deciding which approach is more effective, however, consider that the business world today has become increasingly complex and more intensely competitive. There is less room for error in strategic planning. Recall that Chapter 1 discussed the importance of intuition, experience, and subjectivity in strategic planning, and even the weights and ratings discussed in Chapters 6, 7, and 8 certainly require good judgment. But the idea of deciding on strategies for any firm without thorough research and analysis, at least in the mind of these authors, is unwise. Certainly, in smaller firms there can be more informality in the process compared to larger firms, but even for smaller firms, a wealth of competitive information is available on the Internet and elsewhere and should be collected, assimilated, and evaluated before deciding on a course of action on which survival of the firm may hinge. The livelihood of countless employees and shareholders may hinge on the effectiveness of strategies selected. Too much is at stake to be less than thorough in formulating strategies. It is not wise for a strategist to rely too heavily on gut feeling and opinion instead of research data, competitive intelligence, and analysis in formulating strategies.

The Visible or Hidden Issue

An interesting aspect of any competitive analysis discussion is whether strategies themselves should be secret or open within firms. The Chinese warrior Sun Tzu and military leaders today strive to keep strategies secret because war is based on deception. However, for a business organization, secrecy may not be best. Keeping strategies secret from employees and stakeholders at large could severely inhibit employee and stakeholder communication, understanding, and commitment and also forgo valuable input that these persons could have regarding formulation or implementation of that strategy. Thus, strategists in a particular firm must decide for themselves whether the risk of rival firms easily knowing and exploiting a firm's strategies is worth the benefit of improved employee and stakeholder motivation and input. Most executives agree that some strategic information should remain confidential to top managers, and that steps should be taken to ensure that such information is not disseminated beyond the inner circle. For a firm that you may own or manage, would you advocate openness or secrecy in regard to strategies being formulated and implemented?

There are certainly good reasons to keep the strategy process and strategies themselves visible and open rather than hidden and secret. There are also good reasons to keep strategies hidden from all but top-level executives. Strategists must decide for themselves what is best for their firms. This text comes down largely on the side of being visible and open, but certainly this may not be best for all strategists and all firms. As pointed out in Chapter 1, Sun Tzu argued that all war is based on deception and that the best maneuvers are those not easily predicted by rivals. Business and war are analogous.

Some reasons to be completely open with the strategy process and resultant decisions are these:

1. Managers, employees, and other stakeholders can readily contribute to the process. They often have excellent ideas. Secrecy would forgo many excellent ideas.
2. Investors, creditors, and other stakeholders have greater basis for supporting a firm when they know what the firm is doing and where the firm is going.
3. Visibility promotes democracy, whereas secrecy promotes autocracy. Domestic firms and most foreign firms prefer democracy over autocracy as a management style.
4. Participation and openness enhance understanding, commitment, and communication within the firm.

Reasons why some firms prefer to conduct strategic planning in secret and keep strategies hidden from all but the highest-level executives are as follows:

1. Free dissemination of a firm's strategies may easily translate into competitive intelligence for rival firms who could exploit the firm given that information.
2. Secrecy limits criticism, second guessing, and hindsight.
3. Participants in a visible strategy process become more attractive to rival firms who may lure them away.
4. Secrecy limits rival firms from imitating or duplicating the firm's strategies and undermining the firm.

The obvious benefits of the visible versus hidden extremes suggest that a working balance must be sought between the apparent contradictions. Parnell says that in a perfect world all key individuals both inside and outside the firm should be involved in strategic planning, but in practice particularly sensitive and confidential information should always remain strictly confidential to top managers.[17] This balancing act is difficult but essential for survival of the firm.

The Top-Down or Bottom-Up Approach

Proponents of the top-down approach contend that top executives are the only persons in the firm with the collective experience, acumen, and fiduciary responsibility to make key strategy decisions. In contrast, bottom-up advocates argue that lower- and middle-level managers and employees who will be implementing the strategies need to be actively involved in the process of formulating the strategies to ensure their support and commitment. Recent strategy research and this textbook emphasize the bottom-up approach, but earlier work by Schendel and Hofer stressed the need for firms to rely on perceptions of their top managers in strategic planning.[18] Strategists must reach a working balance of the two approaches in a manner deemed best for their firms at a particular time, while cognizant of the fact that current research supports the bottom-up approach, at least among U.S. firms. Increased education and diversity of the workforce at all levels are reasons why middle- and lower-level managers—and even nonmanagers—should be invited to participate in the firm's strategic planning process, at least to the extent that they are willing and able to contribute.

Special Note to Students

Just Google the words *balanced scorecard images* and you will see more than 100 actual Balanced Scorecards being used as a tool by various organizations to gain and sustain competitive advantage. Note the variation in format. In performing your case analysis, develop and present a Balanced Scorecard that you recommend to help your firm monitor and evaluate progress toward stated objectives. Effective, timely evaluation of strategies can enable a firm to adapt quickly to changing conditions, and a Balanced Scorecard can assist in this endeavor. Couch your discussion of the Balanced Scorecard in terms of competitive advantage versus rival firms.

Conclusion

This chapter presents a strategy-evaluation framework that can facilitate accomplishment of annual and long-term objectives. Effective strategy evaluation allows an organization to capitalize on internal strengths as they develop, to exploit external opportunities as they emerge, to recognize and defend against threats, and to mitigate internal weaknesses before they become detrimental.

Strategists in successful organizations take the time to formulate, implement, and then evaluate strategies deliberately and systematically. Good strategists move their organization forward with purpose and direction, continually evaluating and improving the firm's external and internal strategic positions. Strategy evaluation allows an organization to shape its own future rather than allowing it to be constantly shaped by remote forces that have little or no vested interest in the well-being of the enterprise.

Although not a guarantee for success, strategic management allows organizations to make effective long-term decisions, to execute those decisions efficiently, and to take corrective actions as needed to ensure success. Computer networks and the Internet help to coordinate strategic-management activities and to ensure that decisions are based on good information. A key to effective strategy evaluation and to successful strategic management is an integration of intuition and analysis:

> A potentially fatal problem is the tendency for analytical and intuitive issues to polarize. This polarization leads to strategy evaluation that is dominated by either analysis or intuition, or to strategy evaluation that is discontinuous, with a lack of coordination among analytical and intuitive issues.[19]

Strategists in successful organizations realize that strategic management is first and foremost a people process. It is an excellent vehicle for fostering organizational communication. People are what make the difference in organizations.

The real key to effective strategic management is to accept the premise that the planning process is more important than the written plan, that the manager is continuously planning and does not stop planning when the written plan is finished. The written plan is only a snapshot as of the moment it is approved. If the manager is not planning on a continuous basis—planning, measuring, and revising—the written plan can become obsolete the day it is finished. This obsolescence becomes more of a certainty as the increasingly rapid rate of change makes the business environment more uncertain.[20]

Key Terms and Concepts

advantage (p. 373)
auditing (p. 385)
Balanced Scorecard (p. 381)
consistency (p. 373)
consonance (p. 373)
contingency plans (p. 384)
feasibility (p. 373)
future shock (p. 380)

GAAS, GAAP, and IFRS (p. 385)
management by wandering around (p. 375)
measuring organizational performance (p. 378)
reviewing the underlying bases of an organization's
    strategy (p. 376)
revised EFE Matrix (p. 376)
revised IFE Matrix (p. 376)
taking corrective actions (p. 379)

Issues for Review and Discussion

11-1. BHP Billiton has been very successful in the last decade. What is the major reason for its success?

11-2. Visit BHP Billiton's website and evaluate the firm's strategies, which are currently being implemented.

11-3. Discuss the nature and implications of the upcoming accounting switch from GAAP to IFRS, in the United States.

11-4. Ask the following question to an accounting professor at your college or university, and report your findings back to the class—"To what extent would my learning the IFRS standards, on my own, give me a competitive advantage in the job market?"

11-5. Give an example of "consonance," other than the one provided by Rumelt in this Chapter.

11-6. "Evaluating strategies on a continuous rather than a periodic basis is desired." Discuss the pros and cons of this statement.

11-7. How often should an organization's vision or mission be changed, in light of strategy evaluation activities?

11-8. Compare Mintzberg's notion of "crafting" strategies with the notion of "gathering and assimilating information" to formulate strategies, mentioned in this book.

11-9. Do you believe strategic management is more of an art or science? Explain.

11-10. Do you feel strategic management should be more a top-down or bottom-up process in a firm? Briefly explain your answer.

11-11. Do you think strategic management should be more visible or hidden, as a process in a firm? Explain.

11-12. Develop a balanced scorecard for BHP Billiton.

11-13. Create a balanced scorecard for your college or university.

11-14. Discuss contingency planning.

11-15. Identify some important financial ratios, which are useful in evaluating a firm's strategies.

11-16. How often should a firm formally evaluate its strategies?

11-17. Under what conditions are corrective actions not required in the strategy-evaluation process?

11-18. Define and discuss auditing, as it relates to strategy evaluation.

11-19. List 10 characteristics of an effective evaluation system.

11-20. Go to *Fortune* magazine's website and identify several firms in your city, which are listed among the most admired companies in the world according to *Fortune*.

11-21. Ask the dean of your school to describe how their department evaluates strategies. Present your findings to the class.

11-22. Identify four firms that provide their strategic plans on their websites, and four that do not. Should firms do this? Explain your answer.

MyManagementLab®

Go to **mymanagementlab.com** for the following Assisted-graded writing questions:

11-23. Why is the Balanced Scorecard an important topic both in devising objectives and in evaluating strategies?

11-24. Do you believe strategic management should be more visible or hidden as a process in a firm? Explain.

Current Readings

Aguinis, Herman, Ryan K. Gottfredson, and Harry Joo. "Delivering Effective Performance Feedback: The Strengths-Based Approach." *Business Horizons* 55, no. 2 (March 2012): 105–111.

Lafley, A.G., Roger L. Martin, Jan W. Rivkin, and Nicolaj Siggelkow. "Bringing Science to the Art of Strategy." *Harvard Business Review* (September 2012): 56.

Lux, Sean, T. Russell Crook, and Terry Leap. "Corporate Political Activity: The Good, the Bad, and the Ugly." *Business Horizons* 55, no. 3 (May 2012): 307–312.

Kahane, Adam. "Transformative Scenario Planning: Changing the Future by Exploring Alternatives." *Strategy and Leadership* 40, no. 5 (2012): 19–23.

Mauboussin, Michael J. "The True Measures of Success." *Harvard Business Review* (October 2012): 46.

Peltola, Soili. "Can an Old Firm Learn New Tricks? A Corporate Entrepreneurship Approach to Organizational Renewal." *Business Horizons* 55, no. 1 (January 2012): 43–51.

Stieger, Daniel, Kurt Matzler, Sayan Chatterjee, and Florian Ladstaetter-Fussenegger. "Democratizing Strategy: How Crowdsourcing Can Be Used For Strategy Dialogues." *California Management Review* 54, no. 4 (Summer 2012): 44–68.

ASSURANCE OF LEARNING EXERCISES

EXERCISE 11A

Evaluating BHP Billiton's Strategies

Purpose

BHP Billiton is featured in the opening chapter example as a firm that engages in excellent strategic planning. BHP is a large Australian multinational mining and petroleum company headquartered in Melbourne, Australia. BHP also has major offices in London. BHP is arguably the world's largest mining company and among the top ten largest companies in the world measured by market capitalization. *Fortune* in 2013 ranked BHP as the 115th largest company in the world and the 20th most profitable. BHP is among the world's top producers of iron ore, coal, aluminum, copper, manganese, nickel, silver, uranium, and potash. BHP also has crude oil and natural gas holdings. BHP may soon divest its diamond assets.

This exercise can give you practice evaluating a company's strategies.

Instructions

Step 1   Go to BHP Billiton's corporate website and navigate to the Investors & Media section. Review recent news releases for BHP Billiton.
Step 2   Determine what new strategies BHP is pursuing.
Step 3   Evaluate BHP's newest strategies based on concepts presented in Chapter 11.
Step 4   Prepare a strategy evaluation report for BHP.

EXERCISE 11B

Preparing a Strategy-Evaluation Report for adidas AG

Purpose

This exercise can give you experience locating strategy-evaluation information. Use of the Internet coupled with published sources of information can significantly enhance the strategy-evaluation process. Performance information on competitors, for example, can help put into perspective a firm's own performance.

Instructions

Step 1   Search the Internet for information on adidas. Prepare a strategy-evaluation report for your instructor. Include in your report a summary of adidas' strategies and performance in 2013 and a summary of your conclusions regarding the effectiveness of adidas' strategies.
Step 2   Based on your analysis, do you feel that adidas is pursuing effective strategies? What recommendations would you offer to adidas' chief executive officer?

EXERCISE 11C

Preparing a Balanced Scorecard for adidas AG

Purpose

This exercise can give you experience developing a Balanced Scorecard for a corporation.

Instructions

Step 1   Compile all information that you have collected on adidas.
Step 2   Join with three other students in class. Jointly develop a 20-item Balanced Scorecard for the company.
Step 3   Appoint a spokesperson for your team to give a three-minute overview to the class regarding the substance of your Balanced Scorecard.

EXERCISE 11D
Evaluate My University's Strategies

Purpose

An important part of evaluating strategies is determining the nature and extent of changes in an organization's external opportunities/threats and internal strengths/weaknesses. Changes in these underlying critical success factors can indicate a need to change or modify the firm's strategies.

Instructions

As a class, discuss positive and negative changes in your university's external and internal factors during your college career. Begin by listing on the board new or emerging opportunities and threats. Then identify strengths and weaknesses that have changed significantly during your college career. In light of the external and internal changes that were identified, discuss whether your university's strategies need modifying. Are there any new strategies that you would recommend? Make a list to recommend to your department chair, dean, president, or chancellor.

Notes

1. Karen Talley, "Sales Plunge Another 23% at Penney," *Wall Street Journal* (August 11–12): B3.

2. Dale McConkey, "Planning in a Changing Environment," *Business Horizons*, September–October 1988, 64.

3. Robert Simons, "Control in an Age of Empowerment," *Harvard Business Review*, March–April 1995, 80.

4. Dale Zand, "Reviewing the Policy Process," *California Management Review* 21, no. 1 (Fall 1978): 37.

5. Eccles. 3:1–8.

6. Claude George Jr., *The History of Management Thought* (Upper Saddle River, New Jersey: Prentice Hall, 1968), 165–166.

7. M. Erez and F. Kanfer, "The Role of Goal Acceptance in Goal Setting and Task Performance," *Academy of Management Review* 8, no. 3 (July 1983): 457.

8. D. Hussey and M. Langham, *Corporate Planning: The Human Factor* (Oxford, England: Pergamon Press, 1979), 138.

9. Carter Bayles, "Strategic Control: The President's Paradox," *Business Horizons* 20, no. 4 (August 1977): 18.

10. Robert Waterman, Jr., "How the Best Get Better," *BusinessWeek*, September 14, 1987, 105.

11. Robert Linneman and Rajan Chandran, "Contingency Planning: A Key to Swift Managerial Action in the Uncertain Tomorrow," *Managerial Planning* 29, no. 4 (January–February 1981): 23–27.

12. American Accounting Association, *Report of Committee on Basic Auditing Concepts*, 1971, 15–74.

13. Michael Rapoport, "Delay Seen (Again) For New Rules on Accounting," *Wall Street Journal* (July 6, 2012): C1; Michael Rapoport, "Accounting Panel Expresses 'Regret' Over U.S. Stance," *Wall Street Journal* (July 16, 2012): C5.

14. John Parnell, "Five Critical Challenges in Strategy Making," *SAM Advanced Management Journal* 68, no. 2 (Spring 2003): 15–22.

15. Henry Mintzberg, "Crafting Strategy," *Harvard Business Review*, July–August 1987, 66–75.

16. Henry Mintzberg and J. Waters, "Of Strategies, Deliberate and Emergent," *Strategic Management Journal* 6, no. 2: 257–272.

17. Parnell, 15–22.

18. D. E. Schendel and C. W. Hofer (Eds.), *Strategic Management* (Boston: Little, Brown, 1979).

19. Michael McGinnis, "The Key to Strategic Planning: Integrating Analysis and Intuition," *Sloan Management Review* 26, no. 1 (Fall 1984): 49.

20. McConkey, 72.

GUIDELINES FOR CASE ANALYSIS

Source: Africa Studio/Fotolia

MyManagementLab®

Improve Your Grade!

Over 10 million students improved their results using the Pearson MyLabs.
Visit **mymanagementlab.com** for simulations, tutorials, and end-of-chapter problems.

Guidelines for Case Analysis

CHAPTER OBJECTIVES

After studying this chapter, you should be able to do the following:

1. Describe the case method for learning strategic-management concepts.
2. Identify the steps in preparing a comprehensive written case analysis.
3. Describe how to give an effective oral case analysis presentation.
4. Discuss special tips for doing a case analysis.

ASSURANCE OF LEARNING EXERCISES

The following exercises are found at the end of this chapter.

Oral Presentation—Step 1 Introduction (2 minutes)
Oral Presentation—Step 2 Mission and Vision (4 minutes)
Oral Presentation—Step 3 Internal Assessment (8 minutes)
Oral Presentation—Step 4 External Assessment (8 minutes)
Oral Presentation—Step 5 Strategy Formulation (14 minutes)
Oral Presentation—Step 6 Strategy Implementation (8 minutes)
Oral Presentation—Step 7 Strategy Evaluation (2 minutes)
Oral Presentation—Step 8 Conclusion (4 minutes)

The purpose of this section is to help you analyze strategic-management cases. Guidelines for preparing written and oral case analyses are given, and suggestions for preparing cases for class discussion are presented. Steps to follow in preparing case analyses are provided. Guidelines for making an oral presentation are described.

What Is a Strategic-Management Case?

A *strategic-management case* describes an organization's external and internal conditions and raises issues concerning the firm's mission, strategies, objectives, and policies. Most of the information in a strategic-management case is established fact, but some information may be opinions, judgments, and beliefs. Strategic-management cases are more comprehensive than those you may have studied in other courses. They generally include a description of related management, marketing, finance and accounting, production and operations, research and development (R&D), management information systems (MIS), and natural environment issues. A strategic-management case puts the reader at the scene of the action by describing a firm's situation at some point in time. Strategic-management cases are written to give you practice applying strategic-management concepts. The case method for studying strategic management is often called *learning by doing*.

Guidelines for Preparing Case Analyses

The Need for Practicality

There is no such thing as a complete case, and no case ever gives you all the information you need to conduct analyses and make recommendations. Likewise, in the business world, strategists never have all the information they need to make decisions: information may be unavailable or too costly to obtain, or it may take too much time to obtain. So in analyzing strategic-management cases, do what strategists do every day—make reasonable assumptions about unknowns, clearly state assumptions, perform appropriate analyses, and make decisions. *Be practical.* For example, in performing a projected financial analysis, make reasonable assumptions, appropriately state them, and proceed to show what impact your recommendations are expected to have on the organization's financial position. Avoid saying, "I don't have enough information." Always supplement the information provided in a case with Internet and library research.

The Need for Justification

The most important part of analyzing cases is not what strategies you recommend but rather how you support your decisions and how you propose that they be implemented. There is no single best solution or one right answer to a case, so give ample justification for your recommendations. This is important. In the business world, strategists usually do not know if their decisions are right until resources have been allocated and consumed. Then it is often too late to reverse a decision. This cold fact accents the need for careful integration of intuition and analysis in preparing strategic management case analyses.

The Need for Realism

Avoid recommending a course of action beyond an organization's means. *Be realistic.* No organization can possibly pursue all the strategies that could potentially benefit the firm. Estimate how much capital will be required to implement what you recommended. Determine whether debt, stock, or a combination of debt and stock could be used to obtain the capital. Make sure your recommendations are feasible. Do not prepare a case analysis that omits all arguments and information not supportive of your recommendations. Rather, present the major advantages and disadvantages of several feasible alternatives. Try not to exaggerate, stereotype, prejudge, or overdramatize. Strive to demonstrate that your interpretation of the evidence is reasonable and objective.

The Need for Specificity

Do not make broad generalizations such as "The company should pursue a market penetration strategy." Be specific by telling *what, why, when, how, where,* and *who.* Failure to use specifics is the single major shortcoming of most oral and written case analyses. For example, in an internal audit say, "The firm's current ratio fell from 2.2 in 2013 to 1.3 in 2014, and this is considered to be a major weakness," instead of "The firm's financial condition is bad." But recall from the chapters that selected external and internal factors need to be "*actionable*" to the extent possible, and financial ratios in general are not actionable. Rather than concluding from a Strategic Position and Action Evaluation (SPACE) Matrix that a firm should be defensive, be more specific, saying, "The firm should consider closing three plants, laying off 280 employees, and divesting itself of its chemical division, for a net savings of $20.2 million in 2014." Use ratios, percentages, numbers, and dollar estimates. Businesspeople dislike generalities and vagueness.

The Need for Originality

Do not necessarily recommend the course of action that the firm plans to take or actually undertook, even if those actions resulted in improved revenues and earnings. The aim of case analysis is for you to consider all the facts and information relevant to the organization at the time, to generate feasible alternative strategies, to choose among those alternatives, and to defend your recommendations. Put yourself back in time to the point when strategic decisions were being made by the firm's strategists. Based on the information available then, what would you have done? Support your position with charts, graphs, ratios, analyses, and the like—not a revelation from the library. You can become a good strategist by thinking through situations, making management assessments, and proposing plans yourself. *Be original.* Compare and contrast what you recommend versus what the company plans to do or did.

The Need to Contribute

Strategy formulation, implementation, and evaluation decisions are commonly made by a group of individuals rather than by a single person. Therefore, your professor may divide the class into three- or four-person teams and ask you to prepare written or oral case analyses. Members of a strategic-management team, in class or in the business world, differ on their aversion to risk, their concern for short-run versus long-run benefits, their attitudes toward social responsibility, and their views concerning globalization. There are no perfect people, so there are no perfect strategies. Be open-minded to others' views. *Be a good listener and a good contributor.*

Preparing a Case for Class Discussion

Your professor may ask you to prepare a case for class discussion. Preparing a case for class discussion means that you need to read the case before class, make notes regarding the organization's external opportunities and threats and internal strengths and weaknesses, perform appropriate analyses, and come to class prepared to offer and defend some specific recommendations.

The Case Method versus Lecture Approach

The case method of teaching is radically different from the traditional lecture approach, in which little or no preparation is needed by students before class. The *case method* involves a classroom situation in which students do most of the talking; your professor facilitates discussion by asking questions and encouraging student interaction regarding ideas, analyses, and recommendations. Be prepared for a discussion along the lines of "What would you do, why would you do it, when would you do it, and how would you do it?" Prepare answers to the following types of questions:

- What are the firm's most important external opportunities and threats?
- What are the organization's major strengths and weaknesses?
- How would you describe the organization's financial condition?
- What are the firm's existing strategies and objectives?
- Who are the firm's competitors, and what are their strategies?
- What objectives and strategies do you recommend for this organization? Explain your reasoning. How does what you recommend compare to what the company plans?
- How could the organization best implement what you recommend? What implementation problems do you envision? How could the firm avoid or solve those problems?

The Cross-Examination

Do not hesitate to take a stand on the issues and to support your position with objective analyses and outside research. Strive to apply strategic-management concepts and tools in preparing your case for class discussion. Seek defensible arguments and positions. Support opinions and judgments with facts, reasons, and evidence. Crunch the numbers before class! Be willing to describe your recommendations to the class without fear of disapproval. Respect the ideas of others, but be willing to go against the majority opinion when you can justify a better position.

Strategic-management case analysis gives you the opportunity to learn more about yourself, your colleagues, strategic management, and the decision-making process in organizations. The rewards of this experience will depend on the effort you put forth, so do a good job. Discussing business policy cases in class is exciting and challenging. Expect views counter to those you present. Different students will place emphasis on different aspects of an organization's situation and submit different recommendations for scrutiny and rebuttal. Cross-examination discussions commonly arise, just as they occur in a real business organization. Avoid being a silent observer.

Preparing a Written Case Analysis

In addition to asking you to prepare a case for class discussion, your professor may ask you to prepare a written case analysis. Preparing a written case analysis is similar to preparing a case for class discussion, except written reports are generally more structured and more detailed. There is no ironclad procedure for preparing a written case analysis because cases differ in focus; the type, size, and complexity of the organizations being analyzed also vary.

When writing a strategic-management report or case analysis, avoid using jargon, vague or redundant words, acronyms, abbreviations, sexist language, and ethnic or racial slurs. And watch your spelling! Use short sentences and paragraphs and simple words and phrases. Use quite a few subheadings. Arrange issues and ideas from the most important to the least important. Arrange recommendations from the least controversial to the most controversial. Use the active voice rather than the passive voice for all verbs; for example, say "Our team recommends that the company diversify" rather than "It is recommended by our team to diversify." Use many examples to add specificity and clarity. Tables, figures, pie charts, bar charts, timelines, and other kinds of exhibits help communicate important points and ideas. Sometimes a picture *is* worth a thousand words.

The Executive Summary

Your professor may ask you to focus the written case analysis on a particular aspect of the strategic-management process, such as (1) to identify and evaluate the organization's existing vision, mission, objectives, and strategies; or (2) to propose and defend specific recommendations for the company; or (3) to develop an industry analysis by describing the competitors, products, selling techniques, and market conditions in a given industry. These types of written reports are sometimes called *executive summaries*. An executive summary usually ranges from three to five pages of text in length, plus exhibits.

The Comprehensive Written Analysis

Your professor may ask you to prepare a *comprehensive written analysis*. This assignment requires you to apply the entire strategic-management process to the particular organization. When preparing a comprehensive written analysis, picture yourself as a consultant who has been asked by a company to conduct a study of its external and internal environment and to make specific recommendations for its future. Prepare exhibits to support your recommendations. Highlight exhibits with some discussion in the paper. Comprehensive written analyses are usually about 10 pages in length, plus exhibits. Throughout your written analysis, emphasize how your proposed strategies will enable the firm to gain and sustain competitive advantage. Visit www.strategyclub.com for examples.

Steps in Preparing a Comprehensive Written Analysis

In preparing a *written* case analysis, you could follow the steps outlined here, which correlate to the stages in the strategic-management process and the chapters in this text. (Note—The steps in presenting an *oral* case analysis are given on pages 401–403, are more detailed, and could be used here).

Step 1 Identify the firm's existing vision, mission, objectives, and strategies.

Step 2 Develop vision and mission statements for the organization.

Step 3 Identify the organization's external opportunities and threats.

Step 4 Construct a Competitive Profile Matrix (CPM).

Step 5 Construct an External Factor Evaluation (EFE) Matrix.

Step 6 Identify the organization's internal strengths and weaknesses.

Step 7 Construct an Internal Factor Evaluation (IFE) Matrix.

Step 8 Prepare a Strengths-Weaknesses-Opportunities-Threats (SWOT) Matrix, Strategic Position and Action Evaluation (SPACE) Matrix, Boston Consulting Group (BCG) Matrix, Internal-External (IE) Matrix, Grand Strategy Matrix, and Quantitative Strategic Planning Matrix (QSPM) as appropriate. Give advantages and disadvantages of alternative strategies.

Step 9 Recommend specific strategies and long-term objectives. Show how much your recommendations will cost. Clearly itemize these costs for each projected year. Compare your recommendations to actual strategies planned by the company.

Step 10 Specify how your recommendations can be implemented and what results you can expect. Prepare forecasted ratios and projected financial statements. Present a timetable or agenda for action.

Step 11 Recommend specific annual objectives and policies.

Step 12 Recommend procedures for strategy review and evaluation.

Making an Oral Presentation

Your professor may ask you to prepare a strategic-management case analysis, individually or as a group, and present your analysis to the class. Oral presentations are usually graded on two parts: content and delivery. *Content* refers to the quality, quantity, correctness, and appropriateness of analyses presented, including such dimensions as logical flow through the presentation, coverage of major issues, use of specifics, avoidance of generalities, absence of mistakes, and feasibility of recommendations. *Delivery* includes such dimensions as audience attentiveness, clarity of visual aids, appropriate dress, persuasiveness of arguments, tone of voice, eye contact, and posture. Great ideas are of no value unless others can be convinced of their merit through clear communication. The guidelines presented here can help you make an effective oral presentation.

Organizing the Presentation

Begin your presentation by introducing yourself and giving a clear outline of topics to be covered. If a team is presenting, specify the sequence of speakers and the areas each person will address. At the beginning of an oral presentation, try to capture your audience's interest and attention. You could do this by displaying some products made by the company, telling an interesting short story about the company, or sharing an experience you had that is related to the company, its products, or its services. You could develop or obtain a video to show at the beginning of class; you could visit a local distributor of the firm's products and tape a personal interview with the business owner or manager. A light or humorous introduction can be effective at the beginning of a presentation.

Be sure the setting of your presentation is well organized, with seats for attendees, flip charts, a transparency projector, and whatever else you plan to use. Arrive at the classroom at least 15 minutes early to organize the setting, and be sure your materials are ready to go. Make sure everyone can see your visual aids well.

Controlling Your Voice

An effective rate of speaking ranges from 100 to 125 words per minute. Practice your presentation aloud to determine if you are going too fast. Individuals commonly speak too fast when nervous. Breathe deeply before and during the presentation to help yourself slow down. Have a cup of water available; pausing to take a drink will wet your throat, give you time to collect your thoughts, control your nervousness, slow you down, and signal to the audience a change in topic.

Avoid a monotone voice by placing emphasis on different words or sentences. Speak loudly and clearly, but do not shout. Silence can be used effectively to break a monotone voice. Stop at the end of each sentence, rather than running sentences together with *and* or *uh*.

Managing Body Language

Be sure not to fold your arms, lean on the podium, put your hands in your pockets, or put your hands behind you. Keep a straight posture, with one foot slightly in front of the other. Do not turn your back to the audience; doing so is not only rude, but it also prevents your voice from projecting well. Avoid using too many hand gestures. On occasion, leave the podium or table and walk toward your audience, but do not walk around too much. Never block the audience's view of your visual aids.

Maintain good eye contact throughout the presentation. This is the best way to persuade your audience. There is nothing more reassuring to a speaker than to see members of the audience nod in agreement or smile. Try to look everyone in the eye at least once during your presentation, but focus more on individuals who look interested than on those who seem bored. To stay in touch with your audience, use humor and smiles as appropriate throughout your presentation. A presentation should never be dull!

Speaking from Notes

Be sure not to read to your audience because reading puts people to sleep. Perhaps worse than reading is merely reciting what you have memorized. Do not try to memorize anything. Rather, practice unobtrusively using notes. Make sure your notes are written clearly so you will not flounder when trying to read your own writing. Include only main ideas on your note cards. Keep note cards on a podium or table if possible so that you will not drop them or get them out of order; walking with note cards tends to be distracting.

Constructing Visual Aids

Make sure your visual aids are legible to individuals in the back of the room. Use color to highlight special items. Avoid putting complete sentences on visual aids; rather, use short phrases and then orally elaborate on issues as you make your presentation. Generally, there should be no more than four to six lines of text on each visual aid. Use clear headings and subheadings. Be careful about spelling and grammar; use a consistent style of lettering. Use masking tape or an easel for posters—do not hold posters in your hand. Transparencies and handouts are excellent aids; however, be careful not to use too many handouts or your audience may concentrate on them instead of you during the presentation.

Answering Questions

It is best to field questions at the end of your presentation, rather than during the presentation itself. Encourage questions, and take your time to respond to each one. Answering questions can be persuasive because it involves you with the audience. If a team is giving the presentation, the audience should direct questions to a specific person. During the question-and-answer period, be polite, confident, and courteous. Avoid verbose responses. Do not get defensive with your answers, even if a hostile or confrontational question is asked. Staying calm during potentially disruptive situations, such as a cross-examination, reflects self-confidence, maturity, poise, and command of the particular company and its industry. Stand up throughout the question-and-answer period.

Tips for Success in Case Analysis

Strategic-management students who have used this text over 14 editions offer you the following tips for success in doing case analysis. The tips are grouped into two basic sections: (1) Content Tips and (2) Process Tips. Content tips relate especially to the content of your case analysis, whereas the Process tips relate mostly to the process that you and your group mates undergo in preparing and delivering your case analysis/presentation.

Content Tips

1. Use the www.strategyclub.com website resources. The free excel student template provided there is especially useful as are the sample PowerPoint case analyses on a couple of companies.
2. In preparing your external assessment, use the S&P *Industry Survey* material in your college library.
3. Go to http://finance.yahoo.com or http://money.msn.com and enter your company's stock symbol.
4. View your case analysis and presentation as a product that must have some competitive factor to favorably differentiate it from the case analyses of other students.
5. Develop a mind-set of *why*, continually questioning your own and others' assumptions and assertions.
6. Because strategic management is a capstone course, seek the help of professors in other specialty areas when necessary.
7. Read your case frequently as work progresses so you do not overlook details.
8. At the end of each group session, assign each member of the group a task to be completed for the next meeting.
9. Become friends with the library and the Internet.
10. Be creative and innovative throughout the case analysis process.
11. A goal of case analysis is to improve your ability to think clearly in ambiguous and confusing situations; do not get frustrated that there is no single best answer.
12. Do not confuse symptoms with causes; do not develop conclusions and solutions prematurely; recognize that information may be misleading, conflicting, or wrong.
13. Work hard to develop the ability to formulate reasonable, consistent, and creative plans; put yourself in the strategist's position.
14. Develop confidence in using quantitative tools for analysis. They are not inherently difficult; it is just practice and familiarity you need.
15. Strive for excellence in writing and in the technical preparation of your case. Prepare nice charts, tables, diagrams, and graphs. Use color and unique pictures. No messy exhibits! Use PowerPoint.
16. Do not forget that the objective is to learn; explore areas with which you are not familiar.
17. Pay attention to detail.
18. Think through alternative implications fully and realistically. The consequences of decisions are not always apparent. They often affect many different aspects of a firm's operations.
19. Provide answers to such fundamental questions as *what, when, where, why, who,* and *how.*
20. Do not merely recite ratios or present figures. Rather, develop ideas and conclusions concerning the possible trends. Show the importance of these figures to the corporation.
21. Support reasoning and judgment with factual data whenever possible.
22. Your analysis should be as detailed and specific as possible.
23. A picture speaks a thousand words, and a creative picture gets you an A in many classes.
24. Emphasize the Recommendations and Strategy Implementation sections. A common mistake is to spend too much time on the external or internal analysis parts of your paper or presentation. The recommendations and implementation sections are the most important part.
25. Throughout your case analysis, emphasize how your proposed strategic plan will enable the firm to gain and sustain competitive advantage.

Process Tips

1. When working as a team, encourage most of the work to be done individually. Use team meetings mostly to assimilate work. This approach is most efficient.
2. If allowed to do so, invite questions throughout your presentation.
3. During the presentation, keep good posture, eye contact, and voice tone, and project confidence. Do not get defensive under any conditions or with any questions.
4. Prepare your case analysis in advance of the due date to allow time for reflection and practice. Do not procrastinate.
5. Maintain a positive attitude about the class, working *with* problems rather than against them.
6. Keep in tune with your professor, and understand his or her values and expectations.
7. Other students will have strengths in functional areas that will complement your weaknesses, so develop a cooperative spirit that moderates competitiveness in group work.
8. When preparing a case analysis as a group, divide into separate teams to work on the external analysis and internal analysis.
9. Have a good sense of humor.
10. Capitalize on the strengths of each member of the group; volunteer your services in your areas of strength.
11. Set goals for yourself and your team; budget your time to attain them.
12. Foster attitudes that encourage group participation and interaction. Do not be hasty to judge group members.
13. Be prepared to work. There will be times when you will have to do more than your share. Accept it, and do what you have to do to move the team forward.
14. Think of your case analysis as if it were really happening; do not reduce case analysis to a mechanical process.
15. To uncover flaws in your analysis and to prepare the group for questions during an oral presentation, assign one person in the group to actively play the devil's advocate.
16. Do not schedule excessively long group meetings; two-hour sessions are about right.
17. Push your ideas hard enough to get them listened to, but then let up; listen to others and try to follow their lines of thinking; follow the flow of group discussion, recognizing when you need to get back on track; do not repeat yourself or others unless clarity or progress demands repetition.
18. Develop a case-presentation style that is direct, assertive, and convincing; be concise, precise, fluent, and correct.
19. Have fun when at all possible. Preparing a case is frustrating at times, but enjoy it while you can; it may be several years before you are playing CEO again.
20. In group cases, do not allow personality differences to interfere. When they occur, they must be understood for what they are—and then put aside.
21. Get things written down (drafts) as soon as possible.
22. Read everything that other group members write, and comment on it in writing. This allows group input into all aspects of case preparation.
23. Adaptation and flexibility are keys to success; be creative and innovative.
24. Neatness is a real plus; your case analysis should look professional.
25. Let someone else read and critique your presentation several days before you present it.
26. Make special efforts to get to know your group members. This leads to more openness in the group and allows for more interchange of ideas. Put in the time and effort necessary to develop these relationships.
27. Be constructively critical of your group members' work. Do not dominate group discussions. Be a good listener and contributor.
28. Learn from past mistakes and deficiencies. Improve on weak aspects of other case presentations.
29. Learn from the positive approaches and accomplishments of classmates.

Sample Case Analysis Outline

There are musicians who play wonderfully without notes and there are chefs who cook wonderfully without recipes, but most of us prefer a more orderly cookbook approach, at least in the first attempt at doing something new. Therefore the following eight steps may serve as a basic outline for you in presenting a strategic plan for your firm's future. This outline is not the only approach used in business and industry for communicating a strategic plan, but this approach is time-tested, it does work, and it does cover all of the basics. You may amend the content, tools, and concepts given to suit your own company, audience, assignment, and circumstances, but it helps to know and understand the rules before you start breaking them.

Depending on whether your class is 50 minutes or 75 minutes and how much time your professor allows for your case presentation, the following outlines what generally needs to be covered. A recommended time (in minutes) as part of the presentation is given for an overall 50-minute event. Even if you do not have time to cover all areas in your oral presentation, you may be asked to prepare these areas and give them to your professor as a written case analysis. Be sure in an oral presentation to manage time knowing that your recommendations and associated costs are the most important part. You should go to www.strategyclub.com and use that information and software in preparing your case analysis. Good luck.

Current Readings

Kearney, Eric, Diether Gebert, and Sven Voelpel. "When Diversity Benefits Teams: The Importance of Team Members' Need for Cognition." *Academy of Management Journal*, June 2009, 581–598.

STEPS IN PRESENTING AN ORAL CASE ANALYSIS

ORAL PRESENTATION—STEP 1
Introduction (2 minutes)

a. Introduce yourselves by name and major. Establish the time setting of your case and analysis. Prepare your strategic plan for the three years 2014–2016.
b. Introduce your company and its products or services; capture interest.
c. Show the outline of your presentation and tell who is doing what parts.
d. Let your audience know that the primary motivation, rationale, or intent of every slide is to reveal how the firm can best gain and sustain competitive advantage.

ORAL PRESENTATION—STEP 2
Mission and Vision (4 minutes)

a. Show existing mission and vision statements if available from the firm's website, annual report, or elsewhere.
b. Show your "improved" mission and vision and tell why it is improved.
c. Compare your mission and vision to a leading competitor's statements.
d. Comment on your vision and mission in terms of how they support the strategies you envision for your firm.

ORAL PRESENTATION—STEP 3
Internal Assessment (8 minutes)

a. Give your financial ratio analysis. Highlight especially good and bad ratios. Do not give definitions of the ratios and do not highlight all the ratios.
b. Show the firm's organizational chart found or "created based on executive titles." Identify the type of chart as well as good and bad aspects. Unless all white males comprise the chart, peoples' names are generally not important because positions reveal structure as people come and go.
c. Present your improved or recommended organizational chart. Tell why you feel it is improved over the existing chart.
d. Show a market positioning map with firm and competitors. Discuss the map in light of strategies you envision for firm versus competitors' strategies.
e. Identify the marketing strategy of the firm in terms of good and bad points versus competitors and in light of strategies you envision for the firm.

f. Show a map locating the firm's operations. Discuss in light of strategies you envision. Also, perhaps show a value chain analysis chart.

g. Discuss (and perhaps show) the firm's website and Facebook page in terms of good and bad points compared to rival firms.

h. Show your "value of the firm" analysis.

i. List 20 of the firm's strengths and weaknesses. Go over each one listed without "reading" them verbatim.

j. Show and explain your Internal Factor Evaluation (IFE) Matrix.

ORAL PRESENTATION—STEP 4
External Assessment (8 minutes)

a. Identify and discuss major competitors. Use pie charts, maps, tables, or figures to show the intensity of competition in the industry.

b. Show your Competitive Profile Matrix. Include at least 12 factors and two competitors.

c. Summarize key industry trends citing Standard & Poor's *Industry Survey* or Chamber of Commerce statistics, and so on. Highlight key external trends as they impact the firm, including trends that are economic, social, cultural, demographic, geographic, technological, political, legal, governmental, and to do with the natural environment.

d. List 20 of the firm's opportunities and threats. Make sure your opportunities are not stated as strategies. Go over each one listed without "reading" them verbatim.

e. Show and explain your External Factor Evaluation (EFE) Matrix.

ORAL PRESENTATION—STEP 5
Strategy Formulation (14 minutes)

a. Show and explain your SWOT Matrix, highlighting each of your strategies listed.

b. Show and explain your SPACE Matrix, using half of your "space time" on calculations and the other half on implications of those numbers. Strategy implications must be specific rather than generic. In other words, use of a term such as *market penetration* is not satisfactory alone as a strategy implication.

c. Show your Boston Consulting Group (BCG) Matrix. Again focus on both the numbers and the strategy implications. Do multiple BCG Matrices if possible, including domestic versus global, or another geographic breakdown. Develop a product BCG if at all possible. Comment on changes to this matrix as per strategies you envision. Develop this matrix even if you do not know the profits per division and even if you have to estimate the axes information. However, make no wild guesses on axes or revenue/profit information.

d. Show your Internal-External (IE) Matrix. Because this analysis is similar to the BCG, see the preceding comments.

e. Show your Grand Strategy Matrix. Again focus on implications after giving the quadrant selection. Reminder: Use of a term such as *market penetration* is not satisfactory alone as a strategy implication. Be more specific. Elaborate.

f. Show your Quantitative Strategic Planning Matrix (QSPM). Be sure to explain your strategies to start with here. Do not go back over the internal and external factors. Avoid having more than one 4, 3, 2, or 1 in a row. If you rate one strategy, you need to rate the other because that particular factor is affecting the choice. Work row by row rather than column by column on preparing the QSPM.

g. Present your recommendations page. This is the most important page in your presentation. Be specific in terms of both strategies and estimated costs of those strategies. *Total your estimated costs.* You should have 10 or more strategies. Divide your strategies into two groups: (1) Existing Strategies to Be Continued and (2) New Strategies to Be Started.

ORAL PRESENTATION—STEP 6
Strategy Implementation (8 minutes)

a. Show and explain your earnings per share/earnings before interest and taxes (EPS/EBIT) analysis to reveal whether stock, debt, or a combination is best to finance your recommendations. Graph the analysis. Decide which approach to use if there are any given limitations of the analysis.

b. Show your projected income statement. Relate changes in the items to your recommendations rather than blindly going with historical percentage changes.

c. Show your projected balance sheet. Relate changes in your items to your recommendations. Be sure to show the retained earnings calculation and the results of your EPS/EBIT decision.

d. Show your projected financial ratios and highlight several key ratios to show the benefits of your strategic plan.

ORAL PRESENTATION—STEP 7

Strategy Evaluation (2 minutes)

a. Prepare a Balanced Scorecard to show your expected financial and nonfinancial objectives recommended for the firm.

ORAL PRESENTATION—STEP 8

Conclusion (4 minutes)

a. Compare and contrast your strategic plan versus the company's own plans for the future.

b. Thank audience members for their attention. Genuinely seek and gladly answer questions.

Glossary

Acquisition When a large organization purchases (acquires) a smaller firm; a merger.

Actionable factors Meaningful in terms of having strategic implications; reveal potential strategies to capitalize or compensate.

Activity ratios Inventory turnover and average collection period measure how effectively a firm is using its resources.

Advantage A way to evaluate strategies, i.e. to determine if a particular strategy creates or extends a firm's competitive superiority in a selected area of activity.

Aggressive quadrant In a SPACE matrix analysis, when the firm's directional vector points in the upper right quadrant, the firm should pursue aggressive strategies.

Annual objectives Desired targets to achieve; used to focus/direct/channel efforts and activities of organization members. They (1) represent the basis for allocating resources; (2) are a primary mechanism for evaluating managers; (3) are the major instrument for monitoring progress toward achieving long-term objectives; and (4) establish organizational, divisional, and departmental priorities.

Annual objectives Short-term milestones, usually one year, that organizations must achieve to reach long-term targets/goals.

Attractiveness scores (AS) In a QSPM, the numerical value (rating) that indicates the relative attractiveness of each strategy given a single internal or external factor.

Auditing The accounting process that firms undertake to have their financial statements reviewed for accuracy in order to assure compliance with the law and IRS code.

Avoidance A method for reducing conflict through such actions as ignoring the problem in hopes that the conflict will resolve itself or physically separating the conflicting individuals (or groups).

Backward integration A strategy seeking ownership or increased control of a firm's suppliers, such as a manufacturer acquiring its raw material source firms.

Balanced scorecard A framework of desired objectives; derives its name from the need of firms to "balance" quantitative (such as financial ratios and percentages) with qualitative (such as for employee morale and business ethics) objectives that are oftentimes used in strategy evaluation.

Balanced Scorecard A strategy evaluation tool utilized to establish, monitor, and evaluate both qualitative and quantitative (hence the word balanced) objectives in order to improve organizational effectiveness and performance.

Bankruptcy A legal document that allows a firm to avoid major debt obligations and void union contracts in order to survive and regroup as a firm. There are five major types: Chapter 2, Chapter 10, and Chapter 11.

Benchmarking A management technique associated with value chain analysis, whereby a firm compares itself on a wide variety of performance-related criteria against the best firms in the industry, thus establishing standards of excellence.

Benchmarking An analytical tool used to determine how a firm's value chain activities compare to rival firms in order to better gain and sustain competitive advantages.

Board of directors A group of individuals above the CEO, who have oversight and guidance over management and who care for shareholders' interests.

Bonus system A form of incentive compensation whereby employees and/or managers receive a year-end or period-end reward, usually cash, based on some organizational performance criteria such as sales, profit, production efficiency, quality, and safety; used to motivate individuals to support strategy-implementation efforts.

Book value Number of shares outstanding times stock price.

Boston Consulting Group (BCG) Matrix A four quadrant, strategic planning analytical tool that places an organization's various divisions as circles in a display (similar to the IE Matrix) based on two key dimensions: 1) relative market share position and 2) industry growth rate. The diagram's four quadrants (Stars, Question Marks, Cash Cows, Question Marks) each have different strategy implications.

Breakeven (BE) point The quantity of units that a firm must sell in order for its total revenues (TR) to equal its total costs (TC).

Bribe A gift bestowed to influence a recipient's conduct.

Bribery Offering, giving, receiving, or soliciting of any item of value to influence the actions of an official or other person in discharge of a public or legal duty.

Business analytics An MIS technique designed to analyze huge volumes of data to help executives make decisions; sometimes called predictive analytics or data mining.

Business ethics Principles of behavior/conduct a firm may institute to minimize wrongdoing among employees/managers.

Business portfolio Autonomous divisions (or profit centers or segments) of an organization as represented by circles in a BCG and IE matrices.

Business-Process Outsourcing (BPO) When a firm contracts with an outside firm(s) to take over some of their functional operations, such as human resources, information systems, payroll, accounting, or customer service.

Capacity utilization The extent to which a manufacturing plant's output reaches its potential output; the higher the capacity utilization the better, because otherwise equipment may sit idle.

Capital budgeting A basic function of finance; the allocation and reallocation of capital and resources to projects, products, assets, and divisions of an organization.

Cash budget The most common type of financial budget; developed to forecast future receipts and disbursements of cash in operations, investments, and financing.

Cash cows A quadrant in the BCG Matrix for divisions that have a high relative market share position but compete in a low-growth industry; they generate cash in excess of their needs, they are often milked, this is the lower left quadrant.

Champions Individuals most strongly identified with a firm's new idea/product/service, and whose futures are linked to its success.

Chief Information Officer (CIO) Is more an external manager compared to a CTO; focuses on the firm's technical, information gathering, and social media relationship with diverse external stakeholders.

Chief Technology Officer (CTO) Is more of an internal manager than the CIO; focuses on technical issues such as data acquisition, data processing, decision-support systems, and software and hardware acquisition.

Code of business ethics A written document specifying expected employee/manager behavior/conduct in an organization.

Combination strategy The pursuit of a combination of two or more strategies simultaneously.

Communication Perhaps the most important word in strategic management, because gathering, assimilating, and evaluating information in an interactive, effective manner can lead to enhanced understanding and commitment so vital in strategic planning.

Competitive advantage Anything a firm does especially well, compared to rival firms. For example, when a firm can do something that rival firms cannot do, or owns something that rival firms desire, that can represent a competitive advantage.

Competitive analysis The process of gathering and analyzing data about competitors and disseminating the data (intelligence) on a timely basis to who needs to know in order to gain and sustain a firm's competitive advantages.

Competitive Intelligence (CI) "A systematic and ethical process for gathering and analyzing information about the competition's activities and general business trends to further a business's own goals" (SCIP website).

Competitive Position (CP) One of four dimensions/axes of the SPACE Matrix; determines an organization's competitiveness, using such factors as market share, product quality, product life cycle, customer loyalty, capacity utilization, technological know-how and control over suppliers and distributors.

Competitive Profile Matrix (CPM) A widely used strategic planning analytical tool designed to identify a firm's major competitors and its particular strengths and weaknesses in relation to a sample firm's strategic position.

Competitive quadrant In a SPACE Matrix analysis, when the firm's directional vector points in the lower right quadrant it suggests that the firm should pursue competitive strategies such as horizontal integration.

Concern for employees A component of the mission statement; are employees a valuable asset to the firm?

Concern for public image A component of the mission statement; is the firm responsive to social, community, and environmental concerns?

Concern for survival, growth, and profitability A component of the mission statement; does the firm strive to survive, grow, and (if for-profit) be profitable?

Conflict A disagreement between two or more parties on one or more issues.

Confrontation A method for reducing conflict exemplified by exchanging members of conflicting parties so that each can gain an appreciation of the other's point of view, or holding a meeting at which conflicting parties present their views and work through their differences.

Conservative quadrant In a SPACE Matrix analysis, when the firm's directional vector points in the upper left quadrant it suggests that the firm should pursue conservative strategies such as market penetration.

Consistency A way to evaluate strategies, i.e. to determine if a particular strategy is supportive of overall strategies/objectives/policies of the firm.

Consonance Refers to the need for strategists to examine sets of trends, as well as individual trends, in evaluating strategies.

Contingency plans Alternative plans that can be put into effect if certain key events do not occur as expected.

Controlling A basic function of management; includes all of those activities undertaken to ensure that actual operations conform to planned operations.

Cooperative arrangements Includes joint ventures, research and development partnerships, cross-distribution agreements, cross-licensing agreements, cross-manufacturing agreements, and joint-bidding consortia.

Core competence A value chain activity that a firm performs especially well.

Cost leadership One of Michael Porter's strategy dimensions that involves a firm producing standardized products at a very low per-unit cost for consumers who are price-sensitive.

Cost/benefit analysis An activity that involves assessing the costs, benefits, and risks associated with marketing decisions. Three steps are required to perform this: (1) compute the total costs associated with a decision, (2) estimate the total benefits from the decision, and (3) compare the total costs with the total benefits.

Creed statement Another name for mission statement; a declaration of an organization's "reason for being." It answers the pivotal question, "What is our business?"

Cultural products Include values, beliefs, rites, rituals, ceremonies, myths, stories, legends, sagas, language, metaphors, symbols, heroes, and heroines. These products are levers that strategists can use to influence and direct strategy formulation, implementation, and evaluation activities.

Culture The set of shared values, beliefs, attitudes, customs, norms, personalities, heroes, and heroines that describe a firm.

Culture The set of shared values, beliefs, attitudes, customs, norms, personalities, heroes, and heroines that describe a firm. Strategists should strive to preserve, emphasize, and build upon these aspects.

Customer analysis Examination and evaluation of consumer needs, desires, and wants; involves administering customer surveys, analyzing consumer information, evaluating market positioning strategies, developing customer profiles, and determining optimal market segmentation strategies.

Customers A component of the mission statement; individuals who purchase a firm's products/services.

Data mining Analyzing huge volumes of information in order to determine trends and garner information to make decision making more effective.

Data Raw facts and figures; "data" becomes "information" only when they are evaluated, filtered, condensed, analyzed, and organized for a specific purpose, problem, individual, or time.

De-integration Reducing the pursuit of backward integration; instead of owning suppliers, companies negotiate with several outside suppliers.

Decentralized structure Also called a divisional structure, this type of organizational design is based on having various profit centers or segments by geographic area, by product or service, by customer, or by process. With a divisional structure, functional activities are performed both centrally and in each separate division.

Decision stage Stage 3 of the strategy formulation analytical framework that involves development of the Quantitative Strategic Planning Matrix (QSPM). A QSPM uses input information from Stage 1 to objectively evaluate feasible alternative strategies identified in Stage 2. A QSPM reveals the relative attractiveness of alternative strategies and thus provides objective basis for selecting specific strategies.

Defensive quadrant In a SPACE Matrix analysis, when the firm's directional vector into the lower left quadrant it suggests that the firm should pursue defensive strategies such as retrenchment.

Defusion A method for reducing conflict includes playing down differences between conflicting parties while accentuating similarities and common interests, or compromising so that there is neither a clear winner nor loser, or resorting to majority rule, or appealing to a higher authority, or redesigning present positions.

Delayering Reducing the number of divisions or units or hierarchical levels in a firm's organizational structure.

Demand void Areas in a perceptual map where there is not a cluster of ideal points indicating an unattractive group of potential customers.

Differentiation One of Michael Porter's strategy dimensions that involves a firm producing products and services considered unique industry-wide and directed at consumers who are relatively price-insensitive.

Directional vector In a SPACE Matrix analysis, this line begins at the origin and goes into one of four quadrants, revealing the type of strategies recommended for the organization: aggressive, competitive, defensive, or conservative.

Director of competitive analysis The person who gathers and analyzes data about competitors, and disseminates data (intelligence) on a timely basis to who needs to know in order to gain and sustain a firm's competitive advantages.

Discount If an acquiring firm pays less for another firm than the firm's stock price times its # of shares of stock outstanding (book value or market value), then that # less the actual purchase price is called a discount.

Distinctive competencies A firm's strengths that cannot be easily matched or imitated by competitors.

Distribution The process of getting goods and services to market; includes warehousing, distribution channels, distribution coverage, retail site locations, sales territories, inventory levels and location, transportation carriers, wholesaling, and retailing.

Diversification strategies When a firm enters a new business/industry, either related and unrelated to their existing business/industry. Related diversification is when the old vs. new business value chains possesses competitively valuable cross-business strategic fits; unrelated diversification is when the old vs. new business value chains are so dissimilar that no competitively valuable cross-business relationships exist.

Divestiture Selling a division or part of an organization.

Dividend decision A basic function of finance; concerns issues such as the percentage of earnings paid to stockholders, the stability of dividends paid over time, and the repurchase or issuance of stock.

Dividend recapitalizations When private-equity firms especially, but other firms also, borrow money to fund dividend payouts to themselves.

Divisional structure This type of organizational design is based on having various profit centers or segments by geographic area, by product or service, by customer, or by process. With a divisional structure, functional activities are performed both centrally and in each separate division.

Dogs A quadrant in the BCG Matrix for divisions that have a low relative market share position and compete in a low-growth industry, this is the lower right quadrant.

Downsizing Reducing the number of employees, number of divisions or units, and/or number of hierarchical levels in the firm's organizational structure.

Educative change strategy A management technique to facilitate a firm adapting to new strategies/policies/situations by presenting to employees/managers information that reveals why the firm needs to do what is to be done; this approach can be slow but oftentimes yields high commitment.

Empirical indicators Refers to three characteristics of resources (rare, hard to imitate, not easily substitutable) that enable a firm to gain and sustain competitive advantage.

Employee Stock Ownership Plans (ESOP) A tax-qualified, defined-contribution, employee-benefit plan whereby employees purchase stock of the company through borrowed money or cash contributions.

Empowerment The act of strengthening employees' sense of shared ownership by encouraging them to participate in decision making and rewarding them for doing so.

Environment The surroundings in which an organization operates, including air, water, land, natural resources, flora, fauna, humans, and their interrelation.

Environmental Management System (EMS) When a firm or municipality operates utilizing "green" policies/practices/procedures as outlined by ISO 14001.

Environmental scanning Another term for external audit; conducting research to gather and assimilate external information.

Environmental scanning Process of conducting research and gathering and assimilating external information.

EPS/EBIT analysis A financial technique to determine whether debt, stock, or a combination of debt and stock is the best alternative for raising capital to implement strategies.

Establishing annual objectives The managerial activity that determines appropriate/desired targets to achieve by region/product/service.

External audit Process of identifying and evaluating trends and events beyond the control of a single firm, in areas such as social, cultural, demographic technology, economic, political, and competition; reveals key opportunities and threats confronting an organization, so managers can better formulate strategies.

External Factor Evaluation (EFE) Matrix A widely used strategic planning analytical tool designed to summarize and evaluate economic, social, cultural, demographic, environmental, political, governmental, legal, technological, and competitive information.

External forces (1) Economic forces; (2) social, cultural, demographic, and natural environment forces; (3) political, governmental, and legal forces; (4) technological forces; and (5) competitive forces.

External opportunities Economic, social, cultural, demographic, environmental, political, legal, governmental, technological, and competitive trends/events/facts that could significantly benefit an organization in the future.

External threats Economic, social, cultural, demographic, environmental, political, legal, governmental, technological, and competitive trends/events/facts that could significantly harm an organization in the future.

Feasibility A way to evaluate strategies, i.e. to determine if a strategy is capable of being carried out within the physical, human, and financial resources of the firm.

Feng shui In China, this term refers to the practice of harnessing natural forces, which can impact how you arrange office furniture.

Financial budget A financial document that details/reveals how funds will be obtained and spent for a specified period of time in the future.

Financial objectives Include desired results growth in revenues, growth in earnings, higher dividends, larger profit margins, greater return on investment, higher earnings per share, a rising stock price, improved cash flow, and so on.

Financial Position (FP) One of four dimensions/axes of the SPACE Matrix that determines an organization's financial strength, considering such factors as return on investment, leverage, liquidity, working capital, and cash flow.

Financial ratio analysis Quantitative calculations that reveal the financial condition of a firm and exemplify the complexity of relationships among the functional areas of business. For example, a declining return on investment or profit margin ratio could be the result of ineffective marketing, poor management policies, research and development errors, or a weak management information system. Ratios are usually compared to industry averages, or to prior time periods, or to rival firms.

Financing decision A basic function of finance; determines the best capital structure for the firm and includes examining various methods by which the firm can raise capital (for example, by issuing stock, increasing debt, selling assets, or using a combination of these approaches).

First mover advantages The benefits a firm may achieve by entering a new market or developing a new product or service before rival firms.

Fixed Costs (FC) A key variable in breakeven analysis; includes costs such as plant, equipment, stores, advertising, and land.

Focus One of Michael Porter's strategy dimensions that involves a firm producing products and services that fulfill the needs of small groups of consumers.

Force change strategy A management technique to facilitate a firm adapting to new strategies/policies/situations by simply giving orders and enforcing those orders; this approach has the advantage of being fast, but it is plagued by low commitment.

Forward integration A strategy that involves gaining ownership or increased control over distributors or retailers, such as a manufacturer opening its own chain of stores.

Franchising An effective means of implementing forward integration whereby a franchisee purchases the right to own one or more stores/restaurants of a chain firm.

Friendly merger If the merger/acquisition is desired by both firms.

Functional structure A type of organizational design that groups tasks and activities by business function, such as production/operations, marketing, finance/accounting, research and development, and management information systems.

Functions of finance/accounting The basic activities performed by finance managers; consists of three decisions: the investment decision, the financing decision, and the dividend decision.

Functions of management Consist of five basic activities: planning, organizing, motivating, staffing, and controlling.

Functions of marketing The basic activities performed by marketing managers, including (1) customer analysis, (2) selling products/services, (3) product and service planning, (4) pricing, (5) distribution, (6) marketing research, and (7) opportunity analysis.

Furloughs Temporary layoffs.

Future shock High anxiety that results when the nature, types, and speed of changes overpower an individual's or organization's ability and capacity to adapt.

GAAS, GAAP, and IFRS Generally accepted auditing standards, generally accepted accounting principles, and international financial reporting standards.

Gain sharing A form of incentive compensation whereby employees and/or managers receive bonuses when actual results exceed some pre-determined performance targets.

Generic strategies Michael Porter's strategy breakdown; consists of three strategies: cost leadership, differentiation, and focus.

Glass ceiling A term used to refer to the artificial barrier that women and minorities face in moving into upper levels of management.

Global strategy Designing, producing, and marketing products with global needs in mind, instead of solely considering individual countries.

Globalization A process of doing business worldwide, so strategic decisions are made based on global profitability of the firm rather than just domestic considerations.

Goodwill If a firm acquires another firm and pays more than the book value (market value), then the additional amount paid is called a premium, and becomes goodwill, which is a line item on the assets portion of a balance sheet.

Governance The act of oversight and direction, especially in association with the duties of a board of directors.

Grand Strategy Matrix A four-quadrant, two axis tool for formulating alternative strategies. All organizations can be positioned in one of this matrix's four strategy quadrants, based on their position on two evaluative dimensions: competitive position and market (industry) growth. Strategy suggestions ensue depending on which quadrant the firm is located.

Growth ratios Measures such as the percent increase/decrease in revenue or profit from one period to the next are important comparisons.

Guanxi In China, business behavior is based on "personal relations".

Halo error The human tendency to put too much weight on a single factor.

Horizontal consistency of objectives Objectives need to be compatible across functions; for example if marketing wants to sell 10% more than production must produce 10% more.

Horizontal integration Acquiring a rival firm.

Hostile takeover If the merger/acquisition is not desired by both firms.

Human resource management Also called personnel management; a basic function of management; includes activities such as recruiting, interviewing, testing, selecting, orienting, training, developing, caring for, evaluating, rewarding, disciplining, promoting, transferring, demoting, and dismissing employees, as well as managing union relations.

Industrial Organization (I/O) An approach to competitive advantage that advocates that external (industry) factors are more important than internal factors for a firm in striving to achieve competitive advantage.

Industry analysis Another term for external audit; conducting research to gather and assimilate external information.

Industry Position (IP) One of four dimensions/axes of the SPACE Matrix that determines how strong/weak a firm's industry is, considering such factors as growth potential, profit potential, financial stability, extent leveraged, resource utilization, ease of entry into market, productivity and capacity utilization.

Information Technology (IT) The development, maintenance, and use of computer systems, software, and networks for the processing and distribution of data.

Information Data that has been evaluated, filtered, condensed, analyzed, and organized for a specific purpose, problem, individual, or time.

Inhwa A South Korean term for activities that involve concern for harmony based on respect of hierarchical relationships, including obedience to authority.

Initial public offering When a private firm goes public by selling its shares of stock to the public in order to raise capital.

Input stage Stage 1 of the strategy-formulation analytical framework that summarizes the basic input information needed to formulate strategies; consists of an EFEM, CPM, and IFEM.

Integration strategies Includes forward integration, backward integration, and horizontal integration (sometimes collectively referred to as vertical integration strategies).

Intensive strategies Includes market development, market penetration, and product development.

Internal audit The process of gathering and assimilating information about the firm's management, marketing, finance/accounting, production/operations, R&D, and MIS operations. The purpose is to identify/evaluate/prioritize a firm's strengths and weaknesses.

Internal Factor Evaluation (IFE) Matrix A strategy-formulation tool that summarizes and evaluates a firm's major strengths and weaknesses in the functional areas of a business, and provides a basis for identifying and evaluating relationships among those areas.

Internal strengths An organization's controllable activities that are performed especially well, such as in areas that include finance, marketing, management, accounting, MIS, across a firm's products/regions/stores/facilities.

Internal weaknesses An organization's controllable activities that are performed especially poorly, such as in areas that include finance, marketing, management, accounting, MIS, across a firm's products/regions/stores/facilities.

Internal-External (IE) Matrix A nine quadrant, strategic planning analytical tool that places an organization's various divisions as circles in a display (similar to the BCG Matrix) based on two key dimensions: 1) the segment's IFE total weighted scores on the x-axis and 2) the segment's EFE total weighted scores on the y-axis. The diagram is divided into three major regions that have different strategy implications: 1) grow and build or 2) hold and maintain, or 3) harvest or divest.

International firms Firms that conduct business outside their own country.

Internet A global system of interconnected computers that serve billions of users worldwide; provides a vast range of information resources and services; enables billions of businesses and individuals globally to communicate instantly with each other by email, tweets, etc.

Intuition Using one's cognition without evident rational thought or analysis; based on past experience, judgment, and feelings; essential to making good strategic decisions but must not relied upon heavily in lieu of objective analysis.

Investment decision Also called capital budgeting; a basic function of finance; the allocation and reallocation of capital and resources to projects, products, assets, and divisions of an organization.

ISO 14000 A series of voluntary standards in the environmental field whereby a firm minimizes harmful effects on the environment caused by its activities and continually monitors and improves its own environmental performance.

ISO 14001 A set of standards adopted by thousands of firms worldwide to certify to their constituencies that they are conducting business in an environmentally friendly manner. These standards offer a universal technical standard for environmental compliance that more and more firms are requiring not only of themselves but also of their suppliers and distributors.

Joint venture A strategy that occurs when two or more companies form a temporary partnership/consortium/business for the purpose of capitalizing on some opportunity.

Just-In-Time (JIT) A production approach in which parts and materials are delivered to a production site just as they are needed, rather than being stockpiled as a hedge against late deliveries.

Leverage ratios The debt-to-equity ratio and debt-to-total assets ratio measure the extent to which a firm has been financed by debt.

Leveraged Buyout (LBO) When the outstanding shares of a corporation are bought by the company's management and other private investors using borrowed funds.

Linear regression A quantitative statistical technique often used for forecasting, but based on the assumption that the future will be just like the past. To the extent that historical relationships are unstable, linear regression is less accurate.

Liquidation Selling all of a company's assets, in parts, for their tangible worth.

Liquidity ratios The current ratio and quick ratio measure a firm's ability to meet short-term cash obligations.

Long-range planning Deciding upon future actions/objectives/policies with the aim to optimize for tomorrow the trends of today; less effective and comprehensive than strategic planning.

Long-term objectives Specific results that an organization seeks to achieve (in more than one year) in pursuing its basic vision/mission/strategy.

Long-term objectives The specific results expected from pursuing various strategies.

Management by wandering around A part of strategy evaluation whereby managers simply walk around facilities and operations in order to observe and talk with employees, thus garnering information useful in evaluating strategies.

Management Information System (MIS) A system that gathers, assimilates, and evaluates external and internal information to facilitate decision-making.

Management information system A computer-based process for obtaining and utilizing external and internal facts/figures/trends to support managerial decision-making. Includes gathering and utilizing data about marketing, finance, production, and personnel matters internally, and social, cultural, demographic, environmental, economic, political, governmental, legal, technological, and competitive factors externally.

Market capitalization Number of shares outstanding times stock price.

Market commonality The number and significance of markets that a firm competes in with rivals.

Market development Introducing present products or services into new geographic areas.

Market penetration Increasing market share for present products or services in present markets through greater marketing efforts.

Market segment Areas in a perceptual map where there is a cluster of ideal points indicating an attractive group of potential customers to target.

Market segmentation The marketing technique of subdividing consumers into distinct subsets according to needs and buying habits in order to more effectively and economically direct marketing efforts.

Market value Number of shares outstanding times stock price.

Marketing research The systematic gathering, recording, and analyzing of data about problems/practices/issues related to the marketing of goods and services.

Markets A component of the mission statement; geographic locations where a firm competes.

Marking mix variables Product, place, promotion, and price.

Matching stage Stage 2 of the strategy-formulation framework that focuses upon generating feasible alternative strategies by aligning internal with external factors by utilizing five matrices: BCG, IE, SWOT, GRAND, SPACE.

Matching When an organization matches its internal strengths and weaknesses with its external opportunities and threats using, for example, the SWOT, SPACE, BCG, IE, or GRAND Matrices.

Matrix structure This type of organizational design places functional activities along the top row and divisional projects/units along the left side to create a rubric where managers have two bosses – both a functional boss and a project boss, thus creating the need for extensive vertical and horizontal flows of authority and communication.

Measuring organizational performance Activity # 2 in the strategy evaluation process; includes comparing expected results to actual results, investigating deviations from plans, evaluating individual performance, and examining progress being made toward meeting stated objectives.

Merger When two organizations of about equal size unite to form one enterprise; an acquisition.

Mission statement components 1) Customers, 2) products and services, 3) markets, 4) technology, 5) concern for survival, growth, and profitability, 6) philosophy, 7) self-concept, 8) concern for public image, 9) concern for employees.

Mission statement A declaration of an organization's "reason for being." It answers the pivotal question, "What is our business?" Is essential for effectively establishing objectives and formulating strategies; consists of nine components.

Mission statement An enduring statement of purpose that distinguish one business from other similar firms; several sentence statement that identifies the scope of a firm's operations in product and market terms and addresses the question "What is our business?"

Motivating A basic function of management; the process of influencing and leading people to accomplish specific objectives.

Multidimensional scaling The same as product positioning (perceptual mapping), except encompasses three or more evaluative criteria simultaneously.

Multinational corporations Firms that conduct business outside their own country.

Nemaswashio U.S. managers in Japan have to be careful about this phenomenon, whereby Japanese workers expect supervisors to alert them privately of changes rather than informing them in a meeting.

Organizational culture A pattern of behavior developed by an organization over time as it learns to cope with its problem of external adaptation and internal integration, and that has worked well enough to be considered valid and to be taught to new members as the correct way to perceive, think, and feel in the firm.

Organizing A basic function of management; the process of arranging duties and responsibilities in a coherent manner in order to determine who does what and who reports to whom.

Outstanding shares method A method for determining the cash worth of a firm by multiplying the number of shares outstanding by the market price per share; also called book value, market value, or market capitalization.

Perceptual map Also called product-positioning map; a two-dimensional, four quadrant marketing tool designed to position a firm vs. its rival firms in a schematic diagram in order to better determine effective marketing strategies.

Personnel management Also called human resource management; a basic function of management; includes activities such as recruiting, interviewing, testing, selecting, orienting, training, developing, caring for, evaluating, rewarding, disciplining, promoting, transferring, demoting, and dismissing employees, as well as managing union relations.

Philosophy A component of the mission statement; the basic beliefs, values, aspirations, and ethical priorities of the firm.

Planning A basic function of management; the process of deciding ahead of time strategies to be pursued and actions to be taken in the future.

Policies The means by which annual objectives will be achieved. Policies include guidelines, rules, and procedures established to support efforts to achieve stated objectives. Policies are guides to decision making and address repetitive or recurring situations.

Policy Specific guidelines, methods, procedures, rules, forms, and administrative practices established to support and encourage work toward stated goals.

Porter's Five-Forces Model A theoretical model devised by Michael Porter, who suggests that the nature of competitiveness in a given industry can be viewed as a composite of five forces: 1) Rivalry among competing firms, 2) Potential entry of new competitors, 3) Potential development of substitute products, 4) Bargaining power of suppliers, and 5) Bargaining power of consumers.

Premium If an acquiring firm pays more for another firm than that firm's stock price times its # of shares of stock outstanding (book value or market value), then the overage is called a premium.

Price-earnings ratio method This method involves dividing the market price of the firm's common stock by the annual earnings per share and multiplying this number by the firm's average net income for the past five years.

Pricing A basic function of marketing; determining the appropriate value for products and services to be charged to customers, given associated costs and competitor's prices.

Product and service planning A basic function of marketing; includes activities such as test marketing; product and brand positioning; devising warranties; packaging; determining product options, features, style, and quality; deleting old products; and providing for customer service.

Product development Increased sales by improving or modifying present products or services.

Product positioning Also called perceptual mapping; a two-dimensional, four quadrant marketing tool designed to position a firm vs. its rival firms in a schematic diagram in order to better determine effective marketing strategies.

Production/operations function Consists of all those activities that transform inputs into goods and services; including issues such as inventory control and capacity utilization.

Products or services A component of the mission statement; commodities or benefits provided by a firm.

Profit sharing A form of incentive compensation whereby some of a firm's earnings are distributed to employees/managers based on some pre-determined formula; used to motivate individuals to support strategy-implementation efforts.

Profitability ratios The profit margin ratio and return on investment ratio measure the profitability of a firm's operations.

Projected financial statement analysis A financial technique that enables a firm to forecast the expected financial results of various strategies and approaches; involves developing income statements and balance sheets for future periods of time.

Protectionism When countries impose tariffs, taxes, and regulations on firms outside the country to favor their own companies and people.

Quantitative Strategic Planning Matrix (QSPM) An analytical technique designed to determine the relative attractiveness of feasible alternative actions. This technique comprises Stage 3 of the strategy-formulation analytical framework; it objectively indicates which alternative strategies are best.

Question marks A quadrant in the BCG Matrix for divisions that have a low relative market share position but compete in a high-growth industry; this is the upper right quadrant; firm's generally must decide whether to strengthen such divisions or sell them (hence a question is at hand).

Rational change strategy A management technique to facilitate a firm adapting to new strategies/policies/situations, whereby employees/managers are given incentives to be supportive while at the same time are educated as to the need to change.

Reconciliatory In regard to mission statements, the need for the statement to be sufficiently broad to "reconcile" differences effectively among diverse stakeholders, ie appeal to a firm's customers, employees, shareholders, creditors – rather than alienate any group.

Reengineering Reconfiguring or redesigning work, jobs, and processes in a firm, for the purpose of improving cost, quality, service, and speed.

Related diversification When a firm acquires a new business whose value chain possesses competitively valuable cross-business strategic fits.

Relative market share position It is the horizontal axis in a BCG Matrix, which is the firm's particular segment's market share (or revenues or #stores) divided by the industry leader's analogous number

Research and Development (R&D) Spending money to develop new and improved products and services.

Research and development Monies spent by firms to enhance existing products/services and/or create new and improved ones.

Reshoring Refers to American companies planning to move some of their manufacturing back to the USA.

Resistance to change A natural human tendency to be wary of new policies/strategies due to potential negative consequences; if not managed then this could result in sabotaging production machines, absenteeism, filing unfounded grievances, and an unwillingness to cooperate.

Resource allocation A central strategy implementation activity that entails distributing financial, physical, human, and technological assets to allow for strategy execution.

Resource similarity   The extent to which the type and amount of a firm's internal resources are comparable to a rival.

Resource-Based View (RBV)   An approach that suggests internal resources to be more important for a firm than external factors in achieving and sustaining competitive advantage.

Restructuring   Modifying the firm's chain of command and reporting channels to improve efficiency and effectiveness.

Retreats   Formal meetings commonly held off-premises to discuss and update a firm's strategic plan; done away from the work site to encourage more creativity and candor from participants.

Retrenchment   When an organization regroups through cost and asset reduction to reverse declining sales and profits.

Reviewing the underlying bases of an organization's strategy   Activity #1 in the strategy evaluation process; entails a firm developing a revised EFE Matrix and IFE Matrix to determine if corrective actions are needed.

Revised EFE Matrix   Part of activity #1 in the strategy evaluation process whereby a firm reassesses its previously determined external opportunities and threats.

Revised IFE Matrix   Part of activity #1 in the strategy evaluation process whereby a firm reassesses its previously determined internal strengths and weaknesses.

Rightsizing   Reducing the number of employees, number of divisions or units, and/or number of hierarchical levels in the firm's organizational structure; also called downsizing.

Secondary buyouts   When private-equity firms buying companies from other private-equity firms.

Self-concept   A component of the mission statement; the firm's distinctive competence or major competitive advantage.

Self-interest change strategy   A management technique to facilitate a firm adapting to new strategies/policies/situations by attempts to convince individuals that the change is to their personal advantage. When this appeal is successful, strategy implementation can be relatively easy. However, implementation changes are seldom to everyone's advantage.

Selling   A basic function of marketing; includes activities such as advertising, sales promotion, publicity, personal selling, sales force management, customer relations, and dealer relations.

Sexual harassment (and discrimination)   Unwelcome sexual advances, requests for sexual favors, and other verbal or physical conduct of a sexual nature; this activity is illegal, unethical, and detrimental to any organization, and can result in expensive lawsuits, lower morale, and reduced productivity.

Six Sigma   A quality-boosting process improvement technique that entails training several key persons in techniques to monitor, measure, and improve processes and eliminate defects in a firm; trained persons can earn black belts.

SO strategies   Strategies that result from matching a firm's internal strengths with its external opportunities.

Social policy   Guidelines and practices a firm may institute to guide its behavior towards employees, consumers, environmentalists, minorities, communities, shareholders, and other groups.

Social responsibility   Refers to actions an organization takes beyond what is legally required to protect or enhance the well-being of living things

ST strategies   Strategies that result from matching a firm's internal strengths with its external threats.

Stability position (SP)   One of four dimensions/axes of the SPACE Matrix that determines how stable/unstable a firm's industry is, considering such factors as technological changes, rate of inflation, demand of variability, price range of competing products, barriers to entry into market, competitive pressure, ease of exit from market, price elasticity of demand and risk involved in business.

Staffing   Includes activities such a recruiting, interviewing, testing, selecting, orienting, training, developing, caring for, evaluating, rewarding, disciplining, promoting, transferring, demoting, and dismissing employees.

Stakeholders   The individuals and groups of individuals who have a special stake or claim on the company, such as a firm's customers, employees, shareholders, and creditors.

Stars   A quadrant in the BCG Matrix for divisions that have a high relative market share position and compete in a high-growth industry; this is the upper left quadrant.

Strategic Business Unit (SBU) Structure   This type of organizational design groups similar divisions together into units; widely used when a firm has many divisions/segments in order to reduce span of control reporting to a COO.

Strategic management   The art and science of formulating, implementing, and evaluating cross-functional decisions that enable an organization to achieve its objectives.

Strategic objectives   Desired results such as a larger market share, quicker on-time delivery than rivals, shorter design-to-market times than rivals, lower costs than rivals, higher product quality than rivals, wider geographic coverage than rivals, achieving technological leadership, consistently getting new or improved products to market ahead of rivals.

Strategic planning   The process of formulating an organization's game plan; in a corporate setting, this term may refer to the whole strategic-management process.

Strategic Position and Action Evaluation (SPACE) Matrix   Indicates whether aggressive, conservative, defensive, or competitive strategies are most appropriate for a given organization. The axes of this matrix represent two internal dimensions (financial position [FP] and competitive position [CP]) and two external dimensions (stability position [SP] and industry position [IP]). These four factors are perhaps the most important determinants of an organization's overall strategic position.

Strategic-management model A framework or illustration of the strategic-management process; a clear and practical approach for formulating, implementing, and evaluating strategies.

Strategic-management process The process of formulating, implementing, and evaluating strategies as revealed in the comprehensive model, that begins with vision/mission development and ends with strategy evaluation and feedback.

Strategies The means by which long-term objectives will be achieved. Business strategies may include geographic expansion, diversification, acquisition, product development, market penetration, retrenchment, divestiture, liquidation, and joint ventures.

Strategists The person(s) responsible for formulating and implementing a firm's strategic plan, including the CEO, President, Owner of a Business, Head Coach, Governor, Chancellor, and/or the top management team in a firm.

Strategy evaluation Stage 3 in the strategic-management process. The three fundamental strategy-evaluation activities are (1) review external and internal factors that are the bases for current strategies, (2) measure performance, and (3) take corrective actions; strategies need to be evaluated regularly because external and internal factors constantly change.

Strategy formulation Stage 1 in the strategic-management process; includes developing a vision/mission, identifying an organization's external opportunities/threats, determining internal strengths/weaknesses, establishing long-term objectives, generating alternative strategies, and choosing particular strategies to pursue.

Strategy implementation Stage 2 of the strategic-management process. Activities include establish annual objectives, devise policies, motivate employees, allocating resources, developing a strategy-supportive culture, creating an effective organizational structure, redirecting marketing efforts, preparing budgets, developing and utilizing information systems, and linking employee compensation to organizational performance.

Strategy-formulation analytical framework A three stage, nine matrix, array of tools widely used for strategic planning as a guide: (stage 1: input stage; stage 2: matching stage; stage 3: decision stage).

Strengths-Weaknesses Opportunities-Threats (SWOT) Matrix The most widely used of all strategic planning matrices; matches a firm's internal strengths/weaknesses with its external opportunities/threats to generate four types of strategies: SO (strengths-opportunities) Strategies, WO (weaknesses-opportunities) Strategies, ST (strengths-threats) Strategies, and WT (weaknesses-threats) Strategies.

Sum Total Attractiveness Scores (STAS) In a QSPM, this is the sum of the Total Attractiveness Scores in each strategy column; value reveals which strategy is most attractive in each set of alternatives.

Sustainability The extent that an organization's operations and actions protect, mend, and preserve, rather than harm or destroy, the natural environment.

Sustained competitive advantage Maintaining what a firm does especially well, compared to rival firms – by (1) continually adapting to changes in external trends and events and internal capabilities, competencies, and resources; and (2) effectively formulating, implementing, and evaluating strategies that capitalize upon those factors.

Synergy The $1 + 1 = 3$ effect; when everyone pulls together as a team, the results can exceed individuals working separately.

Takeover If the merger/acquisition is not desired by both firms.

Taking corrective actions Activity # three in the strategy evaluation process; involves a firm making changes to competitively reposition a firm for the future.

Technology A component of the mission statement; the firm technologically current?

Test marketing An activity to determine ahead of time whether a certain product or service or selling approach will be cost effective; also used to forecast future sales of new products.

Total Attractiveness Scores (TAS) In a QSPM, the product of multiplying the weights by the Attractiveness Scores in each row. The values indicate the relative attractiveness of each alternative strategy, considering only the impact of the adjacent external or internal critical success factor.

Treasury stock An item in the equity portion of a balance sheet that reveals the dollar amount of the firm's common stock owned by the company itself.

Turbulent, high-velocity markets Industries that are changing very fast, such as telecommunications, medical, biotechnology, pharmaceuticals, computer hardware, software, and virtually all Internet-based industries).

Tweet Posted messages of 140 characters or less on Twitter.com.

Unrelated diversification When a firm acquires a new business whose value chains are so dissimilar that no competitively valuable cross-business relationships exist.

Vacant niche In product/market positioning (perceptual map), this is an area in the perceptual map that reveals a customer segment not being served by the firm or rival firms.

Value Chain Analysis (VCA) The process whereby a firm determines the costs associated with organizational activities from purchasing raw materials to manufacturing product(s) to marketing those products, and compares these costs to rival firms using benchmarking.

Value chain The business of a firm, where total revenues minus total costs of all activities undertaken to develop, produce, and market a product or service yields value.

Variable Costs (VC) A key variable in breakeven analysis; includes costs such as labor and materials.

Vertical consistency of objectives Compatibility of objectives from the CEO (corporate level) down to the Presidents (divisional level) on down to the Managers (functional level).

Vertical integration A combination of three strategies: backward, forward, and horizontal integration, allowing a firm to gain control over distributors, suppliers, and/or competitors respectively.

Vision statement A one sentence statement that answers the question, "What do we want to become?"

Vision statement Answers the question, "What do we want to become?"

Wa In Japan, this stresses group harmony and social cohesion.

Whistle-blowing The act of telling authorities about some unethical or illegal activities occurring within an organization of which you are aware.

White knight When a firm agrees to acquire another firm at a point in time when that other firm is facing a hostile takeover by some company.

Wikis Websites that allows users to add, delete, and edit content regarding frequently asked questions and information across the firm's whole value chain of activities.

WO strategies Strategies that result from matching a firm's internal weaknesses with its external opportunities.

Workplace romance An intimate relationship between two truly consenting employees, as opposed to sexual harassment, which the EEOC defines broadly as unwelcome sexual advances, requests for sexual favors, and other verbal or physical conduct of a sexual nature.

WT strategies Strategies that result from matching a firm's internal weaknesses with its external threats.

Name Index

Subject Index

Comprehensive Model of the

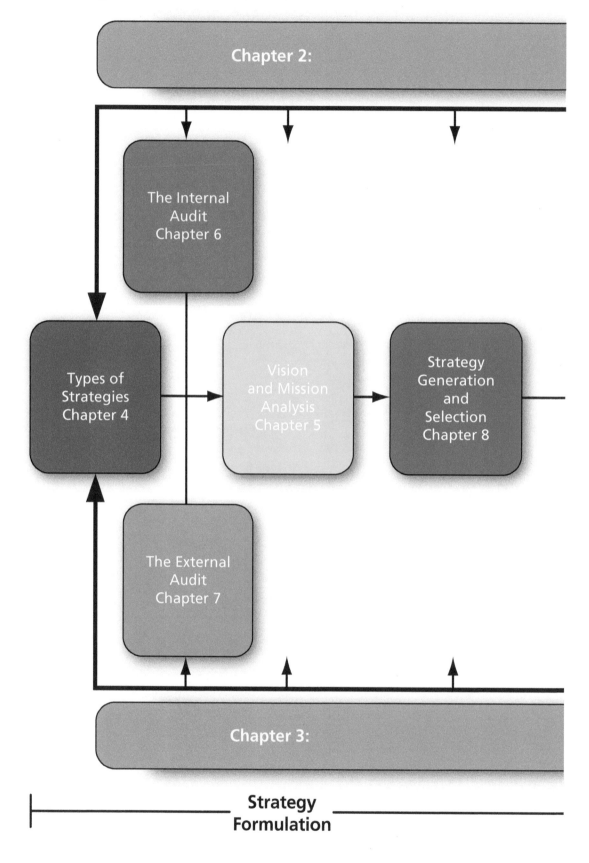

Chapter 2:

The Internal Audit
Chapter 6

Types of
Strategies
Chapter 4

Vision
and Mission
Analysis
Chapter 5

Strategy
Generation
and
Selection
Chapter 8

The External
Audit
Chapter 7

Chapter 3:

Strategy
Formulation

USED WIDELY AMONG BUSINESSES
AND ACADEMIA WORLDWIDE

Strategic-Management Process

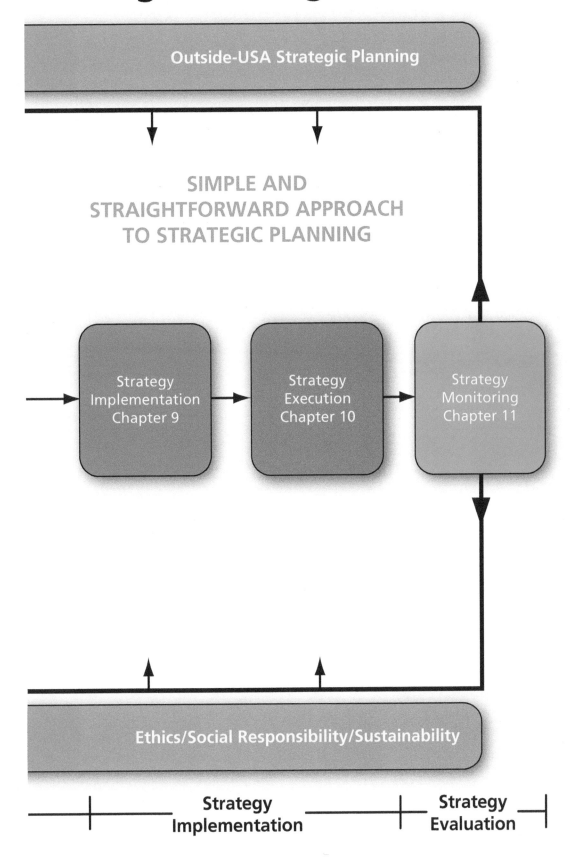

Outside-USA Strategic Planning

SIMPLE AND
STRAIGHTFORWARD APPROACH
TO STRATEGIC PLANNING

Strategy
Implementation
Chapter 9

Strategy
Execution
Chapter 10

Strategy
Monitoring
Chapter 11

Ethics/Social Responsibility/Sustainability

Strategy
Implementation

Strategy
Evaluation

USED TO INTEGRATE AND ORGANIZE
ALL CHAPTERS IN THIS TEXT